AF213809

THE COURT OF JUSTICE AND EUROPEAN CRIMINAL LAW

The aim of this book is to provide an insight into the landmark rulings of the Court of Justice of the European Union (CJEU) in European Criminal Law (ECL). As in other areas of EU law, the decisions of the CJEU have been a driving force for development and integration. By analysing the impact of these leading cases on EU and national law, the book provides a diachronic and multifaceted picture of the Court's approach to criminal law.

Volume 91 in the Series Modern Studies in European Law

Modern Studies in European Law

Recent titles in this series:

The European Union and Social Security Law
Jaan Paju

The Rule of Law in the European Union: The Internal Dimension
Theodore Konstadinides

The Division of Competences between the EU and the Member States: Reflections on the Past, the Present and the Future
Edited by Sacha Garben and Inge Govaere

Unity in Adversity: EU Citizenship, Social Justice and the Cautionary Tale of the UK
Charlotte O'Brien

The Use of Force and Article 2 of the ECHR in Light of European Conflicts
Hannah Russell

Environmental Crime in Europe
Edited by Andrew Farmer, Michael Faure and Grazia Maria Vagliasindi

Questioning EU Citizenship: Judges and the Limits of Free Movement and Solidarity in the EU
Edited by Daniel Thym

The European Union under Transnational Law: A Pluralist Appraisal
Matej Avbelj

Illegally Staying in the EU: An Analysis of Illegality in EU Migration Law
Benedita Menezes Queiroz

Social Legitimacy in the Internal Market: A Dialogue of Mutual Responsiveness
Jotte Mulder

The EU Better Regulation Agenda: A Critical Assessment
Edited by Sacha Garben and Inge Govaere

Administrative Regulation Beyond the Non-Delegation Doctrine: A Study on EU Agencies
Marta Simoncini

The Interface Between EU and International Law: Contemporary Reflections
Edited by Inge Govaere and Sacha Garben

The Rise and Decline of Fundamental Rights in EU Citizenship
Adrienne Yong

For the complete list of titles in this series, see 'Modern Studies in European Law' link at www.bloomsburyprofessional.com/uk/series/modern-studies-in-european-law

The Court of Justice and European Criminal Law

Leading Cases in a Contextual Analysis

Edited by
Valsamis Mitsilegas
Alberto di Martino
and
Leandro Mancano

• HART •
OXFORD • LONDON • NEW YORK • NEW DELHI • SYDNEY

HART PUBLISHING

Bloomsbury Publishing Plc

Kemp House, Chawley Park, Cumnor Hill, Oxford, OX2 9PH, UK

HART PUBLISHING, the Hart/Stag logo, BLOOMSBURY and the Diana logo are trademarks of Bloomsbury Publishing Plc

First published in Great Britain 2019

Copyright © The editors and contributors severally 2019

The editors and contributors have asserted their right under the Copyright, Designs and Patents Act 1988 to be identified as Authors of this work.

All rights reserved. No part of this publication may be reproduced or transmitted in any form or by any means, electronic or mechanical, including photocopying, recording, or any information storage or retrieval system, without prior permission in writing from the publishers.

While every care has been taken to ensure the accuracy of this work, no responsibility for loss or damage occasioned to any person acting or refraining from action as a result of any statement in it can be accepted by the authors, editors or publishers.

All UK Government legislation and other public sector information used in the work is Crown Copyright ©. All House of Lords and House of Commons information used in the work is Parliamentary Copyright ©. This information is reused under the terms of the Open Government Licence v3.0 (http://www.nationalarchives.gov.uk/doc/open-government-licence/version/3) except where otherwise stated.

All Eur-lex material used in the work is © European Union, http://eur-lex.europa.eu/, 1998–2019.

A catalogue record for this book is available from the British Library.

Library of Congress Cataloging-in-Publication data

Names: Mitsilegas, Valsamis, 1971-, editor. | Di Martino, Alberto, editor. | Mancano, Leandro, 1989-, editor.

Title: The Court of Justice and European criminal law : leading cases in a contextual analysis / edited by Valsamis Mitsilegas, Alberto di Martino, Leandro Mancano.

Description: Chicago : Hart Publishing, 2019. | Series: Modern studies in European law | Includes bibliographical references and index.

Identifiers: LCCN 2019021098 (print) | LCCN 2019021910 (ebook) | ISBN 9781509911189 (EPub) | ISBN 9781509911172 (hardback)

Subjects: LCSH: Court of Justice of the European Union. | Criminal law—European Union countries—Cases. | BISAC: LAW / International. | LAW / Criminal Law / General.

Classification: LCC KJE5461 (ebook) | LCC KJE5461 .C677 2019 (print) | DDC 345.24/01—dc23

LC record available at https://lccn.loc.gov/2019021098

ISBN: HB: 978-1-50991-117-2
ePDF: 978-1-50991-120-2
ePub: 978-1-50991-118-9

Typeset by Compuscript Ltd, Shannon

To find out more about our authors and books visit www.hartpublishing.co.uk. Here you will find extracts, author information, details of forthcoming events and the option to sign up for our newsletters.

FOREWORD

If there is one area of law that has been associated with national sovereignty, that is without a doubt criminal law. Traditionally, criminal law has been considered to be one of the 'crown jewels' of national sovereignty. That is because criminal law establishes the rules that enable the state to defend itself and its citizens against actions that are repugnant to the values on which democratic societies are founded. Criminal law is thus a powerful tool that gives true meaning to the idea that only the state may lawfully deprive a person of his or her liberty.

That is why, without a clear mandate from the EC Treaty itself, Member States were initially hostile to the very idea that the EU (then the Community) could enjoy the legislative power to adopt criminal penalties as a means of enforcing substantive EU policies,[1] let alone to harmonise substantive criminal law.

That did not mean, however, that criminal law 'constitute[d] an island beyond the reach of [EU] law'.[2] As some scholars noted, '[n]ational criminal [law] [has always been] restricted either "passively" [by the substantive law of the EU] or "actively" through the imposition of specific criminal sanctions deemed necessary to ensure the proper implementation of [EU law]'.[3] Passively, whilst criminal law was seen as a matter for which the Member States were responsible, that branch of the law was circumscribed by the fundamental freedoms where it constituted an obstacle to free movement. Actively, since the Member States are obliged to penalise infringements of EU law in an effective, proportionate and dissuasive fashion, such an obligation may sometimes require the adoption of criminal penalties.

That said, over the past 60 years, the EU has changed. Its remit is no longer confined to imposing 'active' and 'passive' limits to the criminal laws of the Member States, but has evolved with successive Treaty reforms to cover substantive and procedural aspects of those laws.

[1] See Michael Dougan, 'From the Velvet Glove to the Iron Fist: Sanctions and Penalties for the Enforcement of Community Law' in Marise Cremona (ed), *Compliance and Enforcement of EU Law* (Oxford University Press, 2012) 90.

[2] See, by analogy, Opinion of Advocate General Tesauro in Case C-120/95 *Decker* EU:C:1997:399, para 17. See also Koen Lenaerts, 'Federalism and the Rule of Law: Perspectives from the European Court of Justice' (2009–10) 39 *Fordham International Law Journal* 1338.

[3] Andrea Biondi and Roberto Mastroianni, Case Note on *Berlusconi e.a* (2006) 43 *CML Rev* 553, at 559.

With the Maastricht Treaty[4] and, to a greater extent, the Amsterdam Treaty,[5] the Member States established the objective of maintaining and developing the EU as an area of freedom, security and justice (the 'AFSJ'). In order for the EU to attain that objective, cooperation in criminal matters among national judiciaries was deemed necessary. That is because in a globalised world where organised crime and terrorism know no borders, it is of paramount importance that the Member States, all of which share common values and trust one another, work together and combine their efforts in order to find an effective and unified answer to those threats, whilst upholding the rule of law.

Today, it is safe to say that criminal law is no longer outside the scope of European integration, as the Treaties themselves provide that parts of that law may be subject to EU legislation. In particular, that legislation may seek to facilitate the free movement of judicial decisions in criminal matters by having recourse to the principle of mutual recognition. Additionally, the EU legislator may adopt directives establishing minimum standards governing the definition of criminal offences and sanctions in the area of particularly serious crime with a cross-border dimension resulting from the nature or impact of such offences or from a special need to combat them on a common basis.

For its part, the Court of Justice of the European Union (the 'Court of Justice') has played a leading role in setting out the constitutional principles that underpin EU criminal law. It has also set out the constitutional features that are common to the constitutional traditions of the Member States and that distinguish criminal law – whether at national or EU level – from other branches of the law.

Edited by Valsamis Mitsilegas, Alberto di Martino and Leandro Mancano, this book contains a collection of essays that together make a hugely valuable contribution to the existing literature on EU criminal law. Given the expertise of its contributors, it does not come as a surprise that this book, which brings together their collective wisdom, is an outstanding piece of scholarly work, providing very telling insights into the way in which the Court of Justice interprets EU criminal law.

This book provides a critical assessment of 15 landmark judgments of the Court of Justice. Each judgment is examined by two contributors, the first often examining it from an 'EU law perspective', the second focusing on its impact at national level. Needless to say, readers will greatly benefit from this 'double-perspective', since it illustrates how judicial dialogue works in practice.

Divided into five parts, the book seeks to provide a comprehensive overview of the relevant case law of the Court of Justice in this area of law. First, it looks at three seminal judgments in which the Court of Justice was confronted with

[4] See ex Article K-K.9 of the Treaty on European Union [1992] OJ C191/1.

[5] See ex Article 1, point 11, and Article 2, point 15, of the Treaty of Amsterdam amending the Treaty on European Union, the Treaties establishing the European Communities and related acts [1997] OJ C340/1.

the difficult question of determining whether and if so how, general principles of criminal law – such as the principle of legality – may limit the effectiveness of EU law. The second part of this book focuses on the question of competences. It examines the extent to which the effective implementation of an EU policy may provide a sufficient legal basis for the EU to oblige the Member States to pass legislation providing for criminal penalties. Third, the contributors explore a fundamental right that is part and parcel of EU criminal law, ie the principle of *ne bis in idem*. That principle is examined both in a cross-border context and in purely internal situations. The fourth part of the book is devoted to studying the interaction between national criminal law and other areas of EU law by looking at two specific questions, ie whether irregular migration may be criminalised and whether a Member State may deny a right of residence on grounds of public security. Last, but not least, this book looks at the principles of mutual trust and mutual recognition, which are two defining principles not only of EU criminal law but also of the AFSJ as a whole. In particular, contributors focus on the need to balance those two constitutional principles with the proper protection of fundamental rights.

Written in a clear and entertaining style, this book succeeds in acquainting the reader with the way in which the Court of Justice reads EU criminal law. On all accounts, it is a great pleasure for me to welcome this book. Students, scholars and judges will all benefit immensely from it.

Koen Lenaerts
President of the Court of Justice of the European Union

TABLE OF CONTENTS

Foreword by Koen Lenaerts .... *v*
List of Contributors .... *xiii*

Introduction *1*
Valsamis Mitsilegas, Alberto di Martino and Leandro Mancano

PART I
PRINCIPLES

1. *C-80/86* – Kolpinghuis Nijmegen *7*

   The General Principles of European (Criminal) Law as Limitation to the Enforcement of EU Law: The *Kolpinghuis Nijmegen* Rule 7
   Dr Luisa Marin

   Indirect Effect of EU Law after *Kolpinghuis Nijmegen* (C-80/86): Consistent Interpretation in Dutch Criminal Courts 21
   Jannemieke Ouwerkerk

2. *C-387/02* – Berlusconi and Others *37*

   The *Berlusconi* Judgment: A Cornerstone of European Legality 37
   Frank Meyer

   Allusion, Illusion, Delusion. The Assessment of the *Berlusconi* Judgment in Italy 55
   Alberto di Martino

3. *C-105/03* – Pupino *67*

   Impact of the *Pupino* Decision on EU Law 67
   Maria Fletcher

   Protecting Vulnerable Victims and Beyond: The Duty of Consistent Interpretation in Criminal Matters in Italy after *Pupino* 83
   Grazia Maria Vagliasindi

PART II
COMPETENCE

4. *68/88* – Commission v Greece *107*

Effectiveness, Dissuasiveness, Proportionality of Sanctions and Assimilation Principle: The Long-Lasting Legacy of the *Greek Maize* Case 107
Fabio Giuffrida

The *Greek Maize* Case. From Sincere Cooperation to Criminal Law Integration in the EU 122
Rosaria Sicurella

5. *C-176/03* – Commission of the European Communities v Council of the European Union *137*

The 'Constitutional' ECJ Ruling on the Enforcement of Community Law (Case C-176/03) and its Impact on EU Law 137
M Kaiafa-Gbandi

EU Substantive Criminal Competence and the Court of Justice: Reactions to the Case Law 151
Samuli Miettinen

6. *C-105/14* – Taricco and Others *165*

On Legality in Criminal Matters between Primacy of EU Law and National Constitutional Traditions. A Study of the *Taricco* Saga 165
Silvia Allegrezza

Taricco, Endgame 188
Vittorio Manes

PART III
NE BIS IN IDEM

7. *C-187/01* – Gözütok and Brügge *199*

Comment on CJEU, 11 February 2003, Joined Cases C-187/01 and C-385/01 *Criminal Proceedings v Hüseyin Gözütok and Klaus Brügge* 199
Anne Weyembergh

The Impact of Case C-187/01 [*Gözütok/Brügge*] at the National Level: Inadvertent Legacy 212
Elisavet Symeonidou-Kastanidou and Yannis Naziris

8. *C-486/14* – Kossowski *227*

Judgment (Grand Chamber) C-486/14 *Piotr Kossowski*, 29 June 2016 227
Kai Ambos

Impact of the Case C-486/14 – *Kossowski* at National Level 234
Celina Nowak

9. *C-617/10* – Åkerberg Fransson *245*

Fishing for Better Rights Protection: The Court of Justice on the Application of the Charter in the Member States and the Reach of *ne bis in idem* 245
Tobias Lock

The Impact of Case C-617/10: *Åkerberg Fransson* at National Level – The Swedish Example 259
Maria Bergström

PART IV
MIGRATION AND CITIZENSHIP

10. *C-61/11 PPU* – El Dridi *273*

Criminalisation of Irregular Migration in the EU: The Impact of *El Dridi* 273
Niovi Vavoula

Reshaping Criminalisation of Irregular Migration in Italy: The Impact of EU Law Beyond the *El Dridi* Judgment 290
Alessandra Annoni

11. *C-304/14* – CS *305*

The Intersection of National Criminal Law and EU Citizenship Law: Reflections on the Judgment in *CS* 305
Niamh Nic Shuibhne

Leave at Your Chosen Speed? EU Citizenship and Criminal Convictions: An Insight into the United Kingdom's Approach 319
Leandro Mancano

PART V
MUTUAL RECOGNITION AND MUTUAL TRUST

12. *C-303/05* – Advocaten voor de Wereld *333*

Advocaten voor de Wereld: The Salvation of Mutual Trust 333
Henning Fuglsang Sørensen

The Contribution of *Advocaten voor de Wereld* for the Protection of Human Rights in the Context of Supra-State Law and for the Doctrine of Double Criminality 348
Pedro Caeiro

13. *C-396/11* - Radu *363*

Judgment of the Court of Justice of the European Union, 29 January 2013, *Radu* 363
Rosa Raffaelli

The Implication of *Radu* at a National Level: National Courts' Diversified Response to Conflicting Obligations 380
Irene Wieczorek

14. *C-399/11* - Melloni *393*

Melloni: Primacy versus Rights? 393
Valsamis Mitsilegas and Leandro Mancano

Bypassing or Intensifying the Dialogue between Courts? The Impact of *Melloni* at the National Level 404
Lorena Bachmaier Winter

15. *Joined Cases C-404/15 and C-659/15 PPU* - Pál Aranyosi and Robert Căldăraru v Generalstaatsanwaltschaft Bremen *421*

Resetting the Parameters of Mutual Trust: From *Aranyosi* to *LM* 421
Valsamis Mitsilegas

Aranyosi and Căldăraru through the Eyes of National Judges 437
Adam Łazowski

The Effect of CJEU Case Law Concerning the Rule of Law and Mutual Trust on National Systems 455
Petra Bárd and Wouter van Ballegooij

Index *469*

LIST OF CONTRIBUTORS

Silvia Allegrezza, Associate Professor in Criminal Law, University of Luxembourg.

Kai Ambos, Chair for Criminal Law, Criminal Procedure, Comparative Law and International Criminal Law, University of Göttingen. Judge, Kosovo Specialist Chamber (KSC), The Hague; advisor (amicus curiae) Special Jurisdiction for Peace, Bogota, Colombia.

Alessandra Annoni, Associate Professor, Law Department, University of Ferrara.

Lorena Bachmaier, Professor of Law, Complutense University Madrid.

Petra Bard, Associate Professor, Eötvös Loránd University, Faculty of Law, Hungary; Visiting Professor, Central European University, Budapest, Hungary.

Maria Bergström, Associate Professor, Faculty of Law, University of Uppsala.

Pedro Caeiro, Assistant Professor at the Faculty of Law of the University of Coimbra; Researcher at the UCILeR.

Alberto di Martino, Professor of Criminal Law, Scuola Superiore Sant'Anna, Pisa.

Maria Fletcher, Senior Lecturer in European Law, University of Glasgow.

Dr Henning Fuglsang Sørensen, Associate Professor, Department of Law, University of Southern Denmark.

Fabio Giuffrida PhD Candidate in EU Criminal Law, Queen Mary University of London; University of Luxembourg.

Maria Kaiafa-Gbandi, Professor of Criminal law, European and International Criminal Law, the Law Faculty, Aristotle University Thessaloniki.

Adam Lazowski, Professor of European Union Law, Westminster Law School, University of Westminster.

Tobias Lock, Professor of Law, Department of Law, Maynooth University.

Dr Leandro Mancano, Lecturer in EU Law, School of Law, Edinburgh Law School.

Vittorio Manes, Professore ordinario di Diritto penale, Dipartimento di Scienze giuridiche, Alma Mater Studiorum – Università di Bologna.

Luisa Marin, Contract Professor in EU Law, Catholic University of the Sacred Heart (Milan-Piacenza), and visiting assistant professor, University of Twente.

Frank Meyer, Professor of International and European Criminal Law, University of Zurich.

Dr Samuli Miettinen, School of Governance, Law and Society, Associate Professor, Tallinn University.

Valsamis Mitsilegas, Professor of European Criminal Law and Global Security, Queen Mary University of London.

Dr Yannis Naziris, Aristotle University of Thessaloniki.

Niamh Nic Shuibhne, Professor of EU Law, School of Law, University of Edinburgh.

Celina Nowak, Professor of Criminal Law, Institute of Law Studies, Polish Academy of Sciences.

Jannemieke Ouwerkerk, Full Professor of European Criminal Law at Leiden University, the Netherlands.

Dr Rosa Raffaelli, Judge, Court of First Instance – Criminal Section, Livorno, Italy.

Rosaria Sicurella, Full Professor in Italian, European and International Criminal Law – Department of Law, University of Catania.

Elisavet Symeonidou-Kastanidou, Professor of Criminal Law at the Law Faculty of the Aristotle University of Thessaloniki.

Grazia Maria Vagliasindi, Associate Professor of Criminal Law, University of Catania (Italy), Department of Law.

Dr Wouter van Ballegooij, Policy analyst, European Parliamentary Research Service.

Niovi Vavoula, Lecturer in Migration and Security, Queen Mary University of London.

Anne Weyembergh, Professor, Faculté de droit et Institut d'Etudes européennes, Université Libre de Bruxelles (ULB).

Irene Wieczorek, Research Associate, University of Cambridge and Université Libre de Bruxelles, FWO Post-Doctoral Fellow.

Introduction

VALSAMIS MITSILEGAS, ALBERTO DI MARTINO
AND LEANDRO MANCANO

As a genre in legal literature, the analysis of the *grands arrêts* is not a new one. Publications on the landmark rulings of higher courts have become masterpieces, with regard to national criminal law and EU law broadly speaking.[1] This is not surprising, as judges and courts do fulfil a key interpretative – if not law-making – role in our legal systems.

This is even more the case when it comes to the Court of Justice of the European Union (CJEU), often referred to as the motor of Union integration. From primacy to direct effect, from effectiveness to non-discrimination and fundamental rights, the rulings of the CJEU have indeed shaped the EU as a legal order. As the years have gone by, even more areas of national law have fallen under the umbrella of EU law; and, as a result, under the jurisdiction of the Court. Criminal law has also been involved. Such a pre-eminent stronghold of national sovereignty has been marked by an incredibly fast growing process of integration at EU level.

Starting with the Maastricht Treaty, the Union has been conferred growing powers in criminal law, resulting in the adoption of many legislative instruments. Furthermore, EU competences have expanded, as shown by the establishment of EU citizenship and the Union action in immigration and asylum law. This has heightened the chance of conflict between state criminal law and EU law.

The two dynamics just described has had a number of consequences. First, new forms of cooperation amongst Member States have led to the unprecedented application of certain principles to criminal law, as is the case of mutual recognition. Second, traditional guarantees (the principle of legality, *ne bis in idem*) have been involved in this interaction, and their content has been thus redefined. This has had a significant impact on sovereignty and fundamental rights. To this end, the legally-binding value taken on by the EU Charter of Fundamental Rights following the Lisbon Treaty has played an important role. Third, judgments in EU criminal law have constitutional importance as they deal with questions of fundamental rights protection standards and the extent of Member States' powers in remits traditionally having a national dimension. Fourth, EU criminal law has displayed

[1] See in particular J Pradel and A Varinard, *Les grands arrêts du droit pénal general* (Paris, Dalloz, 2007); M Poiares Maduro and L Azoulai (eds), *The Past and Future of EU Law* (Oxford, Hart Publishing, 2010).

its significance in a plethora of other areas of EU law, including immigration law, free movement and citizenship.

The key function performed by the Court, when promoting and managing that dynamic, has materialised in landmark decisions. The Luxembourg judges have reshaped traditional principles of criminal law (such as the principle of legality, *ne bis in idem*) and engaged with the interpretation of new ones (mutual recognition in judicial cooperation). Furthermore, they have developed the field in uncharted territory. This is especially the case with post-Lisbon key criminal law judgments having a constitutional flavour.

They have, broadly, outlined a role for crime, criminals and criminal law in the EU. A body of law has thus arisen where principles stated within a new legal order interact with an area historically very close to national sovereignty.

For all these reasons, the time is ripe for a comprehensive analysis of the Court's contribution to the field. The aim of this book is to provide an insight into the great rulings of the CJEU in European criminal law. By analysing the most important judgments of the Court in this area, the volume provides a multifaceted picture of the EU (and the Court in particular) understanding of criminal law.

The project revolves around 15 landmark rulings, and brings together over 30 distinguished scholars in EU, international and criminal law. In the light of the mentioned interplay between different areas of Union and national rules, European criminal law is here understood holistically as including: the decisions on the former 'third pillar' instruments and the post-Lisbon instruments adopted on the basis of EU competences in criminal matters (European criminal law *stricto sensu*); the rulings on pieces of EU law that, in spite of not belonging to European criminal law *stricto sensu*, interact with national provisions of criminal law.

The coverage and structure of the book reflect that holistic approach. The leading cases have been selected on the basis of their pioneering and lasting influence. Each ruling is analysed from two different perspectives. The first chapter discusses the impact of the decision, by looking at the way the Court has interpreted the principle(s) involved. The second chapter outlines the effects of the case law on the Member States' systems. The inclusion of two commentaries per case, is meant to emphasise the relatively unexplored perspective of the impact of these leading judgments on the national systems. European criminal law concerns largely the interaction between EU and national law, as well as the application and impact of the law on the individual at national level.

The judgments have been grouped thematically. First, the volume addresses the issues of principles (Part I). The uniqueness of European criminal law shines brightly, with the CJEU called to interpret the consequences of direct effect, indirect effect and legality on individual criminal liability at state level. On the one hand, cases such as *Kolphinghuis* and *Berlusconi*[2] have established the foundations

[2] Case C-80/86 *Criminal proceedings against Kolpinghuis Nijmegen BV* [1987] ECR 3982; and Joined Cases C-387/02, C-391/02, C-403/02 *Silvio Berlusconi, Sergio Adelchi, Marcello Dell'Utri and others* [2005] ECR I-03565.

of European criminal law, such as the principles that EU law cannot determine directly the individual criminal liability and the retroactivity of more lenient criminal penalties. On the other, *Pupino* and *Taricco*[3] show the difficulty in balancing these safeguards against the effectiveness of EU law. The national laws concerned raise the following key questions: are the rules on statute limitation part of procedural or substantive criminal law? How can this impact on the national constitutional understandings of the principle of legality? To what extent can the uniformity of EU law prevail over state identity? The authors deal with these conundra, and provide a comprehensive picture of the legal issues at stake.

Principles specific to the EU legal order – eg effectiveness – have been key to the growth of EU criminal law. This is where the discussion broadens, and extends to a debate on competences (Part II). The focus here is on the two main authorities: the *Greek Maize* and *Environment Crime* cases.[4] The authors highlight the continuity between the judicial and institutional development concerning the EU competences in criminal law, whereby principles stated by the Court – the requirement for Member States to introduce effective, proportionate, dissuasive penalties, or the 'functional' EU competences in criminal law – have found their way into primary and secondary EU law, as well as into national laws.

The combination of horizontal (as between states) and vertical (EU-state) interaction in criminal law increases the risk of double jeopardy. The complexity is enhanced by the variety of legal sources, with the *ne bis in idem* framed differently in Article 54 of the Convention Implementing the Schengen Agreement *and* Article 50 of the EU Charter of Fundamental Rights (Part III). These issues emerge from the *Gözütok and Brügge*[5] (the first case where the CJEU explicitly refers to mutual trust) and *Kossowski*[6] judgments, centrepieces of the transnational (EU) *ne bis in idem*. By homing in on the national *ne bis in idem* and the scope of application of the Charter, *Fransson*[7] highlights the far-reaching nature of the CJEU's case law.

The broad embrace of EU criminal law is further demonstrated by its impact on other EU policies. In line with the holistic approach adopted in the volume, Part IV focuses on migration and citizenship. Through the *El Dridi* and *CS* judgments,[8] the authors prove the importance of a holistic approach to issues of European criminal law. The *El Dridi* case law constitutes a ground-breaking inroad into national sovereignty, with the Court posing important limits to the criminalisation of migration

[3] Case C-105/03 *Maria Pupino* ECR [2005] I-5285; and Case C-105/14 *Ivo Taricco and Others* Grand Chamber, Judgment of 8 September 2015 (*Taricco I*) and Case C-42/17 *MAS & MB* Grand Chamber, Judgment of 7 December 2017 (*Taricco II*).

[4] Case C-68/88 *Commission v Greece* EU:C:1989:339; and Case C-176/03 *Commission v Council* [2005] ECR I-07879.

[5] Joined cases C-187/01 and C-385/01 *Gözütok and Brügge* ECLI:EU:C:2003:87.

[6] Case C-486/14 *Kossowski* ECLI:EU:C:2016:483.

[7] Case C-617/10 *Åklagaren v Hans Åkerberg Fransson* ECLI:EU:C:2013:105.

[8] Case C-61/11 *El Dridi* [2011] ECR I-03015; and Case C-304/14 *Secretary of State for the Home Department v CS* ECLI:EU:C:2016:674.

by Member States. The analysis of the CJEU jurisprudence is complemented by a specific case study on the Italian law and policy. The chapters built around the *CS* judgment reveal the dangerous liaison between criminal conviction and (EU) citizenship rights. The authors elaborate on the problems associated with (quasi)legal presumptions in the area of wrongdoing and rights withdrawal.

Inextricably linked to the above discussion is the development of judicial cooperation between EU Member States (Part V). The dilemma concerning the impact of legality on individual rights and standard of protection clashes between Union and states, are here connected to the nature of the cooperation in this area. The principles of mutual trust and mutual recognition come under the spotlight, and are assessed through the rulings that have most marked the life of the European Arrest Warrant. The diachronic structure of this section lets the evolution of the CJEU's understanding emerge. While in *Advocaten voor de Wereld*, *Radu* and *Melloni*[9] the Court's focus was dramatically placed on the effectiveness of law enforcement at the expense of fundamental rights protection, *Căldăraru* and *LM*[10] show a more mature approach on the part of the EU's supreme judge. By taking into account the specificity of the EU legal order, the book aims to provide a reliable account of the mutual influence between EU, and state, criminal law. The holistic approach and the multilevel analysis show how these key judgments have shaped the EU approach to an area historically prerogative of states power.

[9] Case C-303/05 of 3 May 2005, *Advocaten voor de Wereld VZW v Leden van de Ministerraad* ECLI:EU:C:2007:261; Case C-396/11 *Ciprian Vasile Radu* [2013] ECR I; and Case C-399/11 *Melloni v Ministerio Fiscal* ECLI:EU:C:2013:107.

[10] Joined Cases C-404/15 and C-659/15 PPU *Pál Aranyosi and Robert Căldăraru* ECLI:EU:C:2016:198; and Case C-216/18 PPU *LM* ECLI:EU:C:2018:586.

PART I

Principles

1

C-80/86 – *Kolpinghuis Nijmegen*

The General Principles of European (Criminal) Law as Limitation to the Enforcement of EU Law: The Kolpinghuis Nijmegen *Rule**

DR LUISA MARIN

I. Introduction: *Kolpinghuis Nijmegen* as a First Encounter between EU Law and National Criminal Law(s) Principles

In the same year in which Michael Jackson released his famous 'Bad' album (1987), the Court of Justice of the EU (CJEU or CJ) delivered, on the 8th of October 1987, the judgment in the case *Criminal Proceedings against Kolpinghuis Nijmegen BV* (hereinafter: *Kolpinghuis Nijmegen*), in which it gave its contribution to the edification of European criminal law, by deciding that the principles of legal certainty and non-retroactivity limited the enforcement of EU law into the legal orders of the Member States (MSs).[1] This chapter focuses on this ruling.

The judgment can be considered one of the cornerstones of EU criminal law for several reasons: from one perspective, it indicates how EU law can and cannot influence national law enforcement systems, with specific reference to

* This chapter was written during my stay as Visiting Scholar at the Department of Legal Studies 'A Sraffa' of Bocconi University, Milan, Italy, which I wish to thank.

[1] Case C-80/86 *Criminal Proceedings against Kolpinghuis Nijmegen BV* (hereinafter: *Kolpinghuis Nijmegen*) [1987] ECR 3982.

the interaction between EU law and national criminal law. Two years before the leading '*Greek Maize*' case,[2] the CJ was building the edifice of EU law, unravelling the implications of its famous doctrines of direct effect and indirect effect, in particular for directives.[3]

From another perspective, the *Kolpinghuis Nijmegen* case represents a contribution to the edification of the principles of EU law, namely of legal certainty and non-retroactivity. These principles have a special significance for European criminal law, a field of law which has developed, first, thanks to the adjudication of the CJ and, later on, with the treaties and with the legislation.

The common element within both perspectives is the strong protective dimension developed for individuals by the CJ, with a judgment where EU law is deployed to protect citizens against the state, but also where the CJ resorts to general principles of national criminal justice systems in order to forge this protective dimension. EU law functions like a 'shield' against criminal law.[4]

Kolpinghuis Nijmegen is therefore, and for different reasons, a judgment of crucial importance in both EU law and EU criminal law, with a deep constitutional significance. It contributes to shape EU law as the house built upon the foundational *Van Gend en Loos* case, where the CJ stated that the EU legal order was 'more than an agreement which merely creates mutual obligations between the contracting parties'.[5] As 'a new legal order of international law for the benefit of which the states have limited their sovereign rights (…) and the subjects of which comprise not only Member States but also their nationals,[6] *Kolpinghuis Nijmegen* develops a new declination of this core feature of EU law on the precise juncture of the relations between states and individuals. It is one of those judgments in which EU law emerges not simply as a law to be enforced, but also as a shield for individuals, and as such it shapes the EU as a system based on the 'rule of law'. In a nutshell, it is one of the first encounters between European law and national criminal law principles, which then became European criminal law principles.

The chapter is organised as follows: after this short introduction (I), the judgment will be presented and discussed in relation to the case law of that time (II). In a following section (III), the legal issues at the core of the case will be analysed, and the chapter will move forward on the legacy (IV) of *Kolpinghuis Nijmegen* in the subsequent case law of the Court of Justice, showing how the knots of the direct effect(s) of EU law provisions continue to animate the debate on

[2] Case C-68/88 *Commission v Greece* (hereinafter: *Greek Maize* case) [1989] ECR 2695.

[3] B de Witte, 'Direct Effect, Primacy and the Nature of the Legal Order' in P Craig and G De Burca (eds), *The Evolution of EU Law* (Oxford University Press, 2011) 335.

[4] Y Cartuyvels et al (eds), 'Les droits de l'homme, bouclier ou épée du droit penal?' (Brussels, 2007).

[5] Case 26/62 *Van Gend en Loos* [1963] ECR 1.

[6] *Ibid.*

European, criminal law and constitutional law scholarship, as the recent *Taricco* saga[7] demonstrates, before concluding (V).

II. The Facts of the Case and the Judgment of 8 October 1987

A. The Café Run by *Kolpinghuis Nijmegen*

The case dealt with a preliminary reference from the district court (*arrondissement bank*) of Arnhem, in the Netherlands, in which the referring court asked questions on a directive that, at the time, had not yet been implemented in national legislation.

Council Directive 80/777/EEC[8] on the approximation of the laws of the MSs relating to the exploitation and marketing of natural mineral waters (hereinafter: the Directive) required MSs to take measures necessary to ensure that only waters extracted from the ground and recognised by the national responsible authority as 'mineral waters' could be marketed as such.

The deadline for the implementation of the Directive expired on the 17 July 1984, but the Dutch state amended its legislation with effect from 8 August 1984, whereas the facts of the case took place precisely on 7 August 1984, one day before the entry into force of the legislation implementing the Directive. The facts therefore took place before the state had implemented the Directive, which was already due for transposition.

The facts of the case concerned a prosecution against a company running a café which used to sell a mixture of tap water and carbon dioxide under the label

[7] The '*Taricco* saga' refers to a case of 'dialogue among courts', the Court of Justice (CJ) and the Italian Constitutional Court (ICC), on the compatibility with EU law of Italian provisions on time limitations for criminal proceedings. In '*Taricco I*', the CJ answered a request for a preliminary ruling where the referring judge framed the Italian legislation on time limitations as creating a 'de facto impunity' for VAT 'carousel frauds'. The CJ answered that effectiveness of EU law required the disapplication of national provisions, drawing direct effect from treaty provisions (Art 325 (1) and (2) of the TFEU). This '*Taricco I*' judgment has triggered the reaction of the ICC, which, in a request for a preliminary reference (Order 24 of 2017), threatened the use of its 'counter-limits' doctrine, which would have created a systemic clash between EU law and Italian law. The CJEU moderated its '*Taricco I*' position in the so-called '*Taricco II*' judgment (*MAS and MB*), where it left discretion for the national court not to disapply national law in case this would have entailed a breach of the legality principle, as interpreted by the ICC. The ICC terminated this 'saga' with its judgment of 2018, no 115. The references are as follows: CJEU, Case C-105/14 *Criminal Proceedings against Ivo Taricco and others* [2015] ECLI:EU:C:2015:555; ICC, Order of 26 January 2017, no 24, at www.cortecostituzionale.it; CJEU, Case C-42/17 *Criminal Proceedings against MAS and MB* [2017] ECLI:EU:C:2017:936; ICC, judgment of 31 May 2018, no 115, at www.cortecostituzionale.it.

[8] Council Directive 80/777/EEC of 15 July 1980 on the approximation of the laws of the Member States relating to the exploitation and marketing of natural mineral waters [1980] OJ L229/1–10.

of 'mineral water'. Tap water mixed with carbon dioxide, as one can easily agree, could not be considered as mineral water for the purpose of the Directive, and therefore could not be marketed with that indication. At a domestic level, the undertaking was charged with the infringement of the Inspection Regulation of the Municipality of Nijmegen, prohibiting the stocking and delivery of goods of unsound composition intended for trade and human consumption.

The public prosecutor also relied on the Directive on natural mineral waters in his request for conviction.

In this situation, the judge referring the case questioned the applicability of the Directive for the solution of the case at stake. Therefore, the core of the referral boiled down to the issue of whether an authority of the MS, such as a prosecuting entity, could invoke against a national a provision of a directive in a case which is not covered by the MS's own legislation or implementing provision. It covered, in a nutshell, the question of whether a directive could bring about detrimental direct effects for individuals and how they could do so; second, it covered the issue of whether the Court can be bound to directives via the instrument of consistent interpretation.[9]

B. The Judgment of the Court

This referral gave the Court the chance to dig into the issue of direct effects of directives not yet implemented and their relationship with criminal liability, a subject which was highly dynamic at that time.

After the seminal *Van Gend en Loos* of 1963, EU law history was made in the 1970s with the ramification of the doctrine of the direct effect of treaty provisions into the direct effect of directives following *Van Duyn*[10] and its progenies. In the 1980s, the CJ continued to further develop this complex doctrine.

In this judgment, confronted with the direct effect of directives and an individual's criminal liability, the CJ had examined the first two questions together, since they both referred to the issue of 'detrimental direct effects', ie, direct effects which are detrimental for the individual concerned and do not confer on her/him any right, as was the situation in the classical *Van Gend en Loos* case.

Starting from its case *Becker*,[11] on tax collection and VAT, the Court stated that provisions of directives, sufficiently precise and unconditional, may be relied upon by an individual against the MS where the MS fails to implement the directive by the end of the implementation period or if it has been implemented incorrectly.

This means that a MS which has not adopted the implementing measures required by the directive may not plead, as against individuals, its own failure to perform the obligation the directive entails. This results from the nature of the

[9] In this chapter, the terms consistent interpretation and indirect effect will be used interchangeably.
[10] Case 41/74 *Van Duyn* [1974] ECR 1337.
[11] Case 8/81 *U Becker v Finanzamt Münster-Innenstadt* [1982] ECR 53.

obligation of the then Article 189 of the Treaty (now Article 288 of the Treaty on the Functioning of the European Union (TFEU)), which is of a binding nature toward states, and therefore entails that the individuals concerned should be able to rely on that binding nature.

The Court then moves on to analyse whether a directive can impose obligations on individuals, an issue that was tackled in *Marshall*,[12] which concerned the case of a dietician dismissed from the national health authority on the ground that she had reached retirement age. In *Marshall*, the Court held that the direct effect of directives can be invoked against the state irrespective of whether it acts as an employer or as *autorite' publique*. However, direct effect cannot operate against other individuals, thus denying that directives can have a so-called 'horizontal direct effect'. The logic of the CJ is 'to prevent the State from taking advantage of its own failures to comply with Community Law'.[13]

Developing its *Marshall* doctrine in *Kolpinghuis Nijmegen*, the Court held that 'a directive may not *of itself* impose obligations on an individual and that a provision of a directive may not be relied upon as such against such a person before a national court'.[14] Thus, as long as direct effect is concerned, a directive cannot display horizontal direct effect.

The second question tackled in *Kolpinghuis Nijmegen* concerned whether the Directive could bear indirect effect, in the sense that the national court 'may or must take into account of a directive as an aid to the interpretation of a rule of national law'.[15] In other words, if EU law could not work as a foundation of a duty of incrimination, can the national law, interpreted in harmony with or in light of the Directive, be used to establish such criminal liability? Must it be interpreted in such a way?

The CJ first recalled the *Von Colson* case,[16] where the doctrine of indirect effect or consistent interpretation was first posited, exactly 10 years after *Van Duyn*.

With the doctrine of consistent interpretation, the CJ further expanded the enforcement of EU law via the first European judges, ie, national courts. Consistent interpretation entails that, when a national court cannot derive direct effect from

[12] Case 152/84 *MH Marshall v Southampton and South-West Hampshire Area Health Authority* [1986] ECR723.

[13] *Cf ibid*, para 48: 'In either case it is necessary to prevent the State from taking advantage of its own failure to comply with Community law'. This clearly recalls the 'estoppel' argument; put forward in Case 148/78 *Criminal proceedings against Tullio Ratti* [1979] ECR 1629 as a rationale for direct effect. The lack of horizontal direct effect was also recently confirmed in the cases *Carp* and *Pfeiffer* quoted in de Witte (n 3) 335.

[14] *Kolpinghuis Nijmegen* (n 1) para 9.

[15] *Kolpinghuis Nijmegen* (n 1) para 11.

[16] Case 14/83 *Sabine von Colson and Elisabeth Kamann v Land Nordrhein-Westfalen* [1984] ECR 1891. This case added another room in the house of EU law enforcement. When direct effect is not an option, the judge should explore consistent interpretation. This means that in applying the national law and in particular the provisions of a national law specifically introduced to implement a directive, the court is required to interpret its national laws in light of the wording and purpose of the directive, on the basis of the principle of loyal cooperation.

a directive, because it is not precise, clear and unconditional enough, then the court can interpret its national law in conformity with EU law. Consistent interpretation is a category of interpretation which is also used by many other courts in Europe, and which echoes the *verfassungskonforme Auslegung* of the German Constitutional Court, for example.

However, in *Kolpinghuis Nijmegen* the CJ confronts the duty of consistent interpretation with the general principles of EU law, in particular the principles of legal certainty and non-retroactivity. In other words, the CJ states that in interpreting national law, the national court is limited by the general principles of EU law, namely the principle of legal certainty and non-retroactivity.

As stated a few months earlier in *Pretore di Salò*:[17]

> a directive cannot, of itself and independently of a national law adopted by a Member State for its implementation, have the effect of determining or aggravating the liability in criminal law of persons who act in contravention of the provisions of that directive.[18]

That is also why in the referring case, the CJ answered that, notwithstanding the duty of consistent interpretation which generally speaking applies (the *Von Colson* rule), 'the directive cannot of itself and independently of a law adopted for its implementation, have the effect of determining or aggravating the liability in criminal law of persons who act in contravention of the provisions of that directive'.[19]

Therefore, the *Von Colson* rule is interpreted together with the rule that a directive cannot display 'detrimental' and 'descendant' direct effect, in order to set the same limitation of direct effect also to consistent interpretation. In so doing, the Court reinforces the protective dimension of EU law toward the individuals.

The third issue of the judgment dealt with the question of whether one can rely upon a directive via consistent interpretation before the expiry of the period prescribed for implementation.

Here the Court states that 'it makes no difference to those answers if on the material date the period which the Member State had in which (sic!) to adapt national law had not yet expired'.[20]

This part of the judgment is not well explained or reasoned, which is why it has been criticised by scholarship, and later on, also clarified.[21]

The next section is devoted to understanding the judgment, by putting it into perspective with the case law of that time and unravelling its meaning for EU law and EU criminal law.

[17] Case 14/86 *Pretore di Salò v Persons unknown* [1987] ECR 2545.

[18] *Kolpinghuis Nijmegen* (n 1) para 13.

[19] *Kolpinghuis Nijmegen* (n 1) para 14.

[20] *Kolpinghuis Nijmegen* (n 1) para 15.

[21] *cf* Case C-212/04 *Konstantinos Adeneler and Others v Ellinikos Organismos Galaktos (ELOG)* [2006] ECR I-06057.

III. Revisiting *Kolpinghuis Nijmegen*. Direct Effect and Consistent Interpretation of Directives as a One-Way Road: The Limitation of 'Descendant' and 'Detrimental' Vertical Direct and Indirect Effects

Together with primacy, direct effect is one of the main pillars of EU law. Since *Van Gend en Loos* in 1963, it has contributed in carving out European and MSs' legal systems in a way that nobody could have imagined.[22] Later on, other doctrines were added to this system of enforcement of EU law into the legal orders of the MSs, namely consistent interpretation and the residual state liability doctrine.

In 1987, the Court was building the doctrine of direct effect of directives, and also the doctrine of consistent interpretation. Among the recently posited bricks, we have recalled *Becker*, *Marshall*, *Von Colson* and *Pretore di Salò*, which are the four judgments referred to by the CJ in *Kolpinghuis Nijmegen*. Earlier, the CJ had tackled the issue of direct effect of directives with milestone cases such as *Van Duyn* and *Ratti*,[23] next to *Becker* and *Marshall*.

The direct effect of directives has triggered fierce criticism in many corners: in academic circles;[24] from other courts;[25] and also within the same CJ.[26] What appeared particularly problematic was the case law on the rationale and the scope of direct effect. Interestingly, it is one of the most vivid areas EU law, which is also highly debated these days.[27]

Five years after *Van Duyn*, the CJ in *Ratti* took the opportunity to express a new rationale to justify the direct effect of directives, in the so-called estoppel argument.[28] The estoppel argument entails that a state is precluded, estopped, by its failure to properly implement a directive from refusing to recognise its

[22] de Witte (n 3) and M Dougan, 'When Worlds Collide! Competing Vision of the Relationship between Direct Effect and Supremacy' (2007) 44 *Common Market Law Review*, Issue 4, 931–63.

[23] *Ratti* (n 10).

[24] T Tridimas, 'Black, White and Shades of Grey: Horizontality Revisited' (2002) 21 *Yearbook of European Law* 237; A Albors-Llorens, 'The Direct Effect of EU Directives: Fresh Controversy or a Storm in a Teacup?' (2014) 39 *European Law Review* 850–62, at 3–4, fn 15, and the literature there referred to.

[25] French *Conseil d'Etat*, judgment 20 octobre 1989 – Nicolo – Rec. Lebon p 190, at www.conseil-etat.fr/Decisions-Avis-Publications/Decisions/Les-decisions-les-plus-importantes-du-Conseil-d-Etat/20-octobre-1989-Nicolo (last accessed 11 February 2019).

[26] F Mancini wrote that this judgment goes beyond the letter of Article 189 of the EC Treaty. GF Mancini and D Keeling, 'Language, Culture, and Politics in the Life of the Court of Justice' (1995) *Columbia Journal of European Law* 397, 401.

[27] For the most recent case law, see Case C-385/17 *Hein* [2018] ECLI:EU:C:2018:1018 and a comment from L S Rossi, 'The Kücükdeveci Ambiguity: "Derivative" Horizontal Direct Effects for Directives?', available at http://eulawanalysis.blogspot.com (last accessed 5 March 2019).

[28] This argument articulates that since MSs are bound to transpose directives, they are prevented, or estopped, from exploiting the effects of their failure to implement a directive, once the time limit for the implementation has expired. *Cf Ratti* (n 10).

direct effect. Had the state in question implemented the directive properly, then the individual would have been capable to invoke it before a national court. Had it not been the case, then the state cannot rely on the individual's wrongdoing, with the consequence that the national law in conflict with it should have been disapplied, because of the force of direct effect. In *Ratti*, the CJ recognised the 'ascendant' vertical direct effect, ie, from the individual towards the state, and not vice versa. The direct effect of EU law is therefore an enrichment of the legal sphere of the individual, and not a detriment to it.

Kolpinghuis Nijmegen is a landmark case in EU law for several reasons: it stated the lack of direct effect *in malam partem*, or detrimental and descendant direct effects, consistently with the *Pretore di Salò* case, but in addition to that, it also stated that indirect effect or consistent interpretation undergoes the same limitations. It therefore strengthens the protective dimension of EU law enforcement and consolidates it into limitations for direct and indirect effects.

Compared to *Pretore di Salò*, where the conclusion was reached on the basis of the nature of directives, in *Kolpinghuis Nijmegen* the CJ motivates its position on the general principles of EU law, in particular legal certainty or legality and non-retroactivity.[29] And this is precisely what makes *Kolpinghuis Nijmegen* a foundational case for European criminal law. This is indeed what turns it into a constitutional milestone, because it integrates national constitutional traditions into the European composite constitution.

The Court configured direct effect and consistent interpretation, in this case, as a one-way road: from the individual towards the state. The other direction, ie, from the state against individuals (so-called 'reverse direct effect'), has not proved to be acceptable by the CJ. The logic behind it is that the CJEU has never established that a state could use EU law it did not implement to invoke it against its citizens. This situation is in conflict with the idea of the social pact between the (then, European Economic Community, and now) EU and individuals established in *Van Gend en Loos*. This relationship, though mediated by the state, would never accept that a state could invoke against its own citizens a breach of EU law to its own benefit. This explains also part of the criticism raised against the '*Taricco I*' rule.[30]

One of the criticisms of the case is that the time factor of the expiry of the transposition period for directives appears to be irrelevant for the Court. In this way the Court first of all does not seem to pay attention to the powers and constitutional prerogatives of the national legislatures; second, by differentiating the temporal regime of the direct effect from consistent interpretation, the CJ does create an 'unnecessary complexity', which makes it more difficult for practitioners to enforce EU law.[31]

[29] S Coutts, 'Supranational Public Wrongs: The Possibilities and Limitations of European Union Criminal Law (2017) *Common Market Law Review* 771–804, at 781.

[30] The '*Taricco I* rule' seems to accept reverse direct effect, but in that case the provisions at stake were Art 325 (1) and (2) TFEU. See section IV below and the commentaries given in Chapter 15.

[31] G Betlem, 'The Doctrine of Consistent Interpretation – Managing Legal Uncertainty' (2002) *Oxford Journal of Legal Studies* 397–418, at 403.

Betlem, for example, observed that there is no justified difference between direct effect and indirect effect: recalling Van Gerven, who argued that if the rationale for consistent interpretation is the same as for direct effect, ie, a punishment against incorrect, delayed or non-implementation, Betlem concluded that the functioning should be the same, ie, to operate only after the expiry of the period of implementation.[32]

The solution to this dilemma arrived many years later, with *Adeneler*,[33] where the Court deployed the principle of loyal cooperation in order to create a duty to refrain from interpreting national law in a way that could jeopardise the attainment of the goals of the directive, also before the expiry of the transposition period.

Another criticism towards the CJ concerns the overall coherence of its case law on 'horizontal' direct and indirect effects; indeed, in *Faccini Dori*,[34] the Court, whilst repeating the *Marshall* rule, accepted that consistent interpretation can create duties upon one individual in a procedure started by another individual.[35] In short, while direct effect of directives is still not admitted in so-called horizontal situations, with the caveat of a broad interpretation of state authorities,[36] it is established that in horizontal situations EU law can create duties towards individuals, since in that situation the legal basis is given by the domestic law interpreted consistently with a directive, and not the directive itself. Though it is not possible here to deepen this issue, it has to be noted that direct effect of EU law has been enriched with cases such as *Mangold* and followers,[37] and has been revitalised in the last few years as direct effect of provisions of the Charter of Fundamental Rights,[38] which now has the same status as Treaty provisions, ex Art 6(1) TEU.

In the next section, we turn our attention to the case law following *Kolpinghuis Nijmegen*.

IV. The Legacy of *Kolpinghuis Nijmegen* in the Case Law

Kolpinghuis Nijmegen has left an important legacy in EU law. In the 1996 *Luciano Arcaro* (hereinafter: *Arcaro*) ruling,[39] the CJ confirmed that consistent interpretation is a duty descending from the principle of loyal cooperation.

[32] G Betlem, 'The Principle of Indirect Effect of Community Law' (1995) *European Review of Private Law* 1–19, at 12.

[33] Case C-212/04 *Konstantinos Adeneler and Others v Ellinikos Organismos Galaktos* (ELOG) [2006] ECR I-06057.

[34] Case C-91/92 *Paola Faccini Dori v Recreb Srl* [1994] ECR I-03325.

[35] L Squintani and H Vedder, 'Toward Inverse Direct Effect? A Silent Development of a Core European Law Doctrine' (2014) *RECIEL* 145.

[36] Case C-188/89 *A. Foster and others v British Gas Plc* [1990] ECR 1990 I-03313.

[37] Case C-144/04 *W Mangold v R Helm* [2005] ECLI:EU:C:2005:709.

[38] Case C-414/06 *Vera Egenberger v Evangelisches Werk für Diakonie und Entwicklung e.V.* [2018] ECLI:EU:C:2018:257.

[39] Case C-168/95 *Criminal Proceedings against Luciano Arcaro* [1996] ECR 1996 I-04705.

In *Arcaro* the Court was confronted with a question that arose after *Marshall*, ie, the issue of the effects of directives, after that the Court denied horizontal direct effects. That position, motivated by the estoppel doctrine, proved to be a difficult one to hold on to. But the Court tried to smooth out the consequences of that doctrine, by finding other channels to enforce EU law, by-passing horizontal direct effects.

In *Marleasing* and *Dominquez*, the Court accepted that if national law and the national legal system allow room for interpretation, then directives can govern the dispute and also disputes between private parties. The legal sources are therefore a combination of European and national legal acts, where the European one 'jumps in' to integrate the national legal acts.[40]

However, the Court was once again faced with the problems seen in *Kolpinghuis Nijmegen* while deciding on a preliminary reference raised by a local court in Vicenza, Italy, where Mr Arcaro, a legal representative of an undertaking working precious materials, was being prosecuted for discharging cadmium into the river Bacchiglione, without having submitted an application for the relevant authorisation, as provided for in the Directive.

This was a typical *Kolpinghuis Nijmegen* situation, ie, a national law not being compliant with a European directive aiming at protecting the environment: could the State therefore rely on such a European provision against an individual, even though this would impair that individual's position?

Here the Court did not even examine whether the provision was sufficiently clear, precise and unconditional, but stated that 'a directive may not by itself create obligations for an individual and that a provision of a directive may not therefore be relied upon as such against such a person'.[41] Once excluding direct effect, the CJ confirmed that neither via consistent interpretation a directive 'cannot (…) have the effect of determining or aggravating the criminal liability of an individual who acts in contravention of the provisions of that directive'.[42]

Another ruling that ran along the same lines as *Arcaro*, and which was decided shortly after in the same year, was *Criminal Proceedings against X (re: Display Workers)*,[43] in which the CJ applied the *Kolpinghuis Nijmegen* rule to a case where the issue at stake was about the analogical interpretation of pre-existing crimes.[44] The issue in *Criminal proceedings against X* was about the extent of liability in criminal law arising under legislation adopted for the purpose of implementing a directive; the principle that a provision of the criminal law may not be applied extensively to the detriment of the defendant, which is the corollary of the principle of legality in relation to crime and punishment and more generally of the

[40] Betlem (n 31).

[41] *Arcaro* (n 39), para 36.

[42] *Arcaro* (n 39), para 37.

[43] Joined cases C-74/95 and C-129/95 *Criminal Proceedings against X* [1996] ECR I-06609.

[44] R Sicurella, 'Art. 49. Principi della legalità e della proporzionalità dei reati e delle pene' in R Mastroianni et al (a cura di), *Carta dei diritti fondamentali dell'Unione Europea* (Giuffrè, 2017) 976.

principle of legal certainty, precludes bringing criminal proceedings in respect of conduct not clearly defined as culpable law.

This position of the CJ has been criticised by Betlem since in both cases the Court acknowledged that the duty of consistent interpretation is limited in criminal law situations, but the CJ did not reach the same conclusion in civil and administrative cases.[45] This constitutes a disparity of treatment which is not well justified.

Another application of the case in question was represented by another ruling called *Criminal Proceedings against X (re: Counterfeited Goods)*,[46] which should be interpreted as an extension of the *Kolpinghuis Nijmegen* rule to regulations. Of course, it does apply to those specific regulations that empower the MSs to adopt penalties to punish the infringements established in those same regulations.[47]

Perhaps the most famous progenies of *Kolpinghuis Nijmegen* are two more recent cases, *Berlusconi* and *Pupino*.[48]

Without going into these cases in depth,[49] it is worth mentioning that *Berlusconi* was a case where the State created a manifest breach of EU law, by passing new legislation, allegedly more favourable for the suspect, Mr Berlusconi, who was the Prime Minister of Italy at the time.

The *Berlusconi* case represents the link between the legality principle and the principle of the *favor rei*. Before the entry into force of the Charter of Fundamental Rights, the CJ ascribed the principle to the common constitutional traditions, and used it to rule the case.[50]

With the judgment in *Pupino*, the Court transferred the logic of the *Kolpinghuis Nijmegen* rule to framework decisions, which were the 'counterparts' of the directives for the Third Pillar.

In the *Pupino* case the issue at stake concerned the interpretation of a framework decision which did not have an impact on the criminal liability of the individual, but on the rules of procedure to be followed for the acquisition of testimony of minor victims of crimes. In this case, we also see the influence of the principle of legality interpreted as procedural legality, in contrast to substantive legality.

Interestingly, in *Pupino* the CJ does not mention the classical limitations of the *Kolpinghuis Nijmegen* rule, but it states that consistent interpretation cannot entail an interpretation *contra legem*. The Court acknowledges that the substantive dimension of criminal law is not significant in this case, but rather the procedural dimension. In *Pupino* we are therefore confronted with the procedural dimension of the legality principle. That is why the domestic court has to assess, in light of

[45] Betlem (n 31) 406.

[46] Case C-60/02 *Criminal Proceedings against X* [2004] ECR I-00651.

[47] *Ibid*, para 62.

[48] Joined cases C-387/02, C-391/02 and C-403/02 *Criminal Proceedings against Silvio Berlusconi, Sergio Adelchi and Marcello Dell'Utri and Others* [2005] ECR I-03565.
Case C-105/03 *Criminal Proceedings against Maria Pupino* [2005] ECR I-05285.

[49] See, chapters 4 and 5 of this book.

[50] Sicurella (n 44) 989.

the principle of fair trial of the European Convention on Human Rights, whether the results of the interpretation process still respect the fundamental rights of the accused person, in particular the principle of fair trial. The CJ leaves this assessment to the national court.

In this case law, the Court therefore also used direct effect and consistent interpretation to forge a protective dimension in the context of EU law enforcement, and this is to be read in the several declinations of the *Kolpinghuis Nijmegen* rule discussed above.

The *Taricco* case, however, finds the *Kolpinghuis Nijmegen* rule put 'under stress'.

If the *Kolpinghuis Nijmegen* rule entails that a directive or a regulation, cannot, of itself and independently of a national law adopted by a MS for its implementation, have the effect of determining or aggravating the liability in criminal law of persons who act in contravention of the provisions of the directive, one logically could think that the same should apply to a treaty provision.

However, for the Court in *Taricco*, the disapplication of the national rule of time limitation would in no way lead to a conviction of the accused for an act or omission which did not constitute a criminal offence under national law at the time when it was committed … nor to the application of a penalty which, at that time was not laid down by national law.[51]

The CJ apparently saves the *Kolpinghuis Nijmegen* rule, because it does not frame the time limitation as having a substantive nature, but it interprets it as a merely procedural institute. In practice, it does not pay attention either to the fact that this would represent a factual denial of the *Kolpinghuis Nijmegen* rule.

Years before *Taricco*, this problem of framing situations as procedural or substantive had already been discussed as a possible risk for the individual concerned: a change of laws considered as procedural could have had a 'detrimental effect for the defendant, amounting in practice to determining or aggravating his/her criminal liabilities, in a manner which undermines the spirit if not even the letter of the safeguards developed in the *Kolpinghuis Nijmegen* case law'.[52]

The *Taricco* case has represented a sort of 'denial' of the *Kolpinghuis Nijmegen* rule, in the sense that it admitted in practice, based on direct effect of treaty provisions, a detrimental and descendent direct effect, based on the disapplication of the national law. So, in a sense, it is not such a surprise that, after solicitations of the Italian Constitutional Court, the CJ mitigated its *Taricco I* rule in its *MAS and MB* case, also known as *Taricco II*, by allowing the national court to assess whether the disapplication of national law would entail a breach of the legality principle, as claimed by the Italian Constitutional Court, but also calling upon the duties of the legislature to take the necessary measures.[53]

[51] *Taricco* (n 7), para 56.

[52] A Dashwood, M Dougan, E Spaventa and D Wyatt, 'European Union Law' (Hart Publishing, 2011) 244 ff.

[53] Case C-42/17 *Criminal Proceedings against MAS and MB* ECLI:EU:C:2017:936, paras 59–62.

V. Conclusions: The Emergence of the General Principles of a Protective European Criminal Law

The *Kolpinghuis Nijmegen* judgment represents one of the milestone cases of the CJEU. It is a judgment in which the CJ started to build its catalogue of principles and fundamental rights that have contributed to shape EU law as the law of a unique polity, based on the rule of law, whose members are not simply the Member States but also their citizens, who are also EU citizens.

Two years before the '*Greek Maize*' case, the Court stated that the enforcement of EU law, taking place thanks to European legal instruments, via direct effect, or via their interpretation by domestic courts, could not have detrimental effects from the states towards the individuals. As such, it descends directly from the *Van Gend en Loos* logic, but complements it with a new perspective.

By enshrining the principles of legality and non-retroactivity among the general principles of EU law, the CJ gave a crucial contribution in creating the protective dimension of European criminal law, which later on found expression in the Charter of Fundamental Rights of the EU, in particular in Article 49. The Court was already developing the so-called shield dimension of fundamental rights and principles of European criminal law, before the '*Greek Maize*' case, which is to be understood as an expression of the sword dimension of EU enforcement apparatus, via the '*longa manus*' of the Member States.

Kolpinghuis Nijmegen, its legacy and the subsequent evolution of European criminal law,[54] has developed in the sense that if the EU has a competence in criminal law, as the Lisbon Treaty eventually decided, it is not EU law as such to establish criminal liability. The legality principle in the EU is based on the legality of the MSs' legal orders. In *Advocaten voor de Wereld*,[55] the CJ stated that the legality principle is to be assessed with reference to national law. In *Berlusconi*, the Court stated that the principle of *favor rei* was against the application of the more stringent regime, in compliance with EU law. The Union legislation was not deemed to be able to establish criminal liability. In Article 83(1) and (2) of the TFEU, the Union can adopt directives that the MSs have to transpose.

To conclude, the European integration process has given a criminal law competence to the EU, that dimension is still, to some extent, limited to a few supranational and core areas, and also functional to the fulfilment of other regulatory goals.[56] In spite of this, the CJ had started to define a protective dimension

[54] Case C-176/03 *Commission of the European Communities v Council of the European Union (re: Environmental Crimes)* [2005] ECR I-07879; Case C-440/05 *Commission of the European Communities v Council of the European Union (re: Ship Source Pollution)* [2007] ECR I-09097.

[55] Case C-303/05 *Advocaten voor de Wereld VZW v Leden van de Ministerraad* [2007] ECR I-03633.

[56] Coutts (n 29) 801 ff.

of EU law from 1987, with the foundational case of *Kolpinghuis Nijmegen*, which enshrined the legality in criminal law as a limit to the enforcement of the same EU law into the legal orders of the MSs. It is therefore important to recall the constitutional nature of this case and of its legacy, because it contributed to the construction of the EU edifice, whose main component is the respect of the rule of law, and also helped shape the process of integration through fundamental rights and principles, and not only through law.

Indirect Effect of EU Law after Kolpinghuis Nijmegen *(C-80/86): Consistent Interpretation in Dutch Criminal Courts*

JANNEMIEKE OUWERKERK

I. Introduction

The aim of this chapter is to discuss the impact of the 1987 *Kolpinghuis Nijmegen* judgment[1] on national law, with specific attention on criminal law. This will be done by reflecting on how courts in the Netherlands have been performing their duty of directive-conform interpretation in matters relating to criminal law since the case, and on the role of EU minimum rules in that regard. This chapter therefore starts with a general outline of Dutch post-*Kolpinghuis* case law on consistent interpretation and the limits thereto (section II). Subsequently, it will be discussed whether and how the doctrine of consistent interpretation has actually been functioning in criminal courts in the Netherlands. The discussion will then move on to whether the increasing impact of minimum rules may have reduced the importance of consistent interpretation in the field of criminal law (section III). The chapter then concludes with some final remarks (section IV).

II. Directive-Conform Interpretation in the Netherlands Post-*Kolpinghuis*

In order to solve potential clashes and discrepancies between EU norms and national (implementing) legislation, the EU Court of Justice (CJEU) has developed the principles of *direct effect* – enabling individuals to directly invoke EU norms in domestic courts[2] – and *indirect effect* – requiring courts to interpret domestic norms in line with EU law.[3]

[1] Case C-80/86 *Kolpinghuis Nijmegen BV* [1987] ECR 3982.
[2] Case C-26/62 *Van Gend en Loos* [1963] ECR 1, para II.B.
[3] Case C-14/83 *Sabine von Colson and Elisabeth Kamann v Land Nordrhein-Westfalen* [1984] ECR 1891, para 26.

This chapter deals solely with the principle of *indirect effect* and the resulting duty of directive-conform interpretation of national law – it specifically aims to deal with the boundaries to that duty. And while the previous commentary on the case examines the impact of *Kolpinghuis* on EU law and EU principles,[4] this commentary seeks to discuss its impact on national law. It therefore relies primarily on national sources of law; follow-up CJEU case law on the matter will only be referred to where necessary.

The precise facts and the details of the CJEU ruling in the *Kolpinghuis* case have already been expounded in the preceding commentary.[5] It therefore suffices here to briefly call to mind that in the *Kolpinghuis* case, the CJEU held that the general principles of EU law, and particularly the principles of legal certainty and non-retroactivity, do limit a national court's duty to take into account a directly applicable directive as an aid with which to interpret national law – that is to say where this would have the effect of determining the criminal liability of individuals on the basis of an EU norm itself, and independently of a national act adopted to transpose this EU norm.[6]

As a prelude to the subsequent section on directive-conform interpretation in Dutch criminal courts, the following provides a general outline of how in various fields of law the highest courts in the Netherlands[7] have been acting on the duty of consistent interpretation after *Kolpinghuis*. This outline is far from comprehensive, although shares the most principled and telling considerations concerning directive-conform interpretation in the Dutch legal order.

A. The *Kolpinghuis* Doctrine and Administrative Fines in the Netherlands

A first case that deserves to be mentioned concerns the 2009 *Mandemakers* case in which the Administrative Jurisdiction Division extended the *Kolpinghuis* rule to cover administrative fines.[8] The dispute in this case was about a fine imposed by the Dutch Minister of Social Affairs on the kitchen centre 'Mandemakers' for having disregarded the working hours as prescribed in the Dutch Act on working hours. The fine was based on the European interpretation of the term 'working hours', as included in Article 2 of Directive 2003/88/EC.[9] But before the Court, the question arose whether the Minister was competent to impose this fine at all.

[4] See the previous commentary in chapter 1 by Luisa Marin.

[5] *Ibid.*

[6] See *Kolpinghuis* (n 1) para 13.

[7] The Supreme Court of the Netherlands (*Hoge Raad der Nederlanden*, HR) is the highest court in the areas of civil law, criminal law and tax law. The court of last instance in matters of administrative law is the Administrative Jurisdiction Division of the Council of State (*Afdeling Bestuursrechtspraak van de Raad van State*, RvS).

[8] RvS 4 maart 2009, ECLI:NL:RVS:2009:BH4621 (*Mandemakers*).

[9] Council and Parliament Directive 2003/88/EC of 4 November 2003 concerning certain aspects of the organisation of working time [2003] OJ L299/9.

After all, the Administrative Jurisdiction Division had held that the Directive's definition of the term was wrongfully not implemented into the Dutch Act on working hours.

It was argued, from the viewpoint of the Minister, that by means of a directive-conform interpretation of the Dutch Act on working hours, the imposition of the fine could nevertheless be upheld. This argument was, however, rejected. The Administrative Jurisdiction Division has ruled that the *Kolpinghuis* doctrine applies in this case too – even though the dispute at hand was not related to the scope of criminal liability, but to the scope of liability for an administrative fine. This decision can be considered to logically fit in with the position of the administrative fine in the Dutch legal order. The phenomenon of administrative fines in the Netherlands dates back to the 1990s and has significantly expanded since. In comparison with criminal fines, the imposition of administrative fines aims to result in a more effective system of sanctioning violations. But because of the nature of violations that qualify for administrative fines to be imposed (eg road traffic offences), considered also in relation to the nature of the corresponding sanction (ie punitive), it is standing case law of the European Court of Human Rights (ECtHR) that punitive fines such as those allowed under Dutch administrative law[10] constitute a 'criminal charge' in the sense of Article 6 of the European Convention on Human Rights (ECHR) (right to a fair trial).[11] The Court's concise reasoning in the *Mandemakers* case may well be assumed to be implicitly based on this line of ECtHR case law.

B. General Guidelines on Directive-Conform Interpretation Post-*Kolpinghuis*

The 2007 Supreme Court's judgment in the *Wandelvierdaagse* case[12] is considered to be a turning point in its case law on the duty of consistent interpretation and the role of legal certainty in that regard.[13] In this tax case the question was raised whether the organisation of a public, four day walking event had to be charged with a low or high tax rate. The applicable national provisions contravened the provisions in the relevant EU directive in the sense that national law suggested the low tax rate, whereas EU law seemed to require the high rate. However, to interpret the national provisions in conformity with the rules of the EU directive was held to

[10] In contrast to reparatory administrative fines.

[11] See especially: *Öztürk v Germany* App no 8544/79 (ECtHR, 21 February 1984). T Barkhuysen and ML van Emmerik, 'Het EVRM als inspiratiebron en correctiemechanisme voor de Awb' in T Barkhuysen, W den Ouden and JEM Polak (eds), *Bestuursrecht harmoniseren. 15 jaar Awb* (Boom Juridische Uitgevers, 2010) 565–67.

[12] HR (Tax Chamber) 10 August 2007, ECLI:NL:HR:2007:AZ3758, *AB* 2007, 291, m.nt. Widdershoven (*Wandelvierdaagse*).

[13] See S Haket, 'Coherence in the Application of the Duty of Consistent Interpretation in EU Law' (2015) *Review of European Administrative Law* 215, 242 and accompanying footnotes. See also Widdershoven's case note to the *Wandelvierdaagse* judgment, n 12 above.

be impossible by the Court of Appeal; such an interpretation would deviate from what the Dutch legislature intended according to parliamentary history, and would therefore violate the principle of legal certainty. For in the continental legal system of the Netherlands, the principle of legal certainty significantly limits the courts' powers to change the scope of legal provisions, this is to ensure that individuals can rely on the law as determined by the democratically legitimised legislature.[14]

In the *Wandelvierdaagse* case, the Supreme Court would eventually hold that the Court of Appeal's decision was wrong in law, although the Court of Appeal's line of reasoning did correspond to the then prevailing approach in both the Supreme Court and the Administrative Jurisdiction Division of the Council of State (hereinafter: The Administrative Jurisdiction Division). After all, up until its ruling in the *Wandelvierdaagse* case, the Supreme Court in a number of private law cases used to heavily rely upon parliamentary history and national legislative intent, the consultation of which in fact constitutes significant methods of statutory interpretation within the legal order of the Netherlands.[15] In the 1995 *Asseldonk/Ter Schure* case, this led the Supreme Court to rule that national implementing legislation containing an unambiguous exclusion for women to get access to ecclesiastical offices could not be interpreted in line with the then prevailing Equal Treatment Directive. This Directive only allowed for an exemption from the rule of gender equality where the worker's gender is a determining factor for the occupational activities concerned, either because of their nature, or because of the context in which they are carried out. But because the wording of the national provision as well as the accompanying legislative history were unambiguously expressing the intent of excluding women from these offices, the Supreme Court considered it outside its discretion to set aside the national provision.[16] A similar line of reasoning was followed in the 1996 *Pink Floyd/Rigu Sound* case – dealing with the consequences of the then prevailing Rental Directive which even after the expiration of its transposition deadline was at the time not yet implemented into Dutch legislation conflicting with it – where it was added that a consistent interpretation of the unambiguously worded national rule would violate the principle of legal certainty.[17]

[14] There is no general codification of the principle of legal certainty in Dutch law. As to specific fields of law, however, eg criminal law, the principle of legal certainty is considered to be codified as it falls under the scope of the written principle of legality in Art 1 of the Dutch Criminal Code and Art 1 of the Dutch Code of Criminal Procedure. On the roots and interpretation of legal certainty in Dutch administrative law, see: G ten Berge and RJGM Widdershoven, *The principle of Legitimate Expectations in Dutch Constitutional and Administrative Law. Netherlands Report to the Fifteenth International Congress of Comparative Law* (1998) 421–52.

[15] See, eg, MJ Borgers, 'Wetshistorische interpretatie in de strafrechtspraak' in MS Groenhuijsen and JBHM Simmelink (eds), *Glijdende schalen. Liber amicorum J. de Hullu* (Wolf Legal Publishers, 2003) 51–69; Asser/Scholten, *Algemeen deel** 1974/11 (Tjeenk Willink) (book volume with commentaries on Dutch civil law).

[16] HR 20 October 1995, ECLI:NL:HR:1995:ZC1846, *NJ* 1995, 330 m.nt. Alkema (*Asseldonk/Ter Schure*) para 3.5.

[17] HR 25 October 1996, ECLI:NL:HR:1996:ZC2177, *NJ* 1996, 649 m.nt. Verkade (*Pink Floyd/Rigu Sound*) para 3.4.

The same approach was followed in the context of administrative law. In a 2002 case concerning the Dutch Interim Act on Ammonia and Livestock Farming, the Administrative Jurisdiction Division stated that this Interim Act exclusively and exhaustively provided the grounds on which a farmer could be refused a stock farm licence. For that reason, it considered itself unable to interpret the Interim Act in a manner that would make it consistent with the integrated pollution prevention and control (IPPC) Directive,[18] which was requiring the application of the 'best available techniques' for preventing environmental pollution.[19] And in the 2007 *Fortis* case, the Administrative Jurisdiction Division ruled correspondingly with regard to the framework for granting licences under the Dutch Nature Conservation Act. It was held that an interpretation of this act in line with the Habitat Directive[20] would amount to an extensive interpretation of the national Act which was considered contrary to the principle of legal certainty.[21]

In the *Wandelvierdaagse* judgment, however, the tax chamber of the Dutch Supreme Court ruled otherwise, thereby changing its traditional line of case law on the matter: In this case, it was held that if a national provision allows for an interpretation in conformity with the relevant EU directive, the national judge cannot rely on legislative history leading to an opposite interpretation. In fact, and contrary to previous case law, the Supreme Court stated that even the principle of legal certainty cannot be invoked to justify such an opposite interpretation based on parliamentary history, because that would deny the binding force of EU directives.[22] The foregoing applies even where consistent interpretation would be a detriment to individuals – like in the *Wandelvierdaagse* case in which an interpretation of national law in conformity with the relevant EU directive required the Netherlands to charge the organisers of the walking event with the higher tax rate. As such, it ties in with CJEU case law which over the years has demonstrated that a directive-conform interpretation of national law can result in imposing obligations upon individuals.[23]

In the *Wandelvierdaagse* judgment, as well as in subsequent judgments, the Supreme Court formulated two grounds to exempt from the obligation of consistent interpretation. The first ground relates to the standing rule that in the course of interpreting national law consistently, the national judge must presume the legislature's intention to fully comply with EU law.[24] Obviously, such a presumption cannot persist if parliamentary history unambiguously expresses the legislature's intention to divert national law from EU law; then parliamentary

[18] Council Directive 96/61/EC of 24 September 1996 concerning integrated pollution prevention and control [1996] OJ L257/26.

[19] RvS 13 November 2002, ECLI:NL:RVS:2002:AF0308, para 2.2.6.

[20] Council Directive 92/43/EEC of 21 May 1992 on the conservation of natural habitats and of wild fauna and flora [1992] OJ L206/7.

[21] RvS 28 February 2007, ECLI:NL:RVS:2007:AZ9494 (*Fortis*) para 2.10.

[22] *Wandelvierdaagse* (n 12) para 3.4.

[23] Joined cases C-397/01 and C-403/01 *Pfeiffer et al* [2004] ECR I-8835, para 110.

[24] This rule has been developed by the CJEU in Case C-334/92 *Wagner Miret* [1993] ECR I-6911, para 20.

history may be relied upon nevertheless to prevent the consistent interpretation of national law.[25]

The second ground to exempt from the duty of directive-conform interpretation generally applies where the very wording of the applicable national rule does not allow for such an interpretation.[26] Although very implicitly, this exception presumably refers to the *contra legem* restriction that follows from CJEU case law on the matter[27] and which aims to preserve the separation of legislative and judicial powers.[28] It should be noted, though, that in the 2013 *Albron* case (a private law case), the Supreme Court stated that the incompatible wording of the national provision cannot always be invoked to exempt from the duty of consistent interpretation; this may be different especially where the applicable national rule was adopted to implement an EU directive that aims to confer rights upon individuals, or where the case concerns a situation that, as evident from parliamentary history, was not yet foreseen by the legislature.[29] It remains to be seen whether and how this *Albron* adjustment to the *contra legem* prohibition will be applied by courts in the Netherlands.

We will also have to wait and see whether in matters of administrative law the Administrative Jurisdiction Division will follow the Supreme Court's line of reasoning in *Wandelvierdaagse* and beyond[30] – though that seems quite likely since the Supreme Court has in fact been following CJEU case law.

Be that as it may, based on what precedes it can, first, fairly be concluded that as time goes on, the importance of legislative history and national legislative intent have significantly been reduced in the fields of private law and tax law in the Netherlands. As a matter of principle, if a national provision allows for a directive-conform interpretation, the national judge cannot rely on national legislative history or intent leading to an opposite interpretation. Secondly, this means that the principle of legal certainty no longer necessarily functions as a limit to indirect effect of EU law, for the Supreme Court ruled that where national legislative history points in the direction of such an opposite interpretation, courts

[25] See *Wandelvierdaagse* (n 12), para 3.4. See also, in the field of private law, eg HR 21 September 2012, ECLI:NL:HE:2012:BW5879, *AB* 2012, 367, m.nt. Widdershoven (*Thuiskopie*), para 5.1.3; and HR 17 January 2014, ECLI:NL:HR:2014:88 (*Ryanair/PR Aviation*), para 3.5.2.

[26] See *Wandelvierdaagse* (n 12), para 3.

[27] Case C-105/03 *Maria Pupino* [2005] ECR I-5285. The prohibition of an interpretation *contra legem* has been invoked several times by courts in the Netherlands, but most of the time this was done very implicitly, merely referring to the incompatible wording of the national provision. See for instance the previously mentioned *Pink Floyd* and *Fortis* cases, nn 17 and 21 respectively. An example of a more recent case in which the Administrative Jurisdiction Division referred explicitly to the *contra legem* prohibition in relation to the wording of the national rule is RvS 11 June 2014, ECLI:NL:RVS:2014:2120, para 2.7.

[28] FGH Kristen, 'Hoe Europa de strafrechter dirigeert. Over de betekenis van de richtlijnconforme interpretatie voor het strafrecht en de uitbreiding daarvan tot kaderbesluit en kaderwet' in MS Groenhuijsen and JBHM Simmelink (eds), *Glijdende schalen. Liber amicorum J. de Hullu* (Wolf Legal Publishers, 2003) 395–96.

[29] HR 5 April 2013, ECLI:NL:HR:2013:BZ1780, *NJ* 2013, 389, m.nt. Verhulp (*Albron/FNV*) para 3.7.

[30] See also Haket (n 13) at 242.

can no longer easily escape their duty of consistent interpretation by relying on this fundamental legal principle.

Now we have seen that in the *Kolpinghuis* case it is exactly the principle of legal certainty that has to function as a limit to directive-conform interpretation, that is to say in cases where the doctrine of indirect legal effect comes into view in relation to EU directives which were implemented either too late, or incorrectly, or where transposition into national law did not take place at all. If in such cases a directive-conform interpretation would have the effect of determining or aggravating the criminal liability of individuals, the very duty of directive-conform interpretation does not apply as this would violate general principles of EU law, in particular the principles of legal certainty and non-retroactivity.[31] Therefore, while the previous outline only mentions cases outside the criminal law context, the next section seeks to demonstrate how *criminal* courts in the Netherlands have shaped their duty of consistent interpretation and the limits thereto.

III. Consistent Interpretation in Dutch Criminal Courts

In the absence of principled and guiding Supreme Court rulings on (the limits to) consistent interpretation in the area of criminal law, this section mainly has to rely on judgments from lower criminal courts, ie district courts and courts of appeal. It will, first, be shown, whether and how these courts have been performing their duty of directive-conform interpretation in relation to substantive criminal law, similar matters thus as in the *Kolpinghuis* case (subsection A). It will follow that the principle of legal certainty has not been functioning as a significant limiting factor, even though one might have expected otherwise. In an attempt to account for some of the inconsistencies and contradictions, the second part of this section will discuss why the duty of consistent interpretation seems to make less sense where the relevant EU norms constitute so-called minimum norms (subsection B).

A. Consistent Interpretation of Dutch Substantive Criminal Law: A Fragmented Picture

Not very long ago, in 2014, the Court of Appeal Arnhem-Leeuwarden was confronted with an issue almost equal to the issue in the *Kolpinghuis* case. The Court of Appeal had to decide whether the Dutch Act on Plant Protection Products and Biocides had to be interpreted as also prohibiting the possession and

[31] See *Kolpinghuis* (n 1). See also the third paragraph of section II and accompanying footnotes.

use of products containing the active substance carvone. An interpretation on the confirmative would probably be in line with Directive 91/414/EC;[32] with the adoption of Directive 2008/44/EC,[33] carvone was added to the list of unauthorised active substances of plant protection products. However, Directive 2008/44/EC had not yet been implemented – while it ought to be – at the time when the criminal acts took place (2010–2011) and when criminal proceedings were initiated against the defendant (2012). The Court of Appeal was therefore right in rejecting a directive-conform interpretation; a decision otherwise would have expanded the scope of the national criminal prohibition on the basis of the relevant directive itself, which would run counter to the *Kolpinghuis* doctrine.[34]

Despite the fact that to my knowledge no other typical *Kolpinghuis*-like cases have been brought before criminal courts in the Netherlands, it is still interesting to see how these courts have been dealing with the duty of consistent interpretation in other substantive criminal law cases, for the interpretation of definitions of crime in light of a higher ranked norm remains a sensitive issue *per se*.

The first category of cases that deserves attention concerns cases in which courts have rejected a directive-conform interpretation, while such an interpretation would have been to the suspects' benefit. It should be noted that these cases date from before the Supreme Court's judgment in the *Wandelvierdaagse* case and its successors – that might explain why in the 1992 *Chinese Konijnenbouten* case the Court of Appeal in 's-Hertogenbosch merely relied on a separation of powers argument to justify its rejection of a directive-conform interpretation. While it recognised the existence of a clear difference between the relevant directive and national legislation – meaning that pursuant to national law criminal liability occurred sooner than was required under EU law – it stated that such differences had to be solved through the adoption of legislation.[35]

Albeit implicitly, a similar argument was used in two related cases in 2004. These cases differ from the previous one in that the transposition of the relevant EU directive had not yet taken place, despite the expiration of its implementation deadline. It remains unclear from the verdicts for what exact reason the defendants' lawyers requested the Amsterdam District Court to interpret Dutch criminal law on insider trading in conformity with Directive 2003/6/EC[36] – though the fact that the request was done by defence lawyers suggests that in these cases a directive-conform interpretation would have been beneficial to their clients.

[32] Council Directive 91/414/EEC of 15 July 1991 concerning the placing of plant protection products on the market [1991] OJ L230/1.

[33] Commission Directive 2008/44/EC of 4 April 2008 amending Council Directive 91/414/EEC to include benthiavalicarb, boscalid, carvone, fluoxastrobin, Paecilomyces lilacinus and prothioconazole as active substances [2008] OJ L94/13.

[34] Court of Appeal Arnhem-Leeuwarden 23 April 2014, ECLI:NL:GHARL:2014:3361.

[35] See the Court of Appeal's considerations in HR 3 March 1992, ECLINL:PHR:1992:AB8369 (*Chinese Konijnenbouten*) para 6.1.2.

[36] European Parliament and Council Directive 2003/6/EC of 28 January 2003 on insider dealing and market manipulation [2003] OJ L96/16.

But the Amsterdam District Court referred to an extensive ongoing parliamentary debate on the exact interpretation and scope of the norms included in the relevant EU directive, the outcome of which was uncertain at the time. The Court considered itself incompetent to anticipate the outcome and therefore rejected a directive-conform interpretation of Dutch criminal law in these cases.[37]

A consistent interpretation was also rejected in a 1993 criminal case, this time by the Supreme Court. Directive 91/439/EEC[38] stipulated the mutual recognition of driving licences, but the then prevailing national legislation still required the exchange of a foreign driving licence to a national one after one year of residence in another Member State. If the national rule would have been interpreted in conformity with the directive, the suspect in this case would have gone unpunished. But, although the implementation deadline of Directive 91/439/EEC had not yet expired, the Supreme Court chose a systematic legal argument to reject a directive-conform interpretation of national law. It considered a directive-conform interpretation of national law impossible because of the foundational and systematic differences between both mechanisms.[39]

The aforementioned judgments demonstrate the orientation Dutch courts traditionally have towards legislative history and legislative intent, and how this orientation closely connects to a strict view of the doctrine of the separation of powers. It needs no explanation that such a strict view has gradually become influenced by the increasing amount of EU norms that may have direct or indirect effect. Therefore, and in view of developments in Dutch case law over the past decade (as described in section II), it can be seriously doubted whether the above arguments and alike would presently be invoked to justify a rejection of directive-conform interpretation – all the more since in these cases a directive-conform interpretation would have been to the individual's advantage.

The following demonstrates why in other, more recent, cases (the second category) the Court decided to actually apply the method of consistent interpretation. In one case, dating from 2000, the scope of a Dutch criminal prohibition seems to have broadened as a direct result of consistent interpretation. The Supreme Court upheld a lower court's interpretation of the term 'to destroy' in the sense of the Dutch Game Act. The suspect in this case, a building company, was prosecuted for having destroyed the nests of rooks. It was claimed that rather than destroying these nests, the company merely rendered them useless by having cut the trees in which the rooks' nests were built. This argument was rejected. Because the provision on the Dutch Game Act was adopted to implement the former Birds Directive, the Supreme Court approved the lower court's decision to interpret the Game Act in line with this Directive and to apply a broader definition of the term

[37] District Court Amsterdam 3 December 2014, ECLI:NL:RBAMS:2004:AR6884, para 3.1; and District Court Amsterdam 3 December 2014, ECLI:NL:RBAMS:2004:AR6888, para 3.1.

[38] Council Directive 91/439/EEC of 29 July 1991 on driving licences [1991] OJ L237/1 (no longer in force).

[39] HR 19 January 1993, ECLI:NL:HR:1993:ZC9192, para 6.3.

'to destroy' – encompassing the suspect's acts – than is commonly used in Dutch criminal law.[40]

Of course, the method of consistent interpretation can also have the result of limiting the scope of criminal liability, examples of which were easier found in Dutch case law. It is worth underlining that in some of these cases, courts have found themselves obliged to (also) rely on norms of primary law of the EU. Already in 1990, the Supreme Court held a Dutch criminal prohibition incompatible with an EU Directive read in conjunction with primary EU law. The then applicable Dutch Law on Birds prohibited the buying and selling of red grouse on the domestic market, even where it concerned red grouse lawfully killed in another EU Member State. The criminalisation of these acts offered a wider protection of wild birds than required under Directive 79/409/EEC,[41] and the question arose whether this national prohibition on imports could be justified under the former EC Treaty (former Article 36) on grounds of the protection of animals' health and life. In line with the CJEU's preliminary ruling on the matter,[42] the Supreme Court ruled in the negative. Indeed, the Directive as such did allow Member States to introduce stricter protective measures, but only where it concerned a migratory species or a seriously endangered species, neither of which applies to red grouse. The national criminal prohibition therefore had to be qualified as an unjustified restriction on imports.[43]

A similar reasoning can be found in three related criminal cases from 2006, although in these cases the District Court in 's-Hertogenbosch *only* relied upon the primary law of the EU, and not at all on norms in secondary legislation, such as a directive. The District Court had to try a general practitioner, a pharmacist, and a director of a pharmaceutical wholesale business. The three of them were inter alia suspected of the selling, delivering, or trading in unregistered – and therefore illegal – pharmaceutical products, prohibited under the then prevailing Dutch Medicines Act. But the Court observed that as an actual consequence of the criminal prohibition at hand, Dutch pharmaceutical businesses were prevented from putting on the internal market products that are illegal under Dutch law, though possibly legal under the laws of other EU Member States. This prohibition was therefore qualified as a measure of having equivalent effect as quantitative restrictions on exports, forbidden under the former EC Treaty (former Article 29), ie in so far as it applied to putting unregistered products on the *internal* market. In its own words, the Court applied the method of 'EC law-conform interpretation' of the Dutch Medicines Act, as a consequence of which the acts of the three suspects were declared as not criminally prohibited.[44]

[40] HR 11 July 2000, ECLI:NL:HR:2000:ZD1900, *NJ* 2000/606 (*Vernielen vogelnesten*), paras 3.3–3.4.

[41] Council Directive 79/409/EEC of 2 April 1979 on the conservation of wild birds [1979] OJ L103/1.

[42] Case C-169/89 *Van den Burg* [1990] ECR I-2143.

[43] HR 20 November 1990, ECLI:NL:PHR:1990:AD1286.

[44] District Court 's-Hertogenbosch 7 December 2006, ECLI:NL:RBSHE:2006:AZ3897; District Court 's-Hertogenbosch 7 December 2006, ECLI:NL:RBSHE:2006:AZ3934; District Court 's-Hertogenbosch 7 December 2006, ECLI:NL:RBSHE:2006:AZ3935.

In a case concerning human trafficking, the District Court of Maastricht seemed to rely on a kind of 'international law-conform' interpretation of national law, which in this area of crime also implies directive-conform interpretation – although an explicit reference to the relevant EU directive is lacking.[45] The District Court partly cleared the suspect of charges of 'sexual exploitation', criminalised under the Dutch 'human trafficking-provision' (Article 273f of the Dutch Criminal Code). The Court stated that to legally qualify sexual abuse as 'sexual exploitation', it is required that sexual desires are repeatedly taken out on victims over a longer period of time. Because the Court's statement is preceded by general remarks on the international legal background of the criminalisation of human trafficking, it is suggested that the Court's restrictive interpretation of the term 'sexual exploitation' is based on its interpretation of international norms.[46]

Be that as it may, the restrictive interpretation displayed by the District Court of Maastricht is a little surprising, for it seems to contrast with both the legislature's and the Supreme Court's viewpoint that, generally spoken, the international legal framework on human trafficking would stipulate an extensive interpretation of Article 273f of the Dutch Criminal Code.[47] This has brought several lower courts to convictions for human trafficking in cases that in common parlance would probably not be considered trafficking in human beings and exploitation. For instance, in 2013, the District Court of Midden-Nederland convicted a grandfather on the basis of Article 273f(2) of the Dutch Criminal Code for letting his granddaughter commit a single theft, an act that was qualified as 'exploitation of criminal activities' as laid down in Directive 2011/36/EU.[48] The question has been raised whether this Directive really means to refer to a situation as in the aforementioned case, especially since the preamble to Directive 2011/36/EU suggests a certain duration of activities.[49]

A third category of cases worth mentioning here concerns cases in which for no apparent reason courts have refrained from referring to higher ranking norms in EU directives which possibly could have clarified the scope of the applicable

[45] The international legal framework regarding the definitions of human trafficking offences encompasses both international treaties (eg Council of Europe conventions) and EU secondary legislation (such as directives).

[46] District Court Maastricht 22 March 2012, ECLI:NL:RBMAA:2012:BV9705, para 4.3.

[47] For instance, it is standing case law of the Supreme Court that to fulfill the definition of 'exploitation' the duration of the alleged exploitation activities constitutes merely one of the several relevant factors, rather than a strict requirement, see most recently HR 5 April 2016, ECLI:NL:HR:2016:554, *NJ* 2016, 315, m.nt. Van Kempen.

[48] District Court Midden-Nederland 9 July 2013, ECLI:NL:RBMNE:2013:2679. For the text of the Directive, see: European Parliament and Council Directive 2011/36/EU of 5 April 2011 on preventing and combating trafficking in human beings and protecting its victims, and replacing Council Framework Decision 2002/629/JHA [2011] OJ L101/1.

[49] PHPHMC van Kempen, 'Mensenhandel?' (2017) *Delikt and Delinkwent* 407. Recital 11 states: 'The expression "exploitation of criminal activities" should be understood as the exploitation of a person to commit, inter alia, pick-pocketing, shop-lifting, drug trafficking and other similar activities which are subject to penalties and imply financial gain.'

Dutch criminal prohibition. Over the past few years, this has occurred in money laundering cases particularly, in which the question arose whether the criminal prohibition of money laundering in Article 420bis of the Dutch Criminal Code should also cover so-called self-laundering (eg the acquisition or possession of property that derives from the suspect's *own* criminal activities). In defiance of its literal wording, the Dutch Supreme Court repeatedly held that the mere acquisition or possession of the proceeds of an individual's own crime could not be qualified as money laundering under Article 420bis of the Dutch Criminal Code. Later on, it was held that under these circumstances the same rule had to apply to the conversion, transfer, or use of such criminal proceeds. Such a restrictive interpretation of the national anti-money laundering provision was considered necessary to avoid ordinary crimes such as theft automatically falling under the scope of Article 420bis of the Dutch Criminal Code. The Supreme Court's activism was both welcomed and condemned, but many agreed that the Supreme Court was wrong in *not* referring at all to EU Directive 2005/60/EC[50] – either to find a more convincing justification for such a restrictive interpretation of money laundering, or to learn that such a restrictive interpretation was contrary to the obligations resulting from this Directive.[51] But to date, it remains unclear why the Supreme Court refused to involve in its reasoning the wording and aims of the relevant Directive. In the meantime, the Dutch legislator – unhappy with the Supreme Court's line of case law on the matter – has adopted new provisions that explicitly criminalise the mere acquisition or possession of property that derives from an individuals' own criminal activity (Articles 420bis.1 and 420quater.1 of the Dutch Criminal Code).

Under the category of cases in which courts fail to consult the relevant EU instruments, one could also group the several human trafficking cases in which references to EU norms are entirely lacking.[52] The absence of such references are probably the result of the Supreme Court's standing case law that in order to determine whether a matter constitutes 'exploitation', the court's frame of reference for the weighing of all relevant factors in this regard (eg duration) is composed of standards that apply in the Dutch society.[53] Commentators have argued that such an emphasis on national standards is likely to ignore the fact that international and European norms on the criminalisation of human trafficking are primarily

[50] European Parliament and Council Directive 2005/60/EC of 26 October 2005 on the prevention of the use of the financial system for the purpose of money laundering and terrorist financing [2005] OJ L309/15.

[51] See, eg, HR 27 May 2014, ECLI:NL:HR:2014:1237, *NJ* 2014/305, m.nt. Keijzer; HR 7 October 2014, ECLI:NL:HR:2014:2913, *NJ* 2014, 500, m.nt. Keijzer. See also SS Buisman, 'Witwassen – het enkele verwerven en voorhanden hebben en richtlijnconforme interpretatie' (2013) *Delikt en Delinkwent* 53.

[52] For some relatively recent examples, see: Court of Appeal The Hague 24 May 2017, ECLI:NL:GHDHA:2017:1524; Court of Appeal Arnhem-Leeuwarden 16 March 2017, ECLI:NL:GHARL:2017:2189; Court of Appeal Amsterdam 5 October 2016, ECLI:NL:GHAMS:2016:3891.

[53] In Dutch: 'Bij de weging van deze en andere relevante factoren dienen de in de Nederlandse samenleving geldende maatstaven als referentiekader te worden gehanteerd', HR 27 October 2009, ECLI:NL:HR:2009:BI7099, para 2.6.1.

rooted in a commitment to protect human rights, for which reason national criminal prohibitions regarding human trafficking should not be stretched too far, ie encompass minor offences or offences that lack a clear link with serious human rights violations in the sense of Article 4 ECHR.[54] Van Kempen has therefore argued that *international* standards, rather than national standards, should function as courts' frame of reference in interpreting Article 273f of the Dutch Criminal Code – not only because that would do better justice to the aims of the international and European legal instruments on the matter, but also because wide divergences between the Dutch interpretation and the interpretation of human trafficking provisions in other (EU Member) States is likely to hinder transnational cooperation.[55] But, even if the application of an international frame of reference would indeed be in conformity with the aims of the relevant higher ranking norms – such as the norms in Directive 2011/36/EU – it is highly questionable whether courts can held to apply this interpretation, for Directive 2011/36/EU and the other relevant international instruments envisage *minimum* harmonisation.[56]

The above account of directive-conform interpretation in Dutch criminal courts shows a fragmented picture. In the absence of guiding Supreme Court judgments in the criminal law field, courts have explicitly referred to the relevant EU norms sometimes, but refrained from doing so at other times. And where they do, it strikes that the principle of legal certainty does not seem to play a very significant role; in the abovementioned judgments the courts have not explicitly relied on it. Moreover, where references to EU norms do occur, the differing outcomes often seem irreconcilable.

On several occasions the diverging approaches are thus not so easy to explain. As to some other cases, however, divergences may have their roots in differing degrees of harmonisation that EU directives aim for in different areas. Therefore, the following paragraphs aim to discuss the (potential) impact of EU minimum norms on the duty of directive-conform interpretation in matters of substantive criminal law.

B. Directive-Conform Interpretation: Maximum vs Minimum Norms

In the pre-Lisbon era, the European Union had fewer powers to enact criminal law provisions. Where EU norms made their way to national penal codes it was usually because of the discretionary choices of Member States to enforce EU norms through national criminal law while they were often free to opt for other ways of

[54] See, eg, Buruma's note attached to HR 27 October 2009, ECLI:NL:HR:2009:BI7099, *NJ* 2009/598, para 5, where he also refers to *Rantsev v Cyprus and Russia* App no 25965/04 (ECHR, 7 January 2010) where the Strasbourg Court connected human trafficking with a violation of Article 4 ECHR.

[55] See n 49 above, at 408–409.

[56] As is also recognised by Van Kempen, n 49 at 408–409.

enforcement, such as through administrative law. In such cases, the underlying EU instrument has been adopted outside the criminal law sphere and the required implementation has therefore not been restricted to minimum rules. In three of the previously discussed cases, the Dutch criminal court indeed had to deal with EU directives prescribing maximum rules (one relating to plant protection, and two others in the field of animal protection), leaving no room for a stricter or more lenient enforcement at the national level and, thus, eliminating purely national standards. That probably explains why the courts in these cases have been so keen to closely follow the wording and aim of these respective directives in the interpretation of the applicable national laws, either to the detriment, or to the benefit of the individual involved.[57]

Already with maximum rules, application of the method of directive-conform interpretation could be very demanding, but the situation becomes even more complicated when the relevant EU directive contains minimum norms. Especially since the entry into force of the Lisbon Treaty, the phenomenon of minimum harmonisation has become of growing importance in the area of substantive criminal law. Pursuant to Article 83 of the Treaty on the Functioning of the European Union (TFEU) – which provides the main legal basis for the adoption of common definitions of crime – the EU legislature can only adopt *minimum* norms concerning the definitions of crime and sanctions in the listed areas (money laundering, terrorism, human trafficking, etc, see para 1) as well as in other areas in which shared minimum norms are considered necessary for the effective implementation of previously adopted harmonisation measures (eg the area of environmental protection, see para 2). As the term itself already suggests, criminalisation provisions adopted on the basis of Article 83 TFEU require Member States to at least criminalise the envisaged behaviour, but leaves it to the Member States' discretion to provide for more extensive criminal prohibitions at the national level.

Such EU minimum rules also apply in the areas of human trafficking and money laundering, the scope of which crimes have been under discussion in the other criminal cases mentioned above. It has been observed that in several human trafficking cases, courts in the Netherlands have followed an extensive interpretation of the Dutch criminal prohibitions in the field of human trafficking, either without referring to EU norms at all,[58] or with only a general reference to the relevant directive provision, but without really interpreting it in the light of the directive's aims.[59] Although commentators have recommended a stricter interpretation in order to avoid an interpretation too far removed from what the international and European norms were originally meant for, it has also been recognised that under the applicable EU directive Member States are indeed allowed to criminalise more than mandatorily required.[60] In such a case, courts may no longer be

[57] See nn 34, 40, and 43 above.
[58] See n 52 above.
[59] See n 48 above.
[60] See Van Kempen (n 49).

obliged to apply a directive-conform interpretation; according to Kristen, consistent interpretation is not prescribed in so far as the interpretation of national law relates to legal elements that exceed the mandatory minimum floor.[61] Courts are therefore held to examine whether or not the legislature has chosen to implement broader provisions than it was strictly held to do, and whether the prosecuted criminal activity at hand falls under the extended scope of the national criminal prohibitions.

It is quite possible that the existence of minimum norms also explains the lack of references to EU law in the Supreme Court's decisions on money laundering. Whereas the relevant Dutch criminal prohibitions did include self-laundering activities, it was by no means certain that the criminalisation of self-laundering was required by the anti-money laundering EU norms – in fact, a majority of Dutch scholarly experts on the anti-money laundering legal framework have convincingly argued that the former and current anti-money laundering directives do not require such a broad scope of criminal prohibitions.[62] It may well be that the Dutch Supreme Court has been of the same opinion and therefore considered it unnecessary to consult the relevant EU minimum norms.

Come what may – and before jetting off into the realm of speculation – the previous account suggests that the growing importance of minimum norms in the criminal law domain have further complicated the courts' duty of directive-conform interpretation – not only because the Member States' discretion may blur the line between EU dictated norms and national choices, but also because the very existence of national discretion is likely to lessen the significance of directive-conform interpretation in this field – that is to say *if* courts across the EU would hold the viewpoint that where EU law stipulates minimum rules, a consistent interpretation of national law is *not always* required. As rightly pointed out by Altena-Davidsen, such a viewpoint may 'greatly diminish[es] the harmonizing potential' of EU legal instruments in the field of substantive criminal law.[63]

IV. Final Remarks

At the time the CJEU delivered its judgment in the famous case of *Kolpinghuis Nijmegen*, the EU's impact on national criminal law was still very limited. Where EU law prescribed the adoption of national prohibitions, Member States were

[61] Kristen (n 24) 391–92, 401. See also: FGH Kristen, *Misbruik van voorwetenschap naar Europees recht* (Wolf Legal Publishers, 2004) 77. Against: JGH Altena-Davidsen, *Het legaliteitsbeginsel en de doorwerking van Europees recht in het Nederlandse materiële strafrecht* (Kluwer, 2016) 279–84.

[62] See, eg, MJ Borgers in his note under HR 2 July 2013, ECLI:NL:HR:2013:121, *NJ* 2013, 425, para 4; see also: T Kooijmans, 'Witwassen: communicatie tussen rechter en wetenschap, maar waar is de wetgever?' (2014) *Delikt and Delinkwent* 413–14. Against: SS Buisman, 'Witwassen – het enkele verwerven en voorhanden hebben en richtlijnconforme interpretatie' (2013) *Delikt en Delinkwent* 53.

[63] JGH Altena-Davidsen, 'The Netherlands: Principles of Consistent Interpretation' in CNK Franklin (ed), *The Effectiveness and Application of EU & EEA Law in National Courts* (Intersentia, 2018).

usually free to decide through which area of law they wanted to enact those prohibitions. And where Member States failed to (correctly) transpose EU-level prohibitions, courts could be held to give effect to those norms nevertheless, ie through the method of directive-conform interpretation.

Because at earlier times EU law mostly concerned maximum obligations, the boundaries to the duty of consistent interpretation were relatively clear, especially in the criminal law domain. In the *Kolpinghuis* judgment, the principles of legal certainty and non-retroactivity have been held to limit the national court's duty to interpret national law in conformity with higher ranking EU norms – namely where such an interpretation would have the effect of determining or aggravating criminal liability.

Now the inconsistencies that follow from the previous account already disclose the difficulties and obscurities judges may encounter in applying the method of directive-conform interpretation in practice. But as claimed in this commentary, the rise of EU minimum norms in the field of substantive criminal law has complicated the application of directive-conform interpretation even more. Where the national legislator has decided to go beyond what is minimally required and to broaden the scope of the EU-level criminal prohibition, the question arises whether and to what extent courts can still be bound to interpret national implementation legislation in conformity with the relevant EU norms. As argued above, it may well be that the frequent lack of references to EU law in Dutch criminal courts in cases on human trafficking and money laundering does relate to the very fact that in these areas of crime national legal provisions have transposed *minimum norms* in EU directives. Would that be the case indeed it suggests that, in addition to existing limitations, the duty of consistent interpretation is further restricted in cases where EU norms constitute minimum norms, as to which the national legislature has decided to go beyond what is at least required.

2

C-387/02 – *Berlusconi and Others*

The Berlusconi *Judgment: A Cornerstone of European Legality*

FRANK MEYER

I. Introduction

The *Berlusconi* judgment is commonly portrayed as a landmark case of European legality. It has firmly established the *lex mitior* principle in EU criminal law. The Court of Justice of the European Union (CJEU) held that 'the retroactive application of the more lenient penalty that came into effect ex post facto was part of the common constitutional heritage of the Member States', from which it 'follows that this principle must be regarded as forming part of the general principles of Community law which national courts must respect when applying the national legislation adopted for the purpose of implementing Community law'.[1] To date, this judgment ranks as main precedent in this regard. The *Berlusconi* judgment is also frequently referenced as a leading case regarding the direct effect of directives in the field of criminal law. It is often cited alongside the *Kolpinghuis Nijmegen* ruling of the CJEU from 18 years earlier. In the *Kolpinghuis* case the CJEU developed its jurisprudence on the direct application of directives in the field of criminal law. The Court held that a

> national authority may not rely, as against an individual upon a provision of a directive whose necessary implementation in national law has not yet taken place. … [A] directive cannot, of itself and independently of a law adopted for its implementation, have the effect of determining or aggravating the liability in criminal law of persons who act in contravention of the provisions of that directive.[2]

This chapter has a twofold mission. It will sketch a brief historiography of the *Berlusconi* case and its quintessential propositions. From here the text will proceed

[1] Joined Cases C-387/02, C-391/02, C-403/02 *Silvio Berlusconi, Sergio Adelchi, Marcello Dell'Utri and others* [2005] ECR I-03565.
[2] Case C-80/86 *Kolpinghuis Nijmegen BV* [1987] ECR 3969.

to take a look at its reception in legal practice and academia. It will be scrutinised whether the widespread understanding of the case is actually accurate. Taking a closer look at the case and its premises might reveal that the conclusions drawn by the Court were much less obvious than one would infer from its (attributed) status as major precedent. It could turn out that this perception is, at least partly, misplaced. Finally, the CJEU's main arguments will be put to the test in the new constitutional environment of the area of freedom, security and justice. It is argued that the legality principle in the Charter of Fundamental Rights (CFR) lends much less support to the CJEU's position in *Berlusconi* than one would expect.

The analysis in this chapter proceeds in four steps. The first section summarises the facts of the case. The second section repeats the main arguments of the Court. The standing and interpretation of the decision in national courts and by criminal lawyers will be traced in the third section. The fourth and major section is dedicated to a deeper exploration of the judgment. Source and justification of the *lex mitior* principle will be illuminated and placed within the context of EU (criminal) law. The chapter then concludes with several suggestions on how the *lex mitior* principle and the supremacy of EU law should be reconfigured within the framework of a multilevel area of freedom, security and justice.

II. The Facts

The case originated in criminal proceedings which had been brought against the former Italian Prime Minister, Silvio Berlusconi, and others for alleged breaches of the provisions governing false information on companies (false accounting) between 1986 and 1989, punishable under Articles 2621 and 2622 of the Italian Civil Code. He was accused of drawing up and publishing false documents relating to the annual accounts of companies in the Fininvest group in responsible capacity in order to increase hidden reserves earmarked for the financing of certain allegedly unlawful transactions.[3] The substantive accounting and reporting requirements, as well as sanctions in the pertinent provisions of the Italian Civil Code both sought to implement EU law, namely, the First, Fourth and Seventh Company Law Directives.[4] After commencement of the proceedings, Italian law-makers passed Legislative Decree No 61/2002 introducing the new Articles 2621 and 2622 in the Italian Civil Code. With the Decree's entry into force on 16 April 2002 they replaced the corresponding old provisions. The new provisions provided for considerably higher liability thresholds ('margins of tolerance'), lower sentences (which led to a shorter limitation period) and new prosecution requirements (precondition of individual complaint in Article 2622). The national courts rightly concluded that the effect of applying those new provisions rather

[3] *Berlusconi et al* (n 1) para 27.
[4] See nn 5, 6 and 7.

than those applicable at the material time would be that criminal prosecution of the accused would no longer be possible. The charges would be time-barred or lack a complaint from a member or a creditor who regarded himself as having been adversely affected by the false documentation. The accused parties argued that the new provisions ought to be applied to them. Article 2 paragraph 4 of the Italian Criminal Code stated that

> if the legislation in force when the offence was committed and the later legislation differ, the legislation which is to apply shall be that which is more favourable in its provisions to the accused person, unless a final and irreversible judgment has been delivered in the case.

The Italian courts sensed the tensions between the said statutory demand and their legal obligations under the then EC law, specifically:

- First Council Directive 68/151/EEC of 9 March 1968 on coordination of safeguards which, for the protection of the interests of members and others, are required by Member States of companies within the meaning of the second paragraph of Article 58 of the Treaty, with a view to making such safeguards equivalent throughout the Community (the First Company Law Directive),[5] in particular Article 6 thereof;
- Fourth Council Directive 78/660/EEC of 25 July 1978 based on Article 54(3)(g) of the Treaty on the annual accounts of certain types of companies (the Fourth Company Law Directive),[6] in particular Article 2 thereof; and
- Seventh Council Directive 83/349/EEC of 13 June 1983 based on Article 54(3)(g) of the Treaty on consolidated accounts (the Seventh Company Law Directive),[7] in particular Article 16 thereof.

The Italian judiciary referred the case to the CJEU. In particular, they inquired whether Article 6 of Directive 68/151/EEC (directly or in conjunction with Article 5 EEC, which later became Article 10 TEC) required the Italian legislature to criminalise the alleged conduct and whether they were supposed to disapply the new provisions if they could not be considered adequate in this regard.[8]

The Commission argued that the incompatibility of later adopted, more lenient national provisions with Community law could indeed force national courts to set

[5] Directive 68/151/EEC on coordination of safeguards which, for the protection of the interests of members and others, are required by Member States of companies within the meaning of the second paragraph of Article 58 of the Treaty, with a view to making such safeguards equivalent throughout the Community [1968] OJ L65/8, 41.

[6] Directive 78/660/EEC based on Article 54 (3)(g) of the Treaty on the annual accounts of certain types of companies [1978] OJ L222/11.

[7] Directive 83/349/EEC based on Article 54 (3)(g) of the Treaty on consolidated accounts [1983] OJ L193/1.

[8] They sought further advice as to whether the principles on annual and consolidated accounts set out in the Fourth and Seventh Company Law Directives are to be interpreted as precluding national legislation setting thresholds below which inaccurate statements would no longer be punishable.

aside the application of those national provisions in order to maintain the applicability and effects of national implementing legislation in force at the time of commission. In the Commission's view, the primacy of Community law precluded the application of *leges mitior* if the new provisions did not ensure that infringements of Community law were punished in an appropriate manner. Advocate General (AG) Kokott concurred. In her view the referring courts had an obligation under Community law to give effect to the provisions of the Company Law Directives in the criminal proceedings pending before them.[9] AG Kokott emphasised that directives cannot be relied upon directly in order to determine or aggravate liability in criminal law since a directive may not of itself give rise to obligations against individuals.[10] But no such situation was present in the case at hand as the directives in conjunction with Article 10 TEC did not render individuals criminally liable. On the contrary, they ensure that the 'national legislation as it existed at the material time none the less remains applicable'. In the present case, it was not the Community legislation which determined or increased criminal liability. Union law would merely command that the effects of the national legislation in force at the time of the acts and in conformity with Community law be maintained ('by refraining from the application of later legislation which is more favourable but contrary to Community law').

III. The CJEU's Judgment in a Nutshell

The CJEU reviewed the new legislation for its appropriateness under Union law. The Court specified the obligations arising from the First, Fourth and Seventh Company Law Directives in light of its case law on Article 10 TEC.[11] Their enforcement nevertheless ought not to infringe on general principles of Union law. Forming part of the constitutional traditions common to all Member States, the rule of retroactive application of the more lenient penalty also fell into this category.[12] Although the Court raised the obvious question that this principle might be at variance with other central elements of Union law, it concluded straightforwardly that it was not necessary to further address this aspect since the community rule concerned in the case at hand was contained in a directive, an instrument which cannot be relied upon against an individual directly to establish or increase that individual's criminal liability.[13] The CJEU acknowledged that, in theory, national courts would have to set aside new measures which threaten the effectiveness of EU law. In the present setting, however, not applying new,

[9] AG Kokott, *Berlusconi et al* (n 1), Opinion delivered on 14 October 2004, para 136.
[10] AG Kokott, *Berlusconi et al* (n 1), Opinion delivered on 14 October 2004, para 142.
[11] *Berlusconi et al* (n 1) paras 53 ff.
[12] *Berlusconi et al* (n 1) paras 68 ff.
[13] *Berlusconi et al* (n 1) paras 74 ff.

unsatisfactory legislation would be contrary to this tenet of EU law and have the effect of determining or aggravating the liability in criminal law of persons who act in contravention of the Company Law Directives.[14]

It was this effect that the CJEU saw looming on the horizon in *Berlusconi*. For the Court to set aside the application of more lenient provisions provided for by the new articles would have been tantamount to rendering applicable a manifestly more severe criminal penalty (and liability requirements) based on a directive.[15]

IV. Reception and Interpretation by National Criminal Courts and Scholars

While many commentators have criticised the erratic approach the CJEU had adopted and the obvious inconsistencies with its prior case law,[16] the decision has been well received by the criminal law community; not least because it curbs the influence of EU law on national criminal justice systems. It confirmed the predominant view that a directive cannot by itself have the effect of determining or increasing the criminal liability of those who act in breach of the directive. The *Berlusconi* judgment seems to extend the said *Kolpinghuis* jurisprudence to the context of legislative changes ex post facto, even though it compromised EU law's primacy and effectiveness. The recognition of the *lex mitior* safeguard has raised more eyebrows. Although the principle is well-known in national systems, it has been argued that it is not one of constitutional law.[17] But overall, the content and foundation of *lex mitior* have not been discussed thoroughly by either CJEU or criminal lawyers.

Further discrepancies have come to the fore in academic comments on the case. Some scholars argue that the case did not involve a primacy problem in the first place. Hecker, for instance, explains that such conflicts could arise where

[14] *Berlusconi et al* (n 1) paras 78 and 74 citing *Kolpinghuis Nijmegen* (n 2) para 13 and Case C-60/02 *X* [2004] ECR I-00651, para 61 and the case law there cited.

[15] *Berlusconi et al* (n 1) paras 75 and 76; confirmed in Joined Cases C-23/03, C-52/03, C-133/03, C-337/03, C-473/03 *Mulliez and Others* [2006] ECR I-03923, para 45.

[16] A Biondi and R Mastroianni, 'Joined Cases C-387/02, C-391/02 and C-403/02, Berlusconi and Others' [2006] *Common Market Law Review* 563; according to E Herlin-Karnell, *The Constitutional Dimension of European Criminal Law* (Oxford and Portland, Hart Publishing, 2012) 21, the CJEU should have clarified how to resolve confrontations between positive and negative obligations in EU law.

[17] I Gross, 'Keine Strafverfolgung wegen Bilanzfälschung auf Grund einer Richtlinie – Berlusconi' [2005] *Europäische Zeitschrift für Wirtschaftsrecht* 371, 372; H Satzger, 'EuGH, 3.5.2005 – Rs. C-387/02, C-391/02 u. C-403/02 Berlusconi u. a. – Zum Lex-mitior-Grundsatz im Gemeinschaftsrecht' [2005] *Juristenzeitung* 998, 1000. Dannecker, on the other hand, views *lex mitior* as a basic principle of substantive justice, *cf* G Dannecker, 'Der zeitliche Geltungsbereich von Strafgesetzen und der Vorrang des Gemeinschaftsrechts' [2006] *Zeitschrift für internationale Strafrechtsdogmatik* 309, 315.

EU law stipulates directly applicable conflicting rules.[18] Since directives cannot have such (direct) effect they cannot claim priority over national law (so-called *Scheinkollision*).[19] It was considered unpersuasive and arbitrary that AG Kokott relied on the older Italian provisions as anchor points of primacy. These could not be equated with EU law since they were set by the Italian legislature which deliberately opted to change them. To hold otherwise would also imply criminal law-making powers of the Union which had not been recognised then. Given the absence of such authority at the time, EU law could not dictate the continued validity of implementing national legislation. Some authors explicitly tie the primacy of EU law to its legislative powers in the field of criminal law.[20] The application of *lex mitior* would, as a consequence, become a simple matter of national law even where it defied EU law obligations.

However, after the entry into force of the Lisbon Treaty, this position is moot for the most part. The argument that EU directives cannot command that the older (implementing) criminal legislation persist (for lack of legislative competence) has lost its legal backbone. Furthermore, this line of thought overlooks that there actually was a collision, namely between the national implementing legislation (to the extent that it had to be interpreted as an expression of the principles of loyalty and effectiveness) and the newly introduced criminal provisions (or, alternatively, the *lex mitior* clause of the Italian Criminal Code). One is left to wonder whether deeper cleavages with respect to the scope and concept of primacy are lurking at this point. A later section will address this aspect. At this stage, it suffices to note that, up to now, the *Scheinkollision* remains a commonly shared position among criminal lawyers.

Other voices, critiquing the CJEU's ruling, have focussed on the *lex mitior* safeguard and present it as a main outcome of the case.[21] However, the bad faith of the legislature in the cases at issue gave them reason to pause. In a rather pragmatic, though creative fashion possible exceptions to the general rule were pondered. From this perspective, the key question that presented itself in *Berlusconi* was whether and to what extent *lex mitior* constrains primacy.[22] Klip argues that legislative changes initiated by the party of an accused should be treated as void of any legal effect vis-à-vis EU law and implementing domestic criminal provisions. This proposition is based on an analogy to Article 7, paragraph 2 of the European Convention on Human Rights (ECHR), which is arguably not regulating a

[18] B Hecker, *Europäisches Strafrecht*, 5th edn (Heidelberg, Springer Verlag, 2015) § 9 no 15 ff; in the same vein G Dannecker and J Bülte, 'Die Bedeutung des Unions- und Gemeinschaftsrechts für das nationale Wirtschaftsstrafrecht' in H-B Wabnitz and Th Janovsky (eds), *Handbuch Wirtschafts- und Steuerstrafrecht*, 4th edn (Munich, CH Beck, 2014) no 251, 254; Satzger (n 17) 998, 1000.

[19] Hecker, *ibid*, § 9 no 15 ff.

[20] Dannecker (n 17) 313.

[21] Biondi and Mastroianni (n 16) 553; A Klip, *Substantive Criminal Law of the European Union*, 3rd edn (Antwerpen, Maklu, 2016) 203.

[22] Biondi and Mastroianni (n 16) 553.

sufficiently similar situation, however. Article 17, paragraph 1 of the Rome Statute ('unwillingness' to prosecute crimes within the jurisdiction of the International Criminal Court) could *prima vista* be a better fit. In any case, the remaining uncertainties testify to the fact that neither the foundation nor the permissible restrictions of *lex mitior* are well-articulated in EU law.

Overall, the discussion has done very little to advance our understanding about legality, *lex mitior* and the legal effects of directives in criminal law. *Berlusconi* is remembered for being an important addition to the *Kolpinghuis* jurisprudence which, however, sits uncomfortably with the factual background of the case and other rulings of the CJEU in comparable cases. Yet, much more could have been learned from the *Berlusconi* case. It is time to revisit this landmark case to tap into its full potential.

V. Perspectives on *Berlusconi*

The case can be approached from three different perspectives: *lex mitior*, primacy and effects of criminal law directives. The CJEU presents its solution as a clear-cut case that does not warrant resolving the tensions between primacy and *lex mitior* or clarifying the relationship between direct effect and primacy. Supposedly, the *Kolpinghuis* doctrine had done the entire job already. AG Kokott presented an entirely different view, according to which *Kolpinghuis* did not apply and *lex mitior* had to yield in light of the bad faith of the authors of the new laws.[23] Who is right hinges on two theoretical questions. First, what type of EU law does primacy presuppose? Second, at what moment does the impact of primacy start to unfold? Notwithstanding these highly intricate theoretical matters, what appears to be missing the most is an integrated solution under the umbrella of the legality principle (understood as a fundamental principle of EU law). However, one should not blame the CJEU for offering no clear vision of legality as a fundamental principle of EU criminal justice in *Berlusconi*. The judgment predates the recognition of the Union's criminal law competences, the emergence of the Union's goal of establishing an area of freedom, security and justice, as well as the entry into force of the CFR. But this does not absolve us from understanding legality as a multilevel concept that integrates multiple legal actors and layers of legal sources today. This section therefore seeks to answer both preliminary questions and to bring these findings in line with the *lex mitior* concept within the framework of the legality principle.

[23] AG Kokott, *Berlusconi et al* (n 1), Opinion delivered on 14 October 2004; A Biondi and R Mastroianni (n 15) 553, 561, 562, agree that Berlusconi is distinguishable from Kolpinghuis and presented no problem of direct effect of a directive.

A. The Concept of Primacy

The case raises the question whether directives enjoy primacy or, in more abstract terms, whether direct effect is a precondition of primacy. The relationship between primacy and direct effect is indeed not beyond controversy.[24] It has been suggested that immediate direct effect is a condition precedent for EU law to have primacy ('trigger model').[25] Primacy would then characteristically operate through a substitutionary effect. For EU law to claim primacy it would therefore, at least, have to produce independent effects within national legal systems (that could replace national law-based legal effects and allow parties to invoke EU law before national courts).[26]

The dominant strand in the field appears to follow a more flexible line ('primacy model').[27] In this model supremacy is conceived of in a conceptually broader sense, as a constitutional function of EU law rather than just a mechanism to resolve individual disputes between inconsistent provisions. Enforcement of directly applicable norms is not the real concern behind primacy, but effectiveness and consistency (of the application of common-market provisions in this particular case) is.[28] To this end the principle of primacy produces certain legal (exclusionary) effects whenever an incompatibility between a rule of EU law and a rule of domestic law appears, irrespective of the former's direct effect or self-executing specificity. The EU rule may take the place of the yielding national rule (substitution) but this is not a mandatory requirement. An exclusionary effect, nonetheless, presupposes that EU law has a specific, identifiable and binding legal impact. Such legal effects could (among others) emanate from the interplay of EU-induced national norms and EU enforcement principles or directives,[29] provided they put forward an identifiable legal result which must not be thwarted by incompatible national measures. The primacy effect would be limited to the extent of the actual conflict with domestic rules in this model.

Primacy therefore would, after all, not presuppose directly applicable EU norms. Rather, direct effect should be seen as an alternative form of invoking EU law

[24] P Craig and G De Búrca, *EU Law, Text, Cases and Materials*, 6th edn (Oxford, Oxford University Press, 2015) 276; K Lenaerts and T Corthaut, 'Of Birds and Hedges: The Role of Primacy in Invoking Norms of EU Law' (2006) 31 (3) *EL Rev* 287, 290–91, 303.

[25] M Dougan, 'When Worlds Collide! Competing Visions of the Relationship between Direct and Supremacy' [2007] *Common Market Law Review* 931, 932.

[26] See *ibid*, 931, 932 ff; also for *Berlusconi* B Wegener and T Lock, 'Die Kleinen "hängt" man, die Großen lässt man laufen? Berlusconi und Niselli – Ungleiche vor dem EuGH' (2005) 6 *Europarecht* 802, 807.

[27] Craig and De Búrca (n 24) 277; Lenaerts and Corthaut (n 24) 287, 289–91.

[28] Lenaerts and Corthaut (n 24) 287, 290.

[29] Lenaerts and Corthaut (n 24) 287, 290–91, 303; see Case C-285/98 *Tanja Kreil* [2000] ECR I-00069, where Directive 76/207/EEC on the implementation of the principle of equal treatment for men and women as regards access to employment, vocational training and promotion, and working conditions [1976] OJ L 39/40 precluded the application of national provisions. The CJEU expresses the same understanding in *Berlusconi et al* (n 1) para 72.

which becomes necessary where exclusion is not enough and empowerment and private enforcement are needed. Even if one would argue with the trigger model that primacy *stricto sensu* requires two potentially applicable, yet irreconcilable norms to exist, the principle of effectiveness would cause the same result.[30] The *Scheinkollision* solution is, thus, at odds with the prevailing opinion in EU law. Although it conflates arguments on direct effect and primacy[31] it can (unwittingly?) be understood as an expression of the trigger theory. If a direct collision would require a directly applicable conflicting EU norm, claiming primacy would inevitably presume attributing direct effect to a directive. While this view cannot be dismissed as indefensible it needs to be emphasised, however, that the special characteristics of (EU) criminal law do not lend it further support either. As we have seen above it is not in conflict with the EU's allocation of law-making competences (anymore). Moreover, directives (in conjunction with EU enforcement principles and) in combination with national transposition measures may very well produce independent legal effects that directly expand or limit individual freedoms. This does not turn the directive into a direct source of criminal liability though. The second main theoretical question in the *Berlusconi* case was rather whether the national object of interpretation (and effective enforcement) was still valid when the question of primacy arose.

To conclude, not only directly applicable EU rules may enjoy primacy, even in criminal law.[32] The recent *Taricco* judgment is a case in point. In this case, the requirement of effective implementation of EU tax law justified the refusal to apply pre-existing statutes of limitation. There is no apparent doctrinal difference between newly introduced legislation and pre-existing law; also, it does not make a difference in terms of legal effects and the concept of primacy whether substantive or procedural provisions are affected. Under the given circumstances of the case at hand it could be argued anyway that it would have been sufficient to disapply the procedural *lex mitior* rule in the Italian Code of Criminal Procedure instead of the new substantive provisions. This brings us to the central issue of the case: the intricate and unresolved relationship between primacy and *lex mitior*. Since the CFR became effective, the Italian procedural rule must be interpreted as (partly) embodying a fundamental right of the Union, namely Article 49, paragraph 1, clause 3 of the CFR. As such it may channel and curtail the enforcement of EU law. Admittedly, the application of the *lex mitior* safeguard logically presupposes that a *lex mitior* exists.

[30] See Case C-105/14 *Taricco* [2015] ECLI:EU:C2015:555; see in this sense Biondi and Mastroianni (n 16) 553, 564 ff, who suggest that the principle of loyalty be applied. This could, of course, lead to the next academic debate, ie whether the principle of effectiveness triggers supremacy, is a means to enforce supremacy, or produces comparable results independent of the principle of supremacy.

[31] eg H Satzger, *Internationales und Europäisches Strafrecht*, 7th edn (Baden-Baden, Nomos, 2016) § 9 no 88.

[32] Also Biondi and Mastroianni (n 16) 553, 569.

B. The Temporal Dimension of Primacy

The specific facts of the *Berlusconi* case call for a deeper reflection of the onset of the primacy effect. From a theoretical standpoint primacy could kick in automatically once a conflict between EU and national law arises or later upon determination of a competent authority. Hence, the impact of a national court decision to leave certain provisions unapplied by reason of their incompatibility with EU law, could be constitutive or declaratory. Only in the former case would the *Kolpinghuis* doctrine apply; since it would indirectly result in the inapplicability of the *lex mitior* rule. This presupposes, however, that *lex mitior* actually had the effect of commanding the application of the new provisions. This contribution will turn to the question of whether *lex mitior* really would have led to this result in the subsequent section.

In the latter case the new provision would have never become applicable to prior wrongdoing. That said, it would not have been necessary to rely on the directives directly to reanimate the former provisions. The CJEU's precedents imply that primacy sets in immediately once a conflicting national law or decision is passed and renders that measure inapplicable.[33] This interpretation finds additional support in the telos behind this development.[34] The CJEU has continuously fostered a dynamisation of the application of EU law. And, last but not least, it corresponds with the theoretical justification of supremacy which, from the standpoint of EU law, is an effect inherent in the respective EU norm.[35]

It could be argued, however, that indirect conflicts[36] call for a differential treatment since they depend on legal determinations to a considerably greater extent than other manifestations of primacy. To the knowledge of the author, such proposition does not find any support in the jurisprudence of the Court. It emerges from the case law (including criminal cases) that decisions of the referring court would merely confirm the inapplicability of conflicting rules or practices. Hence, referring to the enforcement obligations flowing from the directive would not be tantamount to having a direct incriminating or exacerbating effect.

[33] Case 11/70 *Internationale Handelsgesellschaft GmbH v Einfuhr- und Vorratsstelle für Getreide und Futtermittel* [1970] ECR 01125, para 3; Case C-399/11 *Melloni* [2013] ECLI:EU:2013:107, paras 59 ff; Case C-10/97 to C-22/97 *Ministero delle Finanze v IN.CO.GE.'90 and others* [1998] ECR I-06307, para 21; Case C-8/88 *Deutschland v Kommission* [1990] ECR I-2321: Primacy is to be respected by any authority charged with applying EU law. This duty includes both courts and administrative agencies; Case C-13/91 and C-113/91 *Debus* [1992] ECR I-03617; M Ruffert, 'Art 1 AEUV' no 22 in Ch Calliess and M Ruffert (eds), *EUV/AEUV: Das Verfassungsrecht der Europäischen Union mit Europäischer Grundrechtecharta,* 5th edn (Munich, CH Beck, 2016); M Nettesheim, 'Art 288 AEUV' no 52 in E Grabitz, M Hilf and M Nettesheim (eds), *Das Recht der Europäischen Union*, 60th supplement (Munich, CH Beck, 2016).

[34] See for instance Nettesheim, *ibid*, 'Art 288 AEUV' no 49.

[35] Nettesheim (n 33) 'Art 288 AEUV' no 51.

[36] German literature on EU law distinguishes between direct and indirect collisions, see Ruffert (n 33) 'Art 1 AEUV' no 22. With respect to primacy they are generally being treated the same. They block any introduction, interpretation or application of domestic law that challenge the validity or effectiveness of EU law.

Since, after all, the primacy effect logically sets in one ominous (legal) second (*juristische Sekunde*) earlier than *lex mitior*, one could be tempted to argue that the matter is settled for good in this fashion. And it is, indeed, recognised that primacy also takes precedence over the *lex posterior* rule.[37] This view, nevertheless, seems objectionable for it dodges the key problem of the case: the relation of primacy and effectiveness on the one hand and *lex mitior* on the other.[38] Article 51 CFR makes it clear that the application of EU enforcement principles needs to comply with fundamental principles. It continues to be an open question that needs to be satisfactorily answered whether *lex mitior* constrains the primacy effect of EU law. The outcome has potentially far-reaching consequences in light of the dynamic legal development in the EU and the growing awareness for effective enforcement. It must be clarified how far a national legislator is empowered to rearrange implementing legislation to which directives apply or whether EU law firmly stands in its way.

C. The Legality Principle in the CFR

The legality principle is a general principle of Union law and explicitly guaranteed by Article 49 CFR.[39] Modelled on Article 7 ECHR, this safeguard comprises the classic elements of legality, namely: *lex scripta*; *lex stricta*; *lex certa*; and *lex praevia*. Going beyond the text of the ECHR, Article 49, paragraph 1, clause 3 also contains a *lex mitior* rule. Although it explicitly refers to subsequent introductions of 'a lighter penalty', it is widely recognised that paragraph 1, clause 3 encompasses any change in the scope of liability or punishment to the benefit of a defendant.[40] The CJEU refers to this guarantee as the 'principle of retroactivity of the more lenient criminal law'.[41] While the European Court of Human Rights (ECtHR) has, nonetheless, interpreted Article 7 ECHR as to include a *lex mitior* rule, their legality concepts diverge in an important (not yet fully appreciated) aspect. In EU law legality must be understood as a multilevel concept.[42] Preserving legality is a shared responsibility. This insight has a number of considerable consequences.

[37] Nettesheim (n 33) 'Art 288 AEUV' no 52.

[38] Under the CFR, legality is supposed to act as a limit to direct effect, V Mitsilegas, 'Art 49' no 22 in S Peers, T Hervey, J Kenner and A Ward (eds), *The EU Charter of Fundamental Rights* (Baden-Baden and Oxford, CH. Beck, Hart Publishing and Nomos, 2014).

[39] *Ibid* 'Art 49' no 19; A Eser, 'Art 49' no 9 ff in J Meyer (ed), *Charta der Grundrechte der Europäischen Union*, 4th edn (Baden-Baden, Nomos, 2014); Herlin-Karnell (n 16) 20; K Karsai, 'The Legality of Criminal Law and the New Competences of the TFEU' [2016] *Zeitschrift für internationale Strafrechtsdogmatik* 24, 35.

[40] Eser, *ibid* 'Art 49' no 34; Case C-218/15 *Paoletti and Others* [2016] ECLI:EU:C:2016:748, para 27.

[41] *Paoletti*, *ibid*, paras 25 and 27.

[42] Instructive Ch Peristeridou, *The Principle of Legality in European Criminal Law* (Cambridge, Intersentia, 2015) 295 ff.

i. Legality as a Multilevel Concept

As a multilevel concept, legality first of all protects the system of shared competences in the area of freedom, security and justice.[43] Legality requires that the EU and national bodies stay within the confines of their respective law-making powers. In this sense and in stark contrast with the ECHR, EU legality serves democratic self-determination. It guarantees that decisions are taken at the right political level and by those organs that have been designated as responsible democratic actors in the EU treaties. Otherwise, legislative acts would lack democratic legitimacy.

Furthermore, legality allocates the (shared) responsibility to ensure throughout the law-making process that a new criminal provision is sufficiently foreseeable and accessible. A similarly shared responsibility exists with a view to the implementation of EU law. This insight is particularly important in areas of indirect enforcement such as criminal law. The EU treaties, with the exception of Article 325 of the Treaty on the Functioning of the European Union (TFEU), do not provide for criminal legislation by regulation. Union level and national level are to guarantee legal certainty in an integrated two-step process that combines EU directives and national implementation. The EU directive must be sufficiently clear and specific to allow a coherent and foreseeable implementation. For their part, national law-makers and courts are then to further substantiate and specify the content throughout the implementation process in order to reach the compulsory level of legal certainty.

Finally, EU legality comprises a *lex mitior* rule. Its codification in the CFR has confirmed its status as a special constitutional safeguard. However, no details are elaborated on in Article 49 CFR.[44] And there is little, if any, guidance from the CJEU. The Court does not say anything substantial about the justification and content of *lex mitior* in the *Berlusconi* case. It merely postulates its normative provenance from the common constitutional tradition of the Member States.[45] More has been said about origin and scope of the doctrine advocated by AG Kokott. She understands *lex mitior* as an exception to the principle of legality (legal certainty) that is ultimately 'based on considerations of fairness'.[46]

The characterisation of *lex mitior* as an exception to the legality principle does not hold up as the following section will show. *Lex mitior* must be conceived of and explained as an expression of legality. In this regard, the concept of *lex mitior* has remained obscure after *Berlusconi*. In the meantime, the ECtHR has recognised an unwritten *lex mitior* rule in Article 7 ECHR. To illuminate the meaning of *lex mitior*, one may therefore draw on the ECtHR's explorations in several recent decisions.

[43] *Ibid* 296, 297.
[44] Karsai (n 39) 24, 35.
[45] *Berlusconi et al* (n 1) para 68.
[46] AG Kokott, *Berlusconi et al* (n 1), opinion delivered on 14 October 2004, para 160.

ii. The Meaning of Lex Mitior

Unlike Article 15 of the International Covenant on Civil and Political Rights (ICCPR), the ECHR did not know a *lex mitior* safeguard until after the *Scopolla (No 2)* judgment of the ECtHR. If, subsequent to the commission of a criminal offence, the law provides for a lighter penalty or otherwise changes to the benefit of the offender, that new penalty or provision shall be applicable.[47] Either the constituent elements of the crime offence or the regulations in civil or administrative law (stipulating what conduct is prohibited) which they reference must have undergone a change over time. *Lex mitior* does not encompass changes in the legal status of the perpetrator or in the actual circumstances, in which case the unaltered criminal provisions are to be applied.[48]

The retroactive application of a milder criminal provision is obviously compatible with the ban on retroactive introduction of criminal prohibitions or stiffer sentences. But why should an offender benefit from changes in the law after the material time? What is more, many jurisdictions know the category of *Zeitgesetz* (temporary law; frequently used in the areas of commercial or trade law), which from the outset limits the applicability of criminal provisions to a certain period of time with a view to their purpose and substance. It is uniformly accepted that *lex mitior* does not apply to these laws.[49] They are not affected by later changes in the law.

The ECtHR argues that it would be contradictory and unequitable to hold a perpetrator accountable to standards that had already been repealed or abolished at the time of judgment.[50] To deny retroactive application of more lenient provisions would result in treating the same kind of conduct differently just because of different times of commission. The Strasbourg Court adds that the application of the more recent laws is also a matter of foreseeability under Article 7 ECHR.[51] While the latter argument is not beyond any doubt, the former one deserves a closer look. It is not the later change in the scope and degree of criminal punishability as such that calls for its application to earlier cases. It is neither contradictory nor unjust to hold perpetrators accountable according to the standards that they (foreseeably) had to obey when they committed the crime. The equity argument gains substance only when the reasons behind the legislative changes are taken into account. If the legislature changed a criminal statute for reasons of constitutional law, humanity

[47] *Scoppola v Italy (No 2)* App no 10249/03 (ECtHR, 17 September 2009) para 108 f; *Maktouf and Damjanović v Bosnia Herzegovina* App no 2312/08 and 34179/08 (ECtHR, 18 July 2013); *Gouarré Patte v Andorra* App no 33427/10 (ECtHR, 12 January 2016) para 28; see also *Schmitt v France* App no 52118/99 (ECtHR, 19 June 2001).

[48] *Paoletti and Others* (n 40) para 33; *Rosanò*, 'Principle of lex mitior, Is that you? – Case note on C-218/15, Paoletti and others' (2017) 8 *New Journal of European Criminal Law* 6, 12.

[49] T Fischer, *Strafgesetzbuch mit Nebenbestimmungen*, 64th edn (Munich, CH Beck, 2017) § 2 no 13.

[50] *Scoppola v Italy (No 2)* (n 47) para 108; in the same vein Herlin-Karnell (n 16) 20; in *Paoletti and Others* (n 40) para 27, the CJEU apparently also views the change in the position of the legislature as the pivotal aspect.

[51] *Scoppola v Italy (No 2)* (n 46) para 108.

or in reaction to changes in societal attitudes and preferences, it would, indeed, be unfair to judge a case based on standards that the sovereign has ex post facto found to be no longer acceptable for one of the aforementioned reasons. Viewed from this perspective, *lex mitior* is a procedural transmission belt for the implementation of normative change. It is only this normative dimension that justifies considering the *lex mitior* rule as an act of justice and proportionality.[52]

Recent case law implies that the ECtHR does not insist on mechanical compliance with the rule but pays attention to the reasons behind legislative changes, in particular if they affect only shorter interim periods (for technical reasons).[53] Overall, it emerges that *lex mitior* primarily applies when the competent national bodies (sometimes dictated by their constitutional courts) have changed their penal attitudes in favour of more lenient sanctions or have decided to increase the requirements of criminal liability. As a consequence, *lex mitior* does not establish a most-favoured-treatment clause. It knows certain implicit limits flowing from its normative foundations. Hence, the interests and reasons behind each change in the law need to be verified before *lex mitior* is applied.

VI. Reassessing Key Elements of *Berlusconi* in the Light of Multilevel Legality

In the final section the impact of such an updated understanding of legality on the contentious aspects of the *Berlusconi* case shall be tested, most importantly the relationship between primacy and *lex mitior*. However, whether the direct effect of directives would be compatible with or excluded by legality also deserves a second look.

A. Direct Effect

The rule that directives cannot be directly relied upon in order to determine or aggravate liability in criminal law is widely accepted. It is much less clear whether this limitation flows from the essential nature of the directive[54] or whether it is dictated by the legality principle. In terms of classical legality, a criminal provision

[52] Dannecker (n 17) 309, 315: 'Ausprägung verhältnismäßiger Gerechtigkeit'; see G Radbruch and E Wolf, *Rechtsphilosophie* (Stuttgart, Koehler, 1956) 123. G Dannecker, *Das intertemporale Strafrecht* (Tübingen, JCB Mohr, 1993) 410 ff; F-Ch Schroeder, 'Der zeitliche Geltungsbereich der Strafgesetze' in P Bockelmann and A Kaufmann (eds), *Festschrift für Bockelmann zum 70. Geburtstag 1978* (Munich, CH Beck, 1979); K Tiedemann, 'Zeitliche Grenzen des Strafrechts' in J Baumann and K Tiedemann (eds), *Einheit und Vielfalt des Strafrechts: Festschrift für Karl Peters zum 70. Geburtstag* (Tübingen, Mohr Siebeck, 1974).

[53] *Ruban v Ukraine* App no 8927/11 (ECtHR, 12 July 2016).

[54] Mitsilegas (n 38) 'Art 49' no 22.

must be sufficiently accessible and foreseeable. According self-executing direct effect to a criminal law directive would not be incompatible with this principle as long as the directive's contents are sufficiently clear and predictable. In a case like *Berlusconi*, a different assessment could be called for if the crime was committed after the entry into force of the new legislation. In these circumstances the scope of criminal liability might not be foreseeable in light of two potentially applicable sets of criminal law. The foreseeability is severely impaired by the fact that any potentially exclusionary effect does not extend beyond the scope of the conflict which, for its part, is staked out by the requirements of effectiveness. It is barely possible, at least for ordinary citizens, to determine the extent to which the older legislation would remain in force.

Directives and their direct effect also appear to qualify as 'law' for the purposes of the legality test. Human rights law requires that criminal liability is stipulated 'by law' but interprets this criterion as a matter of national constitutional law and takes account of the characteristics of the domestic legal order. In this light direct effect of criminal law directives becomes a matter of the EU legal order whose treaties generally do not allow for the introduction of directly applicable criminal provisions. EU law recognises direct effect of directives only in so far as it does not give rise to obligations against individuals. However, the key argument underlying this pillar of EU doctrine is not legality-driven. Direct effect was derived as an empowerment tool meant to enhance private enforcement of EU law.[55] There is no equivalent to that particular rationale in the field of criminal law. Direct effect would equip the prosecutor with a new basis of authorisation rather than bestow a subjective right.

But one could argue from a functional perspective that it would serve the interests of the Union to enlist courts and prosecutors to enforce EU law vis-à-vis recalcitrant national governments and parliaments. In this sense prosecutions based on directives would become means of indirect enforcement. In a criminal law environment, a prosecutor would nevertheless still pursue public (supranational) interests and not subjective rights that national bodies are (illegally) trying to withhold. In such a situation, it is reasonable to hold Member States accountable for their failure to implement EU law; it is much less convincing to shift the burden of non-compliance of states to their citizens.

Finally, in a multilevel system approving direct effect of criminal law directives would run counter to the system of shared competences. Since implementation at the national level adds vitally to the democratic legitimacy of EU criminal law, direct effect of criminal directives is irreconcilable with the notion of self-determination. As a consequence, the *Kolpinghuis* doctrine may also be interpreted as an imperative of EU legality.

Nevertheless, in the case at hand, direct effect was not the central issue. As was explained above, it was the indirect effect of various directives that would have

[55] Ruffert (n 33) 'Art 1 AEUV' no 29.

justified maintaining the applicability of national implementing legislation in the face of later legislative incursions. It needs to be analysed now whether such an outcome can be reconciled with the principle of legality.

B. *Lex Mitior*

In a supranational, multilevel context the concept of *lex mitior* needs to be adjusted to these constitutional structures. This transformation is particularly important with respect to the future application of EU law. While *lex mitior* has been incorporated in Article 49, paragraph 1 of the CFR, there are clear signs at the EU level that stronger enforcement should be expected.[56] It is only a question of time until courts will need to reconsider what limits the principle of legality sets on the enforcement of EU law. So far it remains an open question whether *lex mitior* applies when it contradicts Union law.[57]

In the words of AG Kokott:

> the retroactive application of a more lenient criminal provision is justified only where the primacy of Community law is preserved, that is to say, where the value judgements of the Community legislature are also taken into account and the (revised) opinion of the national legislature is in conformity with the provisions laid down by the Community legislature.[58] I do not see why the defendant should retroactively benefit from the national legislature's revised assessment of the punishability of his conduct where that assessment runs counter to the unchanged provisions of Community law.

Of course, her reasoning was based on the assumption that *lex mitior* is a concept of fairness, not of legality, and as such 'cannot have the same high status'.[59] From this point of view, there is, of course, no reason to make an exception to a fundamental constitutional principle such as legality based on considerations of fairness when a national legislature infringes the provisions of Union law.[60] On the contrary, it jeopardises both the uniform application of Union law and the coherence of national legal systems.

But despite the mischaracterisation of *lex mitior*, AG Kokott has a point. The introduction of the new legislation was not based on considerations of justice or humanity but a blunt attempt to hamstring the bringing to justice of a powerful politician. It had been adopted in clear violation of binding EU law for the

[56] *cp Taricco* (n 30).

[57] See HD Jarass, 'Art 49', no 15, *Charta der Grundrechte der EU*, 3rd edn (Munich, CH Beck, 2016); Biondi and Mastroianni (n 16) 553, 562–63, exclude its application when the lex *mitior* is in conflict with EU law. In support of their position they refer to the *Tombelli* and *Niselli* decisions of the CJEU: Joined Cases C-304/94, C-330/94, C-342/94, C-224/94 *Tombesi* [1997] ECR I-03561, para 43; Case C-457/02 *Niselli* [2004] ECR I-10853, para 30.

[58] AG Kokott, *Berlusconi et al* (n 1), opinion delivered on 14 October 2004, para 162.

[59] AG Kokott, *Berlusconi et al* (n 1), opinion delivered on 14 October 2004, para 160: It does not serve the rule of law.

[60] AG Kokott, *Berlusconi et al* (n 1), opinion delivered on 14 October 2004, para 163.

purpose of shielding the person concerned from criminal responsibility. Referring to the implicit limitations of *lex mitior* explained above it could be argued that it is reasonable not to apply it in this case since the applicants could not rely on any of the normative reasons underlying the concept.

But even assuming that Italian law-makers were truly motivated by concerns over the harshness of the earlier implementation, it would have remained a contentious question how to resolve the divide between national and European attitudes. From the standpoint of EU law the answer seems clear. EU law prevails as long as national legislation is incompatible with Union law. The legality principle does not command a diverging conclusion. Understood as a multilevel concept, it underscores that the Union view takes precedence over the national one (as long as it does not infringe on EU law, in particular the CFR, itself). The legality principle allocates authority to set policy goals and targets (of effectiveness) which are binding on other authorities further down the implementation stream. In this respect, it deserves mention that more lenient laws prevailed in several cases where the changes in the legal framework were in line with or required by Union law.[61] These examples highlight the multilevel dimension of the issue. The changes were brought about by the (according to primary EU law) competent supranational bodies and had to be followed even against differing perceptions at the national level.

To conclude, legality may limit primacy but only under the condition that it protects interests of proportionality and equity that are themselves grounded in or compatible with EU law. If, for instance, new domestic laws that repeal older implementation acts have properly satisfied EU requirements, the *lex mitior* rule must be observed in favour of the accused. Conflicts of assessment and interpretation are to be resolved through the mechanisms installed by the treaties. Where Member States are found liable of deliberate infringements of Union interests their legal actions must be disregarded for the determination of the *lex mitior*. This was the situation in *Berlusconi*. *Lex mitior*, therefore, had not forced national courts to afford the defendants the legal benefits intended to be brought about with the legislative changes.

VII. Conclusions

The *Berlusconi* judgment has left many crucial questions unanswered. The CJEU has done very little to clarify either the effects of directives or the notion of *lex mitior*. This contribution has sought to expose the many weaknesses and

[61] Case C-341/94 *Allain* [1996] ECR I-04631; Case C-230/97 *Awoyemi* [1998] ECR I-06781: crime inconsistent with directive before the end of the implementation period; Case C-193/94 *Skanavi* [1996] ECR I00929, paras 16, 17: more favourable criminal law takes retroactive effect to the extent to which it is contrary to the provisions of the Treaty (Eastern European workers without valid work permit may not be punished for prior illegal conduct after the date of accession that legalises said conduct).

shortcomings hidden behind the façade of this landmark ruling. It has tried to achieve this objective by exposing the premises of the ruling and confronting it with an advanced interpretation of the principle of legality. To date the Court has shown no initiative to reformulate its understanding of legality to fit the present constitutional structure of the EU.

Against the background of the *Berlusconi* case, this contribution therefore set out to develop and promote a multilevel notion of legality that understands the interpretation and implementation of EU directives as an exercise of public EU authority bound by supranational fundamental rights. Discussing the main argumentative pillars of *Berlusconi* based on these insights it emerged that denying the direct effect of criminal law directives finds strong support in a multilevel legality principle. By contrast, the *lex mitior* rationale behind the judgment collapsed. The legality principle lends no support to this key aspect of the *Berlusconi* ruling. Its landmark status should be scrapped. These findings and propositions may not be uncontroversial but they are necessary to revive a debate that is long overdue.

Allusion, Illusion, Delusion. The Assessment of the Berlusconi *Judgment in Italy*

ALBERTO DI MARTINO

I. Ambiguities

Many Italian scholars, after having expressed harsh criticism[1] against the Opinion of the Advocate General in the case of *Berlusconi and Others*,[2] should have felt relieved by the judgment of the Court on the limits of European law's prevalence on domestic law whenever fundamental principles of criminal law are at stake.[3] Nonetheless, it has left the impression that a fundamental issue explicitly raised by the Advocate General has been avoided, as to whether the principle of retroactivity of the more lenient penalty (the so-called *lex mitior* principle, newly enshrined in Article 49 of the Charter of Fundamental Rights of the European Union (CFREU)) is applicable whenever it would lead to the application of domestic rules that are incompatible with Community (now European) law.

Apart from the result, the reasoning of the Court has appeared ambivalent, if not inconsistent indeed.

[1] See especially the essays contained in R Bin, G Brunelli, A Pugiotto and P Veronesi (eds), *Ai confni del 'favor rei': Il falso in bilancio davanti alle Corti Costituzionale e di Giustizia* (Milano, Giuffrè, 2004), and in particular the harsh criticisms raised by N Mazzacuva, 'A proposito di "interpretazione creativa" tra diritto penale, principi costituzionali e direttive comunitarie' (but see S Riondato, 'Falso in bilancio e Corte di Giustizia CE (causa Berlusconi). Non è un rigetto', *ibid*). Specifically after the Opinion of the Advocate General and before the European Court of Justice's (ECJ) judgment, see L Mezzetti, 'Il falso in bilancio fra Corte di Giustizia e Corte Costituzionale italiana (passando attraverso i principi supremi dell'ordinamento costituzionale)', www.giurcost.org/studi/mezzetti.html (labelling that Opinion as 'more a pladoyer of a public prosecutor than an Opinion of an Advocate General in front of the European Court of Justice'). On the topic of the impact of European obligations to criminalise certain types of behaviour on the safeguards set out by the Italian Constitution (criminalisation only through parliamentary law – '*riserva di legge*'), see generally G Insolera, *Democrazia ragione e prevaricazione* (Milano, Giuffrè, 2003), especially 59–64.

[2] Opinion of the Advocate General (AG) Kokott delivered on 14 October 2004 [2004] OJ I3568.

[3] 'To uphold the conclusions of the Advocate General would have been tantamount to abandon the *lex mitior* principle': A Rossi, 'Reati ed illeciti amministrativi societari' in F Antolisei (C F Grosso), *Manuale di diritto penale. Leggi complementari*, 13th edn (Milano, Giuffrè, 2007) Vol I, 174.

It begins by pointing out that 'the principle of the retroactive application of the more lenient penalty forms part of the constitutional traditions common to Member States'[4] and therefore 'must be regarded as forming part of the general principles of Community law which national courts must respect' even when they apply domestic legislation implementing Community law – here, the directives on company law.[5] After this demanding statement of principle, the core question consequently and unavoidably arises, 'as to whether the principle … applies in the case in which that penalty is at variance with other rules of Community law'.

But once the problem is put on the table in such frank terms, it appears no more than the object of an allusion, since the implacable pace of this question is stopped, the issue dropped immediately as if it were swept under the carpet. The answer to that question is suddenly deemed to be 'unnecessary … for the purpose of the disputes in the main proceedings as the Community rule in issue is contained in a directive on which the law-enforcement authorities have relied against individuals'.[6]

According to the consistent case law of the Court, 'a directive cannot of itself impose obligations on an individual and cannot therefore be relied on as such against that individual'.[7] In particular, a directive cannot of itself and independently of a national legislation adopted for its implementation 'have the effect of determining or aggravating the liability in criminal law of persons who act in contravention of the provisions of that directive'.[8]

The reasoning of the Court revolves around the general principles of Community law (preference); it is not based on assumptions that take into account the rationale of the legality principle. The core question therefore remains unanswered and the judgment is substantially deluding.[9]

The main thrust of this commentary is to provide a new reading of the subject matter of the judgment. In fact, the strange ambiguities and silence on the core issue might suggest that the right issue has not really been focussed on. The subject matter of the *Berlusconi* judgment is only seemingly the retroactivity of more lenient penalties even though contrary to European law; it lies in a deeper divide (see section IV).

[4] C-387/02 *Berlusconi and Others* [2005] ECR I-03565, no 68.

[5] *Ibid* no 69.

[6] *Ibid* no 71.

[7] *Ibid* no 73 and the case law there cited. This point is highlighted in the authoritative textbook by G Tesauro, *Diritto dell'Unione Europea* (Padova, Cedam, 2012) 185.

[8] *Berlusconi* (n 4) no 74. The Court further observes that 'reliance on Article 6 of the First Companies Directive for the purpose of assessing' the compatibility of new domestic legislation with that provision 'could have the effect of setting aside application of the system of more lenient penalties' provided for by the new articles.

[9] G Insolera and V Manes, 'La sentenza della Corte di giustizia sul "falso in bilancio": un epilogo deludente?' (2005) *Cassazione penale* 2768–83.

II. Against the Advocate General: a) Retroactivity vs Effectiveness

Many commentators argue that the fundamental principle of *lex mitior* should prevail against any conflicting interests, even against the principle of sincere cooperation and prevalence of Community law.[10]

Moreover, it has been underscored that national judges, even if the domestic criminal law was deemed to be contrary to Community law, could never of their own motion set aside domestic provisions most favourable to the accused. They would have to submit a motion to the Constitutional Court asking to declare the provisions unconstitutional because they are contrary to Community law (however, it is only when legal rules can be easily interpreted in conformity with the Constitution that the ordinary judge is entitled to avoid asking the Constitutional Court).[11] Relevant to that effect is the revised provision of Article 117 of the Italian Constitution which sets out the mandatory compliance of domestic legislation with the European (Community) legal order[12] and other international law obligations.

The Constitutional Court has therefore maintained that, on the one hand, as a matter of principle it is vested with jurisdiction on the matter of the conformity of domestic legislation with the constitutional rules providing for the mandatory compatibility of domestic legal order with the (Community) Union law. On the other hand, however, it has been stressed that the Court cannot create 'additional' offences ('*in via additiva*'), nor aggravate penalties through its judgments, which would amount to the erosion of the scope of parliamentary discretion.[13] This is the case even when European legislation requires Member States to effectively penalise certain behaviours, but domestic legislation omits implementing it in an effective way.

Without going into much detail, I shall underline that at the root of this account is the strong belief that individual fundamental rights can never be affected by an effectiveness-oriented, functionalist view of criminal law as an accessory tool for enforcing (here: European) policies. Such prevalence would lead to the result of overcoming one of the main aims of criminal law, ie the protection of individuals from the arbitrariness of otherwise legitimate powers.[14] It is mainstream opinion that the principle of legality and in particular the *lex mitior* principle should therefore prevail against the duty of loyal cooperation (*fidélité communautaire*).

[10] Insolera (n 1) 63: 'If the sincere cooperation principle prevailed against the principle of parliamentary sovereignty to create criminal offences, it would amount to the punishment through criminal law of the mere slight disobedience to European rules'.

[11] Corte Costituzionale, 10 July–22 October 1996, n 356, GU 30 Oct 1996 no 44.

[12] '*Ordinamento comunitario*' is the literal wording of Article 117 of the Italian Constitution.

[13] Corte Costituzionale, 26 May–1 June 2004 no 161, para 7.1.

[14] See, eg, KS Gallant, *The Principle of Legality in International and Comparative Criminal Law* (Cambridge, Cambridge University Press, 2009) 22: 'legality can provide a bare minimum of protection against arbitrariness in the exercise of state power'.

This argument explains why a number of Italian scholars have harshly criticised the conclusions of the Advocate General. Criticism is focused primarily on two main areass: the foundation and content of the retroactivity principle, on the one hand, and the superfluousness of any 'prior completion of proceedings before the Italian Constitutional Court' on the other.[15]

The Advocate General maintained that the principle of legality in its specification of retroactivity was not affected in the present case, since

> The national legislation as it existed at the material time none the less remains applicable. The criminal liability of the defendants is therefore determined by the national legislation in force at the material time, that is to say, the old Article 2621 of the Italian Civil Code.[16]

The limits of the legislative discretion are clearly set in the Advocate General's account:

> For, since the obligation to ensure that provision is made for effective, proportionate and dissuasive penalties still obtains, Community law precludes the national legislature from simply repealing the existing rules governing penalties without at the same time replacing these with other effective, proportionate and dissuasive penalties.[17]
>
> The situation could be assessed otherwise only if the facts forming the subject of the charges had taken place after the adoption of Legislative Decree No 61/02. If Legislative Decree No 61/02 were set aside in relation to acts committed after its adoption, the application of a directive or of Article 10 EC could more readily be said to create obligations directly.[18]

Against this background, scholars have criticised the misconception of the Advocate General, who holds the *lex mitior* principle to be an exception to the legality principle. They stressed the fundamental reason underpinning the constitutional rank of the retroactivity rule, despite its not being enshrined as such in a constitutional provision. First of all, it is an expression of the principle of equal treatment: it would be unacceptable that a person be sanctioned at all, or subjected to a harsher penalty, when, due to a change in the law, the same conduct which was formerly criminalised becomes allowed (and therefore none shall be punished for that) or subjected to lesser penalties. It is true that derogations are allowed on reasonable grounds, as the Constitutional Court has pointed out when referring to the necessity of safeguarding competing interests (eg, temporary laws, exceptional laws, *res iudicata*). But it is firmly established case law that neither ordinary judges nor the Constitutional Court are allowed to expand offence definitions beyond the

[15] Opinion of AG Kokott (n 2) no 61: domestic 'courts have an obligation under *Community law* to set aside *of their own motion* any provision of national law which infringes Community law. The prior completion of proceedings before the Italian Constitutional Court is unnecessary for this purpose' (emphasis in original).

[16] Opinion of AG Kokott (n 2) no 145.

[17] Opinion of AG Kokott (n 2) no 146.

[18] Opinion of AG Kokott (n 2) no 152.

boundaries set forth by the legislature, and to draw lines of criminal policy that are autonomous and contrary to that devised by the legislature's discretion.[19]

Secondly, and contrary to the opinion of the Advocate General, the principle at hand is not only of a procedural nature and therefore a synonym of 'fairness',[20] but pertains to the most fundamental tenet of a legal order in a democratic society: the equality principle.

Finally, the construction of retroactivity of more lenient provisions as an exception to the principle of legality[21] is more than a mischaracterisation: it is a mistake, since non retroactivity is an integral part of the legality principle,[22] being at the same time 'a general principle of law accepted by the community of nations'.[23]

However, a new trend in the constitutional case law is worth mentioning. In recent judgments[24] the Constitutional Court has contended that the retroactivity of the 'new evaluation' of the 'criminal wrongfulness' (*Unrecht*) of the facts by the legislature is only legitimate if it does not infringe constitutional principles and prescriptive rules (*precetti*) by enacting a 'norm of privilege' (*norma di favore*), that is, by unreasonably and arbitrarily 'subtracting certain groups of individuals or behaviours from the remit of ordinary or more general rules that provide for a heavier punishment or treatment'.[25] One might wonder whether this qualification is able to encompass the violation of said Article 117 because of the indirect violation of the Constitution through the direct violation of Community law. This specific issue[26] has not been subjected to any further, in-depth analysis by legal scholars. This is surely due to the fact that the judgment maintains that a norm of privilege is not deemed to cover the abolition of heavier penalties but only the enactment of a new provision simultaneously in force with the more general one. But one might ask whether this distinction is correct, since the Court stresses that

[19] Corte costituzionale 27 February–15 March 2002, n 49, in GU 20 March 2002 no 12.

[20] 'That exception is based ultimately on considerations of fairness, which cannot have the same high status as, for example, the basis for application of the principle of legality in relation to crime and punishment, that is to say, the principle of legal certainty, which itself flows from the principle of the rule of law': Opinion of AG Kokott (n 2) no 160.

[21] Opinion of AG Kokott (n 2) no 159: 'The application of later, more lenient criminal provisions constitutes an exception to the aforementioned fundamental principle of legality in relation to crime and punishment (nullum crimen, nulla poena sine lege), since it involves the retroactive application of a provision other than that which was in force at the material time'.

[22] eg, Gallant (n 14) 11 under no (1), describes that part of the legality principle in criminal law as follows: 'no act that was not criminal under a law applicable to the actor (pursuant to a previously promulgated statute) … at the time of the act may be punished as a crime'.

[23] Gallant (n 14) 242.

[24] See especially Corte cost 23 October–23 November 2006, no 393, in GU 20 March 2002 no 12; Corte cost 8 November–23 November 2006 no 394, in GU 29 November 2006 no 47.

[25] See Corte cost 8 November–23 November 2006 no 394 (*ibid*).

[26] The more general question of the identity and nature of norms of privilege (*norme penali di favore*) has been extensively discussed (and the Court's holdings criticised) by the legal doctrine: eg L Zilletti and F Oliva (eds), *Il controllo di costituzionalità delle norme di favore. Verso un sindacato di legittimità sulle scelte politico-criminali?* (Pisa, Edizioni ETS, 2007). For further references, see: www.cortecostituzionale.it/actionPronuncia.do.

both norms must be entrusted with validity.[27] If a violation of binding European rules amounted to an inadmissible rule of privilege, and the answer to the question above[28] was positive, one would be able to conclude that a new, more lenient provision incompatible with (Community, now) European law should be legitimately deprived of any retroactive effect.

III. Against the Advocate General (and against the Court): b) Primacy vs Domestic Constitutional Control

Another controversial and highly criticised part of the reasoning of the Advocate General (and the Court) is where the Advocate General elaborates upon the power of ordinary judges to set aside the national legislation of their own motion: 'it is not necessary for the court to request or await the prior setting aside of such provision by legislative or other constitutional means'.[29]

The Court is of the same opinion on that specific point:

> Admittedly, should the national courts which made the references conclude, on the basis of the replies to be given by the Court, that the new Articles 2621 and 2622 of the Italian Civil Code do not, by reason of certain of their provisions, satisfy the Community law requirement that penalties be appropriate, it would follow, according to the Courts well-established case-law, that the national courts which made the references would be required to set aside, under their own authority, those new articles without having to request or await the prior repeal of those articles by way of legislation or any other constitutional procedure.[30]

However, The Italian Constitutional Court holds a different position.[31] If a tension arises between the obligation to interpret national law in conformity with EU law and the obligation to interpret domestic law in conformity with the state's Constitution, the judge must abide by the second obligation. The supreme judges maintain that in such instances exclusively the Constitutional Court – not the ordinary judges – is tasked with evaluating whether European (now Union) law is incompatible with supreme principles of the national Constitution (especially whenever individual fundamental rights are at stake).

[27] 'The lex mitior must be enacted legally' not only from a procedural point of view but also from a substantial one, ie, it complies with constitutional values: Corte cost 8 November–23 November 2006 no 394 (above n 24) para 6.4 (at the end).

[28] Text to n 26.

[29] Opinion of AG Kokott (n 2) no 135.

[30] *Berlusconi* (n 4) no 72.

[31] See, recently, Corte Costituzionale 10 April–31 May 2018, no 115 GU 6 June 2018 no 23, esp at para 8. Among scholars, see Mezzetti (n 1) para 2, p 5.

IV. Is (Only) Retroactivity at Stake? A Deeper Divide

As suggested at the outset of this contribution, I contend that retroactivity is neither exclusively, nor even primarily at stake here.

In spite of the commonly accepted narrative, which is also endorsed by the party concerned, the actual issue here is preliminary to the retroactivity problem. Albeit the interpretation of the structure and content of the criminal offences to be provided for by the domestic legislature encountered no further discussion, the view that I shall argue for is that the key issue here is rather the opposite: the interpretation *in malam partem* of Community law and, more broadly and fundamentally, the way of interpreting criminal statutes[32] on the *Spannungsfeld*, that is, along the line of tension between domestic and European law and even more generally in a multilevel legal order.

The fundamental issue raised by the *Berlusconi* judgment is primarily related to the way the Community (EU) legislature drafts and the competent institutions and Court(s) interpret the constituent elements of an offence definition. The issue is conceptually preliminary to and perhaps more twisted than that revolving around the retroactivity of more lenient penalties.

As well as the Advocate General, the Court holds that the penalties set out by Article 6 of the First Company Law Directive[33] must be 'extended' to the violation of obligations which are not explicitly provided for by the first Directive: under the plain wording of the said article, the offence definition for which the penalties are explicitly set forth is *only* the 'failure to disclose the balance sheet and profit and loss account as required by Article 2(1)(f)', which in turn requires such documents for each financial year, as subjected to 'compulsory disclosure' (number 1 first proposition).

Therefore, a different, more general and extended offence definition may be 'drafted' only through a twofold assumption: on the one hand, by way of a teleological interpretation in light of the purpose of the Directive(s); on the other hand, by making specific reference to the safeguard of the fundamental interest referred to by the general provision of Article 2(3) and (5) of the Fourth Company Law Directive.[34]

[32] Here: rules providing for a duty to criminalise.

[33] Directive 68/151/EEC on coordination of safeguards which, for the protection of the interests of members and others, are required by Member States of companies within the meaning of the second paragraph of Article 58 of the Treaty, with a view to making such safeguards equivalent throughout the Community [1968] OJ L65/8.

[34] Directive 78/660/EEC based on Article 54 (3)(g) of the Treaty on the annual accounts of certain types of companies [1978] OJ L222/11.

As to the teleological interpretation on the one hand, it is grounded on two basic purposes explicitly set forth by the First Company Directive, namely those of

a) protecting the interests of third parties;
b) compulsorily giving ('annual accounts must give') 'a true and fair view of a company's' economic and financial situation (duty of transparency in annual accounts).

On the other hand – reference to transparency in annual accounts not simply as a 'legal good'[35] but as a constituent element of an autonomous offence to be dealt with through the appropriate penalties referred to in Article 6 of the First Directive – the Court holds that 'annual accounts of companies coming within the scope of that [fourth] directive must give a true and fair view of the company's assets and liabilities, financial position and profit or loss'.[36]

Considering Article 6 of the First Company Directive in light of the whole system, the Court holds that:

> *the wording of that provision in itself* indicates that that system is to be understood as covering not only the case of absence of any disclosure of annual accounts but also the case of disclosure of annual accounts which have not been drawn up in accordance with the rules prescribed by the Fourth Companies Directive in regard to the content of such accounts.[37]

Actually, though, the Court infers the intention of the Community legislature

> 'to extend the system of penalties referred to in Article 6 of the First Companies Directive to cover infringements of the obligations contained in the Fourth Companies Directive' not from the wording but from the broad *purpose* of the 4th Directive. The extension is due to the '*absence* in that directive of general rules on penalties'.[38]

The fact that the penalties are not explicitly provided for as the consequence of violating the obligations set out by Article 2(3) and (5) of the Fourth Company Directive is recognised by the Court, which acknowledges that '*by contrast*, the Seventh Companies Directive does provide for such a general rule'.[39]

In spite of the struggle between the reference to the (supposed) univocal import of the black letter, on the one hand, and the acknowledgment of a need for systematic interpretation fastened on the Directive's purpose on the other, the line of reasoning drawn by the Court is clear. The fundamental principle that the annual accounts must give a true and fair view of the economic situation of the company follows from both the aim of the directives (fourth proposition

[35] On this concept, which is more familiar to continental criminal lawyers, see especially C Roxin, 'The Legislation Critical Concept of Goods-in-law under Scrutiny' (2013) *European Criminal Law Review* 3 ff.

[36] *Berlusconi* (n 4) no 54.

[37] *Berlusconi* (n 4) no 56 (italics added).

[38] *Berlusconi* (n 4) no 58 (italics added).

[39] *Berlusconi* (n 4) no 59 (italics added).

of the preamble of the Fourth Company Directive) and the specific content of Article 2(3) and (5) of the same Directive.

Accordingly, the wording of Article 6 of the Fourth Company Directive has to be interpreted in light of the context and objectives of the directives.

> It follows from the *purpose* of the Fourth Companies Directive, which supplements, for the same types of companies, the obligations laid down by the First Companies Directive, and *in the absence in that directive of general rules on penalties*, that ... the Community legislature did *intend to extend* the system of penalties referred to in Article 6 of the First Companies Directive to cover infringements of the obligations contained in the Fourth Companies Directive and, in particular, the failure to publish annual accounts which, in respect of their content, satisfy the rules laid down in that regard.[40]

The question arises whether the 'intention' to extend a rule explicitly set forth for a literally different situation should really be able to satisfy the requirement of a *lex stricta* – that the law be narrowly construed – as a constituent part of the legality principle in criminal matters.[41] One might bear in mind that the same requirement is mentioned even for the most serious crimes of international concern, such as those over which jurisdiction is conferred on the International Criminal Court (ICC) (Article 22 ICC-Statute): 'The definition of a crime shall be strictly construed and shall not be extended by analogy. In case of ambiguity, the definition shall be interpreted in favour of the person being investigated, prosecuted or convicted'.

The main concern for criminal lawyers worried about the content of the legality principle as requiring, first and foremost, a strict definition of offences and penalties, is the extension of penalties to obligations for which the penalties are not strictly, clearly and explicitly provided for. This concern appears at least as a key problem to be put on the table from the point of view of the Italian legal order, where the requirement is enshrined in the Constitution as a fundamental human rights principle and especially in its Article 25(2), thus operating as a counter-limit (*controlimite*) against the otherwise automatic primacy of the European rules over incompatible provisions laid down by the domestic legislature.

V. Overcoming the Divide? Analogy in Interpreting a State's Duty to Criminalise

The logic of counterlimits may lead the topic to a dead end. Slightly shifting the visual angle, though, one has to recognise that at stake here is a broader, preliminary

[40] *Berlusconi* (n 4) no 58 (italics added).

[41] On the origins of that requirement in the culture of the common law, from a historical-comparative perspective, see GP Fletcher, *Basic concepts of Criminal Law* (New York–Oxford, Oxford University Press, 1998) 208 and fn 5 (statutes in derogation of the common law must be strictly construed).

methodological issue that cannot be dealt with by invoking any authoritative text pertaining to a single domestic, supranational or international legal order. The question arises, in fact, how the legality principle operates in a multilevel legal order, and – as an even more overarching issue – what a criminal law should look like which, on the one hand, is based on that principle but, on the other, is certainly part of supranational legal orders and subjected to international law.

We may (reluctantly) still admit that criminal law is, or may be treated as, a tool among others through which the Union pursues the effectiveness of European policies, being consequently effective or policy-oriented.[42] However, since it potentially curbs the fundamental right to personal liberty however defined,[43] it must operate according to the *extrema ratio* principle. Not every attack against a protected interest can be subjected to criminal penalties: criminalisation encompasses only the types of behaviour which are strictly described within (= 'typified' by) the offence definition (*Tatbestandsmäßigkeit*).

I dare to remind people how deep the principle of 'precision' (*précision* in French) in criminal matters is rooted, not only in the exclusive clubs of pundits but also in the European culture, by quoting excerpts from one of the most famous pieces of world literature:

> This bond doth give thee here no jot of blood;
> *The words expressly are 'a pound of flesh'.*
> Take then thy bond, take thou thy pound of flesh,
> But in the cutting it if thou dost shed
> One drop of Christian blood, thy lands and goods
> Are by the laws of Venice confiscate
> Unto the state of Venice.[44]

What has been said above on the strict-description principle, as we may name it, holds true moreover for the 'fundamental principle … that annual accounts of companies coming within the scope of that directive must give a true and fair view of the company's assets and liabilities, financial position and profit or loss', as it is enshrined in the fourth recital of the Preamble and in Article 2(3) and (5) of the Fourth Directive.

One might consider that the Fourth Directive, on the one hand, expresses the general principle of the true and fair view. On the other hand, the Directive explicitly and more specifically prescribes to this end (the purpose of implementing that general principle), as the *specific* content of the State's obligation, a 'mandatory

[42] On that topic see, eg, an interesting article written by J Horder, 'Bureaucratic "Criminal" Law. Too Much of a Bad Thing?' in RA Duff, L Farmer, SE Marshall, M Renzo and V Tadros (eds), *Criminalization* (New York–Oxford, Oxford University Press, 2014), 101 esp 114 ff.

[43] Personal liberty is not an uncontroversial concept, but the philosophical foundations of that premise cannot be dealt with in this short contribution. See MS Moore, 'Liberty's Constraints on What Should be Made Criminal' in Duff, et al, *ibid*, 182 esp 194 ff.

[44] W Shakespeare, *The Merchant of Venice*, IV, 1 (italics added).

layout … for the balance sheet and the profit and loss account' as well as laying down 'the minimum content of the notes on the accounts'.

At the forefront of this obligation there is, as the Court itself acknowledges, an absence of explicit criminalisation, the latter being limited to the very specific behaviour of 'failure to disclose'. This is not irrational, from the point of view of the *extrema ratio* principle: only the modal criteria of the safeguarding of the protected interests are criminally relevant – in other words, requirements relating to the general and abstract *mode or form* of the companies' annual documents (structure, content, valuation methods and disclosure). This is the content, but also the limit of the State's obligation under a strict reading of the offence definition.

Admittedly, when Article 2(3) of the Fourth Directive provides for the rule that 'the annual accounts shall give a true and fair view of the company's assets' etc, it sets a twofold obligation, with different legal content and status: the first – although indirectly – towards individuals, who must abstain from false accounting; the second towards the State. The content of the first and the second type of obligation are closely connected, but they do not overlap. The exact content of the State's obligation has yet to be determined. According to a strict legality principle (narrow construction of criminal offences), the obligation to criminalise – the duty to recur to adequate sanctions against false accounting – might at most be extended *within the limits of the modal obligation to adopt harmonized schemes of accounting* intended to enable members and third parties to gain a true and fair view of the company's economic and financial situation. In other words, the State shall penalise the failure to adopt and respect the mandatory layout prescribed by the Fourth Directive.

However, the view that I shall argue for is that extension by analogy (ie by way of judicial interpretation) is admissible even *in malam partem* whenever at stake is not the content of the individual duties, but the content of the obligation is incumbent upon the States, given the allocation of powers within the European legal order. In other words, in a multilevel legal order analogy is a legitimate way of interpreting States' duties to act even in criminal matters, provided that people are not adversely affected by that. Individuals cannot suffer for States' failure to comply with their own obligation.

For the case at hand, therefore, it is fully legitimate to interpret the directives as imposing on the Member States the duty to criminalise both the failure to disclose and false accounting.

But it should be clear that we face here an entirely different issue than that of the retroactivity of a more lenient penalty. Rather the contrary: even if we admit judicial interpretation *in malam partem* of the content of the State's obligation, that interpretation cannot be retrospective. At stake is the (universally accepted)[45] rule of non-retroactivity of crime and punishment.

[45] Gallant (n 14) 241.

3

C-105/03 – *Pupino*

Impact of the Pupino *Decision on EU Law*

MARIA FLETCHER

I. Introduction

Well over a decade on from the decision, this chapter considers the significance of the *Pupino*[1] judgment of the Court of Justice of the European Union ('CJEU or 'the Court') today from an EU perspective. *Pupino* is (in)famous for having extended the EC constitutional principle of 'indirect effect' to the then third pillar, which dealt with Police and Judicial Cooperation in Criminal matters (PJCC). More precisely, it held that 'the principle of conforming legislation' was 'binding in relation to framework decisions adopted in the context of Title VI of the Treaty on European Union'.[2] This chapter will recall the key features of the principle as outlined by *Pupino*; identify how that principle has evolved in later case law; and evaluate its place in the considerably different post-Lisbon context of EU PJCC and in light of the peculiar qualities of the field of criminal law. It is well known that the changes effected by the Treaty of Lisbon were transformative in the field of EU crime and policing, particularly in the sense of absorbing the agenda into a largely Communitarian constitutional framework and it is equally well recognised that *national* criminal justice systems represent and actively reinforce the sovereign authority of the State.

A review of cases in which the Court considers the indirect legal effects of PJCC instruments post *Pupino* and post-Lisbon essentially reveal both a continued commitment to this principle, and a full alignment of its fleshed out terms – scope and limits – with the principle as developed more generally in EU law. From one perspective, the continuation of application of the principle is less controversial in the post-Lisbon era of enhanced constitutional legitimacy

[1] C-105/03 *Maria Pupino* [2005] ECR I-5285.
[2] *Ibid*, para 43.

and rights protection,[3] especially when compared to the *Pupino* era when it appeared that the Court had effectively ignored the added sensitivity of criminal law matters as reflected in the third pillar constitutional and institutional framework. For EU lawyers, it is hardly surprising that the Court has confirmed the continued validity of this constitutional tool for achieving an understanding and application of the EU that coheres with domestic law. It is by its very nature, a flexible and limited tool which allows for inconsistencies between two connected legal orders to be ironed out gently and quietly at the behest of national authorities 'as far as possible'. Nevertheless, another perspective is that national criminal law remains a highly sensitive field imbued with uniquely protected principles and safeguards for individuals. Any constitutional principle which compels national judges to adopt an interpretation of national criminal law that it would otherwise not have to, but for EU law – the primary rationale of which is to make EU law more effective in national legal orders – is likely to be met with some resistance. This tension is bound to be further exaggerated where criminal law itself is being 'Europeanised' because not only is there more scope for EU law to impinge on domestic criminal law, there is more scope for substantial clashes, where for instance cornerstone principles, such as legality, diverge or emerge at the EU level only incrementally.

As predicted by many commentators, serious disruption to the balance of rights in national criminal justice systems as a direct consequence of EU level intervention would almost certainly provoke direct challenges from national courts as to the authority of EU instruments adopted in this field and to the scope and exercise of EU competences.[4] To some extent this has played out,[5] but through this direct dialogue there are some tentative but important signs that the Court is mindful of the national sensitivities and peculiarities of criminal law and further, that it is recognising its own enhanced responsibility in this field. These tentative conclusions emerge from a reading of two cases in particular – the *Caronna*[6] case and the *Taricco* 'saga'[7] – where we see, first, the CJEU attributing particular

[3] The Treaty of Lisbon for instance enhanced the role of the European Parliament and the CJEU in the field of PJCC and confirmed the legal status, equivalent to the EU treaties, of the EU Charter of Fundamental Rights [2010] OJ C83/2. The Charter includes the right to liberty and security (Art 6); the right to an effective remedy and to a fair trial (Art 47); the presumption of innocence and right of defence (Art 48); principles of legality and proportionality of criminal offences and penalties (Art 49); and the right not to be tried or punished twice in criminal proceedings for the same criminal offence (Art 50).

[4] See, for instance, Jo Shaw, 'One or Many Constitutions?: The Constitutional Future of the European Union in the 2000s from a Legal Perspective' (2007) 52 *Scandinavian Studies in Law* 393.

[5] For instance the various constitutional challenges to the European Arrest Warrant at both the national and EU level; See, eg, E Guild (ed), *Constitutional Challenges to the EAW* (TMC Asser, 2006) and C-303/05 *Advocaten voor de Wereld* [2007] ECR I-3633. More recently see C-105/14 *Ivo Taricco and Others* Grand Chamber, Judgment of 8 September 2015 (*Taricco I*) and C-42/17 *M.A.S & M.B* Grand Chamber, Judgment of 7 December 2017 (*Taricco II*).

[6] Case C-7/11 *Caronna* [2012] OJ C80 /26.

[7] *Taricco I* and *Taricco II* (n 5).

importance to the position and scope of fundamental rights and safeguards in EU law and between EU law and national law and, second, an acknowledgement of the pressures on national judges and the limits of what can be achieved through national judiciaries when the legal worlds of EU (criminal) and national criminal law collide.

These developments indicate an evolving relationship between the EU and domestic legal orders in the field of criminal law, as well as articulating a fuller understanding of EU criminal law and crucially, the place of rights within it. Through direct, constructive and co-operative dialogue – possible thanks to the now full jurisdiction of the CJEU over PJCC and heeding the new and extended duties and principles articulated in Article 4(2) and 4(3) Treaty on European Union (TEU)[8] respectively – one might hope to see more mutual understanding and accommodation as between EU and national law and constitutional and criminal law. This, would certainly helpfully inform our understanding of the limits of the scope of the consistent interpretation duty upon national judges and probably also encourage a more active use of it. Today then, the *Pupino* principle remains valid in theory but poses significant challenges to national judges in practice. We need to look beyond it to better understand its scope and contribution.

II. *Pupino*: The Judgment, the Critique, the Context

The *Pupino* judgment of June 2005 addressed for the first time the question of the effects within national legal orders of measures adopted under the powers of Title VI of the TEU dealing with police and judicial cooperation in criminal matters (also known as the 'third pillar'). In holding that national judges have a duty to interpret national law so far as possible in conformity with third pillar instruments, known as framework decisions – and in this case specifically a Framework Decision on the Standing of Victims in Criminal Proceedings[9] – the Court transposed a relatively mature constitutional doctrine developed within the framework of the first 'Community' pillar to the 'third pillar'. This doctrine of

[8] Art 4(2) TEU reads: 'Pursuant to the principle of sincere cooperation, the Union and the Member States shall, in full mutual respect, assist each other in carrying out tasks which flow from the Treaties.

The Member States shall take any appropriate measure, general or particular, to ensure fulfilment of the obligations arising out of the Treaties or resulting from the acts of the institutions of the Union.

The Member States shall facilitate the achievement of the Union's tasks and refrain from any measure which could jeopardise the attainment of the Union's objectives.' Art 4(3) TEU reads: 'The Union shall respect the equality of Member States before the Treaties as well as their national identities, inherent in their fundamental structures, political and constitutional, inclusive of regional and local self-government. It shall respect their essential State functions, including ensuring the territorial integrity of the State, maintaining law and order and safeguarding national security. In particular, national security remains the sole responsibility of each Member State.'

[9] Council Framework Decision 2001/220/JHA of 15 March 2001 on the standing of victims in criminal proceedings [2001] OJ L82/1 (no longer in force).

conforming interpretation is often referred to as the principle of 'indirect effect'. It was first espoused by the Court in the case of *Von Colson*[10] in 1984 and fleshed out in a number of ways by later cases.

A brief reminder of the facts and queries in this case might be useful at this point. Ms Pupino, a children's nursery teacher in Italy, was prosecuted for having allegedly used physical violence against children in her care. At the initial stage of the criminal proceedings the public prosecutor asked for the children to be heard out of court considering their age and vulnerability. Such special arrangements for taking evidence were permitted pursuant to the Framework Decision on the Standing of Victims in Criminal Proceedings, but not permitted according to the relevant provisions of the Italian code of criminal procedure. Unhappy with the limited scope of national law, the Italian Court sought to question its compatibility with the EU Framework Decision bearing in mind its duty to 'interpret its national law in the light of the letter and spirit of Community provisions'. It consequently stayed national proceedings and requested a preliminary ruling from the CJEU, in the course of which the CJEU confirmed that the duty of conforming interpretation applies in respect of framework decisions.

The Court based its finding on two familiar foundations, plus two more. The 'binding character' of framework decisions together with the duty of loyal or sincere cooperation provided the familiar Community law justificatory bases of the principle of conforming interpretation. These were supplemented by an *effet utile* argument linked to the limited jurisdiction of the Court to give preliminary rulings under the third pillar, namely that that jurisdiction would 'be deprived of most of its useful effect if the duty of conforming interpretation did not exist'. And finally, it held that is 'perfectly comprehensible' that the authors of the EU Treaty designed third pillar instruments to have similar legal effects to first pillar instruments in order to contribute effectively to the pursuit of the Union's objectives.

This was remarkable indeed at the time. Prior to the *Pupino* judgment it had been assumed that third pillar instruments were not capable of giving rise to any legal effects in domestic regimes, in part because of the distinctive institutional features of the third pillar and in part because the Treaty expressly declared that Framework Decisions 'shall not entail direct effect'.[11] So, although framework decisions were similar in character to the Community legislative instrument – directives – in that they were binding on Member States and the manner in which they were to be implemented in domestic law was left to the Member States, they differed fundamentally from directives in that they did not give rise to rights or obligations which individuals could enforce before their national courts. Nonetheless, the *Pupino* judgment made clear that national courts *were* required to 'take consideration of all the rules of national law and to interpret them, so far as possible, in the light of the wording and purpose of the Framework Decision'.[12]

[10] Case 14/83 *Von Colson and Kamann v Land Nordrhein-Westfalen* [1984] ECR 1891.
[11] Art 34 (2)(b) TEU Treaty.
[12] *Pupino* (n 1) para 62.

In terms of the scope of the principle, the Court provided a relatively comprehensive and familiar outline. The national courts were to consider 'the whole of national law' in order to assess how far it can be applied in such a way as not to produce a result contrary to that envisaged by the framework decision[13] thereby reflecting the *Pfeiffer*[14] case, which itself absorbed the *Marleasing*[15] extension to interpretative duty to national provisions whether adopted before or after the relevant EU law. The 'so far as possible' construction also reflects the *Marleasing* reformulation of the *Von Colson* principle, and reminds us that national courts are ultimately its gatekeepers. But the limits of what is possible are then articulated by the Court in what were by then familiar terms.[16] First, that the obligation is limited by the general principles of law, particularly those of legal certainty and non-retroactivity. And more specifically still, 'those principles prevent that obligation from leading to the criminal liability of persons who contravene the provisions of a framework decision from being determined or aggravated on the basis of such a decision alone, independently of an implementing law'.[17] Later in the judgment the Court confirmed that the Framework Decision must be interpreted in such a way that fundamental rights, including in particular the right to a fair trial as set out in Article 6 of the Convention and interpreted by the European Court of Human Rights, are respected.[18]

A second, familiar limit identified was that the obligation cannot serve as the basis for an interpretation of national law *contra legem*.[19] In other words, the obligation on the national court ceases when the contents of the national law provision are not open to interpretation in conformity with the norm of EU law. The national judges need only apply interpretative methods recognised by it and national law should not be improperly distorted; ultimately it is for the national judges to decide on what is possible.[20]

Applying these limits to the query at issue in the case, the Court held that 'the provisions which form the subject-matter of this reference for a preliminary ruling do not concern the extent of the criminal liability of the person concerned but the conduct of the proceedings and the means of taking evidence'.[21] And in relation to the *contra legem* limitation the Court noted that it was 'not obvious' that an interpretation of national law in conformity with the framework decision is

[13] *Pupino* (n 1) para 47.

[14] Joined Cases C-397/01 to C-403/01 *Bernhard Pfeiffer and Others* [2004] ECR I-8835.

[15] Case 106/89 *Marleasing SA v La Comercial Internacional de Alimentacion SA* [2004] ECR I-8835.

[16] Case 80/86 *Kolpinghuis Nijmegen BV* [1987] ECR 3969 and C-212/04 *Adeneler and Others* [2006] ECR I-6057.

[17] *Pupino* (n 1) paras 44 and 45.

[18] *Pupino* (n 1) para 59.

[19] *Pupino* (n 1) para 47. By analogy with *Kolpinghuis Nijmegen* (n 16), para 13 and *Adeneler and Others* (n 16) para 110.

[20] For an interesting exposition on the *contra legem* limit, see M Brenncke, 'Hybrid Methodology for the EU Principle of Consistent Interpretation' (2017) *Statute Law Review*.

[21] *Pupino* (n 1) para 46.

impossible, before finally conceding that it is for the national court to determine whether such a conforming interpretation is indeed possible.[22] The upshot of all this was that EU law should be interpreted to enable special evidence-gathering procedures to be used for children in Italian criminal trials, something that was not previously possible as a matter of national law.

This case, reviewed extensively at the time, was a remarkable assertion of the constitutional quality and legal effects of a field of EU law that had retained significant features of inter-governmentalism, precisely because States wished to reflect the centrality of criminal justice issues to their own sovereign power. The explicit bar to framework decisions creating direct effect; the limited jurisdiction of the CJEU; the limited role of the European Parliament and the unanimity requirement to pass legislation were all distinctive features of the third pillar. Should EU level action in this field be capable of producing independent legal effects in the national context – albeit indirect – that could be a game changer in terms of the vertical power balance between the EU and States in relation to criminal law matters? *Pupino* was that game changer.

From an EU constitutional law perspective, this was another notable act of judicial constitutional activism on the part of the CJEU. Certainly, dubiety surrounded the legitimacy of the ruling given the pillar distinctions, the Court's reasoning was subject to critique and interesting constitutional questions were pondered, such as whether the Community principles of supremacy and State liability might also apply to the third pillar.[23] Cautious optimism was expressed to the extent that the principle of conforming interpretation might be a route to securing the protection of individual rights in the PJCC field and to the extent that the ruling enhanced judicial scrutiny over an EU field of cooperation with relatively impoverished democratic credentials.[24] And we were reminded of the wider political context of the day, namely that the EU's political actors and the Member States had already laid out a 'Communitarised' constitutional vision for the field of EU criminal law in the then Draft Constitutional Treaty – the features of which would ultimately come to fruition in the Lisbon Treaty. It had been suggested that the Court was boldly flexing its transformative constitutional muscles[25] at a time of gathering political storm clouds *vis a vis* the draft Constitutional Treaty, but it might equally have been the case that the Court in *Pupino* simply anticipated what it had reason to believe was going to happen in any case.[26]

From another perspective, this ruling was seen as an entirely inappropriate incursion into sovereign territory, requiring well-established national criminal

[22] *Pupino* (n 1) para 48.

[23] See, for instance, E Spaventa, 'Opening Pandora's Box: Some Reflections on the Constitutional Effects of the Decision in Pupino' (2007) 3(1) *European Constitutional Law Review* 5; M Fletcher, 'Extending "Indirect Effect" to the Third Pillar: The Significance of Pupino?' (2005) 30(6) *European Law Review* 862; JSpencer, 'Child Witnesses and the EU' (2005) 64(3) *Cambridge Law Journal* 569.

[24] Fletcher and Spaventa, *ibid.*

[25] Fletcher (n 23).

[26] Spaventa (n 23) 24.

procedures to be revised at the behest of EU law. National constitutional courts were among those enjoining the EU treading carefully in this field. For instance in its judgment reaffirming the constitutionality of the act adopting the Lisbon Treaty 2007, the *Bundesverfassungsgericht* (BVerfG) observed that the European Union should proceed with caution given the potential encroachment on competences primarily reserved to the Member States on the basis of special constitutional sensitivity, [including] 'decisions on substantive and formal criminal law [and] on the disposition of the police monopoly on the use of force towards the interior …'.[27]

III. The Principle after *Pupino*, after Lisbon

As things transpired, the 'pillarised' critiques of, and queries arising from, *Pupino* lost their salience with the entry into force of the Treaty of Lisbon, as of 1 May 2009. But what did this mean for the application of the conforming interpretation principle to the PJCC sphere in practical terms? It will be recalled that the Lisbon Treaty changes were particularly transformative in the field of EU crime and policing both in terms of its substance and its constitutional framing. Most prominently, the pillar structure of the EU came to an end and PJCC was incorporated into the Treaty on the Functioning of the European Union (TFEU), complete with the application of many 'Community law features' to the field, including democratic and (full)[28] judicial oversight by the European Parliament and the Court of Justice, respectively. Of particular note, another *Communitarising* feature introduced was that henceforth, the only legislative instruments to be adopted in the field of police and criminal law matters were to be the traditional Community 'directives', replete with direct and indirect legal effect potential.[29] What then of the already adopted third pillar framework decisions? They survived the entry into force of the Lisbon Treaty due to the Transitional Provisions in Protocol 36, according to which the legal effect of acts adopted pursuant to the third pillar before 1 May 2009 were 'preserved until those acts are repealed, annulled or amended in implementation of the treaties'.[30] So, framework decisions until such time as they were *Lisbonised*, would continue to lack direct effect, but would be able to have indirect legal effects in a given national legal system *a la Pupino*. This has been confirmed by the Court in relation to enduring post-Lisbon framework decisions as we will

[27] BVerfG, 2 BvE 2/08, para 252–253. See B Davies, 'EU Criminal Law in National Courts: Breaking the Monopoly?' (2013) 34(3) *Liverpool Law Review* 241.

[28] Protocol No 36 on transitional arrangements.

[29] Article 83 TEU.

[30] Article 9 of Protocol (No 36) on transitional provisions, annexed to the EU treaties [2012] OJ C326/322.

see in more detail below.[31] The principle would almost certainly apply following their amendment to, presumably, a directive.[32] The extent to which such amending (or repealing) directives acquire direct effect is more contested.[33] However the principles of supremacy, direct effect and indirect effect would apply to any new post-Lisbon legislative measures adopted in the field of police and judicial cooperation in criminal matters.[34]

The CJEU has, on a number of occasions since the entry into force of the Treaty of Lisbon, considered the legal effects of enduring framework decisions, including for the first time, mutual recognition instruments that are assumed to be underpinned by mutual trust between Member States. Compliance with the duty of conforming interpretation in this context might be more challenging for national judges as the limits of that mutual trust are exposed. Nonetheless, as we shall now see, in these cases, it has taken the opportunity to reiterate the principle of conforming interpretation in identical terms to cases previously handed down in different fields, so that it is fully absorbed into a single EU articulation of the principle.

In ruling on the scope of a Member State to implement a ground for non-execution of the European arrest warrant,[35] the Grand Chamber in *Lopes Da Silva Jorge*,[36] reiterated the interpretative duty on national judges in these more expansive terms: the principle

> requires national courts to do whatever lies within their jurisdiction, taking the whole body of domestic law into consideration and applying the interpretative methods recognised by it, with a view to ensuring that the framework decision in question is fully effective and to achieving an outcome consistent with the objective pursued by it.

In relation to the *justificatory* foundations of the principle, we also see alignment with more recent cases on the principle of conforming interpretation. The Court in *Lopes Da Silva Jorge* justified the duty on national judges with reference first, to the 'binding character' of framework decisions and second, by claiming that

[31] C-42/11 *Lopes Da Silva Jorge* [2011] ECR C103/16; C-554/14 *Ognyanov* [2015] ECR C73/17; the fullest summary of the principle in a case concerning EU criminal justice matters can be found in Case C-579/15 *Daniel Adam Popławski* Judgment of the Court (Fifth Chamber) of 29 June 2017 at paras 26–36. All the cases concerned mutual recognition instruments.

[32] The victims' rights framework decision at issue in *Pupino* has now been replaced by Directive 2012/29/EU of 25 October 2012 establishing minimum standards on the rights, support and protection of victims of crime [2012] OJ L315/57.Note also that although the duty of consistent interpretation is most commonly applied in the context of directives, the duty also applies in relation to the EU Treaties, general principles of EU law, regulations, recommendations and potentially even to the EU Charter of Fundamental Rights. See Sim Haket, 'Coherence in the Application of the Duty of Consistent Interpretation in EU Law' (2015) 8(2) *Review of European Administrative Law* 215 at fn 11.

[33] H Satzger, 'Legal Effects of Directives Amending or Repealing Pre-Lisbon Framework Decisions' (2015) 6(4) *New Journal of European Criminal Law* 528.

[34] Steve Peers, *EU Justice and Home Affairs*, 3rd edn (Oxford, Oxford University Press, 2011) 42.

[35] Council Framework Decision 2002/584/JHA of 13 June 2002 on the European arrest warrant and the surrender procedures between Member States [2002] OJ L190/1.

[36] C-42/11 *Lopes Da Silva Jorge* [2011] ECR C103/16.

the duty 'is inherent in the system of the TFEU, since it permits national courts, for matters within their jurisdiction, to ensure the full effectiveness of EU law when they determine the disputes before them'.[37]

The first of these justifications – the binding nature of framework decisions – can be found in *Pupino*. Missing now, of course, is the justificatory argument in *Pupino* connected to ensuring the *effet utile* of the limited third pillar preliminary reference jurisdiction; that being unnecessary given the extended judicial oversight introduced by the Treaty of Lisbon. Missing too, also logically, is the argument drawn from the implied intention on the part of the authors of the EU Treaty concerning the legal effect of framework decisions. More conspicuous however, is the absence of any explicit reference to the principle of loyal cooperation as the foundation for the effectiveness argument, and hence the principle of conforming interpretation. It will be recalled that the pre-Lisbon principle of loyal or sincere cooperation has been a clear basis for the duty of consistent interpretation from its original development in *Von Colson*. Found only in Article 10 EC and therefore presumed by some to extend only to the Community pillar, the Court in *Pupino*, somewhat controversially, ruled that it also applied in respect of the third pillar, thus providing a by then well-established foundation for the extension of the principle of indirect effect. In its post-Lisbon iteration,[38] the principle of loyalty now appears as a strengthened, reciprocal and general principle of 'sincere cooperation'[39] between the Union and the Member States in Article 4(3) TEU, clearly applicable to all policy fields.[40] Reference to it would have been easy and perhaps expected and yet it is not there.[41] Instead the Court, as noted above, refers to the principle of conforming interpretation as being 'inherent in the system of the TFEU …' which first emerged in the *Pfeiffer* judgment[42] in relation to ensuring the full effectiveness of *Community* Law and was extended to

[37] *Ibid* paras 53 and 54.

[38] Article 4(3) TEU reads: 'Pursuant to the principle of sincere cooperation, the Union and the Member States shall, in full mutual respect, assist each other in carrying out tasks which flow from the Treaties.

The Member States shall take any appropriate measure, general or particular, to ensure fulfilment of the obligations arising out of the Treaties or resulting from the acts of the institutions of the Union.

The Member States shall facilitate the achievement of the Union's tasks and refrain from any measure which could jeopardise the attainment of the Union's objectives.'

[39] Contrast this with the more limited and one-way duty of Article 10 EC: 'Member States shall take all appropriate measures, whether general or particular, to ensure fulfilment of the obligations arising out of this Treaty or resulting from action taken by the institutions of the Community. They shall facilitate the achievement of the Community's tasks. They shall abstain from any measure which could jeopardise the attainment of the objectives of this Treaty.'

[40] Although note that a separate duty of cooperation is maintained in Article 24(3) TEU in specific relation to Common Foreign and Security Policy.

[41] Herlin-Karnell reminds us that in the terrorist sanctions judgments of T-256/07 *OMPI* C-354/04 P *Gestoras Pro Amenstia* and C-355/04 P *Segi*, the notion of loyalty was recognised as being 'especially binding' in the third pillar. See Ester Herlin-Karnell, 'In the wake of *Pupino*: *Advocaten voor der Wereld* and *Dell'Orto*' (2007) 8(12) *German Law Review* 1147.

[42] *Pfeiffer* (n 14), para 114.

cover *European Union* law in the post-Lisbon case of *Dominguez*,[43] concerning the Working Time Directive.[44] In *Pfeiffer* the duty of sincere cooperation was also explicitly recalled as a foundation for the duty of consistent interpretation, whereas it did not appear in *Dominguez*. Are we to assume that the sincere cooperation principle is still a central foundation for the duty but that it is now simply part of the 'inherent in the system of the Treaty' argument? It is not clear. On the one hand, its absence might be welcomed given the argued overreliance and ambiguous impact of the *effet utile/effectiveness* argument used by the Court as both an enforcement mechanism and a competence parameter.[45] On the other hand, emphasising the importance of sincere cooperation in its fleshed out and *reciprocal* Lisbon version, might be of rejuvenated and richer value today, particularly in relation to EU criminal law, where there is a greater likelihood of, and potentially more at stake in terms of individual rights in, clashes between the EU and Member States. It is suggested that Article 4(3) TEU, especially when read with Article 4(2) TEU – the respect for national identities provision[46] – provides a constitutional framework that allows for a more sophisticated development and understanding of criminal law *at* and *by* EU and national levels; it should be capable of embracing more than a narrow *effet utile* route to achieving – indeed, insisting on – the coherence of EU law above all else. As promising as this might sound, it is also ambiguous, at least in the current stage of development of EU criminal law. Perhaps, the Court is sensitive to this; nevertheless it still feels odd to eschew direct reference to the sincere cooperation duty as a primary rationale for the principle of conforming interpretation.

In *Ognyanov*[47] another instrument of mutual recognition was considered, this time Framework Decision 2008/909.[48] The Grand Chamber pursued a similar alignment of the principle in this case. Here, it confirmed that the duty on

[43] C-282/10 *Dominguez* Judgment of the Court (Grand Chamber), 24 January 2012 at para 24. For a critical commentary of this case, see M De Mol, 'Dominguez: A Deafening Silence' (2012) 8(2) *Electronic Communications Law Review* 280.

[44] Directive 2003/88/EC of the European Parliament and of the Council of 4 November 2003 concerning certain aspects of the organisation of working time. [2003] OJ L 299/9.

[45] For a full exposition of this thesis in the context of EU criminal law, see E Herlin-Karnell, *The Constitutional Dimension of European Criminal Law* (Oxford, Hart Publishing, 2012).

[46] Introduced for the first time by the Treaty of Lisbon, Article 4(2) TEU reads: 'The Union shall respect the equality of Member States before the Treaties as well as their national identities, inherent in their fundamental structures, political and constitutional, inclusive of regional and local self-government. It shall respect their essential State functions, including ensuring the territorial integrity of the State, maintaining law and order and safeguarding national security. In particular, national security remains the sole responsibility of each Member State.'

[47] *Ognyanov* (n 31).

[48] Framework Decision 2009/909/JHA of 27 November 2008 on the application of the principle of mutual recognition to judgments in criminal matters imposing custodial sentences or measures involving deprivation of liberty for the purpose of their enforcement in the EU [2009] OJ L327/27. In this case Bulgarian law governing the enforcement of criminal sentences, and its settled interpretation by the Bulgarian Supreme Court, allowed for a reduction in custodial sentence on account of work carried out by the sentenced person while detained in the issuing Member State. The relevant EU Framework Decision made no such provision for reduction of sentence.

the national court arises from the date of expiry of the implementation deadline identified in the Framework Decision by analogy with *Adeneler*.[49] It further confirmed that the requirement to interpret national law in conformity with EU law includes the expansive obligation, on all national courts, to alter, where necessary, settled case law if that case law is based on an interpretation of national law that is incompatible with the objectives of a framework decision.[50] As such, the principle of consistent interpretation also requires that a lower national court disapplies, on its own authority, settled domestic case law achieved by the national court of last resort, if that case law is not compatible with the objective of EU law. The Court further clarified that a contrary interpretative judgment cannot be the *sole* reason for claiming that an EU-compatible interpretation is impossible.[51]

IV. An Evaluation of the Principle in the Field of Criminal Law

Having identified that the principle first established in *Pupino* has been absorbed into the mainstream understanding of the principle in EU law (as formerly developed in the Community context), this section briefly reflects on its peculiar challenges in the context of PJCC today and suggests that two recent cases offer some welcome developments and guidance to national judges on the limits of their interpretative duty to give effect to EU law.

First, it is recalled that while the interpretative duty on national judges is broad, the precise scope of the stated limits to that duty are not foreseeable in every case, and ultimately the national judges themselves are the final arbiters as to whether an EU-friendly interpretation of national law is 'possible'.[52] As we have seen, the CJEU has articulated two explicit limits to the principle of conforming interpretation and has apparently further directed national courts in more general terms as to the scope of what is possible; for instance that national legislation specifically implementing EU law should be capable of a conforming interpretation and a duty for lower courts to disapply rulings of higher courts. The Court in that sense reinforces the superiority of EU law within the confines of a plural system and encourages national courts to go and reach the outer limits of their scope

[49] *Adeneler and Others* (n 16) paras 115 and 124. One might also suggest that before the deadline for transposition there is an obligation to refrain from interpreting national law in a way that would seriously compromise the attainment of the objective of the framework decision by analogy with C-129/96 *Inter-Environnement Wallonie ASBL v Région wallonne* [1997] ECR I-07411.

[50] By analogy with *inter alia* C-441/44 *Dansk Industri (DI)* Judgment of the Court (Grand Chamber) of 19 April 2016 concerning the general framework directive relating to the principle of non-discrimination (also see Case C-456/98 *Centrosteel* [2000] ECR I-6007).

[51] *Ognyanov* (n 31) paras 69 and 70.

[52] K Sawyer, 'The Principle of "*interprétation conforme*": How Far Can or Should National Courts Go when Interpreting National Legislation Consistently with European Community Law?' (2007) 28(3) *Statute Law Review* 165; S Haket, 'Coherence in the Application of the Duty of Consistent Interpretation in EU Law' (2015) 8(2) *Review of European Administrative Law* 215.

in finding an interpretation that is compatible with EU law. Ultimately though, national judges sitting in courts across the length and breadth of the EU must determine whether an interpretation will be *contra legem* (further than possible) ostensibly based on a view as to the limits of canons of construction/interpretation (understood to be) available to it. The extent to which there are or even can be objective limits to meaning and interpretation is surely relevant here.[53] Certainly, wider pragmatic and socio-legal perspectives that emphasise other factors as determinative of the limits of the duty (or indeed of engaging it at all) are certainly persuasive. These have been noted to include legal cultural perspectives, power dynamics within the judiciary and between the judiciary and legislature. All of these might predetermine what are acceptable interpretations.[54] And where significant constitutional norms are put at risk by EU law, it is surely hardly surprising that national judges choose not to pursue the conforming interpretation duty.[55]

What about the specific criminal liability proviso as a limit to the application of the principle? The well-established position that EU law cannot in and of itself either determine or aggravate the criminal liability of the individual, was reiterated by the Court in *Pupino* as a specific expression of the general principles limitation, of which the principles of legal certainty and non-retroactivity were highlighted.[56] This extension to the field of PJCC puts the criminal liability proviso under the spotlight. As Spaventa pointed out in 2007,

> in the Community law context, the application of the criminal liability exception has not proven to be particularly difficult nor particularly controversial. However, the transposition of the same doctrine in the field of co-operation in criminal matters might be more difficult, since the consistent interpretation in this field is more likely to centre on the interpretation of criminal law.

And, the Court's particular finding on this proviso in *Pupino* arguably put it 'under significant strain'.[57] In essence the Court had indicated that where provisions of national law are procedural in nature, they could and should be interpreted so as to conform with framework decisions; in other words national rules on criminal procedure cannot 'determine or aggravate' criminal liability. This is contentious, as although such rules (for instance relating to evidence gathering or time limits

[53] See L Rodak, 'Objective Interpretation as Conforming Interpretation' (2011) 1(9) *Oñati Socio-Legal Series* 11.

[54] J Bengoetxea and H Jung, 'Autonomy and Heteronomy of the Judiciary in Europe' (2011) 1(9) *Oñati Socio-Legal Series* 1.

[55] See Albi's summary and critique of the commentary which accuses certain national constitutional courts of going against the spirit of *Pupino* and undermining loyal cooperation in their consideration of the European Arrest Warrant; A Albi, 'The European Arrest Warrant, Constitutional Rights and the Changing Legal Thinking: Values Once Recognised Lost in Transition to the EU Level' in M Fletcher, E Herlin-Karnell and C Matera (eds), *The European Union as an Area of Freedom, Security and Justice* (Routledge, 2017) 137, 139 ff.

[56] *Pupino* (n 1) paras 44 and 45.

[57] Davies (n 27) 253. Davies usefully highlights that the underpinning rationale for the liability proviso has varied in EU law and outlined why a more coherent logic is needed, and made more necessary by the expansion of EU competences and activity in the criminal law domain.

for prosecution) are not constitutive of criminal liability, they might well determine the outcome of the case to the detriment of the defendant. Moreover, the particular constitutional value that is attributed by states to specific aspects of the criminal law can vary. The Court's ruling on the liability proviso can consequently be read as imposing a particular and narrow understanding of the principle of legality on national courts, that might well be at odds with the national conception of the same.

So, if the question of what amounts to the determination and aggravation of criminal liability goes to the heart of fundamental safeguards that are recognised for individuals uniquely in the field of criminal justice *and* the EU's conception of these safeguards (including within the specific scope of EU criminal justice) appears at odds with those of the States, is a national judge still required to interpret domestic law so as to achieve the objectives and obligations laid down in EU legislation? A formal application of the principle of conforming interpretation viewed through a narrow *effet utile*/loyalty lens might elicit a positive response to this question, but some recent CJEU cases might be signalling otherwise, perhaps reflecting a greater comprehension on the part of the Court of the constitutional *and* criminal law sensitivities at stake.

In *Caronna*, which concerned Directive 2001/83/EC on medicinal products for human use[58] and the relevant national implementing law, the Court confirmed the interpretative limits of EU secondary law as lying in the determination or aggravation of criminal liability without a national legal basis. But in so doing, it also suggested that fundamental rights considerations trump the duty to interpret domestic law in conformity with secondary EU law obligations. It held that respect for the principle of legality as enshrined in Article 49 EU Charter of Fundamental Rights would prevail even where national law is contrary to EU law and in so doing permitted the non-compliance of national law with an EU directive on fundamental rights grounds.[59]

The *Taricco* saga[60] is also worth a brief mention. This litigation before the CJEU and the Italian Constitutional Court has generated a number of fundamental questions about the relationship between European criminal law and national constitutional law and about the impact that EU law has on domestic criminal justice systems. Like *Pupino*, it will likely be remembered most for its constitutional significance, both actual and potential. One eminent commentator describes the ensuing dialogue between the two courts in *Taricco* as having ultimately resulted in 'a considerable degree of pragmatism and mutual accommodation, while leaving a number of issues unresolved'.[61]

[58] Directive 2001/83/EC of 6 November 2001 on the Community code relating to medicinal products for human use [2001] OJ L311/67.

[59] On how this case law can be used to enhance protection of individuals in other spheres of EU criminal law, see L Mancano, 'Another Brick in the Whole. The Case-Law of the Court of Justice on Free Movement and Its Possible Impact on European Criminal Law' (2016) 8(1) *Perspectives on Federalism* 1.

[60] *Taricco I* and *Taricco II* (n 5).

[61] V Mitsilegas, 'Judicial Dialogue in Three Silences: Unpacking *Taricco*' (2018) 9(1) *New Journal of European Criminal Law* 38.

In *Taricco I*, Mr Taricco and other individuals had been under criminal investigation in Italy over allegations that they had committed serious VAT fraud between 2005 and 2009. The Italian Criminal Code provides strict time limits for the prosecution of crimes and in the case of serious financial crimes – which take a considerable time to investigate – such a statute of limitations regime could effectively become a guarantee of impunity for Mr Taricco and his like. The Italian judge, unhappy about this state of affairs, effectively sought to challenge national criminal law on the basis that it breached Italy's commitments under EU law. The CJEU was therefore asked to rule on the compatibility of Italian law with the obligations of Member States pursuant to Article 325 (1) and (2) TFEU concerning the combatting of fraud affecting the financial interests of the EU. The CJEU in its judgment asserted that the national provisions should indeed enable an effective and dissuasive penalisation of VAT fraud, but left it up to the referring court to decide if they should be disapplied because they impede the effectiveness of protection of the financial interests of the EU.[62] Furthermore the CJEU says that the national court should ensure that its decision to put aside national law is compatible with the suspect's fundamental rights. In particular, the national court should observe the principles of legality and proportionality of criminal offences and penalties enshrined in Article 49 of the EU Charter of Fundamental Rights. However, in the CJEU's view, a disapplication of the Italian rules relating to the statute of limitations period would *not* infringe the suspect's fundamental rights, thus implying (as it had done in *Pupino*) that the principle of legality (Article 49 of the Charter) doesn't apply in the context of national procedural rules pertaining to time limits for criminal prosecution. This was controversial, not least because a feature of the domestic, Italian legality principle was that it did also apply to limitation periods. In fact the disapplication of the provisions of national law by national judges would have breached the prohibition of retroactive effects (as for the crimes which had not been time-barred before the time the *Taricco I* judgment came out), the sufficient precision of criminal law and the separation of powers. The judgment therefore exposed national judges to a serious conundrum – effectiveness of EU law versus fundamental rights enshrined in domestic law, leading to the critique that too much was left to national judges by the CJEU in *Taricco I*, thereby also opening up the prospect of disparate application.[63] These overly high expectations on national courts to 'cure' national legislation from any incompatibility with EU Law were apparently later 'corrected'[64] by the

[62] More precisely, national judges should disapply if they consider that the 'national rule prevents the imposition of effective and dissuasive penalties in a *significant number of cases* of *serious* fraud affecting the financial interests of the European Union' (emphasis added): *Taricco I* (n 5) para 58.

[63] On this point and for a wider critique of *Taricco I*, see for instance, E Billis, 'The European Court of Justice: A "Quasi-Constitutional Court" in Criminal Matters? The *Taricco* Judgment and Its Shortcomings' (2016) 7(1) *New Journal of European Criminal Law* 21–38.

[64] See analysis by C Peristeridou and J Ouwerkerk, 'A Bridge over Troubled Water – a Criminal Lawyers Response to Taricco II' (*Verfblog*, December 2017) https://verfassungsblog.de/a-bridge-over-troubled-water-a-criminal-lawyers-response-to-taricco-ii/ (last accessed 18 February 2019).

Grand Chamber of the CJEU in *Taricco II* – this time a reference from Italy's Constitutional Court on the same matter – where the CJEU actually said 'it is primarily for the national legislature to lay down rules on limitation that enable compliance with the obligations … [of EU law]'.[65] If nothing else this is a welcome acknowledgement that national judges can be put in very difficult situations by EU law; situations that strain and disturb well-established national constitutional practices and potentially undermine rules and central tenets of national criminal law. In such circumstances it is just too simple to suggest that national judges are being 'disobedient' or 'unfriendly' towards the EU and the matter should not simply be viewed through a narrow EU loyalty and *effet utile* lens. In actual fact, the Italian Constitutional Court in *Taricco II* showed considerable respect to the EU by asking it for further guidance. It actively sought a more balanced and more directive judgment from the EU in light of domestic constitutional values and adopted language and style that was authoritative[66] but not threatening. The judgment of the CJEU ultimately did show deference to the domestic understanding of the scope of the principle of legal certainty. In light of that principle, it allowed Italian judges *not to* disapply the time-bar norms set out in national law which had previously been declared incompatible with EU law by the CJEU in *Taricco I*. The Court here gave an indication of how to adapt the principle of legality to a multi-level governance system. The challenge is clear; in the absence of clarity and uniformity around policy and principles of the EU's PJCC agenda, it must do enough to avoid overt clashes of authority while preserving, or rather accommodating pluralism.

To summarise, the role of national judges to secure the indirect effect of EU criminal law must be understood within the wider setting of the, as yet, uncomfortable 'fit' between EU Law with the *effet utile* and internal coherence imperatives used to justify the extension of the principle and the national criminal law replete with its own internal coherence, peculiarities and sensitivities.[67] While the consistent interpretation duty should be valued for its potential to neutralise or soften constitutional conflicts, and its recognition of the role of national judges as guardians of EU law, the degree, extent and cost of the asymmetries here is such that national judges cannot and should not be expected to offer anything like a comprehensive solution. And yet the developments identified in these cases might

[65] *Taricco II* (n 5) para 41.

[66] As it might be in the light of the '*controlimiti* doctrine' which it could invoke to buttress supreme national constitutional principles. See more generally M Dani, 'National Constitutional Courts in Supranational Litigation: A Contextual Analysis' (2017) 23 *European Law Journal* 189 who argues that constitutional courts can 'still exert a strategic influence in supranational litigation and encourage considerate handling of national constitutional claims by the Court of Justice. National constitutional courts, however, cannot be expected to embark on rights-based constitutional resistance against supranational technocratic and intergovernmental encroachment. If faithful to their task, they can only correct Union policy measures in the light of national constitutional principles and proportionality. This approach may have the disturbing paradoxical effect of reinforcing a legal and political order corroding the idea of constitutional democracy'.

[67] On this see, for instance, Albi (n 55).

perhaps serve to embolden national judges to engage more readily with the duty of conforming interpretation and enable them to do so more easily.

V. Conclusion

Leaving aside the concerns relating to judicial activism and law-making on the part of the CJEU in *Pupino*, the upshot of the ruling at the time was that it brought national judiciaries into the picture at a time when judicial and democratic oversight of this area of law was woefully lacking. This was remarkable at the time because of the distinctiveness of the third pillar, but it was also broadly accepted by EU law scholars, even welcomed, as a mechanism through which individual rights might be upheld. Today, within the confines of markedly different constitutional settings, the *Pupino* principle endures in the PJCC field and has been fully aligned with the by now expansive duty of conforming interpretation developed in other fields of law. Far from these factors providing for a more legitimate and rights-based 'Europeanisation' of criminal law which can be smoothly applied in domestic contexts with the minimum of interpretative gymnastics, in fact, a much more contentious picture prevails. The *Pupino* judgment gave us the first hint of the challenges that would lie ahead in term of the substantive clashes between EU law and national law (particularly around the crucial question of individual rights and safeguards). In such a context, the conforming interpretation principle saddles national judges with a considerable and uncomfortable burden. Meanwhile the EU, and in particular the Luxembourg judges, have the unenviable but (within the confines of the multi-level, supranational EU legal order) ultimately inevitable task of articulating more thoroughly the contours of EU criminal law and the legal relationship between EU and national law. There are some signs here that the CJEU recognises the uniqueness of domestic criminal law regimes and the fundamental principles and safeguards upon which they are built, and that the effective interpretation and application of EU law – including via conforming interpretation of national law – is bound up with that. The challenges that fall to judges, at all levels (probably inappropriately so), have arguably never been greater in the history of the EU; certainly the stakes have never been higher.

Protecting Vulnerable Victims and Beyond: The Duty of Consistent Interpretation in Criminal Matters in Italy after Pupino

GRAZIA MARIA VAGLIASINDI

I. Preliminary Remarks

This chapter explores the impact at national level of the principles expressed by the European Court of Justice (ECJ) in *Criminal Proceedings against Maria Pupino* (the case *Pupino*).[1]

In the case *Pupino*, the ECJ for the first time interpreted a framework decision adopted under the former so-called third pillar, ie Title VI of the Treaty on European Union (TEU) entitled 'Provisions on Police and Judicial Cooperation in Criminal Matters'.

Framework decisions were the main legal means in the third pillar, where most instruments aiming at approximating Member States' substantive and procedural criminal law were adopted under the pre-Lisbon constitutional structure. From a merely definitional point of view, the only difference between framework decisions, on the one side, and directives adopted under the former first pillar, on the other, is that the principle of direct effect, which the ECJ has long recognised with regard to directives,[2] does not apply to framework decisions: Article 34 (2)(b) TEU

[1] ECJ (Grand Chamber), 16 June 2005, Case C-105/03 *Criminal Proceedings against Maria Pupino* [2005] ECR I-5285.

[2] According to this principle, directives, if phrased clearly and precisely and free of all ambiguity, have vertical direct effect, ie individuals can claim their applicability whenever the State did not transpose the directive within the established timeframe (or transposed it incorrectly), and the national judge – as in the case of direct applicability (which concerns treaties' provisions, regulations and ECJ rulings on directly applicable provisions) – should apply the community rule, disapplying the conflicting national one in the light of the principle of supremacy of Community law; see ECJ, 17 December 1970, Case C-33/70 *SACE* [1970] ECR 01213; ECJ, 4 December 1974, Case C-41/74 *van Duyn* [1974] ECR 01337; ECJ, 26 February 1986, Case C-152/84 *Marshall* [1986] ECR 00723. However, the principle of direct effect cannot lead to the criminal liability of persons who contravene a provision of EC law to be determined or aggravated on the basis of such provision alone, independently of an implementing law. See, for instance, ECJ (Grand Chamber), 3 May 2005, Joined Cases C-387/02, C-391/02 and C-403/02 *Criminal Proceedings against Silvio Berlusconi et al* [2005] ECR I-03565; recently, ECJ (Grand Chamber), 5 December 2017, C-42/17 *Criminal Proceedings against MAS and MB* ECLI:EU:C:2017:936.

expressly stated that framework decisions 'shall not entail direct effect'. However, directives and framework decisions lived in the wider constitutional context of different rules respectively governing the supranational component (the first pillar) and the intergovernmental component (the third pillar) of the EU construction in terms of applicable legislative procedures, role of the EU institutions (including a more limited jurisdiction of the ECJ on third pillar subject matters) and enforcement remedies in case of non-implementation by Member States. In turn, this determined differences as to the respective level of democratic legitimation of the above mentioned instruments as well as to the attitude of national institutions towards their implementation. Thus, despite a structure that was largely similar to directives, framework decisions were an expression of a different level of integration as compared to first pillar instruments. Correlatively, the applicability to framework decisions of case law principles developed by the ECJ with regard to directives, such as that of indirect effect,[3] was not obvious.

In this context, in the case *Pupino* the ECJ was called upon by an Italian court to interpret Framework Decision 2001/220/JHA on the standing of victims in criminal proceedings.[4] In the preliminary ruling delivered on 15 June 2005, the ECJ stated that the principle of interpretation of national law in conformity with European Community (EC) law is binding in relation to framework decisions adopted in the context of police and judicial cooperation in criminal matters. The decision has been taken on the grounds of the binding nature of framework decisions and the implied applicability of the duty of loyal cooperation also to the third pillar TEU.

The extremely intense academic debate on the ruling[5] shows its relevance in the EU constitutional perspective in general, and specifically in relation to the developments concerning 'European criminal law'.[6]

[3] According to this principle – which is also known as 'conforming interpretation' or 'harmonious interpretation' and is based on the binding nature of directives and on the principle of loyal cooperation between Member States and the Community – national authorities and judges, once the deadline for transposition has expired, must interpret their national law in conformity with the letter and scope of the directive in order to meet the objectives pursued by the directive, even if the directive at stake is not of direct effect; see ECJ, 10 April 1984, Case C-14/83 *von Colson and Kamann* [1984] ECR 01891; ECJ, 13 November 1990, Case C-106/89 *Marleasing* [1990] ECR I-04135; ECJ, 16 December 1993, Case C-334/92 *Wagner Miret* [1993] ECR I-06911; ECJ, 7 January 2004, Case C-60/02 *Criminal Proceedings against X* [2004] ECR I-00651; ECJ (Grand Chamber), 5 October 2004, Joined Cases C-397/01 to C-403/01 *Pfeiffer et al* [2004] ECR I-08835. However, the obligation on the national court to refer to the content of a directive when interpreting the relevant rules of its national law cannot have the effect, on the basis of the directive and independently of legislation adopted for its implementation, of determining or aggravating the criminal liability of persons; see, for instance, ECJ, 12 December 1996, Joined Cases C-74/95 and C-129/95 *Criminal Proceedings against X* [1996] ECR I-06609.

[4] Council Framework Decision 2001/220/JHA of 15 March 2001 on the standing of victims in criminal proceedings [2001] OJ L82/1.

[5] See, for instance, M Fletcher, 'Extending 'Indirect Effect' to the Third Pillar: The Significance of Pupino?' (2005) *European Law Review* 862; J Spencer, 'Child Witnesses and the European Union' (2005) *The Cambridge Law Journal* 569; C Lebeck, 'Sliding Towards Supranationalism? The Constitutional Status of EU Framework Decisions after Pupino' (2007) 8 *German Law Journal* 501.

[6] This chapter does not address these profiles, since they are dealt with in chapter 3(a) by Fletcher.

Equally important are the consequences of the case *Pupino* at national level.[7]

From this specific standpoint, it is first of all worth exploring how the principles expressed by the ECJ in the case *Pupino* impacted on the specific area of law directly concerned by the ruling, ie the standing of vulnerable victims in criminal proceedings under Italian law.[8]

Moreover, the ruling further enhances the ECJ tendency (already underpinning the elaboration of the duty of consistent interpretation)[9] towards making national judges the cornerstone of a system where their role trespasses the typical (and traditionally legitimate) function of law application, to encompassing the maximising of the integration of EU law into national law.[10] From this perspective, it is worth exploring the practical attitude – and consequences thereof – of national judges towards interpreting their national substantive and procedural criminal law in conformity with framework decisions in other areas of law after the case *Pupino*. While with the entry into force of the Treaty of Lisbon the distinction into pillars has been abolished and new framework decisions can no longer be adopted, framework decisions adopted under the former third pillar shall be

[7] In Italy, an extremely vast literature flourished with regard to both the EU constitutional relevance and the impact at national level of the case *Pupino*. See, among others, F Cherubini, 'L'obbligo di interpretazione conforme "sconfina" nel terzo pilastro: note a margine della sentenza Pupino' (2006) *Studi sull'integrazione europea* 157; V Manes, 'L'incidenza delle "decisioni-quadro" sull'interpretazione in materia penale: profili di diritto sostanziale' (2006) *Cassazione penale* 1151; E Aprile, 'I rapporti tra diritto processuale e diritto dell'unione europea, dopo la sentenza della Corte di Giustizia sul "caso Pupino" in materia di incidente probatorio (2006) *Cassazione Penale* 1165; F Sgubbi and V Manes (eds), *Interpretazione conforme al diritto comunitario in materia penale* (Bononia University Press, 2007); C Sotis, 'Il caso "Pupino": profili sostanziali' in Sgubbi and Manes, *ibid*, 33; S Allegrezza, 'Il caso "Pupino": profili processuali' in Sgubbi and Manes, *ibid*, 53; M Caianiello, 'Il caso "Pupino": riflessioni sul nuovo ruolo riconosciuto al giudice alla luce del metodo adottato dalla Corte di Giustizia' in Sgubbi and Manes, *ibid*, 89; F Viganò, 'Il giudice penale e l'interpretazione conforme alle norme sovranazionali' in P Corso and E Zanetti (eds), *Studi in onore di Mario Pisani* (La Tribuna, 2010) Vol 2, 617; Alessandro Bernardi (ed), *L'interpretazione conforme al diritto dell'Unione europea. Profili e limiti di un vincolo problematico* (Jovene, 2015).

[8] On the protection of victims, including vulnerable ones, see for instance G Mannozzi, *La giustizia senza spada. Uno studio comparato su giustizia riparativa e mediazione penale* (Giuffrè, 2003); MV Del Tufo, 'La vittima di fronte al reato nell'orizzonte europeo' in G Fiandaca and C Visconti (eds), *Punire Mediare Riconciliare. Dalla giustizia penale internazionale all'elaborazione dei conflitti individuali* (Giappichelli, 2009) 107; M Bargis and H Belluta (eds), *Vittime di reato e sistema penale. La ricerca di nuovi equilibri* (Giappichelli, 2017).

[9] See, with general reference to the duty of consistent interpretation, Cherubini (n 7) 170–71.

[10] In general, on the enhanced role of the judge in the context of multilevel legislation, see, among others, O Di Giovine, *L'interpretazione nel diritto penale. Tra creatività e vincolo alla legge* (Giuffrè, 2006); A Gargani, 'Verso una democrazia giudiziaria? I poteri normativi del giudice tra principio di legalità e diritto europeo' (2011) *Criminalia* 99; A Di Martino, 'Una legalità per due? Riserva di legge, legalità CEDU e giudice fonte' (2014) *Criminalia* 91; V Manes, 'Metodo e limiti dell'interpretazione conforme alle fonti sovranazionali in materia penale' in Bernardi (n 7) 391; M Donini, 'Il diritto giurisprudenziale penale' (No 3-2016) *Diritto penale contemporaneo Rivista trimestrale* 13; CE Paliero, S Moccia, G De Francesco, G Insolera, M Pelissero, R Rampioni and L Risicato (eds), *La crisi della legalità. Il "sistema vivente" delle fonti penali* (Edizioni Scientifiche Italiane, 2016).

preserved until they are repealed, annulled or amended.[11] Moreover, the limits to conforming interpretation in criminal matters expressed in *Pupino* are deemed of relevance also with regard to directives adopted in criminal matters under the post-Lisbon constitutional framework.[12] Thus, the implementation by national judges of their duty of consistent interpretation in relation to framework decisions is still an issue of scientific and practical relevance.

This chapter is structured as follows. First, an overview is given of the case *Pupino* from the viewpoint of providing a background for the analysis of its impact at national level. On these grounds, the impact of the principles expressed by the ECJ on the policy area concerned at national level is described and analysed. Then, the wider consequences of the case *Pupino* at national level are explored. Critical considerations conclude.[13]

II. The Case *Pupino*: An Overview

The order for reference for a preliminary ruling[14] concerned the scope of Articles 2, 3 and 8 of Framework Decision 2001/220/JHA, which Italy had not implemented within the established deadline.

The reference occurred within the criminal proceedings, at the preliminary enquiry stage before the *Tribunale di Firenze*, against Mrs Pupino, a nursery school teacher charged with several offences of 'misuse of disciplinary measures' ('*abuso dei mezzi di correzione o di disciplina*', Article 571 of the Italian Criminal Code (*Codice Penale*, CC)) against a number of her pupils aged less than five years at the time and with the offence of causing aggravated 'injuries' ('*lesione personale*' *aggravata*, Articles 582, 585 and 576 CC, in relation to Article 61, paras 2 and 11, CC) to one of the pupils.

The reason for the reference was linked to the fact that, under Italian law, criminal procedure comprises two distinct stages, namely that of the preliminary

[11] Article 9 of 'Protocol (No 36) on transitional provisions' attached to the Treaty of Lisbon [2008] OJ C115/01.

[12] See Manes (n 10) 401–402, 408 (fn 61), 413. In general, on the innovations (directly or indirectly) relevant to criminal matters introduced by the Treaty of Lisbon, see, among an extremely vast literature, G Grasso, 'Il Trattato di Lisbona e le nuove competenze penali dell'Unione Europea' in M Bertolino, L Eusebi and G Forti (eds), *Studi in onore di Mario Romano* (Jovene, 2011) Vol IV, 2307; L Picotti, 'Limiti garantistici delle incriminazioni penali e nuove competenze europee alla luce del Trattato di Lisbona' in G Grasso, L Picotti and R Sicurella (eds), *L'evoluzione del diritto penale nei settori d'interesse europeo alla luce del Trattato di Lisbona* (Giuffrè, 2011) 207; R Sicurella, 'EU Competence in Criminal Matters' in V Mitsilegas, M Bergström and T Konstadinides (eds), *Research Hanbook on EU Criminal Law* (Edward Elgar Publishing, 2016) 49.

[13] No official English translation is available of the national provisions and judgments analysed in this chapter. The translation has been made by the author and it is not meant to be official. All the decisions of the Italian Constitutional Court mentioned in this chapter are available (in Italian) at www.cortecostituzionale.it.

[14] G.i.p. Tribunale di Firenze (dr.ssa Mori), ordinanza 3 February 2003, Pupino (2004) Il Foro Italiano II-54.

enquiry and that of the adversarial stage. The trial technically begins only with the adversarial stage, where, as a rule, evidence must be taken at the initiative of the parties and in compliance with the adversarial principle.

However, Article 392 of the Italian Code of Criminal Procedure (*Codice di Procedura Penale*, CCP), lays down exceptions to that rule, allowing a limited number of forms of evidence to be gathered during the preliminary enquiry stage (and with the same probative value as that gathered during the adversarial stage of the proceedings) through the special inquiry procedure for early gathering of evidence (*incidente probatorio*), on a decision of the judge in charge of the preliminary enquiries and in compliance with the adversarial principles.[15] The *rationale* underpinning the special inquiry procedure is to gather (and secure) unpostponable perishable evidence, ie evidence that might vanish or deteriorate if it is gathered during the adversarial stage.[16]

Even outside the cases of perishable evidence provided for in Article 392, para 1, CCP, Article 392, para 1-*bis*, CCP, in the formulation into force at the time of order for reference to the ECJ,[17] allowed the special procedure to be used when taking the testimony from minors aged less than sixteen years with regard to listed sexual (or with a sexual background) criminal offences. Article 392, para 1-*bis*, CCP, concerned cases of 'presumed vulnerability', ie cases where the peculiar nature of the listed crimes is an index of vulnerability and, as such, justifies the special inquiry procedure in order to ensure the genuineness of the testimony and to minimise the traumatic effects arising from the examination.[18]

With regard to the same offences listed in Article 392, para 1-*bis*, CCP,[19] Article 398, para 5-*bis*, CCP, allowed the special inquiry procedure to be performed according to special arrangements (or 'protected modalities') established by the judge in charge of the preliminary enquiries, when minors aged less than sixteen years are involved in the evidence gathering and the special arrangements are necessary and appropriate to ensuring their protection.[20] This provision aims to protect the minor, while at the same time ensuring the genuineness and reliability of the evidence.[21]

The offences allegedly committed by Mrs Pupino did not fall within the listed offences for which the special inquiry procedure for the early gathering of evidence was permitted or the special arrangements for gathering evidence could be used.

[15] The Italian Constitutional Court (*Corte Costituzionale*), with the judgment No 77 of 23 February–10 March 1994, has declared the illegitimacy of Article 392 CCP in that it did not allow the special inquiry procedure to be also used in the phase of the preliminary hearing.

[16] See T Magno, 'The Pupino Case: Background in Italian Law and Consequences for the National Judge' (2007) ERA Forum 215, 217; S Recchione, 'Articolo 392' in G Canzio and R Bricchetti (eds), *Codice di Procedura Penale* (Giuffrè, 2017) 2767, 2769.

[17] On subsequent amendments to Article 392, para 1-*bis*, CCP, see section III.C below.

[18] See Recchione (n 16) 2786.

[19] In the formulation into force at the time of the order for reference to the ECJ; on subsequent amendments, see section III.C below.

[20] See Recchione 'Articolo 398' in Canzio and Bricchetti (n 16) 2817.

[21] Recchione (n 20) 2823.

Nevertheless, in August 2001 the Public Prosecutor's Office had asked the judge in charge of the preliminary enquiries to take the testimony of eight children, witnesses and victims of the offences for which the defendant was under investigation, pursuant to Articles 392, para 1-*bis*, and 398, para 5-*bis*, CCP. The defendant had opposed that request.

The referring Court acknowledged that, under the national provisions in question, the application of the Public Prosecutor's Office would have to be dismissed. However, the referring Court noted that there was no reason to preclude those provisions covering other offences, like those allegedly committed by the defendant, in which the victim is a minor, since these offences might prove more serious for the victim than those referred to in Article 392, para 1-*bis*. Having doubts as to the compatibility of Articles 392, para 1-*bis*, and 398, para 5-*bis*, CCP, with Framework Decision 2001/220/JHA, the judge in charge of the preliminary enquiries at the *Tribunale di Firenze* decided to stay the proceedings and ask the ECJ to rule on the scope of Articles 2, 3 and 8 of Framework Decision 2001/220/JHA.

As mentioned above (section I), the ECJ in its ruling extended the principle of conforming interpretation to framework decisions, so that

> When applying national law the national court that is called upon to interpret it must do so as far as possible in the light of the wording and purpose of the framework decision in order to attain the result which it pursues and thus comply with Article 34(2) (b) EU.[22]

Important limits apply to this obligation on the national court to refer to the content of a framework decision when interpreting the relevant rules of its national law, namely the 'general principles of law, particularly those of legal certainty and non-retroactivity'.[23] These principles '(…) prevent that obligation from leading to the criminal liability of persons who contravene the provisions of a framework decision from being determined or aggravated on the basis of such a decision alone, independently of an implementing law (…)'.[24] However, according to the ECJ, the provisions forming the subject matter of the reference for a preliminary ruling '(…) do not concern the extent of the criminal liability of the person concerned but the conduct of the proceedings and the means of taking evidence'.[25] Importantly, the ECJ stressed that

> The obligation on the national court to refer to the content of a framework decision when interpreting the relevant rules of its national law ceases when the latter cannot receive an application which would lead to a result compatible with that envisaged by that framework decision. In other words, the principle of conforming interpretation cannot serve as the basis for an interpretation of national law *contra legem*. (…).[26]

[22] *Pupino* (n 1) 43.
[23] *Pupino* (n 1) 44.
[24] *Pupino* (n 1) 45.
[25] *Pupino* (n 1) 46.
[26] *Pupino* (n 1) 47.

This being the general framework of the ECJ reasoning, on the question referred for a preliminary ruling, the ECJ moved from the consideration that, in the specific case at stake, children of a young age who have allegedly been repeatedly maltreated by a school teacher have to be considered vulnerable victims for the purpose and objectives of Framework Decision 2001/220/JHA, and should therefore benefit from the specific protection required by the latter. Thus, according to the ECJ,

> (…) achievement of the aims pursued by the abovementioned provisions of the framework decision require that a national court should be able, in respect of particularly vulnerable victims, to use a special procedure, such as the Special Inquiry for early gathering of evidence provided for in the law of a Member State, and the special arrangements for hearing testimony for which provision is also made, if that procedure best corresponds to the situation of those victims and is necessary in order to prevent the loss of evidence, to reduce the repetition of questioning to a minimum, and to prevent the damaging consequences, for those victims, of their giving testimony at the trial.[27]

The ECJ introduced, however, two important caveats.

In particular, it noted that 'according to Article 8(4) of the Framework Decision, the conditions for giving testimony that are adopted must in any event be compatible with the basic legal principles of the Member State concerned'.[28]

The ECJ also added that:

> The Framework Decision must thus be interpreted in such a way that fundamental rights, including in particular the right to a fair trial as set out in Article 6 of the Convention and interpreted by the European Court of Human Rights, are respected.[29]

On these grounds, the ECJ concluded that:

> (…) Articles 2, 3 and 8(4) of the Framework Decision must be interpreted as meaning that the national court must be able to authorise young children, who, as in this case, claim to have been victims of maltreatment, to give their testimony in accordance with arrangements allowing those children to be guaranteed an appropriate level of protection, for example outside the trial and before it takes place. The national court is required to take into consideration all the rules of national law and to interpret them, so far as possible, in the light of the wording and purpose of the Framework Decision.[30]

III. The Practical Consequences of *Pupino* in the Relevant Policy Area at National Level

With its ruling in *Pupino*, the ECJ made it clear that Framework Decision 2001/220/JHA (which had not been implemented in Italy) expressed a wider principle of protection of the victims in criminal proceedings than the one expressed

[27] *Pupino* (n 1) 56.
[28] *Pupino* (n 1) 57.
[29] *Pupino* (n 1) 59.
[30] *Pupino* (n 1) 61.

by national law (which had been adopted previous to the enactment of Framework Decision 2001/220/JHA).

Thus, the national judge had to explore the possibility of interpreting internal legislation in such a way as to ensure its compatibility with the obligations arising from Framework Decision 2001/220/JHA.[31]

The judge in charge of the preliminary enquiries admitted the special inquiry procedure and the special arrangements for hearing testimony in the criminal proceedings against Mrs Pupino.[32] In so doing, through the means of 'consistent interpretation' the national judge overcame the legislative obstacle represented by the fact that the crimes of misuse of disciplinary measures and aggravated injuries were not included in the list of crimes for which Articles 392, para 1-*bis*, and 398, para 5-*bis*, CCP, allowed special timing and modalities of evidence gathering.[33]

It is worth adding that, a few days later, the same judge admitted in a distinct proceedings the special inquiry procedure with regard to a victim who carried a serious disability, but was not of minor age and, as such, was not included (at the time) in the list of recipients of the special inquiry procedure.[34] Thus, the judge, in invoking the concept of 'vulnerability' – at that time neither mentioned in Article 392, para 1-*bis*, CCP, nor elsewhere in the CCP – and interpreting it in conformity with Framework Decision 2001/220/JHA, overcame the statutory limits concerning the applicability of the special inquiry procedure only to victims who were minors of age.

With all evidence, in both cases the national judge contributed in ensuring that the application of Italian national law conformed to the objectives of Framework Decision 2001/220/JHA, thus enhancing the legal standing of vulnerable victims.

Whether the above described judicial operations were a mere application of national law interpreted in conformity with Framework Decision 2001/220/JHA is, however, doubtful, as is the compatibility of the (allegedly) interpretative operations with the same limits to consistent interpretation in relation to framework decisions.

A. Direct versus Indirect Effect and Limits to Indirect Effect in Substantive and Procedural Criminal Matters

As a matter of fact, framework decisions lack direct effect. Consequently, in case of contrast between national law and a framework decision, the national court cannot apply the latter and disapply national law; it is worth adding that the same

[31] See Viganò (n 7) 621.

[32] G.i.p. Tribunale di Firenze (dr.ssa Mori), ordinanza 12 September 2005, Pupino, unpublished; this reference is provided by Viganò (n 7) 621 and Magno (n 16) 221.

[33] Viganò (n 7) 621.

[34] G.i.p. Tribunale di Firenze (dr.ssa Mori), ordinanza 14 September 2005, Nicolais, unpublished; this reference is provided by Viganò (n 7) 621.

principle of direct effect – again, not applicable to framework decisions – cannot determine or aggravate the criminal liability of individuals independently of an implementing law.

As to the duty of consistent interpretation – ie indirect effect – in criminal matters, it is subject to the limit of the general principles of law, and particularly those of legal certainty and non-retroactivity, which prevent that duty to determine or aggravate the criminal liability of a person independently of an implementing law. Moreover, the duty of consistent interpretation cannot serve as a basis for an interpretation *contra legem* of national law, or however incompatible with the basic legal principles of the legal system, and must respect fundamental rights as guaranteed by the European Convention on Human Rights (ECHR) and interpreted by the European Court of Human Rights (ECtHR).

A correct assessment of the implications of the above at national level implies a separate consideration of substantive criminal law and procedural criminal law.

Substantive criminal law enjoys a strict application of the *nullum crimen, nulla poena sine praevia lege poenali*, as set out in Article 25, para 2, of the Italian Constitution.[35] This implies the following corollaries: only the law can provide for criminal offences and criminal penalties; criminal law must be clear and precise; analogy *in malam partem* for the offender is prohibited;[36] retroactive application of criminal law *in malam partem* for the offender is prohibited. Retroactive application of criminal provisions *in bonam partem* for the offender is provided for by Article 2 CC, but not considered to be covered by Article 25, para 2, of the Constitution; however, retroactivity of favourable criminal law is deemed to have constitutional coverage under Article 3 of the Constitution (Principle of equality) and is considered as a fundamental principle by the ECJ[37] and the ECtHR.[38]

As far as procedural criminal law is concerned, Article 111 of the Italian Constitution, in the formulation entered into force in 1999, stipulates on the fair trial (*giusto processo*) and is read as having brought constitutional coverage to procedural legality since the fair trial is the one that is 'regulated by the law';[39] however, it has been noted that procedural legality at national level lives 'in a weak

[35] As to the ECHR, see for instance *Scoppola v Italy (No 2)* App no 10249/03 (ECtHR, 17 September 2009).

[36] As to an extensive interpretation *in malam partem*, in criminal matters it is allowed under national law, but banned according to ECJ case law: see for instance C-74/95 and C-129/95 *X* (n 3) 25–26. However, the distinction between extensive interpretation and analogy is a difficult one and carries the risk of introducing, under the umbrella of extensive interpretation, a prohibited analogical application. In any case, the admissible extensive interpretation *in malam partem* should be a 'reasonably foreseeable' one, following the general indications of the ECtHR; see Manes (n 10) 420–21.

[37] *Berlusconi et al* (n 2) 66–69.

[38] According to the ECtHR, Article 7 §1 of the ECHR guarantees not only the principle of non-retrospectiveness of more stringent criminal laws but also, and implicitly, the principle of retrospectiveness of the more lenient criminal law; see for instance *Scoppola v Italy (No 2)* (n 35).

[39] See, for instance, O Mazza, 'I diritti fondamentali dell'individuo come limite della prova nella fase di ricerca e in sede di assunzione' (*Diritto penale contemporaneo*, 18 December 2012) 1, available at www.penalecontemporaneo.it (last accessed 25 February 2019).

or mobile dimension'.[40] As far as non-retroactivity *in malam partem* and retroactivity *in bonam partem* are specifically concerned, Italian criminal procedure is traditionally governed by the *tempus regit actum* principle.[41] Analogy is a particularly delicate issue in procedural criminal law, since it raises a tension between the rights of the defendant and the rights of the offended person: an analogical application of a procedural provision *in malam partem* for the defendant would negatively affect his rights while enhancing those of the offended person; an analogical application of a procedural provision *in bonam partem* for the defendant would enhance his rights while negatively affecting those of the offended person.[42] However, it should be borne in mind that Article 14 of the Italian 'Dispositions of the law in general' (*Disposizioni sulla legge in generale*) prohibits analogy for criminal law – a prohibition which is interpreted as referring only to substantive incriminating criminal provisions – and for provisions which lay down exceptions to a general rule; therefore, procedural criminal provisions which lay down exceptions to a rule cannot be applied analogically.

These peculiarities respectively concerning substantive and procedural criminal law are of extreme relevance when assessing the impact of *Pupino* at national level (see sections III.B and IV), since the duty of consistent interpretation (and limits thereof) apply not only to procedural criminal law, but also to substantive criminal law. However, the following can be considered a common denominator. Interpretation in conformity, whose logical premise is the need to solve an antinomy between rules, can be performed only to the extent that it does not alter the meaning of the national provision,[43] also taking into account the consolidated interpretation of the same provision by national courts (*diritto vivente*).[44] If the meaning of the national provision is altered, the interpretation is *contra legem* and would become a 'masked judicial creation of the rule':[45] in such a case, the judge, under the umbrella of conforming interpretation, undertakes a 'crypto-disapplication' of the national provision (illegitimate when the involved Union provisions lack direct effect, and in any case when it leads to determining or aggravating the criminal responsibility of individuals independently of

[40] V Valentini, 'La ricombinazione genica della legalità penale: bio-technological strengthening o manipolazione autodistruttiva?' (*Diritto penale contemporaneo*, 20 June 2016) 1, 4, available at *ibid*.

[41] According to the ECtHR, the rules on retrospectiveness set out in Article 7 ECHR apply only to provisions defining offences and the penalties for them, while it is reasonable for domestic courts to apply the *tempus regit actum* principle with regard to procedural laws; see for instance *Mione v Italy* App no 7856/02 (ECtHR, 12 February 2004); *Rasnik v Italy* App no 45989/06 (ECtHR, 10 July 2007); *Martelli v Italy* App no 20402/03 (ECtHR, 12 April 2007); *Scoppola v Italy (No 2)* (n 35). For an in-depth analysis of the *tempus regit actus* principle in the light of the Constitutional Court and ECtHR case law, see M Chiavario, 'Norme processuali penali nel tempo: sintetica rivisitazione (a base giurisprudenziale) di un principio sempre attuale' (*La legislazione penale*, 31 July 2017) 1, available at www.lalegislazionepenale.eu (last accessed 25 February 2019).

[42] Mazza (n 39) 5–6.

[43] See, with general regard to interpretation in conformity with supranational sources, Manes (n 10) 407–408.

[44] See Manes (n 10) 408; Corte Costituzionale, Judgment No 227 of 21–24 June 2010.

[45] Manes (n 10) 408–409; C Grandi, *Riserva di legge e legalità penale europea* (Giuffrè, 2010) 41–48.

an implementing law) or a 'crypto-analogy' (prohibited for substantive incriminating criminal provisions and for provisions laying down exceptions to a rule).

B. Assessing the Immediate Consequences of *Pupino* in the Policy Area Concerned

In this framework, it is now possible to assess the immediate consequences of *Pupino*, where procedural provisions on the standing of vulnerable victims were concerned.

As seen above, the national court extended the special timing and modalities for taking evidence beyond the textual scope of Articles 392 and 398 CCP. This happened, despite the fact that the Constitutional Court had previously deemed the exclusion of the special inquiry procedure with regard to the crimes at stake in *Pupino* not to be constitutionally illegitimate.

In fact, in the same criminal proceedings against Mrs Pupino, an order for reference had been previously made by the same judge in charge for the preliminary enquiries at the *Tribunale di Firenze* to the Constitutional Court. In particular, the judge had challenged the constitutional legitimacy of Articles 392, para 1-*bis*, and 398, para 5-*bis*, CCP, with regard to Articles 2 (Protection of inviolable rights of the person) and 3 (Principle of equality) of the Italian Constitution, in that the abovementioned CCP provisions did not allow the testimony of children under the age of 16, as long as they are the persons offended by the crime, to be taken through the special inquiry procedure and under special arrangements with regard to crimes not listed therein.

The Constitutional Court had rejected these arguments and considered the challenge of constitutional legitimacy of Article 392, para 1-*bis*, CCP, ungrounded.[46] According to the Constitutional Court, Article 392, para 1-*bis*, CCP, is a special rule which refers to a specific category of crimes and cannot be interpreted extensively. The Constitutional Court ruled that this legislative choice is not without justification, since the need to protect the minor's personality, within his or her involvement in the trial, arises with greater intensity and clearness with respect to the listed crimes than with regard to other crimes, as does the need to protect the genuineness of the evidence. According to the Constitutional Court, the arguments raised by the referring judge did not justify, from a constitutional perspective, a derogation to the rule according to which evidence comes into existence only at the adversarial stage and after the parties' cross-examination.[47]

[46] Corte Costituzionale, Judgment No 529 of 6–18 December 2002.

[47] As to the protection of the personality of the minor, the Court found that it is ensured through those CCP provisions which allow for the use of special modalities, suitable to protect the personality of the minor witness and regardless of the type of crime under proceedings, in the trial (examination *in camera*: Article 472, para 4, CCP; examination conducted by the judge, also with the help of a family member or an expert: Article 498, para 4, CCP).

Thus, the Constitutional Court had confirmed the interpretation of Article 392, para 1-*bis*, CCP as establishing a *numerus clausus*[48] or, said in broader terms, as an exception to the general rule that evidence is gathered at trial,[49] as such falling under the prohibition of analogy set out in Article 14 of the 'Dispositions on the law in general'. It is also worth mentioning that, if it is true that a means of taking evidence is *per se* neutral as to the conviction or acquittal, it cannot be neglected that the (retroactive) application of the special timing and modalities for taking evidence could aggravate the procedural position of the defendant.[50] Moreover, as it has been noted, the special inquiry procedure under Article 392 CCP comes at a cost: the reference is to the principles of orality and immediacy, since the evidence is gathered by a judge who is in charge of the preliminary enquiries and not the judge of the trial.[51] Thus, overall, an interpretative extension of the scope of the provisions at stake to crimes not mentioned therein in order to conform to the objectives of Framework Decision 2001/220/JHA appeared as being contrary to national law.

Notwithstanding the above, the judge in charge of the preliminary enquiries, giving paramount (*recte*: exclusive) relevance to the general need to protect minors who are victims (and witnesses) of crimes, in the proceedings against Mrs Pupino as well as in distinct criminal proceedings, admitted the special inquiry procedure under special arrangements. While some authors read this judicial operation as a legitimate *praeter legem* interpretation,[52] others saw it as an illegitimate *contra legem* interpretation.[53] Indeed, the tension between the choice of the national court, from the one side, and the characteristics of framework decisions (lack of direct effect) and the same limits to their indirect effect (particularly, non-contrariety with national law and right to a fair trial), on the other, is evident. The special inquiry procedure under protected modalities has been *de facto* introduced

[48] This is the prevailing interpretation with regard to Article 392, para 1, CCP, also in the literature; see references in Recchione (n 16) 2768.

[49] The Constitutional Court, with Ordinance No 108 of 26 March–1 April 2003, had declared ungrounded the challenge of constitutional legitimacy of Article 392, para 1-*bis*, in that it does not allow the special inquiry procedure with regard to adults affected by mental infirmness and, as such, requiring protection; the Court had stated that Article 392, para 1-*bis*, is an exception to the rule that evidence must be gathered in the trial and, this being the choice of the legislator, no special constitutional needs require the special procedure to be extended to the mentally infirm witness (on subsequent legislative amendments, see section III.C below).
However, the Constitutional Court, with the Judgment No 63 of 13–29 January 2005, has later declared, inter alia, the constitutional illegitimacy of Article 398, para 5-*bis*, CCP, in that it did not allow the judge to proceed according to the modalities set out therein when among the interested persons one is a mentally infirm adult, when the needs to protect the infirm would make this choice necessary and appropriate.

[50] See R Mastroianni, 'Supremazia del diritto dell'Unione e "controlimiti" costituzionali: alcune riflessioni a margine del caso "Taricco"' (Diritto penale contemporaneo, 7 November 2016) 1, 4, available at www.penalecontemporaneo.it (last accessed 25 February 2019).

[51] See Recchione (n 16) 2767.

[52] See, for instance, Viganò (n 7) 655–56.

[53] See, for instance, Allegrezza (n 7) 80 ff; Caianiello (n 7) 89 ff; Manes (n 10) 421–22.

for the crimes at stake by the national judge who, under the umbrella of interpretation of national law in conformity with a framework decision which had not been implemented by the Italian legislator, (retroactively and) directly applied a framework decision that the national Parliament had chosen not to implement or, seen from a different perspective, analogically applied a provision which, also in the interpretation of the Constitutional Court, laid down an exception to a general rule.

It has to be noted that, a few years later, the Supreme Court, in relation to a proceeding for the crime of murder, making express reference to the *Pupino* principles, stated that even in proceedings other than those concerning sexual or sexual-related crimes, there are reasons similar to those that inspired Article 392, para 1-*bis*, CCP, which lead to consider this provision as being the rule in the case of a minor witness, since the sexual component of a crime does not appear as a sufficient ground for a differentiation with other criminal offences concerning different legal protected interests.[54] This judgment of the Supreme Court is clearly opposed (and with an explicit reference to the ECJ ruling in *Pupino*) to the interpretation that the special inquiry procedure can be admitted only in mandatory cases. Thus, the national court opted again for the possibility of an (allegedly extensive) interpretation of Article 392, para 1-*bis*, CCP, as a provision applicable to vulnerable witnesses of crimes not included in the list, based on the identification of the *rationale* of the provision in the protection of the vulnerable witnesses from the negative effects that they could suffer from the adversarial stage of the proceedings.[55]

C. Legislative Developments at National Level on the Protection of Vulnerable Victims after *Pupino*

Indeed, the *Pupino* case enhanced the process of a progressive recognition of the special inquiry procedure as a suitable instrument in protecting the interests of vulnerable witnesses (and victims) whilst ensuring the genuineness of evidence, in a legislative context that did not give explicit relevance to the concept of 'vulnerability' until recently.

In this respect, it has to be noted that the provisions of the Italian CCP which played a role in *Pupino*, were not modified as a consequence of the ECJ ruling.

In fact, Article 392, para 1-*bis*, CCP, has been subject to numerous amendments over the years: extension of the possibility to take the testimony through the special inquiry procedure to the offended persons of the listed sexual and sexual-related crimes who are not minors; inclusion of further sexual or sexual-related crimes; and inclusion of non-sexual related crimes.[56] Specular amendments to the

[54] Cass. Pen., Sez. VI, 11 March–11 June 2008, No 23705, CED Cass. No 240321.

[55] See Recchione (n 20) 2818.

[56] It is interesting to note that the crimes at stake in *Pupino* are not mentioned in the list.

list of crimes have been brought to Article 398, para 5-*bis*, CCP;[57] moreover, a new para 5-*ter* was introduced therein, according to which

> The judge, at the parties' request, applies the rules laid down in para 5-*bis* when among those interested to the taking of evidence there are adults in conditions of particular vulnerability, the latter inferred also from the type of crimes under proceedings.

However, these amendments to Articles 392 and 398 CCP mainly occurred in order to comply with the international obligations set out in the Lanzarote Convention[58] and the Istanbul Convention,[59] as well as in order to transpose Directive 2011/36/EU.[60]

On the contrary, the tension between national law and Framework Decision 2001/220/JHA, highlighted in *Pupino*, had not led to the amendment of the provisions at stake. As a matter of fact, it was only with Law No 96 of 6 June 2010 (the so-called 'Community Law 2009') that the Parliament had delegated the Government to enact, within 12 months, legislative decrees to introduce the provisions necessary to transpose, inter alia, Framework Decision 2001/220/JHA.[61] The Government did not enact the legislative decree, most likely because of the initiatives that, following the entry into force of the Treaty of Lisbon, had meanwhile been taken at the EU level to replace Framework Decision 2001/220/JHA with a directive: something that occurred with the adoption of Directive 2012/29/EU.[62]

Legislative Decree No 212 of 15 December 2015, in the transposition of Directive 2012/29/EU, introduced a statutory definition the 'conditions of particular vulnerability' of the offended person (Article 90-*quater* CCP), as well as several other provisions aiming to ensure that vulnerable victims benefit from adequate protection in the various phases of the criminal proceedings.[63]

Importantly, Legislative Decree No 212/2015 introduced an additional provision in Article 392, para 1-*bis*, CCP, according to which

[57] The Constitutional Court, with Judgment No 63/2005, had declared the constitutional illegitimacy of Article 398, para 5-*bis*, CCP, in that it did not allow the judge to proceed according to the modalities set out therein when among the interested persons one is an adult affected by mental infirmness, when the needs of the infirm would made this choice necessary and appropriate.

[58] CETS No 201, Council of Europe Convention on the Protection of Children against Sexual Exploitation and Sexual Abuse opened for signature in Lanzarote on 25 October 2007, entered into force on 1 July 2010.

[59] CETS No 210, Council of Europe Convention on Preventing and Combating Violence against Women and Domestic Violence opened for signature in Istanbul on 11 May 2011, entered into force on 1 August 2014.

[60] Directive 2011/36/EU of the European Parliament and of the Council of 5 April 2011 on preventing and combating trafficking in human beings and protecting its victims, and replacing Council Framework Decision 2002/629/JHA [2011] OJ L101/1.

[61] Article 52 of Law No 96/2010.

[62] Directive 2012/29/EU of the European Parliament and of the Council of 25 October 2012 establishing minimum standards on the rights, support and protection of victims of crime, and replacing Council Framework Decision 2001/220/JHA [2012] OJ L315/57.

[63] On Legislative Decree No 212/2015, see, for instance, F Delvecchio, 'La nuova fisionomia della vittima del reato dopo l'adeguamento dell'Italia alla Direttiva 2012/29/UE' (Diritto penale contemporaneo, 11 April 2016) 1, available at www.penalecontemporaneo.it (last accessed 25 February 2019).

> In any case, when the offended person is in a condition of particular vulnerability, the public prosecutor, even at the request of the same offended person, or the person under investigations may request that his or her testimony is taken through the special inquiry procedure.[64]

This amendment introduces a so-called hypothesis of 'atypical vulnerability',[65] in conformity with Directive 2012/29/EU which required relevance to be given to the vulnerability of victims regardless of presumptions of vulnerability (such as those referred to in the first part of Article 392, para 1-*bis*, CCP).[66] Legislative Decree No 212/2015 also introduced a new para 5-*quater* in Article 398 CCP, stating that 'Without prejudice to para 5-*ter*, when an offended person in conditions of particular vulnerability must be heard, the provisions laid down in Article 498, para 4-*quater* shall apply' (the reference is to hearing under protected modalities).[67]

In sum, the impact of the *Pupino* case in the relevant policy area – the standing of vulnerable victims in criminal proceedings – can be considered very limited as far as national legislative amendments of national law are concerned, since Framework Decision 2001/220/JHA has never been transposed: and this, even after the ECJ ruling in *Pupino* had made clear the tensions between national law and the same Framework Decision. Only the need to comply with international obligations and with the obligations arising from Directive 2012/29/EU, led to a reform of (inter alia) the national legislation that had been at stake in *Pupino*.

On the contrary, as seen above (section III.B), the impact of *Pupino* can be assessed as relevant when one turns to the (controversial) consequences of the implementation, by national judges, of the duty of consistent interpretation with regard to Framework Decision 2001/220/JHA.

[64] Even after the transposition of Directive 2012/29/EU, the Italian word '*vittima*', with the exception of Article 498, para 4-*ter*, CCP, is never used by the Italian legislator, with the expression '*persona offesa dal reato*' ('person offended by the crime') or the word '*offeso*' ('the offended') being used to refer to the victim. This is due to the willingness of the national legislator to maintain the conceptual distinction between the '*persona offesa*', ie the person to whom the legal interest protected by a violated criminal provision belongs, and the '*danneggiato*', ie the subject which suffers the patrimonial and moral consequences of the crime. While the former has powers and faculties aimed at ensuring participation in the proceedings and the possibility to provide input, only the latter can enjoy the rights and powers of a proper party to the proceedings ('*parte civile*').

[65] See Recchione (n 16) 2786–87.

[66] See Delvecchio (n 63) 27–28.

[67] The 'conditions of particular vulnerability' of the offended person had for the first time gained explicit relevance in the Italian CCP through the introduction, by Law Decree No 93/2013, converted into Law No 119/2013, of para 4-*quater* in Article 498, CCP. Article 498 CCP regulates the direct examination and the cross-examination of the witness in the trial stage. Following the amendments brought by Legislative Decree No 212/2015, Article 498, para 4-*quater*, CCP, states that 'Without prejudice to the previous paras, when an offended person in conditions of particular vulnerability must be heard, the judge, upon request of the offended person or of his or her lawyer, shall order the hearing under protected modalities'. It is also worth recalling that, as mentioned above, Article 498, para 4-*ter*, CCP, is the only provision where the word '*vittima*' is used in the CCP.

IV. Wider Consequences of the Duty of Consistent Interpretation in Other Areas of National Criminal Law

Importantly, the consequences of the implementation by national judges of the duty of consistent interpretation trespassed the area of legal standing of vulnerable victims, to embrace other areas which had been subject of approximation measures through framework decisions.[68]

A few examples will be given in this section, bearing in mind that reference will be made only to judgments in procedural and substantive criminal matters involving the interpretation of framework decisions.[69]

It is important to stress that, in 2010, the Constitutional Court expressly clarified that, in case of contrast between national law and a framework decision, the application of the framework decision and contextual disapplication of national law is excluded, since framework decisions lack direct applicability. Thus, according to the Constitutional Court, the first option that the national court should follow in order to solve the antinomy is conforming interpretation, ie choosing, among those possible, the interpretation of national law that ensures conformity with the framework decision. When the textual formulation of the national law makes interpretation in conformity impossible, the remedy available to the national judge is a reference to the Constitutional Court challenging the violation, by the national law, of Article 11 of the Constitution, which provides the grounds for the relationship between the national legal order and (inter alia) the EU one and consequences and limitations thereof, and Article 117, para 1, of the Constitution, which imposes on the legislator a duty to comply with the Constitution and with the constraints deriving from EU legislation and international obligations.[70] The relevance of the judgment is two-fold: first, the Constitutional Court reinstates

[68] See the various contributions in Sgubbi and Manes (n 7).

[69] Reference will only be made to Union and national provisions in force at the time of the judgment; no reference will be made to subsequent amendments (including abolition of the provisions at stake). On the impact at national level of the principle of interpretation in conformity with directives in various areas of law, see, among others, the contributions in Bernardi (n 7). On interpretation of criminal law in conformity with the ECHR, see Viganò (n 7).

[70] Corte Costituzionale, Judgment No 227/2010. With this judgment, the Constitutional Court declared the constitutional illegitimacy of Article 18, para 1, letter *r*, Law No 59 of 22 April 2005 (implementing Framework Decision 2002/584/JHA on the European arrest warrant) for contrast with Articles 11 and 117, para 1 of the Constitution, in that, in contrast with Article 4 (point 6) of Framework Decision 2002/584/JHA as interpreted by the ECJ, Article 18, para 1, letter *r*, Law 59/2005 did not provide the refusal to also surrender with regard to the citizen of a EU Member State who legitimately and effectively lives in Italy, to the end of the execution of a custodial penalty in Italy in conformity to internal law.

With regard to directives, the sequence: lack of direct effect-conforming interpretation–constitutional review had been elaborated on by the Constitutional Court in Judgment No 28 of 23–28 January 2010; on this judgment, see AM Maugeri, 'La dichiarazione di incostituzionalità di una norma per la violazione di obblighi comunitari ex artt. 11 e 117 Cost.: si aprono nuove prospettive?' (2011) *Rivista italiana di diritto e procedura penale* 1134.

the intrinsic limit to conforming interpretation, ie that this can be performed by national courts only in so far as the letter of the law, also as interpreted by courts ('*diritto vivente*'), does not preclude to do so; second, the Constitutional Court clarified that national law implementing a framework decision is not excluded from constitutional review, thus recognising on framework decisions the role of 'interposed parameters of constitutional legitimacy' (*parametri interposti di legittimità costituzionale*).[71]

This said, as far as criminal procedure is concerned, the duty of interpretation in conformity with framework decisions, as spelled out in *Pupino*, played a relevant role, for instance, with regard to the relationship between Framework Decision 2002/584/JHA on the European arrest warrant[72] and Law No 69 of 22 April 2005 implementing the Framework Decision.

A controversial issue concerned Article 18, letter *e*, Law 69/2005, which established a cause of exclusion of the surrender of a person when the requesting State does not provide for maximum limits of preventive detention. Such an exclusion was not contemplated by Framework Decision 2002/584/JHA, but was introduced in Italy motivated by the need to comply with Article 13, para 5 of the Constitution, requiring that the law shall establish the maximum limits of preventive detention (and, as such, giving constitutional coverage to the aforementioned Article 18, letter *e*, Law 69/2005).

This interpretation has been followed by a judgment of the Supreme Court that, given the clear textual phrasing of national law, excluded that those systems in place in other Member States which are merely 'equivalent' to the explicit provision of maximum limits of preventive detention could fulfil the requirement established by Article 18 letter *e*, Law 69/2005.[73]

However, in a subsequent case concerning the surrender of a defendant to Germany – where a six month limit to preventive detention was provided for, but with the possibility of subsequent reexaminations and extensions without an overall limit to preventive detention – a question was referred to the United Sections of the Supreme Court (*Sezioni Unite*, which in Italy intervene when an interpretative contrast between the single sections arises), and this, despite the Substitute General Public Prosecutor suggesting an order for reference to the Constitutional Court. The United Sections of the Supreme Court, with an explicit reference to the ECJ ruling in *Pupino*, undertook an (deemed) interpretation of national law in conformity with the objectives of Framework Decision 2002/584/JHA, stating that the surrender of a person must be allowed with regard to countries where, like in the case at stake, guarantees are established of the right of the defendant not to be

[71] The same holds true for directives which are not self-executing (see Corte Costituzionale Judgment No 28/2010) and the ECHR provisions and ECtHR case law (see Corte Costituzionale Judgments No 348 and 349 of 22–24 October 2007).

[72] Council Framework Decision 2002/584/JHA of 13 June 2002 on the European arrest warrant and the surrender procedures between Member States [2002] OJ L190/1.

[73] Cass. Pen., Sez. VI, 8–15 May 2006, No 16542, Cusini (2006) Il Foro Italiano II-409.

subject to unreasonably long limitations of personal freedom before conviction, in so far as these guarantees are equivalent, albeit differently modulated, to those provided under Italian law.[74] In so deciding, the United Sections of the Supreme Court gave explicit relevance to the mutual recognition and mutual trust principles, which were mentioned in the Preamble to Framework Decision 2002/584/JHA but were not mentioned by Law No 69/2005. However, the limits to consistent interpretation set out in *Pupino* have been trespassed (interpretation in conformity *in so far as possible*), since the interpretation performed by the United Sections of the Supreme Court was clearly in contrast with the letter and the spirit of national law, with the consequence that the national court once again de facto performed an illegitimate disapplication of national law and application of the Framework Decision 2002/584/JHA. With consistent interpretation being impossible, the correct path would have been an order for reference for constitutional review to the Constitutional Court.[75]

As far as substantive criminal law is concerned, a relevant area is that of confiscation of proceeds of crime.

For instance, a decision of the United Sections of the Supreme Court used, inter alia, Framework Decision 2005/212/JHA[76] to perform an extensive interpretation of national law, which resulted in the inclusion of goods acquired *through the use of* immediate proceeds of crime within the concept of 'profit' (*profitto*) relevant for the preventive seizure finalised to confiscation (*sequestro preventivo finalizzato alla confisca*) under national law.[77] This interpretation in conformity with, inter alia, Framework Decision 2005/212/JHA – which required to apply confiscation to proceeds of crime intended as 'any economic advantage from criminal offences' (Article 1), thus even if of a merely indirect nature – is opposed to a restrictive one, which would consider falling under the relevant notion of 'profit' only the goods obtained through the immediate proceeds of crime. Overall, the chosen extensive interpretation does not seem to be in contrast with the possible literal meanings of the (quite generic) concept of 'profit'.[78] However, it is doubtful whether it respects the limit of a reasonably foreseeable extensive interpretation *in malam partem* or, on the contrary, it integrates an inadmissible analogic interpretation *in malam partem*, due, inter alia, to the existence of previous judgments (*diritto vivente*) adopting a restrictive interpretation that stressed the need for an immediate causal derivation of the economic advantage from the crime.[79]

[74] Cass. Pen., Sez. Un., 30 January–5 February 2007, No 4614, Ramoci (2007) Cassazione penale 1911.

[75] See Viganò (n 7) 621–622, 644, 654.

[76] Council Framework Decision 2005/212/JHA of 24 February 2005 on Confiscation of Crime-Related Proceeds, Instrumentalities and Property [2005] OJ L68/49.

[77] Cass. Pen, Sez. Un., 25 October 2007–6 March 2008, No 10280, Miragliotta (2008) Cassazione penale 3167.

[78] See Viganò (n 7) 669.

[79] See Manes (n 10) 421.

Also concerning confiscation, the United Sections of the Supreme Court excluded the possibility to extend to the 'profit' (*profitto*) of the crime of misappropriation (*peculato*) the confiscation of an equivalent amount of money (*confisca per equivalente*) that Article 322-*ter*, para 1, CC, with regard to the crime of misappropriation, provided only for the 'price' (*prezzo*) of that crime.[80] The United Sections of the Supreme Court stated that the judicial attempt to perform such an extension by means of interpretation of national law in conformity with Framework Decision 2005/212/JHA,[81] would violate the principle of legality of criminal punishments. According to the United Sections of the Supreme Court, due to the lack of a clear legislative indication differentiating the meaning of the terms '*profitto*' and '*prezzo*' in Article 322-*ter* from their usual meaning, these terms have to be interpreted in conformity with the consolidated Italian case law, which in particular excludes that the term '*prezzo*' can be extended to encompass any proceeds or economic advantage from criminal offences. Importantly, the Court stressed that a different conclusion would result in an inadmissible judicial corrective intervention of the legal provision *in malam partem*, adding that it is only on the legislator to intervene in order to bring order and coherence into the provision at stake.

Another area of substantive criminal law, where the principles expressed by the ECJ in *Pupino* played a significant role, is child pornography. As recently as 2012, a definition of child pornography was introduced in the CC (Article 600-*ter*, para 7). Before 2012, the lack of a statutory definition had caused interpretative difficulties in the application of the criminal offence of child pornography provided for in the same Article 600-*ter* CC.[82] During that period, the Supreme Court, with an express reference to the duty of consistent interpretation as spelled out in *Pupino*, interpreted the (at the time) undefined notion of child pornography in light of Article 1 of Framework Decision 2004/68/JHA.[83] In particular, the Supreme Court inferred from the definition of child pornography provided for by the Framework Decision (ie the representation of a child involved or engaged in sexually explicit conduct), that a person who, at the beach, had taken numerous pictures of children in bathing-suits (asking the children to bend and repeatedly taking pictures of the children's backsides), cannot be convicted of the criminal offence under Article 600-*ter* due to a lack of lascivious exhibition or sexually

[80] Cass. Pen., Sez. Un., 25 June–6 October 2009, No 38691, Caruso. This was probably an oversight on the part of the legislator, since in the case of the crime of misappropriation the correct qualification/wording should have been '*profitto*' and not '*prezzo*'. It is worth adding that, with regard to the '*profitto*' of the crime, Article 322-*ter*, para 2, CC, provided for confiscation of an equivalent amount of money only for the crime of active bribery (*corruzione attiva*).

[81] Which defined the 'proceeds of crime' in broad terms (see Articles 1 and 2).

[82] Which at the time, punished whoever, using minors under the age of eighteen, facilitated pornographic performances, produced pornographic material or recruited minors in order to participate in pornographic performances.

[83] Council Framework Decision 2004/68/JHA of 22 December 2003 on combating the sexual exploitation of children and child pornography [2004] OJ L13/44.

allusive behaviour.[84] This decision is of particular interest from a methodological point of view, because the Supreme Court, after interpreting national criminal law in conformity with Framework Decision 2004/68/JHA, double-checked the consistency of this interpretation with constitutional principles in criminal matters (precision and offensiveness); the Supreme Court found that the interpretation of the concept of child pornography – a constitutive element of the criminal offence at stake – in conformity with Framework Decision 2004/68/JHA increased the precision of the concept and helped avoid encompassing inoffensive behaviour.[85]

These merely exemplificative cases confirm that, as it has been noted, the duty of consistent interpretation is at the core of the relationship between EU law and national criminal law.[86]

With *Pupino*, the ECJ entrusted national courts with new responsibilities as to ensuring the effectiveness of EU law. Overall, the impression is that national courts in Italy proved to be willing to perform their duty of interpretation of national law in conformity with framework decisions.[87] On some occasions (and, as one would have expected, particularly in substantive criminal law matters), national courts proved to be capable of taking into account the limits to consistent interpretation which had been set out by the ECJ in the same *Pupino* ruling.

V. Concluding Remarks

The ECJ ruling in the *Pupino* case was certainly of great relevance in terms of EU constitutional developments, marking a step towards overcoming differences between the EU pillars. The fact that the ECJ adopted the ruling in its Grand Chamber composition shows that the issues at stake – the Court's competence on interpreting framework decisions, the binding nature of these instruments and the applicability, limits and implications of the indirect effect principle – were perceived as being of particular complexity and importance.

However, the analysis conducted so far has also shown that *Pupino* has been of utmost significance in terms of its consequences at national level.

First of all, the ECJ ruling is relevant for its impact on ongoing criminal proceedings, specifically by leading to the application of the special inquiry procedure for the early gathering of evidence under special arrangements in cases that,

[84] Cass. Pen., Sez. III, 4–22 March 2010, No 10981, Khan (2011) Cassazione penale 1412. See also, in the context of a different formulation of Article 600-*ter* CC, Cass. Pen., Sez. III, 9 January–6 February 2013, No 5874, L.D. (No 2-2013) Diritto e Giustizia 79.

[85] See Manes (n 10) 427–28.

[86] See Sotis (n 7) 34.

[87] See for instance, with regard to conforming interpretation to supranational sources in general, Viganò (n 7) 619. This opinion is not uncontroversial; see for instance Bernardi, 'Presentazione. Nei meandri dell'interpretazione conforme al diritto dell'Unione Europea' in Bernardi (n 7) VII–XXXIV.

at the time, were not included in the scope of the applicable national legislation; and this legislative choice had been previously deemed not to be constitutionally illegitimate by the Constitutional Court. Despite the relevance of the objective of protecting vulnerable victims (and witnesses) pursued by the national judge, the possibility of an interpretation of applicable national law in conformity with Framework Decision 2001/220/JHA collided with the same limits set out by the ECJ, ie that the interpretation in conformity should be performed only *in so far as possible* and it cannot be *contra legem*. The implementation of the objectives pursued by Framework Decision 2001/220/JHA as interpreted by the ECJ would have required the national legislator to step in, in order to formalise a necessary legal change: a change that finally occurred only following the need to comply with the obligations arising from Directive 2012/29/EU.

From this standpoint, *Pupino* is an expression of a (questionable) 'judicial activism'[88] of national courts. At the same time, and correlatively, the ECJ ruling in *Pupino* has enhanced at national level a sort of 'judge's justice model' where consistent interpretation – a methodological and theoretical tool and practice to ensure compatibility and consistency between systems of law – has potential implications on the same separation of powers, while simultaneously challenging (in the substance) the role of the Constitutional Court as the national judge exclusively in charge of constitutional review of legislation, whenever the same legislation regulates an area which has been subject to an EU approximation measure through framework decisions.

Thus, following the ECJ ruling in *Pupino*, judges enjoyed a much wider discretional power than in the past; a power that, while contributing to the creation of a common area of justice whose essential component is a uniform application, to the maximum extent possible, of Union law, may be seen as exceeding the limits of the judicial interpretative function and trespassing into a quasi-creative one.

Beyond the policy area originally involved in the *Pupino* case, ie the standing of vulnerable victims within criminal proceedings, national courts performed their duty of interpretation of national procedural and substantive criminal law in conformity with framework decisions in other relevant areas. The analysis of national judgments concerning the European arrest warrant, confiscation of proceeds of crime and child pornography shows the complexity of the task of national courts when they are called upon to perform their duty of consistent interpretation. A task that, while in some cases resulted in (at the least) questionable decisions, in other cases, and particularly as far as substantive criminal law is concerned, has been performed through a rigorous application of the limits to consistent interpretation.

Correlatively, the ECJ ruling in *Pupino* contributed to what can be qualified as an adaptation at national level of the traditional interpretative criteria and a

[88] Caianiello (n 7) 94.

new equilibrium among these criteria in criminal matters, in order to embed the peculiar logic, needs and limits underpinning interpretation in conformity with supranational sources.[89] The reference made in several national judgments to the principles and limitations in criminal matters expressed by the ECJ in *Pupino*, shows the real 'power' of the *Pupino* case and its persistent relevance: a ruling whose long-term, post-Lisbon impact consists in establishing limitations to conforming interpretation applicable to all cases of non-transposition or incomplete transposition of EU directives in criminal matters.

[89] See, in general, Manes (n 10) 398; Bernardi (n 87) XII–XV.

PART II

Competence

4

68/88 – *Commission v Greece*

Effectiveness, Dissuasiveness, Proportionality of Sanctions and Assimilation Principle: The Long-Lasting Legacy of the Greek Maize *Case*

FABIO GIUFFRIDA

I. Introduction

The importance of the *Greek Maize* case for the development of EU (criminal) law can hardly be underestimated, as it laid the foundations of some key principles concerning the enforcement of EU policies in Member States.

Delivered in 1989, the *Greek Maize* judgment deals with the exportation of some maize from Greece to Belgium.[1] Originally, the maize had been imported into Greece from Yugoslavia, but it was declared as having a Greek origin when exported to Belgium. This fraudulent operation, which was facilitated by the complicity of certain Greek civil servants, withheld from the Community budget the agricultural levies that should have been paid when the Yugoslav maize crossed the Community's borders in the first place. Furthermore, the competent Greek authorities had not taken any appropriate measures to investigate this case.

After an unsuccessful exchange of correspondence between the Commission and Greece, the former brought the latter before the European Court of Justice (ECJ),[2] pursuant to Article 169 of the Treaty establishing the European Economic Community (EEC) (now Article 258 TFEU), since the Hellenic Republic had failed to fulfil its obligations under Community law. Building on the principle of sincere cooperation, enshrined in Article 5 of the EEC Treaty (now Article 4(3) TEU), the ECJ held that Member States shall ensure that

[1] Case 68/88 *Commission v Greece* ('*Greek Maize*') EU:C:1989:339.

[2] For the post-Lisbon era, the acronym 'CJEU' (Court of Justice of the European Union) will instead be used.

> infringements of Community law are penalized under conditions, both procedural and substantive, which are *analogous* to those applicable to infringements of national law of a similar nature and importance and which, in any event, make the penalty *effective*, *proportionate* and *dissuasive*.[3]

The Court added that 'the national authorities must proceed, with respect to infringements of Community law, with the same diligence as that which they bring to bear in implementing corresponding national law'.[4] Whereas this principle has been overlooked in the further development of EU policies,[5] one cannot help but notice that the *Greek Maize* ruling introduced two fundamental concepts of EU law, namely the assimilation principle and the requirement for penalties to be effective, proportionate and dissuasive. The following section discusses the assimilation principle in more detail, while section III deals with the three-fold mantra concerning sanctions. Section IV concludes by summarising the main findings of the analysis.

II. The Assimilation Principle before and after the *Greek Maize* Case

When EU law does not specify what kind of penalties should follow from its violation, the principle of sincere cooperation obliges Member States to take 'all measures necessary to guarantee the application and effectiveness'[6] of EU law.[7] In the *Greek Maize* case, the ECJ singled out the obligation for Member States to treat analogous violations of EU and national law in an analogous way.[8] Thus, *if* national legal orders provide for a system of *criminal* liability for breaches of domestic law, the analogous breaches of EU law should be punished in the same way. Although the ECJ did not spell this consequence out in *Greek Maize*, it nonetheless concluded that Greece had failed to 'institute *criminal* or disciplinary proceedings against the persons who took part in the commission and concealment of the fraud'[9] at issue. Less than one year after, however, the ECJ held that Member States could be obliged to punish infringements of EU law 'if necessary by instituting *criminal* proceedings'.[10]

[3] *Greek Maize* (n 1) para 24 (emphasis added).
[4] *Greek Maize* (n 1) para 25.
[5] A Klip, *European Criminal Law. An Integrative Approach*, 3rd edn (Intersentia, 2016) 81–82.
[6] *Greek Maize* (n 1) para 23.
[7] Although the *Greek Maize* case concerned the 'Community'/'Communities' (law/budget), the following analysis will refer to the 'EU'/'Union' (law/budget), unless where inappropriate.
[8] This principle has been restated in several judgments of the ECJ, such as Case C-70/90 *Vandevenne and others* EU:C:1991:363, para 11.
[9] *Greek Maize* (n 1) para 26 (emphasis added).
[10] Case C-2/88 *Imm Zwartveld and others* EU:C:1990:315, para 17 (emphasis added).

The assimilation principle represented a significant inroad into Member States' sovereignty, especially since, at that time, the dominant narrative was that '[i]n principle, criminal legislation and the rules of criminal procedure are matters for which the Member States are still responsible'.[11] The assimilation principle is a typical example of the Member States' 'positive obligations' descending from EU law, as opposed to 'negative obligations', such as those requiring Member States to not adopt criminal measures that may hamper the free movement of goods and persons.[12]

Before the *Greek Maize* case, and beyond the field of criminal law, the *Rewe* and *Comet* cases had already introduced a similar principle, with regard to the procedural conditions governing legal actions intended to ensure the protection of the rights that citizens derived from Union law. As the ECJ clarified, pursuant to the general principle of sincere cooperation, 'such conditions cannot be less favourable than those relating to similar actions of a domestic nature'.[13] As for criminal law, Article 27 of the 1957 Statute of the Court of Justice of the EEC (now Article 30 of the Statute) required Member States to treat violations of oath by witnesses and experts examined by the Court as if these offences had occurred in national civil proceedings. That provision also obliged Member States to prosecute the offender before the competent domestic courts. Likewise, in accordance with the Treaty establishing the European Atomic Energy Community (Euratom), each Member State had to consider the Euratom's staff violations of professional secrecy as acts 'prejudicial to its rules on secrecy and as [ones] falling, both as to merits and jurisdiction, within the scope of its laws relating to acts prejudicial to the security of the State or to disclosure of professional secrets'.[14]

There is no reference to criminal law in the provision of the Statute of the ECJ and in the Euratom Treaty, perhaps because rules on the violation both of professional secrecy and of oaths by experts and witnesses were (and are) commonly to be found in national criminal justice systems, so that no further specification was necessary.[15] However, the just mentioned rules had a limited scope of application, while the assimilation principle laid down in the *Greek Maize* case concerns the protection of the Union budget, and thus imposes much broader obligations upon Member States.

It is not a coincidence that such a principle was introduced in the field of the protection of the Union's financial interests (hereinafter 'PIF'[16]), since already at that time most EU funds were given to European citizens and legal entities by *national* bodies through *national* procedures on behalf of the EU,[17] in a system

[11] Case 203/80 *Casati* EU:C:1981:261, para 27.

[12] P Asp, 'European Criminal Law and National Criminal Law' in V Mitsilegas, M Bergström and T Konstadinides (eds), *Research Handbook on EU Criminal Law* (Edward Elgar, 2016) 315ff.

[13] Case 33/76 *Rewe* EU:C:1976:188, para 5; Case 45/76 *Comet* EU:C:1976:191, para 13.

[14] Art 194(1) of the Euratom Treaty. See also Asp (n 12) 319.

[15] S Miettinen, *Criminal Law and Policy in the European Union* (Routledge, 2013) 12–13.

[16] This acronym stands for '*protection des intérêts financiers*'.

[17] See, of many, V Covolo, *L'Émergence d'un Droit Pénal en Réseau. Analyse Critique du Système Européen de Lutte Antifraude* (Nomos, 2015) 692.

of 'shared management'.[18] As Member States are competent to implement large portions of the EU budget, the ECJ obliged them to protect the Union's financial interests, by assimilating the latter to the national financial interests. As early as 1976, the Commission had tabled a draft Treaty, which required Member States to punish PIF offences in the same way the domestic *penal* legislations sanctioned fraud to the detriment of the national budget. Together with this proposal, the Commission also suggested an amendment of the Treaties to introduce the assimilation principle with regard to the criminal liability of officials of the European Communities for crimes such as bribery and forgery.[19] Pairing the PIF sector with the protection of the European civil service is justified by the fact that, in both cases, purely European legal interests are concerned.[20] It would be appropriate for the Member States to introduce penalties that were equivalent to those laid down at the national level for offences against the national budget and the national civil service. Nevertheless, the proposals at stake were never adopted, being formally withdrawn in 1994, and the assimilation principle would have been eventually introduced by the ECJ in the *Greek Maize* case.[21]

This principle was later enshrined in the Treaty of the European Community (TEC), which replaced the EEC Treaty as of the entry into force of the Treaty of Maastricht. In accordance with Article 209a(1) TEC, which fell within the then first pillar, 'Member States shall take the same measures to counter fraud affecting the financial interests of the Community as they take to counter fraud affecting their own financial interests'. On the one hand, this provision confirms that the assimilation principle is coterminous with the PIF sector. On the other hand, it does not include any reference to criminal law, since matters concerning criminal justice were relegated into the then third pillar.

Indeed, the first ever instrument of EU substantive criminal law, namely the Convention on the protection of the European Community's (EC's) financial interests ('PIF Convention'),[22] was adopted by the Member States within the frame of the third pillar in 1995. The Convention introduced an obligation for the Member States to sanction with *criminal* penalties some illegal conducts amounting to fraud. The PIF Convention did not aim at the assimilation between the EU and the national budget, but rather at the harmonisation of national legislations on PIF offences. However, Article 4 of the first Protocol to the Convention expressly required the Member States to assimilate active and passive corruption, damaging, or likely to damage, the EC's financial interests, to the corresponding offences

[18] Commission, 'EU Budget 2016. Financial Report' (2017) 19 http://ec.europa.eu/budget/library/biblio/publications/2017/financial-report_en.pdf (last accessed 2 March 2019).

[19] Both these draft Treaties can be found in [1976] OJ C222/13.

[20] G Grasso, 'Relazione Introduttiva' in G Grasso and R Sicurella (eds), *Per un Rilancio del Progetto Europeo. Esigenze di Tutela degli Interessi Comunitari e Nuove Strategie di Integrazione Penale* (Giuffrè, 2008) 3–4.

[21] See also R Sicurella, 'EU Competence in Criminal Matters' in Mitsilegas, Bergström and Konstadinides (eds) (n 12) 64ff.

[22] [1995] OJ C316/49.

provided for by national criminal codes.[23] An almost identical obligation can be found in Article 4 of the 1997 Convention on the fight against corruption involving officials of the EC, which introduced the duty to penalise corruption beyond the cases where damage to the common budget had occurred, or was likely to occur.[24] The legislation mentioned so far confirms that, almost ten years after the *Greek Maize* case, the assimilation principle was still a key principle of the (newborn) EU criminal policy, especially when properly European, 'federal', legal interests were to be protected.

The Treaty of Amsterdam later amended Article 209a TEC, which became Article 280 TEC. This provision restated the principle of assimilation and added various rules to enhance the protection of the Union's financial interests. Furthermore, the ECJ continued to refer to the principle under analysis in various judgments.[25] Eventually, with the Treaty of Lisbon, Article 325 TFEU replaced Article 280 TEC. Article 325(1) TFEU lays down the obligation of the Union and its Member States to counter fraud through deterrent measures affording effective protection, whereas Article 325(2) TFEU reiterates the principle of assimilation.

The Treaty of Lisbon ushered in a new phase of EU criminal policy, since Article 83 TFEU empowers the European Parliament and the Council to adopt directives setting out minimum rules concerning the definition of criminal offences and sanctions.[26] As EU directives can now harmonise national criminal laws, requiring Member States to criminalise certain conducts, the role of the assimilation principle in the development of EU criminal law is likely to be less important.[27] Furthermore, the assimilation principle has shown to be a rather unsatisfactory avenue for the enforcement of EU law, for at least four reasons.

First, it may sometimes be difficult to make a valid comparison between national offences and offences affecting the EU budget, so that the assimilation principle does not always apply straightforwardly.[28] The recent ruling of the CJEU in *Scialdone* is a case in point. The case concerns the Italian legislation on failure to pay correctly declared VAT, namely an offence that Advocate General (AG) Bobek argues is not covered by Article 325(2) TFEU.[29] The latter provision only refers to 'fraud', and the failure to pay correctly declared VAT does not seem to fall within this notion. The AG posits that the assimilation principle nonetheless applies, since it is imposed by Article 4(3) TEU (the principle of sincere cooperation), read in conjunction with Article 325(1) TFEU. After all, in line with the *Greek Maize* findings, 'Article 325(2) TFEU represents an area-specific codification of the case-law

[23] [1996] OJ C313/2.
[24] [1997] OJ C195/2.
[25] See, for instance, Case C-460/06 *Paquay* EU:C:2007:601, para 52.
[26] See V Mitsilegas, *EU Criminal Law after Lisbon. Rights, Trust and the Transformation of Justice in Europe* (Hart Publishing, 2016) 7ff.
[27] Klip (n 5) 76.
[28] *Ibid*; Asp (n 12) 318.
[29] Case C-574/15 *Scialdone*, Opinion of AG Bobek, EU:C:2017:553, paras 70–73.

of the Court on the principle of loyal cooperation'.[30] Against this backdrop, the AG examines whether the VAT offence at stake in *Scialdone* is comparable to the offences concerning direct taxation regulated by Italian law.[31] He advocates a broad approach to the assessment of such comparability, which should not rely on the 'complete identity' between offences, for this would 'make it very difficult to find equivalent sources of revenue or expenditure in the Member States'.[32] Should this restrictive interpretation be followed, AG Bobek argues that VAT offences – due to the specificity of the system of collection of this tax – 'could never be considered as analogous to infringements of any other tax'.[33] The Court did not share the stance of the AG and submitted that failure to pay correctly declared VAT is not comparable to the allegedly similar Italian offence concerning direct taxation, as they 'can be distinguished by both their constituent elements and the difficulty involved in their detection'.[34] The difference between the views of the AG and of the Court captures the inherent complexity flowing from the interpretation and application of the assimilation principle. Incidentally, it is worth noting that the Court seems to extend the assessment of the 'similar nature and importance'[35] of infringements of EU and national law so as to include external factors such as the difficulty in their detection. This arguably runs counter to the traditional understanding of the assimilation principle and may even jeopardise the application of the latter: the comparison between different crimes on the basis of the difficulty in their detection is an admittedly complex task, which seems to leave ample room for largely discretionary assessments.

Second, the assimilation principle does not guarantee that the measures adopted by the Member States to protect EU (financial) interests are effective; if those measures are insufficient to safeguard national interests, such ineffectiveness will inevitably expand to the protection of European interests.[36] Third, the assimilation principle does maintain the existing differences among Member States' legislations, unlike the harmonisation measures that aim to reduce the discrepancies among national criminal justice systems.[37] Almost 25 years after *Greek Maize*, the Commission stated that, as for fraud, corruption, and money laundering, 'Member States have adopted diverging rules and consequently often diverging levels of protection within their national legal systems. This state of affairs shows

[30] *Ibid*, para 75.

[31] The offence at issue is failure to pay withholding tax by the substitute of the taxpayer, which Italian law defines as the conduct of whoever 'fails to pay, within the period fixed for the filing of the withholding agent's annual tax return, the withholding tax resulting from the certification issued to the taxpayers in respect of whom tax is withheld' (Art 10 *bis* of Legislative Decree 74/2000).

[32] *Scialdone*, Opinion of AG Bobek (n 29), para 101.

[33] *Ibid.*

[34] Case C-574/15 *Scialdone* EU:C:2018:295, para 57.

[35] *Greek Maize* (n 1) para 24.

[36] See 'Explanatory Memorandum' in M Delmas-Marty (ed), Corpus Juris *Introducing Penal Provisions for the Purpose of the Financial Interests of the European Union* (Economica, 1997) 16.

[37] Grasso (n 20) 13–16.

that there is *no equivalent protection of the Union's financial interests*'.[38] Finally, the assimilation principle may potentially oblige Member States to introduce criminal sanctions even when the latter are not formally required at the EU level, so increasing the risk of over-criminalisation.[39]

Albeit problematic as a principle that should drive the EU and national *legislatures*, the assimilation principle has recently gained attention as a *judicial* device to cope with Member States' violations of EU law. In *Taricco*,[40] and the follow-up case *MAS, MB*,[41] the CJEU ruled that Italian legislation on the statute of limitation of VAT offences runs counter not only to Article 325(1) TFEU, but also to the principle of assimilation enshrined in Article 325(2) TFEU. In particular, the offence of criminal association with a view to smuggling foreign manufactured tobacco, regulated by a 1973 piece of Italian legislation, was subject to longer limitation periods than comparable offences at issue in the main proceedings before the CJEU (conspiracy to commit various offences in relation to VAT). As a consequence, Italy violated the principle of assimilation, since it did not provide for an analogous treatment of analogous offences affecting national and EU financial interests.[42] The clash of national legislation with Article 325(2) TFEU may lead to the disapplication of that legislation, since Article 325 TFEU lays down 'a precise obligation as to the result to be achieved that is not subject to any condition'.[43]

In *MAS, MB*, the CJEU has confirmed its stance, yet it has clarified that disapplication does not take place when national courts come to the view that the obligation to disapply violates the principle that offences and penalties must be defined by law.[44] One of the most debated issues of the *Taricco* saga concerns precisely the disapplication of national law flowing from the incompatibility with Article 325 TFEU. Whereas Article 325(2) TFEU – enshrining the assimilation principle – would be clear and unconditional enough to allow national courts to disapply conflicting national law, a similar conclusion seems much more debatable with regard to Article 325(1) TFEU.[45] Be that as it may, the assimilation principle could become a key instrument in the hands of national authorities dealing with (unsatisfactory national legislation on) PIF offences, thanks to the *Taricco* and *MAS, MB* cases of the CJEU.

[38] Commission, 'Proposal for a Directive of the European Parliament and of the Council on the fight against fraud to the Union's financial interests by means of criminal law' COM(2012) 363 final, 2 (emphasis added).

[39] Mitsilegas (n 26) 74–75.

[40] Case C-105/14 *Taricco and others* EU:C:2015:555.

[41] Case C-42/17 *MAS, MB* EU:C:2017:936.

[42] *Taricco* (n 40) para 48. For some critical remarks on whether the crimes at hand can truly be regarded as analogous, see G Grasso, 'Evoluzione del Diritto Penale Europeo e Tutela dei Diritti Fondamentali alla Luce della «Saga Taricco»' [2018] *Legislazione Penale* 1, 14–15, available at www.lalegislazionepenale.eu/wp-content/uploads/2018/10/Grasso-Studi.pdf (last accessed 2 March 2019).

[43] *Taricco* (n 40) para 51.

[44] *MAS, MB* (n 41) para 62.

[45] See R Sicurella, 'Effectiveness of EU Law and Protection of Fundamental Rights: The Questions Settled and the New Challenges after the ECJ Decision in the *MAS and MB* Case (C-42/17)' (2018) 9 *New Journal of European Criminal Law* 24, 25–26.

III. Effectiveness, Proportionality and Dissuasiveness of Penalties

Already in the *Greek Maize* ruling, the ECJ seems to imply that the assimilation principle may be insufficient to adequately cope with infringements of Union law. Hence, it adds that the substantive and procedural conditions under which those infringements have to be penalised shall, 'in any event, make the penalty effective, proportionate and dissuasive'.[46]

The *Greek Maize* case is in line with the previous case law of the ECJ, which had acknowledged that Member States enjoy a broad discretion in deciding the measures that should follow the infringements of EU law, and which may 'even be criminal in nature'.[47] However, the *Greek Maize* judgment adds that penalties shall be effective, dissuasive and proportionate but it does *not* require the penalties to be of a *criminal* nature. Scholars and Advocates General have elaborated on the concept of effective, dissuasive and proportionate penalties, which the Court did not define.

The starting point for the analysis is often represented by the Opinion of AG Kokott in the *Berlusconi* case,[48] where she argued that rules laying down criminal penalties are *effective* when 'they are framed in such a way that they do not make it practically impossible or excessively difficult to impose the penalty provided for (and, therefore, *to attain the objectives pursued by Community law*)'.[49] AG Kokott thus draws a clear connection between the 'effectiveness' of penalties and the more general principle of effectiveness that underpins EU law.[50] In her words, moreover, a penalty is *dissuasive* if 'it prevents an individual from infringing the objectives pursued and rules laid down by Community law'.[51] She also highlights that the deterrent effect of a penalty does not depend on its severity *in abstracto* but rather on the certainty that it will be served. Finally, AG Kokott submits that a sanction is *proportionate* when it is 'appropriate (…) for attaining the legitimate objectives pursued by it, and also necessary. Where there is a choice between several (equally) appropriate penalties, recourse must be had to the least onerous'.[52]

Despite this and other analyses of the three-fold *Greek Maize* requirement,[53] it is undisputed that the formula used by the ECJ 'imposes duties upon the member

[46] *Greek Maize* (n 1) para 24.

[47] Case 50/76 *Amsterdam Bulb* EU:C:1977:13, para 32.

[48] See, for instance, J Öberg, *Limits to EU Powers. A Case Study of EU Regulatory Criminal Law* (Hart Publishing, 2017) 85. See also Klip (n 5) 78ff.

[49] Joined Cases C-387/02, C-391/02 and C-403/02 *Berlusconi and others*, Opinion of AG Kokott, EU:C:2004:624, para 88 (emphasis added).

[50] In the same vein see, among many, S Melander, 'Effectiveness in EU Criminal Law and Its Effects on the General Part of Criminal Law' (2014) 5 *New Journal of European Criminal Law* 274, 285–86.

[51] *Berlusconi and others*, Opinion of AG Kokott (n 49) para 89.

[52] *Ibid*, para 90.

[53] See, for instance, Case C-326/88 *Hansen*, Opinion of AG Van Gerven, EU:C:1989:609; Case C-176/03 *Commission v Council*, Opinion of AG Ruiz-Jarabo Colomer, EU:C:2005:311.

state which are relatively clear in the abstract yet often vague in their specifics'.[54] For instance, one may wonder whether a penalty can be proportionate to the offence at the same time as being effective and dissuasive.[55] Furthermore, it could be difficult to claim that a given sanction is truly dissuasive, as one may support an extreme argument according to which, as far as a crime does not cease to be committed, the penalties thereof are not deterrent enough.[56] Some authors have also looked in more detail at the 'effectiveness' of sanctions, wondering whether this principle overlaps with 'deterrence', and how, more broadly, the effectiveness can be assessed in the field of criminal law.[57]

Nevertheless, the *Greek Maize* requirements for penalties have significantly contributed to the development of EU criminal law, and have been restated in several following judgments of the Court of Justice. In *Hansen*, for example, the ECJ endorsed the system of strict criminal liability provided for in Denmark to sanction the violations of an EEC Regulation on road transport.[58] As for the impact on legislation, the *Greek Maize* formula on penalties had a somehow opposite destiny when compared with the assimilation principle. On one hand, the Treaty of Maastricht did not replicate the words of the ECJ, although Article 325(1) TFEU – in line with the previous Article 280(1) TEC (Amsterdam version) – now requires Member States and the Union to adopt 'deterrent' measures (not necessarily penalties) that shall afford 'effective' protection to the Union's financial interests.

On the other hand, the 'effectiveness, dissuasiveness and proportionality' of sanctions has become a mantra of EU *secondary* law. Looking at the pre-Lisbon scenario, several EU substantive criminal law instruments provide an obligation for Member States to: i) adopt effective, proportionate and dissuasive *criminal* penalties for *natural* persons who are responsible for the offences addressed in those instruments; ii) introduce some kind of *imprisonment* penalty for the most serious offences; and iii) ensure that legal persons are punishable by effective, proportionate and dissuasive sanctions. The nature of penalties for legal persons is not further specified, since some Member States had, and still have, some reservations about the *criminal* liability of entities and companies.[59]

[54] M Dougan, 'From the Velvet Glove to the Iron Fist: Criminal Sanctions for the Enforcement of Union Law' in M Cremona (ed), *Compliance and the Enforcement of EU Law* (Oxford University Press, 2012) 84.

[55] E Herlin-Karnell, 'Is Administrative Law Still Relevant? How the Battle of Sanctions Has Shaped EU Criminal Law' in Mitsilegas, Bergström and Konstadinides (eds) (n 12) 236.

[56] See, for instance, Klip (n 5) 80.

[57] Among the many, A Suominen, 'Effectiveness and Functionality of Substantive EU Criminal Law' (2014) 5 *New Journal of European Criminal Law* 388.

[58] Case C-326/88 *Hansen* EU:C:1990:291.

[59] See M Delmas-Marty, 'Necessity, Legitimacy and Feasibility of the *Corpus Juris*' in M Delmas-Marty and JAE Vervaele (eds), *The Implementation of the* Corpus Juris *in the Member States* (Intersentia, 2000) Vol 1, 74–75.

This pattern may be found, for instance, in the PIF Convention,[60] and in most framework decisions adopted within the frame of the previous third pillar, such as those on fraud and counterfeiting of non-cash means of payment,[61] and on trafficking in human beings.[62] Some other framework decisions do not replicate the mantra on effective, dissuasive and proportionate criminal sanctions for *natural* persons, since they only provide an obligation to introduce imprisonment penalties, as is the case with instruments concerning child pornography[63] and organised crime.[64]

After the Lisbon Treaty, some of the previous framework decisions have been, or are in the process of being, replaced by directives adopted in accordance with Article 83 TFEU. This provision is also the legal basis for directives addressing certain forms of crime that were not covered by third pillar instruments, such as market abuse.[65] Nevertheless, despite the changes brought about by the Lisbon Treaty, the pattern does not change and the post-Lisbon instruments still lay down a general obligation to provide for effective, proportionate and dissuasive criminal penalties for natural persons, and more specific imprisonment penalties for the most serious crimes.[66] Likewise, the directives do not require the liability of legal persons to be of a criminal nature.[67]

Against this backdrop, four remarks are necessary. First, although in *Greek Maize* the ECJ did not refer to criminal penalties, the Member States – acting within the frame of the third pillar – soon interpreted the three-fold formula of that ruling as requiring criminal sanctions. Almost by definition, the latter are believed to be more effective and dissuasive than other penalties, eg administrative ones. The need for relying, in any circumstance, on criminal penalties has however been questioned in the literature,[68] especially in those fields where there is a relevant component of administrative law, such as environmental

[60] The liability of legal persons for PIF crimes is provided for by the First Protocol to the PIF Convention.

[61] Council Framework Decision 2001/413/JHA of 28 May 2001 combating fraud and counterfeiting of non-cash means of payment [2001] OJ L149/1.

[62] Council Framework Decision 2002/629/JHA of 19 July 2002 on combating trafficking in human beings [2002] OJ L203/1.

[63] Council Framework Decision 2004/68/JHA of 22 December 2003 on combating the sexual exploitation of children and child pornography [2004] OJ L13/44.

[64] Council Framework Decision 2008/841/JHA of 24 October 2008 on the fight against organised crime [2008] OJ L300/42.

[65] Directive 2014/57/EU of the European Parliament and of the Council of 16 April 2014 on criminal sanctions for market abuse (Market Abuse Directive) [2014] OJ L173/179.

[66] See, for instance, Art 4 of Directive 2011/36/EU of the European Parliament and of the Council of 5 April 2011 on preventing and combating trafficking in human beings and protecting its victims, and replacing Council Framework Decision 2002/629/JHA [2011] OJ L101/1 and Art 15 of Directive (EU) 2017/541 of the European Parliament and of the Council of 15 March 2017 on combating terrorism and replacing Council Framework Decision 2002/475/JHA and amending Council Decision 2005/671/JHA [2017] OJ L88/6.

[67] See Art 6 of Directive 2011/36/EU and Art 18 of Directive (EU) 2017/541.

[68] See, of many, Öberg (n 48) 192–93.

criminal law.[69] Precisely in this field, the ECJ itself seems to have endorsed the presumption that criminal law is always better suited to guarantee effective and dissuasive sanctions. In the *Environmental Crime* case, the ECJ ruled that the lack of competence of Community in the field of criminal law

> does not prevent the Community legislature, when the application of effective, proportionate and dissuasive criminal penalties by the competent national authorities is an essential measure for combating serious environmental offences, from taking measures which relate to the criminal law of the Member States which it considers necessary in order to ensure that the rules which it lays down on environmental protection are fully effective.[70]

In the pre-Lisbon scenario, the *Environmental Crime* case opened the doors to the adoption of first pillar instruments harmonising criminal law, such as Directive 2008/99/EC on environmental crime[71] and Directive 2009/123/EC on ship-source pollution.[72] The marked preference for criminal law measures has led some authors to argue that the main driving force behind EU criminal law legislation is the 'symbolic',[73] 'emotional'[74] aim to create a common sense of justice.[75]

Second, the EU harmonisation instruments adopted so far do not cover financial criminal penalties for individuals, because they exclusively concern sanctions implying deprivation of liberty. It is true that most of the offences defined at the EU level are of such gravity that financial penalties would be too lenient, yet this argument seems less convincing when it comes to purely economic crimes. Financial penalties may also be imposed in addition to imprisonment in some cases, as it emerges from the Preamble of the Directive on combating child pornography, according to which Member States 'are invited to consider providing for the possibility to impose financial penalties in addition to imprisonment',[76] when the offences are committed with the purpose of financial gain.

[69] M Faure, 'European Environmental Criminal Law: Do We Really Need It?' (2004) 13 *European Energy and Environmental Law Review* 18. On the relationship between criminal and administrative sanctions in EU law, see Herlin-Karnell (n 55).

[70] Case C-176/03 *Commission v Council* EU:C:2005:542, para 48. See Dougan (n 54) 101–102.

[71] Directive 2008/99/EC of the European Parliament and of the Council of 19 November 2008 on the protection of the environment through criminal law [2008] OJ L328/28.

[72] Directive 2009/123/EC of the European Parliament and of 21 October 2009 amending Directive 2005/35/EC on ship-source pollution and on the introduction of penalties for infringements [2009] OJ L 280/52. This Directive and the Directive on environmental crime (previous n) replicate the three-fold mantra on criminal sanctions for natural persons, but they do not specify the type and level of penalties, as the ECJ had made it clear that the Community was not competent to rule on that issue (Case C-440/05 *Commission v Council* EU:C:2007:625).

[73] Suominen (n 57) 408.

[74] T Elholm, 'Does EU Criminal Cooperation Necessarily Mean Increased Repression?' (2009) 17 *European Journal of Crime, Criminal Law and Criminal Justice* 191.

[75] See also E Herlin-Karnell, *The Constitutional Dimension of EU Criminal Law* (Hart Publishing, 2012), who discusses the 'over-reliance on the "magic" of the criminal law' (*ibid* 60) at the EU level.

[76] Recital No 16 of Directive 2011/92/EU of the European Parliament and of the Council of 13 December 2011 on combating the sexual abuse and sexual exploitation of children and child pornography, and replacing Council Framework Decision 2004/68/JHA [2011] L335/1.

Third, both in the framework decisions and in the post-Lisbon directives, the EU legislator only sets out a *minimum maximum penalty of imprisonment* for natural persons ('a maximum penalty of at least X years of imprisonment'). As far as they respect the minimum maximum laid down in the directives, Member States enjoy a wide margin of discretion in choosing the amount of penalties. The Commission's proposal for the Directive on the fight against fraud to the Union's financial interests by means of criminal law ('PIF Directive') had attempted to introduce, for the first time, a provision on the harmonisation of *minimum* penalties.[77] It required Member States to introduce a minimum penalty of at least six months imprisonment for some PIF offences. This rule was eventually removed from the final text of the Directive, confirming that the EU intervention in harmonising national criminal legislations is still confined to maximum penalties. It is thus not surprising that the most recent of the Commission's proposals for two further substantive criminal law directives did not even envisage such a rule on minimum penalties, since there is no political will to make this step forward in the path of harmonisation.[78] The issue is, in fact, extremely sensitive, given that some Member States do not provide for specific minimum thresholds of imprisonment penalties.[79]

Fourth, the framework decisions and directives have so far regulated mostly the so-called special part of criminal law, while they have barely touched upon issues of the general part of criminal law, such as the *mens rea*, the definition of what is meant by incitement, aiding and abetting, and attempt, and so on.[80] This is imposed by the current political and legal scenario, where the EU has limited competences in the field of criminal justice. Nonetheless, it is evident that the effective and dissuasive response to crime needs to be more comprehensive, and to take into account further aspects of criminal law.

In that regard, it is worth noting that, in the negotiations of the Commission's proposal for a Directive on countering money laundering by criminal law, some additional penalties for natural persons were added to the text, such as a temporary or permanent ban on entering into contracts with public authorities, a temporary disqualification from the practice of commercial activities, and a long-term ban on running for elections.[81] However, this provision would not envisage mandatory harmonisation, since Member States 'may also take'[82] such measures. On the

[77] Commission (n 38).

[78] See the proposals for the Directives on money laundering (Commission, 'Proposal for a Directive of the European Parliament and of the Council on countering money laundering by criminal law' COM(2016) 826 final) and on fraud and counterfeiting of non-cash means of payment (Commission, 'Proposal for a Directive of the European Parliament and of the Council on combating fraud and counterfeiting of non-cash means of payment and replacing Council Framework Decision 2001/413/JHA' COM(2017) 489 final).

[79] Melander (n 50) 297.

[80] *Ibid* 290ff, who argues that the general part of criminal law has already been affected by some judgments of the Court of Justice.

[81] See Art 5(3) of the proposal in the version of January 2018 (Council doc 5504/18).

[82] *Ibid.*

contrary, and as usual, they 'shall take the necessary measures'[83] to guarantee that criminal penalties are effective, dissuasive and proportionate, and that the most serious offences are punished with imprisonment penalties. In the text eventually approved, however, those additional penalties are mentioned in the Preamble,[84] whereas Article 5 of the Directive simply provides that 'Member States shall (…) take the necessary measures to ensure that natural persons (…) are, where necessary, subject to additional sanctions or measures'.[85] The Directive at issue could have been the first instrument of EU criminal law introducing the (optional) harmonisation of penalties for natural persons which are different from imprisonment,[86] yet the sensitivity of the matter led Member States to confine such a new kind of harmonisation in the (not binding) Preamble.

Even more importantly, the PIF Directive has laid down, for the first time in EU criminal law, some rules on the harmonisation of the *statute of limitation* (or 'prescription') of crimes.[87] The prescription of offences is a crucial issue to consider when effective and dissuasive protection of legal interests is to be afforded by means of criminal law. As for the PIF sector, this became obvious in the *Taricco* case, where the CJEU concluded that the Italian legislation on the statute of limitations of some VAT offences might lead to a *de facto* impunity of the offenders. The effective and dissuasive protection of the Union budget required by Article 325(1) TFEU would be endangered by the lax Italian rules on the prescription of crimes.

Therefore, there seems to be a growing awareness of the need to raise the bar of harmonisation to include other issues of the general part of criminal law.[88] This bodes well for the slow, but continuous, development of EU criminal law. Such an evolution should however not neglect the fundamental role that human rights play in any domestic criminal justice system, and in the EU legal order. In the context of the present analysis, this means that the third limb of the *Greek Maize* formula – the 'proportionality' of the penalty, which is now enshrined in

[83] *Ibid.*

[84] Recital No 14 of Directive (EU) 2018/1673 of the European Parliament and of the Council of 23 October 2018 on combating money laundering by criminal law [2018] OJ L284/22.

[85] Art 5(3) of Directive (EU) 2018/1673.

[86] Art 5(5) of Directive 2014/62/EU of the European Parliament and of the Council of 15 May 2014 on the protection of the euro and other currencies against counterfeiting by criminal law, and replacing Council Framework Decision 2000/383/JHA [2014] OJ L151/1 likewise states that Member States '*may* provide for effective, proportionate and dissuasive criminal sanctions *other than* [imprisonment] (…) if the counterfeit currency was received without knowledge but passed on with the knowledge that it is counterfeit' (emphasis added). Unlike the Directive on money laundering, however, the Directive on counterfeiting does not clarify what the other criminal sanctions could be, not even in its Preamble.

[87] Art 12 of Directive (EU) 2017/1371 of the European Parliament and of the Council of 5 July 2017 on the fight against fraud to the Union's financial interests by means of criminal law [2017] OJ L198/29. See more in F Giuffrida, 'The Protection of the Union's Financial Interests after Lisbon' in R Sicurella, V Mitsilegas, R Parizot and A Lucifora (eds), *General Principles for a Common Criminal Law Framework in the EU. A Guide for Legal Practitioners* (Giuffrè, 2017) 265–67.

[88] In some criminal justice systems, such as the French one, the statute of limitation falls within the remit of procedural criminal law.

Article 49(3) of the Charter of Fundamental Rights of the European Union – shall always be taken into account when the EU and Member States determine the amount of criminal sanctions.

IV. Conclusions

Building on the principle of sincere cooperation, the *Greek Maize* case introduced the assimilation principle and required that the penalties adopted by Member States to enforce EU law have to be effective, proportionate and dissuasive. Although it did not formally impose on the Member States any obligation to adopt criminal law measures, this judgment became a milestone in the history of EU criminal law.

The assimilation principle represented a relevant inroad into Member States' sovereignty, since the latter were obliged to extend the remit of their national (criminal) legislation so as to cover analogous infringements of EU law. From the Treaty of Maastricht onwards, the principle of assimilation has become a key component of the EU action against fraud to the detriment of the Union's financial interests, and it is currently enshrined in Article 325(2) TFEU. The application of this principle may, however, turn out to be rather complicated, for it may be difficult to assess the analogous nature of violations of national and EU law. Moreover, in addition to the risks of over-criminalisation it raises, the assimilation principle does not guarantee the effectiveness of Member States' responses to infringements of EU law, and it does not help to overcome the existing differences among their criminal justice systems. The post-Lisbon EU powers of harmonisation of criminal legislation seem to have further constrained the role of the assimilation principle in the development of EU criminal policy. Nevertheless, thanks to the *Taricco* saga, the principle at hand has become a key instrument in the hands of national courts, which may rely on it to disapply national legislation on PIF offences, if the latter affords less protection to the Union's financial interests than to the national budget.

While the assimilation principle soon migrated to EU primary law, the requirement for penalties to be effective, proportionate and dissuasive has instead become a mantra of secondary EU law. Former third pillar conventions and framework decisions, as well as pre- and post-Lisbon directives, lay down an obligation for Member States to adopt effective, proportionate and dissuasive sanctions, which shall be, for natural persons, of a criminal nature. The requirements singled out by the ECJ in the *Greek Maize* case have thus been interpreted as calling for penal measures. The presumption that, almost by definition, criminal sanctions are more effective and dissuasive than other punitive measures is however subject to fierce debate in the literature. Furthermore, this presumption risks jeopardising the likewise crucial principle of proportionality of penalties, which is now enshrined in the Charter of Fundamental Rights. In any case, the harmonising intervention of the European Union in the field of criminal law has been limited mostly to imprisonment penalties, and to the so-called special part of criminal law. Some recent pieces of EU legislation and the negotiations thereof have nonetheless acknowledged – implicitly or explicitly – that some issues of the general part of criminal law need to be addressed as well, if sanctions are to be truly effective and dissuasive.

The Greek Maize *Case. From Sincere Cooperation to Criminal Law Integration in the EU*

ROSARIA SICURELLA

I. Preliminary Remarks

The *Greek Maize* case[1] is undoubtedly the leading case on effective enforcement of EU law (EC law at the time when the decision was issued), and especially with respect to the constraints stemming from the EU legal order on the Member States when acting to guarantee effectiveness of European law.

Apart from the area of competition where a competence – including a significant sanctioning power of the Commission – has been conferred, since 1957, to the European Community (EC), the founding treaties lacked any specific provision dealing with the enforcement of rules established by the EC in those fields where the same had been conferred already at that time with the normative competence. This is what scholars refer to as the 'European enforcement deficit'.

Indeed, effective enforcement is vital for the success of any legal order. As the European Court of Justice (CJEU) soon cleared up, the enforcement of EC/EU rules is based on the principle of national procedural autonomy. The latter dictates that the enforcement of European law is largely up to the Member States and their authorities, which are entrusted with ensuring compliance with EC/EU law and sanctioning infringements. Then, European rules are created at a European level, but implemented and enforced at a national level.

However, this implies that Member States have extensive freedom to select and shape the enforcement instruments, which leads to different enforcement regimes throughout Europe and subsequently to regulatory competition. In order to prevent or reduce disparities between different enforcement regimes within the EU, the imposition of some limits on the national procedural autonomy of Member States soon appeared to be necessary. By building on the general principle of sincere cooperation, then, the CJEU has progressively laid down more and more

[1] Case 68/88 *Commission v Greece* ('*Greek Maize*') [1989] ECR 2979.

intrusive obligations on the Member States to comply with when implementing EU law. Indeed, sincere cooperation implies both a 'negative' integration mechanism, according to which national authorities must refrain from adopting measures that could represent an obstacle for the EC/EU in achieving its goals, and also a positive one establishing the adoption of adequate measures to prevent obstacles in the EU's path.[2]

Following an earlier jurisprudence established with respect to judicial protection of individuals in the twin rulings *Rewe*[3] and *Comet*,[4] in its decision in the *Greek Maize* case the Court further develops the basic framework that has been consistently served ever since when addressing issues relating to the decentralised enforcement of EC/EU law.

The present contribution will first give an overview of the main achievements of the *Greek Maize* case (section II), followed by a presentation of the major developments of domestic legislation (especially with respect to the Italian legal order) as the consequence of the impact of the principles established by the CJEU in its decision in this case (section III). Some concluding remarks will finally be formulated with the aim of focusing on the main challenges for the EU institutions and especially the CJEU in further developing the principle of effective protection of EU interests (section IV).

II. Main Achievements and Developments

The *Greek Maize* case marks (at least) three major achievements, two of a general character; the third one regarding the specific area concerned by the case, the protection of the financial interests of the Union – the PIF. First and foremost, in its decision in this case the Luxembourg Court established the guiding criteria for the enforcement of EU law by the national authorities, and consequently also the method through which it will assess the compliance by the Member States of the obligations stemming from the European legal order (subsection A). Furthermore, the practical implementation of these criteria triggered in fact a dynamic impact of European law on the sanctioning systems of the Member States, thus leading to the progressive approach of European law with Criminal law (subsection B). Finally, it brought the topic of the protection of the financial interests of the EU under the spotlight, as the crucial area entailing a quite intrusive control by European institutions on national legal orders (subsection C).

[2] Case C-265/95 *Commission v French Republic* [1997] ECR I-6990 (the so-called *Spanish Strawberries* case).

[3] Case 33/76 *Rewe-Zentralfinanz eG and Rewe-Zentral AG v Landwirtschaftskammer für das Saarland* [1976] ECR 1989.

[4] Case C-45/76 *Comet BV v Produktschap voor Siergewassen* [1976] ECR 2043.

A. The Constraints on the National Authorities

The Court made it clear that national procedural autonomy applies whenever harmonisation measures in a given field have yet to be taken, by establishing that

> whilst the choice of penalties remains within their discretion, they [the Member States] must ensure in particular that infringements of Community law are penalized under conditions, both procedural and substantive, which are analogous to those applicable to infringements in national law of a similar nature and importance and in which in any event, make the penalty effective, proportionate and dissuasive'.[5]

The CJEU points out that in the absence of EC/EU legislation, enforcement of rights and obligations stemming from EC/EU law will take place in accordance with national procedural rules. However, those rules are subject to two requirements: the principle of equivalence and the principle of effectiveness. More precisely, the equivalence of protection of European interests and the national interests of a similar nature and relevance is to be considered as the minimum threshold of protection, which means it could result in being insufficient and inadequate. Consequently, Member States will not be considered as fulfilling EU obligations just by extending existing national provisions. They are under an obligation to achieve the precise result of providing an adequate protection to the interests of the EU by adopting effective, proportionate and sufficiently deterrent measures.

Moreover, the Court of Justice also requires the national authorities to proceed by using 'the same diligence as that which they bring to bear in implementing corresponding national laws'.[6] This implies that, in addition to the need to adopt the necessary legal provisions, obligations on the Member States also cover the way Member States implement them.

B. The Progressive Approach of EC Law to Criminal Law

A literal construction of the EC and EU Treaties suggests that their draftsmen intended to exclude the positive competence of the Community, first, and the Union, after the Maastricht Treaty, in the field of criminal law. Indeed, criminal law was always regarded as the symbol and last rampart of national sovereignty, which the Member States were extremely reluctant to give up.

Therefore, the European Communities originally did not have the legal competence in criminal matters and the founding treaties did not contain any express provision in connection with criminal law. However, through its rigorous test of necessity and effectiveness of measures adopted by the Member States imposed since the *Greek Maize* case, the European Court of Justice has progressively developed a reasoning clearly aiming at limiting the discretion of the national authorities

[5] *Greek Maize* (n 1) § 24.
[6] *Greek Maize* (n 1) § 25.

with respect to the choice of which conducts deserve to be sanctioned through criminal measures; thus in fact imposing on the Member States its assessment on the necessity of criminal sanctions. Indeed, the decision in the *Greek Maize* case clearly shows the abandon by the Luxembourg Court of its position in the early ruling in the *Amsterdam Bulb* case leaving the Member States a very wide margin of discretion,[7] by establishing, on the contrary, the framework for a more intrusive scrutiny of domestic legislation.

While the decision in the *Greek Maize* case never refers to the criminal nature of the measures to be provided by the Member States, the obligation stemming from the principle of equivalent protection can indeed imply an indirect obligation to penalise, whenever criminal law measures are adopted in the domestic legal order to protect legal interests whose nature and relevance can be considered as equivalent to the EC interest at stake. Moreover, the obligation to guarantee an effective protection can also result, finally, in an indirect obligation to penalise whenever the adoption of measures of a criminal nature is the only one to be considered proportionate and effective. This was confirmed in an order issued by the CJEU in the *Zwartveld* case,[8] shortly after *Greek Maize*. Here, the European Court, when referring to the decision in *Greek Maize*, mentioned the obligation to provide all the measures necessary to guarantee the application and effectiveness of EU law 'if necessary by instituting criminal proceedings' which was not expressed in the first decision.

The general relevance of the criteria established in the *Greek Maize* case has been definitively confirmed by a Communication of the European Commission especially devoted to this judgment. Here, the Commission took care in stating that the principles established by the CJEU in the *Greek Maize* case were of a general nature and consequently they were supposed to apply in all sectors, and so regardless of the fact that EC measures were provided for to counter infringements of EC law.[9]

Further developments in the jurisprudence of the CJEU with respect to this topic are quite well-known. In particular, the decision issued by the European Court of Justice on the 13th September 2005 in *Commission v Council* (the so-called '*Environmental Crime case*') can be considered as the main achievement of the Court.[10] Here the Court switched from an obligation on the Member States to provide for effective measures (regardless of their formal nature) into the obligation to provide for criminal law sanctions. By stating so, the CJEU expressly acknowledges the existence of a competence of the European legislature in criminal matters, though limited to the adoption of directives implying that criminal provisions to be applied to individuals are ultimately established by domestic implementing legislation according to Constitutional rules for criminal

[7] Case 50/76 *Amsterdam Bulb Bv v Produktschap voor Siergewassen* [1977] ECR 138.

[8] Case C-2/88 *Zwartveld and Others* [1990] ECR I-04405.

[9] Commission notice concerning the judgment of the Court of Justice of 21 September 1989 in case 68/88 [1990] OJ C147/3.

[10] Case C-176/03 *Commission v Council* [2005] ECR I-7907.

law regulation in each Member State. This achievement was finally enshrined in the Lisbon Treaty by the provision in Article 83 TFEU empowering the EU legislature to adopt, by means of directives, 'minimum rules concerning the definition of criminal offences and sanctions [...]'. In particular Article 83.2 TFEU refers such competence of EU legislature to situations where 'approximation of laws and regulations of the Member States proves essential to ensure the effective implementation of a Union policy [...]'. It is worth stressing that the wording in Article 83 TFEU goes a step further on what had been established by the CJEU in the *Environmental Crime* case, and above all in the subsequent '*Ship-source Pollution* case' shortly after, where the Luxembourg Court had expressly denied that the competence of EU legislature to establish the obligation on the Member States to adopt provisions of a criminal nature also includes the competence to establish any obligation about the type and measure of the criminal sanctions to be adopted by the Member States.[11] According to Article 83 TFEU, minimum rules established by EU legislature may concern both the offence and the sanction to be provided by the Member States.

Moreover, by adopting Directive 2017/1371 on the fight against fraud to the Union's financial interests (the PIF Directive),[12] the EU legislature has taken a decisive path on the debated issue whether directives adopted under Article 83 TFEU can also provide for minimum rules concerning crucial topics of the general part of criminal law. Article 6 of the Directive establishes some general criteria dealing with liability of legal entities following the commission of an offence by natural persons in the company. But one must especially look at Article 12 of the Directive, which establishes some minimum common rules on limitation period. By doing so, the EU legislature has followed the most reasonable interpretation of the provision in Article 83 TFEU. Indeed, while a literal interpretation of the latter takes us inevitably to the conclusion that a directive adopted under this Article can never deal exclusively with issues of the general part, the principle of effective and equivalent protection of legal interests of the EU implies that a certain level of harmonisation also in issues of the general part of criminal law is pursued and achieved. Solutions adopted by the Member States to regulate, for example, participation and conspiracy, attempt, mistake, mens rea, circumstances, etc, all have an evident impact on the practical enforcement – and then the concrete scope – of offences established at the domestic level implementing obligations established by EU legislature in order to raise the goal of an effective and equivalent protection of EU legal interests. By adopting common provisions on issues of the general part of criminal law, EU legislature appears to have removed the critics generally opposed by the domestic legal doctrine concerning acceptability of the existence of different rules of the general part in the same legal order respectively applicable to offences implementing EU rules and other offences.

[11] Case C-440/05 *Commision v Council* [2007] ECR I-9128.

[12] Directive (EU) 2017/1371 of the European Parliament and of the Council of 5 July 2017 on the fight against fraud to the Union's financial interests by means of criminal law [2017] OJ L198/29 f.

C. The PIF as a Crucial Area of EU Law and Integration

The decision of the European Court of Justice in the *Greek Maize* case gave an essential impetus for the protection of the budget of the EC/EU to become a crucial topic in the European agenda. Indeed, a 'due diligence' had been launched by President Delors after the publication of the decision of the Court of Justice requiring all the Heads of State and Government to inform about the relevant domestic legislation employed to counter offences affecting EC financial interests, showing the great variety of solutions giving rise to a quite disparate and ineffective protection. A special meeting of the Ministries of Justice was held in Brussels on 13 November 1991 which ended up with the adoption of a resolution which showed that the PIF had finally become a crucial topic.[13] The European Parliament went much further by adopting a resolution requiring the Commission and the Council to take advantage of the (at that time) on-going negotiations in the Intergovernmental Conference to amend the treaty (that ended with the adoption of the Maastricht Treaty) to introduce the necessary provisions in order to empower the European legislature to adopt criminal law measures in the field of the protection of the EC financial interests, to be implemented through regulations and directives aiming at harmonising the legislation of the Member States in this area.[14]

However, the very significant achievements of the decision of the European Court of Justice in the *Greek Maize* case, and the consequent intrusive dynamics concerning the sanctioning powers of the Member States, have only very partially been enshrined in Article 209A ECT of the Treaty of Maastricht that indeed only establishes the principle of equivalence of protection of the EU budget. Notwithstanding, the obligation stemming from the principle of sincere cooperation, to provide for effective, proportionate and dissuasive measures, remained crucial in the future case law of the European Court of Justice. Moreover, one must also stress the special input of the *Greek Maize* case on the adoption of legal instruments in the field of PIF. Some crucial legal texts in the PIF sector were adopted in the 1990s through acts of the third pillar – the Convention on the protection of the financial interests of the European Union, and the two additional Protocols[15] – with the precise aim of harmonising the

[13] Resolution of the Council and of the representatives of the Governments of the Member States, meeting within the Council of 13 November 1991 concerning the protection of the financial interests of the Communities [1991] OJ C328/1.

[14] Resolution on the legal protection of the European Community's financial interests [1991] OJ C305/106.

[15] Convention drawn up on the basis of Article K. 3 of the Treaty on European Union, on the protection of the European Communities' financial interests [1995] OJ C316/48; Protocol drawn up on the basis of Article K. 3 of the Treaty on European Union to the Convention on the protection of the European Communities' financial interests [1996] OJ C313/2; Protocol drawn up on the basis of Article K. 3 of the Treaty on European Union to the Convention on the protection of the European Communities' financial interests (Second Protocol) [1997] OJ C221/12.

criminal law of the Member States in this area. This set of texts shortly became the acquis in the PIF sector with respect to criminal law sanctions, and were only replaced by Directive 2017/1371 (the PIF Directive) adopted on 5th July 2017.[16] In addition to that, the amendment introduced by the Treaty of Amsterdam replacing Article 209 A TEC with Article 280 TEC reflects the progressive 'communitarisation' of the matter of the protection of financial interests of the EU since it expressly establishes the competence of the EU legislature to adopt 'the necessary measures [...] with a view to affording effective and equivalent protection in the Member States'.

Despite the ambiguity of the last sentence in the provision – 'These measures shall not concern the application of national criminal law [...]' – which has given rise to divergent interpretations as to whether measures adopted by EU legislature can directly affect Member States' criminal law, the provision in Article 280 TEC has significantly re-directed the issue of the PIF by clearly establishing PIF as a sector falling within the competence – and responsibility – of both the legislature of the Member States (already under the intrusive obligations stemming from the *Greek Maize* case) and the EC/EU legislature.

The entry into force of the Treaty of Lisbon, and especially of the provision in Article 325 TFEU replacing Article 280 TEC has inaugurated a new phase in the history of PIF, and also in the history of the impact of EU law on the criminal law of the Member States. Article 325 TFEU essentially reproduces the wording of Article 280 TEC of the Amsterdam Treaty, though erasing the hotly debated last sentence of this provision of the Amsterdam Treaty (together with a few other amendments). Focusing on this new wording exclusively, one could easily come to the conclusion that by adopting Article 325 TFEU the drafters of the Treaty had agreed on the conferral to the EU legislature of a quite significant competence in the field of the prevention and fight against fraud to the EU budget, empowering it to adopt 'the necessary measures' in this field, including, presumably, also measures of a criminal law nature. However, such an innovative reading was drastically refused by the Council when adopting its General Approach on the proposal by the Commission for a directive introducing penal provisions in the PIF sector. Thus, the Council expected the legal basis of Article 325 TFEU proposed by the Commission to be replaced by Article 83 TFEU considered as the exclusive legal basis to adopt measures of a criminal law nature in a field whatsoever among the ones where the EU enjoys a normative competence. Indeed, the issue cannot be considered as definitively settled. The reasoning of the CJEU in its decision in the *Taricco* case,[17] establishing Article 325 TFEU as the key provision in the PIF sector, could reasonably imply that the same provision is the basis not only for obligations on the Member States, but also for EU institutions to act with the aim

[16] [2017] OJ L198/29.
[17] Case C-105/14 *Taricco and others* EU:C:2015:555.

to enhance the effectiveness of the fight against PIF offences. Since it establishes a shared competence in these matters, one could reach the conclusion that the same legal basis should apply with respect to any initiative in this field, regardless of whether it comes from the Member States or EU institutions. However, even after the CJEU decision in the *Taricco* case, the Commission has not questioned the legal basis of Article 83 TFEU before the Luxembourg Court.

III. The Impact of the Greek Maize Case on Domestic Legislation

A. The Impact of the Principle of 'Equivalent Protection' on the Italian Criminal Law

The Italian legislature has promptly engaged in the necessary amendments to comply with principles established by the Court of Justice in the *Greek Maize* case. In particular, it has sought to implement the principle of equivalence in the wording of the provision in Article 640 bis of the Penal Code introduced on 19 March 1990 by Law No 55 dealing with frauds against public grants. This provision, labelled as '*Truffa aggravata per il conseguimento di sovvenzioni pubbliche*' (Aggravated fraud for the obtainment of public grants), expressly covers frauds committed for the obtaining of subventions and aids granted by the State or other national public entities, as well as by the European Communities, through '*artifici e raggiri*' (artifice and deception). The offence requires the grant to be effectively obtained by the applicant and it is sanctioned with a penalty of one year (minimum) up to six years' imprisonment.

An earlier provision had been adopted by the Italian legislature on 23 December 1986 by Law No 898 (hereinafter 'Law 898/86') (the so-called '*legge comunitaria*' – the Community statute –, which, since 2012, has been replaced by the 'Legge di delegazione europea' and the '*Legge europea*' which are adopted every year with the specific aim of implementing EC/EU provisions adopted so far).

Article 2 of Law 898/86 already established penal sanctions against frauds affecting the European Agriculture Guarantee Fund (EAGGF). However, the level of sanction was much more lenient than the one provided for by Article 640 bis of the Penal Code with respect to EC subventions and aids. In order to guarantee the most effective protection and the best implementation of Article 640 bis of the Penal Code, the Italian legislature subsequently amended Article 2 of Law 898/86 by adding a subsidiarity clause aiming at excluding the application of the more lenient provision of Article 2 whenever the requirements of Article 640 bis of the Penal Code are met. By doing so, the Italian legislature avoided the risk of providing a lower degree of protection to frauds affecting the EAGGF because of the 'ordinary' prevalence of Law 898/86 being *lex specialis* with respect to the provision in Article 640 bis of the Penal Code.

With the adoption of Law No 86 on 26 April 1990, another important provision was introduced in the Penal Code, Article 316 bis, dealing with the misappropriation of funds. It is aimed at completing the protection of the public grants since it covers behaviours subsequent to the granting of the subventions which in principle could have been legally obtained.[18] However, Article 316 bis originally referred only to subventions and other public contributions granted by the State and any other national public entity. It was most probably an inadvertent oversight which the Italian legislature promptly corrected with the adoption of Law No 181 of 7 February 1992 adding the express reference to the subventions and aids granted by the European Communities. This provision is of particular relevance especially for the protection of the structural funds since aids granted on that basis fall into the scope of the notion of subventions and aids especially 'destined to activities of a public interest' employed in Article 316 bis of the Penal Code.

It is worth mentioning that on 29 September 2000 a new provision was introduced through Law No 300 ratifying the Convention on the protection of the financial interests of the EU (together with some other EU legal texts and the Organisation for Economic Cooperation and Development (OECD) Convention on Combating Bribery of Foreign Public Officials in International Business Transactions). Article 316 ter of the Penal Code establishes the '*Indebita percezione di erogazioni a danno dello Stato*' (Undue receipt of public funds) as an offence, legislating against anyone obtaining public (including EU) funds by using or exhibiting false documents or omitting to inform about facts that the individual was under an obligation to provide.

Through this provision, which reproduces the list of behaviours in Article 1 of the PIF Convention (except for the undue retention), the Italian legislature aimed to provide a complete implementation of this provision of the PIF Convention, including the reference to the €4000 threshold as the divide between the criminal and the administrative offence (which is quite peculiar for a provision in the Penal Code). Indeed, the different structure seen in the offence of aggravated fraud in Article 640 bis of the Penal Code focusing on the description of a fraudulent modus operandi (through '*artifici o raggiri*') instead of listing specific conducts (as in Article 1 of the PIF Convention) could create the risk that some of the behaviours covered by the PIF Convention were not covered by Article 640 bis. In particular the issue arose with respect to the conduct of omission that could hardly fall within the notion of '*artifici o raggiri*' which generally refers to 'positive' behaviours.

However, the result somehow betrayed the original intent, since according to well-established jurisprudence about Article 640 bis of the Penal Code some of the conducts listed in Article 316 ter were already covered by the first provision

[18] In a recent decision, the Supreme Court confirmed the concurrent nature of offences established in Articles 640 bis and 316 bis of the Penal Code respectively. This implies that, whenever they are both established in the concrete case, the author will be sentenced with the addition of punishment corresponding to each offence. Corte di Cassazione – Sezioni Unite 23 February 2017, n. 20664.

which provides for a harsher penalty. In its decision in the *Carchivi* case issued in 2007, the Grand Chamber of the Supreme Court (Corte di Cassazione – Sezioni Unite) provided a criterion to help the judge when qualifying the concrete facts as an aggravated fraud according to Article 640 bis or an undue receipt of public funds according to Article 316 ter depending on whether the behaviour had led to a 'mistake' or not.[19] However, the practical implementation of such a criterion appears quite uncertain, since it depends on the fact of whether the granting procedure provides for a previous control of statements by the applicant or not. Only in the first case can the public agent deciding the granting of the subvention be considered as having incurred a 'mistake', provoked by the fraudulent conduct (*artifici o raggiri*) of the applicant. Notwithstanding, the same criterion has been confirmed by the Supreme Court in later decisions, while trying to make its assessment in the concrete case more precise.[20]

B. The Impact of the Principle of 'Effective Protection' of EU Interests in the Domestic Legal Orders

The reasoning above shows the limits of the principle of equivalence and the need for a constant assessment of the concrete 'effectiveness' of the protection provided at the domestic level by national authorities. Generally speaking, one might say that the most relevant achievement of the *Greek Maize* case consists indeed in having established the principle of the 'effective protection' of the interests of the EU. While the latter has been formally enshrined in the Treaty of Amsterdam with respect to the protection of the financial interests of the Union – since Article 280 TEC (replacing Article 209A TEC) expressly states that 'The Community and the Member States shall counter fraud and any other illegal activities affecting the financial interests of the Community through measures […] which shall act as a deterrent and be such as to afford effective protection in the Member States' – for EU interests other than the financial ones the decision in the *Greek Maize* case still remains the main reference.

More precisely, the latter triggered a special impetus to the protection of EU interests. This can be seen just by looking at the many references for preliminary ruling put forward by national judges to the European Court of Justice where the request for the interpretation of EU law is often a way of obtaining the opinion of the European Court with respect to the compliance of EU obligations by domestic legislation. This was the case, for example, in the *Berlusconi* case, where the national courts took the view that the proceedings at stake raised questions as to whether the penalties provided for under Articles 2621 and 2622 of the Italian Civil Code (as amended by d.lgs (Legislative decree) No 61/2002 after the

[19] Corte di Cassazione, Sezioni Unite 19 April 2007, *Carchivi* n. 16568.

[20] Corte di Cassazione, Sezioni Unite 16 December 2010, *Pizzuto*, n. 7537.

facts were committed) were 'appropriate' when considered in light of, either, Article 6 of the First Companies Directive[21] [....], or Article 5 of the Treaty,

> from which, according to case law which has been well established since Case 68/88 Commission v Greece [1989] ECR 2965, paragraphs 23 and 24, it follows that penalties for infringements of provisions of Community law must be effective, proportionate and dissuasive.[22]

The conclusion raised by the Court was that indeed Italian legislation as amended by d.lgs No 61/2002 (significantly reshaping the legal regime in the field, with the view of reducing the scope of criminal liability) had failed to properly implement EU legislation in the field concerned. However, this did not provoke, in fact, the consequence for the domestic judge to disapply the national low infringing EU law since the same decision the CJEU also established the principle of retroactive application of the more lenient regime (the principle of *favor rei*) as a fundamental right in the EU legal order.

More generally, the relevance of the *Greek Maize* case can be seen particularly with respect to those legal systems where no specific amendments were made after this ruling, but a special dynamism can be detected specifically in the PIF area. This is the case for the Spanish legal system. In 1985, fraud offences had been amended. In fact, the preparation for the entry of the Spanish Kingdom into the European Community (which occurred in 1986) was one of the reasons for this amendment to the Spanish legislation, since Spain was going to become an important recipient of the European budget. However, no express reference could be found in terms of grants or other aid from the European funds. Notwithstanding any precise reference to national Public Administration could be found neither. Consequently, a strictly literal interpretation of these provisions could not prevent the application of the same to frauds affecting the EU budget. Indeed, following the publication of the decision in the *Greek Maize* case, most scholars, as well as the Spanish courts, considered those provisions as applicable to European subventions. The express reference to some of the PIF offences can only be found in the Criminal Code, adopted in 1995. This was more a consequence of the impact of provisions in the PIF Convention that was negotiated at the same time as the Criminal Code. However, the decision in the *Greek Maize* case was very present during all the discussions in Parliament. But above all, it was decisive in boosting the effective investigation and prosecution of frauds affecting the EU budget. Proceedings concerning frauds affecting EU funds were brought, essentially starting from the 1990s. Before that time, the Spanish Administration limited its action essentially to the recovery of funds illegally obtained.[23]

[21] First Council Directive 68/151/EEC of 9 March 1968 on coordination of safeguards which, for the protection of the interests of members and others, are required by Member States of companies within the meaning of the second paragraph of Article 58 of the Treaty, with a view to making such safeguards equivalent throughout the Community [1968] OJ L65/8.

[22] Joined cases C-387/02, C-391/02 and C-403/02 *Criminal Proceedings against Silvio Berlusconi, Sergio Adelchi and Marcello Dell'Utri and Others* [2005] ECR I-03565, §36.

[23] A Nieto Martín, *Fraudes comunitarios. Derecho penal económico europeo* (Praxis, 1995); A Nieto Martin/Arroyo Zapatero, *El fraude de subvenciones en la UE y en el CP, en Derecho penal económico* (Manuales de Formación Continuada, Consejo General del Poder Judicial, 2001).

IV. Concluding Remarks

What has been said in the paragraphs above makes clear the crucial relevance of the decision of the CJEU in the *Greek Maize* case, in particular because of the consequences of a general character flowing from the principles established, that have not been fully rooted [thrashed] out yet, and which are able to very significantly affect the discretion of the domestic authorities and some consolidated assets in the domestic legal order of the Member States, especially where criminal law is concerned.

In particular, the so-called 'negative' side of the obligation to provide effective protection, engaging the obligation to refrain from adopting measures that could represent an obstacle to guaranteeing such protection, can result in being extremely intrusive and disruptive. This is especially true whenever the obligation to provide for effective protection is enshrined in a EU law provision having direct effect; as is the case for the provision in Article 325 TFEU as it was interpreted by the CJEU in its decision in the *Taricco* case, and then confirmed in the following decision of the same in *M.A.S & M.B.*[24] When confronted with an EU provision of such nature, the domestic judge is under the obligation to disapply the relevant national law whenever its effect would be to prevent the Member State concerned from fulfilling its obligation to provide for an effective protection of the EU interest at stake. When no provision having direct effect can be singled out in a given situation, only the ordinary procedure of a deferral by the European Commission to the CJEU of the concerned Member State can be activated, which can lead to a judicial obligation on the domestic legislature to amend existent legislation in order to fulfil EU obligations.

With respect to the Italian system, generally speaking, the *Taricco* saga has shown how far reaching the principle of effective protection of EU legal interests can be. Indeed, because of the obligation on the domestic judge to disapply national provisions incompatible with EU law – and precisely in the *Taricco* case the obligation to disapply national rules on time limitation whenever they become an obstacle to the effective protection of EU financial interests because of the insufficient limitation period for complex cases,[25] – the principle of effective protection ended up clashing with the well-established position of the Italian Constitutional Court holding that provisions on time limitation are of a substantive nature, and are then subject to the legality principle. Consequently, they would be subject to the prohibition of retrospective application of any solution that would entail a detrimental effect for the accused (as it would be the case whenever a provision establishing a shorter limitation period is disapplied in favour of another one establishing a longer period), and also the principle of foreseeability of punishment. The fierce reaction by the Italian Constitutional Court,[26] followed by the ambiguous

[24] Case C-42/17 *M.A.S, M.B* [2017] ECR 936.

[25] Cases such as those concerning VAT fraud realised by a criminal association acting on the territory of more than one Member State.

[26] Corte cost., order n 24/2017,

decision of the CJEU in *M.A.S & M.B*, resulted in a sort of 'flexibilisation' of the principle of legality at EU level in order to meet some of the claims of the first. This, together with a tortuous and quite unclear solution with respect to the principle of effective protection, clearly demonstrates how highly sensitive the practical implementation of the principle of effective protection can be.[27]

However, the practical implementation of the principle of effective protection and the principle of assimilation is far from straightforward. The latter relies on a sensitive assessment by the domestic authorities – that can fall then under the scrutiny of the Court of Justice – with respect to the comparable nature and importance of a given national interest and a European interest that could be assimilated to the first and then protected by extending the same measures and conditions. Although this issue was not particularly debated by scholars commenting on the decision of the CJEU in the *Taricco* case, the fact to consider VAT-related fraud and smuggling of tobacco products as offences affecting comparable interests – that implies the obligation on the Italian authorities to extend to the first the much longer limitation period provided for by the Italian legislation with respect to the latter, according to the assimilation principle enshrined in Article 325.2 TFEU, is far from being unquestionable.[28] The sensitivity of the issue was finally brought under the spotlight in the *Scialdone* case,[29] where Article 325 TFEU was again the object of a request for a preliminary ruling by an Italian judge who had to decide whether the VAT system could be assimilated to direct taxation for the purpose of assessing analogous sanctioning regimes. However, the decision of the Court does not seem to have definitively settled the question. Indeed, the latter appears not to follow the reasoning of Advocate General (AG) Bobek, who in his Opinion reached the conclusion that offences relating to the failure to pay VAT can be considered as 'analogous' to offences to pay income tax,[30] relying on a broad approach to the comparability assessment as a logical development of the general obligation of sincere cooperation.[31] The Court appears to follow a wide approach itself to the comparability assessment, including in the assessment of the 'similar nature and relevance' of the offences concerned 'the difficulty involved in their detection', which the Court denied in the specific case.[32] Evidently, this last criterion can give rise to divergent solutions, and above all it may seriously affect the foreseeability of punishment and also the principle of the reserve of law.

The effects of disruptive dynamism triggered by the principles first established in the *Greek Maize* case on the ever growing integration between the EU and the Member States' legal orders is far from being exhausted. In particular,

[27] *M.A.S, M.B* (n 24).
[28] Among the few authors raising this point, see M Donini, *Le sentenze Taricco come giurisdizione di lotta*, in www.penalecontemporaneo.it (3 April 2018).
[29] Case C-574/15 *Scialdone* [2018] ECR 295.
[30] Case C-574/15 *Scialdone*, Opinion of AG Bobek, [2017] ECR:553, § 104.
[31] *Ibid*, §93 *ff*, especially §101 *ff*.
[32] *Scialdone* (n 29) § 59.

the CJEU needs to handle the practical implementation of these principles in criminal matters carefully because of the concrete and constant risk of a clash between principles and solutions that are considered to reflect the constitutional identity of a given legal order, or a fundamental aspect of the criminal justice system of the same. While keeping its consolidated and quite demanding approach with respect to the implementation of these principles by the Member States, the CJEU should also engage in the development of a well-founded reasoning which is able to guarantee coherence to its decisions and also show the utmost consideration of the sensitivity of issues involved in the process of integration of criminal law systems of the Member States. The best implementation of these principles needs to rely on a general acceptance by the domestic authorities, although such an achievement could be hard to acquire.

5

C-176/03 – *Commission of the European Communities v Council of the European Union*

The 'Constitutional' ECJ Ruling on the Enforcement of Community Law (Case C-176/03) and its Impact on EU Law

M KAIAFA-GBANDI

I. The Essentials of the Decision and its Broader Historical Context

The European Court of Justice (ECJ) ruling in *Commission v Council* (the *Environmental Crime* case),[1] on the Commission's request for annulment of the Framework Decision on the protection of the environment through criminal law (2003/80/JHA)[2] is one of the most consequential in the historical development of both the European Union's (EU) institutional framework and its criminal legislation.[3]

In particular, the ruling of 13 September 2005 together with the antecedent *Pupino*[4] decision, essentially redefined the nature, and thus the dynamics of EU interventions in the field of criminal law in general. To the extent that the ECJ's relevant construal of the EU's founding Treaties once more interpreted the current institutional framework outside its mere wording and spurred decisive practical consequences on the issue of EU competence as regulated in its Treaties, it

[1] Case C-176/03 *Commission v Council* (the *Environmental Crime* case) [2005] ECR I-07879.

[2] Council Framework Decision 2003/80/JHA on the protection of the environment through criminal law [2003] OJ L29/55.

[3] See, eg, V Mitsilegas, 'Constitutional Principles of the European Community and European Criminal Law' (2006) 8 *European Journal of Law Reform* 301, 306.

[4] Case C-105/03 *Criminal proceedings against Maria Pupino* [2005] ECR I-05285.

yet again corroborated that the Court reserves for itself a role of 'the integration process locomotive',[5] whenever it considers necessitous.

Hitherto, EU interventions in national substantive and procedural criminal laws bore two distinguishing key elements. First, the third pillar was their sole legal foundation, ie they were subject to intergovernmental cooperation, since – at least according to the predominant outlook[6] – European Communities were not awarded any competence in criminal matters, not even under the notion of criminal law harmonisation amongst Member States. Second, as a result of the post-Amsterdam Treaty ascendancy of unanimity-bound framework decisions with respect to the third pillar, such EU statutes could not have a direct impact in Member States, as then explicitly excluded by the Treaty on European Union (TEU) (Article 34, paragraph 2b final clause). In fact, this exclusion had been envisaged precisely to prevent the recognition of such an (direct) effect of framework decisions via ECJ case law,[7] as occurred with the first pillar directives to which framework decisions were similar.

With the two abovementioned judgments (*Environmental Crime* and *Pupino*), the ECJ downright overturned this state of affairs. It acknowledged the Community's competency to impose upon its Member States the obligation to criminalise certain behaviour and outline the limits of punishability through EU provisions (ie via directives), at least in some key areas of its policy-making. With its ruling in the *Environmental Crime* case, the Court has broken the political stalemate which has been in evidence since 1993,[8] when the Commission came to diametrically oppose the Council and defended its position on the existence of criminal law competence for the effective implementation of EC (European

[5] See, eg, T Horsley, 'Reflections on the role of the Court of Justice as the "Motor" of European Integration: Legal Limits to Judicial Lawmaking' (2013) 50 *Common Market Law Review* 931 ff; RD Kelemen and SK Schmidt, 'Introduction – the European Court of Justice and Legal Integration: Perpetual Momentum?' (2012) 19 *Journal of European Public Policy* 1 ff; M Cappelletti, 'Is the European Court of Justice "Running Wild"?' (1987) 12 *European Law Review* 3, 8; see also V Murschetz, 'The Future of Criminal Law within the European Union – Union Law or Community Law Competence?' (2007) 38 *Victoria University of Wellington Law Review* 145, 153.

[6] See, eg, inter alia PA Albrecht, *Die vergessene Freiheit: Strafrechtsprinzipien in der europäischen Sicherheitsdebatte* (Berlin, Berliner Wiss.-Verlag, 2003) 166; G Corstens and J Pradel, *European Criminal Law* (The Hague; New York, Kluwer Law International, 2002) 530–33; H Satzger, *Internationales und Europäisches Strafrecht* (Baden-Baden, Nomos, 2006) §7, Rn 25 ff; J Pradel, 'Avis sur la sanction des violations du droit communautaire par le droit penal' in M Kaiafa-Gbandi (ed), *Compénce et imposition des sanctions pénales pour violation du droit communautaire* (Athens-Komotini, Ant. N. Sakkoulas Publishers, 2004) 35 ff; M Kaiafa-Gbandi, 'À la recherché d' une compétence commuautaire en matière de répression pénale – Un tournant essentiel des développments du droit pénal dans le cadre de l' Union européenne' in Kaiafa-Gbandi (ed), *ibid*, 11 ff.

[7] *cf* Mitsilegas (n 3) 309, who notes: 'It is interesting that, while the judge-made principle of direct effect makes its appearance in the EU Treaty in this "negative" manner'.

[8] See R Hefendehl, 'Der EuGH stellt die strafrechtliche Kompetenz auf den Kopf- und wundert sich über Kritik' in J Joerden and A Szwarc (ed), *Europäisierung des Strafrechts in Polen und Deutschland – rechtsstaatliche Grundlagen* (Berlin, Duncker & Humblot, 2007) 44 ff; JAE Vervaele, 'The European Community and Harmonization of the Criminal Law Enforcement of Community Policy. A Cessio Bonorum from the Third to the First Pillar?' in K Nuotio (ed), *Festschrift in Honour of Raimo Lahti* (Helsinki, Faculty of Law, University of Helsinki, 2007) 130.

Community) law. Since that period and up to 2005 the legislative conflicts between the EC and the EU concerning criminal law harmonisation, which came to the fore under different forms,[9] were not apparently solved in a way that enhances EC law. Thus, the Court's judgment has been a landmark ruling concerning the enforcement of Community law.[10] Furthermore, with its earlier judgment in *Pupino*, the Court granted framework decisions a guiding role for the interpretation of national criminal laws, thus implicitly acknowledging their 'direct' effect, at odds with the relevant unambiguous prohibition foreseen in the Treaty.[11] Through these two judgments, the EU assumed a substantially more dynamic role in the relevant field. It made criminal law subject to Community competence, at least in some areas and to some extent, with whatever (decisive) consequences implied, and – despite leaving criminal law to whatever extent to intergovernmental cooperation between Member States (third pillar) – it also acknowledged the Union's decisive prowess through the guiding role attached to framework decisions with respect to the interpretation of national criminal laws.

In other words, the two judgments carry a 'constitutional' importance.[12] One of them operated towards a partial convergence between the third and the first pillar on criminal law issues (substantive and procedural), even bestowing upon framework decisions some limited effects pertinent to directives, therefore affecting national laws to some extent without transposing them to Member States (via interpretation of national law, and therefore without the intervention of national parliaments). Along these lines, transnational cooperation under the third pillar approximates the characteristics of supranational interventions under the first pillar. The subsequent judgment, which is the focal topic of this chapter, took a more radical step. It established Community competence in the field of substantive criminal law with the aim of imposing an obligation on Member States to criminalise, and confirmed the EU's aptitude to delineate elements of punishability for behaviour violating essential EC policy activities. Thus, the Community was granted distinct capacity to impose its outlook upon Member States with respect to key elements of punishability in policy areas it handled.

Two years later, in 2007, the ECJ used the same token (breach of Community competence), annulled Council Framework Decision 2005/667/JHA of 12 July 2005 to strengthen the criminal-law framework for the enforcement of the law

[9] See Vervaele, *ibid*, 126–30, who highlights three types of such conflict: a) warding off, ie the Commission submits proposals for criminal law harmonisation of Community law, which the Council rejects or at best neutralises, stripping off its criminal law packaging; b) 'hijacking', ie the Commission and the Member States take turns to hijack the content of each other' s proposals by packaging it in a different legal instrument; and c) cohabitation forcée, ie two proposals are elaborated alongside each other and in harmony with each other, the substantive provisions are included in a proposal for a directive or a regulation, while the criminal law harmonisation aspects are incorporated in a framework decision.

[10] See *ibid*, 130.

[11] See M Kaiafa-Gbandi, 'Modern Criminal Law Developments in the EU and the Rule of Law Challenges (in Greek)' (2006) *Poinika Chronika* 577, 579 ff and the citations therein.

[12] See M Kaiafa-Gbandi, 'The ECJ Jurisprudence and New Possibilities for EU Interventions in the Field of Member States Criminal Law (in Greek)' (2006) *Poiniki Dikaiosyni* 476, 482.

against ship-source pollution,[13] and further clarified the boundaries between Union and Community competence, stressing in any case that the Community had no competence in determining the type and intensity of imposable criminal sanctions, contrary to the Commission's arguments.[14]

Whether this stance adhered to the rule of law will be examined in detail below, especially with regard to the – more radical – ECJ judgment acknowledging Community competence to intervene in the field of criminal law for certain key EU policy areas. At this point the following observation is significant: the two above-mentioned ECJ judgments were issued after the negative outcome of the French referendum on the European Constitution, and in view of the tension created by Member States either not transposing framework decisions or transposing them in a substandard manner compared to Union standards, as framework decisions could not have direct effect according to the letter of the then valid Treaty. The interpretation adopted by the ECJ on the framework decisions it assessed obviously contemplated upon the adversities faced by the Union for its interventions on Member States' criminal laws, to which a constantly growing role was attributed to support the effectiveness of EU actions. This hardship would not be resolved in the near future through the institutional capacities envisaged within the proposed Constitutional Treaty, as this project seemed to fail.[15] Therefore, the only reasonable solution to the Union law efficiency problem seemed to lie within the then effective institutional framework of the Treaties and its interpretation thereof.

Following the presentation of the ECJ judgment's arguments and critical assessment thereof, this commentary will attempt to outline the impact of the particular judgment at the EU-law level.

II. The ECJ Judgment and its Supporting Argumentation

The Court was called to determine whether the framework decision on the protection of the environment through criminal law was founded – as the Commission claimed – on an erroneous legal basis (Articles 34 in conjunction with 29 and 31 subparagraph e TEU), and therefore arrogated Community competence with respect to the EU policy on environmental protection (Articles 3 paragraph 1 and 174–176 TEC), which – in the form of the then applicable founding Treaties – preceded its acknowledged competences under the third (intergovernmental) pillar, concerning interventions in the field of criminal law. The priority of Community competence was expressly envisaged in Articles 47 and 29 TEU. After contemplating on the particular content of the Framework Decision and the relevant views

[13] Council Framework Decision 2005/667/JHA of 12 July 2005 to strengthen the criminal-law framework for the enforcement of the law against ship-source pollution [2005] OJ L255/164.

[14] Case C-440/05 *Commission of the European Communities v Council of the European Union* [2007] ECR I-09097, para 80.

[15] See also Mitsilegas (n 3) 306.

expressed by the European Parliament (in support of the Commission) and the Council (disputing the Commission's view), the ECJ decided to entirely annul the Framework Decision, thus vindicating the Commission, which had already submitted a similar proposal in September 2001.

The legal issue that pertained to the Commission's claim to annul the Framework Decision had never been brought up before the Court. According to the ECJ's wording,[16] it specifically questioned whether Articles 1–7 of the Framework Decision (which bade Member States to adopt a minimum level of criminalisation of certain environmentally abusive behaviours and link them to corresponding penalties) affect the powers of the Community under Article 175 EC, inasmuch as those articles could have been adopted on the basis of the last-mentioned provision. After emphasising that environmental protection is one of the essential Community objectives (Article 2 and 6 EC) and that the EC Treaty provides for the establishment of 'a policy in the sphere of the environment' (Article 3, paragraph 1 EC), setting at the same time the framework within which Community environmental policy must be carried out (Articles 174–176 EC),[17] highlighted first of all the Court's settled caselaw, according to which the choice of the legal basis for a Community measure must rest on *objective* factors, including in particular the *aim* and the *content* of the measure,[18] on which the Commission based its decision. With respect to the *content* of the Framework Decision, the ECJ found that Articles 2–7 do indeed entail partial harmonisation of the criminal laws of the Member States (constituent elements of various criminal offences committed to the detriment of the environment), and highlighted that as a general rule neither criminal law nor the rules of criminal procedure fall within the Community's competence.[19] However, the ECJ also underlined that the last-mentioned finding does not prevent the Community legislature, when the application of effective, proportionate and dissuasive criminal penalties by the competent national authorities is an *essential* measure for combating serious environmental offences, from taking measures which relate to criminal law of the Member States which it considers *necessary in order to ensure that the rules which it lays down on environmental protection are fully effective*.[20] Thus, given that the protection of the environment has been the aim of the Framework Decision and Article 2 thereof contained violations of its protective measures,[21] the ECJ concluded that on account of both their aim and their content, Articles 1–7 of the Framework Decision have as their main purpose the protection of the environment and they could have been properly adopted on the basis of Article 175 EC. It even felt the need to highlight that this finding is not called into question by the fact that Articles 135 EC and 280, paragraph 4 EC reserve to the Member States, in the areas of customs cooperation and the protection of the Community's financial interests

16 *Environmental Crime* case (n 1) para 40.
17 *Environmental Crime* case (n 1) paras 41–44.
18 *Environmental Crime* case (n 1) para 46.
19 *Environmental Crime* case (n 1) para 47.
20 *Environmental Crime* case (n 1) para 48.
21 *Environmental Crime* case (n 1) paras 46, 50.

respectively, the application of national criminal law and the administration of justice. According to the Court it is not possible to infer from those provisions that, for the purpose of the implementation of environmental policy, any harmonisation of criminal law, even as limited as that resulting from the Framework Decision, must be ruled out even where it is necessary to ensure the effectiveness of Community law.[22] Thus, the Court held that the entire Framework Decision, being indivisible, infringes Article 47 EU as it encroaches on the powers which Article 175 EC confers on the Community, and must be annulled.[23]

From the abovementioned ECJ deliberations, one observes that it essentially based its decision on three arguments: (i) *the elements by which the selection of legal basis is assessed* for a measure taken by the Community (objective elements: aim and content of the measure); (ii) the escalation of the *necessity to adopt punitive measures for the effectiveness of a Community policy* to an *independent* vehicle that can (exceptionally) support the Community's (criminal) competence even where it is generally not foreseen; and (iii) the *reading of Articles 135 and 280, paragraph 4 TEC* – as then in force – in a way that did not prohibit the expansion of Community competence to harmonise *criminal* provisions of the Member States in any of its key policy fields (eg environmental protection), whenever required for the effectiveness of Community law.

III. Critical Evaluation of the Judgment

The above ECJ ruling excusably became subject to jurists' criticism.[24] Its essential points, upon which one's attention should briefly be focused, are:

- Invoking the primacy of Community over Union competence under the then Articles 29 and 47 TEU requires a prior substantiation that the Community

[22] *Environmental Crime* case (n 1) para 52.

[23] *Environmental Crime* case (n 1) paras 53, 55.

[24] See inter alia contra: K Ambos, *Internationales Strafrecht: Strafanwendungsrecht – Volkerstrafrecht – Europaisches Strafrecht* (München, Beck, 2006) §11 para 33; St Braum, 'Europäische Strafgesetzgebung: Demokratische Strafgesetzlichkeit oder administrative Opportunität – Besprechung des Urteils des EuGH vom 13. September 2005' (2006) *Wistra* 121, 121 ff; Hefendehl (n 8) 56 ff; M Heger, 'Anmerkung' (2006) *Juristenzeitung* 311–13; M Kaiafa-Gbandi, 'Aktuelle Strafrechtsentwicklung in der EU und rechtsstaatliche Defizite' (2006) *Zeitschrift für Internationale Strafrechtsdogmatik* 521, 523 ff; Murschetz (n 5) 153, N Neagu, 'Entrapment between Two Pillars: The European Court of Justice Rulings in Criminal Law' (2009) 15 *European Law Journal* 536, 536 ff; H Nilson, '25 Years of Criminal Justice in Europe' (2012) 2 *European Criminal Law Review* 106, 114; T Pohl, 'Verfassungsvertrag durch Richterspruch. Die Entscheidung des EuGH zu Kompetenzen der Gemeinschaft im Umweltstrafrecht' (2006) *Zeitschrift für Internationale Strafrechtsdogmatik* 213 ff; H Satzger, 'The Future of European Criminal Law between Harmonization, Mutual Recognition and Alternative Solutions' (2006) *Journal for European Criminal Law* 27, 27 ff; M Böse, 'Die Zuständigkeit der Europäischen Gemeinschaft für das Strafrecht. Zugleich Besprechung von EuGHUrteil vom 13.9.2005' (2006) *Goldtammer's Archiv* 211, 211 ff; W Frenz and H Wübbenhorst, 'Die Europäisierung des Strafrechts nach der Lissabon-Entscheidung des BVerfG' (2009) *Wistra* 449, 450; O Suhr, 'Strafrechtsharmonisierung in der Europäischen Union: Neue Grenzziehungen und zusätzliche Kontrollaufträge' (2008) *Zeitschrift für Europarechtliche Studien* 45, 57 ff.

was indeed competent to oblige Member States to criminalise various behaviours under the first pillar.

- Similar Community competence never derives from TEC provisions,[25] nor in particular from Articles 135 and 280, paragraph 4 which referred to two of the most fundamental areas of its competence (customs cooperation and protection of the Community's financial interests). Lack of criminal competence in these areas – even for the stipulation of basic behavioural elements that could constitute offences and be punishable – was not immaterial, as the ECJ claimed,[26] as it precisely indicates that in so far as the Community was not granted any competence for criminal protection of its financial interests, it was much more irrational for the opposite to ensue in other areas of its actions, such as the environment.[27]
- On the other hand, the general TEC clauses on 'taking necessary measures' or 'deciding actions' to be assumed by the Community to implement *special* material competences conferred (eg Article 175 TEC), may under no circumstances denote that the Community was granted criminal competence, even to delineate basic behavioural elements that require criminalisation. Refraining from such an assignment was unambiguous according to the parties' intentions, the systematic interpretation of the Treaty of Rome and – much more – of the Amsterdam Treaty, which explicitly classified criminal repression under a separate (third) pillar.
- Moreover, Community competence for criminal matters could not stem from Article 10 TEC referring to Member States' duty of loyalty, as this provision could only operate *within the scope of competence already granted to the Community*. Otherwise, it would establish Community competence for its competence, which – of course – would be impossible to maintain.
- The ECJ's principal argument that the Community legislature may take measures with respect to the criminal laws of its Member State when it considers it crucial to ensure full effectiveness of the rules it establishes in policy areas it handles and despite this being essentially outside its competence, is utterly incompatible with the characteristics of the bestowed, specific and limited nature of Community capacities. This is so because 'the need for efficiency' turns out to be the driving force that establishes such competence

[25] This was apprehensibly the opinion expressed by the majority of jurists. See, eg, Albrecht (n 6) 166; Ambos, *ibid* §11, Rn 1, Kaiafa-Gbandi, *ibid*, 523; Satzger (n 5) §7, Rn 25 ff. For the minority's opinion mainly expressed by advocates of the Corpus Juris project, see, eg, Vervaele (n 8) 139 ff. For the relevant clashing argumentations, see Zeitschrift für die gesamte Strafrechtswissenschaft, Europäisches Strafprozessrecht, 2004, 275 ff, with contributions by Th Weigend, W Hassemer, M Wasmeier, E Bacigalupo, C Nestler, S Gleß, H Fuchs, EG Makoruk, B Schünemann, J Vogel, Y Buruma, V Militello, C Kreß, H Jung, K Ambos, E Malarino, E Weigend, B Namyslowska-Gabrysiak and B Schünemann, *Alternativentwurf für die Europäische Strafrechtspflege* (Köln-Berlin-München, Carl-Heymanns Verlag, 2004).

[26] *Environmental Crime* case (n 1) para 52.

[27] See also Heger (n 24) 312.

for the Community.[28] Within this institutional framework, the *exceptional* acknowledgement of a competence (in this case, to take criminal measures by harmonising environmental offences in Member States) is only possible through a *specific* and *explicit* provision, precisely because it is exceptional and, therefore, not implicitly inferable. Consequently, the judgment contains a logical leap, by claiming that the Community could *exceptionally* acquire a competence it does not otherwise hold, for reasons of key policy effectiveness. However, this exact necessity calls for a corresponding pre-acknowledged competence that the Community cannot generate of its own accord. On the other hand, this Court's stance is rejectable also because it refers specifically to criminal repression. In doing so, it disconnected the legitimisation of the relevant competence – with the excessive distinguishing requirements it includes[29] – from a distinct legal basis and annexed it as a corollary to any other legal basis that envisages special material competences in various key Union policy areas to achieve Community objectives.

- Communitisation of actions in the field of criminal enforcement was then provided exclusively through Article 42 TEU, the infamous 'catwalk provision'. This provision made clear that competence for criminal matters could never be granted implicitly to the Community, given the specific procedure foreseen and the additional prohibition to consider the exercise of criminal competence by the Community as a necessary complementary action which it could predict and autonomously assume under Article 308 TEC, as this required a field in which the Community already had competence.

These arguments show that the ECJ was based on expediency rather than an existing legal basis to promote the expansion of Community competences.[30] It thus acknowledged a competence envisaged only in the Treaty Establishing a Constitution for Europe (Article III – 271 paragraph 2 final subparagraph), which was not then applicable law and could not become such by means of an ECJ ruling.[31] Maybe that is why its rationale was so weak, if not essentially non-existent.

IV. The Consequences of the ECJ Judgment and its Impact on EU Law

As already mentioned, the ECJ's ruling was linked to corollaries of 'constitutional' importance. In particular, the framework decisions required unanimity while

[28] *cf* E Herlin-Karnell, 'Commission v. Council: Some Reflections on Criminal Law in the First Pillar' (2007) 13 *European Public Law* 69, 80. For the ECJ's activism and the substitution of institutional legitimisation by the lack of action on behalf of Community instruments, see the interesting outlook by M Cappelletti, 'Is the European Court of Justice "Running Wild"?' (1987) 12 *European Law Review* 3, 3–17.

[29] On the peculiarities of criminal law, see, eg, Hefendehl (n 8) 43 ff.

[30] See n 24.

[31] See also Hefendehl, (n 8) 52.

directives only qualified majority, making it thus much easier to reach a decision for a criminal law legal instrument. Besides this, directives could have direct effect, while the Commission could initiate infringement proceedings against a Member State, which could be also held financially liable for non-compliance with the Court rulings.[32] However, the acknowledgement of Community competence to issue directives defining basic elements of behaviour that breach community policies and should, therefore, constitute punishable offences predominantly modified the substance of the third pillar, as the harmonisation of substantive criminal laws relating to violations of Community policies – to whatever extent this could be considered to have belonged to this pillar – was transferred in its entirety to the first pillar.

Subsequently, at least on a theoretical level, the harmonisation of substantive criminal laws against breaches of EU policies was significantly boosted, on the one hand because Member States could now be much more effectively obligated to transpose the directives issued by the majority, and on the other because the pretrial Court's competence to interpret directives no longer required its acceptance by Member States.

It is obvious that these after-effects would not remain unexploited, at least by the Commission. As of November 2005, the Commission dispatched a Communication to the Council and the European Parliament[33] on the consequences of the judgment in the Environmental Crime case.[34] Therein, beyond its assessment of the content, the scope, the consequences of the judgment, and the conditions for criminal harmonisation using the Community competence, the Commission also discussed the consequences of the Court's judgment for actual legislative practice. The latter was one of the more noteworthy parts of the Communication. At its core, it ascertained that the Commission was ready to take action not only to modify pending legislative proposals under the new competence acknowledged by the ECJ (under which the criminal law protection of the Community financial interests and the criminal law enforcement of intellectual property rights[35] were only exemplarily cited), but also to amend a large number of already existing framework decisions that called on Member States to criminalise various behaviours and envisage corresponding sanctions. Specifically, beyond Framework Decision 2005/667/JHA to strengthen the criminal-law framework

[32] See Vervaele (n 8) 130; S White, 'Harmonisation of Criminal Law under the First Pillar' (2006) 31 *European Law Review* 81, 82, 90.

[33] Commission (EC), 'Communication from the Commission to the European Parliament and the Council on the implications of the Court's judgment of 13 September 2005 (Case C-176/03 Commission v. Council)' COM (2005) 583 final/2, 24 November 2005.

[34] *Enironmental Crime* case (n 1).

[35] However, a wide array of additional fields was included in a footnote: The Greek proposal concerning the fight against trafficking in human organs and tissues (Proposal for a framework decision of 26 April 2003 [2003] OJ C100/27); and the German proposal concerning criminal law protection against fraudulent or other unfair anti-competitive conduct in relation to the award of public contracts in the common market (Proposal for a framework decision of 4 September 2000 [2000] OJ C253/3).

for the enforcement of the law against ship-source pollution (the annulment of which the Commission had already requested by the ECJ), an Annex to the Communication included six other framework decisions in force,[36] and the legal basis as well as the argument(s) by which the Commission justified its competence to establish criminal measures, the main being that legality in the Community's legal order had to be restored after the ECJ judgment.

Of course, the Council and Member States had a different – cautious, to say the least – reaction to the Court's decision.[37] In some Member States responses were even acidic. For example, in a procedure initiated by the French national Parliament itself, it was argued that the ECJ had acted beyond its powers and had demonstrated a certain '*fédèralisme judiciaire*', while it was also stressed that it was high time that it ended the '*gouvernement des juges*' and restore the power to the entities to whom it belongs, namely the governments and the Member States.[38] Furthermore, the Justice and Home Affairs (JHA) Council has been of the opinion that there was no urgency to enact rectifying legislation, because many adopted framework decisions had already been implemented in national law. Besides, the Council was not prepared to conclude a general 'transfer' agreement in favour of the first pillar, as the Commission wished. According to the Council's position[39] and its understanding of the Court's judgment, Community competence in criminal law was an exception that had to be interpreted restrictively. Such an exception should moreover be no more than the tailpiece of detailed Community policy, while by the harmonisation of criminal sanctions the Community had to leave room for the Member States to define the requirements of effectiveness and proportionality and was not allowed to regulate everything in detail and exclusively. Thus, the position of the JHA Council has been more moderate than the views of some of the Member States, but at the same time it has also been more restrictive than that of the Commission as far as the content of the Court's judgment was concerned, highlighting the exceptional character of the Community's competence in criminal law and the need for a restrictive interpretation of such an exception.

It seems that this has been the reason why the Member States and the Council did not really contribute to a shift of legal instruments from the third to the first pillar. The only three directives enacted in the field of Community competence in criminal law, as recognised by the Court, since the Court's judgment and up until the entry into force of the Lisbon Treaty (December 2009), have been the ones that

[36] Namely, the Commission referred to the criminal enforcement of the environmental protection, the Euro and non-cash means of payment, money laundering, freezing, seizing and confiscation, unauthorised entry transit and residence, corruption in the private sector, attacks against information systems and serious ship-source pollution, see 'Commission Communication (n 33) 7–8.

[37] *cf* L Krämer, 'Environment, Crime and EC Law' (2006) 18 *Journal of Environmental Law* 277, 284–85.

[38] For Member States' reactions, see, eg, Vervaele (n 8) 137–38, as well as the relevant French Parliament resolution in www.assemblee-nationale.fr/12/ta/ta0560.asp, which referred to a need to utilise the procedure under Art 42 TEU when competence on criminal matters is acknowledged to the Community.

[39] See Council of the European Union, 'Procedural consequences of the judgement of the Court of Justice in case C-176/03' Doc 6466/06, 16 February 2006.

replaced the two annulled framework decisions by the Court's judgments in 2005 and 2007, which are as follows:

- the Directive on the protection of the environment through criminal law (2008/99/EC);[40]
- the Directive on ship-source pollution and on the introduction of penalties for infringements,[41] including criminal penalties for pollution offences (2005/35/EC, as amended by Directive 2009/123/EC[42] after the Court's decision);
- lastly, a directive referring to a characteristic field of Community competence (migration policy), ie the Directive providing for minimum standards on sanctions and measures against employers of illegally staying third-country nationals (2009/52/EC).[43]

So, it could be argued without any exaggeration that the effect of the Court's decision was not that extraordinary *in practice*, and certainly not proportional to the Court's radical interpretation, given that, up until the amendment brought to the institutional status by the Lisbon Treaty, only one piece of legislation was passed in the form of a directive on Community competence on criminal matters beyond those imposed by the ECJ with its rulings that annulled the framework decisions on environmental protection. De facto, therefore, the Court's ruling could not in fact convince Member States and the Council to yield their reservations with respect to the proclaimed Community competence in the field of criminal law. Essentially, based on the above argumentation to assess the decision, the criticism on '*gouvernement des juges*' and '*fédèralisme judiciaire*' delivered by the French side appears to be justified. Undeniably, the ECJ opted for broad interpretations in other past decisions by taking a functional approach,[44] but this in itself cannot justify the Court's stance when it exceeds the spirit of the Treaties itself by its interpretation, as revealed above. Two years later (2007), when it annulled the Framework Decision on pollution from ships using the same feasibility logic for the foundation of Community competence in the field of criminal law,[45] the Court felt the need to exclude the delineation of sanctions from Community competences.[46] The reactions that had sprung up in the meantime with respect to the 2005 decision made it clear that this would constitute an apparent misuse of the Treaties.[47]

[40] Directive 2008/99/EC of the European Parliament and of the Council of 19 November 2008 on the protection of the environment through criminal law [2008] OJ L328/28.

[41] Directive 2005/35/EC of the European Parliament and of the Council of 7 September 2005 on ship-source pollution and on the introduction of penalties for infringements [2005] OJ L255/11.

[42] Directive 2009/123/EC of the European Parliament and of the Council of 21 October 2009 amending Directive 2005/35/EC on ship-source pollution and on the introduction of penalties for infringements [2009] OJ L280/52.

[43] Directive 2009/52/EC of the European Parliament and of the Council of 18 June 2009 providing for minimum standards on sanctions and measures against employers of illegally staying third-country nationals [2009] OJ L168/24.

[44] Vervaele (n 8) 140.

[45] See *Commission of the European Communities v Council of the European Union* (n 14).

[46] *Commission of the European Communities v Council of the European Union* (n 14) para 70.

[47] *cf* Kaiafa-Gbandi (n 24) 522–27; Murschetz (n 5) 151–53; Herlin-Karnell (n 28) 80–81.

Of course, it is accurately underscored that a legal interpretation of a judgment and a judgment's conversion into political practice are two different things,[48] especially in a case where the Council was negatively dispositioned. However, one must not overlook the fact that the substantial lack of reasoning (ie the fact that with its 13 September 2005 judgment the ECJ acknowledged Community competence to impose on Member States the obligation to take criminal measures on a wide range of Community activities resulting from Articles 2 and 3 TEC) without any essential arguments or other criteria or contextual clarifications[49] beyond the vague invocation of the need for effectiveness of Community action, contributed decisively to the decision's lack of practical impact.[50] At the same time, this lack of impact played a role in the development of the Union's ensuing institutional regime. With respect to the perception that one could conjure regarding the EU competence to introduce minimum rules on the definition of offences and sanctions in key Union policy areas that have been harmonised, the Court turned the relevant provision of the Treaty establishing a Constitution for Europe into enforceable law via the interpretation of the 13 September 2005 judgment,[51] which was copied by Article 83, paragraph 2 of the Treaty on the Functioning of the European Union (TFEU) under the institutional status of the Lisbon Treaty. In other words, it would indeed be dangerous to suppose that the competence granted to the Union under the current Article 83, paragraph 2 TFEU is an unlimited jurisdiction in key policy areas that have been subject to harmonisation measures, aimed at ensuring the effectiveness of EU actions in the exercise of these policies.

Indeed, the Lisbon Treaty currently confers competence on the Union for the approximation of criminal laws and regulations of the Member States, if this proves to be essential to ensure effective implementation of a Union policy in an area which has been subject to harmonisation procedures (Article 83, paragraph 2 TFEU). Thus, it recognises Union competence to harmonise the criminal laws of its Member States to ensure the effectiveness of its policies with the same generalisation, vagueness and lack of established limits, making criminal repression an annex of the relevant action.[52] The ECJ, having made the (erroneous, as argued herein) choice to consider that such a competence was acknowledged to

[48] Vervaele (n 8) 141.

[49] See, eg, White (n 32) 91, noting that 'the Court may in future have to devise reliable tests to define "an essential measure" and "effectiveness"'. In the same vein, see L Kuhl/B-R Killmann, 'The Community Competence for a Directive on Criminal Law Protection of the Financial Interests' (2006) *Eucrim: The European Criminal Law Associations' Forum* 100, 102, who distinguish between abstract and concrete necessity tests and argue for the latter.

[50] The rationale deficiency is admitted even by supporters of the judgment, see, eg, M Foerster, *(Umwelt-) Strafrechtliche Maßnahmen im Europarecht*, 1st edn (Berlin, Berliner Wissenschafts-Verlag, 2007) 66; Vervaele (n 8) 140.

[51] See Arts III-172§2 and III-271§2 of the Draft Treaty establishing a Constitution for Europe [2003] OJ C169/01.

[52] On the relevant criticism, see, eg, H Satzger, *International and European Criminal Law*, 1st edn (Munchen, CH Beck, Hart, Nomos, 2012) 76–78.

the Community based on the then applicable Treaty of Amsterdam, did not even bother to at least set out specific criteria by which the Community could make use of such competence or its limits thereof, although this was, at best, a competence that resulted merely through the Court's interpretation.[53] Thus, the ECJ missed out on the opportunity to provide guidelines on the exact substance of the competence it acknowledged to the Community and on when exactly it could be exercised. However, this would be crucial for the interpretation of the relevant provision of the Draft for a European Constitution, which essentially rendered it 'applicable' law and which was later included in the Lisbon Treaty.

Advocate General (AG) Ruiz-Jarabo Colomer's Opinion[54] suggested that such explanatory deliberations were necessary for the Court's judgment, but also shortly discussed whether for Community law to be effective it is only necessary for the sanction to be a criminal penalty. In this debate, the AG first stated that 'the power to impose civil, administrative or criminal sanctions must be classified as an instrumental power in the service of the effectiveness of Community law', and then underlined that 'where the integrity of (the Community law) system requires a correctional dimension, the Member States must define the mechanisms required to that end, and their nature must be determined by the Community, *provided that it is in the position to analyse how useful they are for the aim pursued*, since otherwise the task falls to the national legislative authorities'.[55] The importance of this issue (even if one accepted Community competence on criminal matters as the Court did) surfaced later, especially when the German Constitutional Court (GCC) assessed the compatibility of the Lisbon Treaty with the German Constitution. In its judgment, the GCC meticulously examined the provision of Article 83, paragraph 2 TFEU which corresponds – and is substantially identical – to Article III-271, paragraph 2 of the Draft European Constitution, and which was rendered 'valid' law via the ECJ judgment. In other words, it was no coincidence that when the GCC evaluated the 'annexed' competence to employ criminal law for reasons of ensuring the effectiveness of the Union's various policies, it noted that:

> Because this competence in criminal law-making carries the threat that it could be without limits, a provision granting such competence is, as such, just as incompatible with the factually determined and only limited transfer of sovereign powers as with the required protection of the national legislature which is democratically especially bound by the majority decision of the people.[56]

[53] See D Spinellis, 'Judgment of 13 September 2005, (Case C-176/03, Commission v. Council) annulling the Council Framework Decision 2003/80/JHA of 27 January 2003 on the protection of the environment through criminal law' (2006) *European Constitutional Law Review* 2 293, 300, who notices that 'the judgment establishes that Community action with respect to criminal measures must be based on *implicit* powers connected with a specific legal basis' (emphasis added).

[54] C-176/03 *Commission v Council* [2005] ECR I-07879, Opinion of AG Ruiz-Jarabo Colomer, paras 84 ff.

[55] *Ibid*, para 84.

[56] Bundesverfassungsgericht, Urteil vom 30.Juni 2009 (2 BvE 2/08, 2BvE 5/08, 2 BvR 1010/08, 2BvR 1022/08, 2 BvR 1259/08, 2 BvR 182/09) para 361.

> The Treaty of Lisbon, however, provides sufficient indications for an interpretation in conformity with the constitution. On the one hand, the constituent element that grants law-making powers in criminal law is narrowly worded. Accordingly, the harmonisation of corresponding legal provisions of the Member States must prove '*essential to ensure the effective implementation of a Union policy*' in the harmonised area of the law (Article 83.2 first sentence TFEU). *Only if it is demonstrably established that a serious deficit as regards enforcement actually exists and that it can only be remedied by a threat of sanction, this exceptional constituent element exists and the related power to legislate in criminal law may be deemed conferred. These conditions also apply to the existence of a related competence for criminal law that has already been assumed by the European courts.*[57]

In other words, although the ECJ could utilise its judgment in order to leave its mark for the future, at least on the interpretation it invoked, it failed to do so, precisely because its ruling lacked substantial reasoning for a radical step it took on such a core issue as Community versus Union competence in the field of criminal law.

V. Conclusion

The analysis above makes it clear that the ECJ judgment of 13 September 2005 was very significant at the theoretical level, as it attributed Community competence in criminal matters for the effective exercise of its policies which was not envisaged in the Treaties, and thus reallocated the institutional arrangement of boundaries between the first and the third pillar as to the leeway for EU intervention in the field of criminal law. However, the judgment failed to convince and unify all EU legislative bodies, obviously also due to the absence of a sound rationale regarding key issues it should have addressed, and which the AG had already underlined in his Opinion. As a result, the judgment's impact was practically quite limited and it left no substantial interpretative legacy for an issue that proved crucial in future developments with respect to the enforcement of the Lisbon Treaty, ie when the harmonisation of Member States' criminal laws may be considered essential in ensuring the effective implementation of a Union policy. In this sense, one could say that it is not wise for the Court to try to play the role of an 'EU integration process locomotive' without strongly rooted positions, since a lack of rationale logically triggers a lack of persuasion. Moreover, the Court is asked to *interpret* and not *produce* Union law, eventually respecting the principle of separation of powers, which is a key element of European legal culture and EU Treaties.[58]

[57] *Ibid*, para 362 (emphasis added). For the exact same viewpoint with criticism of the 2005 ECJ judgment for exceeding the then valid Treaties, see Satzger (n 52) 77–78.

[58] See Arts 14 para 1, 16 para 1, 17, 19 para 1b TEU.

EU Substantive Criminal Competence and the Court of Justice: Reactions to the Case Law

SAMULI MIETTINEN[1]

I. Introduction

For much of its history, the European Union's (EU) competence or predecessors have been subject to severe constitutional limitations in the field of criminal law. As a consequence of these limits, the EU operated, until relatively recently, very much like any other international organisation in this field, even whilst integration developed a supranational character in many other fields of EU action. The establishment of the EU in 1993 developed intergovernmental cooperation in criminal justice at EU level, but the powers of the more supranational European Community, according to conventional wisdom, remained limited to non-criminal law matters. The judgments of the Court of Justice of the European Union (CJEU) shattered this illusion in two cases. The *Environmental Crime*[2] and *Ship-Source Pollution*[3] cases established that the Community could require Member States to also enact measures of criminal law. After the judgments, the Member States consented to Treaty change which introduced an express provision to this effect. Nevertheless, debate continues whether that provision must be invoked whenever (what is now) the EU requires its Member States to criminalise action that is contrary to its policies. That debate is particularly important for those States that have secured special arrangements exempting them from cooperation in the field of criminal law, but also has implications on the extent of the Union's powers in the field in all the Member States.

This commentary considers some prominent, documented examples of the Member States' reactions to the first judgment. These include in particular parliamentary scrutiny which reflects on the case law or on similar changes proposed in the Constitutional Treaty or the Lisbon Treaty. These reactions also include the Member States' involvement in subsequent litigation and the involvement of Member States in invoking later, similar provisions introduced by the Lisbon Treaty.

[1] Thanks to Maria Bergström, Graham Butler and Petri Freundlich for comments and suggestions, and the *Uppsala Forum* for its kind invitation to present an earlier version of this paper during my tenure as a Visiting Research Fellow.

[2] Case C-176/03 *Commission v Council* [2005] ECR I-07879.

[3] Case C-440/05 *Commission v Council* [2007] ECR-I-09097.

Many reactions are sceptical, but critical reactions should be seen in their broader context. The 2005 judgment and, more precisely, broad readings of that judgment were controversial at that time. However, the Lisbon Treaty introduced express powers similar to those recognised by the Court of Justice in 2005; indeed powers broader than provided in the later 2007 judgment. Their reception suggests what was once controversial has since become conventional wisdom.

In the *Environmental Crime* case, the Court clarifies a pre-existing constitutional framework during a period in which more extensive powers proposed under the Constitutional Treaty become accepted. In 2003, the Convention on the Future of Europe published a draft of the Constitutional Treaty (CT). The CT proposed collapsing the pillar structure and revised several specific, express powers linked to criminal law so that they would be exercised similarly to the pre-Lisbon Community powers.[4] The proposed substantive criminal law competence in the CT was rejected following failed referenda in 2005, but reappeared in substantially identical form following the success of the 2007 Lisbon Treaty. The provisions in force since December 2009 are thus in substance identical to the controversial CT proposals. The powers are more extensive than those recognised in the judgments, albeit with some geographic limitations. They have also been ratified in accordance with national constitutional requirements of the Member States. Thus, any discussion of Member State reactions to the case law on criminal law competence should begin with a reminder that the outcome achieved by Treaty reform is in many areas a greater breadth and depth of powers at EU level than those developed by the Court of Justice in its 2005 and 2007 judgments. In the meantime, the special arrangements now under Protocols 21 and 22 have been re-examined at the political level. The United Kingdom has declared its intention to leave the EU, including those instruments and policies in the area of criminal cooperation to which it has opted in. Denmark, meanwhile, held a referendum in December 2015 in which the electorate chose not to join those areas of cooperation in which they currently participate under the international law arrangements in Protocol 22.

The text in force from 1 December 2009 reads:

> 2. If the approximation of criminal laws and regulations of the Member States proves essential to ensure the effective implementation of a Union policy in an area which has been subject to harmonisation measures, directives may establish minimum rules with regard to the definition of criminal offences and sanctions in the area concerned. Such directives shall be adopted by the same ordinary or special legislative procedure as was followed for the adoption of the harmonisation measures in question, without prejudice to Article 76.[5]

This text corresponds to Article III-271 of the CT with only cosmetic changes: The CT envisaged replacing directives with substantially similar 'framework laws', and

[4] Treaty Establishing a Constitution for Europe [2004] OJ C310/1.
[5] Treaty on the Functioning of the European Union (TFEU) [2012] OJ C326/1, Art 83(2).

contained a reference to Article III-264 which is similar to Article 76 of the Treaty on the Functioning of the European Union (TFEU). This was not, however, the position in 2005 when the Court delivered its judgment in the *Environmental Crime* case. In that case, the Commission argued that even in the absence of an express provision such as Article 83(2) TFEU, the European Community had powers to require criminal law measures on the basis of its other substantive competences. If the Community had the competence to approximate laws to protect the environment, the Commission argued it also had the competence to approximate *criminal laws* for that purpose.

In its September 2005 ruling, the CJEU accepted this argument. As a consequence, the CJEU declared EU third pillar measures invalid when they overlapped with this implied competence to require criminal law measures. According to the Court of Justice, even though neither criminal law nor the rules of criminal procedure fall within the Community's competence, this

> does not prevent the Community legislature, when the application of effective, proportionate and dissuasive criminal penalties by the competent national authorities is an essential measure for combating serious environmental offences, from taking measures which relate to the criminal law of the Member States which it considers necessary in order to ensure that the rules which it lays down on environmental protection are fully effective.[6]

The third pillar measures in that case overlapped and thus infringed the EC treaties under Article 47 TEU because, according to the Court, the European Community had implied powers in the field of criminal law when these were necessary for the effectiveness of its other policies.[7]

Shortly after the judgment, several EU institutions published their own interpretations of the implications of its consequences.[8] The Commission in particular suggested that areas of EC action far beyond the protection of the environment, which was the subject of the first case, involved implied criminal law powers. In subsequent litigation, concluded in 2007, on the extent of those powers, the Court of Justice clarified some limits to this ancillary competence.[9] The EC also passed measures which drew on the Commission's ideas,[10] whilst others were rejected.[11] In the same time period, the Member States reaffirmed the settlement

[6] *Environmental Crime* case (n 2) para 48.

[7] The impact of this case on EU law is discussed in the first part of this chapter by Kaiafa-Gbandi.

[8] Commission, 'Communication from the Commission to the European Parliament and the Council on the implications of the Court's judgment of 13 September 2005 (Case C-176/03 *Commission v Council*)' COM(2005)583 final; Council document 6210/06, 14 February 2006; Council document 6466/06, 16 February 2006; European Parliament resolution on the consequences of the judgment of the Court of 13 September 2005 (C-176/03 Commission v Council) 2006/2007(INI).

[9] *Ship-Source Pollution* case (n 3).

[10] Directive 2009/52/EC of the European Parliament and of the Council of 18 June 2009 providing for minimum standards on sanctions and measures against employers of illegally staying third-country nationals [2009] OJ L168/24.

[11] See, eg, the amended proposal for a Directive of the European Parliament and of the Council COM/2006/0168 final – COD 2005/0127 on criminal measures aimed at ensuring the enforcement of intellectual property rights [2006] OJ C49/37.

first expressed in the Constitutional Treaty by ratifying the substantially similar changes proposed in the Lisbon Treaty. The powers granted to the European Community under this judgment were in many ways similar to what was proposed in the earlier draft Constitutional Treaty.[12]

II. Why Did the Choice of Legal Basis Matter?

The *Environmental Crime* case was a dispute between the Council, supported by intervening Member States, and the Commission regarding *how* particular legal rules should be enacted at European level. The decision effectively awarded the European Community powers in the field of criminal law that overlap with the institutionally more fragile EU third pillar arrangements. But this dispute has significant practical consequences, if the answers to the following questions matter. Should only the Commission carry the initiative, or should the Council, where Member State interests are strongly represented, also draft proposals? Does the European Parliament have a role as a co-legislator or is it merely consulted on proposals? Should these measures use the legal instruments of the European Community, directives and potentially even regulations, or should they be cast as EU framework decisions with all of the attendant limitations in judicial control and legal effects? Should each Member State hold a veto in the Council, or should the European Community's legislative procedures, including qualified majority voting, apply?

Before the 2005 judgment, three countries had special positions in relation to the EC rules on visas, asylum and immigration.[13] Cooperation in criminal law remained primarily in the third, EU pillar, and subject to intergovernmental arrangements distinct from ordinary EC law. When criminal cooperation was fully integrated into the post-Lisbon supranational EU structure, these three countries also received further special treatment in the post-Lisbon criminal law arrangements to complement their prior position in relation to Title IV and Schengen.

As a consequence of the Treaty of Amsterdam which entered into force in 1999, part of the intergovernmental arrangements in the EU Treaty and extra-EU initiatives, the EU policies on visas, immigration and asylum as well as the Schengen acquis that had been developed outside even the EU context were integrated into the first, EC pillar. As cooperation in these fields intensified and became subject to the supranational legal framework, the UK, Ireland and Denmark received special treatment in order to secure their support for transferring some cooperation from the intergovernmental arenas to the new Title IV of the post-Amsterdam EC Treaty. The UK and Ireland were exempt from many measures but could opt

[12] Treaty Establishing a Constitution for Europe [2004] OJ C310, Art III-271.

[13] See, eg, S Peers, *EU Justice and Home Affairs Law*, 2nd edn (New York, Oxford University Press, 2006) 55–62.

in to Title IV measures and measures that built on the Schengen acquis. They had agreed to even take part in criminal law-related Schengen cooperation with the exception of provisions in hot pursuit.[14] Denmark maintained that cooperation should take place outside the supranational framework. Under a Protocol on Denmark, it obtained an exemption from most Title IV measures after Amsterdam and a concession that Title IV Schengen measures are binding to it under international law, not under EU law. Denmark could also opt in to adopted measures and often did so in addition to negotiating international treaties with the EC on issues which fell within Title IV. The remaining EU pillar measures on police and judicial cooperation would continue after Amsterdam to be adopted by unanimity and as a consequence no particular special arrangements would be required in order to maintain an unenthusiastic state's sovereignty.

As the Treaty Establishing a Constitution for Europe transformed into the Lisbon Treaty,[15] it became clear that qualified majority voting and other features of the supranational EC framework would apply to new measures in the Union's 'area of freedom, security and justice'. This encompassed both the former Title IV as well as policies in criminal matters and police cooperation which were formerly the province of intergovernmental third pillar measures. The three states which had special arrangements vis-à-vis supranational cooperation received more extensive special treatment under the Lisbon protocols. Under Protocol 21, the UK and Ireland received the right to remain outside a broad range of measures encompassing almost the whole area of freedom, security and justice (AFSJ) with the possibility of opting into selected measures, whereas Denmark was excluded under Protocol 22. Seen from the perspective of the judgments reviewed in this commentary, these states either retained or further developed their exceptional status in relation to the Union's express substantive criminal competence.

III. Reactions during the Proceedings: Member State Interventions in *Environmental Crime*

Member State reactions to the principle proposed in *Environmental Crime* are already evident in the case itself. In 2001, the Council Legal Service (CLS) gave advice that was later well reflected in the CJEU judgment.[16] Asked to comment on what it thought was the relationship between implied EC powers and the express powers of the Union's third pillar, the CLS itself considered that third pillar Union action was pre-empted where rules could be adopted under the Community pillar.

[14] *Ibid* 57.

[15] On this process, see, eg, J-C Piris, *The Constitution for Europe* (Cambridge University Press, 2006) and J-C Piris, *The Lisbon Treaty: A Legal and Political Analysis* (Cambridge University Press, 2010).

[16] Opinion of the Legal Service of the Council doc 6793/01 on the Draft EU Framework Decision on the Protection of the Environment through Criminal Law [2001].

As a consequence, the Council's own legal service had already concluded that the Community legislator – and not the Union's third pillar – could require criminal sanctions. Community powers were, however, according to this advice limited to the power to establish substantive rules and on the other hand the power to require that Member States provide 'effective, dissuasive and proportionate' *criminal* sanctions'. Similar advice had been given long before the EU Treaty was negotiated. The CLS had already taken this view in an earlier, 1990 opinion.[17]

Eleven of the then 15 Member States[18] intervened in the proceedings, all in support of the Council's view that the Community did not have competence over criminal law.

When the case came to trial, the Council and the intervening Member States, with the exception of the Netherlands, argued before the Court that the Community did not have the power to require imposition of criminal penalties.[19] The Netherlands alone considered that the Community could have substantive criminal law competence under certain conditions.[20] Although the Court's eventual findings reflected the legal advice of the Council's own service, intervening Member States sought to restrict Community competence.

IV. Institutional Reactions to *Environmental Crime*

The EU institutions issued their own interpretations of how the judgment would affect the development of criminal law at EU level. According to the Commission, the judgment could be interpreted so that 'provisions of criminal law required for the effective implementation of Community law' regardless of the area of Community law are a matter for the implied competence of the Community, whereas

> horizontal criminal law provisions aimed at encouraging police and judicial cooperation in the broad sense, including measures on the mutual recognition of judicial decisions, measures based on the principle of availability, and measures on the harmonization of criminal law in connection with the creation of the area of freedom, security and justice not linked to the implementation of Community policies or fundamental freedoms fall within the EU pillar.[21]

Its communication suggested appropriate alternative EC legal bases for both passed and pending third pillar measures. This included single policy legal bases: Article 175(1) EC for environmental crime, Article 123(4) EC to deal with Euro counterfeiting, Articles 61(a) and 63(3)(b) on immigration rules, Article 80(2)

[17] Council Document 7161/90 concerning sanctions in the area of the Common Fisheries Policy [1990].

[18] Denmark, Germany, Greece, Spain, France, Ireland, the Netherlands, Portugal, Finland, Sweden and the UK.

[19] *Environmental Crime* case (n 2) para 26.

[20] *Environmental Crime* case (n 2) para 36.

[21] Commission Communication (n 8) 3–4.

transport policy for rules concerning ship-source pollution, and Article 280(4) for fraud against the EC financial interests. During this period, several of these were successfully passed, whilst others were rejected or stalled.[22]

The Council debated the implications of the ruling and the Commission's perspectives in more detail in late 2005 and early 2006.[23] In addition to debates on which areas fell within Community competence, the Council discussed five further developments which might follow from a broad reading of the judgment. Did, in addition to the definitions of offences and the obligation to impose criminal penalties as such, Community competence also include the nature and level of the penalties in more detail, accompanying penalties such as seizure or exclusion from a profession, issues of jurisdiction including dual criminality and parallel proceedings, rules on initiating criminal prosecutions, and rules on cooperation in investigations? The risk of perceiving criminal law measures as ancillary to any policy would, in its view, present a danger of excessive encroachment upon national criminal law systems.

Some solutions were proposed: that proposals for instruments with criminal law content should always be drawn up under the oversight of the Justice Commissioner and that they should also be adopted exclusively by the Council for Ministers for Justice and prepared under the auspices of working parties on criminal law matters. As the Council recognised, this requires provisions with a criminal law content to be proposed as separate directives.

At least the French delegation issued its own paper, in which it emphasised further limits. 'Horizontal' criminal law provisions, relating to the definition and application of general criminal law rules should continue to fall exclusively within the third pillar; there is no ruling on the ability of the Community to harmonise the types and levels of penalties; and finally, the scope of the competence does not involve all Community law, but that environmental protection as a horizontal objective was special in this regard.[24]

The Council, like the Commission, eventually produced a document containing its interpretation of the effects of the *Environmental Crime* judgment.[25] Three points are worth quoting in full. For the Council,

> 1. As a general rule, criminal law as well as the rules of criminal procedure fall outside the Community's competence (see paragraph 47 of the judgment). The Community must therefore interpret and apply any exception to this general rule in a narrow sense.

[22] See, eg, the list in Council Document 10105/07 Rev 1 [2007] 'Review of the procedural Consequences of judgment in the Court of Justice case C-176/03'.

[23] Council Document 15681/05 [2005] 'The further development of European criminal law and the fundamental rights of Citizens', see especially 5–6.

[24] Council Document 5520/06 [2006] 'Consequences of the judgment of the Court of Justice of the European Communities of 13 September 2005 (Case C-176/03)'.

[25] Council Document 6466/06 [2006] 'Procedural consequences of the judgment of the Court of Justice in case C-176/03 Commission of the European Communities v Council of the European Union [2005] ECR I-7879'.

2. The Community legislator is entitled to take the legislative measures which relate to the criminal law of the Member States which it considers necessary in order to ensure that the rules which it lays down are fully effective (see paragraph 48 of the judgment). This implies that the Community legislator cannot oblige Member States to provide for criminal penalties for violations of rules which the Community has not, or not yet, established or which have been established pursuant to national law only.
3. The Community legislator must leave to the Member States the choice of the criminal penalties to apply, as long as they are effective, proportionate and dissuasive (see paragraph 49). Consequently, Community acts cannot determine in detail and exclusively the level of penalties to be introduced; they should leave a discretion to the Member States.[26]

V. Reviews of *Environmental Crime* at National Level

Some national institutions examined the impact of the judgment in reports dedicated to the case or its implications. In the UK, the House of Lords EU Committee published a 2006 report examining *The Criminal Law Competence of the European Community* in considerable detail. The report considered both the implications of the case and the Commission's interpretation of Union competence, as well as the possibility of transferring remaining third pillar powers to the first pillar.[27] The report and its evidence also provide information on reactions in some other states.[28] Whilst the report itself diplomatically requested clarification of several issues, evidence provided by the Government for this report suggests a more limited reading of the judgment than that offered in the Commission's Communication: procedural criminal law and the issue of specified criminal penalties were considered beyond the scope of Community powers.

The French *Assemblée Nationale* produced a 30-page *rapport d'information* on the case.[29] It took a similarly limited view of EC powers and expressed particular concern about the coherence of national criminal laws where EC powers were broadly construed. It was also directly more critical of the Court's judgment, suggesting that the *passerelle* clause should be invoked in order to regain control of the law from judges.[30] A committee of the French *Sénat* also held a hearing

[26] *Ibid* 2.

[27] UK House of Lords, Select Committee on European Union Forty-Second Report, *The Criminal Law Competence of the European Community* [2006].

[28] *Ibid*, para 19 referring to reactions in the Danish and French parliaments.

[29] No 2829 *Rapport d'information déposé par la Délégation de l'Assemblée Nationale pour l'Union Européenne sur les conséquences de l'arrêt de la Cour de justice du septembre 2005 sur les compétences: pénales de la Communauté européenne (COM(2005) 583 final/no E 3022).* UK House of Lords Report (n 27) 12, 35.

[30] See Treaty on European Union [2012] OJ C326/13, Art 42, according to which before the Lisbon Treaty 'The Council, acting unanimously on the initiative of the Commission or a Member State, and after consulting the European Parliament, may decide that action in areas referred to in Article 29 shall fall under Title IV of the Treaty establishing the European Community, and at the same time determine the relevant voting conditions relating to it. It shall recommend the Member States to adopt that decision in accordance with their respective constitutional requirements.'

with Judge Puissochet and Advocate General Léger, both of the Court of Justice, at which the case was discussed.[31] These jurists emphasised the link to environmental protection. In Denmark, the Danish Parliament *Folketing* held a hearing with the Minister of Justice. Its resolution asked that EU criminal law should be developed as far as possible within the third rather than the first pillar.[32] In Finland, where Parliament receives detailed briefs on EU issues falling within its competence, an information letter set out a wide list of issues raised by substantive EC competence. The advice asked whether Article ex-95 EC was too broad as a legal basis for criminal law measures; whether EC criminal law powers should only be used where there was prior EC secondary legislation. Harmonisation of sanctions was thought outside EC competence, and the advice emphasised that the judgment concerned only a single framework decision and that there was no reference to the harmonisation of criminal procedure as part of EC competence.[33]

VI. *Ship-Source Pollution* and further Member State Litigation

Many of these issues resurfaced in the 2007 judgment of the Court of Justice concerning the ship-source pollution Framework Decision.[34] Here, the Commission claimed before the CJEU that a framework decision could not be validly adopted because its constituent elements could be adopted under the EC transport competence. Nineteen of the then 25 Member States intervened in support of the Council,[35] which defended the Framework Decision.[36] The arguments reflected those already raised above in the aftermath to the *Environmental Crime* case.

For the Council and its supporters, transport was not a transversal policy and therefore not comparable to the environmental policy which justified EC action in the *Environmental Crime* case. The 'aim and content' of the measure was in its view 'to approximate the laws of the Member States relating to the fight against ship-source pollution by harmonising the type and level of the applicable criminal penalties'[37] and therefore not within EC competence. Finally, rules on

[31] Réunion de la délégation pour l'Union européenne du mercredi 22 février 2006. UK House of Lords Report (n 27) 12, 18.

[32] See the evidence of Per Lachmann, Published evidence to the House of Lords report, p 39, 7 June 2006.

[33] Information letter to *Eduskunta* (the Finnish Parliament) E 130/2005, 3 January 2006.

[34] *Ship-Source Pollution* case (n 3).

[35] Kingdom of Belgium, Czech Republic, Kingdom of Denmark, Republic of Estonia. Hellenic Republic, French Republic, Ireland, Republic of Latvia, Republic of Lithuania, Republic of Hungary, Republic of Malta, Kingdom of the Netherlands, Republic of Austria, Republic of Poland, Portuguese Republic, Slovak Republic, Republic of Finland, Kingdom of Sweden, United Kingdom of Great Britain and Northern Ireland.

[36] *Ship-Source Pollution* case (n 3) paras 42–52.

[37] *Ship-Source Pollution* case (n 3) para 47.

jurisdiction, extradition and prosecution were in its view outside EC competence on any reading of the previous case.

The Court ruled that EC competence included measures 'to enhance maritime safety and improve protection of the marine environment against ship-source pollution'.[38] Effective, dissuasive and proportionate penalties for this purpose were considered within EC competence where 'necessary to ensure compliance with the Community rules laid down in the field of maritime safety'.[39] However, the 'determination of the type and level of the criminal penalties to be applied does not fall within the Community's sphere of competence'.[40] No judgment was passed on the competence of the Community over criminal procedural issues.[41] At least the question of transversal competence was also left open following this judgment.

As the entry into force of the Lisbon Treaty and Article 83 of the TFEU drew nearer, legislative practice also accepted a broader range of criminalisation powers than that argued by the Council in these cases. For example, the Directive on minimum standards on sanctions and measures against employers of illegally staying third-country nationals[42] was adopted on the basis of Article 63(3)(b) EC. This took place after the Lisbon Treaty was agreed, but before its entry into force. It provided definitions of criminal offences and required effective, proportionate and dissuasive criminal sanctions.

Some of the reactions to developing EU substantive criminal competence, whether in the case law of the Court or of the Lisbon Treaty, also document national constitutional issues concerning the conferral of competence or the precise mechanism that allows this at national level. In Germany, the *Bundesverfassungsgericht's* (or *BVerfG*) Lisbon judgment suggested that certain transfers would be difficult from the perspective of German Constitutional law.[43] In Ireland, it was asked whether the effects of the judgment in *Environmental Crime* might constitute an unauthorised delegation of legislative power from the *Oireachtas*.[44] It was also suggested that the application of the judgment would cause constitutional difficulties in France because the comparable provisions of the Constitutional Treaty would have required constitutional amendment.[45]

[38] *Ship-Source Pollution* case (n 3) para 62.
[39] *Ship-Source Pollution* case (n 3) para 68.
[40] *Ship-Source Pollution* case (n 3) para 70.
[41] *Ship-Source Pollution* case (n 3) para 73.
[42] Directive 2009/52/EC of the European Parliament and of the Council of 18 June 2009 providing for minimum standards on sanctions and measures against employers of illegally staying third-country nationals [2009] OJ L168/24.
[43] *BVerfG*, Judgment of the Second Senate of 30 June 2009 – 2 BvE 2/08, ECLI:DE:BVerfG:2009:es20090630.2bve000208, especially paras 352–66.
[44] E Fahey, 'Commission v Council: EU Legislation and the Irish Constitution' [April 2006] *The Bar Review: Journal of the Bar of Ireland* 44–46.
[45] See the Memorandum of Richard Plender given in evidence to the House of Lords 2006 report (n 27) p 9.

VII. Reactions to Substantive Criminal Competence after the Lisbon Treaty

This discussion continues in the context of the new, Lisbon-era provisions in the TFEU. Under Article 83(2) TFEU, the Union has powers to approximate criminal law 'if the approximation of criminal laws and regulations of the Member States proves essential to ensure the effective implementation of a Union policy in an area which has been subject to harmonisation measures'. The list of 'euro-crimes' in Article 83(1) is also potentially open-ended. Thus, the idea that criminal competence is limited to particular transversal areas has been rejected. However, the new competence poses a number of limitations: measures must take the form of directives, they can contain only 'minimum rules with regard to the definition of criminal offences and sanctions', and Article 83(3) provides an 'emergency break' which in theory can result in a Member State remaining outside the geographic scope of application of a substantive criminal law measure. Denmark, the UK and Ireland have further special arrangements under Protocols 21 and 22. As for criminal procedure, Article 82(1) TFEU provides wide-ranging powers: 'measures' adopted by the Ordinary Legislative Procedure (OLP) rather than unanimity which

> (a) lay down rules and procedures for ensuring recognition throughout the Union of all forms of judgments and judicial decisions; (b) prevent and settle conflicts of jurisdiction between Member States; (c) support the training of the judiciary and judicial staff; (d) facilitate cooperation between judicial or equivalent authorities of the Member States in relation to proceedings in criminal matters and the enforcement of decisions.

Thus, procedural harmonisation can be by regulation and need not necessarily involve the consent of all states bound by the measure. Article 82(2) allows directives for 'minimum rules' necessary for mutual recognition.

After the Lisbon Treaty, national parliaments examined the subsidiarity of legislative proposals in this field.[46] A review of some reasoned opinions shows that several national parliaments remain ill at ease with substantive criminal competence in the new framework. The arguments are rooted in the text of the new Treaty provisions but reflect concerns not unlike those raised during the criminal competence litigation. In 2012, the Swedish *Riksdag* issued a reasoned opinion on the proposal which eventually became the PFI Directive.[47] In its view, both the proposed legal basis of Article 325 and the specific minimum penalties in the

[46] S Miettinen, *The Europeanization of Criminal Law: Competence and Its Control in the Lisbon Era* (University of Helsinki, 2015) 456–66; J Öberg, *Limits to EU Powers: A Case Study of EU Regulatory Criminal Law* (Hart Publishing, 2017) 159–85.

[47] Proposal for a Directive of the European Parliament and of the Council COM (2012) 363 on the fight against fraud to the Union's financial interests by means of criminal law, now passed as Directive of the European Parliament and of the Council 2017/1371 of 5 July 2017 on the fight against fraud to the Union's financial interests by means of criminal law [2017] OJ L198/29.

original proposal raised subsidiarity concerns.[48] During the passage of the 2014 Market Abuse Directive,[49] the German *Bundesrat* raised concerns about whether the measures were 'essential' within the meaning of Article 83(2), because the *BverfG Lisbon* judgment required that 'it must be demonstrated that a significant shortcoming in enforcement actually exists and can only be overcome by the threat of sanctions'.[50] The proposal for a Directive of the European Parliament and of the Council on the Union legal framework for customs infringements and sanctions drew a response from the Swedish *Riksdag*, which considered that 'that the proposal contains features that are reminiscent of criminal law, which normally occur in legal instruments for which the legal basis is article 83 in the TFEU'.[51]

There is very little case law of the CJEU in which these limits are expressly considered. However, litigation on legal bases has continued. The main focus of this litigation is whether ancillary criminal law measures always require reference to an AFSJ legal basis, and therefore in practice impose the limits referred to in these articles.[52] In this respect these arguments mirror those presented in the *Environmental Crime* and *Ship-Source Pollution* cases. The extent of implied ancillary substantive competence has also resurfaced in the legislative procedure which led to the adoption of a directive on the protection of the financial interests of the Union.[53] Here, the original Commission proposal suggested that Article 325(4) could be used to propose a regulation, decided through the ordinary legislative procedure, which defined crimes and specified minimum penalties.[54] This legal basis was unanimously opposed by the Council and the European Parliament and, thanks to this the unanimity of opposition, was changed to Article 83(2).[55]

[48] Statement by the Committee on Justice 2012/13:JuU8, courtesy translation available via IPEX at http://www.ipex.eu/IPEXL-WEB/scrutiny/COD20120193/serik.do.

[49] Directive of the European Parliament and of the Council 2014/57/EU of 16 April 2014 on criminal sanctions for market abuse [2014] OJ L173/179.

[50] Bundesrat Printed matter 646/11 (Decision), courtesy translation available via IPEX at http://www.ipex.eu/IPEXL-WEB/scrutiny/COD20110297/debra.do, 2–3.

[51] Proposal for a Directive of the European Parliament and of the Council COM/2013/0884 final – 2013/0432 (COD) on the Union legal framework for customs infringements and sanctions [2013], Reasoned opinion of the Swedish Riksdag, courtesy translation available at http://www.ipex.eu/IPEXL-WEB/scrutiny/COD20130432/serik.do.

[52] See, eg, Case C-43/12 *European Commission v European Parliament and Council of the European Union* [published in the electronic reports for 2014], on information exchange on road traffic infringements, a transport competence issue, and C-137/12 *Commission v Council* [published in the electronic reports for 2013], in which acceding to the Conditional Access Convention together with its criminal law obligations fell fully within the Common Commercial Policy. This litigation attracts significantly less intervention from Member States, with C-43/12 involving seven interveners and C-137/12 involving five interveners. Sweden and the UK are the common denominators here. S Miettinen, Criminal Competence and the Choice of Legal Basis: Space in the Margins? (2015) 1 *European Criminal Law Review* 222–42.

[53] Directive of the European Parliament and of the Council 2017/1371 of 5 July 2017 on the fight against fraud to the Union's financial interests by means of criminal law [2017] OJ L198/29–41.

[54] See in particular the Commission's impact assessment evaluation of options SWD (2012)195 [2012] 39–40.

[55] Council Document 10729/13 Proposal for a Directive of the European Parliament and of the Council on the fight against fraud to the Union's financial interests by means of criminal law – General Approach [2013].

The Commission maintains the proposal should have been based on Article 325 TFEU.[56] Some states have also continued to claim that legislation pursues aims of criminal policy rather than, for example, the establishment or functioning of the internal market.[57]

VIII. Conclusion

The question is: are there in fact 'national reactions' to the case law on substantive criminal competence? Measuring this is a difficult task complicated by the fact that different institutions and actors at national level govern the different legislative and judicial interactions of the state with the Union. Nevertheless, the research above shows that the Union's substantive competence in the field of criminal law elicits responses from several national-level actors, as well as the Union's own institutions. Before the Treaty of Lisbon, Member States litigated actively at the Court of Justice in order to limit substantive EC competence. Their responses were relatively uniform in this context, whereas legal basis litigation does not often receive such broad-based attention. At the same time, the governments of those Member States agreed and ratified treaty reforms that confirmed many aspects of these judgments and indeed went beyond them in several respects. When in force, the new treaty provisions attracted some limited litigation, led by a handful of Member States, and some national parliaments raised concerns about the way in which the new Treaty powers were exercised. In one case, the Council changed a legal basis to reflect its view of the horizontal division of competences at EU level but equally there are cases where measures of a criminal law nature are included in other legal bases. Dialogue on the extent and limits of EU powers continues in this new, post-Lisbon setting.

[56] Commission, 'Communication from the Commission to the European Parliament pursuant to Article 294(6) of the Treaty on the Functioning of the European Union concerning the position of the Council at first reading with a view to the adoption of a Directive of the European Parliament and of the Council on the fight against fraud to the Union's financial interests by means of criminal law' COM(2017) 246 final.

[57] See for example C-482/17 *Czech Republic v Parliament and Council* [2017] application [2017] OJ L137/22.

6

C-105/14 – *Taricco and Others*

On Legality in Criminal Matters between Primacy of EU Law and National Constitutional Traditions. A Study of the Taricco *Saga*

SILVIA ALLEGREZZA*

I. Shifting Paradigms: The First *Taricco* Decision of the Court of Justice

The *Taricco* case has its origins in a preliminary reference raised in the criminal proceedings pending before the Italian Court of Cuneo against Ivo Taricco and other individuals, who were charged with the offence of conspiracy to commit VAT fraud related to champagne trading in the form of 'VAT carousel' for several million euros.

The referring court, called to commit the accused to trial, noted that the said offences would most likely become time-barred before a final judgment could be delivered, determining the acquittal of the defendant.

In its preliminary reference, the Court of Cuneo thus asked whether the national limitation rules, which in view of the complexity of VAT frauds and of the length of criminal proceedings in Italy 'usually' result in the accused enjoying a de facto immunity for those offences, are compatible with EU law. In the referring court's view, such rules could either amount to a form of unfair competition infringing Article 101 of the Treaty on the Functioning of the European Union (TFEU) or to a forbidden form of State aid in violation of Article 107 TFEU. They could, moreover, create a de facto VAT exemption in breach of Directive 2006/112/EC

* The Author would like to thank Dr Sofia Mirandola for her assistance in the background research and her critical remarks. The usual disclaimer applies.

(hereinafter referred to as the VAT Directive),[1] as well as a violation of the principle of sound public finances laid down in Article 119 TFEU.

In her Opinion, Advocate General (AG) Kokott found that none of the provisions invoked by the referring court was applicable to the case. She observed, nevertheless, that the order for reference implicitly also raised the concern that the described limitation regime might run counter to the Member States' duty to provide effective and dissuasive sanctions against VAT fraud affecting the Union's financial interests.[2]

With this aim, AG Kokott rephrased the question raised by the Italian court in these terms: does EU law require the national judges to refrain from applying certain provisions of their national law on the limitation periods applicable to criminal prosecution in order to guarantee the effective punishment of VAT offences?[3] Once admitted that the issue at stake cannot be assessed by reference to antitrust or State aid law, the AG identifies an 'at least implicit' additional question of whether the Italian limitation regime of criminal offences is compatible with the duty of the Member States to impose effective penalties against VAT frauds: Article 325 TFEU becomes the primary normative reference, shifting the paradigm of the entire case. Consequently, the primacy of EU law and the need to protect EU financial interests via the imposition of effective criminal sanctions for serious VAT frauds justify and support the duty for national courts to set aside any internal provisions that might hinder such a process. National provisions on limitation periods should therefore be also set aside in pending criminal proceedings because they are incompatible with EU law provisions such as Articles 4(3) of the Treaty on European Union (TEU), 325 TFEU, Regulation No 2988/95[4] and Directive 2006/112/EC.

AG Kokott resolutely rules out the existence of any potential conflict with the principle of legality as set up by Article 49 of the Charter of Fundamental Rights on the ground that limitation periods

> say nothing about the criminal liability of an act or the penalty which that act attracts, but deal only with whether a criminal offence may be prosecuted, and, consequently, are not even caught by the rule of *nullum crimen, nulla poena sine lege*.[5]

The case concerns no modification as regards to the criminal liability, the conduct or the penalty provided for tax frauds, as the provisions at stake are merely procedural in nature.[6] Therefore, as stated by the case law of the European Court of

[1] Council Directive 2006/112/EC of 28 November 2006 on the common system of value added tax [2006] OJ L347/1.

[2] Case C-105/14 *Ivo Taricco and others*, Opinion of AG Kokott, EU:C:2015:293, paras 74–79.

[3] *Ibid*, para 1.

[4] Council Regulation (EC, Euratom) No 2988/95 of 18 December 1995 on the protection of the European Communities financial interests [1995] OJ L312/1.

[5] *Taricco*, Opinion of AG Kokott (n 2), para 115.

[6] *Taricco*, Opinion of AG Kokott (n 2), para 118. In this way a distinction is made with the *Berlusconi* case, where the amendments at stake affected substantive criminal law provisions; Case C-387/02, 391/02 and 403/02 *Berlusconi and others*, EU:C:2005:270, para 18–22.

Human Rights (ECtHR), limitation periods can be extended or reduced even after the offence has been committed 'so long as the limitation period has not expired'.[7]

Such view was actually entirely shared by the Court in its first judgment.[8] The question referred by the Italian Court was thus reformulated and the Court of Justice of the European Union (CJEU) focused its analysis on whether the national rules on statutory periods amounted to an obstacle to an effective fight against VAT evasion in a manner incompatible with EU law.[9]

Recalling that VAT revenue belongs to the EU financial interests,[10] the Court emphasised, as it did in the past,[11] that Member States have a duty to provide effective and dissuasive criminal sanctions for serious VAT frauds such as the one at hand. Despite the silence of the VAT Directive on criminal law issues, the Court focuses its reasoning on the interpretation of Article 325 TFEU and Article 1 of the Convention on the protection of the European Community's (EC's) financial interests ('PIF Convention').[12] Article 325 TFEU enshrines a general duty to provide effective deterrent measures against EU frauds. Although such obligation normally leaves discretion to the national authorities in choosing the type of sanctions to apply, the Court clarified that serious VAT frauds do warrant criminal sanctions.[13] In this light, relying on the *Åkerberg Fransson* case,[14] the Court could affirm that EU law imposes on the Member States a specific obligation to effectively criminalise VAT frauds and, at least in serious cases, to make such conducts punishable with deprivation of liberty.[15]

Such obligation therefore would be breached, on the basis of Article 325(1) TFEU, if the prosecution of serious VAT frauds becomes time-barred in a significant number of cases. Moreover, on the basis of Article 325(2) TFEU (according to the so-called assimilation principle), the said obligation would not be fulfilled when the limitation period laid down for such crimes is shorter than the one established by domestic law for analogous cases of fraud affecting the Member State.

The Court did not doubt the dissuasiveness of the criminal penalties provided by Italian law in itself. It considered, nevertheless, that the effectiveness of such penalties could be seriously impaired by the application of the national provisions

[7] *Coëme and others v Belgium* App nos 32492/96, 32547/96, 32548/96, 33209/96, 33210/96 (ECtHR, 22 June 2000) para 149; *Scoppola v Italy (no 2)* App no 10249/03 (ECtHR, 17 September 2009), para 110; *OAO Neftyanaya Kompaniya Yukos v Russia* App no 14902/04 (ECtHR, 20 September 2011), paras 563–64, 570.

[8] Case C-105/14 *Ivo Taricco and others* ('*Tarrico I*') EU:C:2015:555.

[9] *Ibid*, para 35.

[10] Case C-617/10 *Åkerberg Fransson* EU:C:2013:105, paras 26–27.

[11] Case 68/88 *Commission v Greece* EU:C:1989:339.

[12] [1995] OJ C316/49.

[13] *Tarrico I* (n 8), para 39. In Case C-574/15 *Scialdone* EU:C:2018:295, paras 40–44, the Court distinguished other unlawful behaviour, such as the mere failure to pay VAT, that does not constitute fraud and accordingly shall be punished by effective and dissuasive sanctions pursuant to Art 325 TFEU, but not necessarily of a criminal nature.

[14] *Åkerberg Fransson* (n 10).

[15] *Tarrico I* (n 8) para 40.

on limitation periods, if such rules 'have the effect that, in a considerable number of cases, the commission of serious fraud will escape criminal punishment, since the offences will usually become time-barred before the criminal penalty laid down by law can be imposed'.[16]

If this were to be the case, as it is left to the national court to decide, the Court concluded that the sanctions provided would not satisfy the requirement of effectiveness inherent in the said EU law obligation. Therefore, by virtue of the primacy, the national court has the duty to set aside the domestic provisions, including rules on limitation, that, by depriving the sanctions of their effectiveness, conflict with the primary law obligation to punish EU frauds effectively. The provisions of Article 325(1) and (2) TFEU, indeed, have the effect 'in accordance with the principle of the precedence of EU law, in their relationship with the domestic law of the Member States, of rendering automatically inapplicable, merely by their entering into force, any conflicting provision of national law'.[17]

However, the Court stressed that in so doing, the national judge should also be mindful of ensuring respect of the fundamental rights of the defendants,[18] in particular with the principle of legality barring a retrospective *in peius* application of criminal law.[19]

In this respect, nevertheless, the Court considered that the disapplication of the absolute limitation period would not result in a retroactive application of a more severe criminal penalty. Therefore, such disapplication would not breach the legality principle as enshrined in Article 49 of the Charter or Article 7 of the European Convention on Human Rights (ECHR).[20]

The Court thus answered to the question referred by stating that the national judge has the obligation to disapply national limitation periods if such rule is liable to prevent the application of effective and dissuasive criminal sanctions in a significant number of serious frauds affecting the EU financial interests in breach of the obligation under Article 325 TFEU.

II. The Tormented Aftermath of *Taricco I*

The *Taricco* decision sparked partisan reactions. On the one hand, there were the supporters of a strong European response to the – real or presumed – Italian *laissez-faire* in fighting VAT frauds via criminal law.[21]

[16] *Tarrico I* (n 8) para 47.
[17] *Tarrico I* (n 8) para 52.
[18] *Tarrico I* (n 8) para 55.
[19] *Tarrico I* (n 8) para 53.
[20] *Tarrico I* (n 8) paras 55–57. The same conclusion was also reached by the AG, see *Taricco*, Opinion of AG Kokott (n 2), para 115. As for the ECHR, see *Coëme v Belgium* (n 5).
[21] A Klip, *European Criminal law* (Intersentia, 2016) 76–78.

Several scholars, especially outside Italy, welcomed the decision as a step 'to strengthen the constitutional foundations of EU law in the criminal field' because it states clearly that there is an obligation for national courts to disapply incompatible national procedural provisions but they cannot be forced to set aside substantive national criminal law.[22] In other words, scholars from non-continental traditions have considered this decision as a milestone in preventing major intrusions from the EU side on the sensitive field of substantive criminal law policy, at least as far as financial interests are concerned.

But it seems rather unlikely that the Court was moved by these intentions. It seems more probable that the Court intended to support the EU policies on the protection of financial interests under discussion at the time. When the *Taricco I* decision was delivered, tough negotiations relating to the inclusion of VAT frauds in the PIF Directive[23] were indeed ongoing.[24]

Several Member States opposed the Commission and the Parliament regarding their intention to include VAT frauds among the crimes for which the European Public Prosecutor would have become competent as the main EU-wide enforcement agency. The echo of that debate might have reached the plateau of Kirchberg in Luxembourg and might have had an impact on the way the Court answered the question raised by the national court. In particular, the Court extended EU criminal obligations to VAT frauds considering them a pre-existing obligation stemming directly from the Treaties, rather than merely from the PIF Convention. It seems clear that the Court intended to reaffirm the EU competence in the field of VAT frauds and wanted this message to sound loud and clear to the Council engaged, at the time, in the negotiations for the PIF Directive.

The immediate consequence of the principle stemming out of *Taricco I* would have been that the exclusion of VAT frauds from the draft PIF Directive, under negotiation at that time, would have had a limited impact because the EU is grounding its criminal competence on such offences directly on the TFEU.[25] That was a clear signal to the opponents to the inclusion of VAT frauds in the PIF Directive and, as a matter of fact, this has resulted in a successful policy choice: VAT frauds are currently part of the approved PIF Directive and, as such, they fall within the material scope of the EPPO, which will come into force in 2019.[26]

[22] S Peers, 'The Italian Job: The CJEU Strengthens Criminal Law Protection of the EU's Finances' (EU Law Analysis, 2015) http://eulawanalysis.blogspot.com/2015/09/the-italian-job-cjeu-strengthens.html (last accessed on 4 March 2019).

[23] Directive 2017/1371/EU of the European Parliament and of the Council of 5 July 2017 on the fight against fraud to the Union's financial interests by means of criminal law [2017] OJ L198/29.

[24] Highlighting the link, V Franssen, 'EU Criminal Law and *effet utile*: A Critical Examination of the Union's Use of Criminal Law to Achieve Effective Enforcement' in JB Banach-Gutierrez and C Harding (eds), *EU Criminal Law and Policy. Values, Principles and Methods* (Routledge, 2018) 90–91.

[25] Peers (n 22).

[26] Council Regulation (EU) 2017/1939 implementing enhanced cooperation on the establishment of the European Public Prosecutor's Office ('the EPPO') [2017] OJ L283/1, entered into force on 20 November 2017.

In addition, even for those States that opted-out of the PIF Directive, such as Ireland and Denmark, according to *Taricco I* they will still be bound by the PIF Convention and even more by the obligations stemming from the Treaties. Emphasising the role of Article 325 TFEU as a potential direct legal basis to increase EU competence in the field of criminal law was thus crucial at the time of *Taricco I*. In this light, the reasons that inspired that decision are clear: a pan-European, comprehensive, voluntary choice to boost the protection of EU financial interests, whatever it takes. It is not the first time that the Court has supported the policy choices of the Commission, adopting controversial decisions in order to steer the political debate in a certain direction and to force the hand of reluctant Member States.[27] And it is not the first time that this has happened in criminal law. What is new is that in supporting these policy choices the Court directly affects the position of the individuals. For this – and other – reasons, the decision triggered a harsh debate in the literature, highlighting the sensitiveness of the issues at stake.

However, on the other hand, the majority of Italian scholars and some others strongly criticised the decision both in terms of its methodology and content, raising several arguments.[28]

The first relates to the breach of the legality principle, being rules on limitation periods in criminal matters considered in Italy as *substantive in character* and consequently falling within the scope of the principle of legality referred to in Article 25 of the Italian Constitution as part of substantive criminal law.

Legality imposes not only a clear and explicit content of the rule but also its entry into force before the crime is committed (non-retroactive effect of criminal law). Limitation periods cannot be modified by the courts after the commission of the crime and judges are not free to determine the duration of criminal proceedings on a case-by-case basis. To the contrary, in *Taricco I* the Court seemed to impose the disapplication of more favourable rules on time limitation in respect to offences committed prior to the CJEU decision, leading as such to the violation of the principle on non-retroactivity of criminal law, protected by Article 25(2) of the Italian Constitution.[29]

Second, according to the *Taricco I* decision, the duty to set aside national provisions that are incompatible with EU law was not absolute, but rather left to the prudent assessment of national courts. In other terms, the CJEU did not foresee that the disapplication entailed an automatic imprescriptible criminal trial for every VAT fraud, but it obliged internal courts to disapply national rules so far as they prevent effective and dissuasive penalties 'in a significant number of cases of

[27] Case C-176/03 *Commission v Council* ECLI:EU:C:2005:542.

[28] E Billis 'The European Court of Justice: A 'Quasi-Constitutional Court' in Criminal Matters?' (2016) 7 *New Journal of European Criminal Law* 20, 31–32; A Camon, 'La torsione di un sistema. Riflessioni intorno alla sentenza Taricco' (2016) *Archivio della Nuova Procedura Penale* 1–6.

[29] S Manacorda, 'The Taricco Saga: A Risk or an Opportunity for European Criminal Law?' (2018) 9 *New Journal of European Criminal Law* 4–11, 6.

serious fraud affecting the financial interests of the European Union'. As a result, national courts were called to carry out a twofold problematic empirical assessment: first, looking at the seriousness of the fraud and, second, the quantity of cases in which no sanction was imposed out of the effects of limitation periods. The Court did not however, sufficiently detail the rules that national courts should consider in order to determine such issues and thus it allowed a limitless discretion of national judges.[30] As several scholars observed, this assessment cannot be left to the single national court because, first, it lies outside its judicial mandate and, second, the judges do not have the means to reach a plausible and stable result, to the detriment of legality and equality of treatment.[31]

Third, the CJEU identified Article 325 TFEU as the provision that would justify the duty for national courts to disapply conflicting internal rules. By so doing, the Court attached a vertical, direct negative effect to a provision that merely substantiates a general obligation imposing the 'imperative of assimilation'[32] and lacks, at the very least, the requirement of being unconditional.[33] In order to support the weakness of Article 325 TFEU as a potential legal basis, several scholars referred to the long negotiations of the PIF Directive, where the content of Article 325 TFEU triggered a clash between the Commission, suggesting the latter as the optimal legal basis for the new text,[34] and the Council, imposing finally and victoriously Article 83(2) TFEU, emphasising the principle of conferral rather that the *effet utile*,[35] as the Commission wished for.[36] Is it thus convincing to require a national court to set aside national criminal rules conflicting with the duty enshrined in Article 325 TFEU for the Member States to protect the EU financial interests, whilst modifying the same rules to clearly imply a harmonising legal instrument on a different legal basis?

[30] C Sotis, 'Il limite come controlimite. Riflessioni sulla vicenda Taricco, con una postilla sulla ordinanza 24 del 2017 della Corte costituzionale "tra Antigone e Creonte io sto con Porzia"' in M D'Amico and I Pellizzone (eds), *Principio di legalità penale e diritto costituzionale. Problematiche attuali* (Giuffrè, 2017) 185–234.

[31] Sotis, *ibid*; Manacorda (n 29).

[32] DE Khan, R Geiger, 'Art. 325 TFEU' in R Geiger, DE Khan and M Kotzur (eds), *European Union Treaties. A Commentary* (Beck-Hart, 2015) 1009.

[33] G Zaccaroni, F Rossi, 'Settling the Dust? An Analysis of Taricco II from an EU Constitutional and Criminal Law Perspective (European Law Blog, 2018) https://europeanlawblog.eu/2018/04/12/settling-the-dust-an-analysis-of-taricco-ii-from-an-eu-constitutional-and-criminal-law-perspective/ (last accessed on 4 March 2019). LS Rossi, 'Come risolvere la 'questione Taricco' senza far leva sull'Art. 4 par. 2 TUE' (SIDIblog, 2017) www.sidiblog.org/2017/05/17/come-risolvere-la-questione-taricco-senza-far-leva-sullart-4-par-2-tue/ (last accessed on 4 March 2019).

[34] Stronger than its predecessor, the former Article 280 TEC, and not limited by the so-called 'non-affection clause', see IE Fromm, 'Ius puniendi: The Right of the Institutions of the EC to Protect the Financial Interests of the EC from Fraud' (2008) *European Journal of Crime, Criminal Law and Criminal Justice* 16, 125 at 135–38; Franssen (n 24) 89.

[35] See R Schütze, 'Direct Effects and indirect Effects of Union law' in R Schütze and T Tridimas, *Oxford Principles of European Law. Volume I: The European Legal Order* (Oxford University Press, 2018) 265–299.

[36] See Franssen (n 22).

III. Back to Court. Constitutional Gatekeepers Raising their Voices

The harsh debate in the literature was promptly echoed in court decisions.

Immediately after the CJEU decision, the Italian Court of Cassation adopted a decision in a similar VAT fraud case in which it fully adhered to the *dictum* of the European court, setting aside the rules on limitation periods in force at the time of the crime and applying the less favourable ones.[37] Conversely, the Court of Appeal of Milan[38] and thereafter the Court of Cassation,[39] confronted in those very days with the same issue, detected an inconsistency between the *Taricco* decision and the Italian Constitution. Both courts hence raised the issue before the national Constitutional Court, arguing that the duty of setting aside limitation rules, as stemming from the *Taricco* judgment, is incompatible with the constitutional principle of legality and non-retroactivity.

The Italian Constitutional Court honoured the traditional dialogue with the Court of Justice and courageously referred the question back to Luxembourg. The request is a masterpiece of judicial diplomacy:[40] it formally invites the CJEU to a new dialogue[41] while threatening the re-appeal.[42] The Italian Court avoided challenging the Court of Justice's authority in assessing and interpreting the Treaty provisions. Indeed, no reference is made to the correct interpretation of Article 325 TFEU but the request rather focuses on the duty to respect fundamental rights when it comes to criminal law provisions.

The Corte Costituzionale thus foresaw a possible breach of the legality principle which might flow from the obligation stated in the *Taricco* judgment to disapply the limitation periods having regard to two different aspects. First, on the ground that, since limitation rules in the Italian legal system are part of substantive criminal law, those rules shall be defined by law and be reasonably foreseeable by individuals at the time when the alleged offences are committed and cannot be retroactively altered *in peius*. Second, as limitation periods are part of the rules defining criminal liability, their legal basis shall be precise enough to delimit and guide the national court's assessment.

In particular, the Italian Constitutional Court makes clear that a confirmation of the decision in *Taricco* would lead to a clash between the European *dictum* and the internal constitutional rules, to the point of forcing the Italian Constitutional

[37] Consequently, the conviction of the defendants as declared by the lower courts was confirmed by the Court of Cassation, Third Section, 15 September 2015, n 2210.

[38] Court of Appeal of Milan, order of 18 September 2015.

[39] Court of Cassation, Third Section, 8 July 2016, n 28346.

[40] ML Ferrante, 'L'ordinanza della Corte costituzionale sull'affaire Taricco: una decisione "diplomatica" ma ferma' (2017) 1 *Dirittifondamentali.it* 1–23, 22 www.dirittifondamentali.it/media/1836/1-2017-ferrante-caso-taricco.pdf (last accessed on 4 March 2019).

[41] G Rugge, 'The Italian Constitutional Court in Taricco: Unleashing the Normative Potential of 'National Identity'?' (2017) 7 *Questions of International Law* 21–29.

[42] D Paris, 'Carrot and Stick. The Italian Constitutional Court's Preliminary Reference in the Case Taricco' (2017) 37 *Questions of International Law* 5–20, 5.

Court to resort to the so-called counter-limits doctrine and act unilaterally. The counter-limits doctrine refers to the respect of supreme principles of the national constitutional order and inalienable human rights as a prerequisite for the applicability of EU law.[43] In the Italian system, it dates back to the 1973 judgment of the Constitutional Court in the *Frontini* case[44] in which the Italian Court stated its exclusive power to challenge – and eventually exclude – the applicability of EU law where that would encroach upon the supreme principles of the constitutional order.[45] Therefore, even though 'the recognition of the primacy of EU law is an established fact'[46] within the case law of the Italian Constitutional Court, when European law is not compliant with the *Kern* of national constitutional principles, the duty for the Constitutional Court would be to prevent the conflict and to declare the national law authorising the ratification and implementation of the EU Treaties unconstitutional.[47]

Against this background, the national court firmly states that the principle of legality in criminal matters is

> an expression of a supreme principle of the internal legal framework, which has been posited in order to safeguard the inviolable rights of the individual insofar as it requires that criminal rules must be precise and must not have retroactive effect.[48]

Despite the appreciation this decision undoubtedly deserves, none is perfect. The Italian Constitutional Court seems to play the game of the three cards when it comes to the nature of limitation periods. They are flaunted as part of the *noyau dur* of the legality principle defining national identity before the Court of Justice, whereas, more or less at the same time, they are described as 'an irrelevant feature of Italian law'.[49]

The request thus formally reopens the judicial dialogue but, at its very heart, what the Italian judges are asking for is a confirmation of the supremacy of national constitutional rights when dealing with criminal law.[50] Shorn of its kind

[43] On the 'controlimiti' theory, see A Bernardi, 'I controlimiti al diritto dell'Unione europea e il loro discusso ruolo in ambito penale' in A Bernardi, *I controlimiti. Primato delle norme europee e difesa dei principi costituzionali* (Jovene, 2017) VII.

[44] Italian Constitutional Court, judgment of 27 December 1973, no 183.

[45] Sotis (n 30).

[46] See C Amalfitano, O Pollicino, 'Two Courts, Two Languages? The Taricco Saga Ends on a Worrying Note' (VerfBlog, 2018) https://verfassungsblog.de/two-courts-two-languages-the-taricco-saga-ends-on-a-worrying-note/ (last accessed on 4 March 2019).

[47] See the previous decisions of the Italian Constitutional Court in this field, notably judgment of 21 April 1989 no 232; judgment of 8 June 1984 no.170; and judgment of 27 December 1973 no 183.

[48] Constitutional Court, order of 26 January 2017 no 24, available at www.cortecostituzionale.it/documenti/download/doc/recent_judgments/O_24_2017.pdf (last accessed on 4 March 2019), para 2.

[49] See the words of Judge Pinto De Albuquerque referred to the decision of the Italian Constituional Court no 49 of 2015 on non-conviction based confiscations in his partly concurring, partly dissenting Opinion in the case *G.I.E.M. S.R.L. and others v Italy* App no 1828/06 (ECtHR, 28 June 2018) paras 87–88.

[50] C Amalfitano, 'La vicenda Taricco nuovamente al vaglio della Corte di giustizia: qualche breve riflessione a caldo' (Eurojus.it, 2017) http://rivista.eurojus.it/la-vicenda-taricco-nuovamente-al-vaglio-della-corte-di-giustizia-qualche-breve-riflessione-a-caldo/ (last accessed on 4 March 2019).

wording, the gentle invitation to review its previous decision delivered in *Taricco I* sounds more like an *ultimatum*,[51] as some scholars already highlighted. Extremely relevant from the point of view of European law – in particular on the scope of application of Article 53 of the Charter[52] – is the part of the order in which the Italian Constitutional Court draws a distinction between the EU carousel fraud in *Taricco* and the *Melloni*[53] decision. According to the Italian Constitutional Court, the case at stake is 'clearly distinct' from *Melloni* in the sense that the application of the Spanish Constitution would have 'ruptured the unity of EU law within an area based on reciprocal trust that has a uniform legislative framework'.[54] The field of *in absentia* decisions as a solid basis for a European arrest warrant was already harmonised, whereas the rules on limitation periods were not, at least until the recent approval of the PIF Directive. As a consequence, in *Melloni* no discretion was left for the Member State and the more protective standard of the Spanish Constitution was to be set aside, whereas in the current case,

> the Member State has quite a lot of discretion under EU law, and the CJEU recognizes such discretion and allows the Constitutional Court to make full use of it in order to uphold the higher standard of protection under Italian law.[55]

IV. Back to Luxembourg with the Opinion of AG Yves Bot: Confirming *Taricco*, Reaffirming *Melloni*, Reinvigorating *Internationale Handelgesellschaft*[56]

The preliminary ruling asked by the Italian Constitutional Court brought the case back to Luxembourg and in the hands of AG Yves Bot.[57] In its long and cogent

[51] Term used by M Caianiello, 'Processo penale e prescrizione nel quadro della giurisprudenza europea. Dialogo tra sistemi o conflitto identitario?' (2017) 2 *Diritto Penale Contemporaneo* 216–30.

[52] M Condinanzi, P Iannuccelli, 'Articolo 53' in R Mastroianni, O Pollicino, S Allegrezza, F Pappalardo, O Razzolini (eds), *Carta dei diritti fondamentali dell'Unione europea* (Giuffrè, 2017) 1085–97; Peers (n 22).

[53] Case C-399/11 *Melloni* EU:C:2013:107. In that case, relating to a Spanish constitutional provision on procedural safeguards in case of convictions adopted *in absentia*, the Grand Chamber of the CJEU held that no further requirements for the enforcement of a European arrest warrant could be imposed under the terms of a Member State's Constitution in addition to those agreed to by consensus reached by all the Member States regarding the scope to be given under EU law to the procedural rights enjoyed by persons convicted *in absentia*.

[54] Constitutional Court order of 26 January 2017, no 24 (n 48) para 8.

[55] D Sarmiento, 'To Bow at the Rhythm of an Italian Tune' (Despite our Differences Blog, 2017) https://despiteourdifferencesblog.wordpress.com/2017/12/05/to-bow-at-the-rhythm-of-an-italian-tune/ (last accessed on 4 March 2019).

[56] These are the smart labels inspired by J Arlettaz, 'La fin de Taricco. Le juge de l'Union face à la tradition romano-germanique' (2018) 11 *L'Actualité Juridique Droit Administratif* 618–19.

[57] It was its conclusions that inspired the Court of Justice in the aforementioned *Melloni* (n 53).

conclusions, AG Bot goes through all the different issues raised by the Italian Supreme Court, resolutely rejecting all of them.

AG Bot opens his conclusions with several preliminary observations that set up such a strong narrative that will influence the future debate in the field of criminal justice. It is the doctrine of *primauté dure et pure*, where AG Bot seems to define a sort of European counter-limit, opposable to whatever conflict relating to fundamental rights. A revealing indicator of his wish of uniformity can be found in the suggestion to develop, in the future, an autonomous European concept of interruption of the limitation period, to be intended as meaning that 'each investigative act and any act necessarily extending it interrupts the limitation period, that act then causing a new period, identical to the initial period, to run, while the limitation period which has already elapsed will then be cancelled'.[58] We would welcome the pleading in favour of common definitions if it is intended as a wider effort in the field of harmonisation of criminal justice. It seems nevertheless implausible to share a common meaning of 'interruption' without standardising the different statutes of limitation and the penalty amount, according to which the time limits are determined. It seems even more difficult to identify which 'acts' of criminal procedure would determine such effect without a serious understanding of procedural rules. EU criminal policies are far from such an attempt and courts cannot play that substitute role.[59]

As for the core issue at stake, AG Bot entirely reaffirms the *Taricco* decision on the duty for the national courts to disapply the absolute limitation period resulting from the Italian criminal provisions when they prevent the imposition of effective and dissuasive penalties for serious European frauds in a significant number of cases. In this regard, the AG acknowledges as a matter of fact that the criteria imposed by the CJEU decision in order to justify the setting aside of national legislation, *id est* the 'seriousness of the fraud' and the 'significant number of cases' appear to introduce 'an element of subjectivity'[60] in the judicial assessment. As he correctly observes, national courts are called to a delicate operation on the existence of a 'systemic risk of impunity' for which they might not be well-equipped.

Concerning the arguments raised on Article 4(2) TEU and Article 53 Charter of Fundamental Rights (CFR), AG Bot declares to strongly disagree with the Italian Constitutional Court on the interpretation to be given to both provisions. As for Article 4(2) TEU, it should be intended as the duty to respect the self-conception that the single Member State has developed along its history,[61] including the basic political and constitutional structures. It would thus be a mistake to think that modifications of the limitation periods would affect the national identity of the Italian Republic. Less embraceable, however, is AG Bot's formalistic approach on

[58] Case C-42/17 *M.A.S. and M.B.*, Opinion of AG Bot, EU:C:2017:564, paras 108–109.
[59] Arlettaz (n 56) 619–22.
[60] *M.A.S. and M.B.*, Opinion of AG Bot (n 58) para 112.
[61] Khan, Geiger (n 32) 1009.

the constitutional provisions that would define the Italian national identity, that would be composed only by the principles classified as fundamental as set out in Articles 1 to 12 of the Italian Constitution, in the words of AG Bot, with the exclusion of the legality principle. History, culture, social and political features, including the protection of fundamental rights, lie at the very heart of the Italian national identity, even though their Constitutional basis is not part of the first 12 provisions.

Even more problematic is the analysis of Article 53 CFR and its impact on the present case. AG Bot seems to accept the distance between *Melloni* and the present case, as suggested by the request of the Italian Constitutional Court, but he nevertheless considers it possible to deny any margin of discretion to the Member States, even in the fields which have not yet been harmonised at European level, according to the following arguments. First, the European standard of protection of legality in criminal matters would exclude limitation periods, being a procedural 'simple precondition' of the examination of the case,[62] from the core area protected by Article 49 CFR, as stated by the case law of the ECHR, extending the references to the *Previti v Italy*[63] and *Borcea v Romania*[64] cases. That being the European standard of protection, AG Bot emphasises the 'specific nature of EU law'[65] as the main argument to deny any room for national discretion, even when it comes to Constitutional fundamental rights. The

> specific nature of EU law means that the level of protection deriving from the interpretation of a national Constitution cannot be automatically transposed to the EU level, nor can it be relied upon as an argument in the context of the application of EU law.[66]

Allowing the Member States to apply higher standards of protection in the different fields of EU law, however, would be 'tantamount to disregarding the fact that the exercise of determining the level of protection for fundamental rights to be achieved cannot be separated from the context in which it is carried out'.[67] As a consequence, national Constitutions should be 'adjusted depending on the different interests at stake'.[68] This statement does not come as a surprise, being so close to the conclusions AG Bot delivered in the *Melloni* case. What is different is the lack

[62] *M.A.S. and M.B.*, Opinion of AG Bot (n 58) para 138, recalling *Previti v Italy*, App no 45291/06 (ECtHR, 8 December 2009) para 80.

[63] *Previti v Italy*, *ibid.* There seems to be, however, a difference between the ratio of the *Previti* case and the decision in *Taricco*. The first recognised the procedural nature of these rules and submitted them to the *tempus regit actum* instead of the more restrictive principle of legality that informs substantive criminal law. *Tempus regit actum* means the possibility for the legislator to modify procedural rules after the crime has been committed (but before the procedural act should take place and in the lack of arbitrariness), whereas what the CJEU suggested (sic! ordered) in *Taricco* is something completely different. The *dictum* of the Court is to ignore national provisions and ban time limitations of certain crimes, not prescribed by the law but decided by the courts upon assessment of vague requirements.

[64] *Borcea v Romania* (dec) App no 55959/14 (ECtHR, 22 September 2015).

[65] *M.A.S. and M.B.*, Opinion of AG Bot (n 58) para 150.

[66] *M.A.S. and M.B.*, Opinion of AG Bot (n 58) para 153.

[67] *M.A.S. and M.B.*, Opinion of AG Bot (n 58) para 152.

[68] *M.A.S. and M.B.*, Opinion of AG Bot (n 58) para 154.

of a common definition at the EU level of what limitation periods should look like in case of a fraud. But this difference, in the reading of AG Bot, would not impose a different solution, because, first, Article 47(2) CFR refers to 'reasonable time' and would therefore constitute the archetype of the harmonised rule.[69] Second, the Italian Constitution, if applied as suggested by the Italian Constitutional Court, would 'compromise the primacy of EU law', being an obstacle to a duty set up by the CJEU. And third, the interpretation suggested by the Italian Court affects the effectiveness of EU law because the EU frauds would not 'be the subject of a final conviction (…) and will therefore go unpunished'. As a consequence, Article 53 CFR cannot, according to AG Bot, allow the application of a higher standard of protection.

Several reasons militate against the three arguments raised by AG Bot on the interpretation of Article 53 CFR.

First, 'reasonable time', in Article 47 CFR[70] as well as in Article 6§1 ECHR,[71] usually refers to the need for the courts to take a decision within a 'reasonable' timeframe, putting an end to uncertainty.[72] The ECtHR declared 'a war to unreasonable delays',[73] because 'keeping an individual in a protracted state of doubt (…) may be considered akin to a denial of justice'.[74] Even when the ECtHR finds a case complex, the main criterion to justify a certain delay, it rarely considers a reasonable time for a criminal proceedings to go beyond seven and a half years.[75] In the words of the ECtHR,

> limitation may be defined as the statutory right of an offender not to be prosecuted or tried after the lapse of a certain period of time since the offence was committed. Limitation periods (…) serve several purposes, which include ensuring legal certainty and finality and preventing infringements of the rights of defendants.[76]

It would be no more than a *soupçon* of a caricature to use this right as an argument to sustain, first, an accomplished harmonisation of statutes of limitations and, second, its drastic de facto abrogation.

Second, when it comes to the primacy of EU law, the AG emphasises the 'catastrophic consequences' that the primacy would derive from the acceptance of a broader understanding of legality as a general principle of EU law. Again, like his

[69] *M.A.S. and M.B.*, Opinion of AG Bot (n 58) para 165.

[70] See DP Domenicucci, F Filpo, 'La tutela giurisdizionale effettiva nel diritto dell'Unione Europea' in Mastroianni, Pollicino, Allegrezza, Pappalardo, Razzolini (eds) (n 52) 876–78; Peers (n 22).

[71] S Trechsel, *Human Rights in Criminal Proceedings* (Oxford University Press, 2006) 134–52.

[72] P Ricoeur, *Le juste* (Esprit, 1995) 98.

[73] S Galand-Carval, 'The European Court of Human Rights Declares War on Unreasonable Delays' (1996) *St Louis-Warsaw Transatlantic Law Journal* 109–26.

[74] F Edel, *The Length of Civil and Criminal Proceedings in the Case-Law of the European Court of Human Rights* (Council of Europe Publishing, 2007) 6.

[75] *Dementjeva v Latvia* (dec.) App no 17458/10 (ECtHR, 13 March 2012); *Breinesberger and Wenzelhuemer v Austria* (dec.) App no 46601/07 (ECtHR, 27 November 2012); *Ivanovas v Latvia* (dec.) App no 25769/02 (ECtHR, 4 December 2012) para 103; *Krakolinig v Austria* App no 33992/07 (ECtHR, 10 May 2012) para 104.

[76] *Coëme v Belgium* (n 7) para 146.

Opinion in *Melloni*, Bot seems to get confused on the difference between primacy and uniformity.[77] Primacy does not mean banning the differences and it includes the protection of fundamental rights as part of EU law, that being the primary role of criminal procedure. Efficiency cannot overturn every procedural rule that limits the action of enforcement agencies.[78]

V. How to Build up a *Revirement*: The *M.A.S.* Decision of the Court of Justice. *Repetita iuvant*?

Cautious, prudent, accommodating, diplomatic, conciliatory – but also a 'worrying example of a weakly reasoned court decision' bowing to political pressure[79] – are just a few of the definitions used in literature to describe the decision rendered by the CJEU in the case *M.A.S. and M.B.* on 5 December 2017,[80] immediately nicknamed '*Taricco II*'.[81]

Keeping an astonishing silence on several pivotal points – no mention of the notions of constitutional or national identity, no direct reference to *Melloni* or to Article 53 CFR[82] – the decision reaches out to the Italian Constitutional Court and distances itself from the Opinion of AG Bot. No iron fist but rather a politically sensitive *revirement*.[83]

The CJEU first recalls the primary function of the preliminary ruling procedure as provided for in Article 267 TFEU: an instrument of cooperation to set up a dialogue between national and European courts to secure the uniform interpretation of EU law and ensuring its consistency.[84] But suddenly this reference becomes instrumental for the Court in rather highlighting the limits of its first

[77] M Bassini, O Pollicino 'The Opinion of Advocate General Bot in Taricco II: Seven "Deadly" Sins and a Modest Proposal' (*VerfBlog*, 2017) https://verfassungsblog.de/the-opinion-of-advocate-general-bot-in-taricco-ii-seven-deadly-sins-and-a-modest-proposal/ (last accessed on 4 March 2019).

[78] On the inherent function of fundamental rights in criminal law to limit efficiency see infra, last para 7.

[79] D Burchardt, 'Belittling the Primacy of EU Law' (*VerfBlog*, 2017) https://verfassungsblog.de/belittling-the-primacy-of-eu-law-in-taricco-ii/ (last accessed on 4 March 2019).

[80] Case C-42/17 *M.A.S and M.B.* EU:C:2017:936.

[81] M Bassini, O Pollicino, 'Defusing the Taricco Bomb through Fostering Constitutional Tolerance: All Roads Lead to Rome' (VerfBlog, 2017) https://verfassungsblog.de/defusing-the-taricco-bomb-through-fostering-constitutional-tolerance-all-roads-lead-to-rome/ (last accessed on 4 March 2019); C Cupelli, 'Ecce Taricco II. Fra dialogo e diplomazia, l'attesa sentenza della Corte di giustizia' (Diritto Penale Contemporaneo, 2017) www.penalecontemporaneo.it/d/5755-ecce-taricco-ii-fra-dialogo-e-diplomazia-lattesa-sentenza-della-corte-di-giustizia (last accessed on 4 March 2019); R Bin, 'Taricco Tango. Quale sarà il prossimo passo?' (Forum di Quaderni costituzionali, 2018) www.forumcostituzionale.it/wordpress/wp-content/uploads/2018/02/bin.pdf (last accessed on 4 March 2019).

[82] Arlettaz (n 56) 620.

[83] Some scholars rather define it as a '*renoncement*', see E Dubout, 'La primauté du droit de l'Union et la passage au pluralisme constitutionnel' (2018) *Revue Trimestrielle de Droit Européen* 563–86, 565.

[84] *M.A.S. and M.B.* (n 80) paras 22–23, quoting, meaningfully, Opinion 2/13 of the Court of 18 December 2014, EU:C:2014:2454, para 176. See Amalfitano, Pollicino (n 46).

decision – the so-called *Taricco I*. At the time, the CJEU acknowledged that the issue at stake was limited to the 'factual and legislative context of the questions as described in the order for reference'.[85] As a matter of fact, in recalling the questions raised by the Italian Constitutional Court with the second request for preliminary ruling, the CJEU clarifies that those arguments 'were not drawn to its attention in the case in which the *Taricco* judgment was given'.[86] In other words, the CJEU acknowledges how its previous limited knowledge might have affected its first decision.[87]

The *M.A.S.* decision nevertheless confirms the previous *Taricco* principle of September 2015: Article 325(1) and (2) TFEU require the Member States to counter illegal activities affecting the EU financial interests, including the collection of VAT revenues, through effective and deterrent measures, equivalent to those taken to combat fraud affecting their own financial interests. In this light, 'Member States are in breach of their obligations under Article 325(1) and (2) TFEU if the criminal penalties adopted to punish serious VAT fraud do not enable the collection in full of VAT to be guaranteed effectively'. And this duty concerns primarily the national legislature that shall provide for limitation periods that enable compliance with the obligations stemming from Article 325 TFEU.[88] It is clear in these words the echo of the scholars' criticism toward *Taricco I* in as much as it did not sufficiently highlight that the obligations under Article 325 TFEU are first and foremost directed to the national parliaments and governments rather than to national courts.[89] The national courts' duty to disapply internal incompatible rules should in principle play a mere ancillary role.[90]

However, the CJEU clearly reaffirms – in line with *Taricco I* and the ECtHR case law[91] – that a legislative extension of a limitation period even after the crime has been committed and 'its immediate application to alleged offences that are not yet time-barred do not, in principle, infringe the principle that offences and penalties must be defined by law'.[92] This statement might have important consequences in future disputes relating to the legality principle. The CJEU seems to say strong and loud that retroactive application of rules related to criminal law other than the ones strictly relating to criminal liability is perfectly in line with that principle, and that it is for the CJEU itself to decide what falls within the scope of legality *stricto sensu* and what does not. But the strong statement is partially mitigated by the

[85] *M.A.S. and M.B.* (n 80) para 23. See also, Case C-39/16 *Argenta Spaarbank* EU:C:2017:813, para 38. Strong criticism towards this 'excuse' comes from Dubout (n 83) 563–86, 565.

[86] *M.A.S. and M.B.* (n 80) para 28.

[87] A reference to this issue can be found in M Nisticò, 'Taricco II: il passo indietro della Corte di giustizia e le prospettive del supposto dialogo tra le Corti' (2018) 1 *Osservatorio Aic*, 3.

[88] *M.A.S. and M.B.* (n 80) para 41.

[89] C Sotis, 'Obblighi comunitari di tutela e opzione penale: una dialettica perpetua?' (2002) *Rivista italiana di diritto e procedura penale* 171.

[90] *M.A.S. and M.B.* (n 80) para 28.

[91] See *Tarrico I* (n 8).

[92] *M.A.S. and M.B.* (n 80) para 42.

fact that, first, the protection of financial interests is a shared competence within the meaning of Article 4(2) TFEU and, second, the limitation periods were not harmonised at the time of the offence and have only been partially harmonised by Directive 2017/1371. As a consequence, Italy as a Member State was – at the time of the criminal proceedings – still free to provide that limitation periods 'like the rules on the definition of the offences, and the determination of penalties, form part of (Italian) substantive criminal law'.[93] Such a possibility nevertheless expires when a certain degree of harmonisation is introduced at the European level. In the specific field here at issue, the CJEU seems to affirm that harmonisation puts an end to the power for national legislators – and courts – to determine the scope of application of the legality principle. In other words, from the very moment in which an agreement is found at the European level on a specific aspect of criminal justice, it is rather for the EU legislator and for the CJEU to decide the corollaries of those rules.

VI. Mapping the Limits of 'Disapplication' while Defining the European Legality Principle in Criminal Matters

A crucial step to build up the *revirement* focuses on the protection of fundamental rights of the accused persons. The CJEU first recalls *Taricco I* and refers back to the role of the judge:

> It is therefore for the competent national courts to give full effect to the obligations under Article 325(1) and (2) TFEU and to disapply national provisions, including rules on limitation, which, in connection with proceedings concerning serious VAT infringements, prevent the application of effective and deterrent penalties to counter fraud affecting the financial interests of the Union.[94]

But this confirmation comes in *M.A.S.* with a crucial caveat.[95] In deciding on the disapplication of national criminal law, national courts 'are required to ensure that the fundamental rights of persons accused of committing criminal offences are observed'.[96] In other words, setting aside internal incompatible rules is a duty

> unless that disapplication entails a breach of the principle that offences and penalties must be defined by law because of the lack of precision of the applicable law or because of the retroactive application of legislation imposing conditions of criminal liability stricter than those in force at the time the infringement was committed.[97]

[93] *M.A.S. and M.B.* (n 80) para 45.
[94] *M.A.S. and M.B.* (n 80) para 39; *Taricco and others*, Opinion of AG Kokott (n 2) paras 49, 58.
[95] Manacorda (n 29) 7.
[96] *M.A.S. and M.B.* (n 80) paras 46, 48.
[97] *M.A.S. and M.B.* (n 80) para 62.

These statements lead straight to the very heart of the *revirement* of the *Taricco* saga and are worthy of being analysed in detail.

The need to balance defence rights with the duty to set aside national rules, as we previously mentioned, was already affirmed in the first *Taricco I* decision.[98] Some scholars correctly emphasised that the protection of the defendant's rights represented the tool for the Italian courts to avoid a radical conflict with the Court of Justice.[99] They suggested that Article 6(3) TEU could work as a sound reference to apply as a possible limit to the enforcement of *Taricco I* based on the constitutional traditions of Member States, meant as an inherently pluralistic notion. This provision, admittedly, ranks fundamental rights as resulting from the constitutional traditions common to Member States, among the 'general principles of EU law'.

Nevertheless, at the time the Italian Constitutional Court preferred to avoid an open conflict and referred the case back, forcing the CJEU to define the meaning and scope of legality in criminal law. In particular, the principle that offences and penalties must be defined by law entails the right to reasonably foresee the consequences of disapplication. In the present case, the negative effects on the individuals were linked to an uncertain parameter such as the fact that Italian limitation periods were preventing the effective punishment of a 'significant number' of 'serious' EU frauds. This requirement, the Court affirms, is not compatible with the foreseeability, precision and non-retroactivity that should characterise criminal law.[100]

In this way, the CJEU emphasises the principle of legality as part of the common constitutional traditions of Member States as enshrined in Article 49 of the EU Charter.[101] Here the CJEU is defining the European dimension of the legality principle in criminal matters. And it does define it via recalling both common constitutional traditions, international treaties and in particular Article 7(1) ECHR and the related case law.[102]

Foreseeability, precision and non-retroactivity thus represent the inherent *noyau dur* of legality in its European dimension as protected by Article 49 CFR.[103] First, criminal law must grant accessibility and foreseeability as regards both the

[98] *Taricco and others*, Opinion of AG Kokott (n 2) para 53, according to which 'if the national court decides to disapply the national provisions at issue, it must also ensure that the fundamental rights of the persons concerned are respected'.

[99] R Sicurella, 'Effectiveness of EU Law and Protection of Fundamental Rights. The Questions Settled and the New Challenges after the CJEU Decision in the M.A.S. and M.B. Case (C-42/17)' (2018) 1 *New Journal of European Criminal Law* 24–30.

[100] *M.A.S. and M.B.* (n 80) para 51.

[101] *M.A.S. and M.B.* (n 80) para 52. Amalfitano, Pollicino (n 46).

[102] *M.A.S. and M.B.* (n 80) para 52–55. As for the ECtHR case law, see *Cantoni v France* App no 17862/91 (ECtHR, 15 November 19969) para 29; *E.K. v Turkey* App no 28496/95 (ECtHR, 7 February 2002) para 51; *Achour v France* App no 67335/01 (ECtHR, 29 March 2006) para 41; and *OAO Neftyanaya Kompaniya Yukos v Russia* (n 7) paras 567–70.

[103] See R Sicurella, 'Art. 49. Legalità e proporzionalità nel diritto penale sostanziale' in Mastroianni, Pollicino, Allegrezza, Pappalardo, Razzolini (eds) (n 52) 972–1001; M Panzavolta, 'Art. 49. Legalità e proporzionalità nel diritto penale processuale' in *ibid*, 1001–14.

definition of the offence and the determination of the penalty.[104] Second, the law must be precise and define offences and penalties clearly; this condition

> is met where the individual is in a position, on the basis of the wording of the relevant provision and if necessary with the help of the interpretation made by the courts, to know which acts or omissions will make him criminally liable.[105]

Third, the

> principle of non-retroactivity of the criminal law means in particular that a court cannot, in the course of criminal proceedings, impose a criminal penalty for conduct which is not prohibited by a national rule adopted before the commission of the alleged offence or aggravate the rules on criminal liability of those against whom such proceedings are brought.[106]

With no further specification, the CJEU acknowledges that the Italian system considers limitation periods as part of substantive criminal law. And this happens without any comparative analysis confirming a common constitutional tradition – which would have given a potential negative result.[107] It is therefore clear that the Court shows tolerance towards a higher standard of protection provided by a single Member State, and offers an appalling silence on the open denial of the *Melloni* doctrine. In the light of the *M.A.S.* judgment, in no way can limitation periods be considered as part of European substantive criminal law. This area is exclusive pertinence of rules defining offences and penalties. Nevertheless, the CJEU accepts the possibility of a variable geometry in the way legality should be intended and Article 49 of the Charter applied: when the European integration process did not lead to a common understanding, a national *marge d'appréciation* is still possible.[108] And this is the case for limitation periods.[109]

Furthermore, the CJEU emphasises how the precision and non-retroactivity of criminal law or judicial decisions worsening the position of the individuals prevents the full application of the *Taricco I* rule to crimes committed before the 8th September 2015, ie the date of publication of that decision. As a consequence, national courts should not disapply internal provisions on statute of limitations if the defendants 'could thus be made subject, retroactively, to conditions of criminal

[104] *M.A.S. and M.B.* (n 80) para 55.

[105] *M.A.S. and M.B.* (n 80) para 56, citing Case C-72/15 *Rosneft* EU:C:2017:236, para 162.

[106] *M.A.S. and M.B.* (n 80) para 57, referring, by analogy, to Case C-554/14 *Ognyanov* EU:C:2016:835, paras 62–64.

[107] M Lassalle, 'Taricco Kills Two Birds with one Stone for the Sake of the PIF' (European Law Blog, 2017) https://europeanlawblog.eu/2015/10/27/taricco-kills-two-birds-with-one-stone-for-the-sake-of-the-pif/ (last accessed on 4 March 2019).

[108] M Delmas-Marty, ML Izorche, 'Marge nationale d'appréciation et internationalisation du droit. Réflexions sur la validité formelle d'un droit commun pluraliste' (2000) 52-4 *Revue International de Droit Comparé* 753–80.

[109] Some scholars emphasised the uncertainty stemming from this shift from European to national level, see K Wegner, 'Vorhang zu und alle Fragen offen? – Zum Verhältnis von nationalem Verfassungsrecht und unmittelbar anwendbarem Unionsrecht nach "Taricco II"' (Junge Wissenschaft in Öffentlichesrecht, 2017) www.juwiss.de/143-2017/ (last accessed 4 March 2019).

liability that were stricter than those in force at the time the infringement was committed'.[110] The *revirement* is thus completed.

VII. The Art of Uncertainty: Protecting Primacy Accepting Pluralism in the Post-Lisbon and Post-Charter EU Legal Order

The Court 'has thought things twice and its decision is different now. It's wiser too'.[111] But the adjustment to which the CJEU was forced to avoid the clash is clear.

That is why the *M.A.S.* judgment exposes itself, again, to harsh criticism. It can be interpreted as 'an incredible self-inflicted blow on the part of the Court of Justice',[112] having disregarded 'legally problematic questions, seemingly subordinating argumentative consistency to the constraints of legal policy in a climate increasingly critical towards EU law and institutions'. As a consequence, the principle of primacy of EU law suffered a strong relativisation *vis-à-vis* domestic constitutional law.[113]

However, it would be short-sighted to see the *M.A.S.* decision mainly as a *débacle* of the European law primacy, forced by political pressure. There are several reasons to welcome this judgment, even after acknowledging its argumentative weakness and appalling silences.

First and foremost, setting aside internal criminal rules with consequences *in malam partem* for the individuals is an extremely sensitive decision that deserves the full attention of every court at whatever level. In *M.A.S.* the Court complemented – rather than contradicted – its previous harsh position, offering an option to Member States to include other rules, such as the ones on limitation periods, in a wider concept of legality in criminal matters. The analysis is much more detailed and based on a complement of information that was lacking in the first place, as the CJEU openly affirmed.[114]

Instead of firmly rejecting the counter-limits doctrine, the CJEU has been able to transform them into vital and dynamic parts of the judicial dialogue. There has been no demonisation but rather acceptance and centralisation of their analysis, with the additional beneficial effect of preventing many judicial interventions by national courts.

Second, even though the *M.A.S.* judgment does not refer to the *Melloni* case, it seems to apply those same criteria in a reasonable way. When implementing

[110] *M.A.S. and M.B.* (n 80) para 60.

[111] Sarmiento (n 55); referring to a 'lesson of wisdom': V Manes, 'Some Lessons from the Taricco Saga' (2018) 9(1) *New Journal of European Criminal Law* 12–17, 17.

[112] These are the ironic, hyperbolic words of Sarmiento (n 55). The scholar finally comes to far more positive conclusions on the *M.A.S.* judgment.

[113] Burchardt (n 79).

[114] See Sarmiento (n 55).

European provisions in areas in which there is no previous harmonisation, national courts can choose between the standards of fundamental rights protection under national law or EU law. In *Melloni* there was no discretion left for the Member State, so the standard of the Charter was applied and the more protective standard of the Spanish Constitution was set aside. Now, in *M.A.S.*, the Member State can enjoy quite a lot of discretion under EU law, and the Court acknowledges such discretion and allows the Constitutional Court to make full use of it. Where there is not 'enough Europe', while AG Bot suggested a pretorian solution, putting the courts in charge to cover the lacunas, even against their national traditions, the CJEU in *M.A.S.* allows their use.[115]

Third, far and beyond the *querelle* on the substantive or procedural nature of statutes of limitation, it is rather important to highlight how procedural rules also need to be defined by law in a clear way. The CJEU and the ECtHR have on several occasions accepted the principle *tempus regit actum* as of general application for procedural rules, instead of the strict non-retroactivity, as autonomously defined by the ECtHR.[116] It is thus in line with that case law to change procedural rules after the commission of the crime and impose their application from the very moment of their formal entry into force. But this possibility is given to the legislator, not to the courts, all the ECtHR cases being indeed referred to legislative *post factum* amendments.[117] The role of law in a country imbued with principles of the romano-germanic legal family[118] is in line with the continental constitutional tradition that favours formal legality over substantial legality, conferring only to the parliaments a pivotal role in terms of legality.

But even more crucially, in *M.A.S* the Court introduces a methodology to define European fundamental rights that adopts an inclusive approach inspired by pluralism since common constitutional traditions have a supranational, European dimension.[119] '*Ordonner le pluralisme*'[120] is a difficult but unavoidable exercise. The shift is not only terminological but rather ontological as it concerns the real essence of the Charter's principles and their relationship with national Constitutions. There is no space for patriotic – and anachronistic – constitutional identities but rather an inclusive, pluralistic, more tolerant concept of constitutional traditions,[121] developing the new mantra of Constitutional tolerance[122]

[115] Arlettaz (n 56) 621.

[116] The reference goes to the case *Scoppola v Italy (no 2)* (n 7). See F Viganò, *Retroattività della legge penale più favorevole* in *Libro dell'anno del Diritto 2014* (*Treccani*, 2014) 1–16.

[117] See *Coëme v Belgium* (n 7) paras 142–51; *Previti v Italy* (n 62) para 80; *Borcea v Romania* (n 64) paras 62–65.

[118] Arlettaz (n 56) 619.

[119] Dubout (n 83) 569 indicates pluralis as the origin of 'insouciance'. See also F Viganò, 'Melloni Overruled? Considerations on the 'Taricco II' Judgement of the Court of Justice (2018) 9(1) *New Journal of European Criminal Law* 18–23, 22.

[120] M Delmas-Marty, *Les forces imaginaires du droit. Tome II: Le pluralisme ordonné* (Seuil, 2006); N Perlo, 'L'affaire Taricco: la voie italienne pour préserver la collaboration des juges dans l'Union européenne' (2017) *Revue Trimestrielle de Droit Européen* 768.

[121] Delmas-Marty, *ibid.*

[122] Bassini, Pollicino (n 81).

as the only answer to resilient new nationalistic populisms. European Constitutional identity is inherently composed as pluralism.

Strongly criticised by some scholars because of its detrimental effects on the primacy of EU law, the *M.A.S.* case partially rewrote that principle.[123] Primacy, however, needs to be updated to a post-Lisbon and post-Charter context, where fundamental rights are part of the 'primacy of EU law' in a system that seeks unity in diversity. Legitimation and strength of this unity in a system where diverse entities should coexist should stem from the tolerance for the minimum – but necessary – grade of difference.[124]

What is new in the *M.A.S.* decision is the fact that the CJEU does not seem to consider fundamental rights as external and opposed to primacy of EU law. The Italian Constitutional Court chose to refer the case to the CJEU, and instead of reacting abruptly – and disruptively[125] – the CJEU, on its side, opened the doors to cooperative constitutionalism.[126] Scholars observed that 'in this way, Article 6(3) TEU, even if not explicitly mentioned, is definitely preferred to Article 4(2) as reference to let a more elaborated understanding of the principle of legality (than that adopted in *Taricco I*) to emerge'.[127] The consequence will not be the lack of conflict but rather an increase in conflict, because pluralism naturally leads to conflict, whereas dominance of one order imposes the silence of the others. What scholars call judicial dialogue is often a sophisticated form of ordeal, which represents the real lifeblood of EU law. In this forced confrontation, everybody officially – and politely – disagrees, but in the end national supreme courts have followed the CJEU *dicta*.[128]

But in order for this inclusive, plural dialogue to be successful, the CJEU should take into due consideration the specificity of criminal law. Legal uncertainty in criminal law is not compatible with both the European and the national dimension of the legality principle. From a European perspective, this is the most important statement of the *M.A.S.* judgment because it affirms 'the primacy of the principle of legality over the obligation to contrast frauds affecting the financial interests of the Union through criminal measures'.[129]

Even the sceptics of legal continental formalism should consider a further argument: the use of criminal law as the last resort requires prudent assessment and balancing, that the liberal theory of criminal law confers to the

[123] Burchardt (n 79).

[124] L Gradoni, 'Incontro al limite' (SIDIBlog, 2018) www.sidiblog.org/2018/01/29/incontro-al-limite/ (last accessed on 5 March 2019); A Lucifora, 'The Role of National Courts between EU Obligations and National Standards of Protection of Fundamental Rights' (2018) 9(2) *New Journal of European Criminal Law* 216–28, 226.

[125] As it may have done later on with judgment no. 115 of 31 May 2018, and judgment no. 269 of 14 December 2017.

[126] Amalfitano, Pollicino (n 46).

[127] Bassini, Pollicino (n 81).

[128] Gradoni (n 124). See Case C-62/14 *Gauweiler and others* EU:C:2015:400.

[129] Bassini, Pollicino (n 81).

legislator in light of the priorities as listed in national – and now European – Constitutions.[130] Legal interests to be protected via criminal law and the intensity of that protection, mirrored in the severity of the penalty, are still ordered according to their relevance within the Constitutions. Even in the current rupture of Kelsenyan hierarchical models, criminal policies should always prioritise fundamental interests such as life and health, and peace and safety of people. The protection of financial interests is surely crucial for the very existence of the European Union, but every criminal policy relying on Article 325 TFEU appears hyper-legitimised to break through,[131] far more than in any other fields where stronger EU protection would be needed. A huge difference remains between the CJEU approach to Article 325 TFEU and the one suggested by the Italian Constitutional Court. Putting the cards on the table, we do agree with the national court in firmly emphasising the difference between 'means' and 'goals', Article 325 TFEU imposing only the latter, whereas the CJEU, in line with Jean Monnet's functionalism of '*petits pas*',[132] is building up an entire system on that provision. But this mosaic risks being rejected.

Subsidiarity in criminal law, in fact, can hardly cope with the European subsidiarity,[133] because the latter deprives the EU organs of a general power to legiferate in this sensitive field, with the risk of the EU over-criminalising breaches falling within its competence and ignoring the other, major, crimes. Expiration of limitation periods and the resulting impunity of crimes are symptoms of a wider Italian disease: the inefficiency and unfairness (for both defendants and victims) of the internal judicial system. Impunity might unfortunately embrace the most serious crimes, such as murder[134] or torture.[135] As the ECtHR decisions have emphasised, Italy failed in making justice of crimes committed in Genoa on the occasion of the G8 summit in 2001,[136] which was unanimously considered as the biggest breach of human rights in Europe since World War II. It would have been highly unfair for the victims of those tortures to see that EU frauds had become imprescriptible whereas their suffering had no echo.

A last remark is needed: procedural safeguards are set up to protect fundamental rights. As such, they might always represent an obstacle[137] to efficiency and effectiveness of crime repression. And we are not talking theoretically, being

[130] F Bricola, *Teoria generale del reato* (UTET, 1974).

[131] Sotis (n 30).

[132] C Sotis, 'Actualités du droit pénal italien. Réserve du code, valeur du précédent et droits fondamentaux' (2018) *Revue de Sciences Criminelles et de Droit Comparé* 581–90, 590.

[133] M Donini, 'Sussidiarietà penale e sussidiarietà comunitaria' (2003) *Rivista Italiana di Diritto e Procedura Penale* 141–83.

[134] *Alikaj and others v Italy* App no 47357/08 (ECtHR, 29 March 2003).

[135] *Cestaro v Italy* App no 6884/11 (ECtHR, 7 April 2015); *Bartesaghi Gallo and others v Italy* App no 12131/13 (ECtHR, 22 June 2017).

[136] *Cestaro v Italy*, *ibid.*

[137] Herbert Packer famously likened his Due Process model to an 'obstacle course', see HL Packer, *The Limits of the Criminal Sanction* (Stanford University Press, 1968) 163.

preliminary references already been brought to the CJEU.[138] The temptation of this new European consequentialism[139] in criminal law is then to balance the respect of fundamental rights with primacy of EU law or the efficiency of its policies. But the balancing metaphor is sometimes misleading and it appears to exude fairness almost to the point of incontrovertibility.[140]

It is the very primary function of fundamental rights to limit the powers of investigative, prosecutorial and adjudicating authorities. From Herbert Packer[141] to Winfried Hassemer,[142] from Miriam Damaska[143] to Andrew Ashworth and Luigi Ferrajoli,[144] fairness should be the dominant interest of criminal proceedings. But rights are essentially anti-consequentialist: the whole point of recognising a right is to uphold the claim of an individual to protection, even when such a treatment would negatively affect the community.[145]

With this aim, the EU and its Court should abandon certain efficiency logics and start including human rights protection within the 'primacy of EU law', because in the post-Lisbon, post-Charter era those rights are now fully-fledged EU law. But they leave no room for the Member States to stoke the flames in Luxembourg with 'national identity' rhetoric spiked up with an anti-cosmopolitan imagery.[146] Member States, on their side, should pick their battles wisely. Statute of limitations is not worth enough.

[138] See Case C-310/16 *Petar Dziev*, in which the punishment for a VAT fraud was hindered by the ban to use conversations among the defendants captured via illegal interceptions. AG Bobek strongly rejected the idea that Article 325 TFEU could preclude national legislation to prohibit the use of illegal evidence, see Case C-310/16 *Petar Dziev*, Opinion of AG Bobek EU:C:2018:623, paras 125–32. See also, F Giuffrida, 'Taricco Principles beyond Taricco. Some Thoughts on Three Pending Cases (Scialdone, Kolev and Menci)' (2018) 9 *New Journal of European Criminal Law* 31–37.

[139] On consequentalistic theories in criminal law, see J Braithwaite, P Pettit, *Not just Deserts. A Republican Theory of Criminal Justice* (Oxford University Press, 1990); A Saunders, R Young, *Criminal Justice* (Oxford University Press, 2007) 44; For a harsh criticism, A Ashworth, M Redmayne, *The Criminal Process* (Oxford University Press, 2010) 45.

[140] A Ashworth, M Redmayne, *Criminal Process*, 4th edn (Oxford University Press, 2010) 41–42, 45: 'Yet talk of "balancing" often assumes a kind of hydraulic relationship between human rights safeguards and the promotion of public safety'.

[141] Packer (n 137).

[142] W Hassemer, 'Menschenrechte im Strafprozess' (1988) 4 *Kritische Vierteljahresschrift für Gesetzgebung und Rechtswissenschaft* 336.

[143] M Damaska, 'The Competing Vision of Fairness: The Basic Choice for International Criminal Tribunals' (2010) 36 *North Carolina Journal for International Law and Commercial Regulation* 365.

[144] L Ferrajoli, *Diritto e Ragione. Teoria del garantismo penale* (Laterza, 2009).

[145] Ashworth, Redmayne (n 140).

[146] Paraphrasing Judge Pinto de Albuquerque in his flaming opinion in *G.I.E.M. S.R.L. v Italy* (n 49).

Taricco, *Endgame**

VITTORIO MANES

I. *Taricco* through the Labyrinth of Jurisprudence

The Constitutional Court's Decision no 115 of 2018 concludes the '*Taricco* saga', apparently preventing further interpretative disputes.

The possibility of disapplying national provisions on limitation periods (according to the limited extension of interruptions ruled by Arts 160 and 161 of the Criminal Code)[1] gave rise to controversy in order to ensure effective and deterrent criminal penalties against serious VAT frauds and to protect the financial interests of the Union under Art 325 of the Treaty on the Functioning of the European Union (TFEU).

The judicial case is intricate and entangled, attracting great attention from both Italian[2] and European[3] scholars. After the first preliminary ruling, the judgment of the Court of Justice[4] brought about two questions of constitutionality (referred by the Court of Appeal of Milan and the Court of Cassation).

* The commentary is to be part of C Amalfitano (ed), *Primato del diritto dell'Unione europea e controlimiti alla prova della 'saga Taricco'* (Milan, 2018).

[1] The rules on limitation of criminal proceedings have been entirely modified by Law no 103 of 2017.

[2] Among several works, see, on one hand, the volume published after the first *Taricco* judgment: A Bernardi (ed), *I controlimiti. Primato delle norme europee e difesa dei principi costituzionali* (Naples, 2017) and, on the other hand, the one published after the Constitutional Court's decision no 24 of 2017: A Bernardi and C Cupelli (eds), *Il caso Taricco e il dialogo tra le Corti. L'ordinanza 24/2017 della Corte costituzionale* (Naples, 2017).

[3] As for the Court of Justice's first judgment, see, *ex multis*, E Billis, 'The European Court of Justice: A "Quasi-Constitutional Court" in Criminal Matters? The Taricco Judgment and Its Shortcomings' (2016) *New Journal of European Criminal Law* 20 ff; M Timmermann, 'Balancing Effective Criminal Sanctions with Effective Fundamental Rights Protection in Cases of VAT Fraud: Taricco' (2016) *Common Market Law Review* 779 ff; J Bülte, *Anwendungsvorrang und Gesetzlichkeitsprinzip im europäisierten Strafrecht und Strafverfahrensrechts, Anmerkung zu EuGH, Urt. v. 8.9.2015 – C 105/14* (2015) *NZWiSt* 390 ff. On the second judgment, see, in particular, F Meyer, *EuGH, 5. 12. 2017-C-42/17 M.A.S. und M.B., Europäisches Strafrecht zwischen unionsrechtlichem Effektivitätsprinzip und nationalem Verfassungsrecht, Anmerkung* (2018) *JuristenZeitungJZ* 304 ff; V Mitsilegas, *Judicial Dialogue in Three Silences: Unpacking Taricco* (2018) *New Journal of European Criminal Law* 38 ff; D Burchardt, *Kehrtwende in der Grundrechts- und Vorrangrechtsprechung des EuGH?, Anmerkung zum Urteil des EuGH vom 5.12.2017 in der Rechtssache M.A.S. und M.B. (C-42/17, 'Taricco II')* (2018) *Europarecht* 248 ff.

[4] Case C-105/14 *Ivo Taricco and others* ('*Tarrico I*') EU:C:2015:555.

The Constitutional Court answered firmly and politely (order no 24 of 2017), demanding the Court of Justice a second preliminary ruling. Thus, the Grand Chamber delivered a new decision attenuating contents and effects of the previous 'revolutionary' *Taricco* judgment.[5]

At the end of the course, the Constitutional Court rejected the referred relevant questions and delivered a *tranchant* judgment which clarified the outstanding issues.

Hence, the *Taricco* judgment represents not only an episode of 'judicial adventurism', capable of altering interconnections among different legal orders, but also a decision conflicting with the legality principle.

In particular, the non-retroactivity principle was undermined by a *post factum* expansion of the limitation period; the void of vagueness was hurt by a judge-made law conferring the judge the power to disapply national provisions whether criminal punishments escaped in a 'significant number of cases of serious fraud'. Furthermore, the *nullum crimen sine lege*, the judge subject to the supremacy of law and the separation of powers were recognised as essential elements of Italian constitutional order in accordance with the civil law paradigm.

II. Solved and Unsolved Questions after the 2017 Grand Chamber Judgment

Actually, the Court of Justice had already solved several issues brought before the Constitutional Court: in fact, on the one hand, the Grand Chamber (preliminary ruling, 5 December 2017) specified that the '*Taricco* rule' could not apply to facts committed before the judgment had been delivered (8 September 2015) according to the non-retroactivity principle. On the other hand, the Court stated that national courts had to verify whether the '*Taricco* rule' undermined the legality principle.

Moreover, the EU Court defined the void of vagueness on the ground of Art 49 of the Charter of Fundamental Rights of the European Union, recognising the principle being part of Member States' constitutional tradition, even if not 'common' to all (ie the limitation period is substantive – and not procedural – in nature according to Italian criminal law but in contrast to other European legal orders).

Thus, the Constitutional Court – enhancing the (partial but decisive) *revirement* of the Grand Chamber – could have settled for an *appeasement* or a polite *glissè*, being able to choose among several alternative forms available to decide the constitutional proceedings.

[5] Case C-42/17 *M.A.S and M.B.* EU:C:2017:936. On this issue, see all the papers collected by the *Forum* on '*La saga Taricco ad un svolta: in attesa della decisione della Corte costituzionale*', available at www.diritticomparati.it.

On the contrary, the Court evaluated the political shades of the decision since the alleged excessive vagueness of the '*Taricco* rule' implied relevant consequences conferring the judge 'eccentric' and 'anomalous' powers.

In fact, applying the '*Taricco* rule', judges risked being influenced by general political aims, acting without boundaries in order to affect criminal policy and pursue specific goals on penalties. Therefore, jurisdiction risked assuming those powers that the Constitution reserved to the legislator in accordance with the civil law paradigm (see Arts 25, § 2, and 101, § 2, Constitution).

III. Decision No 115 of 2018: The Nature of the Limitation Period, the 'Determination' of European Obligations and the Tasks of Competent National Courts

Considering the impact of the questions referred to,[6] the Constitutional Court reasonably decided to deliver a significant judgment in terms of substantial and formal content. The Court articulated several arguments underpinning the previous judgment no 24 of 2017 – rather than enforcing dialogue with the European partner[7] – in order to state peremptory conclusions and build a valid benchmark for future disputes.

Thus, it will be useful to focus on some essential aspects of the decision.

First, the Court claims the power to assess whether the obligations imposed by EU law comply with the Constitution, particularly referring to 'fundamental rights of the persons concerned' and counter-limits. The Constitutional Court retains this power – in accordance with the relevant *obiter dictum* stated by judgment no 269 of 2017[8] – and it allows national judges only to refer constitutional questions in case of ambiguous issues.

Therefore, the power of national judges is significantly limited in case of constitutional concerns. In other words, the decision no 115 of 2018 affects the process which has been enhanced by the need to disapply national provisions in order to fulfil EU obligations and which has provided the single judge a direct dialogue with supranational high jurisdictions.[9]

[6] As for the scholars in Constitutional Law, see M Luciani, *Il brusco risveglio. I controlimiti e la fine mancata della storia costituzionale* and R Bin, *Taricco, una sentenza sbagliata: come venirne fuori?* in Bernardi (ed) (n 2) 63 ff, 291 ff.

[7] From this perspective, see the observations of C Amalfitano and O Pollicino, 'Jusqu'ici tout va bien … *ma non sino alla fine della storia. Luci, ombre e atterraggio della sentenza n. 115/2018 della Corte costituzionale che chiude (?) la saga Taricco*' (2018), available at www.diritticomparati.it.

[8] In this *obiter dictum* the Court claimed the power to assess when national provisions comply with the Constitution as well as with the European fundamental rights enshrined in the Charter.

[9] S Cassese, 'Fine della solitudine delle corti costituzionali, ovvero il dilemma del porcospino' (2015) *Ars interpretandi* 21 ff.

Second, plunging *in medias res*, the substantive – and not procedural – nature of the limitation period is strongly reaffirmed, stating that the '*Taricco* rule' departs from constitutional principles. The majority of national case law shares the approach, despite being challenged several times during the 'saga'. In particular, the Advocate General's Opinion[10] as well as the Grand Chamber judgments[11] noticeably contrast with the national perspective.

On this issue, indeed, the Constitutional Court expressly affirms that the limitation period influences the determination of penalties since it prevents the application of criminal sanctions once the proceeding is time-barred. Thus, there are no doubts that the legality principle prescribed by Art 25, § 2, Constitution, applies to the rules on limitation.

Then, the Court analyses the obligation to disapply any provision of national law affecting the fulfilment of EU obligations whether it depends on vague and unclear criteria derived from a norm – Art 325 TFEU – particularly ambiguous and unable to comply with individual autonomy.

As already mentioned, the Court rejects this hypothesis in relation to both the adequacy principle (Art 325, § 1, TFEU) and the assimilation principle (Art 325, § 2, TFEU).

In fact, in the judges' view, Art 325 TFEU as well as the '*Taricco* rule' are so vague that nobody could foresee any eventual criminal liability. Moreover, it is doubtful that the provisions of Art 325 TFEU allow the rules on limitation to be disapplied in criminal matters, even in particular circumstances.

On this premise, the Constitutional Court held that a violation occurs when criminal liability depends on unclear rules (in particular, Art 325 TFEU) barely defined by the Court of Justice's case law (above all, the first *Taricco* judgment).

[10] In addition, see the opinion of Advocate General (AG) Yves Bot, hearing 18 July 2017, Case C-42/17 *M.A.S. and M.B.*, Opinion of AG Bot, EU:C:2017:564.

[11] See the judgment *M.A.S.*, where the Court firstly recalls that 'an extension of a limitation period by the national legislature and its immediate application, including to alleged offences that are not yet time-barred, do not, in principle, infringe the principle that offences and penalties must be defined by law' (para 42) and that 'the protection of the financial interests of the Union by the enactment of criminal penalties falls within the shared competence of the Union and the Member States within the meaning of Article 4 (2) TFEU' (para 43). Then, the judges observe that '[…] at the material time for the main proceedings, the limitation rules applicable to criminal proceedings relating to VAT had not been harmonized by the EU legislature, and harmonisation has since taken place only to a partial extent by the adoption of Directive (EU) 2017/1371 of the European Parliament and of the Council of 5 July 2017 on the fight against fraud to the Union's financial interests by means of criminal law […] The Italian Republic was thus, at that time, free to provide that in its legal system those rules, like the rules on the definition of offences and the determination of penalties, form part of substantive criminal law, and are thereby, like those rules, subject to the principle that offences and penalties must be defined by law' (para 44 and 45). Thus, the Directive seems to affect Member States' discretionary power as if, after the harmonisation of rules on limitation periods concerning VAT offences, it is up to the Directive, not to the Member State, to define the compelling regime of time-barred proceedings. The outline is that this regime would have negative effects for the accused person, as the limitation period is considered to be procedural in nature, in accordance with the first *Taricco* judgment delivered by the Court of Justice.

In other words, the interpretation of EU primary law is not foreseeable and, however, constitutes a hypothesis of judge-made law. Thus, it contrasts with the imperative of civil law jurisdictions, such as Italy, which requires the legislator to assess criminal policy preventing the case law from replacing the *praevia lex scripta* so that legal certainty and individual autonomy are not undermined.

IV. '*Taricco* Rule' before the Constitutional Court: Recommendations 'Behind the Appearances'

Some aspects of the decision could appear too intense and, if not, overwhelming the attributions of the Court of Justice. In fact, the Constitutional Court ensures effective application of EU primary law but, at the same time, the Court states that Art 325 TFEU is so vague that its shortcomings cannot be resolved, neither considering national and supranational case law.[12]

A. Judiciary Discretion Faces the Foreseeability of Criminal Law

In particular, the Court verifies if Art 325 TFEU, para 1 and 2, together with the '*Taricco* rule' – a judge-made law which implies disapplication of national provisions – complies with the void of vagueness even if the judiciary power adopts criminal policy decisions which should be reserved to the legislator.

On this basis, the constitutional questions also involve the assimilation principle: Art 325 TFEU, para 2, is scrutinised on the ground of the void of vagueness although it might not present those shortcomings. Yet, other problematic issues concerning assimilation remain unsolved by the *M.A.S.* judgment.[13]

In this vein, the Court tries to silence the manifold interpretations spread among national courts after the first *Taricco* judgment. The main goal is to prevent a 'patchwork' criminal law, left to the judicial discretion and to the efforts connecting non-criminal provisions in order to pursue contingent scopes.[14]

[12] On this issue, see C Amalfitano and O Pollicino (n 7); otherwise, a different perspective on direct effect and EU law primacy is provided by D Gallo, *L'efficacia diretta del diritto dell'unione europea negli ordinamenti nazionali* (Milan, 2018) 394 ff.

[13] As for the alternatives available to apply the '*Taricco* rule' after the *M.A.S. and M.B.* judgment, on the ground of the assimilation principle, see E Lupo, *La sentenza europea c.d. taricco-bis: risolti i problemi per il passato, rimangono aperti i problemi per il futuro* (22 December 2017), available at www.penalecontemporaneo.it. Criticising the analogical application of an exceptional norm, in order to ensure full effect to Art 325, para 2, see M Donini, *Le sentenze Taricco come giurisdizione di lotta* (3 April 2018), available at www.penalecontemporaneo.it. In addition, as for the improper use of the assimilation principle, see I Pellizzone, *La sentenza Taricco II e il suo ambivalente impatto sui principi di irretroattività e di determinatezza in materia penale* (2018).

[14] Actually, the Constitutional Court had already underpinned this idea in decision no 24 of 2017.

In other words, the purpose is containing judge-made law – detached from interpretative boundaries – rather than void of vagueness. Thus, the Constitutional Court aims to control and reduce the expansion of new rights enhanced by interconnections among Charters and Courts. In fact, the '*floraison de la fondamentalité*'[15] and the development of positive obligations into 'multi-level' jurisdictions have brought about an increase in different rights even in the criminal field, requiring the Court to handle that phenomenon.

However, judgment no 115 of 2018 – despite enforcing void of vagueness and foreseeability in accordance with decision no 24 of 2017 – requires further compliant judgments in order to overrule the self-restraint the Constitutional Court used to adopt in case of alleged violations of the guarantees under Art 25, para 2, Constitution. The development of further constitutional decisions is also necessary to eventually overcome the power conferred to judicial discretion as a sort of 'legality in action'.[16]

In fact, the Court attempts to define judicial discretion towards the subjective standard of foreseeability. In particular, judicial interpretation ensures only an *ex post* assistance, selecting the meaning of law between those which respect the *littera legis* and emerge reading the provision (see para 11 of the judgment).

The Court recalls the debate concerning the predictability of new judicial interpretations, of overruling (not solely *in malam partem*) and, above all, of the principle of individual autonomy which allows one to foresee criminal liability and, thus, freely determine personal behaviour. National courts are admonished whether – as was the case recently – they consider the legislative provision as a mere starting point, venturing interpretations which forget formal boundaries[17] and generate *in malam partem*[18] effects.

[15] Recalling the expression by L Burgorgue-Larsen, *Les concepts de liberté publique et de droit fondamental*, in JB. Auby (dir), *L'influence du droit européen sur les catégories du droit public* (Paris, Dalloz, Thèmes et commentaires, 2010) 395.

[16] It is well-known that the Constitutional Court chose self-restraint when assessing void of vagueness. First, the Court accepted broad expressions and admitted exemplifying or synthetising techniques in relation to explicit analogical interpretation (see judgment no 27 of 1961, no 120 of 1963 and no 79 of 1982). Generally, it stated that vague expressions, together with generic clauses, did not violate the Constitution whether the judge was able to identify the meaning of the provision through systematic readings which took into account, at the same time, the scope of punishment and the legal framework. However, no judge could exceed his competence evaluating the legislative provision so that it is possible to control the arguments and clearly appreciate the relevance of a particular offence (see, recently, judgment no 282 of 2010, recalling the previous decision no 327 of 2008; no 5 of 2004; no 34 of 1995 and no 122 of 1993). That approach – *bon à tout faire* – allowed the Court not to declare void several provisions concerning personal preventive measures (judgment no 282 of 2010).

[17] N Irti, *Il salvagente della forma* (Bari-Rome, 2007).

[18] See, for instance, Court of Cassation, 21 December 2017–22 February 2018, no 8770, analysed by G Caletti and M Mattheudakis, *La fisonomia dell'art. 590-*sexies *c.p. dopo le Sezioni Unite tra 'nuovi' spazi di graduazione dell'imperizia e 'antiche' incertezze* (9 April 2018) available at www.penalecontemporaneo.it.

B. *Nullum crimen sine lege* and Supranational Legislation

In fact, it is uncertain if *Taricco* concerns void of vagueness or, rather, its core issue has remained unsolved, that is to say *nullum crimen sine lege* in relation to supranational legislation, to normative effects of the Court of Justice's decisions and to national legislation.

Dealing with that, the Court might have chosen a more rigid attitude towards the Court of Justice, insisting on the traditional ban on applications *in malam partem* of EU law. The outline would have been noticeable in order to define future relations among national and supranational jurisdictions.

Furthermore, recognising direct effect to Art 325 TFEU – thus, avoiding Art 83 TFEU – risks legitimising innovative provisions adopted (not only by harmonisation directives but also) by regulations which require no implementation at all, worsening the *status quo*, also, in relation to *nullum crimen sine lege*.

C. The Substantive Nature of the Rules on Limitation

From this perspective, a further aspect emerges concerning European harmonisation.[19]

After *M.A.S.*, the Constitutional Court restates the substantive nature of the limitation period without mentioning the PIF Directive.[20] Thus, the Court undermines the approach which considers the rules on limitation to have procedural character and prevents the expansion of harmonisation as envisaged in relation to the general, if not ambiguous, provisions of the Directive.[21]

In fact, the Court suggests that a different complex process is required in order to attach essential rules of criminal law, such as the limitation period, to the EU paradigm. Actually, decision no 24 of 2017 has recalled the notion of 'Member State's national identity' whether it became necessary to ensure sufficient guarantees for time-barred proceedings.[22]

A sole provision, part of a specific and peculiar legislative field, seems unable to reach the goal, even considering its ambiguous meaning. In fact, the judges

[19] M Delmas Marty, L Arroyo, M Pieth, U Sieber (eds), *Les chemins de l'harmonisation pénale* (Paris, Socièté de législation comparé, 2008).

[20] Directive 2017/1371/EU of the European Parliament and of the Council of 5 July 2017 on the fight against fraud to the Union's financial interests by means of criminal law [2017] OJ L198/29.

[21] It is well-known that Art 12 of the PIF Directive provides *minimum* harmonisation on time-barred proceedings, only referring to the relevant crimes.

[22] See decision no 24 of 2017, para 6. In fact, the Court observed that if the limitation period was substantive in nature (as in Italy or Spain), the rules governing the elapsed time needed to be analytically described by the law before the act had been committed. It was necessary to identify a written provision governing offence, punishments and limitation of criminal proceedings in order to appreciate the essential value of the crime. The debate continues about the notion of 'national identity': see G Di Federico, *L'identità nazionale degli Stati membri nel diritto dell'Unione europea. Natura e portata dell'art. 4 par. 2 TUE* (Naples, 2017).

observe that the Directive does not directly involve EU competences or EU law, excluding the need to harmonise Member States' legislations.[23]

V. Conclusion

What lesson can be drawn from the '*Taricco* saga'? The interconnections among different jurisdictions, the process of harmonisation in criminal law and the European *primauté* could never overcome fundamental guarantees which protect the criminal field.

The separation of power and the supremacy of law are not questionable since, in accordance with the civil law paradigm, they represent the main cornerstone of the rule of law, as for the constitutional dimension of punitive power.

In the criminal sphere, the legal certainty and the legality principle exceed the need to protect financial interests and to meet European obligations. The limitation period pertains to substantive criminal law[24] as the effects of criminal sanctions completely depend on (and collapse without) the presumption of innocence.

Therefore, in *Taricco*, the Court concludes rejecting any leap forward when it aims to substitute national authority even in dangerous circumstances, such as in relation to VAT fraud.[25]

In fact, this interference generates authoritarian outlines, despite eventual good intentions,[26] affecting the constitutional balance between the legality principle and the rule of law.

Hence, that balance conflicts with judge-made laws: in civil law jurisdictions, penalties shall never be created and, then, imposed by the judicial authority according to the separation of powers and the *nullum crimen sine lege*.

[23] See decision no 24 of 2017, para 4.

[24] P Gaeta, *Rapporti tra fonti europee e Cassazione in tema di legalità: alcune icone* in A Cadoppi (ed), *Cassazione e legalità penale* (Rome, 2017) 169 ff.

[25] See judgment no 115 of 2018, para 14.

[26] D Pulitanò, *Crisi della legalità e confronto con la giurisprudenza* (2015) *Rivista italiana diritto e procedura penale* 29 ff.

PART III

Ne bis in idem

7

C-187/01 – *Gözütok and Brügge*

Comment on CJEU, 11 February 2003, Joined Cases C-187/01 and C-385/01 Criminal Proceedings v Hüseyin Gözütok and Klaus Brügge

ANNE WEYEMBERGH

I. Introduction

The decision of the Court of Justice of the European Union (CJEU) of 11 February 2003 in the joined *Gözütok and Brügge* cases was the first time that the Court interpreted the *ne bis in idem* principle as enshrined in Article 54 of the Convention Implementing the Schengen Agreement (CISA).[1]

The preliminary questions asked by the *Oberlandesgericht Köln* and the *Rechtbank van eerste aanleg te Veurne* respectively boiled down to asking the Court whether the principle of *ne bis in idem* laid down in Art 54 of the CISA also applied to procedures whereby further prosecution was barred following an out-of-court settlement. In its decision of 11 February 2003, the Court replied that the scope of the principle of *ne bis in idem* is not limited to final decisions delivered by criminal jurisdictions, but also covers public prosecutors' decisions in so far as they definitely put an end to the prosecution. The Court thus concluded that the principle of *ne bis in idem*

> also applies to procedures whereby further prosecution is barred […] by which the Public Prosecutor in a Member State discontinues, without the involvement of a court, a prosecution brought in that State once the accused has fulfilled certain obligations and, in particular, has paid a certain sum of money determined by the Public Prosecutor'.[2]

[1] CJEU, 11 February 2003, Joined Cases C-187/01 and C-385/01 *Gözütok and Brügge* ECLI:EU:C:2003:87.

[2] *Ibid*, para 48.

The Court based this extensive and autonomous interpretation of the *bis* on three main arguments:

- The decision concerned comes from an authority required to take part in the administration of criminal justice in the national legal system concerned. In so far as such a decision penalises the unlawful conduct which the accused is alleged to have committed, use has been made of the *ius puniendi*;[3]
- The application of Art 54 of the CISA is not subordinated to the harmonisation or approximation of Member States' criminal laws relating to the procedures whereby further prosecution is barred;[4] this implies that Member States have mutual trust in their criminal justice systems and that each of them recognises the criminal law in force in the other Member States even when the outcome would be different if its own national law were applied;[5]
- This interpretation is the only one that allows the purpose and aim of Art 54 of the CISA and of the EU to prevail, ie free movement and the establishment of an area of freedom, security and justice.[6]

Of course, since 11 February 2003, a lot of water has gone under the bridge. Among the most important changes in these last 15 years are: the growing number of EU instruments implementing the mutual recognition principle in criminal matters;[7] the entry into force of the Treaty of Lisbon; and the submission of cooperation in criminal matters to the EU ordinary method and EU basic principles, all with related consequences. There was also the enshrinement of the mutual recognition principle in the Treaty itself[8] and the enshrinement of the *ne bis in idem*

[3] *Ibid*, paras 27 to 31.
[4] *Ibid*, para 32.
[5] *Ibid*, para 33.
[6] *Ibid*, paras 35 *ff*.
[7] Framework Decision (FD) 2002/584/JHA of 13 June 2002 on the European Arrest Warrant and the surrender procedures between Member States [2002] OJ L190/1; FD 2003/577/JHA of 22 July 2003 on the execution in the European Union of orders freezing property or evidence [2005] OJ L196/45; FD 2005/214/JAI of 24 February 2005 on the application of the principle of mutual recognition (MR) to financial penalties [2005] OJ L76/16; FD 2006/783/JHA of 6 October 2006 on the application of the principle of MR to confiscation orders [2006] OJ L328/59; FD 2008/675/JHA of 24 July 2008 on taking account of convictions in the MSs of the European Union in the course of new criminal proceedings [2008] OJ L220/32; FD 2008/947/JHA of 27 November 2008 on the application of the principle of MR to judgments and probation decisions with a view to the supervision of probation measures and alternative sanctions [2008] OJ L337/102; FD 2008/909/JHA of 27 November 2008 on the application of the principle of MR to judgments in criminal matters imposing custodial sentences or measures involving deprivation of liberty [2008] OJ L327/27; FD 2008/978/JHA of 18 December 2008 on the European Evidence Warrant for the purpose of obtaining objects, documents and data for use in proceedings in criminal matters [2008] OJ L350/72; FD 2009/829/JHA of 23 October 2009 on the application, between MSs of the European Union, of the principle of MR to decisions on supervision measures as an alternative to provisional detention [2009] OJ L294/20; Directive 2011/99/EU of the European Parliament and of the Council on the European Protection Order [2011] OJ L338/2; and Directive 2014/41/EU of the European Parliament and of the Council of 3 April 2014 regarding the European Investigation Order in criminal matters [2014] OJ L130/1.
[8] See Art 67 and 82 of the Treaty on the Functioning of the European Union (TFEU).

principle in Art 50 of the EU Charter of Human Rights, pertaining henceforth to EU primary law.

However, in spite of this evolution, the *Gözütok and Brügge* case remains very topical. When the ruling was delivered, it inspired many comments.[9] Some welcomed the extensive interpretation of the *ne bis in idem* principle given by the CJEU. It has indeed been the point of departure of a series of decisions by the Court that have been rather favourable for individuals' rights or defendant-friendly. It is particularly interesting to analyse what its legacy has been with regard to an extensive interpretation of the *ne bis in idem* principle, which will be examined in section II. As will be seen, some limits have been introduced by the Court. Tensions with the *Gözütok and Brügge*'s line of reasoning have appeared, which have not yet been resolved, which will be discussed in section III. Other comments addressed to the *Gözütok and Brügge* decision were more critical, especially because the Court contents itself with stating the Member States' obligation to have trust in each other's criminal justice system, giving the impression that such mutual confidence would easily be established and should be self-sufficient. Some authors particularly highlighted the fact that the Court overlooked the essential role played by the approximation of legislation in the establishment and legitimacy of such mutual trust.[10] In this respect, the *Gözütok and Brügge* decision has constituted a milestone in the CJEU's case law concerning the mutual recognition principle and its foundation, namely the principle of mutual trust (which will be the focus of section IV).

II. The Legacy of the *Gözütok and Brügge* Case with Regard to the Broad Interpretation of the *ne bis in idem* Principle

Since the *Gözütok and Brügge* case, many other decisions interpreting the *ne bis in idem principle* have been delivered by the CJEU. In most of them, the Court defended a broad interpretation of the *bis* and of the *idem*. In these decisions, the Court frequently referred to its *Gözütok and Brügge* decision.

It did so for instance in the *Van Straaten*[11] and *Gasparini*[12] cases when identifying the kind of decisions that may give rise to the *bis*. In both cases, one of the

[9] See, for instance, M Fletcher, 'Some Developments to the ne bis in idem Principle in the European Union: Criminal Proceedings Against Hüseyn Gözütok and Klaus Brügge (2003) *The Modern Law Review* 769 and ff; JAE Vervaele, 'Joined Cases C-187/01 and C-385/01, Criminal Proceedings against Hüseyin Gözütok and Klaus Brügge' (2004) 41 *Common Market Law Review* 3, 795 *ff*.

[10] A Weyembergh, 'Le principe *ne bis in idem* : pierre d'achoppement de l'espace pénal européen?' (2004) *Cahiers de droit européen* 337 *ff*.

[11] CJEU, 28 September 2006, Case C-150/05 *Van Straaten* ECLI:EU:C:2006:614.

[12] CJEU, 28 September 2006, Case C-467/04 *Gasparini* ECLI:EU:C:2006:610.

questions referred to by the Court was whether an acquittal decision sufficed to establish a *bis*. The reasons underlying the acquittal were, however, different. While in the first case the Dutch Court (the *Arrondissementsrechtbank te 'sHertogenbosch*) had reached its final decision to acquit the accused on the grounds of lack of evidence – therefore following an assessment of the merits of the case – in the *Gasparini* case the Portuguese jurisdiction (the *Supremo Tribunal de Justiça*) had acquitted the defendants on the ground that their prosecution was time-barred – without therefore assessing the merits of the case. In spite of this fundamental difference (assessment or absence of assessment of the merits of the case), the Court concluded that there was a *bis* in both cases. Reference(s) to the Court's decision in *Gözütok and Brügge* was (were) made and elements of its reasoning were repeated, especially those based on the Schengen/EU objectives of freedom of movement[13] and those based on the non-conditionality upon harmonisation or approximation and on trust.[14] In the *Bourquain* case,[15] where the Court ruled that *in absentia* judgments are not excluded from the scope of application of Art 54 of the CISA and may therefore constitute a 'final disposal' within the meaning of that provision, the Court also referred explicitly to *Gözütok and Brügge*, using both the aforementioned arguments.[16] However, references to *Gözütok and Brügge* are not systematic in this group of decisions where the Court interpreted the *bis* broadly, as is illustrated by the *M.* case.[17] Indeed, in its decision of 5 June 2014, the Court considered that a final judgment of 'non-lieu' as provided for by Arts 128 and 246 ff of the Belgian Criminal Investigation Code (the 'CIC'), which terminates criminal proceedings after an extensive investigation but which permits the proceedings to be reopened in the light of new evidence, precludes the initiation or conduct of proceedings in respect of the same facts and the same person in another Member State. Reference is, for instance, made to the *Van Straaten* decision but no reference to the *Gözütok and Brügge* decision is to be found. One of the main elements investigated here by the Court was to establish whether the decision had been taken after an examination of the merits of the case,[18] which seemed to indicate a change in the Court's attitude as to the need or not for such an examination to lead to the existence of the *bis*. The legacy of the *Gözütok and Brügge* case is also clear in the Court's decisions interpreting the outlines of the *idem* broadly. Its landmark ruling in the *Van Esbroeck* case of 9 March 2006 should be mentioned here. The Court declared that the only relevant criterion is that of the 'identity of the material acts, understood in the sense of the existence of a set of concrete circumstances which are inextricably linked together',[19] irrespective of their legal classification

[13] See *Van Straaten* (n 11) para 57; *Gasparini*, *ibid*, para 27.
[14] *Gasparini* (n 12) para 29–30.
[15] CJEU, 11 December 2008, Case C-297/07 *Bourquain* ECLI:EU:C:2008:708.
[16] *Ibid*, paras 36, 37 and 41.
[17] CJEU, 5 June 2014, Case C-398/12 *M.*ECLI:EU:C:2014:1057.
[18] Paras 28–30.
[19] CJEU, 9 March 2006, *Van Esbroeck*, Case C-436/04, ECLI:EU:C:2006:165, para 36.

or the legally protected interest. Explicit references are made to its *Gözütok and Brügge* decision and two of its main arguments are back again, namely the one based on the non-conditionality upon harmonisation or approximation and on mutual trust[20] and the other based on the Schengen/EU objectives of freedom of movement.[21] The Court of Justice has confirmed and detailed its factual approach to the *idem* in subsequent cases.[22]

III. Limits to the Broad Interpretation of *ne bis in idem* and the Appearance of Tensions in the Court's Case Law

In comparison to its first decision relating to Art 54 of the CISA, the Court progressively introduced limits to the principle of *ne bis in idem*. In doing so, it mainly referred to the objective of establishing an area of freedom, security and justice and mainly availed itself of the aspects relating to prevention and the effective fight against crime.

Some of these decisions where the Court restricts the scope of the *ne bis in idem* principle are perfectly logical and did not really suffer from criticism. This is, for instance, the case in its decision in the *Miraglia* case,[23] where criminal proceedings had been instituted against the same person both in Italy and in the Netherlands. The Dutch Queen's prosecutor did not press charges against the defendant because Italy had already done so for the same acts. Availing themselves of this decision, the Dutch authorities refused the request for judicial assistance issued by the Bologna Court on the grounds of the principle of *ne bis in idem*. Referring to *Gözütok and Brügge*, the Court points to its settled case law according to which the objective of Art 54 of the CISA is to ensure that no one is prosecuted on the same facts in several Member States on account of his having exercised his right to freedom of movement. But it continues, considering that the application of Art 54 of the CISA to such a decision to close proceedings – 'adopted by the judicial authorities of a Member State when there had been no assessment whatsoever of the unlawful conduct with which the defendant was charged'[24] – would result in making it more difficult, indeed impossible, to penalise in the Member States concerned the unlawful conduct with which the defendant is charged.[25] It concludes that such a consequence would go against the objective of

[20] *Ibid*, paras 29 and 30.
[21] See *ibid*, para 33.
[22] See *Gasparini* (n 12) paras 53 ff); *Van Straaten* (n 11) paras 49 and 50; *Bourquain* (n 15) paras 23 *ff*) but also CJEU, 18 July 2007, Case C-288/05 *Kretzinger* ECLI:EU:C:2007:441, paras 34 *ff*.
[23] CJEU, 10 March 2005, Case C-469/03 *Miraglia* ECLI:EU:C:2005:156.
[24] *Ibid*, para 34.
[25] *Ibid*, para 33.

establishing an area of freedom, security and justice 'in which the free movement of persons is assured in conjunction with appropriate measures with respect to (…) prevention and combating of crime'.[26] Another example of logical limits to the principle is to be found in the *Turansky* case,[27] where the *Landesgericht für Strafsachen Wien* wished to know whether the principle of *ne bis in idem* laid down in Art 54 of the CISA applies to a decision of a police authority to discontinue criminal proceedings, taken prior to the decision to charge a person but following an examination of the merits of the case. In its ruling of 22 December 2008, the Court refers again to *Gözütok and Brügge* and its settled case law.[28] It did not exclude that a decision taken by a police authority could provide the basis for a *bis*. However, it stated that, in order to assess whether a decision is final for the purposes of Art 54 of the CISA, the national law of the State where the decision originated must consider it to be final and binding and the decision must lead, in that State, to the protection granted by the *ne bis in idem*.[29] Finding that, in the case in hand, the decision taken by the police authority did not preclude the institution of new criminal proceedings in respect of the same acts in the territory of that State under national law, the Court concluded that such a decision could not constitute a decision which finally disposed of the case within the meaning of Art 54 of the CISA.[30]

Other decisions limiting the principle were rather critically welcomed. This is particularly the case for decisions relating to the so-called execution condition of Art 54 of the CISA *in fine*. This provides that the *ne bis in idem* will only apply on the condition that the penalty imposed 'has been enforced, is actually in the process of being enforced or can no longer be enforced under the laws of the sentencing contracting party'. In the *Spacic* case,[31] the Court was questioned in order to establish whether such an execution condition was compatible with Art 50 of the Charter. The Court gave a positive answer to that question, considering that Art 54 of the CISA *in fine* satisfies the four conditions laid down in Art 52(1) of the Charter. Under this provision, any limitation on the exercise of the rights and freedoms recognised in the Charter must be provided for by law and respect the essence of those rights. Limitations must also respect the principle of proportionality and may only be made if they are necessary and genuinely meet objectives of general interest recognised by the Union or the need to protect the rights and freedoms of others. The Court considers that each of these conditions is satisfied. The main argument guiding the Court is the objective pursued by the execution condition, ie the fight against impunity. It concludes that the restrictions laid down in Art 54 of the CISA *in fine* are compatible with Art 50 of the Charter.[32] In reaching this

[26] *Ibid*, para 34.
[27] CJEU, 22 December 2008, Case C-491/07 *Turansky* ECLI:EU:C:2008:768.
[28] *Ibid*, paras 32 to 41.
[29] *Ibid*, para 35.
[30] *Ibid*, paras 39 and 40.
[31] CJEU, 27 May 2014, *Spasic* ECLI:EU:C:2014:586.
[32] *Ibid*, paras 57 *ff*.

decision, the Court departed from the extremely thorough and nuanced position of Advocate General Niilo Jääskinen.[33] He had argued that, in the current state of EU law and among other factors in the light of the principle of mutual recognition, the generalised application of the execution condition does not comply with the proportionality requirement of Art 52 (1) of the Charter. In his view, the execution condition cannot be considered a justified interference into the right not to be tried or punished twice for the same criminal offence. The Advocate General accepted nonetheless that, in limited cases, the application of the execution condition might be necessary to achieve the desired objective.[34] This Court's decision was rather coolly received by several scholars, who especially noticed and regretted the change of spirit when compared with the *Gözütok and Brügge* case law. This was especially the case of Martin Wasmeier, who noticed that, in sharp contrast to settled case law, *Spasic* put an almost exclusive focus on avoiding impunity and avoids other elements of the area of freedom, security and justice such as free movement, legal certainty or mutual trust.[35] However, as is illustrated by its previously mentioned *M.* decision issued just a few days later, the Court did not mean to abandon its previous *Gözütok and Brügge* line of reasoning.[36] The discrepancy between the reasoning in *Spasic* and the Court's case law following *Gözütok and Brügge* remains, however, somehow puzzling.[37] It shows how difficult it is to strike the right balance between the various aspects of the area of freedom, security and justice and among the various concerns at stake.[38]

The *Kossowski*[39] case offered an opportunity to shed more light on how to strike this balance. The first question referred to the Court concerned the compatibility with Art 50 of the Charter of the exceptions that Art 55 of the CISA allows, so that the Contracting Parties can make a declaration by means of which they are not bound by Art 54 of the CISA in one or more of the three cases it foresees. These cases relate to the territory where the offence was committed, the essential public interest in prosecuting the offence and the interest in prosecuting acts committed by officials of that Contracting Party in violation of the duties of their office. As such, they give prevalence to the States' interests and national sovereignty,[40]

[33] View of Advocate General Jääskinen delivered on 2 May 2014, ECLI:EU:C:2014:739.

[34] *Ibid*, paras 91 *ff*.

[35] M Wasmeier, 'Ne bis in idem and the Enforcement Condition: Balancing Freedom, Security and Justice?' (2014) *New Journal of European Criminal Law* 534 *ff*.

[36] *Ibid*.

[37] *Ibid*.

[38] I Armada and A Weyembergh, 'The Principle of *ne bis in idem* in Europe's Area of Freedom, Security and Justice' in V Mitsilegas, M Bergström, T Konstadinides (eds), *Research Handbook on EU Criminal Law* (Edward Elgar, 2016) 189 *ff*.

[39] CJEU, 29 June 2016, C–486/14, *Kossowski* ECLI:EU:C:2016:483.

[40] The Initiative of the Hellenic Republic with a view to adopting a Council Framework Decision concerning the application of the *ne bis in idem* principle, the so-called 'Greek proposal' proposed to repeal these exceptions but its negotiations failed because of the sensitivity of the project (see [2003] OJ C100/24).

rather than to human rights and the establishment of a real EU justice area.[41] If one relies solely on the explanations relating to the Charter, generally declaring that the exceptions permitting Member States to derogate from the *ne bis in idem* are covered by the horizontal clause in Art 52 (1) of the Charter without drawing a distinction between Arts 54 and 55 of the CISA, one is tempted to conclude that Art 55 of the CISA is in line with Art 50 of the Charter. But, if, by contrast, one acknowledges the limited legal value of the explanations and proceeds to an in-depth examination of the conformity of the exceptions of Art 55 of the CISA with the conditions set out in Art 52(1), one can cast doubt on the condition of respecting the essence of the rights and freedoms recognised in the Charter having been fulfilled. Indeed, those exceptions give precedence to States' interests and to national sovereignty considerations over fundamental rights and the establishment of an EU area of criminal justice. In its decision No 1/2011, the Greek Supreme Court (*Arios Pagos*) ruled that Art 55(1) of the CISA is incompatible with Art 50 of the Charter since it cannot be justified pursuant to Art 52(1) of the Charter. It consequently abolished the Greek declaration that sought to avoid the application of the principle to drug trafficking offences.[42] In such a context, it would of course have been extremely interesting to have the Court of Justice's position on the compatibility of the exceptions of Art 55 of the CISA with Art 50 of the Charter. In its conclusions,[43] Advocate General Yves Bot considered that Art 55(1)(a) of the CISA is invalid, not due to the integration of the Schengen acquis into EU law in itself[44] but because its effect is to deprive the *ne bis in idem* principle of its content.[45] In his reasoning, specific emphasis is put on the *Gözütok and Brügge* case law,[46] on the link between the *ne bis in idem* principle and that of mutual recognition and on the fundamental importance of the latter principle for the construction of the area of freedom, security and justice. According to Advocate General Bot, an exception could only be made to this conclusion if it were justified by the need to give the reservation useful effect in favour of a superior interest which would not hinder the development of the area of freedom, security and justice.[47] He then examines whether the reservation is useful or necessary and concludes that it is not.[48] It thus considers it invalid with regard to Art 50 of the Charter. In its judgment of 29 June 2016, the Court did not answer the question of compatibility between Art 55 of the CISA and Art 50 of the Charter. It moved

[41] See especially K Ligeti, 'Rules on the Application of *ne bis in idem* in the EU' (2009) *Eucrim* (1–2) 41.

[42] Following a similar approach, see the judgment of the *Tribunale di Milano* of 6 July 2011. For a critical comment see Chiara Amalfitano 'Il principio del *ne bis in idem* tra caas e carta dei diritti fondamentali del l'Unione Europea' [2012] *Cassazione penale* 3889.

[43] Opinion of Advocate General Bot delivered on 15 December 2015, ECLI:EU:C:2015:812.

[44] *Ibid*, paras 33 *et seq*.

[45] *Ibid*, para 48.

[46] *Ibid*, paras 41 *et seq*.

[47] *Ibid*, para 49.

[48] *Ibid*, paras 50 *et seq*.

immediately to the other preliminary question relating to the definition of the *bis*. This part of the judgment is well known because it confirmed the Court's position in its *M.* judgment as to the importance of the examination of the merits of the case to conclude to the existence of a *bis* or a final decision.[49] Concluding that the decision did not constitute a *bis* (a final decision), it considered that it was no longer necessary to answer the previous question.[50] The question as to whether the Court will extend its reasoning in the *Spasic* judgment relating to Art 54 *in fine* to the reservations of Art 55 of the CISA or whether it will rather come closer to its *Gözütok and Brügge* line of reasoning thus remains so far unanswered. And yet, this a fundamental issue because of the extremely sensitive underlying question of the balance to be struck between mutual trust and national sovereignty.[51]

IV. The General Impact on the Functioning of the Mutual Recognition Principle and on the Mutual Trust Principle

In its transnational dimension, the principle of *ne bis in idem* at the European level leads to the recognition of the *res judicata* of foreign decisions. The work seeking to deepen Art 54 of the CISA was thus motivated by the desire to fully achieve the objective of setting up an area of freedom, security and justice[52] and was logically attached to the principle of mutual recognition.[53] It is indeed in the light of these objectives that Art 54 of the CISA has been interpreted by the Court of Justice.

The *Gözütok and Brügge* judgment was the first decision of the Court of Justice dealing with the principle of mutual recognition in criminal matters and the first in the Court's case law on cooperation on criminal matters to insist on the importance of mutual trust. Since then, the importance of mutual trust has steadily grown such that it has gained the status of a 'principle of

[49] *Kossowski* (n 39) para 42.

[50] *Kossowski* (n 39) para 55.

[51] A Weyembergh, 'Le ne bis in idem en matière pénale dans l'UE: de quelques développements récents et de quelques perspectives' in D Brach-Thiel (dir), *Actes de la 5ème journée franco-belge de droit pénal, Existe-t-il encore un seul non bis in idem aujourd'hui?* (L'Harmattan, 2017) 195 *ff.*

[52] See Action Plan of the Council and the Commission on how best to implement the provisions of the Treaty of Amsterdam on an area of freedom, security and justice (the so-called 'Vienna Plan') [1999] OJ C19/1, point 49 e); the Commission's Green Paper on conflicts of jurisdiction and the principle of *ne bis in idem* in criminal proceedings COM(2005)696final, 23 December 2005 and the Greek proposal (n 40). See also, for example, the Opinion of Advocate General Ruiz-Jarabo Colomer in Case C-436/04 *Van Esbroeck* [2006] ECR I-02333, para 23, who sees in Art 54 of the CISA 'a rule designed to assist European integration by creating a common area of freedom, security and justice'.

[53] See the Programme of measures to implement the principle of mutual recognition of decisions in criminal matters [2001] OJ C12/10; the Commission's Green Paper and the Greek proposal.

fundamental importance' in the Court's Opinion 2/13.[54] Indeed, it is one of the main arguments on which the Court has built its reasoning to conclude on the non-compatibility with the Treaties of the draft agreement on the accession of the European Union to the European Convention on Human Rights (ECHR).[55] However, no explicit reference to its *Gözütok and Brügge* judgment is to be found in this Opinion. Furthermore, although it somehow constitutes its starting point, the *Gözütok and Brügge* judgment is only rarely referred to in the Court's case law dealing with the other EU instruments of mutual recognition in criminal matters, such as the Framework Decision of 13 June 2002 on the European Arrest Warrant (EAW).[56] One of the reasons for this could be that the concerns served by the *ne bis in idem* principle are different from most other EU instruments implementing mutual recognition in criminal matters. Indeed, whereas the main objective of the latter instruments is to strengthen the efficiency of judicial cooperation and the fight against impunity, the *ne bis in idem* principle intends rather to improve defendants' rights. So, although mutual trust is most of the time or at least frequently in tension with the protection of human rights, in the case of the *ne bis in idem* principle, it contributes to/strengthens their protection.[57]

The *Gözütok and Brügge* judgment has nevertheless been explicitly referred to a few times. In this respect, the first judgment of 3 May 2007 of the Court of Justice in the *Advocaten voor de Wereld VZW* case is worth mentioning.[58] As a reminder, in this preliminary ruling, the Court confirmed the validity of the Framework Decision of 13 June 2002 on the EAW and especially the compatibility with the principle of equality and non-discrimination and the principle of legality in criminal matters of its Art 2(2), which limits the verification of the requirement of double criminality for the offences mentioned in it. It is in this respect that the Court referred by way of analogy to the *Gözütok and Brügge* judgment. It indeed considered that, with regard to the fact that the lack of precision in the definition of the categories of offences in question risks giving rise to disparate implementation of the Framework Decision within the various national legal orders, it is not the objective of the Framework Decision to harmonise the substantive criminal law of the Member States. It went on to state that nothing in Title VI of the EU Treaty makes the application of the EAW conditional on harmonisation of the criminal laws of the Member States within the area of the offences in question.[59] So, in this regard, the legacy of the *Gözütok and Brügge* case law is clear here as well: harmonisation is not a

[54] CJEU, 18 December 2014, Opinion 2/13 ECLI:EU:C:2014:2454.

[55] See particularly paras 191 and 194.

[56] FD 2002/584/JHA (n 7).

[57] See E Bribosia and A Weyembergh, 'Confiance mutuelle et droits fondamentaux: "Back to the future"' (2016) *Cahiers de droit européen* 469–521.

[58] CJEU, 3 May 2007, Case C-303/05 *Advocaten voor de Wereld VZW* ECLI:EU:C:2007:261.

[59] *Ibid*, para 59.

condition for mutual trust and for mutual recognition in general. Without going into further details because much has been written about this, let us notice that the complementary relationship between mutual recognition and mutual trust on the one hand and approximation of legislation on the other has been clearly established.[60] The Treaty itself recognises such a link (see Art 82, para 2 TFEU), as do the European Council[61] and the EU legislator.[62]

Another interesting preliminary ruling relating to the Framework Decision on the EAW where the *Gözütok and Brügge* judgment is mentioned is the *Mantello* case.[63] This ruling concerns the interpretation of the mandatory ground for refusal based on the *ne bis in idem* principle which is enshrined in Art 3(2) of the Framework Decision on the EAW. It constitutes, in a way, the meeting point of two types of mutual recognition/mutual trust: one serving the interests of the fight against impunity (execution of the European Arrest Warrant) and the other serving the interests of the individual (ground for refusal based on the *ne bis in idem* principle). After reformulating the question referred,[64] the Court ruled on the *bis*. It held in particular that 'whether a person has been "finally" judged for the purposes of Art. 3 (2) of the Framework Decision is determined by the law of the Member State in which judgement was delivered'. By doing so, it applied by analogy its decision in the aforementioned *Turansky* case.[65] However, the Court goes further and states that, in circumstances such as those at issue in the main proceedings, where the issuing authority, in response to a request for information, has expressly stated and explained that its earlier judgment does not cover the acts referred to in the arrest warrant and therefore does not preclude the criminal proceedings referred to in that arrest warrant, the executing judicial authority is

[60] See for instance A Suominen, 'The Sensitive Relationship between the Different Means of Legal Integration: Mutual Recognition and Approximation' in C Brière and A Weyembergh (eds), *The Needed Balances of EU Criminal Law: Past, Present and Future* (Hart Publishing, 2018); A Weyembergh, *L'harmonisation des législations : condition de l'espace pénal européen et révélateur de ses tensions* (Bruxelles, édition de l'Université de Bruxelles, 2004).

[61] See for instance The Stockholm Programme ([2010] OJ C115/1–38).

[62] See in particular the preamble of the directives implementing the roadmap on the rights of the suspects and accused persons, namely Directive 2010/64/EU of 20 October 2010 on the right to interpretation and translation in criminal proceedings [2010] OJ L280/1–7; Directive 2012/13/EU of 22 May 2012 on the right to information in criminal proceedings [2010] OJ L142/1–10; Directive 2013/48/EU of 22 October 2013 on the right of access to a lawyer in criminal proceedings and in European Arrest Warrant proceedings, and on the right to have a third party informed upon deprivation of liberty and to communicate with third persons and with consular authorities while deprived of liberty [2013] OJ L294/1–12; Directive (EU) 2016/343 of 9 March 2016 on the strengthening of certain aspects of the presumption of innocence and of the right to be present at the trial in criminal proceedings [2016] OJ L65/1–11; Directive (EU) 2016/800 of 11 May 2016 on procedural safeguards for children who are suspects or accused persons in criminal proceedings [2016] OJ L132/1–20; and Directive (EU) 2016/1919 of 26 October 2016 on legal aid for suspects and accused persons in criminal proceedings and for requested persons in European Arrest Warrant proceedings [2016] OJ L297/1–8.

[63] CJEU, 16 November 2010 Case C-261/09 *Mantello* ECLI:EU:C:2010:683 (see para 45).

[64] *Ibid*, para 43.

[65] *Ibid*, paras 46 and 47.

obliged to draw all the appropriate conclusions from the assessments made by the issuing judicial authority in its response.[66] Thus, the Court is no longer simply stating that one must turn to the national law of the State where the decision comes from to check whether that decision puts an end to criminal prosecutions and terminates criminal proceedings. Against the Opinion of Advocate General Yves Bot,[67] it holds that the executing authority must conform to the analysis done by the issuing authority. In other words, it must trust its concrete analysis of the first decision taken. The Court seems to have considerably extended the limitations to the autonomous interpretation of the concept of *bis* established in the *Turansky* case. It confirms the philosophy underpinning the principle of mutual recognition, according to which the bulk of the checks should be carried out in the issuing State and duplicating checks should be avoided to the largest possible extent. The Courts' approach is, however, hard to reconcile with the binding nature of the ground for refusal at stake.[68] But as one knows, in its case law interpreting the Framework Decision on the EAW, the Court has since then introduced some limits to such a high level of trust serving the efficiency of the surrender procedures and it has achieved a better balance between the various interests at stake.[69]

V. Conclusion

The *Gözütok and Brügge* judgment is the first in a long series of rulings by which the Court of Justice has largely contributed to the *ne bis in idem* principle and more generally to the mutual recognition principle. It has been qualified as a visionary or groundbreaking decision.[70] Indeed, the Court's line of argument in which it emphasised the link to free movement and 'the necessary implication that Member States have mutual trust in their criminal justice systems' has become a golden thread of this case law.[71]

However, over the years, the Court's case law has evolved towards a more moderate or finely nuanced approach, but it has also revealed several tensions or even inconsistencies. The latter show how difficult it is to reconcile the various concerns at stake and find the right balance between the different interests to take into consideration in order to build a real area of freedom, security and justice.

[66] *Ibid*, para 50.

[67] Opinion of Advocate General Bot, 7 September 2010, ECLI:EU:C:2010:501.

[68] A Weyembergh, 'Les arrêts de la CJUE du 21 octobre 2010 dans l'affaire I.B. et du 16 novembre 2010 dans l'affaire Mantello' (2011) *Journal de droit européen* 177 *ff*.

[69] See especially CJEU, 5 April 2016, Cases C-404/15 and C-659/15 PPU *Aranyosi and Caldararu* ECLI:EU:C:2016:198.

[70] Wasmeier (n 35).

[71] Wasmeier (n 35).

It is case law in the making/under construction. The search by the Court for the right equilibrium is ongoing. This is thus a story that should be closely monitored. Interesting cases concerning the *ne bis in idem* principle are currently pending, but most of these concern Art 50 of the EU Charter of Human Rights.[72] A few others concern the interpretation of Art 54 of the CISA.[73] These and future preliminary questions will undoubtedly give the Court of Justice the opportunity to sharpen its approach and orientation.

[72] See especially Cases C-596/16 and C-597/16 *Di Puma and Consob* (see Opinion of Advocate General Campos Sánchez-Bordona, 12 September 2017, ECLI:EU:C:2017:669); Case C-537/16 *Garlsson Real Estate e.a.* (see Opinion of Advocate General Campos Sánchez-Bordona, 12 September 2017, ECLI:EU:C:2017:668; Case C-524/15 *Menci* (see Opinion of Advocate General Campos Sánchez-Bordona, 12 September 2017, ECLI:EU:C:2017:667).

[73] See for instance Case C-390/16 *Lada*, which concerns both Art 50 of the Charter and Art 54 of the CISA (see [2016] OJ C350/16).

The Impact of Case C-187/01 [Gözütok/Brügge] *at the National Level: Inadvertent Legacy*

ELISAVET SYMEONIDOU-KASTANIDOU AND YANNIS NAZIRIS

I. Introduction

Few might have predicted that European criminal law would be largely shaped by a judgment delivered on the basis of Article 54 of the Convention Implementing the Schengen Agreement (CISA).[1] Yet the manner in which the European Court of Justice treated the principle of *ne bis in idem* in the joined cases of *Gözütok/Brügge*[2] was destined to have a lasting impact on both the European and the national level.

Both cases entailed criminal proceedings instituted against Messrs Gözütok (in Germany) and Brügge (in Belgium) for offences committed in the Netherlands and Belgium, respectively; those proceedings were instituted despite the fact that the two accused had been subjected to procedures in the Netherlands and Germany, respectively, which had been discontinued upon payment of 'a certain sum of money' determined by the Public Prosecutor as part of an out-of-court settlement barring further prosecution. Thus, a central issue in applying the *ne bis in idem* principle as enshrined in Article 54 of the CISA was the classification of the terms ('obligations') imposed to the accused as 'punitive' in nature.

The Court found that the aforementioned procedure was criminal in nature given that the decision to refrain from prosecution was made by 'an authority required to play a part in the administration of criminal justice in the national legal system concerned',[3] and that it ultimately 'penalises' the conduct in question via the imposition of 'certain obligations prescribed by the Public Prosecutor'.[4]

[1] According to this provision: 'A person whose trial has been finally disposed of in one Contracting Party may not be prosecuted in another Contracting Party for the same acts provided that, if a penalty has been imposed, it has been enforced, is actually in the process of being enforced or can no longer be enforced under the laws of the sentencing Contracting Party'.

[2] Joined Cases C-187/01 and C-385/01 *Criminal proceedings against Hüseyin Gözütok and Klaus Brügge* [2003] ECR I-1345 (hereafter 'Judgment').

[3] *Ibid*, para 28.

[4] *Ibid*, para 29.

In his pertinent Opinion,[5] Advocate General Ruis-Jarabo Colomer more conspicuously argued that the obligations were imposed as 'an alternative sanction which constitutes retribution for the culpable conduct and a deterrent against future transgressions',[6] thereby forming an exercise of the State's '*ius puniendi*'.[7] He further noted that, by providing consent to the out-of-court settlement, the accused 'acknowledges his guilt',[8] thereby 'expiating it',[9] and thus 'need not fear further sanction'.[10]

This was the premise on which the Court unfolded its position on the following themes:

- The elevation of 'mutual trust' to normative status.
- The conditions of applying Article 54 CISA in terms of both substantive and procedural law.
- The method of interpretation which should be applied in discussing principles such as *ne bis in idem*.

These three themes will be discussed below,[11] followed by brief conclusions as to the overall impact of the case in point.

II. Contribution to the Recognition of Mutual Trust as a Normative Tool

The part of the judgment that is widely held to be its most significant contribution relates to the elevation of mutual trust to the status of a normative guide to Member States in their effort towards integration. Undoubtedly, this particular aspect of the case is also closely associated with the impact of *Gözütok/Brügge* on European law.[12] However, one cannot deny that the Court's judgment was a milestone as regards the role of mutual trust within (and between) national jurisdictions.

The Court began by observing that

> nowhere in Title VI of the Treaty on European Union relating to police and judicial cooperation in criminal matters (Articles 34 and 31 of which were stated to be the legal basis for Articles 54 to 58 of the CISA), or in the Schengen Agreement or the CISA itself,

[5] Joined Cases C-187/01 and C-385/01 *Criminal proceedings against Hüseyin Gözütok and Klaus Brügge* [2003] ECR I-1345, Opinion of AG Ruis-Jarabo Colomer, ECR I-1349 (hereafter 'Opinion').

[6] *Ibid*, para 87.

[7] *Ibid*, paras 46 ff.

[8] *Ibid*, para 68.

[9] *Ibid*, para 49.

[10] *Ibid*.

[11] See sections II, III and IV, respectively.

[12] See generally K Lenaerts, 'The Principle of Mutual Recognition in the Area of Freedom, Security and Justice' (The Fourth Annual Sir Jeremy Lever Lecture, All Souls College, University of Oxford, 30 January 2015) 1, 6.

> is the application of Article 54 of the CISA made conditional upon harmonisation, or at the least approximation, of the criminal laws of the Member States relating to procedures whereby further prosecution is barred.[13]

Given this passage, it is rather paradoxical to note that several commentators have read an indirect call to harmonise into the findings of the judgment. Yet it is true that requiring mutual trust in a legal environment lacking uniformity ultimately does a better job in achieving harmonisation compared to direct pleas for approximation.

The Court continued by unreservedly declaring that

> in those circumstances, whether the *ne bis in idem* principle enshrined in Article 54 of the CISA is applied to procedures whereby further prosecution is barred (regardless of whether a court is involved) or to judicial decisions, there is a necessary implication that the Member States have mutual trust in their criminal justice systems and that each of them recognises the criminal law in force in the other Member States even when the outcome would be different if its own national law were applied.[14]

This was a rather bold step, considering the narrow space in which the Court had to navigate. It should indeed be recalled that the judgment in *Gözütok/Brügge* was delivered at a time when cooperation in criminal law matters was still confined to the intergovernmental regime of the third pillar, which largely explains the harsh criticism waged against its conclusions. Yet the Advocate General had provided a theoretical underpinning by invoking the principle of 'sincere cooperation',[15] while other cases had featured a reference to the principle of 'loyalty'. With hindsight, it can be argued that the subsequent movement towards the communitarisation of the former third pillar began with the Court's revolutionary approach in *Gözütok/Brügge*. It would in fact be accurate to say that the Court's judgment presaged the incorporation of *ne bis in idem* as a fundamental right in Article 50 of the Charter of Fundamental Rights (CFR),[16] guiding its demarcation in the post-Lisbon era.

In terms of its impact in other fields pertaining to criminal law, *Gözütok/Brügge* came shortly after the Council's Framework Decision on the European Arrest Warrant (EAW) of 2002,[17] whose preamble expressly alluded to a certain level of trust already achieved.[18] Both the Advocate General and the Court took stock

[13] Judgment (n 2), para 32.

[14] Judgment (n 2), para 33.

[15] See Art 4(3) of the Treaty on European Union (TEU): 'Pursuant to the principle of sincere cooperation, the Union and the Member States shall, in full mutual respect, assist each other in carrying out tasks which flow from the Treaties'.

[16] See D Sarmiento, 'Ne Bis in Idem in the Case Law of the European Court of Justice' in B van Bockel (ed), *Ne Bis in Idem in EU Law* (Cambridge University Press, 2016) 103.

[17] Council Framework Decision 2002/584/JHA on the European arrest warrant and the surrender procedures between Member States [2002] OJ L190/1.

[18] See reference in Presidency Conclusions, Tampere European Council (15–16 October 1999), at para 33: 'Enhanced mutual recognition of judicial decisions and judgments and the necessary approximation of legislation would facilitate cooperation between authorities and the judicial protection of individual rights. The European Council therefore endorses the principle of mutual recognition which, in its view, should become the cornerstone of judicial cooperation in both civil and criminal matters within the Union. The principle should apply both to judgments and to other decisions of judicial authorities'.

of prior developments,[19] and braced them by providing a normative backbone. One indeed notes that the Court's judgment in *Gözütok/Brügge* has probably been the most influential precedent in terms of its impact on national court decisions concerning areas of EU law where mutual trust is of vital importance, having been widely cited in case law concerning EAW matters across Europe.

Besides, placing *ne bis in idem* within a normative context underlined by mutual trust also helps delimit the principle as recognised within the EU from other (parallel) sources, most notably Protocol No 7 to the European Convention on Human Rights (ECHR).[20] The relationship between the two is vital[21] given that all EU Member States are also State Parties to the ECHR.[22]

Clearly, there remain issues to be resolved, which were not touched upon by the Court's judgment in *Gözütok/Brügge*. These include: the position of reciprocity in applying *ne bis in idem*; the rapport between the national and transnational *ne bis in idem*;[23] or the relationship between the substantive aspects of *ne bis in idem* with purely substantive norms, such as the dual criminality requirement. These issues, however, will be better dealt with in the environment created after *Gözütok/Brügge*.

III. Contributions to the Clarification of the Normative Content of the *ne bis in idem* Principle

The wording of Article 54 CISA, coupled with the particular facts of the two joined cases in point, shifted the focus to the interpretation of requirements such as 'finally disposed of' or 'penalty', which are essential for clarifying the normative content of the *ne bis in idem* principle.[24] Still, the Court's contribution was not so much in delimiting the particular conditions of Article 54 but rather in opening up new fields of debate concerning the principle of *ne bis in idem*. It was indeed

[19] Indeed they prompted further developments. A few days after the ECJ judgment in *Gözütok/Brügge*, Greece submitted a proposal for a framework decision on *ne bis in idem* to replace Articles 54–58 CISA. The proposal defined criminal offences as *stricto sensu* offences (Article 1), equating administrative offences thereto on condition of an appeal procedure before a criminal court, and expressly classified extra-judicial mediated settlements as equivalent to 'final judgments', along with any decision producing *res iudicata* under national law.

[20] See Article 4.

[21] See X Groussot and A Ericsson, 'Ne Bis in Idem in the EU and ECHR Legal Orders: A Matter of Uniform Interpretation?' in B van Bockel (ed), *Ne Bis in Idem in EU Law* (Cambridge University Press, 2016) 53.

[22] Although it should be noted that Protocol No 7 has only scantily been ratified.

[23] See indicatively J Vervaele, 'The Transnational *ne bis in idem* Principle in the EU: Mutual Recognition and Equivalent Protection of Human Rights' (2005) 1(2) *Utrecht Law Review* 100, 110.

[24] This was in contrast to other prerequisites, such as the 'idem' prong, which did not become the object of serious discussion in this case. This is partly due to the fact that Article 54 applies to prosecution in respect of the same 'acts', not of the same 'offence', thus allowing less room for interpretative ambiguity as to the content of the 'idem' prong.

the first time that the Court attempted to address issues normally discussed within a national context.

A. The Notion of (Criminal) 'Penalty'

In order to fully appraise the terms 'penalty' or 'guilt', one would necessarily have to begin by placing them in a national context; this is not just because such notions are only definable within the confines of the domestic criminal law jurisdictions that prescribe them, but also because the so-called 'ius puniendi' – even as invoked in *Gözütok/Brügge* – comprises a sovereign prerogative of a given State. Financial 'obligations' of the sort imposed in both *Gözütok and Brügge* can hardly be regarded as criminal sanctions, given that they are typically not classified as such in the domestic criminal legislation of the States imposing them.[25] Besides, these measures do not feature substantive characteristics of a criminal penalty, such as a particular nature or severity.

Adding to the picture, the imposition of these measures does not presuppose a finding of 'guilt' or even an 'acknowledgment' thereof on the part of the accused.[26] Indeed, settlement procedures of the sort discussed in the Court's judgment may even provide leeway for accused individuals who simply desire to avoid burdensome criminal proceedings, regardless of their guilt or innocence. The only criterion suggested by the Advocate General is that the accused must be afforded the 'freedom to accept or reject the settlement'.[27] Yet the optional character of the settlement has nothing to say about substantive notions such as 'penalty' or 'guilt'. Therefore, contrary to the Advocate General's Opinion, no 'expiation' can be traced in the processes carried out.

A proper line of reasoning would begin from the classification of a given measure under domestic law and continue by placing it in a broader (European) perspective. This would in turn call for a demarcation of a 'European *ius puniendi*', to which domestic penalties would subscribe.[28] The Advocate General's Opinion seems to grasp this by stating, in so many words, that

> the construction of a Europe without borders, with its corollary of the approximation of the various national legal systems, including the criminal systems, presupposes that

[25] The problem is compounded given that the 'act' in question may be punishable by totally different standards in various jurisdictions.

[26] Even in the case of Article 153a of the German *Strafprozessordnung* (Criminal Procedure Code) (which gave rise to one of the two joined cases), no recognition of guilt could be read in the plea made by the accused, nor was there a finding of guilt on the authorities' part.

[27] Opinion (n 5), paras 94–95.

[28] In other words, the need arises to establish a common basis for *ius puniendi* across national jurisdictions, while recognising that the legal values protected may not be the same in every jurisdiction (even in areas of the law that fall within the ambit of Article 82 of the Treaty on the Functioning of the European Union (TFEU).

the States involved will be guided by the same values. It is here, in the sphere of values, that the principle under consideration achieves its full significance.[29]

This may be viewed either as a call to EU Member States to achieve further approximation of their national laws or as wishful thinking. Its primary significance, however, lies in the appeal to national courts to place the reading of their legal values in the broader context of Europeanisation. Yet neither the Opinion of the Advocate General nor the judgment of the Court attempt to delineate a set of substantive criteria defining a criminal penalty on the European level, as had been done by the European Court of Human Rights through its Engel criteria;[30] moreover, no discussion is made as to the values protected in the particular instances under scrutiny, which would allow for the conclusion that criminal justice had been definitively meted out via the out-of-court settlements in the Netherlands and Germany.

One may note that the ECJ did not have to resort to an expanded definition of a State's '*ius puniendi*' in order to apply Article 54 CISA; in doing so, it failed to fully engage in substantive law matters, such as the nature or effect of the penalty imposed. The Court was thus left with purely formal criteria, revolving around the 'authority' imposing the measure (even though, interestingly, the Court avowed to steer clear of 'formalism'). This could have presented a missed opportunity to expand the discussion so as to address future challenges, such as the distinction between administrative[31] and criminal sanctions[32] or even the application of the *ne bis in idem* principle in processes alternative to criminal justice, such as restorative justice. Still, the indirect effect of *Gözütok/Brügge* was to spawn a debate concerning the application of the *ne bis in idem* principle on entirely novel terms.

B. Procedural Issues: Competent 'Authority', 'Finality' and 'Enforcement'

The above definition of 'penalty', coupled with the definitive discontinuation of the proceedings, led the Court to find that the case had been 'finally disposed of'.[33] The Court arrived at its conclusion based on the observation that 'following such a procedure, further prosecution is definitively barred' on account of

[29] Opinion (n 5), para 55.

[30] See ECHR, *Engel and Others v The Netherlands* (1976) 1 EHRR 647.

[31] See, inter alia, Case C-617/10 *Åklagaren v Åkerberg Fransson* [2013] ECR I-0000 [EU:C:2013:280]; *cf* Case C-399/11 *Stefano Melloni v Ministerio Fiscal* [2013] ECR I-0000 [EU:C:2013:107].

[32] This matter is of particular significance not only in the ECHR environment, but also under Article 50 CFR: see, for instance, Supreme Court of Sweden (*Högsta domstolen*), Judgment of 29 June 2011, NJA 2011, 444.

[33] The equivalent terms in German and French would be '*rechtscräftig abgeurteilt*' and '*definitivement jugée*', respectively.

a penalty already 'enforced for the purposes of Article 54'.[34] The Advocate General corroborated this view by providing a brief overview of what he termed 'settlement procedures' in various Member States,[35] all of which produce *some form of res iudicata*, barring the reopening of the case.[36]

This line of reasoning is partly erroneous and partly lacking in precision. To begin with, it has already been mentioned that the imposition of a financial obligation on the accused following a 'settlement' can hardly be regarded as the equivalent of a criminal sanction. Accordingly, the better course would have been for the Court to acknowledge that the discontinuation of further (criminal) proceedings in the Netherlands and Germany, respectively, meant that the penalty threatened for the proscribed conduct 'could no longer be enforced', rather than consider the monetary fine a penalty 'already enforced'. This would ensure the fulfilment of the 'enforcement clause' of Article 54 while at the same time respecting the classification of criminal penalties under domestic law. It should be noted, of course, that any finding of the Court regarding 'enforcement' is now of reduced significance,[37] especially given the fact that Article 50 of the EU CFR does not require that a criminal penalty actually be 'enforced'.[38]

Another question which is partly left unanswered concerns the organ which shall be deemed 'competent' to render a final 'disposition' within the meaning of the law. The judgment appears to reduce this question to a mere 'matter of form', contending itself with any authority required to play a part in the administration of criminal justice.[39] At the same time, it stops short of clarifying which particular organs may be classified as an 'authority' of this sort. A combined reading of both the judgment and the Advocate General's Opinion indicates that a prosecutor or an examining magistrate[40] might be regarded as an authority capable of rendering a 'final disposition' in this regard, based on their competence to impose certain terms, such as a fine. However, two questions remain open: first, whether the same treatment must be recognised vis-à-vis settlements which are 'ratified' via a court decision as opposed to those which are not;[41] second, whether police authorities (or even customs officers) might be equated with such status, considering that

[34] Judgment (n 2), para 30.

[35] Opinion (n 5), paras 64 *ff*.

[36] Greece was (and still remains) an exception with respect to this matter for two reasons: a) Greek law does not recognise out-of-court criminal settlements; b) Greece had filed a reservation with respect to Article 54 CISA upon ratification of the Convention.

[37] I Anagnostopoulos, *Ne bis in idem: National and international aspects* (Law & Economy: P.N. Sakkoulas, 2008) 174 [in Greek].

[38] In point of fact, Article 50 of the Charter does not even specifically allude to a 'criminal penalty'.

[39] Judgment (n 2), para 31: 'The fact that no court is involved in such a procedure and that the decision in which the procedure culminates does not take the form of a judicial decision does not cast doubt on that interpretation, since such matters of procedure and form do not impinge on the effects of the procedure'.

[40] Opinion (n 5), para 111.

[41] One might argue that this was deliberately left open in the judgment so as to allow for a broad interpretation that might uphold both kinds of settlement within the ambit of *ne bis in idem*.

they, too, retain the competence to impose certain 'sanctions' in a number of jurisdictions. In essence, one might observe that the Court was correct in pointing out that the application of the *ne bis in idem* principle should not merely hinge on matters of form, but missed the opportunity to set a concrete criterion which would lay emphasis on the substance of the matter, such as the type of the disposition, the nature of the sanction imposed, or even the degree of independence afforded to the competent authority in a given jurisdiction.

The main problem inherent in the Court's reasoning lies with its 'blanket' acceptance of settlement mechanisms as procedures by virtue of which a case is 'finally disposed of'. The Court seems to content itself with the fact that, by virtue of such a settlement, the State refrains from exercising its criminal jurisdiction. In order to dispel any doubts, the Court resorts to an argument *a maiori ad minus*:

> if Article 54 of the CISA were to apply only to decisions discontinuing prosecutions which are taken by a court or take the form of a judicial decision, the consequence would be that the *ne bis in idem* principle laid down in that provision (and, thus, the freedom of movement which the latter seeks to facilitate) would be of benefit only to defendants who were guilty of offences which – on account of their seriousness or the penalties attaching to them – preclude use of a simplified method of disposing of certain criminal cases by a procedure whereby further prosecution is barred, such as the procedures at issue in the main actions.[42]

The contribution of this passage, especially with respect to national law, was the fact that it expands the notion of 'final disposition' of a case so as to extend to not only court judgments (issued at the conclusion of a complete 'trial')[43] but also decisions or rulings by other competent authorities (eg a prosecutor).[44] This would in itself constitute a significant contribution to this matter, provided it proceeded a step further, suggesting a concrete criterion (preferably derived from substantive law) ample to equate out-of-court settlements with trial judgments.

Yet the aforementioned argument fails to reverse the essentially 'passive' character of the Court's position, which remains focused on the discontinuation of the proceedings. However, were it sufficient to find that a State has 'conclusively' exercised its *ius puniendi* by merely stopping short of prosecuting an individual, then the same ought to be true (*a fortiori*, one might add) in cases of States that have not even criminalised a given conduct to begin with: are we simply to assume that they, too, have exercised their *ius puniendi* in such (negative) fashion, thereby precluding other EU Member States from exercising theirs?

[42] Judgment (n 2), para 40.

[43] One might also observe that the Court failed to address the use of the term 'trial' as the process which should be "finally disposed of" under Article 54 CISA. It is true, of course, that expanding the notion of 'trial' so as to encompass out-of-court settlements would have been a plausible interpretation; still, one would expect that a judgment insisting on the rejection of legal nominalism would have something to say about this issue.

[44] One might add that this would also infringe on the sovereign right of Member States to dispose of criminal cases as they please.

The solution would be to distinguish between two kinds of 'settlements': on the one hand, there are settlements by virtue of which the State actually exercises its criminal authority by passing 'judgment' on the merits of the case; this sort of 'settlement' artlessly falls within the purview of Article 54 CISA, since it permanently precludes the reopening of the case (under any legal characterisation) concerning the same act. On the other hand, there are situations where a so-called 'settlement' ensures the 'temporary' discontinuation of the proceedings for reasons of expediency; this latter category of 'settlements' is not premised on a finding concerning the merits of the case, which explains why they do not produce definitive *res iudicata*, but rather allow the possibility of future prosecution of the same act (typically on the condition that new evidence is produced).[45]

The above distinction is not too hard to make, yet it is crucial in order to provide a meaningful basis on which to apply the *ne bis in idem* principle across various judicial systems. National codes of criminal procedure explicitly acknowledge the distinction by conferring the status of *res iudicata* to some judicial/prosecutorial acts and not others.[46] The distinction had in fact been made in pertinent case law: in the *Lacour* case,[47] the German Federal Court of Justice [*Bundesgerichtshof* – BGH] had found that the French ordonnance-de-lieu (issued by the interrogating judge) only bars prosecution when based on legal as opposed to factual grounds; in the latter instance, the case may be reopened upon new evidence.[48] In *Krombach*,[49] the same issue arose with respect to the dismissal of the case by virtue of a decision issued by a pre-trial chamber on the grounds of lack of evidence. Besides, similar problems arise with respect to the Belgian '*transactie*' (applicable to smuggling offences), the out-of-court settlement applicable to tax offences in France, and so forth. Even Article 153(1) of the German Code of Criminal Procedure [*Strafprozessordnung*], which had applied to Mr Brügge, did not have the effect of permanently discontinuing the case, but rather allowed for reopening under certain circumstances, including a finding that the act in question could give rise to a felony as opposed to a misdemeanor.

Nonetheless, neither the Court's judgment nor the Advocate General's overview engaged in this fine distinction between permanent and non-permanent discontinuation of a case. As a result, the ECJ's findings gave rise to a certain legal paradox by applying Article 54 to preclude criminal proceedings in a third State on the grounds of a procedure which does not per se preclude criminal prosecution

[45] In the subsequent case of *Miraglia*, the Court would embrace a more reserved position, holding that not every discontinuation of a case is able to preclude another State's authorities from exercising their power to prosecute: see Case C-469/03 *Criminal proceedings against Filomeno Mario Miraglia* [2005] ECR I-0200.

[46] This is not just pertinent to out-of-court settlements, but also becomes crucial as regards other prosecutorial acts: one example is Article 43 of the Greek Code of Criminal Procedure, which allows the prosecutor to 'close' a case in the absence of evidence (subject to reopening should evidence arise).

[47] BGH [*Lacour*], Urteil vom 10.6.1999, NStZ 2000, 636.

[48] *Arrêt de non-lieu par des raisons de fait.*

[49] BGH [*Krombach*], Urteil vom 4.12.1997, IX ZB 23/97; Urteil vom 29.6.2000, NJW 2000, 3289.

in the State which applied it in the first place. Once more, the legal means by which the Court arrived at its conclusion were deficient, yet the conclusion itself appears to place the principle in new light. It was indeed the first time in which the transnational *ne bis in idem* principle was treated as a different animal than its domestic counterpart.[50] This brings us to the broader questions underlying the judgment of the Court, which may be where its most significant contribution rests.

IV. Contribution to Establishing a Novel Method of Interpretation

In many respects, the significance of *Gözütok/Brügge* lies in the method of interpretation the Court employed in addressing the issues posed. Regardless of the merits or flaws of the particular solutions adopted in the judgment, the methodology which led to them not only inaugurated a new era for the Court itself but also opened up a novel path for national courts to follow (or deviate from, depending on each State's priorities).

It has already been made clear that the Court readily departed from a strict literal interpretation of the terms included in Article 54 CISA either in the form of stretching them to previously unapproachable limits (as in the case of the notion of 'penalty') or in the form of virtually ignoring them (as in the case of the term 'trial'). This in itself is justified due to the import of the questions posed, which far exceeded the scope of the CISA, as well as the inherent vagueness of substantive or procedural terms which are largely dependent on the particularities of each domestic system.[51]

Furthermore, the Court easily dispensed with arguments[52] revolving around the systematic interpretation of Article 54 in relation to Articles 55 and 58 CISA. First, it noted that 'Article 55 of the CISA must logically refer to the same acts and procedures as those by which, in relation to those facts, a case is likely to be "finally disposed of" for the purposes of Article 54', as evidenced by the 'use of the same term when referring to those acts and procedures'.[53] This is a proper reading of both provisions of the CISA, in effect preserving the principle of territoriality. Its impact on the national level is somewhat reduced, however, after the introduction

[50] J Lelieur, '"Transnationalising" *Ne Bis In Idem*: How the Rule of *Ne Bis In Idem* Reveals the Principle of Personal Legal Certainty' (2013) 9(4) *Utrecht Law Review* 198, 209.

[51] One might retort that such pluralism did not justify the piecemeal treatment of terms on behalf of the Court: for instance, one would expect a comparative overview of the term 'trial', 'penalty' or 'enforcement' prior to arriving at conclusions of such importance.

[52] These arguments were made by the governments of Belgium and Germany.

[53] Judgment (n 2), para 44. It is interesting to note that the Court, albeit making that observation, did not stop to consider what the meaning of these terms was.

of the CFR, whose Article 50 recognises no exception to the application of *ne bis in idem*,[54] including any exception linked to territoriality.[55]

Further, the Court held that 'applying Article 54 to procedures whereby further prosecution is barred does not render Article 58 nugatory', since it remains 'possible for Member States to apply national provisions which are broader than those not only of Article 54 of the CISA but also all those of the CISA which relate to the *ne bis in idem* principle', while Article 58 also 'acknowledges their right to implement national provisions giving the principle [of ne bis in idem] a wider scope or to make its application subject to less restrictive conditions, regardless of the nature of the foreign decisions concerned'.[56]

As a final step towards detaching the principle from the strict boundaries of the CISA, the Court released itself from the commitment to the original intent of the Contracting Schengen Parties.[57] Specifically, it noted that these intentions were no longer relevant, 'as they predate the Treaty of Amsterdam's integration of the Schengen *acquis* in the EU'.[58] The Court had made sure to note that the integration of the Schengen *acquis* (which includes Article 54 of the CISA) into the framework of the European Union is aimed at 'enhancing European integration and, in particular, at enabling the Union to become more rapidly the area of freedom, security and justice which it is its objective to maintain and develop'.[59]

The Court thus set the stage for the unfolding of its teleological interpretation on two distinct levels. The first level relates to the teleology of the provision itself. As mentioned above, the Court put forward the argument that if Article 54 were to apply to judicial decisions alone, the *ne bis in idem* principle would be confined to only serious offences for which out-of-court settlements are not available.[60] This line of reasoning evokes the Court's familiar practice of seeking a given provision's *effet utile* as a tool of interpretation. Although the ECJ already had a long record of relying on *effet utile*, *Gözütok/Brügge* is interesting since it was the first time where this method of interpretation was put to use in the framework of the third pillar. In a certain way, the invocation of *effet utile* in this area was less liable to attract criticism that the Court was engaging in active 'policymaking under the guise of interpretation'. If anything, this marked the reversal of a previously

[54] This in effect 'nullifies' any reservations made by State parties to the CISA, in as much as they are now bound by Article 50 CFR: see pertinently the decision of *Areios Pagos*, ie the Greek Supreme Court [Grand Chamber] 1/2011, NOMOS database; *cf* Athens Court of Appeal, 4703/2011, NOMOS database.

[55] For instance, the Charter would in principle bind a State to respect *ne bis in idem* even in the event of an offence committed in a State's own territory, which has been punished with a minor penalty in another jurisdiction.

[56] Judgment (n 2), para 45.

[57] J Vervaele, '*Ne Bis In Idem*: Towards a Transnational Constitutional Principle in the EU?' (2013) 9(4) *Utrecht Law Review* 211, 221.

[58] Judgment (n 2), para 46.

[59] Judgment (n 2), para 37.

[60] Judgment (n 2), para 40.

prevailing tendency: instead of interpreting criminal law provisions in light of their understanding in domestic law, national provisions would from then on have to be read in light of European norms.

It was the second level, however, which was most striking in terms of the selected method of interpretation. In a move typical of its overall practice, the Court shifted the focus from the specifics of applying the *ne bis in idem* principle within the confines of national legal systems to a higher level of generality,[61] explicitly associating Article 54 with the final goal of integration. By abstracting out at such heights, the Court allowed itself to enter a discussion on the 'effectiveness' of EU law, liberated from textual details.[62] One might say that the discussion was no longer focused on the teleology of the particular provision but the teleology of the system in which the provision belongs.

Such line of reasoning is already worthy of note. However, its principal contribution lies in the fact that it lifted *ne bis in idem* from the general pool of 'principles' into the realm of *individual rights*.[63] In point of fact, *ne bis in idem* would no longer be treated as a right of each citizen within a given jurisdiction, but would be viewed as a European citizen's right within an ever-integrating Europe.[64] After *Gözütok/Brügge*, the debate would be centred on whether *ne bis in idem* is merely a corollary to 'freedom of movement' (as the Court's judgment seemed to suggest) or a fundamental right in and of itself.[65] This radical change would have the effect of repositioning national courts vis-à-vis the ECJ, much like constitutionalism affects the interplay between State courts and the US Supreme Court on the other side of the Atlantic.

V. Concluding Remarks and Suggestions

The transnational *ne bis in idem* principle is premised on mutual trust: such trust is not just oriented towards particular legal norms but rather towards the judicial system of each Member State, viewed in its entirety. The judgment of the ECJ in the joined cases of *Gözütok/Brügge* was able to grasp this link at a time when most national courts remained fenced within the confines of their national understanding of the principle. Although one might conclude that this was essentially the

[61] G Conway, 'Judicial Interpretation and the Third Pillar' (2005) 13(2) *European Journal of Crime, Criminal Law & Criminal Justice* 255, 277.

[62] This has aptly been described as an exercise in 'meta-teleology': see M Lasser, *Judicial Deliberations: A Comparative Analysis of Transparency and Legitimacy* (Oxford University Press, 2004) 232.

[63] See B van Bockel, 'The 'European' Ne Bis in Idem Principle Substance, Sources, and Scope' in B van Bockel (ed), *Ne Bis in Idem in EU Law* (Cambridge University Press, 2016) 13.

[64] On the one hand, this approach tends to narrow down the scope of the principle to the extent it is used as a tool of 'Europeanisation'. On the other, however, it effectively introduces the principle in a European context.

[65] See AH Gibbs, *Constitutional Life and Europe's Area of Freedom, Security and Justice* (Routledge, 2016) 112.

Court's contribution, the aforementioned thoughts indicate that the significance of the judgment also lies in its 'inchoate' contribution to the normative content of the *ne bis in idem* principle. The Court indeed opened up new paths for the discussion concerning the principle on several levels. Specifically:

- It purportedly confined itself to the interpretation of Article 54 CISA but ultimately offered a broader understanding of the *ne bis in idem* principle that well exceeded the boundaries of the said instrument.
- It delivered its judgment at a time when cooperation in criminal law matters largely consisted in the intergovernmental regime of the third pillar, yet ended up contributing not only to the communitarisation of the (now former) third pillar but also to the treatment of *ne bis in idem* as a fundamental (individual) right in the post-Lisbon era.
- Although it was limited (by definition) to the EU environment, it spawned a debate concerning the relationship of *ne bis in idem* in the 'legal orders' of the EU and the ECHR, respectively.
- It fell short of providing an adequate definition of (criminal) 'penalty' (based on substantive criteria), but set the stage for a conceptualisation of the term which would radically modify the way national systems viewed each other (and themselves).
- It appeared to expand *ne bis in idem* so as to encompass 'authorities' which do not belong to the (*stricto sensu*) judiciary of a given Member State, but stopped short of clarifying which types of organs might be classified as such, which guarantees should underlie the exercise of their functions, and so forth.
- It vaguely delimited the notion of 'final disposition', yet it managed to place its expansion at the centre of the discussion.
- It discussed *ne bis in idem* at a time when Member States could still reserve for themselves the right to invoke territoriality as an exception to the principle, yet presaged the treatment of *ne bis in idem* at subsequent stages (eg under the CFR), where the significance of territoriality would be undermined.

The new institutional framework in the EU in the post-Lisbon era, coupled with the ever-expanding need to achieve an adequate level of mutual trust, means that national systems are unable to 'absorb' the full extent of *ne bis in idem* as envisaged in *Gözütok/Brügge*. It is now time to clarify notions that the Court's judgment left undecided. Thus, the need arises for a new set of rules (preferably in the form of a pertinent Directive), which shall specifically provide for:

- the guarantees which need to be afforded to a competent organ in order for the latter to be classified as an 'authority required to play a part in the administration of criminal justice in the national legal system concerned';
- the conditions under which a 'decision' rendered by the aforementioned authorities shall be deemed to constitute a (binding) 'final disposition' of the case concerned;

- a set of concrete (substantive) criteria which shall determine the nature of a 'term' or 'sanction' as criminal; and
- possibly even a classification of offences (based on their nature and/or gravity), which shall permit the authorities of each Member State to apply *ne bis in idem* in a manner that is consistent across jurisdictions.

8

C-486/14 – *Kossowski*

Judgment (Grand Chamber) C-486/14 Piotr Kossowski, *29 June 2016*

KAI AMBOS*

I. Factual Background[1]

Mr Kossowski (hereinafter 'K') allegedly committed an aggravated extortion in Hamburg, Germany, on 2 October 2005. The Hamburg Public Prosecutor's Office opened a criminal investigation against him. Polish authorities arrested him on 20 October 2005 on other charges but also opened an investigation for the said offence. This investigation was, however, terminated on 22 December 2006 due to lack of sufficient evidence. The reason given was that the suspect refused to give a statement and the potential witnesses (the victim and a hearsay witness) could not be interrogated since they live in Germany. Further, the victim did not use his right to appeal against the terminating decision within seven days. On 24 July 2009 the Hamburg Public Prosecutor's Office issued a European Arrest Warrant against K and on 4 September 2009 the surrender was requested from the Polish authorities. However, it was refused by the Regional Court of Koszalin on 17 September 2009 in view of the termination of the investigation which that Court considered as final for the purposes of the Polish Criminal Procedural Code.

K was then later arrested in Berlin on 7 February 2014 and charged by the Hamburg Public Prosecutor's Office on 17 March 2014. Yet, the Hamburg Regional Court (*Landgericht*), by decision of 4 April 2014, refused to open trial proceedings invoking the European *ne bis in idem* provision of Art 54 of the Convention Implementing the Schengen Agreement of 14 June 1985 ('CISA')[2] and lifted the arrest

* The views expressed are those of the author and do not necessarily reflect the views of the KSC. I thank Christopher Penkuhn for research assistance and Luca Alexander Petersen for assistance in formatting the text.

[1] CJEU GC Case C-486/14 *Kossowski* ECLI:EU:C:2016:483 [29 June 2016] paras 12–23.

[2] [2000] OJ L239/19.

warrant so that K was released. The Hamburg Prosecutor's Office filed an appeal against this decision at the Hamburg Higher Regional Court (*Oberlandesgericht*). This Court decided to suspend the proceeding in order to request a preliminary ruling of the Court of Justice of the European Union (CJEU) with regard to the following two questions to be summarised as follows: (i) Is the German reservation to Art 54 CISA pursuant to Art 55(1)(a) CISA valid in light of Art 50 of the Charter of the Fundamental Rights of the EU ('CFREU')? (ii) Does the Polish prosecutorial termination decision constitute a final decision within the meaning of Art 54 CISA ('finally disposed of')?

According to Art 54 CISA and Art 50 CFREU, a person cannot be prosecuted for the same conduct anew in a Member State if his/her 'trial has been finally disposed of' in another Member State, ie both Art 54 CISA and Art 50 CFREU have a transnational (transeuropean) effect and are not applicable in purely domestic proceedings.[3] In substance, Art 54 CISA and Art 50 CFREU differ only in that the former contains the so-called enforcement element (omitted in Art 50 CFREU), ie that 'the penalty has been imposed, it has been enforced, is actually in the process of being enforced or can no longer be enforced under the laws of the sentencing Contracting Party'. Apart from this, both rules have a different scope of application. While the CISA applies to all Schengen States,[4] the Charter covers the EU and its Member States, although special rules apply to Poland and the United Kingdom.[5] However, Art 55(1) CISA gives the Contracting Parties the option to declare Art 54 inapplicable in certain situations and for certain crimes.[6]

II. Decision of the Court

The Grand Chamber answered the second question in the negative, thereby making an answer to the first question unnecessary.[7] As to the meaning of 'finally

[3] K Ambos, *European Criminal Law* (Cambridge, Cambridge University Press, 2018) Ch 2 mn 165. For another view with regard to Art 50 CFREU, however, see Tomkin, in S Peers et al (eds), *The EU Charter of Fundamental Rights* (2014) Art 50 mn 50.02; A Eser, in J Meyer (ed), *Charta der Grundrechte der EU* (2014) Art 50 mn 6; Jarass, *Charta der Grundrechte der EU* (2016), Art 50 mn 10. However, these authors do not give convincing reasons, if any at all, for their position.

[4] Ambos (n 3) Ch 1 mn 34–35.

[5] Ambos (n 3) Ch 2 mn 154 with endnote 878.

[6] This declaration may be given for cases: '(a) where the acts to which the foreign judgment relates took place in whole or in part in its own territory; in the latter case, however, this exception shall not apply if the acts took place in part in the territory of the Contracting Party where the judgment was delivered; (b) where the acts to which the foreign judgment relates constitute an offence against national security or other equally essential interests of that Contracting Party; (c) where the acts to which the foreign judgment relates were committed by officials of that Contracting Party in violation of the duties of their office.'

[7] The Advocate General (AG) argued in *Kossowski* (n 1) that the reservation provided for by Art 55(1)(a) CISA 'does not respect the essence of the ne bis in idem principle as expressed in Article 50 of the Charter of Fundamental Rights of the European Union and must therefore be declared invalid' (Opinion of AG Bot, 15 December 2015, para 85(a)); concurring B Hecker, 'Europäisches Strafrecht: Transnationales

disposed of' in Art 54 CISA, the Chamber applied a *two-step test* according to which a final disposition of a case ('trial') requires, first, that a further prosecution – under the law of the (first) prosecuting State – must be definitely barred[8] and, second, that the respective decision 'was given after a determination had been made as to the merits of the case'.[9]

The first requirement was met in the case at hand since the Polish prosecutorial termination decision precludes any further prosecution under Polish law in Poland[10] and a prosecutor constitutes a judicial authority within the meaning of Art 54 CISA.[11] However, the second requirement has not been complied with since the Polish Prosecutor's Office had made its decision 'without a more detailed investigation … for the purpose of gathering and examining evidence'[12] – having failed to interrogate the victim and a further potential witnesses – and thus without a proper 'determination as to the merits of the case'.[13] As a consequence the Court decided that the Polish termination of the investigation did not finally dispose of K's case within the meaning of Art 54 CISA and his prosecution in Germany could not be hindered by this provision.

III. Analysis

The Grand Chamber's summary of the previous, somewhat eclectic case law in the form of the said two-step test[14] is convincing in that it offers a more systematic and consistent approach to the final decision requirement of Art 54 CISA. The Chamber's acceptance – as to the *first element* of this test – of a prosecutorial termination decision as a 'final (national) decision' within the meaning of Art 54 CISA, if that decision has such a final effect in the respective domestic jurisdiction, is in line with the Court's case law. This case law has interpreted this requirement broadly since *Gözütök and Brügge*. In the latter decision the Court considered conditional prosecutorial terminations (without the involvement of a court)[15] as final 'once the accused has fulfilled certain obligations and, in particular, has paid

Doppelbestrafungsverbot, Besprechung von EuGH, Urteil vom 29.6.2016 – C-486/14' (2016) 56 *Juristische Schulung (JuS)* 1133 at 1135; for a different view, see Ambos (n 3) Ch 2 mn 168.

[8] *Kossowski* (n 1), paras 34–41.

[9] *Kossowski* (n 1), paras 42–53.

[10] *Kossowski* (n 1), paras 36–37.

[11] *Kossowski* (n 1), para 39.

[12] *Kossowski* (n 1), para 48.

[13] *Kossowski* (n 1), paras 48, 53.

[14] *cf* K Wegner, 'Entscheidungen zur Verfahrenserledigung im Strafverfahren und ihre transnationale Rechtskraftwirkung gem. Art. 54 SDÜ, Art. 50 GRC' (2016) 17 *Höchstrichterliche Rechtsprechung in Strafsachen (HRRS)* 399.

[15] On the competent authority (not necessarily a judge), see also Ambos (n 3) Ch 2 mn 178–79 with further references.

a certain sum of money determined by the Public Prosecutor'.[16] Subsequent case law has followed this broad approach.[17]

In contrast, the Grand Chamber's take on the *second element* of the test – 'determination as to the merits' – is more interesting and somewhat innovative. First of all, it is important to note that the Chamber effectively limits the transnational *ne bis in idem* by requiring a 'determination as to the merits' by the terminating national authority. In fact, the Court had already argued in a similar fashion in *Miraglia*, holding that a termination of proceedings was not sufficient if it had only been ordered because an investigation had already been initiated in another country but without any determination as to the merits of the case.[18] Developing this approach further in the case of *M.*, the Court clarified that a determination as to the merits had taken place if different means of evidence had been collected and examined.[19]

Taking such a merits-based approach, the Grand Chamber calls for a substantive decision – resulting from a more or less thorough investigation – to trigger Art 54 CISA. This comes close to what has been called a 'qualified termination of proceedings' in academic writings.[20] Yet, such a qualified requirement does not follow from a literal or systematic interpretation of Art 54 CISA.[21] Instead, it can only be the result of a teleological, purpose-oriented interpretation of the provision. The Chamber is going in the right direction if it justifies its merits test by reading into Art 54 CISA a 'prevention and combating of crime' side taking recourse to Art 3(2) of the Treaty on European Union (TEU).[22] In other words, Art 54 CISA has, as Art 3(2) TEU, two sides: one ensuring the free movement of persons in the area of freedom, security and justice; and another one relating to the security in this area, especially 'the prevention and combating of crime'.[23]

[16] CJEU C-187/01 and C-385/01 *Gözütök and Brügge* [2003] ECR 2003 I-1345 [ECLI:EU:C:2003:87] para 48.

[17] *cf* CJEU C-469/03 *Miraglia* [2005] ECR 2005 I-2009 [ECLI:EU:C:2005:156] para 35; C-491/07 *Turanský* [2008] ECR 2008 I-11039 [ECLI:EU:C:2008:768] para 45; C-398/12 *M.* ECLI:EU:C:2014:1057 [5 June 2014] paras 31 *ff*, 41.

[18] *Miraglia* (n 17), paras 28, 35.

[19] *M.* (n 17), para 30 ('… that an order making a finding of "non-lieu" at the end of an investigation during which various items of evidence were collected and examined must be considered to have been the subject of a determination as to the merits …, in so far as it is a definitive decision on the inadequacy of that evidence and excludes any possibility that the case might be reopened on the basis of the same body of evidence.'). The German Federal Court (*Bundesgerichtshof*) adopts the same view (following *Kossowski* (n 1), para 48) in 3 StR 25/16 [28 July 2016], reprinted in (2016) 69 *Neue Juristische Wochenschrift (NJW)* 3044, at 3045 para 16. However, K Wegner, 'Strafklageverbrauch und Verfahrensbeendigung wegen überlanger Verfahrensdauer, Anmerkung zu BGH Urteil vom 28.7.2016 – 3 StR 25/16' (2017) 37 *Strafverteidiger (StV)* 227, 228 criticises the Bundesgerichtshof's rejection of a final decision within the meaning of Art 54 CISA in the concrete case of the termination of proceedings by a Lithuanian Court due to their excessive duration.

[20] M Mansdörfer, *Ne bis in idem im europäischen Strafrecht* (Berlin, Duncker & Humblot, 2004) 168 *ff*, 248 (orig 'Form "qualifizierter Verfahrensbeendigung"').

[21] *cf* Ambos (n 3) Ch 2 mn 174–75, 178.

[22] *Kossowski* (n 1), paras 45–49.

[23] *cf* Art 3(2) TEU *in fine* and *Kossowski* (n 1), para 47: 'Therefore, the interpretation of the final nature, for the purposes of Article 54 of the CISA, of a decision in criminal proceedings in a Member State must be undertaken in the light not only of the need to ensure the free movement of persons but also of the need to promote the prevention and combating of crime within the area of freedom, security and justice.' See previously *Miraglia* (n 17), para 34.

This second, security side of Art 54 CISA would be undermined, so the Chamber's argument goes, if a terminating decision without a merits-based determination would be covered by Art 54 CISA since this would 'make it more difficult, indeed impossible, actually to penalise … the unlawful conduct alleged against the accused' and 'clearly run counter to the very purpose of Art 3(2) TEU'.[24] This, of course, seems to go too far, especially if one takes into account Art 50 CFREU which, as correctly acknowledged by the Chamber, informs the interpretation of Art 54 CISA.[25] Indeed, Art 50 CFREU enhances the 'rights focus' of the European *ne bis in idem* and thus speaks against putting the legal security of Europeans citizen and the interest in crime prosecution on the same footing.[26] It is, contrary to the Chamber's view, the very purpose of a transnational *ne bis in idem* to make prosecutions and thus penalisations more difficult. Indeed, this is the consequence of the rights focus of any *ne bis in idem* provision. Of course, this does not, as such, exclude a substantive limitation of the transnational effect of such provisions but this limitation finds its reason rather in the 'quality of the relationship' between the States part of the respective system of mutual recognition than in vague policy aims of crime prevention and repression.

This brings us to the second, more fundamental argument of the Chamber to justify its restrictive interpretation of Art 54 CISA, namely the fundamental idea of *mutual trust*.[27] Indeed, Art 54 CISA is, as just pointed out, an expression of mutual recognition – being the fundamental cornerstone of post-Lisbon cooperation law in criminal matters[28] – since it presupposes that Member States mutually recognise their criminal justice decisions even if the outcome would be different if they only applied their national laws.[29] Mutual recognition, however, is not automatic but presupposes mutual trust which, albeit difficult to measure,[30] is premised, in turn, upon mutual respect, rights observance and common values.[31] In the context

[24] *Kossowski* (n 1), para 49; previously *Miraglia* (n 17), para 33; see also P Kottek, 'Anmerkung zu EuGH Urteil vom 29.6.2016 – C-486/14' (2016) 35 *Zeitschrift für Wirtschafts- und Steuerstrafrecht (wistra) 355, 356 f.*

[25] *Kossowski* (n 1), para 31 ('Article 54 must be interpreted in the light of Article 50.').

[26] See also K Gaede, 'Staatsanwaltschaftliche Verfahrenseinstellung und SDÜ-Doppelverfolgungsverbot EuGH, Anmerkung zu EuGH Urteil vom 29.6.2016 – C-486/14' (2016) 69 *Neue Juristische Wochenschrift (NJW)* 2942.

[27] *Kossowski* (n 1), paras 50–53.

[28] *cf* Arts 67(3) and 82(1) TFEU.

[29] *Kossowski* (n 1), para 50; previously CJEU C-297/07 *Bourquain* [2008] ECR 2008 I-9425 [EU:C:2008:708] para 37 ('Article 54 of the CISA …, necessarily implies that the Contracting States have mutual trust in their criminal justice systems and that each of them recognises the criminal law in force in the other Contracting States even when the outcome would be different if its own national law were applied.').

[30] See in so far on the project of 'Euro-Justis' (scientific indicators of confidence in justice), www.heuni.fi/en/index/researchareas/confidenceinthecjs/eurojustis-scientificindicatorsofconfidenceinjusticetoolsforpolicyassessment.html (last accessed 7 March 2019).

[31] On mutual trust and rights observance as a basis for mutual recognition, see V Mitsilegas, *EU Criminal Law after Lisbon* (Oxford, Hart Publishing, 2016) 125 *ff* (explaining a lack of trust with 'moral distance' [at 129, 151], and concluding that '[T]his deification of mutual trust … poses, however, significant challenges on the effective protection of fundamental rights, which seems to be subordinated

of Art 54 CISA, the trust of the second prosecuting State in the (terminating) decision of the first prosecuting State requires that this State's decision appears to be correct[32] to the second State and satisfies this State's prosecutorial interest too. Only then this State would see no further need and have no further interest in continuing to proceed with the respective case. To be able to make this assessment, the second prosecuting State needs however some basic information as to the grounds of the first prosecuting State's termination decision. As rightly pointed out by the Chamber,

> mutual trust can prosper only if the second Contracting State is in a position to satisfy itself, on the basis of the information provided by the first Contracting State, that the decision of the competent authorities of that first State does indeed constitute a final decision including a determination as to the merits of the case'[33]

This also makes sense from a rights perspective since only then – when the terminating decision is preceded by a determination as to the merits – a citizen/suspect can truly have the confidence that this decision entails a protection against a second prosecution; otherwise, without a determination as to the merits, confidence in non-prosecution has no factual basis.[34]

to the requirement to respect presumed and uncritically accepted trust' [at 151]); see also F Meyer, 'Der Grundsatz gegenseitigen Vertrauens – Konzeptualisierung und Zukunftsperspektiven eines neuen Verfassungsprinzips' (2017) 52 *Europarecht (EuR)* 163, 164 *ff*, 170 *ff* (for whom mutual trust is 'one of the great mysteries of European criminal law' [orig 'Zu den großen Mysterien des eur. Strafrechts', 161] and who, following an instructive overview of the current debate [164–70], identifies a new approach of the ECJ – since its Opinion 2/13 [thereto Ambos [n 3] Ch 2 mn 9–10] – towards a 'constitutional principle inherent in the Union' [orig 'unionsimmanenten Verfassungsprinzip', 173] and a 'cross-policy' concept [183] with an integrative political function [170 *ff*]); see also P Ronsfeld, *Rechtshilfe, Anerkennung und Vertrauen* (Berlin, Duncker & Humblot, 2015) 211 *ff* [217 *ff*]) (listing a joint reference system, mutual sympathy and coordination, transparency and integrity as trust-founding measures); for a fundamental critique from the perspective of legitimation theory, see G Vermeulen, 'The EU's Mutual Trust and Recognition Bubble – Challenging the Legitimacy of EU Criminal Policy & Judicial Cooperation in Criminal Matters' in K Tiedemann et al (eds), *Die Verfassung moderner Strafrechtspflege* (Baden-Baden Nomos, 2016) 181 ff; on the relationship between mutual recognition and trust, see also T Ostropolski, 'The CJEU as a Defender of Mutual Trust' (2015) 6 *New Journal of European Criminal Law (NJECL)* 167; on trust resulting from harmonisation, see P Asp, *Procedural Criminal Law Cooperation in the EU* (Stockholm, Stiftelsen Skrifter utgivna av Juridiska fakulteten vid Stockholms universitet, 2016) 54; on the indicators for mutual trust, see P Albers, 'Results Survey Contact Points of the European Judicial Network in Criminal Matters' in P Albers et al (eds), *Towards a Common Evaluation Framework to Assess Mutual Trust in the Field of the EU Judicial Cooperation Criminal Matters* (The Hague, Ministerie van Veiligheid en Justitie, 2013) 315; M Böse, 'Comparative Overview of the Country Reports and Surveys' in Albers et al, *ibid* 35761; on the weakening of mutual trust by rights violations, German Constitutional Court (*Bundesverfassungsgericht*), 2 BvR 2735/14 [15 December 2015] in (2016) 69 *Neue Juristische Wochenschrift (NJW)* 1149, paras 73–75, English translation available at www.bundesverfassungsgericht.de/SharedDocs/Entscheidungen/EN/2015/12/rs20151215_2bvr273514en.html (last accessed 3 May 2019); calling for more mutual trust, see E Herlin-Karnell, 'All Roads Lead to Rome: The New AFSJ Package and the Trajectory to Europe 2020' (2014) 9 *eucrim* 30.

[32] On this 'Richtigkeitsgewähr' ('guarantee of correctness') see previously M Böse, 'Der Grundsatz "ne bis in idem" in der Europäischen Union (Art 54 SDÜ)' (2003) 150 *Goltdammer's Archiv für Strafrecht (GA)* 752–53; conc Ambos (n 3), Ch 2 mn 176; furthermore Wegner (n 19) 227 (‚eine Art "Ernsthaftigkeitskontrolle"' – ‚a kind of "seriousness-test"').

[33] *Kossowski* (n 1), para 52.

[34] In a similar vein, see Gaede (n 26) 2942; Wegner (n 19) 228.

One must not overlook, however, that a merits test has ramifications which the Court does not address and which may unduly restrict the transnational *ne bis in idem* effect. First, it is difficult to define *in abstracto* when a *sufficient assessment of the merits* of the case has taken place in the first prosecuting State.[35] This is case- and context-dependent. In practice it is up to the second prosecuting State to assess the terminating decision of the first prosecuting State in light of the merits threshold. This implies a quality statement by that second State with regard to the investigation of the first State but there are obvious limits to such an external quality control. Indeed, it is difficult to imagine a judgment of insufficiency by the second State with regard to the first State's investigation except in extreme cases of a lack of or a totally insufficient investigation. The second State's position is comparable here to the position of the International Criminal Court with regard to the complementarity test where the Court has to assess the willingness and ability of a domestic jurisdiction to investigate and prosecute the crimes within its jurisdiction.[36] At any rate, the second State has three possibilities:

- accepting the first State's investigation as sufficiently detailed and thus ceasing its own investigation;
- considering the first investigation as insufficient and continuing to investigate itself;
- suspending proceedings and making a preliminary reference to the CJEU.

A second issue concerns the *termination* of national investigations *for purely legal reasons*, eg a bar to prosecution on grounds of a statute of limitations or immunities.[37] These kinds of terminations usually do not require a more detailed investigation but it suffices to establish the legal ground which calls for the termination. The decision would normally be final under national law without a further assessment on the merits. Would such a decision nonetheless amount to a final disposition of the respective case within the meaning of Art 54 CISA? It has been suggested that Art 54 CISA should apply if the termination decision amounts to a 'normative statement about the need to prosecute the respective conduct'.[38] While this is difficult to operationalise, it calls for a differentiation between normatively founded and purely formal decisions. In the former case, for example if proceedings are terminated since the prosecuting authority considered that the respective conduct only represented a minor wrong and therefore did not deserve a prosecution, Art 54 CISA should apply; in the latter case, for example if proceedings are terminated because of lack of competence of the prosecuting authority, Art 54 should not apply. Of course, this needs to be further developed with concrete cases in mind.

[35] Crit. see also Wegner (n 14) 401; Gaede (n 26) 2942 (calling for a more precise definition).

[36] *cf* Art 17 ICC Statute and K Ambos, *Treatise on International Criminal Law, Vol III: International Criminal Procedure* (Oxford, Oxford University Press, 2016) 266 *ff*.

[37] *cf* Wegner (n 14) 401–402.

[38] Wegner (n 14) 403 ('normative Aussage über die generelle Verfolgungswürdigkeit der betroffenen Tat' [free translation by the author]).

Impact of the Case C-486/14 – Kossowski *at National Level*

CELINA NOWAK

I. Circumstances of the Case

The preliminary ruling of the Court of Justice of 29 June 2016 in the case C-486/14 *Kossowski*[1] refers to the principle of *ne bis in idem* which is recognised as a general principle of criminal law in the EU Member States, as well as a general principle of the EU law,[2] provided for in both Article 54 of the Convention Implementing the Schengen Agreement of 14 June 1985 ('CISA') and Article 50 of the Charter of Fundamental Rights.

The circumstances of the case, as briefed by the Court in its judgment, are rather straightforward. Mr Piotr Kossowski, a Polish citizen, allegedly, on 2 October 2005 in Hamburg (Germany), committed acts which, under German criminal law, are classified as extortion with aggravating factors. At the time of the crime, the accused fled in a vehicle belonging to the victim in the main proceedings. A criminal investigation was initiated against the accused in Hamburg. On 20 October 2005 the Polish authorities stopped a car driven by the accused in the course of a roadside check in Kołobrzeg (Poland) and arrested him with a view to the enforcement of a term of imprisonment to which he had been sentenced in Poland in a different case. After making enquiries about the vehicle driven by the accused, the District Public Prosecutor's Office in Kołobrzeg opened an investigation against him, accusing him of extortion with aggravating factors, as laid down in Article 282 of the Polish Criminal Code, on account of his actions in Hamburg on 2 October 2005.

As a matter of mutual legal assistance, the Regional Public Prosecutor's Office in Koszalin, Poland, requested copies of the investigation file from the Hamburg Public Prosecutor's Office. Those copies were provided in August 2006. In December 2006, the Kołobrzeg District Public Prosecutor's Office sent to the Hamburg Public Prosecutor's Office its decision of 22 December 2006

[1] CJEU GC C-486/14 *Kossowski* ECLI:EU:C:2016:483.

[2] As claimed by D Sarmiento in D Sarmiento, 'Ne bis in idem in the case law of the CJEU' in B van Bockel (ed), *Ne bis in idem in EU law* (Cambridge, Cambridge University Press, 2016) 108–10.

terminating, for lack of sufficient evidence, the criminal proceedings against the accused. It is common ground that the reasons for that decision were that the accused had refused to give a statement and that the victim in the main proceedings and a hearsay witness were living in Germany, so that it had not been possible to interview them in the course of the investigation and it had therefore not been possible to verify the statements made by the victim, which were, in parts, vague and contradictory. The persons concerned had a right to appeal against that decision within a period of seven days from service of the decision. The victim in the main proceedings does not appear to have brought such an appeal.

In July 2009 the Hamburg Public Prosecutor's Office issued a European arrest warrant against the accused, having already obtained a national arrest warrant against him from the District Court in Hamburg, Germany, on 9 January 2006. Poland was requested to surrender the accused to the Federal Republic of Germany, but execution of the European arrest warrant was refused by decision of the Regional Court in Koszalin, Poland, in view of the decision of the Kołobrzeg District Public Prosecutor's Office terminating the criminal proceedings, which that Court classified as final for the purposes of the Polish Criminal Procedure Code.

In February 2014, the accused, who was still wanted in Germany, was arrested in Berlin. After the Hamburg Public Prosecutor's Office brought charges against him the Regional Court in Hamburg refused to open trial proceedings, basing its decision on the fact that further prosecution had been barred, for the purposes of Article 54 of the CISA, by the decision of the Kołobrzeg District Public Prosecutor's Office terminating the criminal proceedings, and discharged the arrest warrant and released the accused.

The Hamburg Public Prosecutor's Office submitted an appeal against that decision which was recognised by the Higher Regional Court in Hamburg, which eventually decided to stay the proceedings and to refer two following questions to the Court of Justice for a preliminary ruling:

> (1) Do the reservations declared at the time of ratification by the contracting parties to the CISA pursuant to Article 55(1)(a) of the CISA – specifically, the reservation [relating to Article 54 of the CISA] – continue in force following the integration of the Schengen acquis into the legal framework of the European Union by [Protocol (No 2) integrating the Schengen acquis into the framework of the European Union], as preserved by [Protocol (No 19) to the Schengen acquis integrated into the framework of the European Union]? Are these exceptions proportionate limitations on Article 50 of the Charter, within the meaning of Article 52(1) of the Charter?
>
> (2) If that is not the case, are the prohibitions on double punishment and double prosecution laid down by Article 54 of the CISA and Article 50 of the Charter to be interpreted as prohibiting prosecution of an accused person in one Member State – in the present case, Germany – where his prosecution in another Member State – in the present case, Poland – has been discontinued by the public prosecutor's office, without any obligations imposed by way of penalty having been fulfilled and without any detailed investigation, for factual reasons in the absence of sufficient evidence

> for a probable conviction, and can be reopened only if essential circumstances previously unknown come to light, where such new circumstances have not in fact emerged?[3]

The Court stated that the question of the possible applicability of the exception in Article 55(1)(a) of the CISA to the *ne bis in idem* will arise only when that rule applies because a person's trial has been 'finally disposed of' within the meaning of Article 54 of the CISA, and therefore found it appropriate to start by answering Question 2 and eventually abstained from answering Question 1.

II. Ruling of the Court

The Court first raised the fact that the aim of the *ne bis in idem* principle in Article 54 of the CISA is that a person whose trial has been finally disposed of is not prosecuted in several Contracting States for the same acts. However, according to the Court, at the same time the *ne bis in idem* must not be understood as 'intended to protect a suspect from having to submit to investigations that may be undertaken successively, in respect of the same acts, in several Contracting States'.[4] In this respect, the Court submitted that Article 54 of the CISA should be interpreted

> in the light of Article 3(2) TEU, which states that the European Union is to offer its citizens an area of freedom, security and justice without internal frontiers, in which the free movement of persons is ensured in conjunction with appropriate measures with regard to, amongst other matters, the prevention and combating of crime.[5]

In view of the Court, a decision of a Polish public prosecutor, terminating criminal proceedings against Mr P Kossowski – which was adopted in a situation in which the prosecuting authority, without a more detailed investigation having been undertaken for the purpose of gathering and examining evidence, did not proceed with the prosecution solely because the accused had refused to give a statement and the victim and a hearsay witness were living in Germany, so that it had not been possible to interview them in the course of the investigation and had therefore not been possible to verify statements made by the victim – does not constitute a decision given after a determination has been made as to the merits of the case and as such – as it follows from the Court's reasoning – must not be recognised under Article 54 of the CISA, for it would make it difficult, if not impossible, to penalise the unlawful conduct alleged against the accused.[6]

[3] *Kossowski* (n 1) para 23.
[4] *Kossowski* (n 1) para 45.
[5] *Kossowski* (n 1) para 46.
[6] *Kossowski* (n 1), paras 48–49.

The decision of the Court has further touched upon the issue of mutual trust which is undoubtedly fundamental to the cooperation in criminal matters between the EU Member States.[7] The Court followed a line of argumentation presented by the Advocate General in his Opinion and submitted that

> mutual trust requires that the relevant competent authorities of the second Contracting State accept at face value a final decision communicated to them which has been given in the first Contracting State. However, that mutual trust can prosper only if the second Contracting State is in a position to satisfy itself, on the basis of the documents provided by the first Contracting State, that the decision of the competent authorities of that first State does indeed constitute a final decision including a determination as to the merits of the case.[8]

In the case at hand, the Court found that

> a decision of the prosecuting authorities terminating criminal proceedings and closing the investigation procedure, such as the decision in issue in the main proceedings, cannot be held to have been given after a determination as to the merits of the case and, accordingly, cannot be characterised as a final decision for the purposes of Article 54 of the CISA when it is clear from the reasons actually stated in that decision that there was no detailed investigation, as otherwise the mutual trust between the Member States could be undermined. In that regard, the fact that neither the victim nor a potential witness was interviewed is an indication that no detailed investigation was undertaken in the case in the main proceedings.[9]

For those reasons the Court followed the reasoning presented by Advocate General Y Bot and ruled that the principle of *ne bis in idem* laid down in Article 54 of the CISA, read in light of Article 50 of the Charter of Fundamental Rights of the European Union, must be interpreted as meaning that a decision of the public prosecutor terminating criminal proceedings and finally closing the investigation procedure against a person, albeit with the possibility of it being reopened or annulled, without any penalties having been imposed, cannot be characterised as a final decision for the purposes of those articles when it is clear from the statement of reasons for that decision that the procedure was closed without a detailed investigation having been carried out; in that regard, the fact that neither the victim nor a potential witness was interviewed is an indication that no such investigation took place.

[7] As stated by the Court in Joined Cases C-187/01 and C-385/01 *Gözütok and Brügge* [2003] ECLI:EU:C:2003:87, and reiterated by Y Bot, Advocate General, of 15 December 2015, in *Kossowski* (n 1): 'the application of the principle of mutual recognition requires the Member States to place trust in each other regardless of the differences in their respective national laws' (para 43).

[8] *Kossowski* (n 1), paras 51–52.

[9] *Kossowski* (n 1), para 53.

III. Discussion

Following the wording of Art 54 of the CISA, the Court of Justice set to determine whether the case of Mr Kossowski was 'finally disposed of'[10] in Poland in order to establish whether the Polish proceedings constituted a *bis* and thus made it impossible to repeat the proceedings in Germany. This required veryfing two issues: the finality of the case and the determination of the merits of the case.[11]

Considering whether the case was irrevocably closed by competent national authorities, it has already been established by the Court that decisions taken by prosecutorial authorities fall under the scope of the principle of *ne bis in idem*, just like decisions taken by judicial authorities. Therefore, the right of the Polish prosecutor to close the proceedings was not questioned. Also, it is undeniable that according to the Polish law, the decision taken by the Polish prosecutor would be recognised as final and precluding new investigation of the case pursuant to Art 17, § 1, p 7 of the Polish Code of Criminal Procedure, even though the law provided for extraordinary possibilities to reopen the investigation. Following the Court's case law, such decision would qualify as final.[12]

As mentioned above, the second element of the notion of final disposition of a case is related to the substantive side of the procedure. In this context, the Court refers to the notion of 'merits of the case'. It had been used on previous occasions by the Court, although not in a coherent manner,[13] to justify a refusal to apply the principle *ne bis in idem*. And so in 2005 in *Miraglia*, the Court said that Article 54 of the CISA does not apply to

> a decision of the judicial authorities of one Member State declaring a case to be closed, after the public prosecutor has decided not to pursue the prosecution on the sole ground that criminal proceedings have been started in another Member State against the same defendant and for the same acts, without any determination whatsoever as to the merits of the case.[14]

[10] On this notion see: A Klip, *European Criminal Law*, 2nd edn (Intersentia, 2012), 253 *ff*; D Flore, 'Le principe ne bis in idem en droit pénal européen' in D Brach-Thiel (ed), *Existe-t-il encore un seul non bis in idem aujourd'hui* (L'Harmattan, 2017) 20 *ff*.

[11] S Montaldo, 'A New Crack in the Wall of Mutual Recognition and Mutual Trust: Ne Bis in Idem and the Notion of Final Decision Determining the Merits of the Case', *European Papers* www.europeanpapers.eu, ISSN 2499-8249 Vol 1, 2016, No 3, 1186.

[12] See case C-398/12 *M.* [2014] OJ C355/9–10: 'Article 54 of the Convention implementing the Schengen Agreement (…), must be interpreted as meaning that an order making a finding that there is no ground to refer a case to a trial court which precludes, in the Contracting State in which that order was made, the bringing of new criminal proceedings in respect of the same acts against the person to whom that finding applies, unless new facts and/or evidence against that person come to light, must be considered to be a final judgment, for the purposes of that article, precluding new proceedings against the same person in respect of the same acts in another Contracting State'.

[13] See A Weyembergh, 'Le ne bis in idem en matière pénale dans l'UE: de quelques développements récents et de quelques perspectives' in Brach-Thiel (ed) (n 10) 196ff.

[14] Case C-469/03 *Miraglia* ECLI:EU:C:2005:156.

The Court followed the same line of argumentation in *Van Straaten*, stating that

> the *ne bis in idem* principle, enshrined in Article 54 of that Convention, falls to be applied in respect of a decision of the judicial authorities of a Contracting State by which the accused is acquitted finally for lack of evidence.[15]

However, in 2006, in *Gasparini*, it decided that the *ne bis in idem* applied to a time-barred prosecution, even though in such event the merits of the case had not been considered.[16]

As mentioned above, the Court rejected the view of the Hamburg Regional Court by saying that a decision of the public prosecutor closing an investigation does not constitute a final decision since a detailed investigation had not been carried out, and therefore the merits of the case were not considered.

Interestingly, the Polish public prosecutor did consider the merits of the case, as any decision taken based on evidence or lack thereof constitutes a decision on the substance of the case. It was not a decision based on purely procedural grounds – substance of the case had been considered and eventually, due to a lack of sufficient evidence, the proceedings were discontinued.

The decision of the Court of Justice referred not to a situation of complete lack of examination of merits and, specifically, evidence. What the Court questioned and what it was eventually unsatisfied with was in fact how thoroughly the merits had been examined. As it pointed out, a decision taken by the Polish prosecutor terminating criminal proceedings was adopted without 'a more detailed investigation having been undertaken for the purpose of gathering and examining evidence', since the accused refused to give a statement and the victim and a hearsay witness were not heard as they had been living in Germany.

By formulating such an assessment the Court in fact adds a new requirement of a 'sufficiently detailed investigation' to the *ne bis in idem* principle, expecting that the *bis* should constitute a case examined comprehensively and in detail. This condition goes beyond the understanding of *bis* adopted by this Court on previous occasions. In addition, to put it mildly, it seems quite arbitrary – who is to decide at which point an investigation is detailed enough?

The *ne bis in idem* principle is aimed at coordinating proceedings between national jurisdictions, as well as providing legal certainty to the accused who would otherwise face parallel prosecutions and convictions in different states. It is based on mutual trust[17] and mutual recognition[18] of foreign decisions which lie at the very core of the cooperation in criminal matters in the European Union.

[15] Case C-150/05 *Van Straaten* ECLI:EU:C:2006:614, para 61.

[16] Case C-467/04 *Gasparini* ECLI:EU:C:2006:610, para 33.

[17] A Weyembergh, I Armada, 'The Principle of ne bis in idem in Europe's Area of Freedom, Security and Justice' in V Mitsilegas, M Bergstrom, T Konstadinides (eds), *Research Handbook on EU Criminal Law* (Elgar, 2016) 193.

[18] On the notion of mutual recognition, see: C Janssens, *The Principle of Mutual Recognition in EU Law* (Oxford University Press, 2013), particularly on the link between mutual recognition and mutual trust: 141 *ff*.

However, by its decision in *Kossowski*, the Court puts the mutual trust in jeopardy. It directly encourages the judicial authorities of one Member State not to trust foreign decisions, but to the contrary – to distrust the activities undertaken by judicial authorities in another Member State and to deny recognition of the activities of the authority in question therefore of a decision should the decision not meet the test of 'sufficiently detailed examination' required by the Court.

Understandably, the Court struggled to find a balance between the respect for the *ne bis in idem* principle and the requirements stemming from Article 3(2) of the Treaty on European Union (TEU), which guarantees to the Union citizens a creation of an area of freedom, security and justice without internal frontiers, in which the free movement of persons is ensured in conjunction with appropriate measures with respect to, inter alia, the prevention and combating of crime. The Court addressed this issue by saying that recognition of the Polish prosecutor's decision would make it more difficult, if not impossible, to penalise the unlawful conduct alleged against the accused.[19] This dilemma also touched upon the respect of the values underlying the Union. In this context, the Court seems to uphold the statement of the Advocate General that the *ne bis in idem* principle should not prevail over the respect for fundamental rights, particularly rights of the victim.[20]

One of course cannot expect that the mutual trust should be blind.[21] Yet, one may fear that the Court in *Kossowski* has opened the door to a very dangerous reasoning, which may have further negative impact on both the principle of mutual trust in the EU and the perceived value of European cooperation in criminal matters in Poland.

The mutual trust as a fundament of cooperation in criminal matters in the EU has been developing as an alternative to the harmonisation of national criminal laws,[22] despite Member States' reluctance to automatically recognise foreign decisions. Questioning this fragile faith that they have in other Member States' decisions seems a step too far. In *Kossowski*, the Court encourages national authorities to evaluate actions undertaken in another state, which is not only difficult when not knowing the foreign law and foreign circumstances, but also contradicts what it had said itself in *Van Esbroeck* when it emphasised that 'the Contracting States have mutual trust in their criminal justice systems and that each of them recognises the criminal law in force in the other Contracting States even when the outcome

[19] *Kossowski* (n 1), para 49.

[20] Opinion of Advocate General, Y Bot (n 7) 80.

[21] M Munivrana Vajda, 'The Trust is not Blind – Reviewing the Idea of Mutual Trust in the EU in the Context of Conflicts of Jurisdiction and *ne bis in idem* Principle' (2018) 2 *EU And Comparative Law Issues And Challenges Series* 323–37.

[22] V Mitsilegas, 'Mutual Recognition, Mutual Trust and Fundamental Rights after Lisbon' in Mitsilegas, Bergstrom, Konstadinides (eds) (n 17) 149 *ff*.

would be different if its own national law were applied'[23] or in Opinion 2/13, when it noted that the

> principle of mutual trust … requires, particularly with regard to the area of freedom, security and justice, each of those States, save in exceptional circumstances, to consider all the other Member States to be complying with EU law and particularly with the fundamental rights recognised by EU law.[24]

The question then arises if the circumstances of the case in *Kossowski* were indeed exceptional to the extent that the Court had no other way but to find the case not finally disposed of. There is no doubt that the establishment of an area of freedom, security and justice is an important task and one is not encouraging the Court to apply the *ne bis in idem* in order to provide impunity to an accused to the detriment of the security or fundamental rights. Yet the Court's position is surprising, for – having in mind the future of the Union – mutual trust and mutual recognition seem much more valuable than the possible occasional impunity of an accused due to poorly conducted proceedings in one state and the impossibility to repeat them in another state.

The *Kossowski* ruling, setting a new higher, however arbitrary and not well described, standard with regard to the assessment of national proceedings, is perceived by some as a cure for 'severe pathologies affecting national legal orders'.[25] But such a diagnosis as well as the approach towards the Court's case law seems erroneous. First, the case at hand may not be considered proof of a systemic deficiency of national legal systems. It may well be just one accidental case of a poorly conducted transnational investigation. Second, it is not the Court's role to amend national legal systems.

The Court should not and may not expect the national authorities to do the impossible. In the volume of criminal cases recognised at the pre-trial stage of proceedings in the Member States, there may be cases which are not investigated to the fullest extent possible. It seems unquestionable that the pre-trial proceedings conducted by Polish prosecuting authorities against Mr Kossowski were rather superficial – surely more could have been done to investigate the case, although it should be emphasised that the prosecutor did consider the statement of the victim and the accused had the right to remain silent. The decision was communicated to the victim and the deadline for appeal which was seven days was applicable to all interested parties and is typical for prosecutorial decisions in Polish criminal proceedings. But the impact of the Court of Justice case law goes beyond a given case and influences the practice in all Member States. Hence the lack of due diligence of a prosecutor in a small town in Poland translates into a new general standard for the national authorities struggling with transnational cases. And as

[23] Case C-436/04 *Van Esbroeck* [2006] ECR I-2333, 30.
[24] Opinion 2/13 of the Court (Full Court), 18 December 2014, ECLI:EU:C:2014:2454, para 191.
[25] Montaldo (n 11) 1193.

for the *Kossowski* ruling, this struggle implies a twofold challenge. On the one hand the national authorities have to observe themselves the rather vague requirement of 'a detailed examination' of a case set forth by the Court of Justice of the European Union (CJEU), and on the other – they face the responsibility of determining whether the examination of a case conducted in the other Member State complied with the standard of 'detailed examination' as required by the CJEU.

The assessment of the striking position of the Court has to refer to the timing of the Court's ruling. The original decision of the Polish prosecutor had been taken in 2006, 10 years before the Court's ruling, shortly after Polish accession to the EU, at the time when Polish investigative authorities were not yet familiar with transnational cases and when the EU criminal legal framework was not as developed as it is today. The Court therefore evaluates the situation clearly outdated, which however has a considerable impact *pro futuro*.

Considering the national context, it should be emphasised that the Court's decision came at a bad time for mutual trust within the EU in Poland. After a new parliamentary election in 2016, a Government expressing more populist and anti-European views took over which had started to undermine the value of European cooperation and at the same time the independence of judiciary. Any unfavourable decision of European judicial bodies is now perceived as targeting Polish sovereignty and may trigger more negative responses from the governmental officials.

Perhaps it is therefore lucky that the case at hand has so far received limited attention in Poland. Two positions are expressed – authors having a more internally focused research approach[26] just repeat the words of the Court, thus encouraging the Polish authorities to make more effort in investigating transnational cases, whereas authors with a wider, more European, perspective express their critical views on the decision of the Court fearing it may undermine mutual trust within the EU.[27]

The Polish Supreme Court has taken note of the Court's ruling but it did not enter into any dialogue with the CJEU. Actually, in one of its very few decisions on the applicability of the *ne bis in idem* to transnational proceedings, the Supreme Court upheld the CJEU's statements as to the obligation to examine the merits of the case without any further or more profound examination of the CJEU's position.[28]

[26] J Kosonoga, 'Art. 17' in RA Stefański, S Zabłocki (eds), *Kodeks postępowania karnego. Tom I. Komentarz do art. 1-166* (LEX, 2017).

[27] A Lach, 'Effective Investigation of Crime and the European *ne bis in idem* Principle' (2017) *Teisės apžvalga, Law Review* No.2 (16) 5–16: A Sakowicz, 'Glosa do wyroku Trybunału Sprawiedliwości Unii Europejskiej z dnia 29 czerwca 2016 r. w sprawie C-486/14, Postępowanie karne przeciwko Piotrowi Kossowskiemu' (2017) 22 *Białostockie Studia Prawnicze* 1, 133–43.

[28] Judgment of the Supreme Court of 19 July 2017, V KK 92/17, commented by H Kuczynska, EPS 2018, No 7, 26–31.

IV. Conclusion

For now the impact of the *Kossowski* case translates more as an encouragement to the Polish judicial authorities to be better prepared to face challenges stemming from transnational investigations. But considering the value of mutual trust between the EU Member States and the Polish position in this regard, in particular Poland's recent withdrawal from participating in the enhanced cooperation on the establishment of the European Public Prosecutor's Office based on arguments of sovereignty, as well as the many declarations of Polish officials as to the mistrust of the EU, somehow linked to the very recent judgment of the Court in *PPU*,[29] one may fear that the impact of *Kossowski* in Poland will eventually be more powerful, and that the rigid position adopted by the Court of Justice will be read in a purely political context and may eventually contribute to undermining the trust of Poland and Polish citizens with regard to the EU and other Member States.

[29] Case C-216/18 *PPU* ECLI:EU:C:2018:586.

9

C-617/10 – *Åkerberg Fransson*

Fishing for Better Rights Protection: The Court of Justice on the Application of the Charter in the Member States and the Reach of ne bis in idem

TOBIAS LOCK

The *Fransson*[1] decision – though handed down as recently as 2013 – can already be counted among the major constitutional judgments rendered by the Court of Justice. By making it clear that the European Union (EU) Charter of Fundamental Rights – itself only in force since December 2009 – applies to the Member States whenever national legislation falls within the scope of Union law, the Court adopted a wide understanding of the scope of the Charter. It is axiomatic that this results in a greater number of domestic cases having to comply with (a rather large number of) Charter rights. This alone does not, however, capture the full picture. Forming part of EU law, the Charter benefits from the primacy of EU law over conflicting national law,[2] to which every national court – no matter how low down in the hierarchy – is obliged to give effect by setting aside conflicting national law.[3]

Apart from clarifying the scope of the Charter, the *Fransson* decision is further relevant for confirming that the *ne bis in idem* principle contained in Article 50 of the Charter does not as such prohibit a Member State from subsequently imposing an administrative (tax) penalty and a criminal penalty for the same acts. While this finding is fully compatible with the European Convention on Human Rights, the decision in *Fransson* also marks the departure point for a problematic set of cases that water down the *ne bis in idem* guarantee under the Charter and set the Court of Justice on a course which may result in a conflict with the European Court of Human Rights (ECtHR).

[1] Case C-617/10 *Åklagaren v Hans Åkerberg Fransson* ECLI:EU:C:2013:105.

[2] Established since Case 6/64 *Costa v ENEL* ECLI:EU:C:1964:66.

[3] Case 106/77 *Amministrazione delle Finanze dello Stato v Simmenthal SpA* ECLI:EU:C:1978:49, paras 21–22.

I. Facts and Key Legal Questions

The facts of the *Fransson* case are straightforward. Mr Fransson, a fisherman, was summoned to appear before a Swedish criminal court on charges of serious tax offences. He was accused of having provided false information in his tax return, which resulted in lost income tax and value added tax (VAT) revenues for the Swedish exchequer. Furthermore, he was prosecuted for failing to declare employers' contributions, resulting in losses to the Swedish social security bodies.

In 2007 the Swedish tax authorities ordered Mr Fransson to pay tax surcharges (with interest payable) in relation to the falsely provided tax returns and employers' contribution declarations. Proceedings challenging these were not brought before the (competent) administrative courts.

The decision to impose penalties was based on the same acts of providing false information as those relied upon by the Swedish public prosecutor in the criminal proceedings at issue. Mr Fransson therefore argued that the criminal charges had to be dismissed on the ground that he had already been punished for the same acts in other proceedings. Prosecuting him would therefore infringe Article 50 of the Charter, which reads:

> No one shall be liable to be tried or punished again in criminal proceedings for an offence for which he or she has already been finally acquitted or convicted within the Union in accordance with the law.

As the alleged violation of the Charter was attributable to a Member State and not the Union, the first hurdle to clear was the application of the Charter in this case. Article 51(1) of the Charter states:

> The provisions of this Charter are addressed to the institutions, bodies, offices and agencies of the Union with due regard for the principle of subsidiarity and to the Member States only when they are implementing Union law. They shall therefore respect the rights, observe the principles and promote the application thereof in accordance with their respective powers and respecting the limits of the powers of the Union as conferred on it in the Treaties.

The case raised three legal questions of relevance to the field of EU Criminal Law: first, the scope of application of the Charter in the Member States; second, the reach of the *ne bis in idem* principle enshrined in Article 50 of the Charter; and third, the relationship between Charter rights and their equivalents in those protocols to the European Convention on Human Rights that not all Member States are bound by. This commentary will address these three questions in turn. In doing so, it will not only outline the Court's reasoning and in how far it differed from the Advocate General's position, but also point to the broader implications of the ruling and – where appropriate – subsequent pertinent case law.

II. The Application of the Charter in the Member States: Implementing Union Law

Fundamental rights had long been protected in the Union legal order as unwritten general principles of EU law.[4] These general principles applied in two situations: when a Member State was implementing Union rules;[5] and when a Member State chose to derogate from one of the fundamental freedoms.[6] It followed that whenever national rules came within the scope of Union law, they had to comply with EU fundamental rights.

A. The Decision in *Fransson* and the Approach Suggested by the Advocate General

In *Fransson*, the Court confirmed that the Charter continued in this vein, despite the seemingly narrower formulation – 'when implementing Union law' – used. This reading is consistent with the Charter explanations,[7] which expressly incorporate the Court's pre-Charter case law. More importantly perhaps, the Court's express reference to its pre-Charter 'settled case-law'[8] avoids an otherwise odd bifurcation of fundamental rights protection at the EU level: had the Court chosen a narrower interpretation, this would have resulted in the Charter not being applicable in some cases where fundamental rights as general principles would be. Given that according to Article 6(3) on the Treaty on European Union (TEU) the latter continue to apply, this would have contradicted the overall objective of the Charter to reaffirm (and codify) those general principles.[9] Consequently, the Court was right when – somewhat tautologically – stating that the 'applicability of European Union law entails applicability of the fundamental rights guaranteed by the Charter'.[10]

The controversy surrounding *Fransson* stems not so much from this general statement – which mainly begs the question – but from its concrete application. In the *Fransson* case this outcome was not obvious. The Swedish legislation criminalising tax evasion had not been adopted to transpose a specific duty under EU law. Taken alone, this cannot of course be a reason to deny the application of the

[4] First intimated in Case 29/69 *Stauder v Stadt Ulm* ECLI:EU:C:1969:57 and confirmed shortly after in Case 11/70 *Internationale Handelsgesellschaft mbH v Einfuhr- und Vorratsstelle für Getreide und Futtermittel* ECLI:EU:C:1970:114.

[5] Case 5/88 *Hubert Wachauf v Federal Republic of Germany* ECLI:EU:C:1989:321, para 19.

[6] Case C-260/89 *Elliniki Radiophonia Tiléorassi AE (ERT)* ECLI:EU:C:1991:254.

[7] Explanations relating to the Charter of Fundamental Rights [2007] OJ C303/17.

[8] *Åkerberg Fransson* (n 1), para 19.

[9] See Charter preamble.

[10] *Åkerberg Fransson* (n 1), para 21; this was also welcomed by commentators.

Charter as otherwise Member State legislation pre-dating EU membership – such as the legislation at issue – would fall outside the scope of the Charter.

Instead, the Court pointed to Directive 2006/112/EC on the common system of value added tax, which says that 'Member States may impose [...] obligations which they deem necessary for the correct collection of tax and for the prevention of evasion'.[11] Coupled with the duty of sincere cooperation laid down in Article 4(3) TEU, the Court pointed to its earlier case law on VAT that 'every Member State is under an obligation to take all legislative and administrative measures appropriate for ensuring collection of all the VAT due on its territory and for preventing evasion'.[12] Furthermore, the Court relied on Article 325 of the Treaty on the Functioning of the EU (TFEU), which obliges Member States 'to counter fraud and any other illegal activities affecting the financial interests of the Union'.[13] Given that part of the EU's own resources consist of revenue from VAT, 'there is thus a direct link between the collection of VAT revenue in compliance with the European Union law applicable and the availability to the European Union budget of the corresponding VAT resources'.[14]

The Court chose not to follow the more cautious approach put forward by Advocate General Cruz Villalón. He conceptualises the applicability of the Charter in the Member State legal orders as an exception to the rule that the Member States should be responsible to review acts of their public authorities as to their compliance with fundamental rights as protected by their legal orders.[15] The exception, ie the Charter coupled with the effects of Union law, should only apply where there existed a 'specific interest of the Union in ensuring that that exercise of public authority accords with the interpretation of the fundamental rights by the Union'. The mere fact that an exercise of public authority by a Member State has its origin in Union law is not enough.[16]

In applying his test on whether a transfer of responsibility for guaranteeing rights to the Union level had occurred in the factual scenario before the Court, the Advocate General chose to side with the European Commission and all the Member States that had made submissions to the Court by answering this question with a 'no'. His argument is based on the idea that a 'mere finding that the exercise of the power of the State to impose penalties in a particular case is ultimately based on a provision of Union law is not, of itself, sufficient'.[17] Further legitimation is

[11] Council Directive 2006/112/EC of 28 November 2006 on the common system of value added tax [2006] OJ L347/1.

[12] *Åkerberg Fransson* (n 1), para 25 pointing to Case C-132/06 *Commission v Italy* ECLI:EU:C:2008:412, paras 37 and 46.

[13] *Åkerberg Fransson* (n 1), para 26.

[14] *Åkerberg Fransson* (n 1), para 26.

[15] Case C-617/10 *Åklagaren v Hans Åkerberg Fransson* Opinion of Advocate General (AG) Cruz Villalón ECLI:EU:C:2012:340, para 35.

[16] *Ibid*, para 40.

[17] *Ibid*, para 54.

required; and such legitimation cannot arise from an exercise of public authority by a Member State on the mere occasion of EU law being somewhat connected to that exercise. Instead, EU law must be the *causa* – direct or indirect – for this exercise.[18] In this case, the Advocate General found the connection between the EU law obligation – resulting from Directive 2006/112 to be 'extremely weak' and not 'a sufficient basis for a clearly identifiable interest on the part of the Union'.[19]

Although he never directly mentions either, one can suspect that the Advocate General's position was influenced by a desire to comply with subsidiarity and to respect the limits of the Charter as expressed in its Article 51(2).[20] The difference in approach between the Advocate General and the Court of Justice is therefore stark. While the Advocate General tried to develop a constitutionally principled and nuanced approach, the Court opted for the broad view that wherever there is a connection with EU law, the Charter applies. Its reasoning implicitly contradicts the Advocate General's suggestion that there is no Union interest in guaranteeing fundamental rights in a scenario such as this.

Overall, the Court's view is preferable. While the Advocate General's argument would appear to be more principled and nuanced, it would struggle very much in practice as it fails to define concrete criteria which would determine the Union interest. His references to *occasiones* and *causae* tend to obscure things more than they enlighten them; and, if taken literally, would make the Charter applicable in very limited circumstances only, ie where one could show that the Member State act would not have happened without a Union law obligation in the background. But this ignores the reality of law-making in the EU's multi-level Union. The *Fransson* case is a good example: here such a causality test would fail for the simple reason that the criminal law rules on tax evasion pre-dated Sweden's EU membership. Yet this cannot be a reason to deny that they now help to discharge Sweden's obligation to comply with EU law.

In addition, the Advocate General's argument seems based on the idea that fundamental rights are protected either by the Member States' own constitutional rules or by the Charter. This, however, does not reflect the reality of multi-level fundamental rights protection in Union law characterised by overlaps. As Article 53 of the Charter shows, even where it applies Member States can still protect these rights better than the Charter. Admittedly, this role for the Member States' own fundamental rights guarantees is limited on the basis of the *Melloni* decision handed down on the same day as *Fransson*.[21] At the same time, the Court made it clear in *Fransson* that national courts may apply stricter national

[18] *Ibid*, para 61.

[19] *Ibid*, para 57.

[20] This provision reads: 'The Charter does not extend the field of application of Union law beyond the powers of the Union or establish any new power or task for the Union, or modify powers and tasks as defined in the Treaties'. The same formulation can be found in Article 6(1) TEU.

[21] Case C-399/11 *Stefano Melloni v Ministerio Fiscal* ECLI:EU:C:2013:107, which is discussed in chapter 14 of this book.

standards provided that the primacy, unity and effectiveness of EU law are not compromised.[22] That would in particular seem to be the case where the Member State had discretion in how it would discharge its EU law obligation.[23]

B. Criticism of the *Fransson* Decision

It is hardly surprising that the Court's decision attracted criticism. After all, not only did it decide not to follow its own Advocate General's opinion, but it also went against an unusually unified front of Member States and the European Commission, all of whom considered the case not to come within the scope of the Charter.

Concerns that the Court may have overstepped the limits of its own jurisdiction motivated one of the swiftest and most powerful critiques of the *Fransson* decision. Less than two months after *Fransson*, the German Federal Constitutional Court (*Bundesverfassungsgericht*, or BVerfG) responded by clarifying that *Fransson*

> must not be read in a way that would view it as an apparent ultra vires act or as if it endangered the protection and enforcement of the fundamental rights in the Member States […]. The decision must thus not be understood and applied in such a way that absolutely any connection of a provision's subject-matter to the merely abstract scope of Union law, or merely incidental effects on Union law, would be sufficient for binding the Member States by the Union's fundamental rights set forth in the [Charter].[24]

The Federal Constitutional Court's reasoning is a barely veiled warning that the *Fransson* decision comes very close to not being covered by the Court of Justice's jurisdiction. This makes it perhaps the most fundamental critique of the Court's decision. Academic commentators have focused more on doctrinal questions pertaining to the concrete application of the test espoused in *Fransson*, which has been accused of being question-begging[25] or 'adventurous'.[26] Furthermore, commentators have rightly remarked that an overall picture was still missing[27] and

[22] *Åkerberg Fransson* (n 1), para 29.

[23] See, eg, Case C-399/11 *Stefano Melloni v Ministerio Fiscal* Opinion of AG Bot ECLI:EU:C:2012:600, paras 124–27.

[24] BVerfG, 1 BvR 1215/07, para 91 (English translation as provided on the BVerfG website); for a discussion of the divergent views of both courts, see Daniel Thym, 'Separation versus Fusion – or: How to Accommodate National Autonomy and the Charter? Diverging Visions of the Constitutional Court and the European Court of Justice' (2013) 9 *European Constitutional Law Review* 391.

[25] Filippo Fontanelli, 'Implementation of EU Law through Domestic Measures after Fransson: The Court of Justice Buys Time and 'Non-Preclusion' Troubles Loom Large' (2014) 39 *European Law Review* 682, 685.

[26] See, eg Thorsten Kingreen, 'Ne bis in idem: Zum Gerichtswettbewerb um die Deutungshoheit über die Grundrechte' [2013] *Europarecht* 446, 451.

[27] Daniel Sarmiento, 'Who's Afraid of the Charter? The Court of Justice, National Courts and the New Framework of Fundamental Rights Protection in Europe' (2013) 50 *Common Market Law Review* 1267, 1280.

that *Fransson* had left many questions open,[28] even though – as the next section will show – many of these have now been answered.

Others, by contrast, have rightly pointed out that there was not much new in the Court's reasoning. For one, it is in keeping with the Charter explanations, to which the Court must give due regard.[29] The explanations make reference to the Court's pre-Charter case law, with which the *Fransson* ruling complies.[30] Furthermore, the outcome of the case was hardly surprising given the Court's long-standing case law on the scope of Union law. As Dougan points out,[31] it has been well known since the *Greek Maize* decision of 1989 that a Member State can choose how to enforce Union obligations within its territory but that those choices are within the scope of Union law.[32]

C. Consequences and Subsequent Case Law

The Court's confirmation of a broad conception of 'implementing Union law' in Article 51(1) of the Charter is of constitutional importance in that it subjects a larger number of cases to judicial review by EU standards than the more modest approach ostensibly favoured by the Federal Constitutional Court would have done. This means not only that a greater number of domestic legal acts must be compliant with Charter rights as interpreted by the Court of Justice, but it also leads to an empowerment of inferior domestic courts in the field of fundamental rights protection. As EU law, Charter rights take primacy over conflicting domestic law even if that domestic law is laid down in the constitution.[33] Since every domestic court is under an obligation to give effect to EU law,[34] this broad reading of the Charter allows courts lower down the domestic pecking order to circumvent otherwise existing limitations to their jurisdiction and rule on infringements of fundamental rights by domestic legislation. Such restrictions can be found in many legal orders. For instance, in Germany only the Federal Constitutional Court has the jurisdiction to review acts of parliament as to their compatibility with fundamental rights;[35] and in the United Kingdom, only higher courts can

[28] Fontanelli (n 25) 682.

[29] Article 52(7); the explanations pertaining to Article 51 (1) Charter of Fundamental Rights (CFR) say this: 'As regards the Member States, it follows unambiguously from the case-law of the Court of Justice that the requirement to respect fundamental rights defined in the context of the Union is only binding on the Member States when they act in the scope of Union law'.

[30] Sarmiento (n 27) 1277.

[31] Michael Dougan, 'Judicial Review of Member State Action Under the General Principles and the Charter: Defining the "Scope of Union Law"' (2015) 52 *Common Market Law Review* 1201, 1214.

[32] Case 68/88 *Commission v Greece* ECLI:EU:C:1989:339.

[33] *Costa v ENEL* (n 2); *Internationale Handelsgesellschaft* (n 4) 4.

[34] *Amministrazione delle Finanze dello Stato v Simmenthal SpA* (n 3).

[35] Secured through the duty of domestic courts to refer cases to the Federal Constitutional Court where they consider an act of parliament unconstitutional laid down in Article 100 of the Basic Law.

declare acts of parliament to be incompatible with Convention rights under the Human Rights Act 1998 (HRA 1998).[36] The Charter – as construed by the Court of Justice – allows inferior courts to pierce through this praetorian hierarchy and improve the protection of fundamental rights in the domestic context.

A further consequence of the Court of Justice's approach is that there is no rule of domestic law that is immune from review under the Charter.[37] This means that even in areas that are largely within the legislative competence of the Member States – such as criminal law and criminal procedure – Charter rights may sometimes need to be complied with as the *Fransson* case so aptly demonstrates.

The alignment of the scope of the Charter with the scope of Union law may also result in real-life cases being split as regards the fundamental rights regime that governs them. *Fransson* is a case in point. The defendant had been accused not only of VAT evasion – which fell within the scope of Union law – but also tax evasion concerning his income tax and the non-payment of social security contributions. The latter two charges are outside the scope of Union law and thus not governed by the Charter. This means that as far as VAT evasion is concerned, the fundamental rights (minimum) standard is set by the Charter, whereas the standard applicable to the remainder of the case is the domestic Swedish standard.

If these standards diverge, notably if the Charter requires stronger protection, the outcome of the case will differ depending on which part of the case was in the scope of EU law. But even where the standards are identical, EU law may provide stronger remedies than domestic law. In particular in systems that do not allow for a judicial review of legislation, the EU law remedy of dis-application resulting from the doctrine of primacy is much more powerful and can result in the case being decided the other way.[38]

While few would doubt the importance of the *Fransson* decision, it remained relatively thin on the actual criteria for determining whether a given situation falls within the scope of EU law or not. The Court was only clear in that it did not require the domestic rule in question to have been intended by the Member State to implement Union law – as had been intimated in the earlier *Iida* judgment.[39] Hence a domestic rule pre-dating a Member State's EU membership or pre-dating the existence of an EU obligation can be considered a rule implementing EU law. This shows that the Court places an emphasis on the function the rule fulfils in the domestic legal order of the Member State.[40]

Nonetheless, *Fransson* did not reveal much more about the types of situations covered by the Charter. In subsequent case law the Court has slowly begun to

[36] See HRA 1998, s 4.

[37] Sarmiento (n 27) 1278.

[38] This was, eg, the case in the UK decision of *Benkharbouche v Embassy of the Republic of Sudan; Janah v Lybia* [2015] EWCA Civ 33 (since confirmed by the Supreme Court in *Benkharbouche v Secretary of State for Foreign and Commonwealth Affairs; Secretary of State for Foreign and Commonwealth Affairs and Libya v Janah* [2017] UKSC 62).

[39] Case C-40/11 *Yoshikazu Iida v Stadt Ulm* ECLI:EU:C:2012:691, para 79.

[40] Sarmiento (n 27) 1279.

shed more light on this. In particular, the Court completed the continuity picture in the *Pfleger* case in that it confirmed that the Charter – just like the general principles – also applied to situations where Member States derogate from EU free movement law.[41] At the same time the Charter does not apply to Member State activities expressly excluded from the scope of EU law, such as exclusions found in legislation[42] or in case law.[43]

The case law on the Charter has further shown that implementation occurs not only in cases where the Member States are expressly required to act in a certain manner,[44] but also where they are given a certain degree of discretion. This can be discretion as to how they comply with an EU law obligation, eg to set up a monitoring body under a Regulation[45] or the types of social protections offered by a Member State;[46] and there can be discretion as to whether a Member State wishes to act at all, eg whether to process an asylum application despite not being the Member State responsible under the Dublin Regulation.[47] In all of these cases, the Member State is deemed to implement EU law.

Nonetheless, implementation 'requires a certain degree of connection above and beyond the matters covered being closely related or one of those matters having an indirect impact on the other'.[48] It is not sufficient that the EU has legislative competence in an area for it to fall within the scope of EU law.[49] Apart from

[41] Case C-390/12 *Pfleger* ECLI:EU:C:2014:281.

[42] Case C-198/13 *Víctor Manuel Julian Hernández and Others v Reino de España* ECLI:EU:C:2014:2055, para 45; based on an express provision in a Directive, which allowed Member States 'to apply or introduce laws, regulations or administrative provisions which are more favourable'.

[43] Case C-483/12 *Pelckmans Turnhout NV v Walter Van Gastel Balen NV and Others* ECLI:EU:C:2014:304, para 24 based on the European Court of Justice's (ECJ) case law on selling arrangements originating in Joined cases C-267/91 and C-268/91 *Criminal proceedings against Bernard Keck and Daniel Mithouard* ECLI:EU:C:1993:905.

[44] eg the enforcement of a judgment under Council Regulation (EC) No 2201/2003 of 27 November 2003 concerning jurisdiction and the recognition and enforcement of judgments in matrimonial matters and the matters of parental responsibility, repealing Regulation (EC) No 1347/2000 [2003] OJ L338/1, see Case C-92/12 PPU *Health Service Executive v S.C.* ECLI:EU:C:2012:255.

[45] Case C-562/12 *Liivimaa Lihaveis MTÜ v Eesti-Läti programmi 2007–2013 Seirekomitee* ECLI:EU:C:2014:2229, para 64.

[46] Case C-571/10 *Servet Kamberaj v Istituto per l'Edilizia sociale della Provincia autonoma di Bolzano (IPES) and Others* ECLI:EU:C:2012:233, para 80 – though this ruling has recently been called into question by Case C-333/13 *Elisabeta Dano, Florin Dano v Jobcenter Leipzig* ECLI:EU:C:2014:2358; it has been argued that where an EU right is dependent for its realisation upon Member State measures, this should be differentiated from 'implementation' and constitute a third category, see Emily Hancox, 'The Meaning of "Implementing" EU Law under Article 51(1) of the Charter: Åkerberg Fransson' (2013) 50 *Common Market Law Review* 1411, 1418.

[47] Joined Cases C-411/10 and C-493/10 *N.S. v Secretary of State for the Home Department* ECLI:EU:C:2011:865, para 68.

[48] Case C-206/13 *Cruciano Siragusa v Regione Sicilia – Soprintendenza Beni Culturali e Ambientali di Palermo* ECLI:EU:C:2014:126, para 24.

[49] *Víctor Manuel Julian Hernández and Others v Reino de España* (n 41), para 36; this approach has been suggested as a way forward – but one requiring Treaty change – by Case C-34/09 *Gerardo Ruiz Zambrano v Office national de l'emploi (ONEM)* Opinion of AG Sharpston ECLI:EU:C:2010:560, paras 163–73.

an intention to implement,[50] the Court of Justice has formulated a number of further indicators:

> the nature of the legislation at issue and whether it pursues objectives other than those covered by EU law, even if it is capable of indirectly affecting EU law; and also whether there are specific rules of EU law on the matter or rules which are capable of affecting it.[51]

These criteria are problematic, however. They were originally developed in a case specific to the Common Agricultural Policy, so that there are doubts as to whether they can be generalised.[52] In particular, there is the question whether Member State 'implementation' can be deduced from the mere fact that national legislation pursues the same objectives as EU law. In other words, is a mere coincidence of subject matter enough? This would certainly stretch the notion of 'implementing' considerably.[53] It is clear, however, that the Charter does not apply where the Member States are acting outside the EU legal framework in the absence of Union competence.[54]

In its case law since *Fransson* the Court has opted for a piecemeal approach, deciding each case based on its particular facts without elucidating on a broader rationale for requiring Member States to comply with EU fundamental rights. This is somewhat regrettable as it remains the case that individual scenarios are difficult to predict. All domestic courts can rely on is precedent – by its very nature distinguishable – and the overall message that the Court tends to be rather generous in assuming that the Charter applies. The best available explanation remains the idea that Member States – as far as they are implementing Union law – are conceived of as 'agents' of the Union.[55] At the same time, the agency notion suggests a subordination that paints a perhaps unrealistic picture of intricate EU-Member State relations in a pluralist constitutional setting such as the EU's.

Fransson warrants one final observation on the relationship between the two sources of fundamental rights in EU law, the Charter and general principles. By firmly rooting its decision in pre-Charter case law – to which the Charter explanations also make reference – the Court makes it clear that there is very little room left for general principles. They do not have a separate scope of application and there is probably a huge degree of substantive overlap. After all, the Charter was to do nothing more than reaffirm and codify those general principles. Hence the role for fundamental rights contained in the general principles is mainly confined

[50] *Siragusa* (n 48), para 25.

[51] *Víctor Manuel Julian Hernández and Others v Reino de España* (n 42), para 37.

[52] Case C-309/96 *Annibaldi v Sindaco del Comune di Guidonia and Presidente Regione Lazio* ECLI:EU:C:1997:631; for details see Michael Dougan, 'Judicial Review of Member State Action Under the General Principles and the Charter: Defining the '"Scope of Union Law"' (2015) *Common Market Law Review* 1201, 1232–35 (hereafter Dougan, 'Scope of Union Law').

[53] Dougan, 'Scope of Union Law' *ibid*, 1234.

[54] Case C-370/12 *Thomas Pringle v Government of Ireland, Ireland and The Attorney General* ECLI:EU:C:2012:756, para 180; note, however, that the Charter applies to the Union in comparable circumstances, see Joined Cases C-8/15 P to 10/15 P *Ledra* ECLI:EU:C:2016:701 para 67.

[55] *Fontanelli* (n 25) 684.

to their allowing fundamental rights in EU law to develop beyond the text of the Charter. Given the Charter's breadth, this is unlikely to be necessary in the short term, but long term it cannot be excluded that technological and societal developments will prompt such a development.

III. The *ne bis in idem* Principle Enshrined in Article 50 of the Charter

The Court was brief in answering in the negative the question whether the *ne bis in idem* principle laid down in Article 50 of the Charter prohibited the imposition of an administrative penalty coupled with a tax penalty. It is only if the (supposedly administrative) tax penalty turns out to be criminal in nature and has become final that Article 50 of the Charter precludes further criminal proceedings.[56]

In determining the criminal nature of a penalty in question, the Court – without expressly saying so – employed the well-established Engel criteria.[57] In the Court's own words these criteria are as follows:

> The first criterion is the legal classification of the offence under national law, the second is the very nature of the offence, and the third is the nature and degree of severity of the penalty that the person concerned is liable to incur.[58]

It is up to the national court to make that determination in the individual case.

While this aspect of the decision is in tune with the ECtHR's case law on Article 4 Protocol 7 of the European Convention on Human Rights (ECHR),[59] more recent case law suggests a relaxation in protection standards under the Charter compared with the ECHR. In *Spasic* the Court considered that Article 54 of the Convention Implementing the Schengen Agreement (CISA) constituted a justifiable restriction of Article 50 in accordance with Article 52(1) of the Charter.[60] Article 54 CISA makes the applicability of *ne bis in idem* in a cross-border context conditional on whether the first penalty 'has been enforced, is actually in the process of being enforced or can no longer be enforced'. The Court considered this to be justifiable because it aims 'to prevent, in the area of freedom, security and justice, the impunity of persons definitively convicted and sentenced in an EU Member State'.[61] Leaving aside its compatibility with the ECHR, which

[56] *Åkerberg Fransson* (n 1), para 34.

[57] First pronounced by the ECtHR in *Engel and Others v The Netherlands* (1976) Series A No 22.

[58] *Åkerberg Fransson* (n 1), para 35, basing itself on Case C-489/10 *Bonda* ECLI:EU:C:2012:319.

[59] See *A and B v Norway*, ECHR 2016 which upheld the possibility for the combination of administrative fines and criminal sanctions. The prohibition does however apply if both procedures are, by nature, criminal, see: *Johannesson and Others v Iceland* App no 22007/11 (ECtHR, 18 May 2017).

[60] Case C-129/14 PPU *Spasic* ECLI:EU:C:2014:586.

[61] *Ibid*, para 63; a critical analysis of this judgment can be found in John AE Vervaele, 'Schengen and Charter-related ne bis in idem Protection in the Area of Freedom, Security and Justice: *M* and *Zoran Spasic*' (2015) 52 *Common Market Law Review* 1339.

will be discussed in the next chapter, the specificities of the area of freedom, security and justice would seem to constitute a legitimate reason for accepting Article 54 CISA as compatible with the *ne bis in idem* principle.

The Court did not leave it at that, however, but considered the compatibility of further restrictions of Article 50 of the Charter. The facts in *Menci* were very similar to those in *Fransson*: a tax penalty had been combined with a subsequent criminal prosecution based on the same acts. By contrast with *Fransson*, the Court found that due to its punitive character the tax penalty had to be classed not as a purely administrative fine, but as criminal in nature. Hence the Court held that there had been an interference with *ne bis in idem*.

Instead of finding a violation, however, the Court went on to consider that this interference was justifiable according to Article 52(1) of the Charter as it seeks to ensure the collection of VAT so that a duplication of proceedings may be justified if it is proportionate.[62] This would be the case if the national legislation in question ensures 'that the disadvantages resulting, for the persons concerned, from such a duplication are limited to what is strictly necessary in order to achieve the objective referred to in paragraph 44 of the present judgment', ie to ensure the collection of all the VAT due.[63]

This reasoning is highly problematic as it hinges on a dubious legitimate aim. The aim of ensuring VAT collection is as such of course legitimate, but only in so far as it justifies the imposition of penalties in the first place. Yet to employ the same aim – as the Court has seemingly done – to justify the imposition of two penalties for the same offence, is not at all convincing as it has the potential of undermining the entirety of the *ne bis in idem* right.[64] Furthermore, as the following discussion will show it is incompatible with ECHR standards, which according to Article 52 (3) of the Charter must be applied as a floor to the protections offered by the Charter.

IV. The Relationship between Charter Rights and the ECHR

As hinted at in the previous section, the *Fransson* decision raises important questions about the relationship between the rights enshrined in the Charter and their equivalents found in the ECHR. Article 52(3) of the Charter stipulates:

> In so far as this Charter contains rights which correspond to rights guaranteed by the Convention for the Protection of Human Rights and Fundamental Freedoms, the

[62] Case C-524/15 *Luca Menci* ECLI:EU:C:2018:197, para 44 et seq.

[63] *Ibid*, para 52.

[64] A similar reasoning – this time based on the aim of legislation seeking to protect the integrity of the financial markets of the European Union and public confidence in financial instruments – was used to justify double criminality in Case C-537/16 *Garlsson Real Estate SA* ECLI:EU:C:2018:193, para 46 (handed down on the same day as in *Menci*).

> meaning and scope of those rights shall be the same as those laid down by the said Convention. This provision shall not prevent Union law providing more extensive protection.

It follows that Convention rights corresponding to Charter rights provide the minimum standard of fundamental rights protection in the EU. For this reason, corresponding absolute rights contained in the ECHR, such as the prohibition on torture laid down in Article 3 ECHR, result in their Charter equivalents also being absolute in character. The Charter explanations – though not strictly binding – contain an indicative list of corresponding rights and state that 'Article 50 corresponds to Article 4 of Protocol No 7 to the ECHR, but its scope is extended to European Union level between the Courts of the Member States'.[65]

The Advocate General pointed to a doctrinal issue in this regard relevant to the *Fransson* case. While all EU Member States are parties to the ECHR, not all Member States have signed up to Protocol No 7.[66] And some of those that have signed up, have lodged reservations to parts of it. For the Advocate General this fact meant that

> the requirement that the Charter is to be interpreted in the light of the ECHR must be qualified when the fundamental right in question, or an aspect of it [...] has not been incorporated fully into national law by the Member States.[67]

This reasoning is problematic, however. First, it is not reflected in the wording of Article 52 (3) of the Charter and – in the concrete case – ignores that the Charter explanations expressly list Article 50 as corresponding to Article 4 Protocol 7 ECHR. Second, while it is true that not all Member States have signed up to Protocol 7, they nonetheless agreed to be bound by such rights where the Charter applies.[68] Hence the Advocate General's argument fails to convince.

The Court itself chose not to engage directly with this point. Instead it went even further than the Advocate General in distancing the Charter from its Convention origins. It said:

> it is to be remembered that whilst, as Article 6(3) TEU confirms, fundamental rights recognised by the ECHR constitute general principles of the European Union's law and whilst Article 52(3) of the Charter requires rights contained in the Charter which correspond to rights guaranteed by the ECHR to be given the same meaning and scope as those laid down by the ECHR, the latter does not constitute, as long as the European Union has not acceded to it, a legal instrument which has been formally incorporated into European Union law.[69]

[65] Explanations relating to the Charter of Fundamental Rights [2007] OJ C303/17.

[66] Interestingly, Sweden, where *Fransson* originated, has ratified the Protocol.

[67] *Åkerberg Fransson* (n 1), para 85.

[68] This view is shared in Case C-129/14 PPU *Spasic* Opinion of AG Jääskinen ECLI:EU:C:2014:739, para 63.

[69] *Åkerberg Fransson* (n 1), para 44; this has been repeated in both *Menci* (n 62), para 22 and *Garlsson Real Estate* (n 64), para 24.

By conflating the question whether Article 4 Protocol 7 ECHR is applicable in EU law as such, and the question whether Article 50 of the Charter must be interpreted in the same way as its ECHR counterpart, the Court was able to dismiss the latter suggestion despite the clear mandate in Article 52(3) of the Charter.

This has potentially far-reaching consequences and may eventually conjure up a conflict between the two European courts. Article 4 Protocol 7 ECHR is an absolute right. It does not contain a possibility for derogation, not even in times of emergency.[70] If one takes the Court's reasoning seriously, one could therefore conclude that not even the prohibition on torture – which receives the same protection under the ECHR – is now safe from derogation under the Charter. If this were the case, this would not only be a regressive development, but it would also create the potential for serious conflicts with the ECtHR. After all, that Court cannot allow derogations from absolute rights and might thus – in a given case – come to a finding that the Court of Justice did not protect human rights adequately.[71]

V. Conclusion

There is little doubt that the *Fransson* judgment is of great constitutional significance even though it merely confirmed the Court's pre-Charter approach concerning the applicability of EU fundamental rights standards in the Member States' legal orders. While the rather broad reach of EU fundamental rights remained largely uncontroversial in pre-Charter days – with most judgments confined to pronouncements of principle rather than detail – the advent of the Charter has changed this significantly. Member State courts are now more likely to request preliminary rulings on EU fundamental rights as these are now written down and more easily identifiable. Furthermore, the express endorsement of EU fundamental rights by the Member States gives the Court added legitimacy to determine the standard of fundamental rights protection in the Member States in a growing number of cases.

This makes the Court's regressive stance on the interpretation of Article 50 of the Charter with its potential implications for the protection of absolute rights within the EU legal order particularly regrettable. Of course, the Court has not expressly spelled out the conclusions drawn in the third section of this contribution, but it has certainly paved the way. There is, however, still room for it to row back.

[70] See para 3 of Article 4, Protocol 7, which expressly excludes a derogation even in cases where a state has declared an emergency in accordance with Article 15 ECHR.

[71] On the relationship between the two courts in detail, see Tobias Lock, *The European Court of Justice and International Courts* (Oxford University Press, 2015) Ch 4.

The Impact of Case C-617/10: Åkerberg Fransson *at National Level – The Swedish Example*

MARIA BERGSTRÖM*

I. Introduction

The well-known case C-617/10 *Åkerberg Fransson* from February 2013[1] is 'a landmark decision on the scope of the Charter of Fundamental Rights, EU constitutional law, and the relationship between national and EU law in general'.[2] Much has been written about the case and its presumed impact, 'its scope, effects and repercussions',[3] where almost every European Law scholar has provided a commentary or analysis, not least in Sweden where the case originated.[4]

* This chapter builds on a presentation held at the workshop: *The Impact of European Union Law on National Criminal Law – Challenges and Constraints to Individual Liability in the Member* States, organised by the Edinburgh Europa Institute (University of Edinburgh), Queen Mary University of London and Sant'Anna School of Advanced Studies, Edinburgh, 30 June 2017. I am grateful to Ulf Bernitz, Magnus Gulliksson, Hans Sundberg and Ola Zetterquist for helpful comments. The usual disclaimer applies.

[1] C-617/10 *Åklagaren v Hans Åkerberg Fransson* EU:C:2013:105.

[2] Laurens Ankersmit, 'Casting the Net of Fundamental Rights Protection: C-617/10 Åkernberg Fransson' (European Law Blog, 26 February 2013) available at http://europeanlawblog.eu/2013/02/26/casting-the-net-of-fundamental-rights-protection-c-61710-akerberg-fransson (last accessed 11 March 2019).

[3] Ulf Bernitz, 'The Scope of the Charter and its Impact on the Application of the ECHR: The Åkerberg Fransson Case on *Ne Bis in Idem* in Perspective' in Sybe de Vries, Ulf Bernitz and Stephen Weatherill (eds), *The EU Charter of Fundamental Rights as a Binding Instrument. Five Years Old and Growing* (Hart Publishing, 2015) 155, with further references; See also eg Alexandros-Ioannis Kargopoulos, 'Ne Bis In Idem in Criminal Proceeding' in Maria Bergström and Anna Jonsson Cornell (eds), *European Police and Criminal Law Co-operation* (Hart Publishing Ltd, 2014); and Anne Weyembergh and Inés Armada, 'The Principle of ne bis in idem in Europe's Area of Freedom, Security and Justice' in Valsamis Mitsilegas, Maria Bergström, and Theodore Konstadinides (eds), *Research Handbook on EU Criminal Law* (Edward Elgar Publishing, 2016) with further references.

[4] See, eg, Ulf Bernitz, *ibid*, and in Swedish Rättighetsstadgans genomslag i svensk rätt, JT 2016–17 s 789; Katarina Fast, Oklart om Dubbelbestraffningsförbudets innebörd – en kommentar till generaladvokatens förslag i fallet Åkerberg Fransson, Skattenytt 2012, s 593; Katarina Fast, Dubbelbeskattningsförbudet i EU:s rättighetsstadga och det svenska systemet med skattetillägg och skattebrott, Svensk Skattetidning 2013, s 138 *ff*; Magnus Gulliksson, Klart till halvklart – om ne bis in idem och skattetilläggen, SvJT 2013 s 658; several of the contributions in Joakim Nergelius, and Eleonor Kristoffersson (eds) *Human Rights in Contemporary European Law, Swedish Studies in European Law* (Hart Publishing Ltd, 2015) Vol 6; Dominique Ritleng, Lärdomar av EU-domstolens parallella domar i målen Åkerberg Fransson och Melloni, SvJT 2014 s 36.

In Sweden, the case had an enormous impact resulting in two plenary judgments where the Swedish Supreme Court, *Högsta Domstolen*,[5] and the Swedish Supreme Administrative Court, *Högsta Förvaltningsdomstolen*,[6] in June and October 2013 reversed their previous policies. This in turn gave rise to an exceptional number of petitions for a new trial, alleging that about 1,000 persons were wrongly sentenced for tax fraud during 2009–2013.[7] Although focusing mainly on the particulars of the Swedish system, this chapter provides an illustrative example of the massive impact a single CJEU judgment might have not only on one national legal system, but on the relationship between national and EU law in general, and on the development of EU law and the scope of the EU Charter of Fundamental Rights (EU Charter) in particular. Besides, this chapter provides an interesting case study of the interrelationship between various courts on different levels, and how courts were instrumental not only in the settlement of individual disputes, but in changing the legal system: in other words, *pressure through law*,[8] involving in particular national judges and EU law lawyers.

At the same time, this chapter provides a cautious note to Luxembourg, Strasbourg and their national counterparts in considering the enormous impact an individual judgment might have not only for individuals and national legal systems, but consequently, for their respect for EU law and the European Convention on Human Rights (ECHR). Given their enormous impact, the need for clear, well-reasoned and qualitative legal precedents are crucial for the future of EU and ECHR law. In this context, the significance of the principle of legal certainty must not be taken too lightly. Arguably, any development, in order not to challenge this principle, must be transparent, well-reasoned and qualitative in substance, argument and clarity.

II. From Haparanda to Luxembourg – Case C-617/10 – *Åkerberg Fransson*

The underlying facts of the case are now well-known. Mr Hans Åkerberg Fransson was self-employed and engaged in a fishing business in the Kalix River in the north east of Sweden. There he fished whitefish (*Coregonus albula*), also known as vendace, and sold his catch, mainly vendace roe, in Sweden and Finland.[9]

[5] NJA (*Nytt Juridiskt Arkiv*, the Supreme Court's publication of decision) 2013 p 502.

[6] RÅ 2013 ref. 71 (*Swedish Supreme Administrative Court*).

[7] Ola Zetterquist, 'Ne bis in idem and 2013 European Legal Tsunami' in Nergelius and Kristoffersson (eds) (n 4) 134.

[8] Referring to the concept developed by Carol Harlow and Richard Rawlings, *Pressure though Law* (Routledge, 1992) and in Maria Bergström, *Advocacy Groups and Multilevel Governance: The Use of EC Law as a Campaigning Tool* (Doctor of Laws Thesis defended at the European University Institute, Florence, March 2003).

[9] Åkerberg Fransson who conducted his business as a sole trader, sold the valuable vendace roe directly to first-class restaurants. His business operations almost entirely lacked any cross-border aspects. Bernitz (n 3) 156.

By an administrative decision in 2007, the Swedish Tax Agency, *Skatteverket*, ordered Åkerberg Fransson to pay a tax surcharge relating to income from his business not declared properly by which he had failed to pay income and value added tax (VAT) as well as employers' contributions. Since he did not appeal this decision to the administrative court in Luleå, proceedings challenging the administrative penalties were never instigated.

Instead, criminal proceedings were brought against Åkerberg Fransson before Haparanda District Court based on the same acts of providing false information. He was charged with serious tax offences, for which the penalty was imprisonment of a minimum of six months up to six years. The offences were to be regarded as serious, because they related to very large amounts and, because they formed part of a criminal activity committed systematically on a large scale.[10]

Hence, at the national level, the question arose as to whether the charges brought against Åkerberg Fransson had to be dismissed, since he had already been punished for the same acts in other proceedings, 'as the prohibition on being punished twice laid down by Article 4 of Protocol No 7 to the ECHR and Article 50 of the Charter would be infringed'.[11]

III. The Swedish System, the Rise and Fall of Multilevel Rebellion and Reluctance and the Importance of Dissenting Opinions

The traditional Swedish system involved two parallel systems of sanctions for tax fraud including tax surcharges, administrative law and appeal to the administrative law courts on the one hand, and charges for tax fraud under criminal law and the courts of general jurisdiction on the other.

As emphasised by Appeal Court Judge Ola Zetterquist, the parallel system that was introduced in 1972 had been questioned 'more or less from the outset as being incompatible with the principle of *ne bis in idem* in general, and later on, with the right laid down in Article 4 of Protocol 7 to the ECHR in particular'.[12] In fact, two rulings by the European Court of Human Rights (ECtHR) in 2002 clarified that administrative tax surcharges were of a penal nature,[13] and thus fell within the scope of Article 6 ECHR.

On the other hand, the issue had been dealt with differently by the ECtHR. In the *Rosenquist* ruling from 2004,[14] the ECtHR came to the conclusion that the

[10] *Åkerberg Fransson* (n 1), paras 12–13.

[11] *Åkerberg Fransson* (n 1), para 14.

[12] Zetterquist (n 7) 132.

[13] The ECtHR had ruled in 2002, in cases *Janosevic v Sweden* App no 34619/97, and *Västberga Taxi and Vulk v Sweden* App no 36985/97 that administrative tax surcharges were of a penal nature. See further Bernitz (n 3) 167, and (n 4) 802.

[14] *Rosenquist v Sweden* App no 60619/00 (ECtHR, 2004) discussed eg by Zetterquist (n 7) 132.

Swedish system of parallel tax surcharge and tax fraud constituted two different crimes.[15] In 2004, the ECtHR therefore concluded that the penalties had different aims, and that only tax fraud required intent. As a result, the Swedish system did not initially infringe the *ne bis in idem* principle. The same assessment had been made in the relevant Swedish preparatory materials.[16]

Yet, ten years later, in *Lucky Dev v Sweden*, the ECtHR came to a different conclusion than in the *Rosenquist* case.[17] The question now was whether the Swedish procedures were to be considered as dual or as coordinated procedures which implied a combined penalty for the same act. The latter would not have infringed the *ne bis in idem* principle. According to the ECtHR, the procedures did not meet the requirements of close association in substance and time, but were considered parallel and separate and were independent of each other. On 27 November 2014, the ECtHR held that there had been a violation of Article 4 of Protocol No 7 to the Convention due to the fact that the tax proceedings determining the tax surcharges continued after the criminal proceedings had become final, to the extent that the latter involved the determination of a tax offence. This change by the ECtHR closely followed the legal developments by the Court of Justice of the European Union (CJEU) in *Åkerberg Fransson*, and the Swedish Supreme Courts that will be described and analysed briefly below. Yet, the underlying starting point was the fundamental change in the well-known *Zolotukhin* case.[18] The impact of this ECtHR case in the national Swedish order, was however not immediate.

For the purposes of this contribution, it is interesting to note the discussion by three of the judges in a joint concurring opinion in disagreement with the majority's approach to the retroactive application of the Court's case law after it had undergone this fundamental change:

> Legal change and flexibility are essential for a modern human rights protection system. Thus the Convention has always been considered as a living instrument taking up and responding to changes in European societies. At the same time it cannot be ignored that a radical change in the Court's case-law – as in the present case – upsets legal certainty and, more specifically, the interaction between the national courts and the Court. It is disruptive for national courts following the Court's case-law faithfully to find themselves – without any warning – accused of a breach of the Convention.[19]

[15] For recent publications on penalty payments, see, eg, Leena Halila, Veronica Lankinen, Annika Nilsson, '*Administrativa sanktionsavgifter*' (2018) *En Nordisk komparativ studie, TemaNord* 511, 289; and Vladimir Bastidas Venegas and Maria Bergström, 'Report on Sweden' in Katalin Ligeti and Stanislaw Tosza (eds), *White Collar Crime. A Comparative Perspective* (Hart Publishing, 2018).

[16] Government Bill 2002/03:106 pp 102ff, and Committee Report 2002/03:SkU16 s 11f, referred to in Halila, Lankinen and Nilsson, *ibid*, 289.

[17] *Lucky Dev v Sweden* App no 7356/10 (ECtHR, 2014). See further Bernitz (n 3) 170 Bernitz (n 4) 810; and Halila, Lankinen and Nilsson (n 15) 289.

[18] *Zolotukhin v Russia* App no 14939/03 (ECtHR, 2009). See Magnus Gulliksson, '*Ne Bis in Idem* and Effective Sanctions in EU Law' in Nergelius and Kristoffersson (eds) (n 4) 156.

[19] *Lucky Dev v Sweden* App No 7356/10 (ECtHR, 2014) Joint Concurring Opinion of Judges Villiger, Nussberger and de Gaetano ('Joint Concurring Opinion').

The judges thereby underlined that it is necessary to find a good balance between change and flexibility on the one hand and legal certainty on the other. According to *Marckx v Belgium*,[20] the date of the judgment reversing the existing case law 'is the watershed between the old and the new interpretation of the Convention'.[21]

In this respect, the three judges argued that in the present case, the Swedish courts followed this approach and took the date of adoption of the judgment in *Zolotukhin v Russia*,[22] reversing the previous case law of *Rosenquist v Sweden*, as the starting-point for the change in the Swedish case law. They thus took the *erga omnes* effect of the Court's rulings seriously while at the same time setting a clear timeframe.

Nevertheless, the Swedish Government's argument that there had been no violation of Article 4 Protocol No 7, given that the criminal proceedings had been finalised a month before the *Zolotukhin* judgment 'and thus at a time when the Court's case-law indicated that the Swedish system was in conformity with this provision', was rejected by the majority of the Chamber thereby contradicting *Marckx*.[23]

According to the judges in the concurrent opinion, a much more differentiated approach is needed for applications lodged after the reversal of the case law when the national courts' judgments based on the previous approach have already acquired *res judiciata*:

> In those cases there are clearly conflicting interests: on the one hand the trust of the national courts in the reliability and persistence of the Court's case-law, and on the other hand the applicants' trust in the application of the new case-law.[24]

As a result, the three judges argued that it is perfectly legitimate for national courts to apply the Court's new approach only *ex nunc*, ie from now on, unless there are compelling reasons to decide otherwise, 'which would have to be clearly indicated by the Court in its judgment revising the case-law'.[25] This they argued is all the more true when the national courts agree to change their own case law because of the *erga omnes* effects of the Court's judgments. In this respect, they argued that national courts are required to implement the Court's judgments, but not to anticipate changes in the case law.

Yet, since the proceedings of *Lucky Dev* continued after the date of the *Zolotukhin* judgment, the national courts did have a chance to implement the new approach.[26] Still, I strongly agree with the three judges, that the scope of the retroactive effect of the Court's judgments deserves heightened attention and should be

[20] ECtHR case *Marckx v Belgium* (1979) Series A no 31.
[21] *Lucky Dev v Sweden* (n 19).
[22] *Zolotukhin v Russia* (n 18).
[23] *Lucky Dev v Sweden* (n 17).
[24] *Lucky Dev v Sweden* Joint Concurring Opinion (n 19).
[25] *Lucky Dev v Sweden* Joint Concurring Opinion (n 19).
[26] *Lucky Dev v Sweden* Joint Concurring Opinion (n 19).

dealt with very carefully in order not to undermine the national courts' trust in the validity of the Court's authoritative findings.

Similarly, the Swedish Supreme Court set the date for asking for a new trial based on the argument that the verdict is wrong, to the date when the ECtHR's judgment in *Zolotukhin* was delivered, ie on 10 February 2009.[27] Accordingly, the above mentioned change on *ne bis in idem* was initiated by the ECtHR on 10 February 2009.[28]

The well-known *Zolotukhin* case changed the *idem* part, 'same offence', from a legal to a factual definition: 'facts which constitute a set of concrete factual circumstances involving the same defendant and inextricably linked together in time and space ...'[29] This change was later confirmed, eg in *Ruotsalainen*, which was a case against Finland dealing explicitly with 'the relationship between a tax surcharge and a criminal charge for the same act'.[30] In this case,[31] a person had first been sentenced to a criminal charge, and then an administrative sanction charge for the same offence.

Nevertheless, as has been emphasised eg by Appeals Court Judge Ola Zetterquist, a 2009 Supreme Administrative Court judgment and a 2010 Supreme Court judgment ignored this new approach. Whereas the Supreme Administrative Court in 2009[32] disapplied the ECHR, arguing that the Swedish system had 'distinguishing features',[33] the Swedish Supreme Court in 2010 did apply the ECHR and the new definition introduced by the ECtHR in the *Zolotukhin* case,[34] but ruled there was no *clear support* that there was an infringement of the *ne bis in idem* principle.[35]

Accordingly, up until the Supreme Court and Supreme Administrative Court reversed their policies in June and October 2013, some of the lower courts still felt obliged not to disapply provisions contrary to fundamental rights guaranteed by the ECHR, as long as the infringements were not *clear* from the text of the ECHR, or the case law relating to it. What is noteworthy, however, is that their hesitation also rhymed well with previous rulings of the ECtHR itself, such as the *Rosenquist* ruling, mentioned above.[36]

Hence, *Åkerberg Fransson* resulted in reversed policies by the Swedish Supreme Court, and the Swedish Supreme Administrative Court that the *Zolotukhin* case and the ECHR had not managed alone.[37] In its judgment,[38] the Supreme Court

[27] NJA 2013 s 746.
[28] See further Bernitz (n 3) 166, and Bernitz (n 4) 802.
[29] *Zolotukhin v Russia* (n 18), discussed by Zetterquist (n 7) 132.
[30] Zetterquist (n 7) 133, discussing *Ruotsalainen* App no 13079/03 (ECtHR, 2009).
[31] See also Bernitz (n 3) 164, and Bernitz (n 4) 802.
[32] RÅ 2009 ref 94 (the Supreme Administrative Court).
[33] Zetterquist (n 7) 133.
[34] *Zolotukhin v Russia* (n 18), discussed by Zetterquist (n 7) 132.
[35] NJA 2010 s 168 I and II.
[36] *Rosenquist* (n 14).
[37] *Zolotukhin v Russia* (n 18), discussed by Zetterquist (n 7) 132.
[38] NJA 2013 s 502.

'acknowledged simultaneous criminal and tax sanctions, for the same actions, as an illegal violation of *ne bis in idem*, as acknowledged both by the ECHR and the Charter of Fundamental Rights'.[39] This put an end to an open revolt 'unprecedented in Swedish legal history',[40] including massive academic critique,[41] and open defiance by around ten of the lower courts[42] of the two previous judgments by the Swedish Administrative Supreme Court in 2009,[43] and the Swedish Supreme Court in 2010.[44]

The legal issue whether the administrative penalty tax surcharge, and criminal penalty for tax crime should both be allotted to a person based on the same act of providing false information had been discussed in Sweden for some time, and been tried before various courts with diverging outcomes on different levels.[45]

This allegedly meant that the Supreme Court had 'previously made some severe mistakes in its handling of *ne bis in idem* matters',[46] which in relation to EU law and the EU Charter, were specifically addressed by the CJEU in *Åkerberg Fransson*:

> It follows that European Union law precludes a judicial practice which makes the obligation for a national court to disapply any provision contrary to a fundamental right guaranteed by the Charter conditional upon that infringement being clear from the text of the Charter or the case-law relating to it, since it withholds from the national court the power to assess fully, with, as the case may be, the cooperation of the Court of Justice, whether that provision is compatible with the Charter.[47]

It was not until the origin of the *Åkerberg Fransson* case, ie the District Court Judge in Haparanda, that any of the so-called rebellious lower courts, still far from being the majority, argued the EU law dimension of the issue,[48] and the right of *ne bis in idem* contained in Article 50 of the EU Charter. In other words, it was

[39] Joakim Nergelius, *Human Rights in EU Law 2014: Two Key Cases of 2013* in Nergelius and Kristoffersson (eds) (n 4) 1.

[40] Zetterquist (n 7) 133.

[41] See further Zetterquist (n 7)133.

[42] See, eg, Court of Appeal for Western Sweden, in Case B 2432-09 *MO v Ekobrottsmyndigheten*, judgment of 23 June 2010, in which case Ola Zetterquist was the Judge Rapporteur, Zetterquist (n 7) 133. See also Katarina Fast, Tusen skäl att förekomma istället för att förekommas – en kommentar till dubbelbestraffningsfallen i EU-domstolen och Högsta domstolen 2013, JT 2013–14, s 24; and Halila, Lankinen and Nilsson (n 15) 289.

[43] RÅ 2009 ref 94 (*Swedish Supreme Administrative Court*).

[44] NJA 2010 p 168 (*Swedish Supreme Court*) with two judges dissenting.

[45] Concerning the Supreme Court and the Supreme Administrative Court, see, eg, Halila, Lankinen and Nilsson (n 15) 288, referring to NJA 2000 s 622; NJA 2004 s 519; NJA 2004 s 840; NJA 2005 s 856; NJA 2010 s 168 I och II RÅ 2002 ref 79; RÅ 2009 ref 94.

[46] Nergelius (n 39) 6.

[47] *Åkerberg Fransson* (n 1) 48.

[48] Zetterquist (n 7) 134. See however the Dissenting Opinion by Judge Sundberg in case HfÖN B 801-09, judgment of 8 September 2010, arguing that there was no room for 'clear support' if this is a question of EU law since such a method is incompatible with EU law. Even if the case at hand did not involve application of EU law (which it, as it turned out, did), there was in the dissenting judge's Opinion no room for applying a criteria of 'clear support' in any case, since it had to be applied, as a matter of EU law. Hans Sundberg, senior judge, Court of Appeals for Northern Norrland, 'The Åkerberg Fransson Saga', ACTIONES, Uppsala, 14 December 2016.

not until *Åkerberg Fransson* that any Swedish court argued that the tax surcharges concerning VAT, harmonised on the EU level, actually concerns EU law and the EU Charter. By requesting a preliminary ruling, the District Court 'displayed its independence and knowledge of the Charter'.[49]

Yet, as Article 6(3) TEU confirms, fundamental rights recognised by the ECHR constitute general principles of the European Union's law and whilst Article 52(3) of the Charter requires rights contained in the Charter which correspond to rights guaranteed by the ECHR to be given the same meaning and scope as those laid down by the ECHR, the latter does not constitute, as long as the European Union has not acceded to it, a legal instrument which has been formally incorporated into European Union law. Consequently, as pointed out by the ECJ, European Union law does not govern the relations between the ECHR and the legal systems of the Member States, nor does it determine the conclusions to be drawn by a national court in the event of conflict between the rights guaranteed by that convention and a rule of national law.[50] Thus, adding the EU law dimension and Article 50 of the EU Charter was probably what made way for the change. EU law is clear on this point, since it precludes a judicial practice which makes the obligation for a national court to disapply any provision contrary to a fundamental right guaranteed by the Charter conditional upon that infringement being clear from the text of the Charter or the case law relating to it. According to the ECJ, any other practice would withhold from the national court 'the power to assess fully, with, as the case may be, the cooperation of the Court of Justice, whether that provision is compatible with the Charter.'[51]

Subsequently, the national Supreme Courts confirmed the *Zolotukhin* principle, and overruled the Swedish 'clear support' doctrine. Thus, it was not until the preliminary reference brought to the CJEU by a district court judge in Haparanda adding the EU law dimension, in the proceedings between the Swedish Prosecutor and Hans Åkerberg Fransson that finally triggered a change in the Swedish system.

Nevertheless, after the district court proceedings in the *Åkerberg Fransson* case had been stayed and a preliminary reference was sent to the CJEU, the Swedish Prosecutor appealed the decision to stay the proceedings, arguing that the processing of the case had been delayed without reason.[52] The Court of Appeals, however, with reference to *Cartesio*, rightly emphasised that every national court has an unrestricted right to ask for a preliminary reference.[53]

[49] Bernitz (n 3) 157.

[50] *Åkerberg Fransson* (n 1), para 44.

[51] *Åkerberg Frannson* (n 1), para 48. See further in particular Gulliksson (n 4) and Bernitz (n 4).

[52] Swedish Code of Judicial Procedure, Ch 49, s 7. See also Bernitz (n 4) 811.

[53] HfÖN Ö 496-11. The Court of Appeals rejected the appeal with reference to C-210/06 *Cartesio* EU:C:2008:723. See, eg, Ulf Bernitz, Förhandsavgöranden av EU-domstolen. Utvecklingen av svenska domstolars hållning och praxis 2010–2015, Sieps 2016:9, pp 56 ff.: The right for a trial court to make a reference would be rendered illusory if an appeal of the decision to stay the proceedings would succeed; Hans Sundberg, senior judge, Court of Appeals for Northern Norrland, The Åkerberg Fransson Saga, ACTIONES, Uppsala 14 December 2016; See also Bernitz (n 4) 811, with further references.

In addition, shortly after Haparanda District Court asked the CJEU for a preliminary ruling, the Swedish Supreme Court in yet another case decided not only that the EU Charter was not applicable to a similar situation, but also that the issue was *acte clair*, with no need for clarification by the CJEU. Against two dissenting judges, the majority consisting of three Supreme Court judges decided not to ask for a preliminary ruling.[54]

Regardless of these 'obstacles', the CJEU's ruling in *Åkerberg Fransson* put an end to a multilevel saga on *ne bis in idem* involving various national courts, the ECtHR and the CJEU that inspired the Swedish Supreme Courts and the national law-makers to finally change the applicable laws and practices. Since 1 January 2016, there is a joint sanction procedure in the general courts, and a barring regulation for tax surcharges and tax crimes in respect of the same mistake or invalidity regarding the same person.[55]

This change not only embraces the *ne bis in idem* principle as such, but also the criteria for judicial review of Swedish laws. After *Åkerberg Fransson*, there have been several cases involving judicial review of Swedish laws, including the legality of the weapon's law,[56] and a provision in a temporary law relating to asylum seekers allegedly infringing the Swedish Constitution and EU law. After three Migration Courts had ruled differently, the Migration Court in Gothenburg asked the CJEU for a preliminary ruling concerning the temporary law.[57] This was however later withdrawn,[58] after the Migration Court of Appeal ruled that the temporary law did not infringe either the Swedish Constitution or EU law.[59]

IV. The Fisherman, the Special Mobile Task Force of National Judges, and EU Law

As well-known as the guidance on the extent of the field of application of EU law and the EU Charter principle, and most of the underlying facts in the case of the fisherman in *Åkerberg Fransson* are by now, as little known are perhaps some of the underlying facts of the national judges and academics involved in the saga on different levels. As stated in the case *Åkerberg Fransson*, and therefore no secret,

[54] NJA 2011 s 444. See Bernitz (n 4) 811, with further references.

[55] Government Bill 2014/15: 131, introducing a joint sanction procedure in the general courts. A barring regulation for tax surcharges and tax crimes is introduced in respect of the same mistake or invalidity regarding the same person.

[56] Swedish Supreme Court on 28 September 2018, in case B 2646-18.

[57] Migration Court, *Förvaltningsrätten i Göteborg*, 10 August 2018, UM 1123-18.

[58] 'EU-domstolen prövar inte den svenska gymnasielagen – står klart att lagen får tillämpas' (*Dagens Juridik*, 2018), available at www.dagensjuridik.se/2018/10/eu-domstolen-provar-inte-den-svenska-gymnasielagen-star-klart-att-lagen-far-tillampas (last accessed 11 March 2019).

[59] Migrations Court of Appeal, *Migrationsöverdomstolen*, 25 September 2018, MIG 2018:17 and MIG 2018:18.

EU Law Professor Ulf Bernitz at the University of Stockholm was acting (*pro bono*) on behalf of Åkerberg Fransson before the CJEU. Further, and not surprisingly, one of the so-called rebellious appeal court judges, Judge Ola Zetterquist, is in fact also Associate Professor of EU Law at the University of Gothenburg.[60] A perhaps less known fact is that rebellious appeal court Judge Hans Sundberg[61] was in fact the source and ghost writer of the request for a preliminary reference in the *Åkerberg Fransson* case that gave the CJEU the necessary background for its judgment.[62]

Worried about the increasing case load before some of the national courts and anticipated critique not least from the ECtHR, a special mobile task force comprising national judges had been formed. When digging through the old case files that had piled up, the *Åkerberg Fransson* case was found, already overdue by several years. Against this background, it was not an easy decision to delay judgment even further and ask for a preliminary ruling, supposedly adding another year to the already lengthy proceedings.[63]

Little could anyone know how this long delayed and rather routine ruling would change the national and EU law landscape, giving rise to unusual plenary decisions by both the Supreme Court in June 2013[64] and the Administrative Supreme Court in October 2013,[65] upon which followed an unprecedented number of applications for restitution and compensation from individuals sentenced by Swedish courts between 2009 and 2013. These followed after another Supreme Court judgment in June 2013,[66] allowing for applications for new trials for penal sentences decided after 10 February 2009, ie the date of the *Zolotukhin* judgment.[67]

Following the right to use this extraordinary legal remedy, 'a substantial number of individuals were released from prison, where they were serving sentences for tax offences, and many ongoing tax offences prosecutions were terminated.'[68] According to Judge Zetterquist, it was estimated that about 1,000 persons were wrongly sentenced for tax fraud during this period.[69]

In general, the number of applications for new trials made to the Prosecutor-General per year is not that great, but the cases are often very complex and of considerable interest to the mass media. In 2017, there were 27 new registered cases; in 2016, 35 new registered cases; and in 2015, 34 new cases.[70] In stark

[60] Also author of Zetterquist (n 7).
[61] HfÖN B 801-09, Court of Appeals Judgment 8 September 2010.
[62] Hans Sundberg, senior judge, Court of Appeals for Northern Norrland, 'The Åkerberg Fransson Saga', ACTIONES, Uppsala 14 December 2016.
[63] *Ibid.*
[64] NJA 2013 s 502.
[65] RÅ 2013 ref 71 (*Swedish Supreme Administrative Court*).
[66] NJA 2013 s 746.
[67] *Zolotukhin v Russia* (n 18).
[68] Bernitz, (n 3) 166.
[69] Zetterquist (n 7) 134.
[70] Swedish Prosecution Authority, 'Resning', available at www.aklagare.se/om_rattsprocessen/resning/ (last accessed 11 March 2019).

contrast, the corresponding numbers of 2013 and 2014 were much higher due to *Åkerberg Fransson* and the following Supreme Court judgments.

According to a joint report by the Swedish Prosecution Authority and the Swedish Economic Crime Authority,[71] prosecutors at these authorities have reviewed more than 2,700 cases due to the changes in case law. In 580 double penalty cases, public prosecutors have applied for a new trial. To this, an unknown number of applications by convicted persons should be added.[72] Most of these cases have been heard by a court and most of these have been successful. A large part of these cases have been retried by District Courts or Courts of Appeal.[73]

V. Concluding Remarks

The issue of *ne bis in idem* is not of course finally solved with *Åkerberg Fransson*, nor is there an end to legal development through court cases. More recent case law both from the ECtHR such as *A and B v Norway*,[74] and from the CJEU such as *Luca Menci, Garlsson Reasl Estate, Enzo Di Puma*, and *Consob v Antonio Zecca*,[75] show that there is constant development and new solutions to old issues, as well as new issues that need to be answered.

Yet, in Sweden, the *Åkerberg Fransson* case had an enormous impact resulting in two plenary judgments where the Swedish Supreme Court and the Swedish Supreme Administrative Court reversed their previous policies. This in turn gave rise to an exceptional number of applications for a new trial and subsequently a change of the applicable Swedish legislation. As a result, this commentary has provided an illustrative example of the huge impact a single CJEU judgment might have not only on one national legal system, but on the relationship between national and EU law in general, and on the development of EU law and the scope of the EU Charter in particular.

This commentary has also provided an interesting case study of the interrelationship between various courts on different levels, and how courts were instrumental not only for the settlement of individual disputes, but in changing the legal system: in other words, *pressure through law*, involving in particular national judges and EU law lawyers. Adding the EU law dimension and

[71] Swedish Prosecution Authority and Swedish Economic Crime Authority, 'Dubbelbestraffning – åtgärder vid Åklagarmyndigheten och Ekobrottsmyndigheten med anledning av två beslut från Högsta domstolen', available at www.ekobrottsmyndigheten.se/Documents/Rapporter/Dubbelbestraffning-sammanställning-åtgärder.pdf (last accessed 11 March 2019).

[72] Hans Sundberg, senior judge, Court of Appeals for Northern Norrland, 'The Impact of Preliminary Rulings on National Case Law', ACTIONES, final conference, Brussels 24 October 2017.

[73] Swedish Prosecution Authority and Swedish Economic Crime Authority (n 67).

[74] *A and B v Norway* App nos 24130/11 and 29758/11 (ECtHR, 2016).

[75] Cases C-524/15 *Luca Menci* EU:C:2018:197; C-537/16 *Garlsson Real Estate SA and Others v Commissione Nazionale per le Società e la Borsa (Consob)* EU:C:2018:193; and Joined Cases C-596/16 *Enzo Di Puma v Consob* and C-597/16 *Consob v Antonio Zecca* EU:C:2018:192.

Article 50 of the EU Charter was probably what made way for the change, at the same time emphasising the stronger effect the EU Charter has in the Swedish legal order compared to the ECHR in similar non EU-situations.[76]

Although the ECJ in *Åkerberg Fransson* emphasised that EU law does not govern the relations between the ECHR and the legal systems of the Member States, nor does it determine the conclusions to be drawn by a national court in the event of conflict between the rights guaranteed by that convention and a rule of national law,[77] the subsequent judgments by the national Supreme Courts confirmed the *Zolotukhin* principle, and overruled the Swedish 'clear support' doctrine. Thus, it was not until the preliminary reference brought to the CJEU by a district court judge in Haparanda, in the proceedings between the Swedish Prosecutor and Hans Åkerberg Fransson that finally triggered a change in the Swedish system.

This change not only embraces the *ne bis in idem* principle as such, but also the criteria for judicial review of Swedish laws. After *Åkerberg Fransson*, and the abandoning of the clear support doctrine, there have been several cases involving judicial review of Swedish laws, including the legality of the weapon's law, and a provision in a temporary law relating to asylum seekers allegedly infringing the Swedish Constitution and EU law. After three Migration Courts had ruled differently, the request for a preliminary ruling by the Migration Court in Gothenburg was later withdrawn, after the Migration Court of Appeal judged that the temporary law did not infringe either the Swedish Constitution or EU law. As a result, we will most probably not be given a judgment from the CJEU concerning this issue.

In demonstrating the enormous impact an individual judgment might have not only for individuals and national legal systems, but consequently, for their respect for EU law and the ECHR, this chapter also provides a cautious note to Luxembourg, Strasbourg and their national counterparts. Given their enormous impact, the need for clear, well-reasoned and qualitative legal precedents are in fact crucial for the future of EU and ECHR law. This means that the principle of legal certainty must always be upheld. Arguably, any development need therefore be transparent, well-reasoned and qualitative in substance, argument and clarity, irrespective of whether dissenting opinions are allowed or not.

To conclude, traditional guarantees, such as the principle of legality and *ne bis in idem* have been involved in the interaction between criminal liability at the national level, and rights and principles protected by EU law and their content has been redefined. Clearly, given the current legal and political situation, the European Courts' key role in promoting and managing that dialogue is becoming even greater.

[76] See, eg Bernitz (n 3) 168. According to Bernitz, EU law also has effects in the fundamental rights area which go beyond the scope of EU law, since it would be difficult for the Member State to defend and continue to apply a certain legal rule or practice found to be contrary to the protection of fundamental rights under EU law when EU law is applicable (eg concerning VAT where the CJEU has clear jurisdiction), in purely internal situations (e.g. concerning income tax). Bernitz (n 3) 169.

[77] *Åkerberg Fransson* (n 1), para 44.

PART IV

Migration and Citizenship

10

C-61/11 PPU – *El Dridi*

Criminalisation of Irregular Migration in the EU: The Impact of El Dridi

NIOVI VAVOULA

I. Introduction – The EU Involvement in the Criminalisation of Irregular Migration

The past decade has witnessed the growing use of substantive criminal law as a method of tackling irregular migration. At the European level, this trend – commonly referred to as the criminalisation of irregular migration or 'crimmigration'[1] – has been fleshed out by both the EU legislator and the Member States individually. In particular, the EU involvement takes place in a twofold manner; directly, through harmonisation of national legislation and indirectly, through the case law of the Court of Justice of the EU (CJEU). In recent years, the EU has adopted substantive criminal law provisions which treat conduct associated with irregular migration flows as crimes and provide for sanctions for the violation of these provisions. The trafficking of human beings is a prime example in that respect, with Directive 2011/36/EU[2] substituting a pre-Lisbon Framework Decision[3] and Directive 2004/81/EC granting (conditional) residence permits rights to victims of trafficking.[4] Human smuggling, or in more neutral EU terms, the facilitation of unauthorised entry, transit or residence, is regulated by a dual legislative framework, which mirrors the former pillar

[1] Juliet Stumpf, 'The Crimmigration Crisis: Immigrants, Crime, and Sovereign Power' (2006) 56(2) *American University Law Review* 368, 379.

[2] Council Directive 2011/36/EU of the European Parliament and of the Council of 5 April 2011 on preventing and combating trafficking in human beings and protecting its victims, and replacing Council Framework Decision 2002/629/JHA [2011] OJ L101/1.

[3] Council Framework Decision 2002/629/JHA of 19 July 2002 on combating trafficking in human beings [2002] OJ L203/1.

[4] Council Directive 2004/81/EC of 29 April 2004 on the residence permit issued to third-country nationals who are victims of trafficking in human beings or who have been the subject of an action to facilitate illegal immigration, who cooperate with the competent authorities [2004] OJ L261/19.

structure; a Directive which sets out the definitions for the crimes[5] is accompanied by a Framework Decision criminalising the conduct described in the Directive and setting out sanctions.[6] This set of legal instruments is completed by the Employers' Sanctions Directive,[7] which imposes duties to employers of irregular migrants and provides for sanctions if they fail to comply with these duties or they infringe the prohibition of not employing 'illegally staying third-country nationals'.[8]

The primary focus of these instruments is on individuals who act as facilitators or intermediaries of irregular migration in a broad sense. Conversely, any violations of immigration law by irregular migrants themselves are not dealt with by EU law. However, legislation attributing criminal law sanctions to the violations of immigration law committed by irregular migrants has been put in place in most Member States. Key examples in this context are the treatment of irregular entry and stay as criminal offences with penalties varying from imprisonment to fines and to a lesser extent warnings.[9] The EU is not watching from a distance these parallel national developments and in this sense it indirectly influences national legislations. By using as a motor the Directive on the return of 'illegally staying' third-country nationals ('Return Directive'),[10] the CJEU has placed strict limitations on the Member States' power to enforce criminal sanctions to irregular migrants by differentiating treatment and imposing numerous conditions.

The judgment in *El Dridi*, delivered in April 2011[11] has been the first in a series of cases[12] imposing boundaries to Member States in criminalising irregular migrants and the aim of this commentary is to assess its implications for EU law as it set the foundations for an indirect involvement of the EU in a much controversial and heated topic.[13] In this context, this commentary first provides

[5] Council Directive 2002/90/EC of 28 November 2002 defining the facilitation of unauthorised entry, transit and residence [2002] OJ L328/17.

[6] Council Framework Decision 2002/946/JHA of 28 November 2002 on the strengthening of the penal framework to prevent the facilitation of unauthorised entry, transit and residence [2002] OJ L328/1.

[7] Council Directive 2009/52/EC of the European Parliament and of the Council of 18 June 2009 providing for minimum standards on sanctions and measures against employers of illegally staying third-country nationals [2002] OJ L168/24.

[8] For an overview of the aforementioned measures, see Valsamis Mitsilegas, 'The Changing Landscape of the Criminalisation of Migration in Europe: The Protective Function of European Union Law' in Maria João Guia, Maartje van der Woude and Joanne van der Leun (eds), *Social Control and Justice* (Eleven International Publishing, 2013) 87.

[9] For an overview of the Member States' policies in criminalising violations of domestic immigration rules, see Fundamental Rights Agency (FRA), 'Criminalisation of Migrants in an Irregular Situation and of Persons Engaging with Them' (2014) http://fra.europa.eu/en/publication/2014/criminalisation-migrants-irregular-situation-and-persons-engaging-them (last accessed 11 March 2019).

[10] Directive 2008/115/EC of the European Parliament and of the Council of 16 December 2008 on common standards and procedures in Member States for returning illegally staying third-country nationals [2008] OJ L348/98 ('Return Directive').

[11] Case C-61/11 *El Dridi* [2011] ECR I-03015.

[12] See below (section IV).

[13] See among others Thomas Hammarberg, 'It Is Wrong to Criminalise Migration' [2009] 11 *European Journal of Migration and Law* 383; François Crépeau, 'Report of the Special Rapporteur on the Human Rights of Migrants' (Human Rights Council, Twentieth Session, A/HRC/20/24), available at www.ohchr.org/Documents/HRBodies/HRCouncil/RegularSession/Session20/A-HRC-20-24_en.pdf (last accessed 11 March 2019).

a brief overview of the Return Directive; while an in-depth examination of these issues is beyond the scope of the present commentary, a brief overview will inform the subsequent analysis. Then, the CJEU findings in *El Dridi* will be discussed, followed by an analysis of its impact on EU law and an overview of the case law that has further refined the Court's proclamations.

II. The Return Directive as the Stormy Petrel

The Return Directive is the pan-European legal instrument that has been adopted with the aim of providing common standards on the effective removal and repatriation of 'illegally staying third-country nationals'.[14] In a nutshell, the Directive prescribes that in cases where an irregular migrant is detected on national territory, Member States' authorities are obliged to issue a return decision (Article 6). The addressee is in principle granted a period of voluntary departure ranging between seven and 30 days (Article 7). If that period expires and there is no other sufficient but less coercive measure available, the irregular migrants may be detained pending removal in specialised facilities for a period of up to 18 months (Articles 15–18). According to Article 11(1) of the Return Directive, an entry ban must be issued where a return decision was ordered without a period for voluntary departure being granted, or where the obligation to return has not been complied with. In other cases, an entry ban may be issued.

Much ink has been spilt about the Return Directive, with an array of scholars and practitioners[15] raising significant concerns regarding its restrictive character, particularly as regards the rules on detention and the absence of a clear fundamental rights approach to irregular migrants.[16] Civil organisations have been highly critical of the Directive, to the extent that it has been nicknamed as the 'directive of shame'.[17] At the same time, the controversy surrounding its provisions has meant that the CJEU is repeatedly requested to provide guidance and interpretation on its rules.[18] However, there exists a second type of case that

[14] Art 1 of the Return Directive.

[15] For detailed analyses of the Return Directive, see among others Diego Acosta Arcarazo, 'The Good, the Bad and the Ugly in EU Migration Law: Is the European Parliament Becoming Bad and Ugly? (The Adoption of Directive 2008/115 The Returns Directive)' (2009) *European Journal of Migration & Law* 19; Anneliese Baldaccini, 'The Return and Removal of Irregular Migrants under EU Law: An Analysis of the Returns Directive' (2009) *European Journal of Migration & Law* 1.

[16] The Directive is not completely unconcerned with the protection of fundamental rights. See Recital 2.

[17] Anafé, APDHA, Arci, ATMF, La Cimade, Gisti, IPAM, LDH-Belgique, Migreurop, Statewatch, 'The Council of Ministers of the European Union should not Adopt the Outrageous Directive', available at www.migreurop.org/article1333.html (last accessed 11 March 2019). For an optimistic view, see Francesco Maiani, 'Directive de la honte ou instrument de progrès ? Avancées, régressions et *statu quo* en droit des étrangers sous l'influence de la Directive sur le retour' *Annuaire Suisse de Droit Européen 2008/2009* (Stämpfli/Schulthess Bern/Zurich, 2009) 289–315.

[18] Apart from the judgments that are the subject of this commentary, the following cases have been decided: C-357/09 PPU *Kadzoev* [2009] I-11189; C-534/11 *Arslan* ECLI:EU:C:2013:343; C-383/13 PPU

does not directly relate to the interpretation of the Directive's provisions, but engages in the interaction between the Member States' sovereign powers to criminalise violations of national immigration law and the effectiveness of the Return Directive, with the leading case being *El Dridi*.

III. The Judgment in *El Dridi*: A Decisive Step towards the Delimitation of Member States' Power to Criminalise Irregular Migrants

A. Legal and Factual Background

In *El Dridi*, the CJEU was faced with an Italian legislation which assigned criminal sanctions to irregular migrants who had failed to comply with a return decision and remained at the national territory. As is explained by Annoni in the second part of this chapter,[19] the Italian Government had adopted a series of legislative measures, commonly known as the 'Security Package' (*Pacchetto Sicurezza*),[20] including a law that addressed some aspects of the Return Directive. However, the underlying aim was to avoid implementation of the Return Directive[21] by introducing new immigration offences of irregular entry or stay that were punishable with a fine (Art 10 *bis*), whereas failure to comply with a return decision would be sanctioned with imprisonment of one to four years (Article 14.5 *ter* and *quater*). This is because Article 2 of the Return Directive gives leeway to Member States to exclude from its scope persons who have been 'subject to return as a criminal law sanction or as a consequence of a criminal law sanction, according to national law'. By essentially criminalising all irregular migrants, Italy desired to bypass its obligations pursuant to the Directive.

In this context, Mr El Dridi, an Algerian national, had entered Italy irregularly and had never obtained a valid residence permit. In 2004, he was issued an expulsion decree which six years later served as a basis for a deportation order.

G and R ECLI:EU:C:2013:533; C-297/12 *Filev & Osmani* ECLI:EU:C:2013:569; C-146/14 PPU *Mahdi* ECLI:EU:C:2014:1320; C-189/13 *Da Silva* ECLI:EU:C:2014:2043; C-473/13 *Bero* ECLI:EU:C:2014:2095; C-514/13 *Bouzalmate* ECLI:EU:C:2014:2095; C-474/13 *Pham* ECLI:EU:C:2014:2095; C-166/13 *Mukarubega* ECLI:EU:C:2014:2336; C-249/13 *Boujlida* ECLI:EU:C:2014:2431; C-554/13 *Zh and O* ECLI:EU:C:2015:377; C-38/14 *Zaizoune* ECLI:EU:C:2015:260; C-225/16 *Ouhrami* ECLI:EU:C:2017:590; and C-240/17 *E* ECLI:EU:C:2018:8.

[19] See the second part of this chapter entitled 'Reshaping Criminalisation of Irregular Migration in Italy: The Impact of EU Law beyond the El-Dridi Judgment' by Alessandra Annoni.

[20] For an analysis of the 'Security Package' see Alberto di Martino, Fransesca Biondi Dal Monte, Ilaria Boiano and Rosa Rafaellli, *The Criminalization of Irregular Immigration: Law and Practice in Italy* (Pisa University Press, 2013).

[21] Paolo Bonetti, 'La Proroga del Trattenimento e I Reati di Ingresso o Permanenza Irregolare nel Sistema del Diritto degli Stranieri: Profili Constituzionali e Rapporti con la Direttiva Comunitaria sui Rimpranti' [2009] *Diritto Immigrazione e Cittadinanza* 85.

Though he was requested to voluntarily leave the country within five days, in September 2010 he was arrested and sentenced to one year's imprisonment by the District Court of Trento for the crime of failing to comply with a return order on the basis of Article 14.5 ter. Mr El Dridi appealed against that decision before the Appeal Court of Trento. The latter submitted a reference for a preliminary ruling to the CJEU enquiring whether a criminal sanction during administrative procedures concerning his return due to non-compliance with the stages of those procedures complied with the Return Directive, particularly its Articles 15 and 16 on detention.

B. The Judgment

From the outset, the Court highlighted the purpose and character of the Return Directive. It was stressed that according to Recital 2, its aim is 'the establishment of an effective removal and repatriation policy [...] *for persons to be returned in a humane manner and with full respect for their fundamental rights and also their dignity*'.[22] It thus employed a restrictive interpretation of the Directive paving the way on how it should be interpreted at the national level as well.[23] Furthermore, this remark is crucial in the light of the heated debate surrounding the inclusion of fundamental rights references into the Directive.[24] By founding its reasoning on the basis of fundamental rights, the ruling served as a reminder to Member States about the paramount importance of ensuring a high level of fundamental rights protection in the return procedure.

Next, the Court codified the removal process in a series of successive stages. The chronology begins with the issuance of a return decision. Then, the prescription of a period for voluntary departure is prioritised unless particular circumstances dictate otherwise. If the irregular migrant has not voluntarily complied with the decision, national authorities are obliged to carry out the removal by taking all the appropriate measures. However, the principle of proportionality and the respect of fundamental rights must be observed and, therefore, the least coercive measures should be preferred. Deprivation of liberty and detention are allowed after assessing each specific case and only when the enforcement of the return decision in the form of removal risks to be compromised by the conduct of the person at stake. The Court highlighted that the order in which the stages of the return procedure are to take place corresponds to a gradation of the measures to be taken in order to enforce the return decision. This means that the measures become more stringent as the procedure

[22] *El Dridi* (n 11), para 31 (emphasis added).

[23] Mitsilegas (n 8) 101.

[24] See Annaliese Baldaccini, 'The EU Directive on Return: Principles and Protests' (2009) *Refugee Survey Quarterly* 125.

evolves from the less restrictive in regards to the individual's liberty (voluntary departure) to the most constraining (detention in a specialised facility).[25]

Having set out the lens through which the Directive should be interpreted, the next step for the CJEU was to determine whether in the absence of national implementation, Articles 15 and 16 of the Directive were directly effective in the specific case. The Court found no difficulty in granting the relevant provisions direct effect; since they are sufficiently clear and precise,[26] Mr El Dridi could rely upon them. The Court thus sent a gentle reminder to Member States that they could not act on their own motion and evade their obligations under EU law. This was precisely the Italian case, with the adopted legislation providing for a return procedure which significantly deviated from the standards of the Directive.[27]

The core of the judgment is preoccupied with the interplay between the Return Directive on the removal of irregular migrants and the enforcement of national rules imposing criminal sanctions for violation of immigration laws. The Grand Chamber started its analysis by recognising a certain degree of discretion to Member States when adopting measures, including criminal law ones, aimed inter alia at dissuading third-country nationals from remaining illegally on their national territory. However, it imposed two significant restrictions; first, these measures may come into play only when all other measures already employed have failed to attain the objective of removal.[28] Second, it reiterated that although criminal legislation and the rules of criminal procedure are matters for which the Member States are responsible, this area of law is nevertheless affected by EU law.[29] Therefore, although the legal basis of the Directive (and its Lisbon successor) or the Directive itself do not preclude them from having competence in criminal matters in the area of illegal immigration and illegal stays, their legislation must comply with EU law nevertheless.[30] The Court thus justified these limitations on the basis of the principles of effectiveness and loyal cooperation. It prohibited Member States from applying rules, even criminal law ones, which are liable to jeopardise the achievement of the objectives pursued by the Directive and deprive it of its effectiveness. It invoked Article 4(3) of the Treaty on European Union (TEU) which obliges Member States to '[…] refrain from any measure which could jeopardise the attainment of the Union's objectives' and Recital 13 of the Return Directive which makes the use of coercive measures subject to the principles of proportionality and effectiveness.[31]

Consequently, the Grand Chamber opined that Member States may not, in order to remedy their failure of coercive measures adopted during the return procedure, provide for a custodial sentence solely because a third-country national

[25] *El Dridi* (n 11), paras 37–41.
[26] *El Dridi* (n 11), para 47.
[27] *El Dridi* (n 11), para 50.
[28] *El Dridi* (n 11), para 52.
[29] *El Dridi* (n 11), para 53.
[30] *El Dridi* (n 11), para 54.
[31] *El Dridi* (n 11), paras 56.

continues to stay illegally on their territory despite a return decision. Instead, they ought to continue their efforts to enforce the decision, which continues to produce its effects.[32] If a term of imprisonment is imposed, the attainment of the Directive may be compromised because it is liable to frustrate the application of the measures and delay the enforcement of the return decision.[33] Despite these restrictions, the Court recalled Member States that they are still allowed to adopt and employ criminal law provisions in situations when coercive measures did not lead to the removal of an irregular migrant.[34] However, the Court was mindful to note that the adoption of these provisions must occur with respect to the principles and objectives of the Return Directive, which continues to be the benchmark for the adoption of national criminal law.

C. The Value of *El Dridi* for EU Law

El Dridi has made its way in jurisprudential history as a victory for irregular migrants in three main respects. First, the Grand Chamber stressed that the Return Directive must be interpreted in the light of fundamental rights. Thus, notwithstanding the Council's attempts to disassociate the return procedure from the protection of fundamental rights of irregular migrants, the Court succeeded in giving the Preamble a more substantial context and made it clear that references in the Preamble constitute interpretative guides. Second, as regards to Italy's attempt to bypass EU rules, the Court gave a warning to Member States that circumventing the transposition of the instrument and developing an autonomous path in immigration policy will prove extremely hard.

Third, the most important contribution of *El Dridi* involves the Member States' power to impose national criminal law provisions to irregular migrants and the overall relationship between EU law and national criminal law. The judgment confirmed that the former places limits on the adoption of and employability of the latter and that Member States are not entirely free to introduce criminal law rules, but are required to comply with their obligations under EU law when exercising their powers to criminalise, in particular obligations deriving from the principles of loyal cooperation and effectiveness. In the case of prosecuting and penalising irregular migrants, the practical impact of that pronouncement was that as long as the removal process is ongoing, the Member States are not allowed to impose a term of imprisonment to third-country nationals whose sole misconduct is their stay on the national territory contrary to a return order.

This was the first time that an EU immigration law instrument was found to have a delimiting effect on the Member States' power to criminalise. In the framework of free movement, as early as in 1981, the CJEU opined that Community

[32] *El Dridi* (n 11), para 58.
[33] *El Dridi* (n 11), para 59.
[34] Nevertheless, the Court does not explicitly refer to criminal law provisions.

law places boundaries to the application of national criminal law with a view to safeguarding the effectiveness of rights related to free movement.[35] In *Casati*, the Court held that although criminal law is presumed to be a matter for which the Member States are responsible, 'Community law sets certain limits in that area as regards the control measures which it permits the Member States to maintain in connection with the free movement of goods and persons'.[36] As a result, the penalties imposed ought to be strictly necessary and not so disproportionate to the gravity of the infringement that they become an obstacle to the exercise of that freedom.[37] This approach was justified in order to prevent the erosion of Community law freedoms by national criminal rules.[38] Although in the end the Italian legislation in question was found compatible with Community law, the Court based its approach on a strict proportionality test.[39] This approach was confirmed in subsequent cases; in *Skanavi and Chryssanthakopoulos*,[40] the Court ruled that a provision sanctioning persons who had failed to convert their driving licences obtained outside Germany within a prescribed period was incompatible with Community law due to 'the effect which the right to drive a motor vehicle has on the actual exercise of the rights relating to the free movement of persons'.[41] Furthermore, in *Placanica, Palazzese and Sorricchio*, regarding criminal sanctions imputed for the organised activity of collecting bets without obtaining a licence or a police authorisation, the Court held a criminal penalty is incompatible with free movement rights, where the defendants were unable to obtain licences or authorisations because that Member State, in breach of Community law, refused to grant licences or authorisations to such persons.[42] Finally, in *Bickel and Franz*, concerning the language of criminal proceedings, the Court clarified that such specifications may be subject to limitations for the purpose of ensuring non-discrimination as well as free movement rights.[43]

El Dridi must be seen as a consistent application and a successful transplantation of the CJEU's approach in relation to free movement rights. In the present case, the objective pursued shifted from free movement to the establishment of an effective policy of returns of irregular migrants. What is more important is the nature of the instrument the effective implementation of which is safeguarded. Being an enforcement mechanism and arguably the 'black sheep' of EU immigration law, *El Dridi* creates an interesting paradox; the Directive which has been criticised for its restrictive approach and lack of high standards

[35] Case 203/80 *Casati* [1981] ECR 2595.
[36] *Ibid*, para 27.
[37] *Ibid*.
[38] *Ibid*, para 28.
[39] Takis Tridimas, *The General Principles of EU Law*, 2nd edn (Oxford University Press, 2006) 234.
[40] Case C-193/94 *Skanavi and Chryssanthakopoulos* [1996] ECR I-929.
[41] *Ibid*, para 36.
[42] Joined Cases C-338/04, C-359/04 and C-360/04 *Placanica, Palazzese and Sorricchio* [2007] ECR I-1891.
[43] Case C-274/96 *Bickel and Franz* [1998] ECR I-7637.

of fundamental rights protection is used by the Court as a buffer to protect irregular migrants from being imprisoned for the sole reason that they have violated domestic immigration laws.

It has been eloquently argued that criminalisation is not banned in its entirety.[44] The judgment left to the Member States a degree of discretion by stating that the latter retain the power to adopt provisions in cases where coercive measures have failed to lead to the removal of a third-country national. However, the Court went on to state that even in these cases the imposition of the measures must occur with respect to the principles and objective of the Directive. Given the wide divergence of national legislations on the issue and the shared competence between Member States and the EU in immigration matters, it seems that the Court attempted to strike a balance between national interests and the protection of irregular migrants. Importantly, despite the judgment's limited scope, it opened Pandora's Box regarding the application of a wide array of Member States' measures criminalising irregular migrants' conducts. A key question in that respect was whether these pronouncements could apply not only when the criminal offence in question related to a violation of a return order, but more broadly with any violation of national criminal law, which could interfere with the return of third-country nationals. The following section summarises the key judgments released by the Court that further elaborate and develop the *El Dridi* rationale.

IV. Subsequent Case Law: A Comprehensive Approach towards Criminalisation of Irregular Migrants?

A. The Good News: Deepening and Expanding the *El Dridi* Logic

Following the release of *El Dridi*, practitioners and judges in different Member States were faced with legal uncertainty as to whether the classification of irregular stay as a criminal offence was in line with the judgment at least when a return decision had been issued. In France, the problem was particularly acute; at that time, French immigration law criminalised irregular stay foreseeing punishment of imprisonment of up to one year and a fine of 3750 Euros.[45] In addition, third-country nationals were placed in police custody (*garde à vue*) by the French police, which would carry out investigations before transferring irregular migrants to an

[44] Henri Labayle and Philippe de Bruycker, 'Impact de la Jurisprudence de la CEJ et de la CEDH en Matière d' Asile et d' Immigration' (Directorate General for Internal Policies, Policy Department C: Citizens' Rights and Constitutional Affairs, European Parliament, 2012) 91.

[45] Article L-621 of the Code of Entry and Stay of Aliens and Right of Asylum (*Code d' entrée et du sejour des étrangers et du droit d' asile*, CESEDA).

administrative detention centre awaiting their removal.[46] Mr Achughbabian, an Armenian national, was arrested and placed into custody, but his case differed in that he was sanctioned before the return procedure had been set in motion.[47] Therefore, criminalisation of irregular stay took place independently and was not related to the removal process, thus raising the question of whether the Return Directive would apply in the first place.

The CJEU found no difficulty in ascertaining that the case fell within the scope of the Directive. In the Court's view, in order to ensure its effectiveness, national authorities must act with diligence and take a position without delay on the legality, or otherwise of the stay of the person concerned. Upon finding that a third-country national is irregularly staying, in principle a return decision must be issued. Detention is thus inextricably linked with the outcome of the removal of the third-country national concerned.[48] Then, the Grand Chamber compared the return procedures as set out in the Directive and as in French legislation to note the different character of the procedures and conclude that the latter may jeopardise the application of the Directive's rules and thus its effectiveness.[49] The Court went on to dismiss arguments by the French Government regarding the rare imposition of such sanctions unless they had committed another offence apart from their irregular stay;[50] not only such possibility remained open for the courts, but also, the Directive would be deprived of its effectiveness and binding effect as it would be interpreted as making it lawful for Member States not to apply the provisions of the Directive to all third-country nationals whose only crime is their illegal stay.[51] The Court also made it clear that imposing custodial sentences to irregularly staying third-country nationals before carrying out their removal was also not possible;[52] it follows from the duty of loyal cooperation and the principle of effectiveness that once national authorities establish that a third-country national is an irregular migrant they are required to carry out the removal as soon as possible. This will not take place if instead of implementing a return decision (perhaps not even adopting one on time) criminal prosecution is initiated

[46] See Article 62-2 of the French Code of Criminal Procedure. Also see Angela Bolis, 'Ce qui devrait changer avec la fin des gardes à vue des sans papiers' *Le Monde* (7 June 2012) www.lemonde.fr/societe/article/2012/06/07/ce-que-changerait-la-fin-des-gardes-a-vue-des-immigres-sans-papiers_1714475_3224.html (last accessed 11 March 2019. For different views, see Cour d' Appel de Douai, *Ordonnance* (6 May 2011); Cour d' Appel de Toulouse, *Ordonnance* (9 May 2011); Cour d' Appel de Nîmes, *Ordonnance* (6 May 2011). On the other hand, the Ministry of Justice had issued Ministère de la Justice et des Libertés, 'Circulaire du 12 Mai 2011 relative à la portée de l' arrêt de la Cour de justice européenne (CJEU) du 28 avril 2011 portant sur l' interprétation des articles 15 et 16 de la directive 2008/115/CE, dite "directive retour"' (12 May 2011) http://www.gisti.org/IMG/pdf/circ_2011-05-12.pdf; Cour d' Appel d' Aix en Provence, *Ordonnance* (16 May 2011); Cour d' Appel de Paris, *Ordonnance* (7 May 2011).

[47] Mitsilegas (n 8) 106.

[48] *El Dridi* (n 11), para 31.

[49] *El Dridi* (n 11), paras 38–39.

[50] *El Dridi* (n 11), para 40.

[51] *El Dridi* (n 11), paras 41–43.

[52] *El Dridi* (n 11), para 44.

accompanied by a term of imprisonment. This in-between step would delay the removal and besides is not included among the justifications for a postponement of removal as set out in the Directive.[53]

Finally, having in mind the impact of the judgment on national sovereignty and in order to address their concerns as regards the application of national policies to deter and prevent irregular migration, the Court confirmed its finding in *El Dridi* that Member States retain their power to adopt criminal law provisions in situations when the coercive measures did not make it possible to remove the third-country national.[54] However, even in these cases, which are outside the scope of the Directive, the Grand Chamber managed to 'sneak' two further limitations: first, penal sanctions may be imposed in those cases involving a third-country national who has been subjected to a return procedure and is illegally staying in the territory of a Member State 'without there being any justified ground for non-return';[55] and second, the imposition of such penalties must be subjected to full observance of fundamental rights, in particular the European Convention on Human Rights.[56]

Achughbabian is an important follow-up case to *El Dridi*; it clarified that the criminalisation of irregular stay cannot be an aim in itself, but is ultimately linked to the objective of the return of the third-country nationals affected, thus bringing into play the application of EU law. Furthermore, while the Court was careful to leave Member States with a certain degree of flexibility to adopt criminal law in relation to immigration offences, it provided a clearer idea as to the circumstances under which a custodial sentence may be imposed to third-country nationals for violations of domestic immigration laws. In particular, the imposition of a term of imprisonment may take place in cases where the return procedure has been applied but failed and there is no justified ground for non-return. It has been pointed out that the Court seems to refer to two categories of third-country nationals; those whose return is precluded by international law (non-refoulement) and those whose removal cannot take place for reasons outside their sphere of influence. The latter category would include nationals who cannot be returned either because their country of origin does not allow their return (eg by not issuing travel documents) or because the Member State responsible lacks the means for repatriation.[57] Otherwise, it would seem unreasonable to impose and enforce custodial sentences to individuals who – through no fault of their own – cannot be removed. Therefore, irregular migrants could be subjected to imprisonment if their return is obstructed by their

[53] *El Dridi* (n 11), para 45; Article 9 of the Return Directive provides for the reasons for postponing the removal.

[54] *El Dridi* (n 11), para 46–47.

[55] *El Dridi* (n 11), para 48.

[56] *El Dridi* (n 11), para 49.

[57] Rosa Rafaelli, 'Case Note: The Achughbabian Case: Impact of the Return Directive on National Criminal Legislation' [2012] *Diritto Penale Contemporaneo* 11.

personal conduct.[58] In addition, although at first sight the legislation in question did not appear to be directly related to the Directive, the Court managed to bring it within the realms of EU law and apply the *El Dridi* logic. By doing so, it made it highly unlikely for Member States to unlink the Directive from the criminalisation of irregular migrants at the national level. As such, the judgment in *El Dridi*, as further refined and elaborated on in *Achughbabian*, had far-reaching implications for Member States' power to impose criminal sanctions to irregular migrants.[59] This is because the vast majority of Member States treat irregular stay as a criminal offence, ten of which prescribe the imposition of a fine and/or imprisonment.[60] In those cases, imposition of a criminal sanction before or during the return process is found to be incompatible with the Return Directive.

The criminal offence of irregular entry is of a similar nature, as it is punishable with imprisonment and/or a fine in 17 Member States. Although *Achughbabian* refers specifically to the criminal offence of irregular stay, excluding irregular entry could lead to unjust results for irregular migrants. The CJEU had the opportunity to clarify this issue in the case of *Affum*,[61] a Ghanaian national, who was intercepted by French authorities at the entrance of the Channel Tunnel, whilst transiting through French territory on a bus from Belgium to the UK. She was detained for illegal entry, but the prosecutor decided to take no further criminal proceedings against her. An Order was issued deciding her transfer to Belgium in accordance with a readmission agreement between France and the Benelux countries, coupled with a decision on her administrative detention pending removal. Upon appeal, the Court of Cassation submitted a reference for a preliminary ruling to the CJEU on the compatibility of the Return Directive with national law allowing the imposition of a term of imprisonment of a third-country national on the basis of illegal entry and stay. The Court asserted that third-country nationals found 'staying illegally on the territory of a Member State' fall within the scope of the Return Directive.[62] After reiterating its findings in *Achughbabian*,[63] the Court confirmed its application also in the case of illegal stay by opining that 'the concepts of "illegal stay" and "illegal entry" are closely linked, as such entry is one of the factual circumstances that may result in the third-country national's stay on the territory of the Member State concerned being illegal'.[64] As a result, Ms Affum had to be subject to the procedures laid down in the Return Directive for the purpose of her removal and could not be imprisoned merely on account of

[58] *Ibid*.

[59] For the impact of the judgment in France, see Niovi Vavoula, 'The Interplay between EU Immigration Law and National Criminal Law: The Case of the Return Directive' in Valsamis Mitsilegas, Maria Bergström and Theodore Konstantinides (eds), *Research Handbook on European Criminal Law* (Edward Elgar, 2016) 303–304.

[60] FRA (n 9).

[61] Case C-47/15 *Affum* ECLI:EU:C:2016:408.

[62] *Ibid*, paras 45–50.

[63] *Ibid*, paras 51–56.

[64] *Ibid*, para 60.

her illegal entry, resulting in an illegal stay, as this would thwart the application of the Directive and undermine its effectiveness.[65]

B. The Bad News: A Nuanced Approach towards Criminalisation of Irregular Migrants?

The judgments examined above provide a comprehensive approach towards custodial sentences imposed to irregular migrants before or during the return process. However, in numerous Member States, violations of domestic immigration provisions are sanctioned by way of a pecuniary penalty.[66] The extent to which such sanctions could be imposed on third-country nationals was dealt with in the case of Mr Sagor,[67] who was fined after being apprehended for irregularly staying on Italian territory, as prescribed in Italian legislation.[68] The latter further provided that in cases where the third-country national affected could not afford to pay the fine, the fine would be converted to home detention.[69] The judgment in *Sagor* is a faithful application of the *El Dridi* logic, which this time led to the opposite result, as the Court opined that the imposition of a fine as a sanction to irregular migrants is in compliance with the Directive. In particular, the Court contended that a pending criminal prosecution in itself does not delay or otherwise impede the return. This is because the removal of a third-country national can be achieved without requiring that prosecution to have come to an end. Indeed, under the Italian legislation in question, criminal proceedings are discontinued once the national court is informed that the individual concerned has been returned.[70] Similarly, the imposition of a fine does not constitute a hurdle in the procedure, since it does not prevent a return decision from being taken and implemented in full compliance with the Directive. This finding has significant repercussions for a rather large number of Member States that penalise irregular stay with a pecuniary penalty, as such legislation remains applicable throughout the return process. Furthermore, the initiation of a criminal prosecution parallel to the return process also does not jeopardise the attainment of the Directive. Neither an expulsion order without the prescription of a period for voluntary return is forbidden. As a result, the criminalisation of irregular migrants while

[65] *Ibid*, para 63.

[66] FRA (n 9). According to the report, 10 Member States prescribe the imposition of a fine and/or imprisonment, whereas in 15 Member States a fine is only foreseen.

[67] Case C- 430/11 *Sagor* ECLI:EU:C:2012:777.

[68] Article 10a of Legislative Decree No 286/1998 as amended inter alia, by Law No 94 of 15 July 2009 on public security (Ordinary Supplement to GURI NO 170 of 24 July 2009) and by Decree-Law No 89/2011 of 23 June 2011 (GURI No 144 of 23 June 2011), converted into law by Law No 129 of 2 August 2011 (GURI No 181 of 5 August 2011).

[69] Article 53 of Legislative Decree No 274/2000 on the criminal jurisdiction of the magistrates' court, under Article 14 of Law No 468 of 24 November 1999 (Ordinary Supplement to GURI No 234 of 10 October 2000).

[70] *Sagor* (n 67), para 35.

the return procedure is ongoing is still possible as long as the penalty imposed is restricted to a fine and the overarching objective of removing irregular migrants remains the top priority of national authorities. Unless the CJEU had chosen a different line of reasoning on the basis of the principle of proportionality and the respect of fundamental rights, it would have been difficult to rule otherwise. The Court was thus 'trapped' in its own path of thinking and could not have provided a more protective framework for the third-country nationals affected. However, in relation to the conversion of a fine with home detention, the CJEU reiterated that Member States are obliged to carry out the removal as soon as possible.[71] Thus, home detention does not contribute to the achievement of the removal, namely the physical transportation of the relevant individual outside the Member State's territory. In reasoning similar to *El Dridi*, it noted that home detention also does not constitute a 'measure' or a 'coercive measure' within the meaning of the Return Directive.[72] In this context, it imposed a further limitation to national criminal law provisions. However, once again, the Court was mindful not to make general observations, but to leave room for Member States to adjust their legislation accordingly. It noted that non-compliance arises in particular where the applicable legislation does not provide that the enforcement of a home detention order imposed on an illegally staying third-country national must come to an end as soon as it is possible to effect that person's removal.[73]

The second question that the Court had to tackle involves the extent to which the *El Dridi* logic could also apply in cases of entry ban violations. This was dealt with in the case of *Celaj*,[74] which involved an Albanian national staying illegally in Italy and convicted of attempted robbery. In 2012, he was issued a deportation order accompanied by a three-year entry ban, returned to his country of origin and re-entered the Italian territory in breach of a re-entry ban. However, in February 2014 he was arrested for the criminal offence of breaching an entry ban, which is punishable with imprisonment of up to four years under Italian law.[75] Contrary to the previous judgments and the Opinion of Advocate General Szpunar delivered on that case,[76] it was held that the case did not concern the termination of Celaj's first irregular stay, but his subsequent re-entry in violation of the entry ban issued in the return decision.[77] As such, the circumstances in that case were found to be 'clearly distinct' from previous judgments.[78] The Court

[71] *Sagor* (n 67), para 43.
[72] *Sagor* (n 67), para 44.
[73] *Sagor* (n 67), para 45.
[74] Case C-290/14 *Skerdjan Celaj* ECLI:EU:C:2015:64.
[75] Article 13(13) Decreto legislativo No. 286 – Testo unico delle disposizioni concernenti la disciplina dell'immigrazione e norme sulla condizione dello straniero (of the legislative decree No 286 on harmonising the migration laws and concerning the status of third-country nationals) of 25 July 1998 (ordinary supplement to GURI No. 191 of 18 August 1998) (referred to further as Legislative Decree No 286).
[76] Case C-290/14 *Skerdjan Celaj*, Opinion of Advocate General Szpunar delivered on 28 April 2015.
[77] *Celaj* (n 74), para 27.
[78] *Celaj* (n 74), para 28.

supported this view by referring to *Achughbabian*, which, as noted above, permits the imposition of sanctions in cases of failed return procedures which may be impinged on third-country nationals themselves.[79] *Achughbabian* was interpreted in an argument a fortiori[80] – *a minore ad maius* – and the Court concluded that as long as the entry ban is issued in compliance with Article 11 of the Return Directive,[81] the Directive does not preclude the possibility for Member States to impose a custodial sentence for the breach of entry ban. However, it was reiterated that the imposition of such sanction is subject to the full observance of fundamental rights and the Geneva Convention.[82]

Celaj has attracted mixed reviews by legal scholars,[83] not least because it marks the first time that the Court has deviated from pre-existing case law, particularly *El Dridi*, to hold that imprisonment as a criminal law sanction is compatible with the Return Directive irrespective of the existence of a return procedure. As it has been pointed out, the Court seems to suggest that two types of illegal stay can be distinguished; one that has taken place initially and one after the person was removed and returned on national territory. Whereas in the former case, Member States have no choice but to apply the Return Directive, in the latter case a prison sentence may be imposed so as to dissuade the third-country national in question from re-entering the national territory in an irregular manner. That division seems to be ill-conceptualised and so is the justification for abandoning the effectiveness argument and thus derogating from the purpose of the Return Directive. The Court's interpretation of *Achughbabian* as covering situations whereby the person has left the territory and returned, as opposed to a narrow interpretation advocated by the Advocate General which would cover only situations where authorities did not succeed in returning the person concerned who remains on national territory, seems to be overly expansive. In the case of Mr Celaj, the return process as prescribed in the Return Directive was successfully completed leading to his removal, hence the objective of the Directive remains valid. Nevertheless, the Court seems to understand that lack of cooperation on his behalf is extended even after the completion of the return process, throughout the duration of the entry ban. This is a particularly problematic understanding of the nature of the entry ban given that Article 11 of the Return Directive allows Member States wide discretion in issuing and withdrawing entry bans, which in practice may lead to their imposition *en masse* and in a systematic manner. This is more than rhetoric. This discretion is reflected

[79] See above paras 46–48 of the *Achughbabian* judgment. Para 29 of the *Celaj* judgment.

[80] *Celaj* (n 74), para 30. Anna Magdalena Kosińska, 'The Problem of Criminalisation of the Illegal Entry of a Third-Country National in the Case of Breaching an Entry Ban – Commentary on the Judgment of the Court of Justice of 1 October 2015 in Case C 290/14, *Skerdjan Celaj*' [2016] 18 *European Journal of Migration & Law* 243.

[81] *Celaj* (n 74), para 31.

[82] Geneva Convention, Article 31(1).

[83] Kosińska (n 80), who understands the judgment as a clash of values between the effectiveness of the return directive and the rule of law, legal certainty.

in the more recent evaluation of the Return Directive, whereby in no less than 11 Schengen States an entry ban is automatically issued alongside a return decision, whereas in 14 countries irregular migrants are issued with an entry ban on the basis of the criteria set out in Article 11(1).[84] In three states only the entry ban decision is taken on a case-by-case basis.[85] This directly impacts the imposition of criminal sanctions to second-time or repeated irregular migrants, who on the basis of *Celaj*, may be subjected to custodial sentences. However, as highlighted by the Advocate General, imprisonment delays the return process and compromises the purpose and effectiveness of the Return Directive, which was preciously defended in *El Dridi* a few years before. This was hardly discussed by the Court in what is arguably a laconic judgment for the important implications it entails. Overall, the Court seems to tolerate and even support the preventive approach towards the irregular migrants as envisaged by Member States and thus take a significant step back towards protecting national sovereignty[86] in adopting and imposing criminal sanctions against irregular migrants.

V. Conclusion

The aim of this contribution was to highlight the importance attached to the *El Dridi* judgment in delimiting Member States' power to adopt and impose criminal law provisions as a means of tackling irregular migration. The ruling marked the first time that this issue was brought within the auspices of EU law, with the Court utilising the Return Directive to surround irregular migrants with a protective net, while placing significant barriers to the imposition of imprisonment sanctions. The mechanism was old and well-known: Member States are not entirely free to adopt criminal law measures, but are required to comply with their obligations under EU law when exercising their powers to criminalise, in particular obligations stemming from the principles of loyal cooperation and effectiveness. Otherwise, the attainment of the objectives of the Directive and its effective application will be endangered. Thus, by playing the effectiveness card, domestic criminal laws regulating irregular migration are subjected to several limitations and guidelines.

The significance of *El Dridi* should be seen in the context of the subsequent case law that expanded its logic to a wide range of immigration offences. To codify the Court's pronouncements: in principle, the Return Directive does not preclude a Member State from classifying irregular entry and stay as a criminal offence

[84] Commission, 'Evaluation on the application of the Return Directive (2008/115/EC)' (22 October 2013) 165–66. Also see Izabella Mazcher, 'The CJEU's Ruling in Celaj: Criminal Penalties, Entry Bans and the Returns Directive' (*EU Law Analysis*, 6 October 2015), available at http://eulawanalysis.blogspot.co.uk/2015/10/the-cjeus-ruling-in-celaj-criminal.html (last accessed 11 March 2019).

[85] *Ibid.*

[86] Kosińska (n 80) 254.

and attaching penal sanctions to deter and prevent infringement of the national rules on residence. However, criminal provisions may not be applied before or during the return process when their effect would jeopardise the effective removal of the irregular migrant. Nonetheless, as noted in *Sagor*, the effectiveness argument has significant limits, in the cases of pecuniary sanctions and – to a lesser extent – home detention. In cases where coercive measures did not lead to the removal of the person concerned, Member States enjoy a wide degree of discretionary power to impose sanctions. This was concretised in *Achughbabian*, where the CJEU held that penal sanctions may be imposed in cases of third-country nationals to whom the return procedure has been applied and who are illegally staying in the territory of a Member State without there being any justified ground for non-return. In that respect, it was shown that in *Celaj* the Court opted for an expansive reading of this derogation with a view to addressing sovereignty concerns over criminalising repeated violations of immigration laws. This was an unfortunate and controversial change in the mindset of the Court that seems to have forgotten the effectiveness arguments as proclaimed in *El Dridi* in *lieu* of a restrictive approach that required further justification, particularly in the light of the Advocate General's Opinion, who raised more broadly the issue of whether it is a crime to be a foreigner.[87] This change of heart may arguably spark criticism as regards the complicity of the EU in criminalising irregular migrants. A holistic overview of the case law shows that this complicity is a moving target and perhaps the pronouncements in the leading case of *El Dridi* have recently been nuanced and compromised for the sake of protecting national sovereignty. It remains to be seen whether the Return Directive will generate more cases that will further refine or rebut the findings in *El Dridi*. The tenuous relationship between EU immigration law and domestic criminal law is far from being settled and will thus remain in the spotlight.

[87] *Skerdjan Celaj*, Opinion of Advocate General Szpunar (n 76), para 1.

Reshaping Criminalisation of Irregular Migration in Italy: The Impact of EU Law Beyond the El Dridi *Judgment**

ALESSANDRA ANNONI

I. Introduction

Substantive criminal law has long been used as a tool to combat undocumented migration in Italy. Article 17 of the Consolidated Law on Public Security, approved in 1931, made foreign nationals who did not comply with the requirements set in Title V of the Law liable to a term of incarceration of not more than three months or to a fine of not more than 2,000 Lire.[1] Provisions criminalising breaches of immigration requirements have also been included in Law No 40 of 6 March 1998,[2] and confirmed in the first version of the Consolidated Act of Provisions concerning Regulations on Immigration and Rules about the Conditions of Aliens (hereinafter: CIA), adopted on 25 July 1998.[3] Following the prevailing trend in many European States,[4] the Italian Parliament has subjected this Act to a number of amendments, progressively increasing penalties for existing crimes and adding to the list of offences that irregular migrants could be charged with.[5] By the end of 2009, the Italian legal system included six different provisions criminalising conducts amounting to breaches of immigration requirements.[6] While illegal

* This chapter seeks to reflect the case law as it stood in June 2017. Subsequent developments are not taken into account.

[1] Royal Decree No 773 of 18 June 1931, *Testo unico delle leggi di pubblica sicurezza* (*GU 26 June 1931 No 146*).

[2] Laying down provisions governing immigration and regulations concerning the status of foreigners, Law No 40 was the first attempt to provide comprehensive regulation for immigration and asylum in Italy (*GU 12 March 1998 No 59 – Suppl. Ordinario No 40*).

[3] Legislative Decree No 286 of 25 July 1998, *Testo unico delle disposizioni concernenti la disciplina dell'immigrazione e norme sulla condizione dello straniero* (*GU 18 August 1998 No 191 – Suppl. Ordinario No 139*).

[4] See FRA – European Union Agency for Fundamental Rights, 'Criminalisation of Migrants in an Irregular Situation and of Persons Engaging with Them' (March 2014), available at fra.europa.eu/sites/default/files/fra_uploads/fra-2014-criminalisation-of-migrants-1_en.pdf.

[5] R Sicurella (ed), *Il controllo penale dell'immigrazione irregolare: esigenze di tutela, tentazioni simboliche, imperativi garantistici* (Torino, Giappichelli, 2012).

[6] In addition, Article 61(1)(11-*bis*) of the Criminal Code provided for an aggravating circumstance in the case of a crime perpetrated by an illegally staying third-country national. This provision,

entry or residence in the State's territory was punished merely with a fine,[7] refusal to exhibit a valid residence permit could lead to incarceration,[8] and failure to comply with orders issued in the course of a return procedure could be punished with a term of imprisonment.[9]

This punitive approach has posed considerable challenges for European Union Law.[10] Since the entry into force of the Treaty of Amsterdam, the European Community (and afterwards, the EU) has been responsible for adopting measures on illegal immigration, including repatriation of illegal residents. Article 72 of the Treaty on the Functioning of the European Union (TFEU) clarifies that this (shared) competence should not affect the exercise of responsibilities incumbent upon Member States with regard to the maintenance of law and order and the safeguarding of internal security. As a general principle, however, criminal provisions enacted at domestic level should not hinder the achievement of the objectives set by EU law.[11]

The issue of a possible conflict between Italian legislation criminalising breaches of immigration requirements and EU law emerged, in particular, with reference to Directive 2008/115/EC (the Return Directive).[12] This instrument sets common standards and procedures for returning illegally staying third-country nationals in a humane manner and with full respect to their fundamental rights and dignity,[13] and requires Member States to adjust their domestic legislation accordingly. Giving priority to voluntary departure, the Directive allows States to enforce return decisions only in the exceptional circumstances mentioned in Article 7(4),[14] or when an illegally staying third-country national has not complied with the order to leave the State's territory within the period granted for voluntary departure (Article 8(1)). According to Article 15 of the Directive, moreover, a third-country national who is the subject of return procedures may only be kept in detention in order to prepare the repatriation or to carry out the removal process,

however, was declared unconstitutional in 2010 (C Cost 5 July 2010 No 249 (2010) *Rivista penale* 829). See L Degl'Innocenti (ed), *Stranieri irregolari e diritto penale*, 2nd edn (Giuffrè, Milano, 2011).

[7] Article 10-*bis* CIA.

[8] Article 6(3) CIA. According to the Corte di Cassazione, however, this provision applies only to legally staying immigrants (24 February 2011 No 16453 (2011) *Cassazione penale* 2876).

[9] Article 13(13) and (13-*bis*), and Article 14(5-*ter*) and (5-*quater*).

[10] V Mitsilegas, *The Criminalisation of Migration in Europe. Challenges for Human Rights and the Rule of Law* (London, Springer, 2015) 57.

[11] See Case 203/80 *Guerrino Casati* [1981] ECR 2595, para 28; Case 186/87 *Ian William Cowan v Trésor public* [1989] ECR 195, para 19; Case C-226/97 *Johannes Martinus Lemmens* [1998] ECR I-3711, para 19. See also M Delmas-Marty, 'The European Union and Penal Law' (1998) *European Law Journal* 87.

[12] Directive 2008/115/EC of 16 December 2008 of the European Parliament and of the Council on common standards and procedures in Member States for returning illegally staying third-country nationals [2008] OJ L348/98.

[13] Recital 2 in the Preamble.

[14] According to this provision, Member States may refrain from granting a period for voluntary departure if there is a risk of absconding, or if an application for a legal stay has been dismissed as manifestly unfounded or fraudulent, or if the person concerned poses a risk to public policy, public security or national security.

when there is a risk of absconding or if the person concerned avoids or hampers the preparation of return, and unless other sufficient but less coercive measures can be applied effectively. Detention, in this case, shall respect the conditions set out in Article 16 of the Directive, including the need to keep immigrants separated from ordinary prisoners, and should immediately cease when it appears that a reasonable prospect of removal no longer exists, or, in any case, after a maximum period of 18 months.

At the time of the adoption of the Return Directive, in December 2008, the administrative returns procedure in force in Italy was far from being in line with these requirements, and subsequent amendments introduced by Law No 94 of 15 July 2009 failed to provide the necessary adjustments. The approach adopted by Articles 13 and 14 CIA was contradictory to that mandated by EU law, forcible removal being the ordinary means to enforce a return decision, and voluntary departure representing an exception.[15] Pre-removal detention was also the rule, whenever immediate removal was impossible, and irrespective of whether the immigrant concerned was at risk of absconding, or was trying to hamper the procedure. If there were no places available in pre-removal detention facilities, or once the maximum period of detention set by Article 13(5) CIA expired, the law mandated the *questore* (the local chief of the police) to issue a decree, ordering the person to leave the territory of the State within five days. If they failed to do so without due cause, third-country nationals could be charged with an offence as defined in Article 14(5-*ter*) CIA, punishable by imprisonment for up to four years. Once released, immigrants convicted of such an offence could be forcibly returned or subjected to pre-removal detention, but if none of these options was available, they would be issued with another order to leave. If they disobeyed this order,[16] they could be charged with the offence defined in Article 14(5-*quater*) CIA and punished with detention of between one and five years.

Following the expiration of the deadline set by the Return Directive to transpose it, the persistent inaction of the Italian legislative authority led to judicial chaos.[17] Third-country nationals who were on trial for the crimes defined under Article 14(5-*ter*) or (5-*quater*) CIA demanded to be acquitted, and those who had already been convicted filed requests for immediate release, claiming that Articles 8(1), 15 and 16 of the Directive had direct effects, and should be given precedence over the conflicting rules laid down in the CIA. Judges, however, adopted differing views on this issue. While most of them recognised that at least

[15] R Raffaelli, 'Criminalizing Irregular Immigration and the Returns Directive: An Analysis of the *El Dridi* Case' (2011) *European Journal of Migration and Law* 467. According to Article 13(5) CIA, a period for voluntary departure could be granted only to holders of an expired residence permit, and as long as they were not at risk of absconding.

[16] In December 2010, the Constitutional Court declared Article 14(5-*quater*) CIA partially unconstitutional, in so far as it did not provide the accused with a chance to prove that their behaviour was based on a legally significant justification (13 December 2010 No 359 (2011) *Cassazione penale* 1320). A brief summary of the judgment in English is available at revus.revues.org/2176#tocto2n9.

[17] Raffaelli (n 15) 469.

some of the Directive's provisions had direct effects,[18] some rejected that third-country nationals could rely upon these provisions in criminal matters, either recalling that the EU, at that time, had only limited competence in this field,[19] or insisting on a broad interpretation of Article 2(2)(b) of the Directive, which allows Member States to exclude from the scope of application of this instrument individuals who are subject to return as a criminal law sanction or as a consequence of a criminal law sanction.[20] Other courts, however, acceded to the requests of the defendants, considering Article 14(5-*ter*) and (5-*quater*) CIA as no longer applicable. According to one view, return orders issued in the course of the procedure defined by the CIA were incompatible with the Directive and were therefore to be disapplied *ex* Article 5 of Law No 2248 of 20 March 1865,[21] resulting in their violation no longer being punishable.[22] Some of the judges who acceded to this view, however, were not prepared to acquit defendants who ignored orders to leave the territory of the State issued before 24 December 2010, when the deadline for transposing the Return Directive had not yet expired. According to this view, those orders – which were perfectly valid at the time of their adoption – had not been affected by the direct effects of the Directive.[23] A different conclusion was reached by those judges who considered Article 14(5-*ter*) and (5-*quater*) CIA as being themselves incompatible with EU law, in so far as they subjected irregular migrants to a period of detention far longer than that allowed under Article 15 of

[18] *Contra* Tribunale Modica 31 March 2011, www.penalecontemporaneo.it/upload/Trib.%20di%20 Modica.pdf. The judge was not convinced that Article 14(5-*quater*) CIA could have direct effect, and thus preferred to refer the case to the Constitutional Court, lamenting a possible violation of Article 117 of the Constitution, according to which national legislation must comply with obligations stemming from international and EU law. See also TE Epidendio, 'Direttiva rimpatri e articolo 14 t.u. immigrazione, intervento nel dibattito' (*Penale contemporaneo*, 20 January 2011), www.penalecontemporaneo.it/d/332-direttiva-rimpatri-e-art-14-tu-immigrazione.

[19] Tribunale Milano 18 January 2011, www.penalecontemporaneo.it/upload/Trib.%20Milano%20%20Giud.%20Tremolada.pdf.

[20] Tribunale Verona 20 January 2011, www.penalecontemporaneo.it/upload/Sentenza%20Piziali-2.pdf.

[21] According to this provision, judicial authorities shall apply general and local administrative acts and regulations in so far as they are in conformity with primary legislation.

[22] Tribunale Torino 8 January 2011, www.penalecontemporaneo.it/upload/Salvadori%208%20gen%20AS.doc. See also F Viganò, L Masera, 'Inottemperanza dello straniero all'ordine di allontanamento e "direttiva rimpatri" UE: scenari prossimi venturi per il giudice penale italiano' (2010) *Cassazione penale* 1710, 1715–16.

[23] Tribunale Bologna 29 December 2010, www.penalecontemporaneo.it/upload/Sentenza%20Palladino.doc; Corte d'appello Ancona 31 January 2011, www.penalecontemporaneo.it/upload/Corte%20Appello%20Ancona,%2031.1.2011,%20direttiva%20rimpatri.pdf. See, however, Tribunale Milano 19 January 2011, www.penalecontemporaneo.it/upload/Sanchez%20Gomez%20Carlos.pdf; Tribunale Aosta 28 January 2011, www.penalecontemporaneo.it/upload/Sentenza%20Trib.%20Aosta.pdf. According to these decisions, all orders to leave issued before 24 December 2010, albeit valid at the time of their adoption, must be disregarded after that date. This solution is in line with the conclusions reached by the ECJ in Case C-224/97 *Erich Ciola v Land Vorarlberg* [1999] ECR I-2517. According to the Court, the principle of the primacy of EU law applies not only over general rules of national law, but also in respect of specific individual administrative decisions. Consequently, such decisions must be disregarded if in conflict with a rule of EU law, even if they had become final before the conflicting EU provision had entered into force.

the Return Directive, thus preventing the attainment of the objective set by this instrument to swiftly return illegally staying third-country nationals in a humane manner, and with full respect to their fundamental rights. Guided by the principle of retroactivity of more favourable criminal provisions, courts and public prosecutors who acceded to this view allowed for the acquittal (or release) of third-country nationals charged with Article 14(5-*ter*) and 14(5-*quater*) CIA, irrespective of when the administrative order that they had disobeyed had been issued.[24] Given the prevailing uncertainty, several other judges preferred to stay the proceedings and refer to the European Court of Justice (ECJ) for a preliminary ruling.[25] The *El Dridi* judgment originated from one such request.

II. The *El Dridi* Judgment and its Immediate Impact on the Condition of Third-Country Nationals Who Disobeyed an Order to Leave

Hassen El Dridi was a third-country national who had entered Italy illegally and had subsequently been issued with a deportation decree. Because of the unavailability of suitable means of transport, his removal could not be immediately effected, nor could he be detained pending deportation, due to a temporary lack of places in the establishments intended for this purpose. An order was hence issued on 21 May 2010, requiring Mr El Dridi to leave the territory of the State within five days. Having failed to comply with this order, El Dridi was charged with Article 14(5-*ter*) CIA and sentenced to one year's imprisonment. The defendant appealed to the *Corte d'appello di Trento*, and the latter decided to stay the proceeding and refer to the ECJ for a preliminary ruling, asking the Court to clarify, in essence, whether the Return Directive precludes a Member State's legislation such as that in force, at that time, in Italy, which provides for a sentence of imprisonment to be imposed, on an illegally staying third-country national, on the sole ground that she or he does not comply, without valid grounds, with an order to leave the territory of that State within a given period.[26]

In its judgment delivered on 27 April 2011,[27] the ECJ recognised that the situation of Mr El Dridi fell squarely within the scope of application of the Return

[24] Tribunale Torino 28 February 2011, www.penalecontemporaneo.it/upload/Sentenza%20Natale%2028%20feb.doc. See also Procura Firenze 18 January 2011, www.penalecontemporaneo.it/upload/Nota%20procuratore%20Firenze.pdf; Procura Lecce 10 February 2011, www.penalecontemporaneo.it/upload/Rimpatri%20Lecce.DOC; Procura Rovereto 17 January 2011, www.penalecontemporaneo.it/upload/Procura%20Rovereto.pdf; Procura Pinerolo 13 January 2011, www.penalecontemporaneo.it/upload/Amato_Pinerolo.pdf.

[25] *Ex plurimis* Cass pen (1) 8 March 2011 No 11050 (2011) 5 *Rivista penale* 495.

[26] Corte d'appello Trento 2 February 2011, www.penalecontemporaneo.it/upload/Appello%20Trento%20-%20Ordinanza%20Corte%20Giustizia%20UE.pdf.

[27] Case C-61/11 PPU *Hassen El Dridi, alias Karim Soufi* [2011] ECR I-3015.

Directive: he was an illegally staying third-country national and the limitation clause enshrined in Article 2(2)(b) could not apply, since criminal proceedings against El Dridi were not the cause of the return procedure initiated against him but, on the contrary, they were started as a consequence of his failure to comply with an order to leave the territory of the State issued in the course of that procedure.[28] The Court also noted that the Return Directive establishes a clear order in which the stages of the return procedure are to take place, corresponding to a gradation of the measures that can be adopted to enforce a return decision, ranging from a mere order to leave the territory of the State, to pre-removal detention. In light of this, Articles 15 and 16 of the Directive serve the purpose of regulating the most serious constraining measure allowed under EU law in the framework of a removal procedure, ensuring that the right to personal liberty of illegally staying third-country nationals is fully respected, by making sure, inter alia, that the length of their detention does not exceed that required for the purpose pursued.[29] The Court also confirmed that Articles 15 and 16 of the Directive are unconditional and sufficiently precise, and could therefore be relied on by El Dridi against the Italian State, even though the Directive had not yet been transposed into domestic law.[30]

The Court then went on to assess the compatibility of the Italian legislation with the Directive. After noting that the entire removal procedure provided for in the CIA was 'significantly different' from that established by the Directive,[31] it focused on the compatibility with EU law of Article 14(5-*ter*) of the Act. Recalling the principle of effectiveness and loyal cooperation enshrined in Article 4(3) TEU, the Court argued that, although nothing prevents a Member State from adopting criminal law measures aimed at dissuading third-country nationals from remaining illegally on its territory, such measures should not jeopardise the attainment of the objective pursued by EU law and by the Return Directive in particular, namely, the establishment of an effective policy of removal and repatriation of illegally staying third-country nationals.[32] By providing for a term of imprisonment in the event of failure to comply with an order to leave the territory of the State within a specified period, however, Article 14(5-*ter*) CIA risked delaying the enforcement of the return decision, thus depriving the Directive of its practical effect.[33]

On the basis of these findings, the Court instructed the *Corte d'appello di Trento* not to apply 'any provision' of the CIA which is contrary to the result of the Return Directive, including Article 14(5-*ter*), 'taking due account of the principle of the retroactive application of the more lenient penalty', which – as stressed by the Court – forms part of the general principles of EU law.[34]

[28] *Ibid*, para 49. See also *El Dridi* [2011] ECR I-3015 View of Advocate General (AG) Mazák, paras 22–28.

[29] *El Dridi* (n 27), paras 41–43.

[30] *El Dridi* (n 27), paras 45–47.

[31] *El Dridi* (n 27), para 50.

[32] *El Dridi* (n 27), paras 52–58.

[33] *El Dridi* (n 27), para 59. See also view of AG Mazák (n 28) para 42.

[34] *El Dridi* (n 27), para 61.

The judgment produced far reaching consequences in Italy. In light of the principle of cooperation in good faith laid down in Article 4(3) TEU, following a judgment by the Court of Luxembourg on an order for reference which finds that national provisions are incompatible with EU law, it is for all the authorities of the Member State concerned to take the general or particular measures that are necessary to ensure that EU law is complied with. While legislative authorities are responsible for introducing the necessary changes in the national law as soon as possible, all judicial and administrative branches of the State are called upon to ensure that the rights which individuals derive from EU law are given full and immediate effect, setting aside any provision of national law which the Court considered to be inconsistent with EU law.[35] The obligation to ensure primacy of EU law, as interpreted by the ECJ, binds all courts, and not only the referring one.[36]

Guided by these principles, the very day the *El Dridi* judgment was adopted, Italian courts started to dismiss criminal cases involving third-country nationals charged with Article 14(5-*ter*) CIA, and to free those detained on the basis of that provision. The issue was treated, albeit inappropriately, as a sort of *abolitio criminis*.[37] Third-country nationals who had disobeyed an order to leave the territory of the State and were still under trial were acquitted on the grounds that the incident charged no longer constituted an offence,[38] and those who had already been convicted could rely on a broad interpretation of Article 2(2) of the Criminal Code[39] and Article 673 of the Code of Criminal Procedure,[40] to obtain immediate release, and have the judgment against them withdrawn.[41] In keeping with the

[35] Joined Cases C-231 and C-233/06 *National Pensions Office v Emilienne Jonkman* [2007] ECR I-5149.

[36] Case C- 283/81 *CILFIT v Ministero della sanità* [1982] ECR 3415.

[37] On this issue see: C Amalfitano, 'La reclusione degli immigrati irregolari per violazioni dell'ordine di allontanamento del questore non è compatibile con le prescrizioni della c.d. direttiva rimpatri' (2011) *Cassazione penale* 286; G Morgante, 'Le "relazioni pericolose" tra diritto penale dell'immigrazione e fonti dell'Unione europea' (2012) *Legislazione penale* 85; A Natale, 'La direttiva rimpatri, il testo unico immigrazione ed il diritto penale dopo la sentenza El Dridi' (2011) 2 *Diritto, immigrazione e cittadinanza* 17. See in particular C Favilli, 'L'attuazione in Italia della Direttiva rimpatri: dall'inerzia all'urgenza con scarsa cooperazione' (2011) *Rivista di diritto internazionale* 693; M Francaviglia, 'Il Consiglio di Stato e la sentenza "El Dridi": le direttive europee hanno efficacia "abrogativa"?' (2012) *Giurisprudenza costituzionale* 586; and M Gambardella, 'Disapplicazione o *abolitio criminis* per i reati in materia di immigrazione che contrastano con la Direttiva "rimpatri"?' (2012) *Cassazione penale* 1230. All of them rightly insist on the conceptual difference between abolition (that involves the permanent removal of a rule previously in force) and mere disapplication (which does not invalidate the conflicting rule, but merely suspends its application).

[38] See, for instance, Cass pen (1) 29 April 2011 No 18586 (2011) and No 20130 (2011) *Cassazione penale* 3760.

[39] According to this provision, no one shall be punished for an act which, in accordance with a subsequent law, does not constitute an offence, and if he has already been convicted and sentenced, the execution and the penal consequences of such conviction and sentence shall terminate.

[40] According to this provision, the executing judge (*giudice dell'esecuzione*) should withdraw a judgment on the grounds that the acts charged do not constitute an offence, if the relevant penal provision has been repealed or declared unconstitutional.

[41] See, for instance, Tribunale Milano 29 April 2011, www.penalecontemporaneo.it/upload/673%20Milano.pdf and Tribunale Bari 10 May 2011, www.penalecontemporaneo.it/upload/stranieri_revoca_673_cpp.pdf. See also Consiglio di Stato (ap) 2 May 2011 No 7 (2012) *Giurisprudenza costituzionale* 582.

principle of retroactive application of the more lenient penalty, no distinction was made in respect of the date when the crime had been perpetrated, leading to the acquittal (or liberation) of third-country nationals who had disobeyed an order to leave which had expired long before the date of entry into force of the Return Directive.

Similar consequences were seen with respect to migrants charged under Article 14(5-*quater*) CIA.[42] Although the *El Dridi* judgment did not expressly mention this provision, the reasoning of the Court could certainly apply to it.[43] Just like Article 14(5-*ter*), in fact, Article 14(5-*quater*) CIA made illegally staying third-country nationals subject to a term of imprisonment, simply on the grounds that they had failed to comply with an order issued in the course of a return procedure.

III. The (Belated) Implementation of the Return Directive: The Amended Versions of Article 14(5-*ter*) and (5-*quater*) CIA

On 23 June 2011 - six months after the transposition deadline - the Italian Government enacted an urgent decree aimed, inter alia, at implementing the Return Directive, so as to avoid a potential infringement procedure triggered by the Commission.[44] Despite several changes introduced in Articles 13 and 14 CIA, the Italian administrative return procedure is still not fully in line with the requirements of EU law, since it still gives precedence to forcible return over voluntary departure.[45] Under Article 13(5) CIA, in fact, a period for voluntary departure is only granted upon the immigrant's request, and in so far as none of the multiple precluding circumstances defined in Article 13(4) and (4-*bis*) CIA apply.[46]

The amendments introduced in 2011 have also affected the offences under Article 14(5-*ter*) and (5-*quater*) CIA. Both crimes are now punished with a fine,

[42] Cass pen (1) 28 April 2011 No 22105 (2011) *Cassazione penale* 3766.

[43] The Registrar of the Court himself seemed to support this conclusion. On 28 April 2011, he sent a letter to the Corte di Cassazione, asking it to inform the Court whether, in light of the *El Dridi* judgment, it wished to maintain its request for a preliminary ruling in the *Ngagne* case, which concerned the compatibility of Article 14(5-*quater*) with the Return Directive (Cass pen (1), 8 March 2011 No 11050). Since the referring Court decided to withdraw its request, the case was removed from the Register of the Court (Case C-140/11 *Demba Ngagne* ECLI:EU:C:2011:434).

[44] Decree Law No 89 of 23 June 2011 (conv Law 2 August 2011 No 129). See G Savio, 'La nuova disciplina delle espulsioni conseguente al recepimento della direttiva rimpatri' (2011) 3 *Diritto, immigrazione e cittadinanza* 30.

[45] P De Pasquale, 'L'espulsione degli immigrati irregolari nell'Unione europea: a valle di *El Dridi*' (2011) *Il Diritto dell'Unione europea* 927; A di Martino, F Biondi Dal Monte, I Boiano, R Raffaelli, *The Criminalization of Irregular Immigration: Law and Practice in Italy* (Pisa, Pisa University Press, 2013) 21; L Siracusa, 'Il diritto penale dell'immigrato: brevi spunti per una riflessione sul diritto penale della paura' (2013) *Rivista trimestrale di diritto penale dell'economia* 765.

[46] The request can lawfully be dismissed, for example, simply because the immigrant does not possess a valid passport or cannot provide proof of regular accommodation.

rather than with a term of imprisonment. In this respect, the two provisions may be considered in line with the requirements of the Return Directive as interpreted in *El Dridi*, since – at least in principle[47] – criminal prosecution leading to a fine is not liable to delay or impede the implementation of a return measure.[48]

Through an amendment to Article 16(1) CIA, however, Decree Law No 89 of 23 June 2011 has also added Article 14(5-*ter*) and (5-*quater*) to the list of offences in respect of which the sentence can be converted into an order of expulsion. This choice was deliberately made, in order to allow for the immediate forcible removal of third-country nationals already convicted for having disobeyed an order to leave the territory of the State.[49] According to Article 13(4) CIA, in fact, expulsion may be carried out by the *questore* through law enforcement officials, inter alia, whenever return is ordered as a criminal sanction or as a consequence of a criminal sanction.

Doubts have been raised as to the compatibility of this solution with the Return Directive.[50] In *El Dridi*, the Court clearly stated that the criminal penalties referred to in Article 2(2)(b) of the Directive 'do not relate to the non-compliance with the period granted for voluntary departure', thus excluding the possibility for Italy to rely on that exception clause in this case.[51] As a consequence, the procedural requirements set by the Return Directive fully apply to criminal expulsions ordered against immigrants sentenced under Article 14(5-*ter*) or (5-*quater*) CIA, and Italy may refrain from granting a period for voluntary departure only to the extent that this is allowed under Article 7(4) of the Directive, in particular where there is a risk of absconding.[52] Any judgment in that regard, however, must be based on an individual examination of the person's case, avoiding any automaticity (such as 'previous non-compliance with voluntary departure obligation = risk of absconding').[53]

An additional issue relates to the applicability of the new formulation of Article 14(5-*ter*) and (5-*quater*) in respect of acts perpetrated before the date of entry into force of Decree Law No 89/2011. Considering that the previous versions of the two criminal provisions had never been formally repealed, but simply set aside as a consequence of the Return Directive, one would have expected the new, more favourable, formulations of the two offences to apply retrospectively, on the basis of

[47] See, however, Case C-38/14 *Subdelegación del Gobierno en Gipuzkoa – Extranjería v Samir Zaizoune* ECLI:EU:C:2015:260. The Court considered the Directive incompatible with Spanish legislation which provided, in the event of an illegally staying third-country national, depending on the circumstances, for either a fine or removal; the two measures being mutually exclusive.

[48] See *mutatis mutandis*, Case C-430/11 *Md Sagor* ECLI:EU:C:2012:777, paras 34–36. See also, section IV below.

[49] A Di Martino, 'L'intervento penale in materia di immigrazione e i suoi limiti (per un'introduzione)' in E Rosi and F Rocchi (eds), *Immigrazione illegale e diritto penale. Un approccio interdisciplinare* (Napoli, Jovene, 2013) 14.

[50] Favilli (n 37) 720–21; D Manzione, 'Extracomunitari e legge penale: dalla clandestinità alla sentenza El Dridi e al d.l. 23.6.2011 n. 89, ovvero di un singolare caso di eterogenesi dei fini' (2011) *Legislazione penale* 627.

[51] *El Dridi* (n 27), para 49.

[52] See *mutatis mutandis*, *Md Sagor* (n 48).

[53] Commission, 'Recommendation establishing a common "Return Handbook" to be used by Member States' competent authorities when carrying out return related tasks' COM (2015) 625 final, Annex, 11–12.

Article 2(3) and (4) of the Criminal Code.[54] Domestic courts and scholars, however, have almost unanimously reached the opposite conclusion. Some of them have highlighted the 'temporal discontinuity' between the old provisions (suspended on 24 December 2010, when the deadline for transposing the Return Directive expired) and the new ones (enacted on 23 June 2011);[55] others have stressed their apparent 'structural discontinuity', due mainly to the fact that the administrative procedure leading to the adoption of an order to leave the territory of the State has been largely modified.[56] A third view has made a case on a sort of 'substantial discontinuity', alleging the existence of an implicit *mens legis* to abolish the old provisions and simultaneously exclude the application of the new ones to conduct perpetrated before their enactment.[57]

IV. The Impact of *El Dridi* on Other Provisions Criminalising the Conduct of Illegally Staying Third-Country Nationals: Article 10-*bis* CIA

As mentioned above, in *El Dridi* the ECJ instructed the referring Court not to apply 'any provision' of the CIA which is contrary to the result of the Return Directive. The identification of provisions, other than Article 14(5-*ter*), conflicting with EU law, however, was substantially left to the judgment of domestic courts.

A first possible candidate was Article 10-*bis* CIA. This provision penalises the illegal entry or stay of third-country nationals with a fine of between 5,000 and 10,000 Euros, which may be replaced by an expulsion order,[58] or converted into community work or home detention, if the convicted person is unable to pay.[59] Since its enactment in 2009, the offence has been severely criticised, but all attempts to have it declared unconstitutional have so far failed.[60]

[54] According to Article 2(2), if a defendant has been inflicted a sentence of imprisonment, and the subsequent law merely provides for a fine, the sentence of imprisonment must immediately be converted into a fine. Under Article 2(3), moreover, if the law in force at the time an offence was committed and the subsequent law differ, the law which is more favourable to the accused will be applied, unless the conviction and sentence have become final.

[55] L Masera, 'Il riformato art. 14 co. 5 ter d.lgs. 286/98 e la sua applicabilità nei procedimenti per fatti antecedenti all'entrata in vigore del d.l. 89/2011' (*Penale contemporaneo*, 20 July 2011), www.penalecontemporaneo.it/upload/MASERA%20ART%2014.pdf; Tribunale Pinerolo 14 July 2011 (2011) *Corriere del Merito* 957; Cass pen (1) 10 October 2011 No 36446 (2012) 2 *Rivista penale* 187.

[56] Cass pen (1) 26 May 2016 No 36363 *CED Cass* Rv. 268253.

[57] M Gambardella, 'Gli effetti intertemporali della riformulazione del reato di cui all'art. 14, comma 5-*ter*, T.U. Imm. (D.L. N. 89 del 2001)' (2012) *Cassazione penale* 51; Tribunale Torino 29 June 2011 (2011) *Corriere del Merito* 957; Cass pen (1) 11 October 2013 No 47831 *DeJure*.

[58] Article 16 (1) CIA.

[59] Article 55 of Legislative Decree No 274 of 28 August 2000.

[60] *Ex plurimis*, C Cost 8 July 2010 No 250 (2010) *Rivista italiana di diritto e procedura penale* 1349; 11 March 2011 No 84 (2011) *Giurisprudenza costituzionale* 1273; See A Cossiri, 'La repressione penale degli stranieri irregolari nella legislazione italiana all'esame delle Corti costituzionale e di giustizia' (*Forum di Quaderni Costituzionali*, 21 May 2011), www.forumcostituzionale.it/wordpress/images/stories/pdf/documenti_forum/euroscopio/note_europa/0009_cossiri.pdf.

In the aftermath of the *El Dridi* judgment, a few judges suggested that Article 10-*bis* CIA was not only unreasonable and totally ineffective, but also incompatible with the Return Directive, and should thus be disapplied.[61] As openly confirmed by the Minister for Home Affairs, the provision was enacted for the sole purpose of eluding the application of the Return Directive, through the qualification of the removal of illegally staying third-country nationals as a 'criminal expulsion' falling within the scope of the exception provided under Article 2(2)(b) of the Directive.[62] By providing for the possibility of pecuniary sanctions inflicted on those convicted under Article 10-*bis* CIA to be converted into a period of home detention, moreover, Article 55 of Legislative Decree No 274 of 28 August 2000 ran the risk of jeopardising the attainment of the objectives pursued by the Return Directive, delaying the return of illegally staying third-country nationals.

Eventually, the issue of the compatibility of these provisions with EU law was raised before the ECJ. In two different decisions issued, respectively, on 6 December 2012[63] and 21 March 2013,[64] the Court confirmed its intention to interpret Article 2(2)(b) of the Directive in a restrictive manner, considering the European common rules on return as fully applicable to the expulsion of a third-country national charged solely with the crime of illegal entry or stay.[65] According to the Court, however, the Return Directive does not prevent Member States from penalising illegal stays by means of a fine which may be replaced by an expulsion order, as long as such replacement is enacted solely in respect of third-country nationals whose condition corresponds to one of the situations referred to in Article 7(4) of the Directive. Only in such cases, in fact, may a Member State refrain from granting a period for voluntary departure.[66] The Court also pointed out that the enforcement of any form of criminal detention during the course of the return procedure is liable to delay deportation. For this, it concluded that the Directive precludes domestic legislation allowing illegal stays by third-country nationals to be penalised by means of an order of

[61] See Giudice di pace Roma 16 June 2011, www.penalecontemporaneo.it/upload/gdp%20roma%2010%20bis%2016.6.2011.pdf. On this issue see, among others, A di Martino and R Raffaelli, 'La libertà di Bertoldo: "direttiva rimpatri" e diritto penale italiano' (*Penale contemporaneo*, 26 July 2011), www.penalecontemporaneo.it/d/812-la-liberta-di-bertoldo-direttiva-rimpatri-e-diritto-penale-italiano; GL Gatta, 'Il reato di clandestinità (art. 10 bis T.U. Imm.) e la direttiva rimpatri' (*Penale contemporaneo*, 8 February 2012), www.penalecontemporaneo.it/upload/GATTA_2012A.pdf and G Salcuni, 'La pena pecuniaria in materia di immigrazione è euro-compatibile? Note a margine sul futuro del diritto penale dell'immigrazione' (2012) *Diritto pubblico comparato ed europeo* 78.

[62] Speech of Hon Roberto Maroni before the Chamber, 15 October 2008, leg16.camera.it/470?stenog=/_dati/leg16/lavori/stenbic/30/2008/1015&pagina=s020#Maroni%20Roberto%204%202.

[63] *Md Sagor* (n 48). See A Caputo, 'La contravvenzione di soggiorno illegale dello straniero davanti alla Corte di giustizia' (2013) *Cassazione penale* 1775.

[64] Case C-522/11 *Abdoul Khadre Mbaye* ECLI:EU:C:2013:190.

[65] See, in particular, *ibid*, para 21, evoking Case C-329/11 *Alexandre Achughbabian v Préfet du Val-de-Marne* [2011] ECR I-12695, para 41. See also *El Dridi* (n 27), para 49.

[66] *Md Sagor* (n 48), paras 41, 47–48; *Mbaye* (n 64), para 32.

home detention, without guaranteeing that the enforcement of that order would come to an end as soon as the deportation of the individual concerned becomes possible.[67] The Court, however, left it for the referring Court to rule whether there existed in the national legislation in force in Italy at that time, a provision by virtue of which removal could override the enforcement of the home detention order.

The conclusions reached by the Court in the above-mentioned decisions could hardly justify the disapplication of Article 10-*bis* CIA.[68] The incompatibility of this criminal provision with the Return Directive was indeed not affirmed in terms as clear as those used in *El Dridi* in respect of Article 14(5-*ter*) CIA. Nor did the Italian authorities feel compelled to amend Article 16 CIA, so as to exclude the crime of illegal entry or stay from the list of those for which the sentence can be converted into an order of expulsion. The only immediate effect of the Court's decisions was the introduction of Article 13(3-*septies*) CIA, providing that forcible removal overrides the enforcement of home detention or community work, whenever the latter are ordered in substitution for a fine inflicted to a third-country national convicted under Articles 10-*bis*, 14(5-*ter*) or 14(5-*quater*).[69]

V. Criminalisation of Breaches of a Re-entry Ban: Article 13(13) and (13-*bis*) CIA and the Return Directive

Another offence under the CIA, the compatibility of which with the Return Directive was considered doubtful, is the one involving a breach of a re-entry ban accompanying a return decision. The relevant provisions, Article 13(13) and (13-*bis*) CIA, apply to re-entry bans issued, respectively, by administrative and judicial authorities, and make transgressors liable to a term of imprisonment of between one and four years.[70]

According to the law in force in Italy when the deadline for transposing the Return Directive expired, the length of re-entry bans could range from five to ten years. This clearly conflicted with Article 11 of the Directive, according to which the maximum length is five years, unless the third-country national represents a serious threat to public order, public security or national security. In the aftermath of the *El Dridi* judgment, defendants who had re-entered the territory of the State more than five years after their removal started relying on the direct

[67] *Md Sagor* (n 48), para 47.

[68] See Cass pen (1) 11 July 2013 No 29776 (2013) *Rivista penale* 901; Cass pen (1) 15 September 2015 No 45544 (2016) *Cassazione penale* 1741.

[69] Law No 161 of 30 October 2014.

[70] The two provisions applied to entry bans issued, respectively, by an administrative or judicial authority. In both cases, transgressions were punishable by imprisonment of between one and four years.

effects of this provision, in order to have charges brought against them under Article 13(13) or (13-*bis*) CIA dismissed.[71] This prompted the Government to include, in Decree Law No 89/2011, a provision reducing the maximum length of re-entry bans to five years.

From a more general perspective, scholars and judges began to wonder whether the prohibition of custodial penalties, established in *El Dridi*, could also apply to third-country nationals who disobeyed a re-entry ban, leading *tout court* to the disapplication of Article 13(13) and (13-*bis*) CIA.[72] The issue has recently been settled by the ECJ in the *Celaj* ruling.[73] Contrary to the Opinion of Advocate General Szpunar,[74] the Court held that the Return Directive does not preclude the imposition of a custodial sentence in this case. To justify this conclusion, the Court evoked the second indent of the operative part of its previous *Achughbabian* judgment, where it held that the Return Directive does not prevent Member States from imposing custodial sanctions on 'a third-country national to whom the return procedure established by the said directive has been applied and who is illegally staying in [the territory of that Member State] with no justified grounds for non-return'.[75] According to the Court, the condition of individuals charged under Article 13(13) or (13-*bis*) is similar to the one envisaged in this paragraph: in both cases, the interested individual has already been the object of a removal procedure, as required under EU law, but this has not led to the expected result being attained.

The *Celaj* ruling has attracted considerable academic criticism,[76] and rightly so. Although the Court insisted that the situation of illegally staying third-country nationals who disobey a re-entry ban is 'clearly distinct'[77] from that of individuals who are subject for the first time to a return procedure, the Return Directive does not seem to justify any such distinction.[78] Under Article 2 of the Directive,

[71] *Ex plurimis* Cass pen (1) 13 March 2012 No 12220 (2012) *Rivista penale* 750. On this issue see C Renoldi, 'Profili di diritto intertemporale dei reati collegati all'espulsione, tra la scadenza del termine di attuazione della "direttiva rimpatri" e l'entrata in vigore della legge 129/2011' (2012) 1 *Diritto, immigrazione e cittadinanza* 56, 70–71.

[72] C Favilli, 'Il reato di divieto di reingresso alla luce della direttiva rimpatri' (2013) 3 *Diritto penale e processo* 334; A Romano, 'La Corte di giustizia e la direttiva "rimpatri"' (2014) 3 *Questione giustizia* 106, 110–11; Cass pen (1) 13 March 2012 No 12220 (2012) *Rivista penale* 750. But see Cass pen (1) 25 May 2012 No 35871 (2013) *Cassazione penale* 1182.

[73] Case C-290/14 *Skerdjan Celaj* ECLI:EU:C:2015:640.

[74] Case C-290/14 *Skerdjan Celaj* ECLI:EU:C:2015:285, Opinion of AG Szpunar.

[75] *Achughbabian* (n 65).

[76] ME Bartoloni, 'La direttiva rimpatri, il reingresso irregolare e la pena detentiva: una trangolazione dagli esiti … molto incerti' (2016) *Diritti umani e diritto internazionale* 264; L Lebouf, 'La Cour de justice à la poursuite d'une conciliation entre la compétence pénale des Etats membres et l'effet utile de la directive retour' (2015) *Revue des affaires européennes* 745; I Majcher, 'The CJEU's Ruling in *Celaj*: Criminal Penalties, Entry Bans and the Returns Directive' (*EU Law Analysis*, 6 October 2015), eulawanalysis.blogspot.it/2015/10/the-cjeus-ruling-in-celaj-criminal.html. *cf* however M Savino, 'Irregular Migration at the Crossroads, between Administrative Removal and Criminal Deterrence: The *Celaj* Case' (2016) *CML Rev* 1419.

[77] *Celaj* (n 73), para 28.

[78] A Romano, '"Circumstances … are Clearly Distinct": la detenzione dello straniero per il delitto di illecito reingresso nella sentenza *Celaj* della Corte di giustizia' (2015) 2 *Diritto, immigrazione e cittadinanza* 109.

the procedural rules laid down therein are fully applicable to all return procedures, irrespective of whether the interested person has been subjected to a similar procedure before, and one fails to see why the principle laid down in *El Dridi*, whereby Member States should refrain from adopting any criminal sanction which is liable to impede or delay removal, should not apply in this case, too.

VI. Conclusions

The *El Dridi* judgment was just the first act of a long judicial saga, involving the ECJ and national courts, and aimed at assessing domestic provisions which criminalise irregular immigration in the light of EU law. Unsurprisingly, most of the chapters of this saga were set in Italy. Italy is one of the Member States that relies the most on criminal law tools to thwart irregular immigration. This punitive approach is a cause of frustration for judges and prosecutors, who are called to apply a set of criminal provisions often perceived by them as being unfair, disproportionate and totally ineffective. At a time when the Constitutional Court seemed particularly reluctant to criticise criminalisation choices made in this field, domestic courts started to look at the ECJ for guidance.

In *El Dridi*, the Court made it extremely clear that Member States' criminal responsibility in the field of immigration is not unlimited, and that its implementation must not jeopardise the attainment of objectives set by EU law. In this and subsequent decisions, domestic criminal provisions were assessed in the light of the Return Directive. While offences resulting in a custodial sentence *before* or *during* the implementation of a return decision were considered incompatible with EU law, the Court maintained, in *Celaj*, that imprisonment inflicted on illegally staying third-country nationals *after* a first, unsuccessful, return procedure is admissible. In *Md Sagor* and *Mbaye*, moreover, the Court sent a strong message to the Italian Government, making it clear that criminal law could not be used simply as a tool to elude the application of the European common rules on return.

Overall, the '*El Dridi* doctrine'[79] compelled Italy to introduce a number of adjustments to the CIA, but did not force it to completely abandon its immigration control strategy based on the criminalisation of migrants. As a matter of fact, the limitations imposed by the ECJ have often emphasised the unfairness and uselessness of criminal measures enacted by Italy in this field.[80] Thus for instance, one fails to see how an offence punishable solely with a fine could act as a deterrent for illegally staying third-country nationals, who typically lack any means, especially where the law prevents that fine from being converted into home detention.

[79] Lebouf (n 76) 749.

[80] F Biondi Dal Monte, 'La sentenza Sagor: cosa resta del reato di ingresso e soggiorno illegale?' (2013) *Quaderni costituzionali* 157; GL Gatta, 'La criminalizzazione della "clandestinità" fra scelte nazionali e contesto europeo' in V Militello and A Spena (eds), *Il traffico di migranti: diritti, tutele, criminalizzazione* (Torino, Giappichelli, 2015) 195.

On a different note, one may wonder whether further limits to States' power to criminalise breaches of immigration requirements could result from EU instruments other than the Return Directive. It would be interesting, for instance, to assess Articles 10-*bis*, 13(13), (13-*bis*), 14(5-*ter*) and (5-*quater*) CIA in light of the Directive on Trafficking in Human Beings[81] or of the EU Legal Framework against Smuggling of Migrants.[82] Coupled with the obligation to institute criminal proceedings provided under Article 112 of the Italian Constitution, the mere existence of these offences creates an additional challenge for the prosecution of smugglers and traffickers, because it forces Italian authorities to treat victims of these crimes as 'persons accused or tried in joined proceedings',[83] rather than as mere witnesses. As a result, migrants can refuse to answer any questions and, if they decide to cooperate with the authorities, a full set of procedural guarantees applies, making their examination extremely burdensome.[84] These risks have also recently been highlighted by the European Commission,[85] and have prompted the Corte di Cassazione to rely on a strict interpretation of the existing rules on the scope of the Italian criminal jurisdiction, in order to exclude, at least, the obligation to institute proceedings against third-country nationals saved in international waters and subsequently taken to Italy on board a rescue ship.[86]

[81] Directive 2011/36/EU of the European Parliament and of the Council of 5 April 2011 on preventing and combating trafficking in human beings and protecting its victims, and replacing Council Framework Decision 2002/629/JHA [2011] OJ L101/1.

[82] Council Directive 2002/90/EC of 28 November 2002 defining the facilitation of unauthorised entry, transit and residence and Framework Decision 2002/946/JHA [2002] OJ L/328/17; and Framework Decision 2002/946/JHA on the strengthening of the penal framework to prevent the facilitation of unauthorised entry, transit and residence [2002] OJ L328/1.

[83] According to Article 12(1)(c) of the Italian Code of Criminal Procedure, proceedings are joined whenever one of the crimes at stake has been committed to allow the perpetration of the other, or to conceal the perpetration of the other.

[84] See Articles 64(3)(c), 197 and 197-*bis* of the Italian Code of Criminal Procedure.

[85] Commission, 'REFIT evaluation of the EU legal framework against facilitation of unauthorised entry, transit and residence: the Facilitators Package (Directive 2002/90/EC and Framework Decision 2002/946/JHA)' (Staff Working Document) SWD (2017) 117 final, 24.

[86] Cass pen (1) 1 October 2015 No 39719 (2017) *Cassazione Penale* 1169.

11

C-304/14 – *CS*

The Intersection of National Criminal Law and EU Citizenship Law: Reflections on the Judgment in CS

NIAMH NIC SHUIBHNE

I. Introduction

The judgment of the Court of Justice in *CS*[1] perfectly reflects this collection's focus on the interaction between the application of criminal law at national level and the protection of individual rights at EU level, with particular emphasis on the impact and potential of the Charter of Fundamental Rights ('the Charter'). EU citizenship law already has the capacity, in a general sense, to make awkward incisions into fields of sensitive national competence; for present purposes, the competence to secure the expulsion of persons who have committed criminal offences. Merging national criminal law disputes with the application of EU rights adds a further layer of supranational imposition. Moreover, the rights at issue in *CS* concern the particularly contested role of EU citizenship in factual situations confined to a single Member State.

In this chapter, the legal context of the *CS* case is first briefly outlined, summarising the interaction of EU citizenship law and national criminal law, and also between the relevant 'internal' dimension of EU citizenship law and the Charter of Fundamental Rights. Two main themes evident in the *CS* judgment are then discussed. First, further clarifying the scope of the *Ruiz Zambrano* judgment,[2] the *CS* ruling confirms that EU citizenship rights have relevance in internal situations in exceptional circumstances only. However, second, *CS* has added significant clarification on the application of the Charter in such cases, and on respect for private and family life in particular. The approach of the Court demonstrates that

[1] Case C-304/14 *Secretary of State for the Home Department v CS* EU:C:2016:674.
[2] Case C-34/09 *Ruiz Zambrano* EU:C:2011:124.

when decisions taken by national authorities in the context of criminal liability also fall within the scope of EU law, then they must take due account of the wider standards that underpin EU citizenship rights – and these include the protections guaranteed by the Charter.

Finally, the chapter looks at how case law at EU level and also in the UK courts has developed since the decision in *CS*. Perhaps unsurprisingly, we can see some cautious advancing of the judgment's key principles at EU level but less substantive engagement with the implications at national level. It is early days. And the position of the UK vis-à-vis EU rights and EU case law raises altogether bigger questions at the time of writing. Two broad conclusions are nevertheless drawn: first, the Charter is 'handled with caution' in EU case law, since its application can clearly make a material legal difference; second, national courts, too, seem to be acutely aware of that fact and perhaps pull away from national authority in criminal law matters only with some reluctance.

II. The Legal Context

A. EU Citizenship Law and National Criminal Law

The interaction between EU citizenship law and national criminal law can be summarised as reflecting two opposing themes or dynamics prior to the judgment in *CS*. First, building on foundations laid down in legislation and case law since the 1960s and 1970s, EU citizenship law deepened the framework that seeks to *defend* the free movement claim of the individual in the context of criminal liability. However, second, and more recently, there is also evidence of the *denial* of certain EU citizenship rights precisely because of the claimant's criminal activity.

The first theme represents the natural expectation that EU law would bring distinct procedural and substantive guarantees to bear when national authorities seek to restrict the free movement of persons. In particular, EU rules seek to temper the impulse of Member States to expel foreigners as part of their criminal penalty toolboxes. For example, while what is now Article 45(3) of the Treaty on the Functioning of the European Union (TFEU) has always permitted Member States to derogate from the free movement of workers on grounds of public health, public policy and public security, Directive 64/221/EEC set limits around the exercise of national discretion in this respect. Article 3(1) of the Directive required that '[m]easures taken on grounds of public policy or of public security shall be based exclusively on the personal conduct of the individual concerned' while Article 3(2) stated that '[p]revious criminal convictions shall not in themselves constitute grounds for the taking of such measures'.[3] Procedural safeguards to

[3] Council Directive 64/221/EEC of 25 February 1964 on the co-ordination of special measures concerning the movement and residence of foreign nationals which are justified on grounds of public

enhance judicial protection of the individual facing expulsion or other restrictive measures were also specified. The interpretation of these concepts that progressed through case law placed further limitations on the decision-making autonomy of the Member States – or, conversely, further protected the free movement claims of individuals – by, for example, constraining the scope of the public policy justification.[4]

Directive 2004/38/EC codified but also strengthened this framework of protection for the individual,[5] with Chapter VI of the Directive setting out the main legal premises in detail. Case law once again realised the underlying legislative objectives of consolidating but also strengthening rights, with the Court considering that 'a *particularly restrictive* interpretation of the derogations from [freedom of movement] is required by virtue of a person's status as a citizen of the Union' since 'that status is destined to be the fundamental status of nationals of the Member States'.[6]

Both legislation and case law at EU level also evidence the particular significance of proportionality in free movement law. For example, Article 27(2) of Directive 2004/38 codifies earlier requirements that '[m]easures taken on grounds of public policy or public security shall comply with the principle of proportionality and shall be based exclusively on the personal conduct of the individual concerned'. Article 28(1) goes on to require that

> [b]efore taking an expulsion decision on grounds of public policy or public security, the host Member State shall take account of considerations such as how long the individual concerned has resided on its territory, his/her age, state of health, family and economic situation, social and cultural integration into the host Member State and the extent of his/her links with the country of origin.

These provisions illustrate once again the basic objective of ensuring effective protection of individual rights through the super-imposition of EU principles

policy, public security or public health, now repealed and replaced by Directive 2004/38/EC on the right of citizens of the Union and their family members to move and reside freely within the territory of the Member States [2004] OJ L158/77.

[4] eg Case 30/77 *Bouchereau* EU:C:1977:172, para 35: 'recourse by a national authority to the concept of public policy presupposes, in any event, the existence, in addition to the perturbation of the social order which any infringement of the law involves, of a genuine and sufficiently serious threat to the requirements of public policy affecting one of the fundamental interests of society'.

[5] In line with its stated aims of 'codify[ing] and review[ing] the existing Community instruments dealing separately with workers, self-employed persons, as well as students and other inactive persons in order to simplify and strengthen the right of free movement and residence of all Union citizens' (Recital 3); 'remedying this sector-by-sector, piecemeal approach to the right of free movement and residence' (Recital 4); and 'ensur[ing] a tighter definition of the circumstances and procedural safeguards subject to which Union citizens and their family members may be denied leave to enter or may be expelled' (Recital 22). In Recital 31, it is also stated that '[t]his Directive respects the fundamental rights and freedoms and observes the principles recognised in particular by the Charter of Fundamental Rights of the European Union'.

[6] Joined Cases C-482/01 and C-493/01 *Orfanopoulos and Oliveri* EU:C:2004:262, para 65 (emphasis added); citing eg Case C-184/99 *Grzelczyk* EU:C:2001:458, para 31.

onto national immigration competence, which in turn compels decisions that are proportionate and compliant with EU fundamental rights standards.[7]

In contrast, the second theme – *denial* – is more about identifying the limits of EU citizenship rights where, in effect, the protection added by EU standards is displaced or outweighed by the interest of appropriately recognising and/or punishing criminal offences committed in the host State. This dynamic can be seen in two main strands of case law. The first concerns a judicial collapsing of the legislative distinction between public policy and public security effected by the phased approach to protection against expulsion in Article 28 of Directive 2004/38. This provision enables expulsion of a Union citizen on grounds of public policy or public security (subject to the requirements noted above) when periods of residence of up to five years in the host State are at issue (Article 28(1)); on *serious* grounds of public policy or public security for a Union citizen who has gained the right to reside permanently in the host State (Article 28(2));[8] but on *imperative* grounds of public security *only* for a Union citizen who has either resided in the host Member State for the previous ten years or is a minor (Article 28(3)). However, in its controversial ruling in *PI*, the Court departed from its classic definition of public security, thereby enabling consideration of crime committed against a single victim rather than a threat to the functioning and interests of the State. In this way, the Court facilitated the expulsion of a Union citizen who had resided for more than ten years in the host State in the context of a sexual abuse case – a decision that attracted criticism with respect to the Court's methodology.[9]

In a second line of case law, the Court opted to interpret narrowly the conditions of both legal and continuous residence in Article 16(1) of the Directive in cases querying the impact of terms of imprisonment on qualification for permanent residence in a host State.[10] For example, periods spent in prison in the host State are considered to manifest the compromising of an EU citizen's capacity to integrate into that society, on the basis that

> [t]he imposition of a prison sentence by the national court [shows] the non-compliance by the person concerned with the values expressed by the society of the host Member

[7] The same concerns can be seen in case law interpreting the procedural guarantees set out in the Directive; see, eg, Case C-300/11 *ZZ* EU:C:2013:363. That the Charter demands a further level of scrutiny of limitations on rights can be inferred from para 51 of the judgment. An interesting role for EU standards has also been developed recently at the intersection of EU citizenship rights and national responsibility in the context of extradition beyond Union territory; see Case C-182/15 *Petruhhin* EU:C:2016:630.

[8] According to Article 16(1) of the Directive, 'Union citizens who have resided legally for a continuous period of five years in the host Member State shall have the right of permanent residence there'.

[9] Case C-348/09 *PI* EU:C:2012:300; *cf* Case C-145/09 *Tsakouridis* EU:C:2010:708. For criticism of the Court's approach to public security in this case, see, eg, G Anagnostaras, 'Enhanced Protection of EU Nationals against Expulsion and the Concept of Internal Public Security: Comment on the P. I. Case' (2012) 37 *European Law Review* 627; D Kochenov and B Pirker, 'Deporting Citizens within the European Union: A Counter-Intuitive Trend in Case C-348/09 *P. I. v. Oberbürgermeisterin der Stadt Remscheid*' (2013) *Columbia Journal of European Law* 369.

[10] Case C-378/12 *Onuekwere* EU:C:2014:13; Case C-400/12 *MG* EU:C:2014:9.

> State in its criminal law, [so that] taking into consideration of periods of imprisonment for the purposes of the acquisition [of permanent residence] would clearly be contrary to the aim pursued by that directive in establishing that right.[11]

These rulings produced considerable comment on emerging judicial narratives of 'good' and 'bad' Union citizens.[12] They also establish a more general point: while the balance of case law at the intersection of EU citizenship law and national criminal law is motivated by the ambition of securing free movement rights over and above 'normal' immigration practice in the Member States, transgression of host State values, as expressed in particular by that State's criminal law norms, marks a parameter behind which States can retain regulatory autonomy – and for the crossing of which the Union citizen can face consequences beyond those imposed on the State's own nationals.

B. EU Citizenship Law and the Charter of Fundamental Rights

In EU citizenship law, there is an important and material difference between different types of 'internal' situations, ie where the facts are confined to one Member State: first, 'situations which have no factor linking them with any of the situations governed by European Union law and which are confined in all relevant respects within a single Member State' and fall therefore outwith the scope of the Treaty;[13] and, second, 'the situation of a Union citizen who … has not made use of the right to freedom of movement [but] cannot, for that reason alone, be assimilated to a purely internal situation', which, on the contrary, fall within the scope of EU law.[14] In *Ruiz Zambrano*, the Court determined that, as regards the second situation, 'Article 20 TFEU precludes national measures which have the effect of depriving citizens of the Union of the genuine enjoyment of the substance of the rights conferred by virtue of their status as citizens of the Union'.[15]

The dominant context of these cases concerns national measures seeking the expulsion of third country national family members of dependent EU citizens

[11] *Onuekwere, ibid*, para 26.

[12] eg L Azoulai, 'The(mis)Construction of the European Individual – Two Essays on Union Citizenship Law', EUI working papers, LAW 2014/14, at cadmus.eui.eu/bitstream/handle/1814/33293/LAW_WP_ %202014_14.pdf?sequence=1, 2–3 and 17N; Nic Shuibhne and J Shaw, 'General Report – Union Citizenship: Development, Impact and Challenges' in U Neergaard, C Jacqueson and N Holst-Christensen (eds), *The XXVI FIDE Congress in Copenhagen 2014: Congress Publications* (DJØF Publishing, 2014) Vol 2 at 137 and 223–24; S Coutts, 'Union Citizenship as Probationary Citizenship: *Onuekwere*' (2015) 52 *CML Rev* 531. However, in recent case law, the Court's approach is more nuanced; see eg Case C-247/17 *Raugevicius*, EU:C:2018:898.

[13] Case C-256/11 *Dereci* EU:C:2011:734, para. 60.

[14] *Ibid*, para 61.

[15] *Ruiz Zambrano*(n 2), para 42.

residing in the latter's *home* State. The Court has determined that these can constitute

> very specific situations in which, despite the fact that the … Union citizen concerned has not made use of his freedom of movement, a right of residence exceptionally cannot, without undermining the effectiveness of the Union citizenship that citizen enjoys, be refused to a third-country national who is a family member of his if, as a consequence of refusal, that citizen would be obliged in practice to leave the territory of the European Union altogether.[16]

The Court reasons that such situations have 'an intrinsic connection with the freedom of movement of a Union citizen' (even if this is, in reality, a projection to the future) and are thus distinguishable from the first set of situations noted above.[17]

However, notwithstanding the obvious connection between family member residence rights and EU fundamental rights, the Charter was either not referred to in these rulings,[18] or construed so narrowly in terms of scope that the application of its provisions was ruled out. On the latter point, the Court has been particularly reluctant to bring Charter considerations into the determination of whether or not a *Ruiz Zambrano* residence right exists in the first place, ie it has separated consideration of forced departure from the Union territory and fundamental rights connected to the family for the purpose of establishing the necessary relationship of dependency. In that respect, in *Dereci*, the Court did refer to Article 7 of the Charter (respect for family and private life) but it ruled:

> the mere fact that it might appear desirable to a national of a Member State, for economic reasons or in order to keep his family together in the territory of the Union, for the members of his family who do not have the nationality of a Member State to be able to reside with him in the territory of the Union, is not sufficient in itself to support the view that the Union citizen will be forced to leave Union territory if such a right is not granted.[19]

The Court did not reconcile this position with, or even refer to, Article 24 of the Charter, which protects the rights of the child and requires: first, '[i]n all actions relating to children, whether taken by public authorities or private institutions, the child's best interests must be a primary consideration' (Article 24(2)); and, second, that '[e]very child shall have the right to maintain on a regular basis a personal relationship and direct contact with both his or her parents, unless that is contrary to his or her interests' (Article 24(3)). In *O and S, and L*, the Court appeared to have moderated the harder edges of the *Dereci* ruling, noting that

[16] Case C-40/11 *Iida* EU:C:2012:691, para. 71.

[17] *Ibid*, para 72.

[18] eg *Ruiz Zambrano* (n 2); Joined Cases C-356/11 and 357/11 *O and S, and L* EU:C:2012:776 (where the Charter is mentioned only in connection with the Court's analysis of Directive 2003/86/EC on the right to family reunification [2003] OJ L251/12).

[19] *Dereci* (n 13), para 68.

dependency can take legal, financial *or* emotional forms.[20] However, there was no discussion of or reference to the Charter in this part of the ruling.

III. The *CS* Case

A. The Facts

CS is a Moroccan national who married a British national in 2002; she is also the sole carer of their child, a British national, who was born in the UK in 2011. CS was convicted of a criminal offence in March 2012, sentenced to a term of 12 months in prison, and notified that she was liable to be deported. Under the applicable national rules, deportation was, in effect, an automatic consequence of the commission of offences carrying a term of at least 12 months' imprisonment.[21] CS applied for asylum in the UK, but her application was rejected in early 2013, shortly after her release from prison. She then sought to challenge the deportation order on the basis that she had a derived right to reside in the UK, under *Ruiz Zambrano*, as the primary carer of a dependent Union citizen. She argued that her removal from the UK would necessarily entail forced departure of her child from the Union territory – an argument accepted at first instance but appealed by the Home Secretary.[22]

Accepting the premise that expulsion of CS from the UK would necessarily entail, in the circumstances of this case and because of the relationship of dependency at issue, the departure of a British national from the territory of the Union in consequence, the Upper Tribunal, hearing the appeal, asked the Court of Justice:

> whether Article 20 TFEU must be interpreted as precluding legislation of a Member State which requires a third-country national who has been convicted of a criminal offence of a certain gravity to be expelled from the territory of that Member State to a third country notwithstanding the fact that that national is the primary carer of a young child who is a national of that Member State, in which he has been residing since birth without having exercised his right of freedom of movement, when the envisaged expulsion would require the child to leave the territory of the European Union, thereby depriving him of the genuine enjoyment of the substance of his rights as a Union citizen.[23]

[20] *O and S, and L* (n 18), para 56.

[21] The relevant provisions of the UK Borders Act 2007 and the Immigration (European Economic Area) Regulations 2006 (as amended in 2012) are presented and analysed in more detail in the second part of this chapter by Leandro Mancano.

[22] The case attracted political controversy in the UK following the identification of CS by a Member of the UK Parliament, notwithstanding an order banning the media from naming her; see, eg, 'Moroccan Criminal Fighting Deportation is Abu Hamza's Daughter-in-Law, a Tory MP Reveals' *The Telegraph* (5 February 2016); 'Woman Fighting Deportation is Abu Hamza's Daughter-in-Law, says MP' *The Guardian* (6 February 2016).

[23] *CS* (n 1), para 20.

In other words, are *Ruiz Zambrano* residence rights conferred without limits? The case sought therefore to test the respective boundaries of EU citizenship rights and national criminal law competence.

B. The Judgment: Key Themes

For present purposes, two main findings emerge from the *CS* judgment: first, confirmation that *Ruiz Zambrano* residence rights apply in exceptional circumstances only; and, second, since a primary carer residing in a Member State on that basis falls within the scope of Union law, Charter standards must apply when national authorities seek to revoke such residence rights.

i. Ruiz Zambrano*: An Exceptional Source of Rights*

The Court first confirmed the basic premise on which the preliminary reference questions rested:

> [t]he expulsion of that child's mother, who is his primary carer, could result in a restriction of the rights conferred by the status of Union citizen, as he may be compelled, de facto, to go with her, and therefore to leave the territory of the European Union as a whole. In this sense, the expulsion of the child's mother would deprive the child of the genuine enjoyment of the substance of the rights which the status of Union citizen nevertheless confers upon him.[24]

However, recalling *Iida*, the Court reinforced the fact that *Ruiz Zambrano* residence rights apply only in 'very specific situations'.[25] This is not surprising given the acute sensitivity around application of EU rights in situations where the facts to date[26] are confined to one Member State and the consequential overriding of national immigration decisions that can then follow.

Nevertheless, once, as in the circumstances of this case, the threshold into the EU legal environment is crossed, national decisions impacting upon the continuation of a *Ruiz Zambrano* residence right can no longer be taken outwith the broader requirements of that environment. What, more particularly, does this involve?

ii. The Charter

The Court examined that question in *CS* by first acknowledging that *Ruiz Zambrano* residence rights are not absolute. In particular, 'Article 20 TFEU does not affect

[24] *CS* (n 1), para 32.

[25] *CS* (n 1), para 29.

[26] But remembering the prospective limits in the background of the Court's reasoning: 'CS's child has the right, as a Union citizen, to move and reside freely within the territory of the European Union, and *any* limitation of that right falls within the scope of EU law' (para 31, emphasis added); see also *Iida* (n 16).

the possibility of Member States relying on an exception linked, in particular, to upholding the requirements of public policy and safeguarding public security'.[27] The ruling therefore determines that residence rights derived from EU law can be limited as a consequence of committing a crime not only with respect to host States but also with respect to residence within the territory of the Union *per se* – and, in the latter situation, through no criminal fault of the relevant Union citizen. However, the Court then emphasised that

> since CS's situation falls within the scope of EU law, assessment of her situation must take account of the right to respect for private and family life, as laid down in Article 7 of the Charter … an article which must be read in conjunction with the obligation to take into consideration the child's best interests, recognised in Article 24(2) of the Charter.[28]

Noting the absence of the Articles 7/24 link in previous citizenship case law, as noted in section II.B. above, the Court referred instead to case law on judicial cooperation in civil matters to underpin its prioritisation of the rights of the child in this way.[29]

Next, to assess the proportionality of the national decision, and referring to case law from the European Court of Human Rights (ECtHR), the Court directed that '[p]articular attention must be paid to [the child's] age, his situation in the Member State concerned and the extent to which he is dependent on the parent'.[30] This rights-enriched method of analysis is a welcome step beyond the language of 'merely desiring' to keep a family together in *Dereci*, which could be conceived as dismissive. Instead, the decision in *CS* better aligns Luxembourg case law with Advocate General Sharpston's position that 'considerations regarding the exercise of the right to a family life permeate the substance of EU citizenship rights'.[31]

The Court then drew a link between the protective standards that apply where cross-border movement has occurred and deportation decisions made by national authorities linked to citizenship rights in *Ruiz Zambrano* situations. On that basis, the threat to public policy connected with 'criminal offences committed by a

[27] *CS* (n 1), para 36.

[28] *CS* (n 1), para 36.

[29] Case C-403/09 PPU *Detiček* EU:C:2009:810, paras 53 and 54, where respect for maintaining personal contact with both parents per Article 24(3) of the Charter is characterised as 'undeniably merging into the best interests of any child' (para 54). In *O and S, and L* (n 18), the Court had determined that Article 7 of the Charter 'must also be read in conjunction with the obligation to have regard to the child's best interests, recognised in Article 24(2) of the Charter, and with account being taken of the need, expressed in Article 24(3), for a child to maintain on a regular basis a personal relationship with both parents' but only when addressing the requirements of Directive 2003/86 (see para 76 of the judgment).

[30] *CS* (n 1), para 49; citing *Jeunesse v The Netherlands* App no 12738/10 (ECtHR, 3 October 2014), para 118.

[31] Advocate General (AG) Sharpston in Case C-456/12 *O* EU:C:2013:837 and Case C-457/12 *S* EU:C:2013:842, para 62 of the Opinion.

third-country national who is the sole carer of children who are Union citizens' must be 'genuine, present and sufficiently serious';[32] and cannot amount to a conclusion 'drawn automatically on the basis solely of the criminal record of the person concerned'.[33] On the contrary, assessments informing expulsion measures applicable in *Ruiz Zambrano* situations can be drawn only

> from a specific assessment by the national court of all the current and relevant circumstances of the case, in the light of the principle of proportionality, of the child's best interests and of the fundamental rights whose observance the Court ensures.[34]

In other words, the national court must undertake a 'balancing exercise'.[35]

In contrast to such expectations, the Court highlighted the fact that the national legislation applicable in *CS* 'seems to establish a systematic and automatic link between the criminal conviction of the person concerned and the expulsion measure applicable to him or, in any event, there is a presumption that the person concerned must be expelled'.[36] And, in its final summing up, the Court again emphasised that a legitimate – ie Charter-compliant and proportionate – expulsion measure would therefore reflect 'exceptional circumstances'.[37]

IV. After *CS*: First Impressions

At EU level, the openness to the Charter developed in *CS* was further imprinted on subsequent *Ruiz Zambrano*-related judgments. On the same day, the Court reinforced its statements about proportionality and compliance with fundamental rights in *Rendón Marín*, again linking Articles 7 and 24 of the Charter.[38] Even more significantly, in this judgment the Court also signalled greater openness to contemplation of Charter standards when determining the existence of a *Ruiz Zambrano* residence right in the first place, responding to some extent to the critiques of Advocates General Sharpston and Wathelet in particular.[39] In considering whether the third-country national applicant in *Rendón Marín* might have a derived right to reside in Spain as the primary carer of one of his children, a Spanish national (his other child having Polish nationality), the Court of Justice

[32] *CS* (n 1), para 40.
[33] *CS* (n 1), para 41.
[34] *CS* (n 1), para 41. In para 42, the Court provides the more detailed guidance that '[t]hat assessment must therefore take account in particular of the personal conduct of the individual concerned, the length and legality of his residence on the territory of the Member State concerned, the nature and gravity of the offence committed, the extent to which the person concerned is currently a danger to society, the age of the child at issue and his state of health, as well as his economic and family situation'.
[35] *CS* (n 1), para 48.
[36] *CS* (n 1), para 44.
[37] *CS* (n 1), para 50.
[38] Case C-165/14 *Rendón Marín* EU:C:2016:675.
[39] AG Sharpston in *O* and *S* (n 31), para 61 of the Opinion; AG Wathelet in Case C-115/15 *NA* EU:C:2016:259, para 125 of the Opinion.

finally confronted the distinction between a possibility to reside in another State in a legal sense and that possibility in reality. Cases such as *Dereci, Ymeraga*,[40] and *Alokpa and Moudoulou*[41] had previously suggested that possibility in law would suffice to defeat a *Ruiz Zambrano* claim. However, in *Rendón Marín*, the Court is more nuanced:

> Several Member States which have submitted observations have contended that Mr Rendón Marín and his children could move to Poland, the Member State of which his daughter is a national. Mr Rendón Marín, for his part, stated at the hearing that he maintains no ties with the family of his daughter's mother, who, according to him, does not reside in Poland, and that neither he nor his children know the Polish language. In this regard, it is for the referring court to check whether, in the light of all the circumstances of the main proceedings, Mr Rendón Marín, as the parent who is the sole carer of his children, may in fact enjoy the derived right to go with them to Poland and reside with them there, so that a refusal of the Spanish authorities to grant him a right of residence would not result in his children being obliged to leave the territory of the European Union as a whole.[42]

Subsequently, in *Chavez-Vilchez*, the Court ruled:

> [T]he fact that the other parent, a Union citizen, is actually able and willing to assume sole responsibility for the primary day-to-day care of the child is a relevant factor, but it is not in itself a sufficient ground for a conclusion that there is not, between the third-country national parent and the child, such a relationship of dependency that the child would be compelled to leave the territory of the European Union if a right of residence were refused to that third-country national. In reaching such a conclusion, account must be taken, in the best interests of the child concerned, of all the specific circumstances, including the age of the child, the child's physical and emotional development, the extent of his emotional ties both to the Union citizen parent and to the third-country national parent, and the risks which separation from the latter might entail for that child's equilibrium.[43]

The trajectory following *CS* is thus both more realistically attuned to family relations and family circumstances *and* more normatively appealing. There are also further opportunities pending before the Court to consolidate this Charter-engaged approach.[44] As a case law development, the *CS* line of authority undoubtedly

[40] Case C-87/12 *Ymeraga and Others* EU:C:2013:291.

[41] Case C-86/12 *Alokpa and Moudoulou* EU:C:2013:645; here, the French nationality of a Togolese national's children precluded a *Ruiz Zambrano*-based right to reside in Luxembourg, notwithstanding the applicant's submission that 'she was unable to settle with her children in France, or reside with their father on the ground that she had no relations with the latter and that those children required follow-up medical treatment in Luxembourg as a result of their premature birth' (para 15).

[42] *Rendón Marín* (n 38), para 78.

[43] Case C-133/15 *Chavez-Vilchez and Others* EU:C:2017:354, para 71.

[44] See Case C-82/16 *K* [2016] OJ C145/21, which concerns the relevance of the safeguards articulated in *CS* to a third-country national's residence with a Union citizen in the latter's home State in defiance of an entry ban. The judgment of the Court, in which the concept of dependency is further elaborated with respect to both adult and minor Union citizens, has since been delivered (EU:C:2018:308).

constrains the autonomy and discretion of the Member States when they seek to apply sanctions in connection with criminal offences and in the particular context of immigration competence. But it adds, at the same time, a degree of constitutional substance to both citizenship law and fundamental rights standards, as well as to the intersection of these fields. It also ensures a deeper synergy between the standards protected in EU and in European Convention on Human Rights (ECHR) law respectively.[45]

However, while the evidence is necessarily still limited, case law at UK level that mentions the *CS* judgment tends thus far to adhere to the narrower *Dereci* approach. National judges had expressed concern for the welfare of the child when applying *Dereci*,[46] yet there is at least an initial reluctance to embrace the stronger rights-enriched guidance offered in *CS* and subsequent judgments. For example, in *Secretary of State for the Home Department v VM (Jamaica)*, Sales LJ in the Court of Appeal noted the judgments in *Ruiz Zambrano*, *Dereci*, *O and S*, *and L*, *Rendón Marín* and *CS*, but focused on *Dereci* as 'the most important of these judgments' since the children's mother was a British national.[47] Since he did not therefore consider that a *Ruiz Zambrano* residence right could be established, he declined to consider the extent of the applicant's threat to public policy or public security, as required by *CS* and *Rendón Marín*, and later stated that the tribunal at first instance

> had regard, as again it was entitled to do, to the deterrent effect of maintaining the deportation order and its contribution in expressing society's condemnation of serious criminal activity and promoting public confidence in the immigration system in relation to foreign criminals.[48]

There is no mention of the Charter of Fundamental Rights in any part of the judgment.

[45] On this point, see AG Szpunar: 'According to the case-law of the European Court of Human Rights, it must be determined whether there are any exceptional circumstances that warrant a finding that the national authorities have failed to strike a fair balance between the competing interests, in particular the interest of the children in maintaining their family life in the Member State in question, and thus whether the fundamental right of respect for family life guaranteed by Article 8 ECHR has been observed, especially in cases involving an expulsion decision, like the present case. The consequences which such a decision might have for the children must therefore be taken into account. In weighing the interests at stake, the best interests of the children must be taken into account. Particular attention must be paid to their age, their situation in the country or countries concerned and the extent to which they are dependent on their parents' (EU:C:2016:75, para 174 of the Opinion, citing relevant ECtHR case law).

[46] Examining the application of *Dereci* in the UK courts before *CS*, see N Nic Shuibhne, 'Integrating Union citizenship and the Charter of Fundamental Rights' in D Thym (ed), *Questioning EU Citizenship: Judges and the Limits of Free Movement and Solidarity in the EU* (Hart Publishing, 2017) 209–39.

[47] *Secretary of State for the Home Department v VM (Jamaica)* [2017] EWCA Civ 255, para 54.

[48] *Ibid*, para 70. In *R (on the application of Agyarko) v Secretary of State for the Home Department* [2017] UKSC 11, Lord Reed in the UK Supreme Court outlines points from the *CS* judgment (n 1), paras 63–64 but focuses only on *Dereci* in determining the existence of a *Ruiz Zambrano* residence right (paras 65–67).

It is true that there is still some ambiguity around the extent to which the Charter should inform national decisions on the existence of a *Ruiz Zambrano* residence right in the first place, a point which has become somewhat clearer only since the judgment in *Chavez-Vilchez*. However, the broader messages more clearly evident from *CS* onwards – about the centrality of the Charter when national decisions involve, successfully or otherwise, EU citizenship rights – would not yet appear to have filtered through to the UK courts.

V. Conclusion

This chapter has examined the judgment of the Court of Justice in the *CS* case, which demonstrates the extent of a fundamental premise well established in EU case law: that even when competences remain with the Member States, they must be exercised by taking due account of the broader requirements of EU law. Decisions taken in the application of criminal law are not immune from the reach of this obligation.[49] Furthermore, in a development that may signal a new phase of maturity in the life of the Charter, the Court has been much clearer in requiring that standards of EU fundamental rights protection must be infused into decision-making that affects the rights of EU citizens in that context. However, the discussion also suggests that changes in EU case law do not influence national court practice or reasoning with immediate effect. In that light, there may be scope for the Court of Justice to be less subtle, as well as, equally, scope for national courts to reflect more roundly on the principles and standards set by EU law, and on how they evolve – and can change quite significantly – as the Court's case law continually develops.

As the UK Government begins, at the time of writing, to express its negotiating position on the rights of EU citizens in the UK post Brexit, it seeks in part a retraction of this very legacy. In its policy paper, 'Safeguarding the Position of EU Citizens Living in the UK and UK Nationals Living in the EU', the UK Government stated that it intended 'to apply rules to exclude from the UK those who are serious or persistent criminals and those whom we consider a threat to the UK', suggesting a softer standard than currently applies in EU law; as well as to make 'an assessment of conduct and criminality, including not being considered a threat to the UK' in the determination of its proposed 'settled status' for EU nationals seeking (to continue) to reside in the UK after Brexit.[50] Not surprisingly, what are described as 'systematic criminality checks' were therefore marked as an area of

[49] eg emphasising the significance of non-discrimination on nationality grounds, see Case 186/87 *Cowan* EU:C:1989:47, para 19 on national rules allocating compensation for assault; Case C-274/96 *Bickel and Franz* EU:C:1998:563, para 17 on national criminal procedure rules.

[50] Available at www.gov.uk/government/publications/safeguarding-the-position-of-eu-citizens-in-the-uk-and-uk-nationals-in-the-eu, paras 6 and 21 respectively.

disagreement between the EU and the UK after the second round of negotiations in July 2017.[51]

Perhaps the bruise felt at national level through the suppression of autonomy and discretion that the ECJ case law discussed in this chapter entails becomes evident through the UK's concern to reassert precisely that authority over the fate of EU citizens who commit crimes. It may not be just that EU citizens therefore *become* foreigners;[52] but that, notwithstanding appearances – and despite legal efforts – to the contrary, we always really were.

[51] See the joint technical note on the comparison of EU-UK positions on citizens' rights, available at www.gov.uk/government/publications/joint-technical-note-on-the-comparison-of-eu-uk-positions-on-citizens-rights.

[52] D Kostakopoulou, 'When EU Citizens become Foreigners' (2014) 20 *European Law Journal* 447.

Leave at Your Chosen Speed? *EU Citizenship and Criminal Convictions: An Insight into the United Kingdom's Approach*

LEANDRO MANCANO

I. Introduction

Over the last few years, foreign nationals in the United Kingdom (UK) subject to criminal investigations – let alone convictions – have increasingly experienced an (un)happy ending to their residence in Britain. The aftermath of the 2005 London terrorist attacks has resulted in the toughening up of relevant rules concerning protection of foreigners living in the UK. Such development has been inextricably linked to reconsideration of how non-UK people belong to Great Britain. In an inspiring analysis, Lucia Zedner has associated the legislative actions taken by the UK parliament to the construction of a model of probationary citizenship, where foreigners and their rights – but UK nationals as well – are perpetually on trial, with their legal protection being highly dependent on their level of loyalty to law.[1]

In this context, the – even mere allegation of – foreigners being involved in criminal activities can give rise to significant consequences, the most serious of which is deportation to their country of nationality, be it within or outside the European Union (EU). At times, third-country nationals subject to expulsion measures are in charge of full custody of EU citizens, which makes the picture even more complex. This is the factual background of *CS*,[2] the case that inspired this chapter and brought the Immigration Chamber of the Upper Tribunal to ask the EU Court of Justice ('the CJEU' or 'the Court') for a preliminary ruling.

The decision is a perfect showcase for understanding the complexity and multi-layered UK legal framework concerning criminal activities, expulsion and citizenship. This commentary aims to provide an insight into the British system of deportation as a consequence of criminal activity and (EU) citizenship. In order to do so, the chapter is structured as follows. First, the commentary will outline the

[1] L Zedner, 'Security, the state, and the citizen: the changing architecture of crime control', (2010) 13(2) *New Criminal Law Review* 379–403.

[2] Case C-304/14 *Secretary of State for the Home Department v CS* EU:C:2016:674.

Union citizenship rules relevant to the present discussion, and the CJEU's decision in *CS*. Second, the focus will move on to the national law and policy level, showing how these provisions have been implemented, and how potential conflicts may arise from the interaction with other internal norms. Third, some critical aspects of this framework will be addressed, especially in terms of the possible incompatibility with EU citizenship law. Finally, some conclusions will be drawn on how the current UK approach can impact on EU citizens' rights.

II. The EU Citizenship Legal Framework

Though the introduction and development of EU citizenship has granted substantive rights to individuals over the years, its very core lies in the right, for every Union citizen, to move and reside freely within the EU regardless of their nationality,[3] and without requiring links to the performance of an economic activity.[4] Such a 'formula' rests on two main centrepieces. First, the principle of non-discrimination on grounds of nationality: a link established by the Court of Justice, and currently codified in Articles 18, 20 and 21 of the Treaty on the Functioning of the European Union (TFEU).[5] Residence security is the second feature, namely the right to enter and stay in the territory[6] of a polity.

Directive 2004/38/EC (or the 'Citizenship Directive') reflects this logic.[7] With the view to promoting social cohesion and integration among Union citizens, the Directive provides Union citizens with the right to permanent residence after legally residing for a continuous period of five years in the host Member State. On the other hand, protection against the expulsion is granted. According to the Directive, every restrictive measure shall follow an individual assessment of the conduct as a serious threat to one of the fundamental interests of society.[8]

Article 28(2) stipulates that those Union citizens (or their family members) who have the right of permanent residence in the host Member State, may be subject to an expulsion measure as long as there are serious grounds of public

[3] Case C-224/98 *D'Hoop* [2002] ECR 6191, para 28; Case C-184/99 *Grzelczyk* [2001] ECR I-6193, para 31; Case C-138/02 *Collins* [2004] ECR I-2703, para 61 onwards.

[4] *Grzelczyk*, *ibid*, para 36–37; Case C-413/99 *Baumbast* [2002] ECR I-7091, para 81.

[5] See Case C-76/05 *Schwarz* [2007] ECR I-6849, para 89. See also J Shaw, 'Citizenship: Contrasting Dynamics at the Interface of Integration and Constitutionalism' EUI Working Papers RSCAS 2010/60, 2010, 9 onwards.

[6] Loïc Azoulai, 'The (mis)Construction of the European Individual: Two Essays on Union Citizenship Law', EUI Department of Law Research Paper, no 2014/14, available at http://papers.ssrn.com/sol3/papers.cfm?abstract_id=2515889. D Kochenov and B Pirker, 'Deporting the Citizens within the European Union: A Counter-Intuitive Trend in Case C-348/09, PI V Oberburgermeisterin Der Stadt Remscheid' (2012) 2 *Columbia Journal of European Law* 19, 369.

[7] Directive 2004/38/EC on the right of citizens of the Union and their family members to move and reside freely within the territory of the Member States [2004] OJ L158/77.

[8] Citizenship Directive, Art 27(2).

policy or public security. Article 28(3)(a) precludes the expulsion of Union citizens who have resided in the host Member State for the previous ten years, unless imperative grounds of public security, as defined by Member States, justify the measure.[9] Therefore, measures adopted under Article 28(3)(a), by virtue of the reference to the *imperative grounds* (only) *of public security*, are strictly limited to exceptional circumstances.

Member States are entitled to outline the meaning of 'public security' for the purposes of an expulsion decision. Anyhow, where EU citizenship comes across national rules, the latter remain subject to primary and secondary law as interpreted by the CJEU.[10]

Two main conclusions can be drawn from the Citizenship Directive. First, this law should be a means of, rather than (*only*) a reward for, integration. Second, with specific regard to the use of coercive measures: they cannot be triggered just by criminal record; and they require a case-by-case assessment of the seriousness of the threat embodied by the person concerned. Admittedly, these principles are stated in the context of expulsion from the host state. However, these rules convey the idea that denial of citizenship rights sits at odds with abstract categories without any anchors to reality.

III. Expulsion from the EU and Minor Union Citizens: The Case of *CS*

CS regarded the possible expulsion from the Union of a third-country national who has full custody of minor Union citizens. As explained below, UK law provides for the automatic adoption of an expulsion measure against third-country nationals convicted of a criminal offence of certain gravity. In *CS*, the children would be subject to expulsion as well, as they are not autonomous. The Court found that the expulsion would be in compliance with EU law, should the national court consider the individual a present and real threat, giving rise to imperative grounds of public security.

To this end, public security must be understood consistently with CJEU case law (covering terrorism, drug trafficking and sexual exploitation of children). Articles 27 and 28 of the Citizenship Directive make clear that the personal conduct of the individual concerned must represent a genuine and present threat affecting one of the fundamental interests of society or of the Member State concerned.[11]

[9] Citizenship Directive, Art 28(3)(a).

[10] Case C-135/08 *Rottmann* [2010] ECR I-1449, paras 60–63. For a detailed analysis on *Rottmann* and on the 'Citizenship Directive' in particular, see E Guild, S Peers and J Tomkin, *The EU Citizenship Directive: A Commentary* (Oxford, Oxford University Press, 2014) 24 onwards.

[11] See, inter alia, Case C-30/77 *Bouchereau* [1999] ECR 1977, para 28; Case C-33/07 *Jipa* [2008] ECR I-05157, paras 23 and 24; Case C-441/02 *Commission v Germany* [2006] ECR I-03449, para 93.

An expulsion measure in a situation like this at stake has to be based on a specific assessment by the national court of all the current and relevant circumstances of the case,[12] in the light of the principle of proportionality, of the child's best interests[13] and of the fundamental rights whose observance the Court ensures.[14]

The ruling gives some interesting insight into the UK system on the relationship between citizenship rights, on the one hand, and coercive measures as a consequence of criminal convictions. In the following pages, the commentary focuses on the legal background, paying particular attention to possible frictions between the UK framework and the principles of EU citizenship law.

IV. The UK Legal Framework

For the purposes of the present discussion, there are three main UK legislative instruments to be considered: the 1971 Immigration Act (IA); the 2007 UK Borders Act (UKBA); and the Immigration (European Economic Area or EEA) Regulations 2016.[15]

In the UK, deportation is a statutory power of the Secretary of State for the Home Department. The power is applicable to aliens in particular circumstances defined by statute:[16] mainly, the 1971 IA and the 2007 UKBA.

The 1971 IA can be considered the centre of gravity of UK immigration law. In a similar vein to the Citizenship Directive, the right of abode plays a key role for the rights of foreigners in the UK.[17] Indeed, people entitled to that right are free to live in the UK, unless one of the exceptions laid down in the Act applies.[18]

According to 1971 IA, sections 3(5)(a), the Secretary of State can adopt a deportation measure if they deem it conducive to the public good. The same regulation provides the adoption of such a coercive measure in case of criminal convictions. However, the effective margin of application of such a provision has been considerably reduced by the 2007 UKBA.

[12] The personal conduct of the individual concerned, the length and legality of his residence on the territory of the Member State concerned, the nature and gravity of the offence committed, the extent to which the person concerned is currently a danger to society.

[13] The CJEU made reference in particular to his age, his situation in the Member State concerned and the extent to which he is dependent on the parent. See *Jeunesse v the Netherlands* App no 12738/10 (ECtHR, 3 October 2014) para 118.

[14] In particular, the Court referred to the right to respect for private and family life, as laid down in Article 7 of the Charter. See, to this effect Case C-145/09 *Tsakouridis* EU:C:2010:708, para 52.

[15] The Immigration (European Economic Area) Regulations 1052/2016.

[16] *R (Munir) v SSHD* [2012] UKSC 32, [2012] 1 WLR 2192 and *R (Alvi) v SSHD* [2012] UKSC 33, [2012] 1 WLR 2208.

[17] See *R(otao Bancoult) v SSHD* [2008] UKHL 61, [2009] AC 453, per Lord Hoffmann at [45].

[18] 1971 IA, Art 1(1).

The latter Act has introduced the category of the 'foreign criminal'. The Secretary of State *must* make a deportation order in respect of a foreign criminal, namely anyone who is:

1) not a British citizen;
2) convicted in the UK of an offence to a period of imprisonment of at least 12 months;[19]
3) the offence is specified by order of the Secretary of State under section 72(4)(a) of the Nationality, Immigration and Asylum Act 2002 (c. 41) (serious criminal); and
4) the person is sentenced to a period of imprisonment.[20]

As the same UKBA takes care to clarify, where these conditions are met, deportation is presumed to be conducive to the public good.

The UKBA also provides for exceptions to this presumption: inter alia, no automatic deportation applies where the latter would breach the person's rights under the European Convention on Human Rights (ECHR) (Exception 1), or rights of the foreign criminal under the EU treaties (Exception 4).[21] However, the exception: does not prevent the making of a deportation order; neither results in it being assumed that the deportation of the person concerned is conducive to the public good, nor that it is not conducive to the public good; the same provision states that the presumption applies despite the application of Exception 1 or 4.[22]

The Immigration (EEA) Regulations 2016 is the other relevant instrument in this regard. Part 4 transposes Chapter VI of the Citizenship Directive – that concerning restrictions of citizenship rights on grounds of public policy and public security. Regulation 27 incorporates the principle stated by the Citizenship Directive – with an important addition – by stating that: the measure shall comply with the principle of proportionality; the expulsion shall be based exclusively on the personal conduct of the person concerned; the personal conduct of the person concerned must represent a genuine, present and sufficiently serious threat affecting one of the fundamental interests of society; the decision may not be based on matters isolated from the particulars of the case or which relate to considerations

[19] Under 2007 UKBA, s 38(1), the phrase 'person who is sentenced to a period of imprisonment of at least 12 months': 1) (a) does not include a reference to a person who receives a suspended sentence; (b) does not include a reference to a person who is sentenced to a period of imprisonment of at least 12 months only by virtue of being sentenced to consecutive sentences amounting in aggregate to more than 12 months, includes a reference to a person who is sentenced to detention, or ordered or directed to be detained, in an institution other than a prison for at least 12 months, and includes a reference to a person who is sentenced to imprisonment or detention, or ordered or directed to be detained, for an indeterminate period (provided that it may last for 12 months). 2007 UKBA, s 38(2) excludes from the scope people who are subject to a suspended sentence and subject to detention in facilities that are not a prison.

[20] 2007 UKBA, Art 32.

[21] *Ibid*, Art 33.

[22] *Ibid*, Art 33(7).

of general prevention; the decision may not be justified by a person's previous criminal convictions; *the decision may be taken on preventative grounds, even in the absence of a previous criminal conviction, provided the grounds are specific to the person* (emphasis added).[23]

Before taking a relevant decision on the grounds of public policy and public security in relation to a person who is resident in the UK, the decision-maker must take account of considerations such as her age, state of health, family and economic situation, her length of residence and social and cultural integration in the UK and the extent of her links with the country of origin.[24]

V. The UK Policy Approach

An important role in the present discussion is played by the policy documents published by the Home Office: mainly, the Immigration Rules and internal guidance for decision-makers. As to the former, the 1971 IA, s 3(2) provides that the

> The Secretary of State shall from time to time (and as soon as may be) lay before Parliament statements of the rules, or of any changes in the rules, laid down by him as to the practice to be followed in the administration of this Act for regulating the entry into and stay in the United Kingdom of persons required by this Act to have leave to enter, including any rules as to the period for which leave is to be given and the conditions to be attached in different circumstances.

Over the years, the reach of the Immigration Rules has grown significantly. While these rules and relevant amendments are subject to some form of parliamentary control,[25] and UK judges call for a systematic and purposive interpretation thereto, their legal nature and force are controversial. The shared and accepted idea is that they are not legislation, but rather instruments stating the policy of the executive.[26] Pursuant to section 84(1) of the Nationality, Immigration and Asylum Act 2002, however, one may appeal against an immigration decision on the ground that it is not in accordance with the Immigration Rules.

Furthermore,

> Where the Secretary of State has ignored such a general practice, or policy, to waive a requirement of the rules, it may be possible to challenge the resulting decision as being not in accordance with the law on grounds of unfairness, illegality or unreasonableness.[27]

[23] Immigration (EEA) Regulations 2006, Regulation 27(6).

[24] *Ibid*, Regulation 27(7).

[25] *SSHD v Pankina* [2010] EWCA Civ 719, [2011] 1 QB 376 [18].

[26] *AA (Nigeria) v SSHD* [2010] EWCA Civ 773, [2011] 1 WLR 564; *R (Stellato) v SSHD* [2007] UKHL 5, [2007] 2 AC 70. In *Odelola v SSHD* [2009] UKHL 25, [2009] 3 All ER 1061, paras 6–7.

[27] E Fripp, *Law and Practice of Expulsion and Exclusion from the United Kingdom: Deportation, Removal, Exclusion and Deprivation of Citizenship* (Oxford, Hart Publishing, 2014) 224.

The uncertain legal regime of the Immigration Rules has resulted in concerns in terms of democratic legitimacy.[28]

Equally interesting and controversial, especially for their content, are the internal guidelines for decision-makers included in the Modernised Guidance (MG). The Guidance contained within instructions cannot fetter the rights provided for by legislation or the Immigration Rules.

For the purposes of the present discussion, it is important to refer to the visa and immigration operational guidance, and in particular the document devoted to EEA decisions on grounds of public policy and public security.[29] The guidance elaborates on the principles and provisions stated in the Immigration (EEA) Regulations 2016. Broadly, the logic transpiring from the document is one strongly inspired by the assumption that *Member States enjoy considerable discretion to define their own standards of public policy and public security, for purposes tailored to their individual contexts, from time to time.*

The principle of proportionality is understood as requiring the measure to be necessary and appropriate to protect the fundamental interests of society that are threatened. To this end, the threat must be realistic, but it does not need to be imminent. Likewise, it is not necessary to demonstrate that an individual is likely to commit a specific type of offence, or even that a criminal conviction has been delivered. Other circumstances can also be taken into account, such as the existence of cautions and warnings. A low risk can constitute a present threat, especially where the consequences of any offence could be serious. The threat must be serious enough to affect one of the fundamental interests of society but does not need to be a serious threat.

If the guidance seems to worryingly lower the required threshold to be met, in order to claim the presence of a *threat*, the contours of the *fundamental interest of the society* are even more blurred. The instructions offer a number of examples of what the latter concept can include. While there are reasonable references to the need to counter terrorism and extremism, or prevent the evasion of tax and duties, other instances of what could constitute a fundamental interest of the society are much more debatable. Not only are the objectives indicated very broadly-worded in the guidance (p 20 *ff*) – *maintaining public order, preventing social harm, combating the effects of persistent offending* or *protecting the public* – but the specific examples of behaviour contrary to these interests raise serious doubts as to their capacity for representing a *threat* to *a fundamental interest of the society*: amongst the most striking examples we find are low-level criminality such as persistent shoplifting.

As shown above, the decision-maker has to take into account the level of integration of the person concerned when considering the adoption of the

[28] *R (Stellato) v SSHD* (n 26), per Lord Hope at para 12.

[29] See www.gov.uk/government/uploads/system/uploads/attachment_data/file/588969/EEA-Decisions-taken-on-grounds-of-public-policy.pdf (last updated 14 December 2017).

removal measure. In a similar vein to the Court of Justice's case law, the guidance makes an equation between criminal offending and lack of integration – which, however, should be assessed against the type and length of the sentence. In terms of type of penalty, imprisonment is seen as preventing the integration links from being established. The basic assumption is, therefore, that imprisonment does not allow an individual to become integrated in society. Furthermore, positive contributions to society will not weigh strongly in the individual's favour, if undertaken at such a time to suggest an attempt to avoid deportation. To this end, the individual is expected to provide credible evidence of their contribution.

The list of areas covered by the concept of *public interest* are, furthermore, included in Schedule 1 to the Immigration EEA Regulations 2016, as is the statement that little weight is to be attached to the integration of an EEA national or the family member of an EEA national within the UK if the alleged integrating links were formed at or around the same time as, inter alia, the commission of a criminal offence or an act otherwise affecting the fundamental interests of society.

VI. The Debatable Geometry of the UK Approach to Crime and Citizenship Rights

The legal background presented above raises more than one concern. A first, thorny issue regards the relationship between sources of law: between the different legislative acts, on the one hand; and between the latter, and policy documents, on the other. We saw that, according to the 1971 IA, the Secretary of State does enjoy a margin of discretion in adopting a deportation measure, depending on whether the latter would be conducive to the public good. The 2007 UKBA removes such discretion, by establishing the presumption that, in case of a foreign criminal, expulsion is always conducive to the public good.[30] The question arises as to what role is played by the exceptions under section 33 of the UKBA – specifically, that related to the non-application of automatic deportation when this would breach the foreign criminal's EU rights.

To this end, Fripp outlines two main scenarios.[31] The interaction between those provisions may be interpreted as suggesting a 'neutral' view (expulsion neither conducive nor contrary to the public good), thus preventing a new deportation unless new circumstances occur. A second hypothesis is that section 33(7)(b) would leave discretion to the Secretary as to whether the removal measures are still needed. The existence of such an exception would not require, then, the revision of the test of 'conduciveness', even if the deportation has been revoked in the first place.

[30] Section 32(4) 2007 UKBA, s 32(4).
[31] Fripp (n 27) 249.

The same 2007 UKBA provides that, when one of the exceptions applies, it is not assumed that deportation of the person concerned is conducive to the public good or that it is not conducive to the public good. If the applicable exception is Exception 1 (removal would breach ECHR rights incorporated by the Human Rights Act 1998 or the Convention Relating to the Status of Refugees) or Exception 4 (removal would breach EU law under the Treaties), then the deeming provision will continue to apply.[32] This means that if the EU-exception applies, there is no duty for the Secretary of State to make a removal decision, while they retain however discretion to adopt such a decision under section 5(1) 1971 IA. The likelihood for this order to be executed, in case it would effectively breach EU rights, is debatable.

The judicial interpretation of this exception gives rise to mixed feelings. Where the removal of EEA nationals would prima facie interfere with that exercise, it should be for the relevant Member State to justify its action. The person to be deported should not have the burden of showing that the decision is not in accordance with the law.[33] On the other hand, while reflecting public revulsion at the particular offence does not properly have any part to play in making a deportation decision, in exceptionally serious cases 'failure to remove the offender might itself tend to undermine confidence in the state's ability to administer justice'.[34]

The three instruments (the IA, the UKBA and the Immigration (EEA) Regulations) create a sort of legal conundrum. The Citizenship Directive is reluctant to any automatism between criminal offence and coercive measures. Even if we assume that the application of the EU exception removes the presumption established by the UKBA, so reintroducing the discretionary element enjoyed by the Secretary of State under the IA, the following issue remains. The IA refers to the possibility for the Secretary of State to make a removal decision when this is conducive to the public good: the threshold is clearly much lower than that established by the Citizenship Directive and the Immigration (EEA) Regulations, which require *serious* or *imperative grounds of public security*. A possible interpretation is that the Immigration (EEA) Regulations constitute *lex specialis* to the IA, so that the discretion granted to the Secretary of State must be exercised within the limits laid down in EU Citizenship law.

A second problem regards the role of policy instructions and the mentioned acts. Even though not legally binding, they are indeed relied on by the decision-maker when it comes to adopting removal measures, and express a direction of travel as far as the relationship between crime and citizenship is concerned. They flesh out the skeleton of this relationship outlined in the statutes and statutory instruments presented above. What emerges is a sharp contrast between EU citizenship law, on the one hand, and the UK approach, on the other.

[32] Section 32(4) 2007 UKBA, s 33(7)(b).

[33] *Straszewski v Secretary of State for the Home Department, Kersys v Secretary of State for the Home Department* [2016] 1 WLR 1173.

[34] *Ibid.*

The former creates a – flexible – triangle amongst criminal conviction, the notion of threat and the fundamental interest of society. As also confirmed by the CJEU's case law, it seems difficult to envisage a present and actual threat in the absence of criminal behaviour and criminal convictions. In the UK approach, such a triangle is broken. First, the Immigration (EEA) Regulations 2016 get rid of the criminal conviction requirement, accepting the removal also on preventative grounds. Second, the other two sides of the triangle are significantly stretched. There is no requirement for the threat to be imminent, or likely, or even serious. The redefinition of the boundaries of threats has to be jointly read with those of the fundamental interests of the society. In this regard, one should note the combination between: (1) examples of what such an interest could include that are too vague to be true, such as protecting the public; and (2) examples of behaviour considered contrary to these overbroad areas that are not only incredibly specific, but also rather unlikely to result in serious concerns.

The disputable geometry emerging from the UK approach to the relationship between crime and citizenship determines a preoccupying shift in the burden of proof when it comes to coercive measures and rights restriction. As a rule, it is for the state to demonstrate the need for such a measure, as also confirmed by the case law mentioned above. The trend discussed in this commentary is not reversing, but redefining the allocation of the *onus probandi* between the public powers and the person concerned. It is the individual who, not to see his or her rights restricted, has to bring evidence of his or her *genuine* contribution brought to society.

VII. Concluding Remarks

This commentary has analysed the UK law and policy approach to expulsion of EU citizens in relation to criminal activity. The discussion has not focused on what the impact of the UK's withdrawal from the EU will be. Apart from being very difficult to predict, it is indeed argued that law and policy, as they stand at present in the UK, raise concerns per se as to the protection of EU citizens' rights. The most striking issue emerging from the foregoing assessment is the dissociation between removals and the presence of a criminal conviction. While this disconnection is not entirely absent in EU citizenship law, it is clearly regarded as an exception to the general rule that expulsion measures need to be legally anchored to *at least* a finding of guilt; this meaning that not *all* convictions allow for deportation, but only those that result in a serious, present and actual threat. Furthermore, EU law does not allow for presumptive mechanisms between any crime and rights restriction, but require an individual threat-assessment as referred to above.

The interaction between the UK (1) law and (2) policy in this area seems to derail from the track built over the decades by Union law. The introduction of the category of *foreign criminals* seems to conceptually ghettoise groups of people through an unwelcome automatism once again. The legitimacy and lawfulness of expulsion measures mainly rest on two pillars: *threat* and *public interest*. These concepts are given substantive content by the policy approach of the UK Government, which however stretches these concepts to the extent that they are emptied of any reliable content, making it extremely hard to subject them to judicial review. As negotiations between the UK and the EU on protection of both classes of citizens seem to have reached a stalemate, the current state of the art in the UK on expulsion of EU nationals creates areas of worryingly broad discretion for national authorities, prone to arbitrary exercise of power.

PART V

Mutual Recognition and Mutual Trust

12

C-303/05 – *Advocaten voor de Wereld*

Advocaten voor de Wereld: *The Salvation of Mutual Trust*

HENNING FUGLSANG SØRENSEN

I. Introduction

Advocaten voor de Wereld[1] was the first case in which the Court of Justice was given the opportunity to deal with the European Arrest Warrant (henceforth EAW). The Framework Decision had been invoked in two prior cases concerning the concept of *ne bis in idem*,[2] but this case was the first for the Court concerning the Framework Decision itself and therefore also formed the basis for the present case law on the EAW as it is currently developing.

II. The Preliminary Reference

The case originated in Belgium, where Advocaten voor de Wereld had brought an action before the Belgian *Arbitragehof* or *Cour d'arbitrage* (Constitutional Court), seeking the annulment of the Belgian Law on the EAW.

The context of the case was serious. The EAW was the first and most prominent measure introduced after the terrorist attacks of 9/11 and it was the first Framework Decision to implement the principle of mutual recognition, which was declared as the cornerstone of judicial cooperation in both civil and criminal matters.[3] The controversy surrounding the EAW was not only a problem in Belgium in the

[1] C-303/05 *Advocaten voor de Wereld VZW v Leden van de Ministerraad* EU:C:2007:261.

[2] C-467/04 *Criminal proceedings against Guiseppe Francesco Gasparini and Others* EU:C:2006:610 and C-288/05 *Criminal proceedings against Jürgen Kretzinger* EU:C:2007:441.

[3] European Parliament, 'Tampere European Council 15 and 16 October 1999 – Presidency Conclusions', p 33.

present case; similar cases had also been heard in Poland, Germany, Cyprus and the Czech Republic.[4]

The Constitutional Court decided to ask the Court of Justice two questions concerning the validity of the Framework Decision on the EAW,[5] both touching on various sensitive elements of the still very premature cooperation on criminal law with the new powers of the Maastricht Treaty.

The first sensitive element related to the legal basis for a framework decision concerning extradition and surrender of persons. All Member States were also parties to the Council of Europe Convention on Extradition from 1957,[6] but the procedures prescribed by the Convention were cumbersome and slow. The 12 Member States had therefore used the new powers given to the Council by the Maastricht Treaty, and had agreed upon two conventions on extradition. The two conventions were to supplement the Council of Europe Convention, and were opened for signature in 1995 and 1996. The 1995 Convention was supposed to provide a faster procedure for extradition in cases where the wanted person agreed to be extradited,[7] while the 1996 Convention reduced the requirements for double criminality and allowed for extradition of a country's own nationals.[8] However, the Member States refrained from ratifying the conventions. The 1995 Convention was only ratified by 10 of the 15 Member States,[9] while the 1996 Convention was ratified by 11 of the 15 Member States[10] when the Twin Towers were hit on 11 September 2001. The legal framework regarding extradition was thus extremely complicated and varied from case to case, depending upon which Member States were involved in the specific extradition case. The Amsterdam Treaty gave the Council powers to regulate the matter with a framework decision, and the Framework Decision on the EAW was then decided as the seventh Framework Decision in the history of the European Union.

The Constitutional Court asked as the first question whether Framework Decision 2002/584 was compatible with Article 34(2)(b) of the Treaty on European Union (henceforth TEU), under which framework decisions may be adopted only for the purposes of approximation of the laws and regulations of the Member States.

This question could potentially limit or even prevent the further use of framework decisions as the legislative method in regards to criminal law.

[4] C-303/05 *Advocaten voor de Wereld VZW v Leden van de Ministerraad*, Opinion of Advocate General Ruiz-Jarabo Colomer, EU:C:2006:552, delivered on 12 September 2006, para 7.

[5] Council Framework Decision 2002/584/JHA of 13 June 2002 on the European arrest warrant and the surrender procedures between Member States [2002] OJ L190/1.

[6] European Treaty Series, no 24, 'European Convention on Extradition'.

[7] [1995] OJ C78/2.

[8] [1996] OJ C313/11.

[9] www.consilium.europa.eu/en/documents-publications/treaties-agreements/agreement/?id=1995104&DocLanguage=en (last accessed 13 March 2019).

[10] See www.consilium.europa.eu/en/documents-publications/treaties-agreements/agreement/?id=1996063&DocLanguage=en (last accessed 13 March 2019).

Furthermore, the annulment of the Framework Decision on the EAW would set the legal regime for extradition back to the chaotic patchwork of various conventions and states known prior to the adoption of the Framework Decision.

The second sensitive element related to another sensitive element, namely the principle of mutual recognition and mutual trust and its relationship to fundamental rights. This principle was created at the meeting of the head of states in Tampere, and was implemented in the Framework Decision by requiring the executing judicial authority to recognise the decision made by the issuing judicial authority. But the principle was also implemented by introducing a positive list of 32 categories of offences, for which the principle of double criminality was abolished. Implementing the principle by requiring Member States to agree to extradite for offences that were not a criminal offence in the specific Member State, and at the same time precluding the specific Member State from probing the material of the case, created a whole new way of understanding not only the future legal basis for European Union law, but also a whole new way of understanding the relationship between the Member States, being a relationship based on mutual trust in the decisions made by the judicial authorities of any other Member State. The principle of mutual trust may be defined in various ways, but one simple and yet sufficient way to understand the principle is as a principle of 'reciprocal belief that others behaviour will not violate the basic common principles that lay at the heart of the EU legal systems'.[11] An almost official definition was given in the programme of measures to implement the principle of mutual recognition of decisions in criminal matters, published after the principle of mutual recognition was discussed at the Cardiff European Council meeting in 1998, stating that mutual trust between Member States '[…] is grounded, in particular, on their shared commitment to the principles of freedom, democracy and respect for human rights, fundamental freedoms and the rule of law'.[12]

The Constitutional Court asked as the second question whether the Framework Decision was compatible with the requirement of respect for fundamental rights as stated in Article 6(2) TEU, the principle of legality in criminal proceedings, the principle of equal treatment and the principle of non-discrimination when the Framework Decision set aside the verification of requirements of double criminality for the 32 offences on the positive list.

This question could potentially limit the principle of mutual recognition and mutual trust to a degree that would remove any real substance from these principles.

Put together, the potential of these two questions was devastating. The development of European Union criminal law could face a challenging time if the flexible

[11] Massimo Fichera, 'Mutual Trust in European Criminal Law' 2009/10 Edinburgh School of Law Working paper Series 13; Valsamis Mitsilegas, 'The Limits of Mutual Trust in Europe's Area of Freedom, Security and Justice: From Automatic Inter-State Cooperation to the Slow Emergence of the Individual' (2012) 31 *Yearbook of European Law* 319–72, 322.

[12] [2001] OJ C12/10.

and expedient option of legislating by framework decisions rather than conventions under international law and the principle of mutual recognition rather than the traditional sovereign approach to international cooperation were refused by the Court. And this would also call for a complete restructuring of the approach taken on the war on terror, as the Framework Decision on the EAW was the first and thus far the most important part of the EU response to the 9/11 attacks.

Advocate General Ruiz-Jarabo Colomer delivered his Opinion on 12 September 2006 and the Grand Chamber gave its judgment on 3 May 2007 after having heard the submissions of Advocaten voor de Wereld, the Governments of Belgium, the Czech Republic, Spain, France, Latvia, Lithuania, the Netherlands, Poland, Finland and the United Kingdom, the Council of the European Union and the Commission on 11 July 2006.

III. The Decisions of the Court

A. The First Question

i. Admissibility

The Court first had to decide whether the questions were admissible.

The Czech Government had submitted that the first question was inadmissible as it concerned examination of primary law, as the use of framework decisions was regulated by Article 34(2)(b) TEU and as the Court were given only a limited jurisdiction by Art 35 TEU to give preliminary rulings on the validity and interpretation of framework decisions. The first question related to whether Article 34(2)(b) could be used and would thus require the Court to make an interpretation of this Article of primary law, contrary to the jurisdiction given the Court by Article 35 TEU.

The Advocate General found this approach '[…] wholly erroneous […]', as the central responsibility of the Court was to interpret the Treaties and safeguard them vis-à-vis secondary law.[13]

The Court followed the argument of the Advocate General and stated that the Court was given jurisdiction by Article 35(1) to issue preliminary rulings on the validity of framework decisions and thus also on the question of whether the use of a framework decision was properly adopted on the basis of Article 34(2)(b).[14]

Furthermore, the Czech Government asserted that the Belgian reference to the Court lacked reasons for why the Framework Decision should be invalid. The case heard at the Constitutional Court was a case of whether the Belgian

[13] Opinion of Advocate General Ruiz-Jarabo Colomer (n 4) 33.
[14] *Advocaten voor de Wereld* (n 1) para 18.

implementation law was in conformity with the Belgian Constitution, while the first of the two referred questions was a matter of whether the Framework Decision was a suitable instrument for the approximation of national laws. The reasons presented by the Constitutional Court, concerning whether the Framework Decision was unconstitutional according to Belgian law as it was an unsuitable instrument for approximating national laws, did not enable the other Member States to give useful replies as to whether they thought that the Framework Decision was a suitable instrument as such.

The Advocate General also found this argument invalid, noting that the other 12 submitting parties, as well as the Czech Government, had found the information provided by the Constitutional Court sufficient to submit their observations in the proceedings.[15]

Again, the Court followed the arguments of the Advocate General by concluding that the information provided by the Constitutional Court was sufficient to enable the Court, as well as the governments of the Member States, to submit observations on whether the subject matter of the EAW ought to have been implemented by way of a convention rather than a framework decision.[16]

The first question concerning whether or not a framework decision rather than a convention was the proper way to introduce the EAW was thus found admissible.

ii. Substance

The Advocate General started his analysis of the substance of the first question by discussing whether the concept of surrender as given by the Framework Decision was the same as the concept of extradition as given by the traditional cooperation of sovereign states.

This analysis was obviously important, as Article 34(2)(b) TEU only made it possible to adopt framework decisions for the purposes of approximation of the laws and the regulations of the Member States. By a simple interpretation, this would require a body of pre-existing laws in the Member States. It was thus important to consider whether the surrender prescribed by the Framework Decision was a modern version of extradition.

The Advocate General rightly pointed out that there was some confusion on the matter. Surrender and extradition are both pursuing the same goal, the transfer of a sought person from one Member State to another, while the treaties also refer to extradition and not surrender with Article 31(1)(b) TEU. Academics and constitutional courts in Poland and Germany are also cited as using the term 'extradition'. There was thus plenty of reason to consider surrender as defined by the Framework Decision as a modern version of extradition.

[15] Opinion of Advocate General Ruiz-Jarabo Colomer (n 4) 36.
[16] *Advocaten voor de Wereld* (n 1) para 21–22.

However, the move from extradition to surrender was found to be a complete change of direction. Extradition is cooperation between two sovereign states, where one state decides to help another on a case-by-case basis and with regard to grounds beyond the legal grounds, with interventions from politicians and based upon reciprocity and double criminality. Surrender was found to be something else, as the process is based on a supranational, harmonised legal system, where Member States at least partly have renounced their sovereignty, as they share principles, values and objectives, and therefore have decided to establish a special source of law to combat crime in a single area of freedom, security and justice.

In the view of the Advocate General, the change from extradition to surrender was a matter of axiological models; the only similarity was their objective. This could be considered as support for those claiming that the surrender procedure as given by the EAW was not a matter of approximation and the procedure thus could not be introduced by a framework decision, as this could only be used for approximation.

The Advocate General did, however, find the Framework Decision to be a harmonising provision. He based this Opinion on the apparently simple fact that the aim of providing a national arrest warrant with cross-border effect was at the core of the EAW. The use of national arrest warrants was well-known in the procedural laws and practices of the Member States and the Framework Decision was thus only a matter of approximating the procedural laws of the Member States, so that national arrest warrants from other Member States were given the same effect as national arrest warrants from the Member State itself.

The Advocate General ended his analysis in regard to the first question by concluding that the failed conventions of 1995 and 1996 did not bind the legislator to keep using conventions and not framework decisions, as the competence to decide which instrument to use lay with the Council in so far as the choice was between relevant instruments. Conventions and framework decisions were both relevant instruments, so the Council could choose which one to use. The principles of subsidiarity and proportionality would be respected, and the Framework Decision would also meet the demand for greater effectiveness. The Advocate General finally proposed that the Court should reply to the first question by ruling that the Framework Decision did not infringe on Article 34(2)(b) TEU.

The Court also found the Framework Decision to be a measure that approximated national laws in order to give arrest warrants cross-border effect. The Court also concluded that framework decisions could be used for any of the common actions on judicial cooperation as mentioned in Article 31(1) TEU. Cooperation between Member States and facilitation of extradition was mentioned in Articles 31(1)(a) and (b) TEU. The realisation of an area of freedom, security and justice was set as an objective of the Union by Article 2 TEU, and Article 34(2) TEU gave the Council the power to pursue this objective by the measures mentioned in Article 34(2)(a)–(d) TEU. The Council was thus empowered to use a framework decision as mentioned in Article 34(2)(b) TEU to pursue the approximation of national laws on cooperation as defined by Article 31(1)(a) TEU and extradition as defined by Article 31(1)(b) TEU. The Court then found framework decisions, as well as conventions, to be relevant to adopting a EAW, while it was then within the discretion of the Commission to choose which one to use. The conclusion was thus that the Framework Decision on the EAW was not adopted in a manner contrary to Article 34(2)(b) TEU.[17]

B. The Second Question

The second question concerned the positive list of 32 categories of offences for which the requirement of double criminality was abolished. Was this compatible with the principle of legality in criminal proceedings and with the principle of equality and non-discrimination?

The Advocate General started his analysis by examining the role of the Charter of Fundamental Rights, as the Charter at that time was not given legal value. The importance of the Charter nonetheless had to be acknowledged, and the Advocate General then asked the Court to '… break its silence and recognize the authority of the Charter of Fundamental Rights as an interpretative tool at the forefront of the protection of the fundamental rights which are part of the heritage of the Member States'.[18]

The question of whether the Framework Decision was compatible with the principle of equality before the law gave the Advocate General the opportunity to make an important remark on the nature of the positive list and the core content of the new principle of surrendering the sought person. The EAW, according to the Advocate General, had to be understood as a scheme where the surrender of the sought person is required due to the fact that the sought person is charged or convicted in the issuing Member State. The possibility of making the surrender conditional on whether the act was also a criminal offence in the executing Member State was thus an exception to the main rule of surrender without a check for double criminality, but solely because there was an arrest warrant issued in another Member State. The Advocate General thus found that the Constitutional Court had sent the question to the wrong court, as the use of the exception – the check for double criminality – was the responsibility of the national legislators. But even if the Court was the right authority, then the Advocate General found the question lacking logic, as the principle of equality before the law was a matter of making sure that every person had their case processed according to the same rules. The principle of equality before the law was thus a principle requiring that individuals be treated equally and that comparable situations should not be treated

[17] *Advocaten voor de Wereld* (n 1), paras 24–33.
[18] Opinion of Advocate General Ruiz-Jarabo Colomer (n 4) 79.

differently or different situations made subject to the same rules. The decision of whether or not to apply the requirement of double criminality was based solely on the acts in question and not on the subjective circumstances of the individual, and individuals charged with the same offences would thus have their cases processed according to the same rules, while individuals charged with different offences would have their cases processed according to different rules.[19] The risk of violating the principle of equality in the application of law was also rejected, as the application of the provisions of the EAW was solely a matter for the Member States.

Finally, the Advocate General turned to the principle of legality in criminal proceedings. This principle was found to be a part of substantive criminal law and thus came into play during the criminal proceedings. A EAW was not found to be punitive in its nature, and extradition did not contain a punitive element. The Advocate General thus did not find the principle of legality in criminal proceedings applicable when executing a EAW.

The Court first dealt with the argument that the 32 categories of offences lacked clarity to an extent that the individual would not be able to know if the case was covered by the 32 categories of offences. The Court noted that this was a matter of clarity of the law in the issuing Member State as this Member State would be the one to decide whether the case was covered by one or more of the 32 offences. A lack of clarity would thus be the responsibility of the issuing Member State and a problem arising from the substantive criminal law in this Member State. The Framework Decision did not try to harmonise substantive criminal law and a lack of clarity was thus not covered by the EAW. The Framework Decision therefore could not be found invalid for this reason.

The Court also rejected the argument of a violation of the principle of equal treatment and non-discrimination as the offences included on the list of the 32 categories of offences were found to be of a nature where the severity of the offence and the high degree of trust and solidarity between the Member States justifies dispensing with the verification of double criminality.

The Court therefore answered the second question by concluding that the Framework Decision did not breach the principle of legality or the principle of equal treatment and non-discrimination.

The Court thus found no reason to find the Framework Decision on the EAW invalid.

IV. The Implications of the Judgment

The first and most obvious implication of the judgment was of course the salvation of the use of framework decisions and the salvation of the principle of mutual

[19] Opinion of Advocate General Ruiz-Jarabo Colomer (n 4), paras 83–95.

recognition in regards to fundamental rights. The consequences if the Court had reached the opposite result would have been devastating for the further development of the area of freedom, security and justice.

However, the importance of the judgment goes beyond the case itself. The judgment was handed down on 3 May 2007, and thus 12 years have now passed. During those 12 years, the judgment was cited in more than 60 judgments or opinions of various advocate generals, both within criminal law and within other areas of EU law.

It is hardly surprising that the judgment has often been cited in cases concerning the EAW.

Advocate General Kokott used *Advocaten voor de Wereld* to repeat the importance of fundamental rights and the principle of legality when Member States were applying traditional extradition systems rather than the system of surrender prescribed by the Framework Decision.[20] In his Opinion in *Mantello*, Advocate General Bot referred to *Advocaten voor de Wereld* while reiterating that the execution of third pillar instruments, such as a EAW, must respect fundamental rights.[21] Advocate General Vallon referred to *Advocaten voor de Wereld* in his Opinion in *IB*, while reiterating that the purpose of the Framework Decision on a EAW was to replace the multilateral system of extradition between Member States with a system of surrender between judicial authorities,[22] while Advocate General Bobek referred to *Advocaten voor de Wereld* in his Opinion in *Vilkas* when he emphasised that extradition and surrender are two different procedures.[23] Advocate General Bobek also referred to *Advocaten voor de Wereld* in his Opinion in *Grundza*, where he found the requirement of double criminality was to be assessed in abstract rather than specific terms in a case, where Czech authorities were asked to recognise a violation of a Slovak decision on banning a person from driving a car as an offence according to Czech law.[24] And as the latest case, Advocate General Bobek also referred to *Advocaten voor de Wereld* in *Vilkas*, when he again emphasised that the concept of surrender in the EAW is different from traditional extradition,[25] similar to the view of Advocate General Cruz Villalon in *Lanigan*.[26]

[20] C-296/08 PPU *Ignacio Pedro Santesteban Goicoechea*, Opinion of Advocate General Kokott, delivered on 6 August 2008, EU:C:2008:455 paras 38, 42 and 44.

[21] C-261/09 *Criminal proceedings against Gaetano Mantollo*, Opinion of Advocate General Bot, delivered on 7 September 2010, EU:C:2010:501 para 88.

[22] C-306/09 *IB v Conseil de Ministres*, Opinion of Advocate General Cruz Vallón, delivered on 6 July 2010, EU:C:2010:404 para 37.

[23] C-640/15 *Minister for Justice and Equality v Tomas Vilkas*, Opinion of Advocate General M Bobek, delivered on 27 October 2016, EU:C:2016:826 para 47.

[24] C-289/15 *Grundza*, Opinion of Advocate General M Bobek, delivered on 28 July 2016, EU:C:2016:622 para 37.

[25] Opinion of Advocate General M Bobek (n 23), para. 47.

[26] C-237/15 PPU *Minister for Justice and Equality v Francis Lanigan*, Opinion of Advocate General Cruz Villalon, delivered on 6 July 2015, EU:C:2015:509 para 103. See also paras 101, 108 and 1.

The Court itself has also referred to *Advocaten voor de Wereld* when repeating that the objective of the EAW was to facilitate and accelerate judicial cooperation.[27] The Court referred to *Advocaten voor de Wereld* in the reasoned order in *A*, where the Court required the Dutch authorities not to refuse executing a EAW because the criminal offence was only punishable with a fine in the executing Member State, as the Court found it sufficient that the act was an offence in the executing Member State.[28] The objective of the Framework Decision, replacing the multilateral system of extradition by a system of surrender between judicial authorities, was repeated in *Kozlowski*.[29] In this case, Advocate General Bot also referred to *Advocaten voor de Wereld*, when stating that the Framework Decision itself and the implementation had to respect fundamental rights.[30] In *Wolzenburg*, the Court used *Advocaten voor de Wereld* to explain the principle of equal treatment.[31] Advocate General Bot once again used this case to repeat the importance of fundamental rights when the Framework Decision is implemented or applied by the Member States.[32] The purpose of replacement was also repeated in *Leymann and Pustovarov*[33] and in *Jorge*.[34]

The question of admissibility of cases where the Court is asked to at least partly interpret whether the law of a Member State is incompatible with the European Convention on Human Rights (ECHR) and the Charter of Fundamental Rights was also questioned in *Radu*. In this case, Advocate General Sharpston recommended that the Court should reject the objections with a reference to *Advocaten voor de Wereld*.[35]

The principle of equal treatment in the application of the Framework Decision on the EAW has also been explained in *Jorge*.[36]

However, *Advocaten voor de Wereld* has also been widely used in cases relating to the area of freedom, security and justice but not relating to the EAW. When Advocate General Damaso Ruiz-Jarabo Colomer referred to the case, he repeated the authority of the Charter of Fundamental Rights and the principle of legality as a general principle of Community law in his Opinion in *Bourquain*.[37]

[27] C-192/12 PPU *Melwin West* EU:C:2012:404, para 53.

[28] Order of the Court, Case C-463/15 PPU *Openbaar Ministerie v A* EU:C:2015:634, para 29.

[29] C-66/08 *Szymon Kozlowski* EU:C:2008:437, para 31.

[30] C-66/08 *Criminal Proceedings against Szymon Kozlowski*, Opinion of Advocate General Bot, delivered on 28 April 2009, EU:C:2008:253 para 106.

[31] C-123/08, *Dominic Wolzenburg* EU:C:2009:616, para 63.

[32] C-123/08 *Criminal Proceedings against Dominic Wolzenburg*, Opinion of Advocate General Bot, delivered on 24 March 2009, EU:C:2009:183 paras 116 and 148.

[33] C-388/08 PPU *Artur Leymann and Aleksei Pustovarov* EU:C:2008:669, para 42.

[34] C-42/11 *Joao Pedro Lopes Da Silva Jorge* EU:C:2012:517, para 28.

[35] C-396/11 *Minestural Public – Parchetul de pe lânga Curtea de Apel Constanta v Ciprian Vasile Radu*, Opinion of Advocate General Sharpston, delivered on 18 October 2012, EU:C:2012:648 para 30.

[36] C-42/11 *Joao Pedro Lopes Da Silva Jorges*, Opinion of Advocate General P Mengozzi, delivered on 20 March 2012, EU:C:2012:151 para 52.

[37] C-297/07 *Statsanwaltschaft Regensburg v Klaus Bourquain*, Opinion of Advocate General Ruiz-Jarabo Colomer, delivered on 8 April 2008, EU:C:2008:206 paras 50 and 70.

Several Member States questioned the admissibility of the reference for a preliminary ruling in *Giovanni Dell'Orto and Saipem SPA*[38] concerning the interpretation of the Framework Decision on the standing of victims in criminal proceedings[39] and the Directive relating to compensation to crime victims.[40] The Court made a reference to *Advocaten voor de Wereld*, and found the information given by the referring Court to be sufficient, as the parties had actually been able to make their submissions.

The judgment has also been used in a civil case to underline the integration in the area of freedom, security and justice. In *Roda Golf & Beach Resort SL*, Advocate General D Ruiz-Jarabo Colomer used it to show how judicial and police cooperation in criminal cases has led to an increase in joint operations unprecedented in European history.[41] Advocate General Kokott also referred to the case in *Garcia and Cabrera* when showing how the high degree of trust and solidarity between the Member States justifies the principle of mutual recognition.[42]

Advocaten voor de Wereld has also shown its importance outside the area of freedom, security and justice.

The case has been used to emphasise the importance of compliance with fundamental rights in regards to social security,[43] public procurement law,[44] the protection of personal data,[45] competition[46] and staff regulations.[47]

[38] C-467/05 *Criminal proceedings against Giovanni Dell'Orto* EU:C: 2007:395, para 32–49.

[39] Framework Decision 2001/220/JHA of 15 March 2001 on the standing of victims in criminal proceedings [2001] OJ L82/1.

[40] Council Directive 2004/80/EC of 29 April 2004 relating to compensation to crime victims [2004] OJ L261/15.

[41] C-14/08 *Roda Golf & Beach Resort SL*, Opinion of Advocate General Ruiz-Jarabo Colomer, delivered on 5 March 2009, EU:C:2009:134 para 22.

[42] Joined Cases C-261/08 and C-348/08 *Maria Julia Zurita Garcia v Delegacion del Gobierno en Murcia and Aurelio Choque Cabrera v Delegacion del Gobierno en Murcia*, Opinion of Advocate General Kokott, delivered on 19 May 2009, EU:C:2009:322 para 60.

[43] C-268/06 *Impact*, Opinion of Advocate General Kokott, delivered on 9 January 2008, EU:C:2008:2 para 49; C-350/06 *Gerhard Schultz-Hoff v Deutsche Rentenversicherung Bund*, Opinion of Advocate General V Trstenjak, delivered on 24 January 2008, EU:C:2008:37 para 39; C-520/06 *C Stringer et al v Her Majesty's Revenue and Customs*, Opinion of Advocate General V Trstenjak, delivered on 24 January 2008, EU:C:2008:38 para 52; C-232/09 *Dita Dinosa v LKB Lizings SIA* Opinion of Advocate General Bot, delivered on 2 September 2010, EU:C:2010:486 para 107.

[44] Joined Cases C-147/06 and C-148/06 *SECAP SpA v Comune di Torino and Santorso soc. coop. arl v Comune di Torino*, Opinion of Advocate General D Ruiz-Jarabo Colomer, delivered on 27 November 2007, EU:C:2007:711 para 51.

[45] C-533/07 *College van Burgemeester en wethouders van Rotterdam v MEE Rijkeboer*, Opinion of Advocate General Ruiz-Jarabo Colomer, delivered on 22 December 2008, EU:C:2009:34 paras 22 and 35.

[46] C-8/08 *T-Mobile Netherlands and Others*, Opinion of Advocate General J Kokott, delivered on19 February 2008, EU:C:2009:110 para 92; Joined Cases C-628/10 P and C-14/11 P *Alliance One International Inc. and Others v European Commission* Opinion of Advocate General Kokott, delivered on 12 January 2012, para 166.

[47] F-45/07 *Wolfgang Mandt v European Parliament* EU:F:2010:72, para 116.

The case has also been used to explain the principle of equal treatment in regards to social security,[48] freedom of movement of workers,[49] competition,[50] environment[51] and staff regulations.[52]

The question of whether the request for a preliminary ruling must be declared inadmissible because of a lack of necessary information concerning the factual and legislative context of the dispute has also been a question in other areas of law. The question has been answered with a reference to *Advocaten voor de Wereld* in several cases.[53]

Finally, *Advocaten voor de Wereld* has been used to explain the principle of legality in regard to sanctions for violation of custom duties,[54] public procurement,[55] the protection of financial interests of the Union,[56] approximation

[48] C-268/06 *Impact* Opinion of Advocate General Kokott (n 43) paras 67 and 100; C-212/06 *Government of the French Community and Walloon Government v Flemish Government*, Opinion of Advocate General E Sharpston, delivered on 28 June 2007, EU:C:2007:398 para 147.

[49] C-276/07 *Nancy Delay v Università degli studi di Firenze, Istituto nazionale della previdenza sociale (INPS) and Repubblica Italiana* EU:C:2008:282, para 19.

[50] T-299/08 *Elf Equitaine SA v European Commission* EU:T:2011:217, paras 196 and 302; T-154/09 *Manuli Rubber Industries SpA (MRI) v European Commission* EU:T:2013:260, para 224; T-398/10 *Fapricela – Industria de Trefilaria, SA v European Commission* EU:T:2015:498, para 291; T-413/10 *Socitrel – Sociedade Industrial de Trefilaria, SA and Companhia Previdente – Sociedade de Controle de Participacoes Financeiras, SA v European Commission* EU:T:2018:751 para 283; C-550/07 P *Akzo Nobel Chemicals Ltd v European Commission* Opinion of Advocate General J Kokott, delivered on 29 April 2010, EU:C:2010:229 para 78; C-550/07 P *Akzo Nobel Chemicals Ltd v European Commission* EU:C:2010:512, para 55; C-408/12 P *YKK Corporation, YKK Holding Europe BV and YKK Stocko Fasteners GmbH v European Commission*, Opinion of Advocate General Wathelet, delivered on 12 February 2013, EU:C:2014:66 para 135; T-405/06 *ArcelorMittal Luxembourg SA and Others v European Commission* EU:T:2009:90, para 103.

[51] C-2/10 *Azienda Agro-Zootecnica Franchini Sarl and Eolica di Altamura Srl v Regione Puglia* EU:C:2011:502, para 64.

[52] T-10/11 *Gerhard Birkhoff v European Commission* EU:T:2011:699, para 39; C-16/07 P *Marguerite Chetcuti v Commission of the European Communities* EU:C:2008:549, para 40; C-583/08 P *Christos Gogos v European Commission*, Opinion of Advocate General Kokott, delivered on 4 March 2010, EU:C:2010:118 para 73.

[53] C-74/09 *Batiments et Ponts Construction SA and Others*, Opinion of Advocate General Kokott, delivered on 15 April 2010 EU:C:2010:198, para 30; Joined Cases C-128/09, C-129/09, C-130/09, C-131/09, C-134/09 and C-135/09 *Association des Riverains et Habitants des Communes Proches de l'Aeroport B.S.C.A. (Brussels South Charleroi Airport) ASBL – A.R.A.Ch and Bernhard Page, Association des Riverains et Habitants des Communes Proches de l'Aeroport B.S.C.A. (Brussels South Charleroi Airport) ASBL – A.R.A.Ch, Leon L'Hoir and Nadine Dartois*, Opinion of Advocates General Sharpston, Antoine Boxus and Willy Rosa, Guido Dorlet and Others, Paul Fastrez and Henriette Fastrez, Philippe Daras and Bernard Croiselet, EU:C:2011:319 para 33; C-142/07 *Ecologistas en Accion-CODA v Ayuntamiento de Madrid*, Opinion of Advocate General Kokott, delivered on 30 April 2008, EU:C:2008:254 para 59.

[54] C-546/09 *Aurubis Balgaria AD v Nachalnik na Mitnitsa Stolichna* EU:C:2011:199, para 42.

[55] C-454/06 *pressetext Nachrichtenagentur GmbH*, Opinion of Advocate General Kokott, delivered on 13 March 2008, EU:C:2008:167 para 156.

[56] C-367/09 *Belgisch Interventie- en Restitutiebureau v SGS Belgium NV, Firme Derwa NV and Centraal Beheer Achmea NV*, Opinion of Advocate General Kokott, delivered on 15 July 2010, EU:C:2010:440 para 38.

of laws,[57] competition,[58] environment,[59] ship pollution,[60] taxes[61] and external relations.[62]

There is thus little doubt that the case of *Advocaten voor de Wereld* was an important one. Not only was this the first time the Court was asked about matters relating to the Framework Decision of the EAW, it was also the opportunity for the Court to give its support to the principle of mutual recognition rather than the very complex process of complete harmonisation as the basic model for cooperation within the area of freedom, security and justice, just as it was an opportunity for the Court to approve how the level of cooperation between the Member States had developed to a level where the traditional system of extradition could be replaced by a system of surrender with the abolition of the requirement for double criminality as the most profound symbol of this trust.

If the Court had reached the opposite conclusion, then the cooperation within the area of freedom, security and justice would have been in a very difficult position, as a fast and effective model to replace the traditional system of extradition was needed urgently and the only way forward would probably have been the complete harmonisation of criminal procedural law and substantial criminal law of all the Member States. This would have been a task of unbelievable dimensions.

But the case of *Advocaten voor de Wereld* has also been used widely across most EU law to settle basic principles such as the importance of fundamental rights, the principle of equal treatment and the principle of legality, as well as setting a clearer boundary for the information required from the referring court when a request for a preliminary reference is sent to Court.

[57] C-592/14 *European Federation for Cosmetic Ingredients v Secretary of State for Business, Innovation and Skills*, Opinion of Advocate General M Bobek, delivered on 17 March 2016, EU:C:2016:179 para 23.

[58] T-167/08 *Microsoft Corp v European Commission* EU:T:2012:323, para 84; T-343/08 *Arkema France v European Commission* EU:C:2011:218, para 108; T-372/10 *Bolloré v European Commission* EU:T:2012:325, para 33–35; C-550/07 P *Akzo Nobel Chemicals Ltd v European Commission* Opinion of Advocate General J Kokott (n 50) para 93; C-352/09 P *ThyssenKrupp Nirosta GmbH v European Commission* EU:C:2011:191, para 80; C-226/11 *Expedia Inc*, Opinion of Advocate General Kokott, delivered on 6 September 2012, EU:C:2012:544 para 33; C-501/11 P *Schindler Holding Ltd and Others v European Commission and Others*, Opinion of Advocate General Kokott, delivered on 18 April 2013, EU:C:2013:248 paras 136–42; C-105/14 *Ivo Tarocco and Others*, Opinion of Advocate General Kokott, delivered on 30 April 2015, EU:C:2015:293 para 113-115; T-299/05 *Shanghai Excell M&E Enterprise Co Ltd and Shanghai Adeptech Precision Co Ltd v Council of the European Union* EU:C:2009:72, para 238.

[59] C-405/10 *Özlem Garenfeld* EU:C:2011:722, para 48.

[60] C-308/06 *The International Association of Independent Tanker Owners and Others*, Opinion of Advocate General Kokott, delivered on 20 November 2007, EU:C:2007:689 para 143; C-308/06 *International Association of Independent Tanker Owners and Others v Secretary of State for Transport* EU:C:2008:312, para 70–71.

[61] C-574/15 *Mauro Scialdone*, Opinion of Advocate General Bobek, delivered on 13 July 2017, EU:C:2017:553 para 147.

[62] C-72/15 *PJSC Resneft Oil Company v Her Majesty's Treasury and Others* EU:C:2016:381, para 162.

The importance and influence of this case is thus unquestionable, and the basics of the judgment have been an important part of the development of the current legislation within the area of freedom, security and justice as we know it today.

V. Salvation or Curse?

The principle of mutual recognition is still valid and important in present day European Union criminal law measures. That is beyond any doubt.

The principle of mutual recognition is now to be found in the treaties, and must now be seen as a constitutional principle of the European Union. But the curse that followed from the salvation of the principle of mutual recognition was the principle of mutual trust. Mutual recognition requires mutual trust, as one Member State cannot put the principle of mutual recognition to work with the execution of a EAW if there is no mutual trust when it comes to the protection of fundamental rights. The most profound evidence of this was seen in Opinion 2/13, where the Court emphasised that the Union could not accede to the ECHR if this meant one Member State then would have to check if another Member State was protecting fundamental rights on an adequate level.[63]

Mutual trust cannot be blind trust. If one were to consider this position, then the consequences of *Aranyosi and Caldararu*[64] would soon bring one back to reality. Here, the Court repeated that the principles of mutual recognition and mutual trust are both of fundamental importance as they allow an area without internal borders to be created and maintained. The principle of mutual trust requires thus that Member States consider all the other Member States to be complying with fundamental rights. However, the Court also now accepted that in exceptional cases Member States may question whether other Member States are actually complying with fundamental rights. The Court thus accepted for the first time that mutual trust is not the same as blind trust. The result is however that at present, surrendering to at least a portion of the Member States is impossible or very difficult as there is no doubt that prison conditions in many of the prisons of these Member States will give reason to find a violation of Art 3 of the ECHR.

But how can mutual recognition function in an imperfect world, where mutual trust as a more restricted matter than blind trust is a prerequisite for the effectiveness of mutual recognition?

The President of the Court, Koen Lennarts, has explained that mutual trust must be 'earned' by the Member States.[65] But little guidance is offered as to how

[63] Opinion 2/13, EU:C:2014:2454, para 191.

[64] C-404/15, *Aranyosi and Caldararu* EU:C:2016:198.

[65] Koen Lennarts, 'La vie apres l'avis: Exploring the Principle of Mutual (Yet not Blind) Trust' (2017) *CML Rev* 54, 805–40.

a Member State may earn the trust of another Member State. It is concluded that 'Trust must be "earned" by the Member State of origin through effective compliance with the EU fundamental rights standards'.[66]

Perhaps some judicial authorities nowadays sometimes consider the principle of mutual recognition with the underlying requirement of mutual trust as something that has effectively blocked the surrendering of persons to a number of EU Member States. The basic question is of course if it is for the judges or the politicians to decide whether or not another sovereign Member State has earned the trust of a Member State. The salvation of the principle of mutual recognition and the underlying assumption of the respect for fundamental rights has evolved into a curse, where the judicial authorities of the Member States struggle to figure out who to trust and who not to trust. Mutual trust is nowadays a matter of earned trust rather than presumed trust.[67]

[66] *Ibid*, 840.

[67] Valsamis Mitsilegas, *EU Criminal Law after Lisbon: Rights, Trust and the Transformation of Justice in Europe* (Hart Publishing, 2016) 152.

The Contribution of Advocaten voor de Wereld *for the Protection of Human Rights in the Context of Supra-State Law and for the Doctrine of Double Criminality*

PEDRO CAEIRO

I. Introduction

Looking in retrospect at *Advocaten voor de Wereld* (hereinafter, *Advocaten*),[1] uttered more than ten years ago, we realise the considerable number of important issues that the Court of Justice of the European Union (CJEU) – which at that time bore the name 'European Court of Justice' – had to decide then.

Some of them concerned more directly the 'inner' dimension of European law, such as the competence of the Court to interpret provisions of primary law in order to check whether a legislative act has been adopted on a proper basis,[2] as well as the competence to assess the limits of the discretion conferred upon the European legislative bodies to choose between the available types of legal instruments.[3] From the national perspective, the affirmation of the Court's competence to rule on those matters is important only to the extent that it grants Member States the power to challenge the validity of European legal acts on those grounds. Indeed, such *locus standi* has become more relevant in the context of the Lisbon Treaty, since it is now possible to pass a directive on criminal matters against the vote of some of the members of the Council.

Other issues addressed by *Advocaten* have a clearer impact on national legal orders, especially the following two:[4]

a) the distribution of the competence to assess possible violations of the principle of legality by a framework decision (or, by extension, a directive) between the CJEU and national courts;

[1] C-303/05 *Advocaten voor de Wereld VZW v Leden van de Ministerraad* EU:C:2007:261.
[2] *Ibid*, para 18.
[3] *Ibid*, para 37, 41.
[4] *Ibid*, para 44 *f.*

b) whether or not a surrender procedure that in some cases dispenses with the rule of double criminality is valid before the principles of legality, equality and non-discrimination.

Despite the limited reach of the Court's ruling, which is binding only within the scope of EU law, the ideas put forward in the decision might shed some light on similar issues that also arise at an international level. Consequently, this commentary analyses the impact of *Advocaten* from the perspective of the Member States, in the sphere of EU law and beyond.

II. Can a Framework Decision (or a Directive) Violate the Legality Principle? If so, which Jurisdiction is Competent for Ruling Thereupon?

In the action they had brought before the *Arbitragehof* with a view to annul the Belgian law that transposed the Framework Decision on the European Arrest Warrant (FD-EAW),[5] the association Advocaten voor de Wereld submitted that the said Belgian law, which was the 'direct result of the Council's decision to regulate the subject-matter of the European arrest warrant by means of a framework decision', failed 'to satisfy the conditions of the principle of legality in criminal matters in that it lists, not offences having a sufficiently clear and precise legal content, but only vague categories of undesirable behaviour'. As a consequence, the first issue the Court had to answer was whether a framework decision could violate the legality principle and, if so, whether it enjoyed jurisdiction to rule on the matter.

The Court recalled that the principle *nullum crimen, nulla poena sine lege* is 'one of the general principles underlying the constitutional traditions common to the Member States and has also been enshrined in various international treaties, in particular in article 7(1)' of the European Convention on Human Rights (ECHR).[6] Logically, the standard against which the alleged violations of the principle by EU secondary law ought to be measured is the legality principle in its vest of *EU law*, not the one provided for by the national constitution relevant to the case[7] or by a human rights convention as such. However, apart from a quite important aspect that will be dealt with further below, the Court did not elaborate on any specific contents of the principle. Instead, it relied on the commonly accepted definition followed by the European Court of Human Rights (ECtHR): the law 'must define clearly offences and the penalties which they attract', and such condition is

[5] Council Framework Decision 2002/584/JHA of 13 June 2002 on the European arrest warrant and the surrender procedures between Member States [2002] OJ L190/1.

[6] See also Art 15 of the International Covenant on Civil and Political Rights and Art 49 of the Charter of Fundamental Rights of the European Union.

[7] C-399/11 *Stefano Melloni v Ministerio Fiscal* EU:C:2013:107.

met when 'the individual concerned is in a position (…) to know which acts or omissions will make him criminally liable'.[8]

By doing so, the Court stressed the structural relationship between the rationale of the principle and the assignment of criminal responsibility (liability, guilt[9]) for an act or omission. Consequently, one may legitimately wonder whether legislative acts that are not directly applicable to the individuals and hence are no autonomous source of criminal responsibility – such as framework decisions and directives[10] – can violate the legality principle *at all*.[11] To answer this question, it is convenient to recall the particular way in which those acts produce their effects, which implies a mechanism of cooperation between the EU and domestic legislatures.[12]

Framework decisions and directives leave, by their very nature, a wider or narrower leeway for the states to implement them, which helps reduce the risk of violation of the legality principle. In other words, the, for example, very broad description of the prohibited conduct in a directive (in terms that would clearly infringe upon that principle) can be brought in line with the requirement for *lex certa* by national law. Thus, when a European instrument deliberately uses open concepts or vague expressions in order for the Member States to take the options they deem appropriate,[13] the national legislature has not only the prerogative but indeed the duty, under national *and* European law, to draft the implementation provisions in accordance with the legality principle.

[8] *Advocaten* (n 1), para 50.

[9] This relationship is clearly set out in the cited international instruments that enshrine the guarantee: 'No one shall be held guilty (…)'.

[10] Framework decisions have been introduced by the Treaty of Amsterdam (former Art 34(2)(b) Treaty on European Union (TEU) as a legislative tool which somehow replicated directives in the realm of the former third pillar: they are 'binding upon the Member States as to the result to be achieved', but leave to the national authorities 'the choice of form and methods'. However, framework decisions differ from directives in two aspects: individuals do not have the right to invoke any favourable direct effect that might be produced by the norms of the former; and the failure to transpose framework decisions timely and accurately does not give rise to infringement procedures. The Treaty of Lisbon also extended the scope of directives to the field of the former third pillar (see Art 82(2) and 83 Treaty of the Functioning of the European Union (TFEU) and consequently removed framework decisions from the catalogue of EU legislative tools.

[11] C-308/06 *The Queen, on the application of International Association of Independent Tanker Owners (Intertanko) and Others v Secretary of State for Transport* Opinion of Advocate-General Kokott EU:C:2007:689, para 144: 'However, Directive 2005/35 does not have to meet this criterion since it cannot, as a directive, contain directly effective penal provisions. (83) Such provisions must be adopted by the Member States. Where the provisions of the directive are not sufficiently precise to satisfy the requirements relating to legality, it is for the national legislature to rectify the situation at the time of implementation in the light of the circumstances of the national legal system. (84) It is not the validity of the directive but at most its harmonising effect that is thereby brought into question'.

[12] In detail, see Christina Peristeridou, *The Principle of Legality in European Criminal Law* (Intersentia, Dissertation PhD, University of Maastricht, 2015) 199 *f*, 298 *f*.

[13] eg, the duty to provide for sanctions that prove 'effective, proportional and dissuasive'; further support for this idea can be found in C-308/06 *The Queen, on the application of International Association of Independent Tanker Owners (Intertanko) and Others v Secretary of State for Transport* EU:C:2008:312, para 78.

However, it is possible that the alleged violation of the principle of legality by the national law stems originally from the European act, in the cases where the duty to transpose an EU directive necessarily leads to a result that is incompatible with the legality principle. This will happen when any attempt to transpose the directive in a way that will allow for the domestic law to conform to the principle would inevitably amount to an incomplete or defective transposition. In that case, compliance with the duty to transpose EU law (eg, a strict obligation to describe the prohibited behaviour in an impermissibly vague manner) will lead Member States to violate the legality principle and such violation can be legitimately imputed to the European act.

Since framework decisions and directives are not directly applicable, their validity can only be challenged, in a domestic judicial case, via the concomitant challenge brought against the national law that transposes them – which was precisely the case in *Advocaten*. In that context, the question arises of which jurisdiction is competent to entertain the claim.

Arguably, if the national court finds that the domestic law infringes upon the principle of legality by virtue of certain options taken by the national legislature, which were not imposed by the European act, then the validity of the latter is not at stake and the national court will enjoy jurisdiction to rule on the issue on its own by applying national law.[14]

Only then, when the possible violation of the legality principle is a direct consequence of the duty to transpose secondary law, shall the national courts refer the question to the CJEU. According to Article 267 of the TFEU, if a question concerning the validity of secondary law is raised in a case pending before a court or tribunal of a Member State against whose decisions there is no judicial remedy under national law, that court has the *duty* to refer the question to the CJEU.[15]

In *Advocaten*, the CJEU implicitly acknowledged that a legislative instrument which neither imposes direct duties on individuals, nor provides for penalties applicable by the courts, can nevertheless infringe, in the abstract, upon the principle of legality,[16] in as much as it might hypothetically bind the addressees (the Member States) to adopt laws inconsistent with that principle. Moreover, the Court also found that such violation shall be subject to a judicial assessment.

[14] This was the stance taken by the German Constitutional Court in *BVerfGE* 113, 273, of 18 July 2005, which found that the (first) German law transposing the FD-EAW was unconstitutional because it disproportionately restricted the right of German citizens not to be extradited, by not preserving that right to the fullest extent of the leeway conceded by the FD-EAW. See the analysis of the decision by Helmut Satzger and Tobias Pohl, 'The German Constitutional Court and the European Arrest Warrant. "Cryptic signals" from Karlsruhe' (2006) *Journal of International Criminal Justice* 4, 686 *f.*

[15] Before the entry into force of the Lisbon Treaty, it was unclear whether the CJEU had an exclusive competence to rule on the invalidity of third pillar acts (via the 'cross-pillar' application of the *Foto-Frost* jurisprudence: Case 314/85 *Foto-Frost v Hauptzollamt Lübeck-Ost* [1987] ECR 04199, para 17: 'Since Article 173 gives the Court exclusive jurisdiction to declare void an act of a Community institution, the coherence of the system requires that where the validity of a Community act is challenged before a national court the power to declare the act invalid must also be reserved to the Court of Justice'. In *Advocaten* (n 1), the CJEU did not feel the need to clarify the issue, which is now solved by the Treaty.

[16] *Advocaten* (n 1), para 44 *f.*

It might not be too far-fetched to take this reasoning as inspiration in order to deal with other spheres of the criminal law. Although it is outside the reach of the present commentary, it is interesting to speculate on whether it can also apply to international instruments with a similar content.[17] In a situation where the Security Council of the United Nations adopts resolutions that bind states to pass criminal law with quite precise content – eg, criminalising the act of 'travelling or trying to travel' to a state other than one's own[18] –, it would be important to know the following:

(i) whether the Security Council, while acting under Chapter VII of the UN Charter, is bound by the legality principle provided for by international law[19] and other overarching principles that govern the restriction of human rights, such as proportionality and necessity;
(ii) whether a conflict between those principles and the duties of implementation binding on the states is thinkable;[20] and

[17] The following considerations do not refer to the customary norms of international criminal law that are *directly* applicable to international offences.

[18] See, eg, S/RES 2178 (2014), of 24 September 2014, (6)(a): '(…) *decides* that all States shall ensure that their domestic laws and regulations establish serious criminal offenses sufficient to provide the ability to prosecute and to penalize in a manner duly reflecting the seriousness of the offense: (a) their nationals who travel or attempt to travel to a State other than their States of residence or nationality, and other individuals who travel or attempt to travel from their territories to a State other than their States of residence or nationality, for the purpose of the perpetration, planning, or preparation of, or participation in, terrorist acts, or the providing or receiving of terrorist training (…)'.

[19] Namely, Art 11 of the Universal Declaration of Human Rights (1948) and Art 15(1) of the International Covenant on Civil and Political Rights (1976). This question is part of a broader discussion on the relationship between the action of the Security Council and the more general notion of international legality, which cannot be addressed here: see Devon Whittle, 'The Limits of Legality and the United Nations Security Council: Applying the Extra-Legal Measures Model to Chapter VII Action' (2015) *European Journal of International Law* 26–3, 671 f.; and Miguel Manero de Lemos, 'Primary Responsibility for Maintaining Peace: The UN Security's Council Power to Impose a Solution to the Israeli-Palestinian Conflict' in *'One State', 'Two State' and 'Third Way' Solutions to the Israeli-Palestinian Conflict: Paving the Way to a Functional Palestinian State* (King's College London, The Centre for the Study of International Peace and Security, 12 May 2017), available at https://csips.files.wordpress.com/2017/04/consolidated-papers-v-4.pdf.

[20] The case law of the ECtHR has been dodging the issue by affirming that the resolutions of the Security Council must be interpreted in a way that is consistent with fundamental rights, because 'there must be a presumption that the Security Council does not intend to impose any obligation on member States to breach fundamental principles of human rights. In the event of any ambiguity in the terms of a United Nations Security Council resolution, the Court must therefore choose the interpretation which is most in harmony with the requirements of the Convention and which avoids any conflict of obligations' (*Al-Jedda v The United Kingdom* App no 27021/08 (ECtHR, 7 July 2011), para 102; *Nada v Switzerland* App no 10593/08 (ECtHR, 12 September 2012) para 171–17; *Al-Dulimi and Montana Management Inc v Switzerland* App no 5809/08 (ECtHR, 21 June 2016), para 139–42). It is however worth noting that, in terms of the opinions appended to the latter decision, several judges seemed prepared to go way beyond the Court's approach in the protection of human rights, possibly to the detriment of the effectiveness of the UN sanctions system – a line of reasoning closer to the arguably bolder stance taken by the courts of the EU in the '*Kadi* saga' (see Valsamis Mitsilegas, *EU Criminal Law after Lisbon* (Hart Publishing, 2016) 245 *f* and Jørn Vestergaard, 'Restrictive Measures in the Fights against Terrorism: The UN System and the European Courts' (2019) *New Journal of European Criminal Law*, DOI |10.1177/2032284419834361).

(iii) in the absence of an international judicial body to whom the issue might be deferred, whether national courts are competent to assess and solve such conflict in a concrete case.

III. The Nature and Function of the Double Criminality Rule and its Relationship with the Legality Principle

The double criminality rule means that, in order for certain effects to obtain, a given act shall qualify as a criminal offence both under the *lex fori* (sc, the law of the jurisdiction where a decision is to be taken) and a given foreign law (usually, the *lex loci delicti*). This requirement plays a role in two different fields of international criminal law (*lato sensu*): extraterritorial jurisdiction (see section III.A. below) and international judicial cooperation, especially extradition (see section III.B. below).[21] In spite of bearing the same name and arguably the same contents, the rule has a distinct fundament in each of those legal branches.

A. Extraterritorial Jurisdiction

Double criminality is imposed by general international law as a condition for the establishment and exercise of extraterritorial jurisdiction, except where the offence is directed against the fundamental interests of the forum state (protection principle) or amounts to a violation of customary international law (universal jurisdiction). Save for those exceptions, punitive claims concerning acts committed in a foreign state that are not prohibited by the *lex loci* are likely to infringe upon the principle of non-intervention in as much as they interfere with the foreign state's prerogative to regulate exhaustively social life in the territory under its authority.[22] The latter has the right and possibly the duty to ensure that individuals present in its soil may decide freely on their actions, free from any conditioning, as long as they comply with the local (and international) law. In other words, the territorial criminal law serves not only to protect individual freedom against *actual punishment*, by the *lex loci*, for acts that are not prohibited, but also against

[21] See Petter Asp, Andrew von Hirsch and Dan Frände, 'Double Criminality and Transnational Investigative Measures in EU Criminal Proceedings: Some Issues of Principle' (2006) *Zeitschrift für Internationales Strafrecht* 11, 512 *f.*

[22] Christine van den Wyngaert, 'Double Criminality as a Condition to Jurisdiction' in N Jareborg (ed), *Double Criminality. Studies in International Criminal Law* (*geschriften van de rechtsfaculteit van Uppsala*, Iustus Förlag, 1989) 52. This applies even where the forum state endeavours to enforce its law on the basis of the most traditional grounds for extraterritorial jurisdiction, eg, active personality: see Kai Ambos, *Internationales Strafrecht*, 5th edn (CH Beck, 2018) § 3, mn 40, 43.

any unwarranted intervention by the law with an extraterritorial claim on the *very freedom to decide to act in a certain way*.[23]

From a different perspective, the claim to apply national criminal law to extraterritorial acts which are lawful under the *lex loci* is not consistent with the right to freedom that stems from the liberal principle enshrined in the constitutions of the EU Member States, according to which the limits to individual freedom must result from the collective will embodied in the law. Indeed, 'the law' cannot be construed as just 'any law', but rather as the rules of conduct that are legitimately imposed on individuals and *therefore* applicable to their behaviour. In this context, it is submitted that the respect for the right to enjoy the liberties ensured by the territorial state in the exercise of its legitimate (prescriptive) jurisdiction impinges upon the extraterritorial scope of the *lex fori*[24] and prevails over the personal ties of allegiance typical to the feudal system[25] and, later, to authoritarian regimes.[26] This assumption stems directly from the relationship between the individual and the public power in modern times, especially in a political context where the multiplication of personal ties (eg, the residence in a foreign Member State, the citizenship of the EU as an additional personal status) is encouraged.[27]

In sum, extraterritorial jurisdiction has both external and internal limits, respectively, the principle of non-intervention and the right to freedom embedded in the constitutions of liberal states. When double criminality obtains, those limits do not apply.

It flows from the preceding considerations that the requirement for double criminality in the establishment of extraterritorial jurisdiction does not derive from the principle of legality, which produces its effects only in the face of a law that has already been identified as applicable. Logically, the legality principle cannot intervene at a stage where the conditions for the applicability of a given legal order are still being determined.[28]

Whether or not the applicability of the *lex fori* is foreseeable in the absence of a corresponding prohibition in the *lex loci delicti* is a different matter altogether,

[23] In more detail, Pedro Caeiro, *Fundamento, Conteúdo e Limites da Jurisdição Penal do Estado. O Caso Português* (Coimbra Ed./Wolters Kluwer, 2010) 355 *f*; and Frank Zimmermann, *Strafgewaltkonflikte in der Europäischen Union. Eine Regelungsvorschlag zur Wahrung materieller und prozessualer strafrechtlicher Garantien sowie staatlicher Strafinteressen* (Nomos, 2014) 172 *f*.

[24] van den Wyngaert (n 22) 54 has also hinted at the human/fundamental rights dimension of double criminality as a condition for extraterritorial jurisdiction: 'the questions we discuss here with respect to double criminality are inherent to the fundamental issue of the criminal law in general, i.e. the problem of balancing the rights of the individual against the needs of (domestic and/or international) suppression of crime'.

[25] On the jurisdiction of the feudal lord over his *couchans et levans*, see Henri Donnedieu de Vabres, *Introduction à l'Etude du Droit Pénal International* (Sirey, 1922) 93 *f*.

[26] On the regime of the German National Socialist Penal Code of 1940 (RStGB), which has instated active personality as the main connection for establishing jurisdiction (until 1975), see Helmut Satzger, *Internationales und Europäisches Strafrecht*, 7th edn (Nomos, 2016) § 5, 3, 48.

[27] On this, see Martin Böse, 'Fundamental Freedoms of the Union' in M Böse, F Meyer and A Schneider, *Conflicts of Jurisdiction in Criminal Matters in the European Union. Volume II: Rights, Principles and Model Rules* (Nomos, 2014) 72 *ff*.

[28] Caeiro (n 23) 232 *f*.

which, again, does not contend with the principle of legality, but rather with the more general *right to legal certainty* before the *lex fori*. The respect for that right does not depend, at all, on the existence of double criminality, but on the 'meaningfulness' or 'genuineness' of the connection chosen to exert extraterritorial jurisdiction,[29] which should be foreseeable by the perpetrator, thus ruling out obnoxious or manifestly weak connections.

B. Extradition

Double criminality is usually required as a condition for international cooperation in criminal matters, especially for extradition. In this realm, double criminality means that cooperation (extradition) depends on the condition that the relevant acts are a criminal offence both under the requesting and the requested state's law, the latter being, in this sense, the *lex fori*, because it is the law in force in the jurisdiction whose decision (to extradite) is sought.

According to the argument put forward by *Advocaten voor de Wereld*, the FD-EAW did not fully comply with the principle *nullum crimen sine lege* (*lex certa*) because it might lead to the apprehension of individuals for acts that are not punishable in the executing state and are loosely defined in Article 2(2) ('very vaguely defined categories of undesirable conduct'[30]). This regime would not provide for

> the guarantee that criminal legislation must satisfy conditions as to precision, clarity and predictability allowing each person to know, at the time when an act is committed, whether that act does or does not constitute an offence, by contrast to those who are deprived of their liberty otherwise than pursuant to a European arrest warrant.[31]

This reasoning is obscure and, ultimately, founded on the wrong premise.

It starts by correctly establishing a relationship between the conditions required by the principle of legality and the need for the individual to know, '*at the time when an act is committed*, whether that act does or does not constitute an offence'

[29] See Schönke, Schröder and Eser, *Strafgesetzbuch Kommentar*, 29th edn (CH Beck, 2014), Vorbem §§ 3–9, mn 9, with further references.

[30] *Advocaten* (n 1) para 48.

[31] *Advocaten* (n 1) para 49. Similar concerns have been expressed by a number of authors: see, eg, Stefan Braum, 'Der Europäische Haftbefehl – Motor europäischer Strafrechtspflege?' (2007) *wistra* 404 f; Satzger (n 26) § 10, mn 39, 202; Nuno Piçarra, 'A transposição da Decisão-quadro relativa ao mandado de detenção europeu sob escrutínio dos juízes constitucionais nacionais' (2005) *Jurisprudência Constitucional* 8, 71 (fn 23); Ricardo Bragança de Matos, 'O princípio do reconhecimento mútuo e o mandado de detenção europeu' (2004) *Revista Portuguesa de Ciência Criminal* 14, 353 *f*; Ana Rosa Pais, 'A ausência de controlo da dupla incriminação no âmbito da Decisão-Quadro relativa ao mandado de detenção europeu. Breve anotação ao Acórdão do Tribunal de Justiça de 3 de Maio de 2007' in *Estudos em Homenagem ao Prof. Doutor Jorge de Figueiredo Dias* (Coimbra Editora, 2008) Vol I, 818.

(emphasis added). But it then seems to apply the principle to the deprivation of liberty, pursuant to a EAW or otherwise, as if there was a relationship between the principle of legality and the act of apprehending an individual for the purpose of surrender/extradition proceedings. Indeed, as the Court pointed out, the *nullum crimen* requirements certainly apply to the law under which the individual's responsibility is to be assessed (the issuing state's), which necessarily served as 'conduct-regulating' law when the act was committed.[32] However, the conditions under which an individual can be arrested for the purpose of international judicial cooperation proceedings and subsequently surrendered, fall outside the scope of the principle of legality, precisely because such arrest/surrender does not amount to punishment being meted out as a consequence of an offence.[33]

As a matter of fact, all legal systems are familiar with procedures of deprivation of freedom that do not necessarily result from a prison sentence or from the need to apprehend the suspect in a criminal procedure (preventive detention). Some of them – such as the detention of illegal migrants where provided for, or detention for the purpose of identification of an individual – bear no link with the exercise of the punitive power. The same happens with the detention for the purpose of extradition/surrender. The decisions taken by the courts of the requested state in extradition proceedings do not aim to determine the criminal responsibility of the concerned individual, or impose a penalty upon him/her, but rather answer the question of whether or not he or she should be extradited.

In this context, the decision to order the detention of an individual in the context of extradition/surrender proceedings and the decision to actually extradite him/her are *not* subject to the legality principle. The respect for the latter may only come into play if there is evidence that the requesting state is prosecuting/punishing someone for an act that is not punishable *under its own law*. In that case, there may be grounds to deny extradition on the basis that the legal system of the requesting state does not respect the basic principles of the rule of law and human rights.

[32] On the application of K Binding's distinction between conduct-regulating norms (*Verhaltensnormen, regulae agendi*) and sanctioning norms (*Sanktionsnormen, regulae decidendi*) in the context of the theory of criminal jurisdiction, see Caeiro (n 23) 215 *f*, esp 229 *f*, 331 *f*; and Böse (n 27) 31 *f*.

The use of the adverb 'necessarily' in the text calls for further explanation. There are some exceptional instances where a state can apply a norm that has no connection with the act and therefore could not serve as *regula agendi* when it was committed, namely, the cases where adjudicative jurisdiction is exercised on the basis of vicarious jurisdiction or upon the request for a transfer of criminal proceedings by a foreign state. In both cases, though, the presence of the suspect/defendant in the forum state is an essential condition for the establishment of jurisdiction, which means that a request for extradition/surrender is ruled out (except for the very marginal situations where the suspect or defendant flees during the proceedings). In any case, the exercise of jurisdiction based on those grounds is bound by the specific safeguard of dual criminality (as an element of jurisdiction), which means that the application of the *lex fori* is always subject to the condition that the foreign law (*regula agendi*) qualifies the act as a criminal offence.

[33] For a more detailed critique of the alleged relationship between double criminality and the legality principle, see Asp, von Hirsch and Frände (n 21) 514.

In my view, the fundament of double criminality as a requirement for international cooperation is to be found elsewhere, namely in the principle of *proportionality* and in the protection of *legal certainty*, both of which are discussed in the paragraphs that follow.

Double criminality is a specific precipitate of an assessment performed in the abstract, which puts in balance the public interest in international cooperation for the prosecution/punishment of alleged offenders, on the one hand, and, on the other, the individual rights affected by extradition.[34]

In the first place, it ensures that the requesting state pursues a goal relevant enough to justify, from its own perspective, the serious restrictions of individual rights actually or potentially implied in extradition proceedings (liberty, freedom of movement, the right to family life, the right to work, etc). In the second place, the relevance of the goal pursued shall be condoned by the law of the requested state, which shall consider the acts for which the individual is sought as offences as well. In principle, such an 'agreement' between the two laws is necessary to establish extradition as a means of cooperating against *crime*.[35] In this sense, double criminality is a dimension of *proportionality* specific to international judicial cooperation: the requested state deploys its coercive means and limits individual rights in order to assist the requesting state because the relevance of the latter's claims can be acknowledged under the former's set of most important values.

The perspective can change fundamentally when cooperation procedures are framed in the context of a political union such as the EU. For one, the applicable legal common framework on the protection of human/fundamental rights significantly decreases the risk of an individual being prosecuted or convicted for acts that do not bear any legal impact on worthy legal interests from the point of view of the requested state. This allows for the interest in cooperation to weigh more. Most of the time, the lack of double criminality will be the result of 'technical options' taken at the national level that do not really contend with the core

[34] Traditionally, the other pole of this opposition was deemed to be the clause of *ordre public* as a by-product of sovereignty, which would allegedly condition the use of coercive measures by the executing state in cases where it had no autonomous punitive claim against the sought person (in this direction, Robert Zimmermann, *La Coopération Judiciaire Internationale en Matière Pénale* (Staempfli Eds, 1999) 270; Miguel João Costa, 'O princípio da dupla incriminação na extradição' in P Caeiro (Coord), *Temas de Extradição e Entrega* (Almedina, 2015) 48). A more 'substantive', value-laden version of the *ordre public* as an obstacle that might replace double criminality is put forward by Asp, von Hirsch and Frände (n 21) 515 *f*. Nevertheless, it is submitted that the *ordre public* clause should be used as a tool of last resort, a sort of external limit that prevents cooperation for reasons peculiar to the requested state in cases where cooperation would be otherwise possible and advisable – eg, the applicability of the death penalty to someone who is suspected of genocide. On the contrary, double criminality is right at the core of (traditional) judicial cooperation, in that it builds, at the same time, the fundamental scope of the procedure (cooperation for *criminal* offences) and the basic balance between state interests and individual rights.

[35] For a review of the status of double criminality in several domestic laws and in the literature of the early twentieth century, see Paul Fauchille, *Traité de Droit International Public*, Tome I (Ière partie, Lib. Arthur Rousseau, 1922) 1032 *f*.

'criminality' of the act.[36] In the second place, taking part in a common area of freedom, security and justice means that the relevance of the claims from fellow Member States can be acknowledged at a different level, which does not necessarily require an agreement on the criminal nature of the *particular act* that triggers the procedure. Such accord takes place in more abstract terms, whereby Member States simply recognise the worthiness of each other's criminal policy and provide mutual assistance for its execution – even in instances where their own law does not criminalise in the same precise terms the act underlying the request/order for cooperation.

In a sense, the recognition of values acquires a formalistic nature: judicial cooperation no longer refers to the protection of the *common* legal interest harmed or endangered by, eg, murder, or trafficking in human beings, but to the effectiveness of the penal justice system of the requesting (issuing) state. Of course, the extent to which the control of double criminality can be replaced by this formal element – any offence; or any offence with exceptions ('negative list'); or offences included in a catalogue ('positive list') – is mainly a political issue. In any event, it seems appropriate that the new paradigm starts with a positive catalogue that conditions the mandatory abolition of the control of double criminality, thus 'screening' the protection of the issuing Member State's criminal policy programme, even if such catalogue by no means provides an actual guarantee that the offences contained therein are criminalised across the EU in terms that would comply with the requirement for double criminality.[37]

Although the control of double criminality is not imposed by, or even grounded on the principle of legality, the question remains whether, alongside the indirect and generic protection of individual rights embedded in double criminality as a proportionality requirement, the rule should also serve to protect the *expectations* of the sought individual *vis-à-vis* the requested state and his right to legal certainty.

The starting point here is that states are autonomous jurisdictions and their punitive claims are, in principle, local. In this sense, sovereignty works, and rightly so, for the benefit of individuals; there are no universally valid punitive claims, except for offences against international criminal law, which summon up the punitive power of the international community. Otherwise, no one should be deemed a *hostes omnium*, prone to be chased wherever he or she may be found, as if they were in a state of global outlawry. Consequently, individuals have a legitimate expectation of finding a safe haven when they are not under the immediate authority of the state which claims them.[38] Of course, it is also legitimate for the states to agree to cooperate with each other in the pursuit and surrender of persons, in the conditions they deem appropriate. However, as such agreements

[36] See Costa (n 34) 77 f.

[37] See Anabela Miranda Rodrigues, *O Direito Penal Europeu Emergente* (Coimbra Ed., 2008) 200.

[38] In this direction, Fauchille (n 35) 1031 *f.*

run counter to said expectations, the enforcement of the right to legal certainty seems to require that individuals are able to foresee the situations in which they can be legitimately deprived of their freedom and forcibly displaced to another country for the purpose of prosecution/punishment.[39]

The requirement for double criminality is a rather straightforward, commonly accepted way of drawing the limits of a state's hospitality towards people fleeing from other jurisdictions: individuals can be detained for the purpose of being extradited and actually delivered to the requesting state only when they are sought for having committed acts that are *also* deemed criminal offences in the law of the requested state. This basic condition makes detention and extradition foreseeable by the addressees and enables them to manage their expectations.

That being said, does detention/arrest, or extradition/surrender of an individual, for acts that are not criminalised under the law of the requested/executing state impermissibly hamper on his/her right to legal certainty? In other words, if a system of judicial cooperation sets aside the requirement for double criminality, does it violate that right? The answer should be in the affirmative, unless the requested state has in place an alternative mechanism that ensures foreseeability and prevents the individual from being detained and extradited by surprise. For example, if states A and B agree, in an international covenant, to completely abolish the requirement for double criminality, and such covenant is given the same publicity accorded to domestic law (namely, the publication in the relevant official journal), the individual whose extradition is sought by state A will have sufficient notice that he or she will be detained and extradited by state B in the case where he or she enters its territory, even if the act at stake is not a criminal offence in the latter's criminal law.

It is submitted that the regime of the FD-EAW puts in place a mechanism that is fundamentally in line with the concerns for legal certainty.

As a matter of fact, the EAW is implemented across the EU via the national legislation of the various Member States, which means that its regime can be easily known by the addressees.

If a state opts to abolish the control of double criminality for all offences,[40] the national law of transposition will make clear that the authorities of that state will arrest and surrender any person sought by another Member State pursuant to an EAW, irrespective of the nature of the offence committed. This will be sufficient notice from the viewpoint of legal certainty.

If instead a state abolishes the control of double criminality only in respect of the limited catalogue of 'domains of criminality' provided for by Art 2(2) of the FD-EAW, it is necessary to assess whether the implementation of the resulting regime can be done in a satisfactory way. It is true that the indication of those

[39] See Jorge de Figueiredo Dias and Pedro Caeiro, "Comentário ao Acórdão *Advocaten voor de Wereld VZW c. Leden van de Ministerraad*", in EP Ferreira / ML Duarte / MS Ferro (org.), *Jurisprudência. Cunha Rodrigues – Comentários*, AAFDL, 2013, p. 14–29. This reasoning applies whenever the fulfilment of a punitive claim requires the intervention of two jurisdictions, which is also the case in political unions such as the EU.

[40] Art 2(4) FD-EAW (*a contrario sensu*).

'domains' (murder, theft, etc) does not specify the constitutive elements of the offences, which are referred to the law of the issuing state, and some 'domains' are loosely described (eg, 'computer-related crime', or 'swindling'). This method would clearly infringe upon the legality principle, should the transposing law be under the latter's rule – which is not the case, as has been argued above. However, it seems perfectly compatible with the much more flexible nature of legal certainty,[41] especially if we bear in mind that the courts of the executing state retain the power to control, on a case-by-case basis, the correspondence between the act and the 'domain of criminality' to which it is subsumed.[42]

Following the lead of the notorious decision of the German Constitutional Court of 2005,[43] some authors have expressed concerns about the possibility of a Member State being compelled to arrest and surrender, pursuant to a warrant issued by a Member State in the exercise of extraterritorial jurisdiction, a person who has committed, in the territory of the former, an act that is not unlawful under the *lex loci*[44] – for instance, prosecuting and trying for homicide, under the passive personality principle, a doctor who lawfully assists the death of a terminally ill patient in accordance with the *lex loci*. Such possibility arises because the territoriality of the act is only an *optional* ground for non-execution of the EAW.[45] In those circumstances, arrest and surrender would be – so the argument goes – in clear violation of legal certainty and foreseeability (although not, if I may insist, of the legality principle, which would be respected as long as the law of the issuing state would criminalise the act).

Nevertheless, the problem with this awkward situation is not the lack of double criminality as a requirement for judicial *cooperation*, but the exercise of 'wild' *extraterritorial jurisdiction* despite the lack of double criminality.[46] Strict compliance with the principle of non-intervention[47] would avoid this kind of issue.

On the other hand, no objections would be raised against the issuance of an EAW by state A, in order to arrest, in state B, a suspect of attempted sabotage perpetrated in the same state B against state A, even if the *lex loci* does not

[41] On this difference, see Peristeridou (n 12) 195 *f*, with further references.

[42] See Daniel Flore, 'Le mandat d'arrêt européen: première mise en oeuvre d'un nouveaux paradigme de la justice pénale européenne' (2002) *Journal des Tribunaux* 121e. ann, no 6050 276 *f*; and João Pedro Lopes Costa, 'A dupla incriminação no mandado de detenção europeu e o verdadeiro alcance da abolição do seu controlo' in P Caeiro (Coord), *Temas de Extradição e Entrega* (Almedina, 2015) 102 *f*. In the same vein, the Portuguese Supreme Court has decided that, despite the opposite view of the issuing state, a parent who flees her state of residence with a daughter minor of age with a view to preventing her former husband from exercising his parental rights does not commit an offence of 'kidnapping, illegal restraint or hostage taking' to the effects of Art 2(2) FD-EAW: *Acórdão do Supremo Tribunal de Justiça*, proc. 06P4707, of 4 January 2007.

[43] *BVerfGE* 113, 273, of 18 July 2005 (n 14).

[44] See, eg, Braum (n 31) 404 *f*; Satzger (n 26) § 10, mn 39, 202.

[45] See Art 7(4)(a) FD-EAW.

[46] See Pedro Caeiro, 'Jurisdiction in Criminal Matters in the EU: Negative and Positive Conflicts, and Beyond' (2010) *Kritische Vierteljahresschrift für Gesetzgebung und Rechtswissenschaft* 4, 366 *f*.

[47] See section III.A.

criminalise sabotage (against foreign countries). The explanation is of course very simple: in that case, extraterritorial jurisdiction is legitimate (under the so-called protection principle) *also* in the absence of double criminality. Hence, the abolition of the latter as a condition for judicial cooperation for prosecuting that offence emerges as a natural consequence in the context of the doctrine of jurisdiction. Attempts to manipulate or illegitimately extend the concept of 'sabotage' can be prevented by the courts of the executing state, which keep some control over the labelling performed by the issuing state[48] and may ultimately decide that the acts at stake do not correspond to a common (European) notion of 'sabotage'.

IV. Conclusion

In *Advocaten*, the CJEU touched upon several issues that are of interest not only for the relationship between the states and the EU, but also for the justiciability of possible conflicts between supra-state law and the respect for the principle of legality. It also correctly concluded that the latter does not prevent the abolition of the control of double criminality in the realm of international judicial cooperation. Instead, states may freely agree to dispense with such requirement as long as they ensure the respect for the right to legal certainty of the individuals present in their territory, by setting out and publicising the conditions upon which they can be detained and surrendered to a foreign state.

[48] See n 42 and corresponding text.

13

C-396/11 – *Radu*

Judgment of the Court of Justice of the European Union, 29 January 2013, Radu

ROSA RAFFAELLI

I. Introduction

The decision of the Court of Justice (CJEU) in *Radu*[1] has generally been regarded as a missed opportunity.[2] This was one of the first cases in which the Court was asked to take a position on the role of fundamental rights in the European Arrest Warrant (EAW) system,[3] by clarifying whether a violation of fundamental rights, and in particular of the right to a fair trial, could be considered as a ground to refuse execution of a EAW. Advocate General (AG) Sharpston's Opinion[4] had given rise to very high expectations: she had examined the issue in detail, referring to the standards set out in the case law of the European Court of Human Rights (ECtHR) and to the recent Court of Justice's *NS* judgment,[5] and had concluded that a national court could refuse to execute a EAW based on fundamental rights concerns, albeit exceptionally. However, the Court ruled otherwise: by rephrasing the reference for a preliminary ruling, and cutting it to the bones, the Court was able to limit its decision to the bare minimum, avoiding the issue of the relationship between fundamental rights and the EAW. Yet, one thing was clearly stated in the judgment: the grounds for refusal listed in Framework Decision 2002/584/JHA

[1] Case C-396/11 *Ciprian Vasile Radu* [2013] ECR I.

[2] See, eg, John R Spencer, 'Extradition, the European Arrest Warrant and Human Rights' (2013) *Cambridge Law Journal* 72(2); Ilias Anagnostopoulos, 'Criminal Justice Cooperation in the European Union after the First Few "Steps": A Defence View' (2014) *ERA Forum* No 15.

[3] Council Framework Decision 2002/584/JHA of 13 June 2002 on the European arrest warrant and the surrender procedures between Member States [2002] OJ L190/1, as amended in 2009 by Council Framework Decision 2009/299/JHA with regard to *in absentia* trials.

[4] Case C-396/11 *Ciprian Vasile Radu* [2013] ECR I Opinion of AG Sharpston.

[5] Joined Cases C-411/10 and C-493/10 *NS v Secretary of State for the Home Department and ME and Others v Refugee Applications Commissioner and Minister for Justice, Equality and Law Reform* [2011] ECR I-13905.

are exhaustive, and its Art 1(3), with its reference to fundamental rights, cannot be interpreted as allowing for additional discretion on the part of national courts.

Of course, the judgment in *Radu* was not to be the CJEU's last word on the matter: *Melloni*[6] followed soon afterwards, and many more cases have been decided since – including some recent ones where the Court took a much less rigid approach to the role of (certain) fundamental rights in the EAW system.[7] Yet, the Court's position in *Radu* has proven to be a persistent issue, not only in the debate over the EAW, but also in the broader discussion over the role of mutual recognition and mutual trust in the EU legal order and their relationship with fundamental rights – including, most recently, in the debate over EU accession to the European Convention for the Protection of Human Rights and Fundamental Freedoms (ECHR), which followed the adoption of Opinion 2/13 by the CJEU.[8]

II. The Reference for a Preliminary Ruling and the Opinion of AG Sharpston – High Expectations

The reference for a preliminary ruling came from the *Curtea de Apel Constanţa* (Romania) on 27 July 2011. The facts of the case are not very clear, and the reference does not describe them in detail – however, from AG Sharpston's Opinion, we learn that the case had arisen from several EAWs issued by German prosecutors for the arrest of Mr Radu for robbery. Mr Radu did not consent to his surrender and appealed against the initial decisions, taken by the same Court of Appeals, to execute three of the four EAWs, which led the Court of Appeals to refer the case to the CJEU. In its reference, the Court asked several questions concerning fundamental rights and the EAW. In particular, it asked whether Articles 5 and 6 ECHR (which protect the rights to liberty and security and to a fair trial), read in conjunction with Articles 48 and 52 of the Charter of Fundamental Rights of the EU (Charter),[9] are provisions of primary Community law, contained in the founding Treaties. It then went on to ask whether the execution of an EAW, entailing deprivation of liberty and surrender without the consent of the requested person, constitutes an interference with the right to individual liberty of the person which is compatible with EU law. The Court furthermore asked whether

[6] Case C-399/11 *Melloni* [2013] ECR I.

[7] See in particular Joined Cases C-404/15 and C-659/15 PPU *Pál Aranyosi and Robert Căldăraru v Generalstaatsanwaltschaft Bremen* ECLI:EU:C:2016:198 (on the risk of inhuman or degrading treatment contrary to Art 4 Charter); as well as the more recent Case C-216/18 PPU *Minister for Justice and Equality v LM* [2018] ECR I (on the independency of the judiciary).

[8] Opinion 2/13 [2014] ECR I-2454.

[9] Which concern the presumption of innocence and right of defence, and the scope and interpretation of the Charter itself (including the well-known principle according to which, whenever the Charter includes rights that are also incorporated in the ECHR, they shall be intended to have a similar meaning and scope, notwithstanding the Union's power to provide more extensive protection).

the interference of the executing Member State with fundamental rights must satisfy the requirements of necessity in a democratic society and of proportionality in relation to the objective actually pursued. Additional questions concerned the role of the competent judicial authority of the executing Member State: can they refuse to execute the EAW if the conditions set out in Article 5(1) ECHR and Article 6 of the Charter have not been satisfied? Can they refuse execution if the issuing State has failed to transpose or incorrectly transposed Council Framework Decision 2002/584/JHA? The Court finally asked whether national Romanian law was compatible with the ECHR and the Charter and whether it had correctly transposed Council Framework Decision 2002/584/JHA.[10]

Before moving on to examine AG Sharpston's Opinion, it is essential to briefly refer to another CJEU judgment, which constitutes its background: the *NS* decision.[11] The case arose in the context of the Common European Asylum System (CEAS); in particular, it concerned the risk that an applicant for international protection, who had moved away from the State responsible for examining his/her application under the so-called Dublin Regulation,[12] would be subjected to inhuman or degrading treatment (notably, in terms of inadequate reception conditions) if transferred back to that State. In that judgment, the CJEU followed the ECtHR case law, and in particular the specific precedent set out in *MSS v Belgium and Greece*,[13] to delineate the limits to mutual trust in cases of transfers of asylum seekers under the Dublin Regulation. The CJEU concluded that the presumption that Member States comply with fundamental rights – which is required in a system based on mutual trust, such as the area of freedom, security and justice (AFSJ) – is rebuttable, and that it is so even in a context where the first Member State is bound to observe Directive 2003/9/EC,[14] which at the time established minimum standards for the reception of asylum seekers and which should have ensured, if correctly implemented, decent reception standards in compliance with fundamental rights.

In her Opinion, AG Sharpston moves from an analysis of the background of Framework Decision 2002/584/JHA, recalling that it was meant to facilitate the creation of an AFSJ and to implement the principle of mutual recognition, which

[10] The full text of the reference is available on the Official Journal [2011] OJ C282/15–16.

[11] *NS* (n 5).

[12] Currently, Regulation 604/2013/EU of the European Parliament and of the Council of 26 June 2013 establishing the criteria and mechanisms for determining the Member State responsible for examining an application for international protection lodged in one of the Member States by a third-country national or a stateless person (so-called Dublin III) [2013] OJ L180/31–59; at the time of the *NS* facts, the previous version of the Regulation was applicable (Council Regulation 343/2003). The Regulation is currently under recast.

[13] *MSS v Belgium and Greece* App no 30696/09 (ECtHR, 21 January 2011). On this judgment, see Violeta Moreno-Lax, 'Dismantling the Dublin System: M.S.S. v. Belgium and Greece' (2012) *European Journal of Migration and Law*' 14; Francesco Maiani and Emmanuelle Néraudau, 'L'arrêt M.S.S./Grèce et Belgique de la Cour EDH du 21 janvier 2011' (2011) *Revue du Droit des Etrangers* 126.

[14] The Directive has subsequently been replaced by Directive 2013/33/EU laying down standards for the reception of applicants for international protection, which is also currently under recast.

requires a high level of confidence between the Member States. While the main objective of the Framework Decision was to reduce the delays typical of the extradition process by placing mainly procedural obligations on the Member States, the Decision also incorporates reference to fundamental rights. In particular, Recitals 10, 12 and 13 mention respect for fundamental rights, and Article 1(3) states that the Decision does not have the effect of modifying the obligation to respect fundamental rights and fundamental legal principles as enshrined in Article 6 of the Treaty on European Union (TEU). The AG further stresses that the high level of mutual confidence between Member States, referred to in Recital 10 and which constitutes the backbone of the Framework Decision, is predicated on the observance by States of the fundamental rights enshrined in the ECHR and in the constitutional traditions common to the Member States, as well as on the Charter. According to the AG, there can be no automatic assumption that the human rights of the person whose surrender is requested will be guaranteed, merely because the EAW comes from another EU Member State: there can only be a presumption of compliance with human rights, which should be rebuttable with specific and clear evidence.

The AG then proceeds to examine the specific questions asked by the Romanian Court in detail. Fundamental rights do form part of primary EU law, which incorporates both Convention and Charter, regardless of the entry into force of the Lisbon Treaty and of Article 6 TEU[15] – Sharpston considers the latter as a mere codification of the pre-existing case law of the Court of Justice. The arrest and surrender of a requested person under an EAW constitutes an interference with the right to liberty, protected by Article 5 ECHR and Article 6 Charter, and such interference will normally be considered as 'necessary in a democratic society' (thus complying with Art 5(1)(f) ECHR), provided it is not arbitrary. The AG also incidentally recalls the Commission's 2011 Implementation Report,[16] according to which there has been an excessive use of the EAW procedure for minor offences, with a disproportionate effect on the liberty of requested persons.

The Opinion then examines the issue at the core of the reference: can a Member State refuse to execute an EAW, when implementing it would risk infringing the requested person's rights under Articles 5 and 6 ECHR or Articles 6, 48 and 52 Charter? According to the AG, only a cursory reading of the Framework Decision could lead to the conclusion that this is not allowed. It is true that the Court had already found (in *Leymann*[17] and other subsequent judgments) that the grounds for refusal listed in Articles 3 and 4 of the Decision are exhaustive.

[15] Article 6 TEU expressly recognises that the Charter 'shall have the same legal value as the Treaties' – before the Lisbon Treaty entered into force, the Charter did not formally have binding force.

[16] 11 April 2011 Report from the Commission to the European Parliament and the Council on the implementation since 2007 of the Council Framework Decision of 13 June 2002 on the European arrest warrant and the surrender procedures between Member States' COM(2011) 175 final.

[17] Case C-388/08 PPU *Leymann and Pustovarov* [2008] ECR I-08993; there, the Court had clearly stated that Member States 'must or may refuse to execute a warrant only in the cases listed in Articles 3 and 4' of the Framework Decision.

The AG concedes that the objective of the Decision is to reduce the delays that are typical of extradition, by creating a system of surrender based on mutual recognition and a high level of mutual confidence – Member States are therefore, in principle, obliged to act upon an EAW. However, the AG goes on to argue that a narrow approach, which would completely exclude human rights considerations, is not correct. Indeed, such a conclusion would deprive Article 1(3) of the Framework Decision of any meaning, transforming it into 'an elegant platitude'; its sense, however, is to make it implicit that fundamental rights may be taken into account in deciding not to execute a warrant. To support this view, she cites numerous opinions of other AGs,[18] and proceeds to find additional ground in the case law of both the Strasbourg and the Luxembourg courts. For the Strasbourg Court, there is a wide choice – Sharpston therefore cites specifically an extradition case, the well-known *Soering vs UK*[19] case, where the ECtHR set out the standard of 'substantial grounds to believe that the person faces a real risk' of being subjected to inhuman or degrading treatment if extradited. With regard to the CJEU, however, the choice is much more limited, and it leads to a different context, that of asylum: reference is thus made to the *NS* judgment,[20] which the Court of Justice had issued just over one year before, and which – as already mentioned – concerned Dublin transfers. *NS* was the first, and most prominent, case in which the Court of Justice – following the ECtHR,[21] whose decision had left it with little space to decide otherwise, save opting for a clash with Strasbourg – had found that mutual trust is not without boundaries. The standard justifying a decision not to execute a Dublin transfer had been defined by the CJEU in the following terms: where a Member State 'cannot be unaware' of 'systemic deficiencies' in another Member State, amounting to 'substantial grounds' to believe that the person would face 'a real risk' of being subjected to degrading or inhuman treatment.[22]

[18] In particular, Case C-306/09 *IB* [2010] ECR I-10341, Opinion of AG Cruz Villalón; Case C-123/08 *Wolzenburg* [2009] ECR I-09621, Opinion of AG Bot; Case C-261/09 *Mantello* [2010] ECR I-11477, Opinion of AG Bot; and Case C-42/11 *Lopes da Silva Jorge* [2012] ECR I, Opinion of AG Mengozzi.

[19] *Soering v United Kingdom* Series A no 161 (1989) 11 EHRR 439.

[20] *NS* (n 5).

[21] *NS* (n 5).

[22] On the relevant standard, see also the more recent, and less stringent, standard set out in the *CK* case: Case C-578/16 PPU *CK and Others v Republika Slovenija* [2017] ECR I. There, the Court concluded that a Member State should not execute a Dublin transfer when it would imply a real risk of a significant and permanent worsening of the person's state of health – a possibility which the Court considers to be exceptional, and linked to a pre-existing serious illness of the asylum seeker. The *CK* case has thus clarified that proving 'systemic deficiencies' is not essential, and that an individual assessment of the specific case at hand can also lead to a refusal to transfer an asylum seeker, whenever a real risk of significant and permanent harm emerges. However, the *CK* case has a limited bearing on the principle of mutual trust: as the Court itself clarifies (see para 95), it does not affect the presumption that Member States respect fundamental rights, and therefore it fully respects the principle of mutual trust. Indeed, the *CK* case concerns the need to avoid a transfer which would, in and of itself, affect a person's health, regardless of the levels of healthcare and fundamental rights protection offered in the Member State responsible for the examination of the asylum application under Dublin. In the specific circumstances of the case, it was a given that the latter – Croatia – offered sufficient medical care and decent reception standards; the issue was whether the transfer would inevitably affect CK's health, given her pre-existing conditions, and thus whether it should be considered as an inhumane or degrading treatment *on the part of the transferring State, alone.*

The two cases show that both Courts held that fundamental rights may affect the legislative obligation of a Member State to transfer a person. AG Sharpston then goes on to argue that the CJEU should not follow the standard for refusing to execute an extradition set out by the ECtHR, but should design a less stringent test, thus providing a higher level of protection to fundamental rights than that offered by the ECHR, as allowed under Article 52(3) of the Charter. The test that she delineates is one where refusals to execute EAWs would still be exceptional, based on 'substantially well founded' objections: past breaches that fundamentally destroyed the fairness of the trial process would be relevant, including breaches not only of substantive rights, but *also of fundamental procedural requirements* as to the issuing of the warrant.

The most important conclusion of the Advocate General's Opinion is therefore that breaches of fundamental rights – be they substantive or procedural – can, and should, constitute a ground to refuse execution of an EAW, based on the (rather laconic) Article 1(3) of the Framework Decision. This is in line with the case law of the ECtHR, which does not allow for any conclusive presumption that other States parties to the ECHR will, *in concreto* and in every individual case, fully respect fundamental rights. This conclusion seems to be obvious if we see it in the context of the case law of the Strasbourg Court: after all, its task is to assess whether States that have ratified the Convention really abide by it. Its numerous judgments with findings of violations show that no State party (and therefore, no EU Member State, as they all are parties to the ECHR) is perfect: ratification of the Convention does not automatically imply full implementation in every individual case. Yet, the Court of Justice had always been much more reluctant to exclude the possibility of conclusive presumptions of respect for fundamental rights on the part of other EU Member States. *NS* was, in this context, rather exceptional: there, the Court was almost forced to conclude that mutual trust does not mean blind trust, given the precedents in the Strasbourg Court.

The Opinion of AG Sharpston, read together with the judgment in *NS*, gave rise to very high expectations among scholars and practitioners. Indeed, some authors[23] specifically examined the applicability of the *NS* principle to the execution of an EAW, and argued that the limit to mutual trust identified in *NS* could be extended to the context of criminal justice, and stretched so as to cover violations of procedural, as well as substantive, rights. *NS* thus raised hopes as regards the limits of mutual trust and the role of fundamental rights in the area of freedom, security and justice (an area, it is worth recalling, that includes both asylum and criminal law).[24]

[23] See, eg, Alex Tinsley, 'The Reference in Case C-396/11 Radu: When does the Protection of Fundamental Rights Require Non-Execution of a European Arrest Warrant? (2012) *European Criminal Law Review* 3; Fenella Billing, 'The Parallel between Non-Removal of Asylum Seekers and Non-Execution of a European Arrest Warrant on Human Rights Grounds' (2012) *European Criminal Law Review* 2.

[24] See, eg, Valsamis Mitsilegas, 'The Limits of Mutual Trust in Europe's Area of Freedom, Security and Justice: From Automatic Inter-State Cooperation to the Slow Emergence of the Individual' (2012) *Yearbook of European Law* 31. The Author welcomed *NS* as 'the end of automaticity in inter-state cooperation not only as regards the Dublin Regulation, but also as regards cooperative systems in the fields

It is important to highlight, already at this stage, some important differences between *NS* and *Radu*, as they might help to understand the different conclusions reached in the two cases. Of course, the most visible difference concerns the area they refer to: *NS* is an international protection case, while *Radu* regards judicial cooperation in criminal matters. In my view, however, there are two other very relevant divergences. First, the *NS* case concerned an area where EU legislation was already quite developed: indeed, part of the issue at stake was determining whether the persons concerned would be transferred to a Member State where the Common European Asylum System – and more specifically, the Reception Conditions Directive,[25] which forms part of that system – was fully and correctly implemented. The Court concluded that violations of fundamental rights could still take place, notwithstanding the existence of that Directive, and that its incorrect implementation could require a suspension of Dublin transfers, since it affected the CEAS considered as a whole. This conclusion seems to be relevant if we look at the current situation in the field of judicial cooperation in criminal matters, where there now exist numerous directives protecting suspects' procedural rights, which also form a system of some sort – at the time of the *Radu* decision, however, the situation was much more fragmented. Second, and also rather obviously, *NS* concerned a substantive right (freedom from torture and degrading or inhuman treatment) while Mr Radu claimed a violation of his procedural rights (right to a fair trial and specifically, as emerges from the Court's judgment, right to be heard).

III. The Court's Judgment in *Radu*: A Missed Opportunity

In the previous paragraph, I highlighted why the Court of Justice's judgment in *Radu* was awaited with very high expectations. Yet, the Court decided to rephrase the questions addressed to it, restricting them in light of the facts of the individual case, and thus avoided – at least, for the moment – untangling the fundamental issue of the role of human rights in the EAW structure.[26]

The Court moved from an analysis of the facts in the case at hand, where Mr Radu had opposed his surrender by arguing that the issuance of the EAW by the German authorities, without him having been heard, violated his rights under Articles 47 and 48 of the Charter and Article 6 ECHR. The Court consequently

of criminal law and civil law' (making reference to EAW and child return proceedings) – alas, this was not to be the case. Also see Cathryn Costello, *Dublin-case NS/ME: Finally, an End to Blind Trust across the EU?* (Asiel en Migrantenrecht, 2012).

[25] Directive 2013/33/EU of the European Parliament and of the Council of 26 June 2013 laying down standards for the reception of applicants for international protection [2013] OJ L 180/96–116.

[26] In this sense, see also John R Spencer, *Extradition, the European Arrest Warrant and Human Rights* (2013) *Cambridge Law Journal* No 72(2).

rephrased the issue in very limited terms, as a question concerning the need to ensure that the right to be heard, as a part of the rights to a fair trial and of defence, is respected *before* an EAW is issued.[27] It then clarified that the aim of the Framework Decision establishing the EAW is to facilitate and accelerate judicial cooperation, thus contributing to the objective set for the EU to become an area of freedom, security and justice by basing itself on the high degree of confidence which should exist between the Member States. Having reformulated the issue in such terms, and having clarified that the general context is that of creating the AFSJ, the answer of the Court of Justice comes quite easily. Indeed, the Court sticks to its previous position, which it restated numerous times afterwards: the grounds for non-execution of an EAW are exclusively those listed in the Framework Decision. Thus, when an EAW is issued for the purpose of executing a custodial sentence, an alleged infringement of the rights of the defence at trial is a ground for non-execution of the warrant – so much is clear from the amended Article 4a of the Framework Decision. However, in the case of Mr Radu, the EAW had been issued for the purpose of conducting a criminal prosecution; and the fact that the defendant had not been heard by the issuing Court before issuance of the warrant is not listed in the Framework Decision as a possible ground to refuse its execution. This however, in the Court's view, does not imply a violation of Articles 47 and 48 of the Charter. Indeed, an obligation for the issuing authorities to hear the requested person before issuing an EAW would inevitably lead to a failure of the whole system of surrender, since execution of the warrant requires an element of surprise: such an interpretation would prevent the achievement of the AFSJ. In any case, in the Court's view, the right to be heard is fully respected and implemented in the EAW system, since the requested person is entitled, in cases such as the one concerning Mr Radu, to be heard by the executing judicial authority. Thus, the Court concludes that the EAWs against Mr Radu must be executed.

IV. Some Considerations on Mutual Recognition and Mutual Trust, as Interpreted in *Radu*

The *Radu* case has at its heart the difficult relationship between mutual recognition, mutual trust and respect for fundamental rights. The Court, however, decided not to delve into the issue: it avoided ruling on the core points, and thus left the question of the role of fundamental rights within the system of surrender created by the EAW unanswered. Yet, its silence – its reluctance to take a position on this matter – was not without consequences. As several authors have noted, *Radu* made it possible to decide *Melloni*; and *Melloni* followed easily from

[27] *Radu* (n 1), para 31.

Radu, since the latter is essentially a quest for effectiveness and primacy of EU law, to the detriment of case-by-case discretion based on fundamental rights concerns.[28]

Mutual recognition is a traditional tool of EU integration: it allows States that are reluctant to agree on full harmonisation of national substantive and procedural laws to move forward in the direction of easier, speedier cooperation, without requiring too many changes to national rules.[29] In the context of the EU, it was initially developed as a tool to facilitate the establishment of the single market – thus, scholars have questioned the very applicability of this principle, which was meant to facilitate the free movement of goods, to the criminal law field, where the 'goods' whose free circulation is facilitated are judicial decisions affecting fundamental rights.[30] Moreover, when imported into the context of the AFSJ, the concept of mutual recognition undergoes an important transformation. Indeed, this principle has long been instrumental to ensure primacy: the Court of Justice, by affirming the obligation of mutual recognition, has ensured the prevalence of EU norms over national laws. Yet, once it is exported into the context of the AFSJ, the very concept of primacy is transformed: in most cases,[31] the issue becomes 'which branch of EU law should have primacy'? Thus, the Court is called upon to perform a balancing exercise, deciding to what extent the primacy of the Charter, and of the fundamental rights it protects, can be limited by the primacy of the objectives and principles set out in the Treaties (for instance in Article 67 of the Treaty on the Functioning of the European Union (TFEU), which refers to the creation of an AFSJ). Yet, the Court has sometimes tended to give preference to mutual recognition over fundamental rights[32] – seemingly interpreting its role as requiring it to give primacy to mutual recognition tools, which are essential to achieve the objective of creating a single AFSJ with no internal borders, even when they could affect fundamental rights that are also protected by EU primary law. While this is certainly connected

[28] See Leonard Besselink, 'The Parameters of Constitutional Conflict after Melloni (2004) *European Law Review* 39; Paul de Hert, 'EU Criminal Law and Fundamental Rights' in V Mitsilegas et al (eds), *Research Handbook on EU Criminal Law* (Elgar Publishing, 2016); Ermioni Xantopoulou, 'The Quest for Proportionality for the European Arrest Warrant: Fundamental Rights Protection in a Mutual Recognition Environment' (2015) *New Journal of European Criminal Law* 6.

[29] See in particular Valsamis Mitsilegas, 'Mutual Recognition, Mutual Trust and Fundamental Rights after Lisbon' in Mitsilegas et al (n 27); see also Koen Lenaerts, 'The Principle of Mutual Recognition in the Area of Freedom, Security and Justice' (Fourth Annual Sir Jeremy Lever Lecture) at www.law.ox.ac.uk/sites/files/oxlaw/the_principle_of_mutual_recognition_in_the_area_of_freedom_judge_lenaerts.pdf.

[30] Anze Erbeznik, 'The Principle of Mutual Recognition as a Utilitarian Solution, and the Way Forward' (2012) *European Criminal Law Review* 2; Steve Peers, 'Mutual Recognition and Criminal Law in the EU: Has the Council got it Wrong?' (2004) *Common Market Law Review* 41.

[31] With the notable exception of the application of the *ne bis in idem* principle: see Valsamis Mitsilegas, 'The Constitutional Implications of Mutual Recognition in Criminal Matters in the EU' (2006) *Common Market Law Review* 43.

[32] See in particular Wouter Van Ballegooij and Petra Bard, 'Mutual Recognition and Individual Rights – did the Court get it Right?' (2016) *New Journal of European Criminal Law* 7.

to its understanding of mutual trust, it is by no means an exception in the Court's case law on fundamental rights, in particular with regard to their role in the internal market.[33]

Another important aspect to keep in mind is the fact that, once mutual recognition tools evolve and become more and more ambitious, and particularly once they involve the facilitated transfer of persons (be they applicants for international protection under the Dublin regime, abducted children under the Brussels IIa Regulation,[34] or suspects or convicted persons in the criminal law field), mutual recognition requires increasing levels of mutual trust. Indeed, mutual recognition only apparently implies a minimum sacrifice to national sovereignty by requiring each Member State to recognise the decisions of other States, without changes to the national legal order that might be difficult to reconcile with the principle of subsidiarity.[35] This apparently minimalistic approach actually tends to create problems once applied in practice; and such problems originate precisely from the differences and peculiarities of the national legal orders that the principle of mutual recognition is supposed to preserve. This phenomenon was already well known when the concept of mutual recognition was introduced in the area of criminal law, as even in the internal market field, mutual recognition had required minimum harmonisation to function well in practice.[36] Yet, the problem seems to have been further exasperated by the interpretation of mutual trust that the Court of Justice has long endorsed: if mutual trust requires national authorities to assume that foreign decisions have been taken in full respect for fundamental rights, only exceptionally (if ever) allowing them to check the individual circumstances of the case, this eventually requires substantive harmonisation, to ensure that all national authorities have to stick to certain common minimum standards. National courts tend to be reluctant to accept that the very different rules that exist in other European legal systems are as efficient, in terms of ensuring respect for fundamental rights, as their own. Thus, they will find it difficult to apply the

[33] Also see, for instance, the famous *Viking* and *Laval* decisions of the Court, which concerned the right to take collective action as opposed to the freedom to provide services: Case C-438/05 *International Transport Workers' Federation and Finnish Seamen's Union v Viking Line ABP and OÜ Viking Line Eesti* [2007] ECR I-10779; Case C-341/05 *Laval un Partneri Ltd v Svenska Byggnadsarbetareförbundet, Svenska Byggnadsarbetareförbundets avdelning 1, Byggettan and Svenska Elektrikerförbundet* [2007] ECR I-11767. The Court took a traditional internal market approach, finding that the collective actions initiated in the two cases were to be considered as restrictions to free movement rights, and thus presumptively unlawful. It was deemed to be the task of the relevant trade unions to show that the action was proportionate and necessary to protect workers' interests. For this synthesis, see Catherine Barnard, 'The Protection of Fundamental Social Rights in Europe after Lisbon' in S de Vries, U Bernitz and S Weatherill (eds), *The Protection of Fundamental Rights in the EU After Lisbon* (Hart Publishing, 2013).

[34] Council Regulation 2201/2003 concerning jurisdiction and the recognition and enforcement of judgments in matrimonial matters and the matters of parental responsibility, repealing Regulation (EC) No 1347/2000 [2003] OJ L 338/1–29.

[35] See, eg, Erbeznik (n 30); Mitsilegas (n 31); Luisa Marin, 'Effective and Legitimate? Learning from the Lessons of 10 Years of Practice with the European Arrest Warrant' (2014) *New Journal of European Criminal Law* 5.

[36] See Mitsilegas (n 31); also see Commission Communication 'Mutual Recognition of Final Decisions in Criminal Matters' COM(2000) 495 final at 3.1.

presumption that the Court of Justice requires from them without some degree of harmonisation; in some cases, such a presumption could affect fundamental constitutional values and thus lead to a violation of a Member State's national constitutional identity (in breach of Art 4(2) TEU).[37] The Commission itself, in its latest implementation report on the EAW[38] (which dates back to 2011), linked the so-called 'procedural rights' package to the need to facilitate implementation of the EAW by fostering mutual trust.[39] A similar position has been taken by the European Parliament, which in its 2014 Resolution on the mid-term review of the Stockholm Programme, emphasised that mutual trust between the Member States must be strengthened by harmonising fundamental rights compliance in relation to criminal procedures and taking common measures to ensure the proper administration of justice and prisons.[40] National and EU institutions are fully aware that mutual trust is a goal that must be patiently pursued, and numerous programmes and measures are in place to foster mutual trust: from harmonisation of procedural laws to judicial training and judicial exchanges and networks.[41] Yet, the legal consequences of referring to mutual recognition as a tool for the construction of the AFSJ[42] seem to have been under-explored before the concept was exported to the area of criminal law.

Another essential element of the Court's decision in *Radu* is its reasoning in regards to the relationship between mutual trust and fundamental rights in the context of the AFSJ. The basic idea is that mutual trust is essential to achieve the objective of the EU becoming an AFSJ; as a consequence, anything that would

[37] See, eg, Erbeznik (n 30) cited above; Mitsilegas (n 31).

[38] 11 April 2011 Report from the Commission to the European Parliament and the Council 'On the implementation since 2007 of the Council Framework Decision of 13 June 2002 on the European arrest warrant and the surrender procedures between Member States' COM(2011) 175 final.

[39] The procedural rights package includes: Directive 2010/64/EU on the right to interpretation and translation in criminal proceedings [2010] OJ L 280/1–7; Directive 2012/13/EU on the right to information in criminal proceedings [2012] OJ L 142/1–10; Directive 2013/48/EU on the right of access to a lawyer and the right to communicate upon arrest [2013] OJ L 294/1–12; Directive 2016/343/EU on the strengthening of the presumption of innocence and of the right to be present at trial [2016] OJ L 65/1–11; Directive 2016/800/EU on procedural safeguards for children who are suspects or accused persons [2016] OJ L 132/1–20; and Directive 2016/1919/EU on legal aid for suspects and accused persons, and for requested persons in EAW proceedings [2016] OJ L 297/1–8.

[40] See European Parliament Resolution of 2 April 2014 on the mid-term review of the Stockholm Programme (2013/2024(INI)).

[41] See *ibid*, stressing that 'the development of a European judicial culture is a key prerequisite for making the area of freedom, security and justice a reality' and calling for much greater emphasis on, and funding for, EU judicial training for all legal professionals. On the importance of judicial training in terms of building mutual trust, also see the Commission Communication 'Building trust in EU-wide justice – a new dimension to European judicial training' COM/2011/0551 final; the Council conclusions of 27 and 28 October 2011 on European judicial training; the European Parliament Resolution of 14 March 2012 on judicial training; and Regulation (EU) No 1382/2013 of 17 December 2013 establishing a Justice Programme for the period 2014 to 2020 [2013] OJ L/354 73–83.

[42] The reference was made for the first time during the 1999 Tampere meeting, where the European Council endorsed the principle of mutual recognition as 'the cornerstone of judicial co-operation in both civil and criminal matters within the Union'; see the Presidency conclusions of the Tampere European Council of 15 and 16 October 1999.

allow questioning it could be seen as a threat to the AFSJ, and ultimately to the EU. This reasoning was more explicit in *NS* – where the Court allowed for some level of distrust, in the form of refusals to transfer, but did so very cautiously and set a very high threshold in terms of fundamental rights violations before a national authority is entitled to refuse a Dublin transfer. In the Court's own words in *NS*,

> at issue here is the *raison d'être* of the European Union and the creation of an area of freedom, security and justice and, in particular, the Common European Asylum System, based on mutual confidence and a presumption of compliance, by other Member States, with European Union law and, in particular, fundamental rights.

Thus having defined the context, the decision to set a very high threshold of violations of fundamental rights – which must appear to be *systemic* – before a national authority can refuse a Dublin transfer is only logic. Yet, this reasoning appears to be somewhat curious if we look at it from the perspective of classic fundamental rights scrutiny: were it possible to justify a single violation of fundamental rights based on the greater good of whichever political objective a democratic community has given itself, then fundamental rights would be built on very weak foundations.

The Court's reasoning on this point has been clarified – and limited – in some of its more recent decisions, such as the 2017 *CK* judgment[43] in the asylum field and the 2016 *Aranyosi and Căldăraru*[44] decision in the EAW field. Yet, its persistence over the years has had some very important consequences, in particular on the relationship between the EU and the ECtHR.

V. A Few Considerations on *Radu's* Impact over the Relationship between the EU and the ECtHR

The longstanding Court's interpretation of the principle of mutual trust as requiring a very strong – and almost conclusive – presumption that all EU Member States comply with fundamental rights, lies at the basis of another fundamental decision of the Court: Opinion 2/13. The Opinion blocked the EU's accession to the ECHR, and has already been extensively commented on.[45] In the context of the present

[43] Case C-578/16 PPU *CK. and Others v Republika Slovenija* [2017] ECR.

[44] *Aranyosi and Căldăraru* (n 7).

[45] See, among others, Steve Peers, 'The EU's Accession to the ECHR: The Dream Becomes a Nightmare' (2015) *German Law Journal* 16(1), available from www.germanlawjournal.com/volume-16-no-01; Vladimiro Zagrebelsky, *L'UE e il controllo esterno della protezione dei diritti e delle libertà fondamentali in Europa. La barriera elevata dalla Corte di Giustizia*, Diritti Umani e Diritto Internazionale No 9(1) (Bologna, Il Mulino, 2015); Leonard FM Besselink, 'Acceding to the ECHR notwithstanding the Court of Justice Opinion 2/13' (*Verfassungsblog*, 2014), available at https://verfassungsblog.de/acceding-echr-notwithstanding-court-justice-opinion-213-2/; and the papers published in Sejla Imamovic, Monica Claes and Bruno De Witte, 'The EU Fundamental Rights Landscape after Opinion 2/13' (Maastricht Faculty of Law Working Paper 2016/6). On a less critical note, see, eg, Daniel Halberstam, '"It's the

contribution, it seems sufficient to recall that the Court identified the principle of mutual trust as one of the most important obstacles to the EU's ratification of the draft agreement. More specifically, the Court noted that the principle of mutual trust is of fundamental importance in EU law, since it allows the creation of an area without internal borders by requiring – particularly in the AFSJ – each of the Member States to consider all the other Member States to be complying with EU law, including fundamental rights. Only exceptionally are Member States allowed to check whether another Member State has actually, in a specific case, observed such fundamental rights. The Court furthermore stressed that the Member States, by reason of their membership of the EU, have accepted that relations between them as regards matters covered by the transfer of powers from the States to the EU are governed by EU law – to the exclusion, if EU law so requires, of any other law. Yet, accession to the ECHR under the draft agreement would have required considering the EU, and its Member States, as contracting parties not only in their relations with non-EU parties to the ECHR, but also between themselves, requiring them to check that other Member States have observed fundamental rights even when EU law imposes an obligation of mutual trust. Consequently, the Court declared accession to be liable to undermine the autonomy of EU law.[46]

The Court's decision in *Radu* has often come up in the discussions that followed the adoption of Opinion 2/13, particularly as regards the role of mutual trust within the legal order of the EU. For instance, the Deputy Grand Chamber Registrar of the Strasbourg Court, writing about EU accession,[47] stressed that the focus of the recent case law of the CJEU as regards fundamental rights has been mostly on the autonomy of EU law. According to this Author, the Court has an efficiency-oriented thinking, which tends not to take fundamental rights, but the smooth functioning of EU mechanisms (be they mutual recognition or return mechanisms) as the starting point of the balancing exercise that is typical of fundamental rights adjudication. *Radu* is cited in this context, and for good reason: the idea that the right to be heard can be observed in the executing Member State, so as not to compromise the effectiveness of the EAW, is indeed very efficiency-oriented. While the Court's conclusion in *Radu* is very sensible, and may well be the only reasonable one, the issue remains why it decided to answer a different, and much more limited, question than the one that the referring Court had asked. *Radu* (and *NS* as well) have thus been contextualised as examples of an approach according to which fundamental rights can and should be adapted to broader

Autonomy, Stupid!" A Modest Defense of Opinion 2/13 on EU Accession to the ECHR, and the Way Forward' (2015) *German Law Journal* 16(1), available from www.germanlawjournal.com/volume-16-no-01; Jean Paul Jacqué, 'Non à l'adhésion à la Convention européenne des droits de l'homme?' (*Droit de l'Union europeenne*, 2014), available at www.droit-union-europeenne.be/412337458; Catherine Barnard, 'Opinion 2/13 on EU Accession to the ECHR: Looking for the Silver Lining' (EU Law Analysis, 2015), available at http://eulawanalysis.blogspot.it/2015/02/opinion-213-on-eu-accession-to-echr.html.

[46] See in particular paras 191 *ff* of Opinion 2/13 (n 8).

[47] See Johan Callewaert, 'Is EU Accession Still a Good Idea?' in Imamovic, Claes and De Witte (n 45).

objectives, so that their impact can be limited to preserve the efficiency of some other mechanism (such as mutual recognition), to the detriment of the attention that can be paid to specific situations of individual hardship.

Of course, this is not the only possible reading of Opinion 2/13: some authors have given it a more generous interpretation, and recently the CJEU's President himself has offered a reading of mutual trust, in the light not only of the Opinion but also of subsequent decisions such as *CK* and *Aranyosi*, as a constitutional principle which does not, however, need to be absolute nor 'blind'.[48] Yet, accession to the ECHR is currently still blocked, and one of the most prominent reasons for this is the role that the CJEU has given to the autonomy of the EU legal order, and to the principle of mutual trust, over the obligation to accede to the ECHR under Article 6 TEU – a role that had begun to emerge in the *Radu* judgment.

VI. Some Comments on *Radu*'s Impact over the EAW System and the Subsequent Development of Criminal Law Tools

Another long-lasting consequence of *Radu*, and of the case law that immediately followed it, has been a persistent call for the inclusion of a fundamental rights clause in the EAW. Such a clause has been included in the European Investigation Order (EIO) – an instrument that is meant to be much less intrusive than the EAW, since it does not directly affect a person's liberty, but merely aims to facilitate the obtaining and transferring of evidence between the Member States.[49] This inclusion, however, happened for a reason: the Lisbon Treaty had in the meantime entered into force, and the European Parliament acted, in the adoption of the EIO, as a full co-legislator. Indeed, the original proposal for the EIO was also rather laconic as regards human rights: its Article 1(3) contained the only reference, in the text of the Directive, to fundamental rights, and was only slightly more detailed than Article 1(3) of the EAW Framework Decision.[50] However, the Draft Report adopted by the European Parliament's Committee for Civil Liberties, Justice and Home Affairs (LIBE) as a negotiating mandate to be followed during the so-called trilogues between Parliament and Council included numerous references to fundamental rights – including as a ground for refusal to

[48] See Koen Lenaerts, 'La vie après l'avis: Exploring the Principle of Mutual (yet not Blind) Trust' (2017) *Common Market Law Review* 54(3).

[49] Directive 2014/41/EU of the European Parliament and of the Council of 3 April 2014 regarding the European Investigation Order in criminal matters [2014] OJ L 130/1–36.

[50] See Initiative of the Kingdom of Belgium, the Republic of Bulgaria, the Republic of Estonia, the Kingdom of Spain, the Republic of Austria, the Republic of Slovenia and the Kingdom of Sweden for a Directive of the European Parliament and of the Council of regarding the European Investigation Order in criminal matters.

execute an EIO.[51] From this perspective, we must keep in mind that the EAW is an old third pillar instrument, adopted by governments alone, soon after 9/11 – fundamental rights were definitely not at its core. Since *Radu*, however, scholars and the European Parliament have repeatedly called for the inclusion of a ground for non-execution based on fundamental rights concerns.[52] In particular, in 2014 Parliament adopted a Resolution calling on the Commission to reform the EAW, inter alia by introducing a proportionality check (to avoid use of the EAW for petty crimes) and by providing for a mandatory refusal ground

> where there are substantial grounds to believe that the execution of the measure would be incompatible with the executing Member State's obligation in accordance with Article 6 of the TEU and the Charter, notably Article 52(1) thereof with its reference to the principle of proportionality.[53]

The idea at the basis of this call is that national courts should be allowed to refuse the execution of an EAW if they have serious doubts as regards the issuing authority's respect for the basic fundamental rights of the person concerned.

This call on the part of the European Parliament was met with little enthusiasm in the European Commission: in its follow-up to the Resolution,[54] the Commission expressly stated that it did not share the view that a revision of the Framework Decision was necessary. According to the European executive, the (at the time) ongoing work on providing common minimum standards of procedural rights would sufficiently improve the context of mutual recognition instruments by ensuring respect for fundamental rights.[55] In the words of the Commission,

> this work on procedural rights minimum standards is the best approach to finding the right balance in the European arrest warrant system between the essential adherence to fundamental rights and the key principle of mutual recognition. […] This approach is more effective than re-opening the European arrest warrant legislation to insert an explicit refusal ground on the basis of fundamental rights that will have to be considered in each case. Such an approach has the potential to undermine the principle of mutual recognition. It is not warranted in circumstances where the primacy of fundamental rights is already underlined in Article 1.3 of the Framework Decision. As the Commission set out in its 2011 implementation report, a refusal is possible on fundamental rights grounds in exceptional cases.

[51] Indeed, Article 11(1)(f) of Directive 2014/41/EU reproduces, word by word, an identical amendment which had been inserted in the European Parliament's Report: thus, execution of the EIO may be refused when 'there are substantial grounds to believe that the execution of the investigative measure indicated in the EIO would be incompatible with the executing State's obligations in accordance with Article 6 TEU and the Charter'.

[52] See, eg, Anagnostopoulos (n 2).

[53] European Parliament Resolution of 27 February 2014 with recommendations to the Commission on the review of the European Arrest Warrant, adopted following the legislative initiative procedure.

[54] Adopted on 28 May 2014 and available from www.europarl.europa.eu/oeil/spdoc.do?i=24051&j=0&l=en.

[55] The so-called 'procedural rights packages' were meant as tools to facilitate mutual trust, and thus mutual recognition, by increasing and harmonising the level of protection of the rights granted to a suspect or accused before and during trial. A list of the relevant directives can be found at n 39.

On the other hand, the Commission 'agrees with the Parliament's focus on the importance of direct contacts and consultation between judicial authorities, training, networking and access to reliable information'. Given the role of the Commission in putting forward legislative initiatives, its position means that no revision of the EAW can be expected to take place in the near future. It is interesting to note that the Commission has based its position on its own interpretation of Article 1(3) of the Framework Decision: its follow up document does not even acknowledge the possibility (and even less, the actual existence) of a different interpretation of that clause. The European Parliament has not, however, lost interest, and calls to reform the EAW by including a proportionality test and a fundamental rights exception have been reiterated during the current legislature.[56] Yet, for the moment, nothing is expected on this side.

VII. A Final Thought – Does the *Aranyosi* Case Change it All?

The last question that seems to arise is whether the recent judgment in *Aranyosi and Căldăraru* fundamentally changes the situation. On the one hand, we could argue that it does – the Court of Justice has finally reconsidered the presumption of fundamental rights compliance between Member States, admitting that in some cases, execution of an EAW might be refused based on fundamental rights concerns. Yet, what remains to be seen is whether this same line of reasoning will also apply when the fundamental rights at stake are of a procedural nature – the most recent *LM* judgment only partially answers this question, given the very specific context in which it was given (that of a Member State where the independence and impartiality of the judiciary are no longer guaranteed).[57]

In *Aranyosi and Căldăraru*, the question was one of compliance with Article 4 of the Charter (and Article 3 of the ECHR). The idea that a Member State cannot transfer a person to another State where he or she would be at risk of inhuman or degrading treatment is a very well-established principle of European and international law, both in the asylum context (where it's known as *non-refoulement*) and in the context of criminal law (since at least the *Soering* case). In such cases, the general understanding is that if a State transfers a person without sufficient fundamental rights guarantees, and by doing so allows another State to torture or

[56] See, eg, European Parliament Resolution of 16 September 2015 on the Commission Work Programme 2016 (2015/2729(RSP)); European Parliament Resolution of 8 September 2015 on the situation of fundamental rights in the European Union (2013–2014) (2014/2254(INI)); European Parliament Resolution of 13 December 2016 on the situation of fundamental rights in the European Union in 2015 (2016/2009(INI)).

[57] *LM* (n 7). In this case, the Court has found that breaches of the right to a fair trial might lead to non-execution of a EAW, but only if they affect the essence of that right – thus the questions shift to which breaches of the right to a fair trial affect its core, and which ones are instead to be tolerated.

mistreat the person, the first State is complicit with the second in the ill-treatment. The *NS* case itself was based on this same fundamental principle: in a way, we could say that the high hopes it had raised for the criminal law field have finally been met once the Court has been called to resolve a truly similar case, that of *Aranyosi and Căldăraru*, which concerned detention conditions. In the latter case, the Court established a less stringent standard that national judicial authorities must follow to decide whether to execute a EAW: there is no need to prove a *systemic* violation of fundamental rights (as per *NS*), but it is essential to determine that there are *substantial grounds to believe* that the individual concerned by a warrant will be exposed, because of his detention conditions, to *a real risk* of inhuman or degrading treatment. Such a determination must be based on objective, reliable, specific and properly updated evidence as regards detention conditions in the issuing Member State, which are demonstrated to be deficient, either in a systematic or generalised manner or for specific groups of people or places of detention. If that is the case, it is essential to determine whether, in the particular circumstances of the case, there are substantial grounds to believe that the individual concerned, once surrendered, will run a real risk of being subject to inhuman or degrading treatment; to this aim, reassurances must be sought from the issuing Member State, but if the existence of the risk cannot be discounted, execution of the warrant must be suspended or terminated.

The question remains whether this evolution of the Court's interpretation of mutual trust in case of potential breaches of Article 4 of the Charter says anything about a completely different set of cases – those concerning respect for the right to a fair trial, such as *Radu* or *Melloni*. In the recent *LM* case, the Court held – for the first time – that a breach of the right to a fair trial can, in exceptional circumstances, lead to a refusal to execute an individual EAW. Clearly, the case is too context-specific to allow drawing general conclusions from it, since it stems from the well-known problem of the independence of the judiciary in Poland.[58] Thus, what remains to be seen is whether the *LM* ruling will influence decisions to be taken in less extraordinary contexts; and, ultimately, which of the components of the right to a fair trial, apart from the independence of the judiciary, are part of its *essence*, and can thus justify – in the eyes of the CJEU – a decision to postpone or refuse execution of a EAW.[59]

[58] Which led the European Commission to adopt, for the first time, a Reasoned Proposal in accordance with Article 7(1) TEU with regard to respect for the rule of law in Poland: see COM(2017)835 final.

[59] As stressed by AG Tanchev in his Opinion in the *LM* case, the case law of the ECtHR provides some guidance on this point. Indeed, the first case where the Court found that a flagrant denial of justice could require suspension of an extradition procedure was *Othman (Abu Qatada) v the United Kingdom* [2012] ECHR I 159), where it found that use at trial of evidence obtained by torture constitutes such a denial of justice. Subsequently, the Court has taken another three similar decisions, in which it also held that trial by a commission which is neither independent nor impartial would amount to a serious breach of the right to a fair trial, since such a commission cannot be considered to be a tribunal (24 July 2014, *Al Nashiri v Poland* [2014] not published).

The Implication of Radu *at a National Level: National Courts' Diversified Response to Conflicting Obligations*

IRENE WIECZOREK

I. Introduction

In a context of legal pluralism, where nation states are subject to different national and international obligations, national courts can frequently find themselves in the challenging position of having to simultaneously comply with potentially conflicting obligations. This is particularly the case for EU Member States' courts in the field of criminal justice. On the one hand, national courts have to comply with EU law obligations, stemming from the European Arrest Warrant (EAW) Framework Decision (FD) which imposes surrender of suspects and offenders. On the other hand, they are also bound by international law and national constitutional law fundamental rights obligations of protecting individuals from inhuman and degrading treatment. A national court might consider that automatically surrendering a suspect to a foreign authority, as imposed by the EAW, might endanger this person's fundamental rights as protected by the national constitution and the European Convention on Human Rights and Fundamental Freedoms (ECHR). In this case, EU law and national constitutional law, as well as international law obligations appear to conflict. This naturally poses a problem for the national judge which is meant to comply with both.

The problem of conflicting obligations for national courts was raised from the start during the EAW implementation phase. Integrating the new simplified surrender procedure into national legal orders had proven fairly cumbersome as is well illustrated by the number of constitutional courts' decisions on EAW national implementation laws.[1] The respect of fundamental rights, arguably at risk when executing EAWs, was one of the issues raised before national

[1] Elbeth Guild and Luisa Marin (eds), *Still not Resolved? Constitutional Challenges to the European Arrest Warrant* (Wolf Legal Publishers, 2009).

supreme or constitutional courts.[2] Moreover, more than one national legislator has incorporated a specific fundamental rights-based ground for refusal in the relevant national law.[3] The operational functioning of the EAW has then illustrated how national courts routinely face such tensions between conflicting mutual recognition obligations and fundamental rights obligations.

In a spirit of judicial cooperation, national courts have repeatedly brought the issue to the attention of the Court of Justice of the European Union (CJEU).[4] *Radu* is the first of these cases which poses the question in a very explicit manner.[5] As illustrated in the previous commentary,[6] the referral of the Romanian Appeal Court in Constanta first included a number of questions which were specific to the fundamental rights allegedly involved in the case (the right to a fair trial and the right to liberty). Second, the Court also asked more generally if national courts are meant to execute EAWs if this would put the fundamental rights of the concerned individual in danger. The CJEU discarded the potential violations of the specific fundamental rights in the specific case, and did not address the general question.[7]

In the following *Melloni* case, where the Spanish Constitutional Tribunal had addressed a similar set of questions to the CJEU, the Court made its position clearer by clarifying that the instrument for the resolution of the conflict was primacy.[8] EU law obligations, as those stemming from the EAW, were of prime importance over obligations coming from other sources of law.[9] Since then, the position of the European Court has remained relatively consistent on this point.[10]

[2] Respect of fundamental rights in the executing state was an issue raised in the decision of the German Constitutional Court, 18 July 2005, Decision 2 BVR 2236/04, see para 78–84, respect of the principle of legality in particular was raised before the Czech Constitutional Court and discussed in the decision of, 3 May 2006, Decision No Pl. 66/04, para 101, and before the Hungarian Constitutional Court, in the decision of, 8 March 2008, Decision n 733/A/2007.

[3] See section II, para 3 below.

[4] Preliminary ruling requests in *Radu*, *Melloni* and *West* to a certain extent. *Jeremy F*, *Lanigan* and *Aranyosi and Caldararu* all highlight the difficulties encountered by national courts in executing EAWss, while living up to national and international fundamental rights obligations. CJEU, C-396/11 *Ciprian Vasile Radu* [2013] ECR I; CJEU, C-399/11 *Stefano Melloni v Ministero Fiscal*; CJEU, C-192/12 PPU *Melvin West*. CJEU, C-168/13 PPU *Jeremy F v Premier Ministre*; CJEU, Case C-237/15 PPU *Minister for Justice and Equality v Francis Lanigan*; CJEU, Joined Cases C-404/15 and C-659/15 PPU *Pál Aranyosi and Robert Căldăraru v Generalstaatsanwaltschaft.*

[5] Admittedly, the case of *Advocaten voor de Wereld* had already raised the question of compatibility between the EAW and fundamental rights, in particular the principle of legality. However, this case was an annulment decision, and did not concern a specific, concrete case involving a national court. CJEU, C-303/05 *Advocaten voor de Wereld VZW v Leden van de Ministerraad.*

[6] See Rosa Raffaelli's commentary in the first part of this chapter.

[7] *Ibid.*

[8] *Ibid.*

[9] It should be noted that in *Melloni* (n 4) the Court opens up in principle by not rejecting from the outset the possibility of limiting mutual trust in favour of a more extensive protection of human rights, this is however conditional to the fact that the effectiveness of a uniform application of EU law is not jeopardised.

[10] *Jeremy F* (n 4) is another example of a case in which the Court addressed the problem of respect of fundamental rights within the Arrest Warrants procedures. In this context, the Court reiterated the *Melloni* proviso, and allowed for the application of a higher standard of legal protection in principle. It should be noted nevertheless that this case did not involve any distrust towards a foreign judicial system.

A limited amendment of the CJEU doctrine can be appreciated in later case law, such as in *Aranyosi and Caldararu*, but only when particularly serious violations of absolute fundamental rights are involved. If torture or inhuman degrading treatments are at stake, national authorities can suspend surrender procedures.[11] Scholars have speculated on the extent of this mini-revolution in the case law of the Court, and especially if the ruling in *Aranyosi and Caldararu* can be extended to other fundamental rights, eg the right to fair trial, or maybe the right to liberty.[12] The Court has still to express itself on this point. Thus, as per existing case law, outside the specific case of serious violation of absolute fundamental rights, the rule in case of conflict between EU law and national or international fundamental rights obligations remains that expressed in *Radu*, and later *Melloni*.

This chapter investigates how national courts have interpreted and applied the European Court's proviso in *Radu* (and *Melloni*) on how to address the problem of conflict between EAW and fundamental rights. It focuses first on the judicial follow-up in Romania to the *Radu* CJEU ruling. It then speaks more broadly of the approach of national courts to the question of conflicting obligations stemming from the EAW and fundamental rights legal obligations. The chapter aims to highlight the diversity in approach of the national courts.

II. The Implementation of the CJEU *Radu* Ruling by Romanian Courts

The Romanian courts gave diverse interpretations of the CJEU ruling in the *Radu* case.[13] Before digging into the implementation of the European ruling it should be noted that Mr Radu had first invoked an exception of unconstitutionality before the Romanian Constitutional Court, lamenting that the EAW implementing decision was in breach of the constitutional provision on pre-trial detention (Art 23(5) of the Romanian Constitution) and on fair trial (Art 24(1)), as well as the relevant norms of the ECHR, notably Art 6(3) on fair trial. The aspects which he saw as problematic were the reduced room for the executing judge for checking the actual charges against the requested person, and its duty to limit itself to the form and

[11] See the commentaries in chapter 15 on *Aranyosi and Caldararu*.

[12] See, *inter alia*, Emmanuelle Bribosia et Anne Weyembergh, 'L'arrêt de la CJUE du 5 avril 2016, Aranyosi et Caldararu: imposition de certaines limites à la confiance mutuelle dans la coopération judiciaire pénale' 6 (2016) *Journal de droit européen* 225. Georgios Anagnostaras, 'Mutual confidence is not blind trust! Fundamental Rights Protection and the Execution of the European Arrest Warrant: Aranyosi and Caldararu' (2016) 53(6) *Common Market Law Review* 1675.

[13] National case law is reported in detail in the project 'European Judicial Cooperation in the Fundamental Rights Practice of National Courts – the Unexplored Potential of Judicial Dialogue Methodology (JUDCOOP). See the project database at www.eui.eu/Projects/CentreForJudicialCooperation/Projects/EuropeanJudicialCooperationinFR/Europeanjudicialcooperationinthefundamentalrightspractice.aspx.

the content of the warrant. The Constitutional Court was then confronted with the core question of how to solve the potential clash between mutual trust and mutual recognition, and the respect of fundamental rights. The Romanian Court gave a very EU law-oriented response. It insisted that the oversight on the judicial decision giving rise to the EAW remains with the issuing State, and that holding otherwise would run against the principle of mutual recognition.[14]

As is known, the Appeal Court of Constanta then asked a reference to the CJEU, enquiring into the compatibility of surrender with fundamental rights. The latter Court focused on the specific fundamental rights – allegedly – at stake, namely the right to be heard before being arrested and surrendered, and it ruled out that an EAW could not be refused on these grounds.

Very interestingly, the Court of Appeal of Constanta took a different view than the European Court, and it refused surrender.[15] One of the warrants was refused on *ne bis in idem* grounds. As for the other warrants, the Court considered that the application of the EAW FD had to be in compliance with Article 6 on the Treaty on European Union (TEU) and with the Charter of Fundamental Rights. From this it concluded that surrender can be in some exceptional cases refused, even if this is neither included among the grounds for refusal included in the FD, *nor* in national implementing legislation. Risk of failure to respect the concerned person's fundamental rights was one of these exceptional situations, according to the Romanian Court. In the specific case, the Court held that surrender would disproportionately compress Mr Radu's right to private life, as well as his right to liberty. The Court also made an argument related to rehabilitation. It claimed that being tried by a Romanian Court, and especially serving his sentence in Romania would have allowed Mr Radu to maintain a relationship with his family.

The decision of the Court of Appeal was further appealed in the Court of Cassation. The Supreme Court sided this time with the Romanian Constitutional Court and upheld the CJEU decision.[16] It gave precedence to the principle of mutual recognition and ordered surrender, but for the arrest warrant for which the *ne bis in idem* was applicable. Furthermore, it observed that the restrictions of fundamental rights were anyway proportionate, considering the seriousness of the offences Mr Radu was accused of. Surrender was nonetheless subject to the condition that Mr Radu could serve his sentence in Romania if found guilty.

The judicial follow-up to the *Radu* case at the national level is interesting for at least two reasons. First, the different decisions taken by the various Romanian courts show that the dialogue on the primacy of EU law is not only a national versus

[14] Romanian Constitutional Court, 14 October 2010, Decision no 1290.

[15] Remarkably, the reasoning of the Romanian Court is more in line with the Opinion of Advocate General Sharpston, which had recognised the need to leave it to national courts to exceptionally refuse surrender when there was a risk of human rights violation, explicitly answering the Romanian Court's question, which the Court then decided to ignore *Radu* (n 4) Opinion of AG Sharpston.

[16] Romanian Court of Cassation, decision of 17 July 2013, no 2372.

supranational one. National courts do not constitute a uniform block. Conversely, the debate on how to address the question of conflicting obligations bearing on national courts is also the object of an *internal* judicial vertical dialogue.

Second, it is worth reflecting on the reason for the National Court's disregard of the CJEU ruling. It was observed that newer EU members, such as Romania, have been members of the Council of Europe for longer than they have been of the European Union. As a consequence, they might be more sensitive to ECHR fundamental fights obligations than they might be to general EU law ones.

The inexperience of the Romanian referring Court with EU law matters is arguably evident in the breadth and the general tone of the questions which pertain to the relation between EU and ECHR law.[17] This might explain the heightened sensitivity of the Romanian Appeal Court to fundamental rights-based arguments.[18]

It was also observed that countries such as Romania and Bulgaria have often made the object of decision by the Strasbourg Court with respect to, among others, their criminal justice system. This would have arguably made at least Romanian judges particularly cautious when fundamental rights arguments are raised, not only as a matter of tradition, but also instrumentally, so as to avoid further pronounces from the European Court of Human Rights (ECtHR).[19] Incidentally, attempting to avoid further Strasbourg decisions might also be one of the reasons behind the long length and degree of detail in Romanian judicial decisions. Long and detailed explanations would have the objective of providing a sound account for any possible restriction of fundamental rights.[20]

III. National Courts Diversified Solutions to Conflicting Obligations

As stated, the Appeal Court of Constanta in Radu pointed to a very practical issue linked to the implementation in practice of the EAW FD, namely the discretion of the executing State's judges in refusing surrender. What for the Luxemburg Court seemed a pretty straightforward issue, exhaustively dealt with within the listed ground for refusal in the text of the FD itself, has led in practice to very diversified interpretations.

[17] See in particular the first question raised by the National Court, ie which provisions should be considered provisions of EU primary law? The inexperience of the Romanian Court is highlighted in Madalina Moraru, 'Mutual Trust' from the Perspective of National Courts. A Test in Creative Legal Thinking' in Evelien Brouwer and Damien Gerard (eds), Mapping Mutual Trust: Understanding and Framing the Role of Mutual Trust in EU Law, EUI Working Papers, MWP 2016/13 37, 51.

[18] *Ibid.*

[19] *Ibid.*

[20] This observation was raised by Romanian judges at the ERA Conference, 'Alternative to Detention in the EU', 23–24 February, Bucharest.

There are certainly national courts which have proven a very compliant understanding of mutual recognition and mutual trust. The good functioning of the EAW since its adoption attests to this.[21] In a large number of cases, mutual trust seems to work very well, and surrender is authorised. Moreover, in some cases in which surrender would lead to legal problems, several national courts have decided to adopt the very strict CJEU understanding of the duty of mutual recognition, favouring consistent application of EU law over national fundamental rights standards. Examples of this compliant interpretation are discussed in the following paragraph.

Nevertheless, this is only part of the picture, as national courts have also shown less cooperative behaviour. They have in some cases refused surrender on fundamental rights grounds, or they have allowed surrender, but not after having checked further grounds for refusal which are not included in the FD, without referring any request to the Court of Justice. Three different scenarios can be identified. First, there are exceptional cases in which surrender is refused for very understandable reasons, in cases which the FD arguably did not simply foresee and therefore did not regulate upon. Second, there are cases in which further grounds for refusal were envisaged in national legislation, and courts thus disregard their mutual recognition duties due to national ordinary law obligations. Third, there are scenarios in which national courts still reject surrender in cases in which neither the FD or the relevant implementation law envisage any specific ground for refusal, on fundamental rights and related proportionality grounds. Examples for these three scenarios are discussed in the next subsections below.

A. EU law Compliant Interpretation of Mutual Recognition Duties

The Romanian Constitutional and Supreme Court's decisions in the *Radu* case have already been mentioned as examples of interpretation of mutual recognition duties compliant with EU law. To these one could add, by way of example, the decision of the Spanish Constitutional Court in the *Melloni* case.[22] In the referral order the Spanish Constitutional Court had enquired into whether it could maintain its constitutional doctrine of 'indirect violation of fundamental rights' in procedures involving EAWs. Briefly, the latter implies that Spanish authorities giving effect to

[21] See the summaries of the various implementation reports, which define the EAW as a 'success story', summarised in Anne Weyembergh, Chloé Briere and Ines Armada, 'European Added Value Assessment The EU Arrest Warrant_ANNEX I_Critical Assessment of the Existing European Arrest Warrant Framework Decision' 3, available at http://www.europarl.europa.eu/RegData/etudes/etudes/join/2013/510979/IPOL-JOIN_ET(2013)510979(ANN01)_EN.pdf.

[22] Spanish Constitutional Tribunal, 13 February 2014, Decision no 26/2014. For a comment on the Spanish decision, see Mario Garcia, 'The Spanish Constitutional Court Modifies its Case Law in Response to the CJEU's Melloni Judgment (*European Law Blog*, 2014) available at https://europeanlawblog.eu/tag/case-c-39911-melloni/.

a foreign decision which infringes the 'absolute content' of a fundamental right would 'indirectly' violate the Constitution. In the *Melloni* case the content of the right of fair trial was at stake, which as per Spanish constitutional law included a right to ask for re-trial if tried *in absentia*. Having received an answer in the negative by the CJEU, the Spanish Court opted for modifying its own constitutional doctrine, re-interpreting the right to a fair trial. In particular, it held that, also in light of Strasbourg case law, failure to provide re-trial opportunity, where the decision was rendered *in absentia*, but where the person was actually informed of the trial, does not constitute an absolute violation of the right to fair trial.

While the outcome is the same – full compliance with the EU ruling – it is worth mentioning that the judicial strategy of the Romanian and Spanish courts was qualified as slightly different. The first, the Romanian constitutional and supreme courts, embrace the EU doctrine without questioning it, and it was referred as adopting '(EU) strict conforming behaviour'.[23] The Spanish Court on the contrary first attempted to convince the European Court of its own doctrine of conviction *in absentia*, thus challenging the EU approach, and only after having received a negative answer, decided to comply with the European Court's doctrine. This was defined as '(EU) challenging but conforming behaviour'.[24]

Interestingly, while not closely related to the question of mutual trust and fundamental rights, a parallel can be made between the Spanish Constitutional Court's approach and the approach taken by the Italian Constitutional Court in *Taricco*. The latter received a negative answer when it attempted to get the European Court to embrace the Italian interpretation of statutes of limitation. Following that, rather than fully disregarding the Court's proviso, it decided to challenge the European Court's position once again, with a second request for a preliminary ruling.[25] The Court of Justice has responded to this dialogue in a conciliatory manner with its decision of 5 December 2017 trying to accommodate EU principles and Italian national constitutional precepts.[26]

B. Refusal of Surrender due to Exceptional Circumstances (Lack of Substantial Basis to the EAW)

Next to the EU law-compliant behaviour of national courts, as mentioned, there are at least three scenarios in which Member States' courts go beyond the mandate the EAW FD entrusts them with. A polish case is a good illustration of the first scenario. This involves national courts refusing surrender on the basis of reasons

[23] Moraru (n 17) 50.

[24] Moraru (n 17) 50.

[25] For a summary of the referral from the Italian Constitutional Court, see Pietro Faraguna, 'The Italian Constitutional Court in re Taricco: "Gauweiler in the Roman Campagna"' (*VerfBlog*, 2017) available at http://verfassungsblog.de/the-italian-constitutional-court-in-re-taricco-gauweiler-in-the-roman-campagna/.

[26] CJEU, C-42/17 *MAS and MB*.

linked to the merits of the case, which, due to exceptional circumstances, they look into, despite the letter of the FD preventing it.

The facts concerned a Polish citizen whose surrender was demanded by German authorities to Polish authorities for the prosecution of a number of financial crimes, including bankruptcy and misappropriation. Surrender was authorised by a first instance court, which following the letter of the EAW FD only looked at the formal aspect of the arrest warrant. The surrender decision was nonetheless appealed, and the Appeal Court quashed the decision underlining that the executing State has the possibility to refuse surrender on substantial grounds, when in possession of information that the issuing Member State did not have.[27] In this context, the Polish Court relied upon a position expressed by the Polish Constitutional Tribunal, which had already mentioned the possibility of including this exceptional ground for refusal.[28] In the case at stake, the requested person was detained in Poland at the time of the facts for which he would have to be prosecuted by German authorities. The Polish Court underlined that even before looking at the formal validity of a EAW, the court in the executing Member State must also look at whether there are any reasons which cast doubt on the basis for a EAW to be issued in the first place.

C. Refusal of Surrender due to National Law-Based Only Grounds for Refusal

An Italian, a German and a set of Greek cases provide interesting examples of the second scenario of 'non-authorised' refusal. This is when refusal was mandated by national legislation, which went further than what the EAW FD allowed for.

Italy, Greece and Germany have all included in their national legislation fundamental rights-related grounds for refusal. The Italian implementing law allows EAW compliance refusal, for instance when surrender might violate the person's right to non-discrimination, right to association, right to expression, or right to a fair trial.[29] In Greek legislation, a specific ground for refusal was inserted concerning the right to non-discrimination.[30] Surrender can be refused if prosecution is motivated by grounds pertaining to reasons of racial, political, sexual orientation and so forth. Finally, German legislation strictly speaking states that a EAW should be considered illegitimate if it contradicts either 'essential principles of the German legal system' or 'overriding legal principles of the EU'.[31]

[27] Wroclaw Appeal Court, 4 February 2014, Decision no II AKz 50/14.

[28] Polish Constitutional Tribunal, 5 October 2010, Decision SK 26/08 (OTK-A 2010, no 8, item 73).

[29] Respectively Art 18(a), Art 18(d), Art 18(g) of Law 69/2005.

[30] Article 11(e)) of Law 3251(2004).

[31] See respectively para 73, ss 1 and 2 of the European Arrest Warrant Act of 20 July 2006 in German Official Journal [*Bundesgesetzblatt*], I (2006), 1721.

These grounds for refusal are often invoked by defendants. They are admittedly seldom successful. Yet, the fact remains that national courts exercise a control on the respect of fundamental rights by the issuing State which, as per the text of the FD, they are not meant to carry out.

In the 2005 Hussain Osman case, the Italian Supreme Court evaluated whether the applicant would suffer violation of fundamental rights, and especially of his right to non-discrimination, once surrendered to the United Kingdom. The Court held on points of law that the relevant ground for refusal should be interpreted very restrictively, and that surrender should be refused only if specific and objective circumstances prove that the right to non-discrimination of the concerned individual would be in danger. On points of fact the Court retained that the mere presence of the liberal tradition of the United Kingdom, as also manifested by the enactment of the 1998 Human Rights Act were sufficient to dispel any doubt as to possible violation of the surrendered person's fundamental rights.[32]

Greek courts were confronted with similar cases. A first example concerned an Arrest Warrant coming from France concerning a member of the Kurdistan Workers Party, who argued that prosecution was politically motivated. His claim was assessed on the merits, but considered not to be supported by the facts.[33] Similar cases concerned warrants issued by Germany, where the defendants claimed that if they were surrendered, they risked being further extradited to Turkey by Germany, where their fundamental rights would be violated. Greek courts once again looked into the actual validity of the claim. In a 2013 case the judges considered that there were reasons to believe the fundamental rights of the person would be at risk, and therefore, authorised surrender but under the condition that the person would not be extradited to Turkey.[34] In a 2014 case the judges found that the claim was not supported by sufficient evidence.[35]

Finally, a 2013 German case of the *Oberlandesgherit* of Munich can also be given as an example of '*EU-unfriendly*' national fundamental rights scrutiny. The case is interesting to the extent that it came shortly after *Radu* and *Melloni* and presents itself as an application of these two rulings. It concerned a warrant issued by Bulgarian authorities for the prosecution of a Bulgarian national accused of drunk driving. The question was raised as to whether the person's fundamental rights were at stake considering that the decision which commutated a probation order into a custodial sanction had been rendered *in absentia*. The German Court acknowledged that the *Radu* and *Melloni* cases prevented national courts from refusing surrender on the basis of higher national constitutional standards, but it claimed that para 73 of the German implementing law – imposing the requirement to check compliance with Art 6 TEU fundamental rights standards – should

[32] Italian Court of Cassation, 13–14 September 2005, Decision no 33642.
[33] *Areios Pagos* (Criminal law division) [Greek Supreme Court], Decision no 801/2015.
[34] *Ibid*, Decision no 1261/2013.
[35] *Ibid*, Decision no 966/2014.

be applied *notwithstanding*.[36] In doing so the Court took quite a bold statement with respect to the relationship between CJEU case law and national ordinary law. The Court continued in a more conciliatory manner attempting to illustrate how applying German law would not be in breach of the EU law obligation. It stated that, according to the German Court's interpretation of the Luxemburg cases, the Court of Justice did not intend to prevent execution of EAWs which are non-compliant with Art 6 TEU fundamental rights. Moreover, the German Court continued, as per established case law, that national law must be interpreted in light of EU norms, to the extent that this does not lead to a *contra legem* interpretation. If the German Court had to disregard para 73 of the implementing law then that would precisely be a case of *contra legem* interpretation. The Munich Court then investigated whether such a risk for the violation of fundamental rights actually exists in the case at hand, and it concluded in the negative.

D. Refusal of Surrender on the Basis of Case Law-Based Grounds for Refusal

The third 'unauthorised surrender scenario' is that of national courts carrying out fundamental rights, or closely related proportionality, checks before surrender, even though this is not established either in the Framework Decision nor explicitly by the national implementing law.

The Romanian Court of Appeal decision has already been mentioned as an example of this approach. Romanian implementing law does not include any fundamental rights-based ground for refusal, or generally proportionality-based grounds for refusal, for that matter. This has not prevented the Court in Constanta from refusing surrender on these grounds, by relying on general EU fundamental rights provisions. In a similar case, another Romanian Court, the Brasov Court of Appeal, also stated that 'it appears, without any doubt, that the execution of the EAW shall be done under the condition that fundamental rights and liberties (…) are respected'.[37] A plausible interpretation of the Romanian courts' particular attention on fundamental rights was suggested above in section II. Nevertheless, similar, special judicial attention to fundamental rights, independent from EU and national EAW-implementing norms can also be appreciated other, older, Member States.

[36] Superior Regional Court Munich, 1st criminal senate general Public Prosecution Office/K order of 15 May 2013 – olg ausl. 31 ausl. a 442/13 (119/13). An English version has been published in (2013) 4(3) *New Journal of European Criminal Law* 310.

[37] Decision No 30/F/N/24 March 2008, 2 Aug 2010, cited in 'The European Arrest Warrant and the Necessary Balance Between Mutual Recognition and Fundamental Rights in the EU' (Institutul National Al Magistraturii), 11.

Other interesting examples are provided by German and Greek courts, which carried out a proportionality assessment, linked in the case in point to fundamental rights aspects, although not explicitly required to do so by national legislation.

A first case of the High Court in Stuttgart concerned a warrant from Spain for drug possession.[38] The Court recalls that in the field of extradition German courts have introduced an obligation to introduce a proportionality test ensuring that the punishment the person would suffer after extradition is not 'intolerably severe'. Such test is to be also applied in EAW cases, also considering that the EU Charter of Fundamental Rights, with which the execution of a EAW must comply, includes the principle of proportionality of sanctions at Article 49(3). The Court specifies that German implementing law does not explicitly include such proportionality test. However, the national arrest warrant which follows the European one is a national act which must be in compliance with German constitutional law that, in turn, requires a proportionality test. Interestingly, the Court maintains that proportionality must exist between the seriousness of the crime and the burden of arrest both for the requested person *and* for the *executing State*. Proportionality is thus not only a matter of fundamental rights in this context. It would be interesting to investigate how an extradition procedure is more onerous than having to prosecute and then possibly to execute the sanction nationally. The Court then looks at the merits of the case and excludes that proportionality was violated in that context. It should be noted, however, that in previous case law, involving a Lithuanian arrest warrant, the outcome of the proportionality test had been the opposite, and surrender had been refused.[39]

A second line of cases are the decisions of the Athens Court of Appeal on the Italian warrants for the protesters in the anti-Expo demonstrations in Milan.[40] The warrants were issued for prosecution of causation of damage and aggravated resistance during demonstration. However, all surrenders were refused on the basis of, among other aspects, failure to comply with the principle of proportionality. Decision 1/2016 in particular recalled that no EAW execution can have as an effect the violation of fundamental rights as enshrined in the EU Treaties and the Greek Constitution.[41] In the specific case, surrender would imply a violation of the principle of proportionality, as the crimes for which the arrest warrant had been issued were punished much more severely in Italy (as felonies) than they would be in Greece (as misdemeanors). The same reasoning is contained in the other four decisions.[42] Decision 3/2016 in particular underlines aspects such as

[38] The case is discussed and summarised in Vogel Joachim, Introduction to the Ruling of the Higher Regional Court of Stuttgart of 25 February 2010 – The Proportionality of a European Arrest Warrant' (2010) 1(2) *New Journal of European Criminal Law* 145.

[39] High Regional Court of Stuttgart, 18 November 2009, Decision 1 ausl. 1302/99.

[40] For full references and a discussion of the cases, see Antonio E Kourotakis, 'The Italian European Arrest Warrants for the Five Greeks Taking Part in Riots and Their Rejection by the Greek Authorities' (2016) 7(3) *New Journal of European Criminal Law* 295.

[41] Athens Court of Appeal, 8 January 2016, Decision no 1/2016.

[42] Athens Court of Appeal, 8 January 2016, Decision no 2/2016, 3/2016, 4/2016, 5/2016.

the gravity of the offence, the length of the sentence, the presence of a less onerous alternative both for the individual and for *the executing State.* In this context, as it was for the German case also, proportionality is thus not only a matter of individual rights.

Kouroutakis observes with reference to these cases that the tension and lack of surrender derived from the lack of harmonisation.[43] Mutual recognition has often been presented as a valid alternative to harmonisation and emphasis has been put on the opposition between mutual recognition and having the facts punished in both jurisdictions. What these cases show is that harmonisation of penalities, or more generally 'understanding of the seriousness of the conducts', can prove equally problematic in practice.

IV. Conclusions

The *Radu* case is a paradigmatic example of how the decisions of national courts act as the test-field in which the challenges of legal pluralism can be best appreciated. Indeed, when a State is integrated into two different international or supranational legal orders, as per the European Union and the Council of Europe, it might be that different conflicting legal obligations stem from membership to both legal orders. It is here where national judges can have the difficult task of reconciling different mandates. The preliminary question the Romanian Court asked the European Court is exactly how to carry out this complex task. As it was shown, the Romanian Court then opted for a different solution than the one suggested by the European Court.

Starting with the *Radu* case, what this commentary has offered is an overview of how national courts have reacted when faced with the same theoretical, but also practical, problem lying at the heart of *Radu* itself. Some courts have followed the European Court's approach which identifies primacy of EU law as a rule of conflict. Some others have conversely given precedence to fundamental rights obligations, in some cases following a national legislative mandate, in others introducing some judge-made tests.

As was anticipated, the European Court of Justice has recently adopted a slightly more sympathetic approach towards national courts' struggles by admitting in *Aranyosi* that in very exceptional circumstances – when there is a concrete risk of inhuman and degrading treatment – EU law obligations can be attenuated. In particular national courts can suspend surrender and ask for further reassurance.[44] It should be mentioned however, that this does not make the task of national courts necessarily much easier. First, as stated already, the one in *Aranyosi*

[43] Kourotakis (n 40).

[44] See the commentaries in chapter 15 on *Aranyosi and Căldăraru.*

is a very slim opening. For all the other cases the rule in *Radu* and *Melloni* remains valid. Second, for those cases which do fall within the *Aranyosi* type of situation, the wording of the Court still remains quite unspecified. National courts would have to identify for instance what 'suspending the surrender' means, and especially through which national legal procedural constructs are used to implement it. The Amsterdam Court of Appeal was recently confronted with this question and decided to consider the request of the Romanian prosecutor as inadmissible on formal procedural grounds.[45]

Finally, it should be noted that the challenges faced by national courts in solving practical cases in a legally pluralist context naturally do not stop at the criminal justice field. Similar problems are seen in other areas of freedom, security and justice policy areas, where mutual recognition also plays a pivotal role, namely asylum law, as well as civil justice. In these cases, as well, different national courts have interpreted and implemented the concept in different ways.[46] This naturally adds further complexity. Different interpretation and implementation of the same concept materialise not only at various national and supranational levels, but also within different national courts depending on the policy area. Yet, it also offers an occasion for legal creativity. This can be a fruitful resource in addressing similar problems, if national and European Courts want to engage in a constructive dialogue and exercise of cross-fertilisation among policy areas.[47]

[45] Amsterdam Court of Appeal, 26 January 2017, 13/751069-16 RK/1510.

[46] See, for instance, the diversified interpretation of mutual trust of different UK courts in the EM (Eritrea) asylum case discussed in Moraru (n 17).

[47] See, for instance, how the Court of Justice has quoted in asylum cases also cases on the EAW, CJEU, C 578/16 PPU *CK, HF, AS v Republika Slovenija*, para 59.

14

C-399/11 – *Melloni*

Melloni: *Primacy versus Rights?*

VALSAMIS MITSILEGAS AND LEANDRO MANCANO

I. Introduction

Few judgments issued by the Court of Justice of the European Union (CJEU) have sparked as much controversy and debate in academia and legal professions as *Melloni* did.[1] The case regarded an Italian national who had been tried and convicted *in absentia* in Italy. The Italian authorities issued a European Arrest Warrant (EAW) to Spain for enforcement purposes. While the EAW Framework Decision (FD)[2] provides that the executing judge may refuse to recognise a EAW when based on a conviction *in absentia*, it also states at Article 4a(1)(a) and (b) that the warrant must be executed where the person concerned: in due time either was summoned in person and thereby informed of the scheduled date and place of the trial which resulted in the decision, or by other means actually received official information of the scheduled date and place of that trial in such a manner that it was unequivocally established that he or she was aware of the scheduled trial; and was informed that a decision may be handed down if he or she does not appear for the trial; or, being aware of the scheduled trial, has given a mandate to a legal counsellor, who was either appointed by the person concerned or by the state, to defend him or her at the trial, and was indeed defended by that counsellor at the trial. Mr Melloni fell under the scope of those exceptions exactly.

[1] Case C-399/11, *Melloni v Ministerio Fiscal* EU:C:2013:107. Among a plethora of contributions on this judgment, see L Besselink, 'The Parameters of Constitutional Conflict after Melloni' (2014) *EL Rev* 39(4), 531–52; A Torres Pérez, '*Melloni* in Three Acts: From Dialogue to Monologue' (2014) 10(02) *European Constitutional Law Review* 308–31; G Cavallone, 'European Arrest Warrant and Fundamental Rights in Decisions Rendered in absentia: The Extent of Union Law in the Case C-399/11 Melloni v. Ministerio Fiscal (2014) *European Criminal Law Review* 19–40; N de Boer, Addressing Rights Divergences under the Charter: *Melloni* (2013) 50 *Common Market Law Review*, 4, 1083–1103.

[2] Council Framework Decision 2002/584/JHA of 13 June 2002 on the European arrest warrant and the surrender procedures between Member States [2002] OJ L190/1, as amended in 2009 by Council Framework Decision 2009/299/JHA with regard to *in absentia* trials.

The right to be present at a trial is traditionally considered part of the right to a fair trial enshrined in the Spanish Constitution. The legal dispute arrived before the Spanish Constitutional Court, which decided to stay the proceedings and raise for the first time a preliminary question to the CJEU. First, the Constitutional Court asked whether Article 4a(1)(a) and (b) precluded the executing judicial authority to subject the surrender to the possibility, for the person concerned, to apply for a retrial in the issuing Member State. Second, the CJEU was asked as to whether Article 4a(1) is compatible with Articles 47 and Article 48 of the EU Charter of Fundamental Rights (Charter or CFREU).[3] Third, in case of an affirmative answer to the second question, the Constitutional Court asked whether Article 53 of the Charter, interpreted in conjunction with Articles 47 and 48 of the Charter, would allow Spain to apply its own – higher – standard of protection, and make the surrender of a person convicted *in absentia* conditional upon the conviction being open to review in the requesting state.

The present commentary discusses the follow-up to the *Melloni* judgment in EU law. First, the findings of the Court and the immediate reaction thereto are outlined. Second, the chapter analyses the legislative and judicial development connected to the main legal issues addressed by the CJEU in *Melloni*. On the one hand, it assesses the progress made in the case law and legislation with regard to the protection of individual safeguards in criminal proceedings. On the other, it traces the evolution of the CJEU's approach to primacy of EU law and the relationship between the different standards of protection within the EU. The commentary concludes with some final remarks on the state of the art of the post-*Melloni* debate.

II. The Court's Ruling

In *Melloni*, the Court of Justice reiterated the focus on the effective operation of mutual recognition stated in previous judgments.[4] The Court confirmed that third pillar law (the EAW FD as amended by the FD on judgments *in absentia*, interpreted in the light of the Charter) has primacy over national constitutional law providing a higher level of fundamental rights protection. In order to reach this conclusion, the Court followed a three-step approach. The first step for the Court was to demarcate the scope of the FD on the EAW as amended by the FD on judgments *in absentia* (and in particular Article 4a(1) thereof) in order to establish the extent of the limits of mutual recognition in such cases. The Court reiterated its reasoning in the ruling in *Radu*[5] in adopting a teleological interpretation of the EAW FD and stressing that under the latter, Member States are in principle

[3] The two provisions state the right to a fair trial and the presumption of innocence, respectively.
[4] *Melloni* (n 1).
[5] Case C-396/11 *Ciprian Vasile Radu* [2013] ECR I. For an analysis of the impact of *Radu* at EU law level, see Wieczorek's commentary in chapter 13 in this volume.

obliged to act upon a EAW.[6] In the light of these findings, the Court adopted a literal interpretation of Article 4a(1), confirming that that provision restricts the opportunities for refusing to execute a EAW.[7] That interpretation is confirmed by the mutual recognition objectives of EU law.[8] The second step was to examine the compatibility of the above system with fundamental rights and in particular the right to an effective judicial remedy and the right to a fair trial set out in Articles 47 and 48(2) of the Charter. By reference to the case law of the European Court of Human Rights,[9] the Court of Justice found that the right of an accused person to appear in person at his trial is not absolute but can be waived.[10] The Court further stated that the objective of the FD on judgments *in absentia* was to enhance procedural rights whilst improving mutual recognition of judicial decisions between Member States[11] and found Article 4a(1) compatible with the Charter.

Having asserted the compatibility of the relevant provision with the Charter, the third step for the Court was to rule on the relationship between secondary EU law in question with national constitutional law which provided a higher level of protection. The Court rejected an interpretation of Article 53 of the Charter as giving general authorisation to a Member State to apply the standard of protection of fundamental rights guaranteed by its constitution, when that standard is higher than that deriving from the Charter and, where necessary, to give it priority over the application of provisions of EU law.[12] That interpretation of Article 53 would undermine the principle of the primacy of EU law. It would allow a Member State to disapply EU legal rules *which are fully in compliance with the Charter*, where they infringe the fundamental rights guaranteed by that state's constitution.[13] The Court understood Article 53 of the Charter as meaning that national authorities are free to apply higher human rights standards, as long as the level of protection provided for by the Charter and the *primacy, unity and effectiveness* of EU law are not thereby compromised.[14] In the present case, Article 4a(1) of FD 2002/584 does not allow Member States to refuse to execute a EAW when the person concerned is in one of the situations provided for therein.[15] The FD on judgments *in absentia* is intended to remedy the difficulties associated with the mutual recognition of decisions rendered in the absence of the person concerned at the trial arising from the differences as among the Member States in the protection of fundamental rights. Furthermore, the FD reflects the consensus reached

[6] *Radu*, ibid, paras 36–38.

[7] *Radu*, ibid, para 41.

[8] *Radu*, ibid, para 43.

[9] *Medenica v Switzlerland* App no 20491/92 (ECtHR, 14 June 2001); *Sejdovic v Italy* App no 56581/00 (ECtHR, 24 April 2012); *Haralampiev v Bulgaria* App no 29648/03 (ECtHR, 24 April 2012).

[10] *Melloni* (n 1) para 49.

[11] *Melloni* (n 1) para 51.

[12] *Melloni* (n 1) paras 56–57.

[13] *Melloni* (n 1) para 58. Emphasis added.

[14] *Melloni* (n 1) para 60. Emphasis added.

[15] *Melloni* (n 1) para 61.

by all the Member States regarding the scope to be given under EU law to the procedural rights enjoyed by persons convicted *in absentia* who are the subjects of a EAW.[16] Consequently, allowing a Member State to avail itself of Article 53 of the Charter to make the surrender of a person convicted *in absentia* conditional upon the conviction being open to review in the issuing Member State in order to avoid an adverse effect on the right to a fair trial and the rights of the defence guaranteed by the constitution of the executing Member State, by casting doubt on the uniformity of the standard of protection of fundamental rights as defined in that FD, *would undermine the principles of mutual trust and recognition which that decision purports to uphold and would, therefore, compromise the efficacy of that FD.*[17]

III. Standard of Protection and Conviction *in Absentia*

Important in different respects, *Melloni* stands out as a landmark judgment for the role of conviction in absentia in the context of judicial cooperation, on the one hand. On the other, it sets out a controversial relationship between degree of harmonisation at EU law level and states' power to apply higher standards of protection. While such a relationship has broader constitutional implications, it becomes particularly relevant when criminal proceedings are involved.

The CJEU's follow-up to *Melloni* is twofold. It concerns the interpretation of grounds preventing a judge from not executing an EAW following a conviction *in absentia*, and the leeway to rely on their own standards of protection that states enjoy.

As to the former aspect, the Court has been called upon to interpret Article 4a(1)(a)(i) EAW FD in the *Dworzecki*[18] case. The provision states that the execution of an EAW issued following a trial *in absentia* cannot be refused when 'the person in due time, and in accordance with further procedural requirements defined in the law of the issuing state: was summoned in person and thereby informed of the scheduled date and place of the trial; or, by other means, actually received official information of the scheduled date and place of that trial in such a manner that it was unequivocally established that s/he was aware of the trial'. As for Mr Dworzecki, the summons had been handed over, at his address, to an adult from that household, who undertook to pass it on to Mr Dworzecki, although it cannot be determined from the EAW whether – and, if so, when – that adult actually passed that summons on to the person concerned. While the Court clarified once again that the right for the person to appear at the trial can be waived on specific conditions,[19] the person has to be able to prepare his/her defence effectively.

[16] *Melloni* (n 1) para 62.
[17] *Melloni* (n 1) para 63. Emphasis added.
[18] Case C-108/16 PPU *Openbaar Ministerie v Paweł Dworzecki* EU:C:2016:346.
[19] *Ibid*, para 42.

The Court found that the circumstances could not unequivocally establish that the person concerned 'actually' received the information relating to the date and place of his trial, or the precise time when that information was received. Since Article 4a(1)(a)(i) constitutes an exception to an optional ground for refusal of execution, the executing judge must carefully consider whether the rights of defence of the person concerned have been respected and if need be request supplementary information to the issuing judge.[20]

Put in a wider perspective, *Melloni* and conviction *in absentia* offer a privileged observation point to analyse the CJEU's stance on interaction between different standards of protection within the EU. Consistent with earlier case law, the Court has given priority to the effectiveness of mutual recognition based on presumed mutual trust.[21] Secondary pre-Lisbon third pillar law whose primary aim is to facilitate mutual recognition has primacy over national constitutional law which provides a high protection of fundamental rights. In reaching this conclusion, the Court has interpreted fundamental rights in a restrictive manner. It has emphasised the importance of the FD on judgments *in absentia* for the effective operation of mutual recognition, a FD which as the Court admitted restricts the opportunities for refusing to execute a EAW. This aim sits uneasily with the Court's assertion that the *in absentia* FD also aims to protect the procedural rights of the individual. The Court has privileged the teleology of mutual recognition and upheld the text of the FD on judgments *in absentia* and the subsequently amended FD on the EAW – via the adoption also of a literal interpretation – over the protection of fundamental rights. By doing so, it has shown a great – and arguably undue – degree of deference to the European legislator.[22] Furthermore, the Court's reasoning seems to deprive the national executing authorities of any discretion to examine the compatibility of the execution of a EAW with fundamental rights in a wide range of cases involving *in absentia* rulings.[23]

This deferential approach may be explained by the fact that the Court was asked to examine the human rights implications of measures which have been subject to harmonisation at EU level, with the Court arguing that the FD reflects a consensus among EU Member States with regard to the protection of the individual in cases of *in absentia* rulings within the broader system of mutual recognition.[24]

[20] *Ibid*, paras 49–53.

[21] V Mitsilegas, 'The Symbiotic Relationship between Mutual Trust and Fundamental Rights in Europe's Area of Criminal Justice' (2015) 6 *New Journal of European Criminal Law* 4, 460–85.

[22] LFM Besselink, 'The Parameters of Constitutional Conflict after Melloni' (2014) 39(4) *European Law Review* 531–52, 542; A Torres Pérez, '*Melloni* in Three Acts: From Dialogue to Monologue' (2014) *European Constitutional Law Review* 10, 308–31, 317–18.

[23] See also the Opinion of Advocate General (AG) Bot, who linked national discretion to refuse surrender with the perceived danger of forum shopping by the defendant (para 103).

[24] See also the Opinion of AG Bot, according to whom the Court cannot rely on the constitutional traditions common to the Member States in order to apply a higher level of protection (para 84) and that the consensus between Member States leaves no room for the application of divergent national levels of protection (para 126).

It has been argued that national constitutional standards will be more readily applicable in cases where EU law has not been harmonised.[25]

The Court's ruling in the case of *Jeremy F*[26] has been cited as an example of this approach.[27] In *Jeremy F*, the Court found that the FD on the EAW as amended by the FD on judgments *in absentia* did not preclude Member States from providing for appeals with suspensive effect, provided that such appeals comply with the time limits set out in the EAW FD.[28] The Court noted that the absence of an express provision on the possibility of bringing an appeal with suspensive effect against a decision to execute a EAW does not mean that the FD prevents the Member States from providing for such an appeal or requires them to do so.[29] However, *Jeremy F* must be distinguished from *Melloni*: while *Melloni* concerned the possibility of refusing the execution of a mutual recognition request on fundamental rights grounds, *Jeremy F* did not question the essence of the mutual recognition system as fundamentally. Rather, the question in *Jeremy F* was a meta-question, concerning the specific procedural rules which apply in the process of the execution of a Warrant. Even in this case, the discretion left to Member States to protect fundamental rights is limited and circumscribed by the deadlines set out in the mutual recognition instruments aiming at achieving the desired speed linked to the perceived efficiency of the system. The Court's deferential approach gives undue weight to what are essentially intergovernmental choices (the choices of Member States adopting a third pillar measure without the involvement of the European Parliament), which sit even more uneasily in the post-Lisbon, post-Charter era.[30] The emphasis of the Court on the need to uphold the validity of harmonised EU secondary law over primary constitutional law on human rights (at both national and EU level) constitutes a grave challenge for fundamental rights protection.[31] It further reveals in the context of EU criminal law a strong focus by the Court on the need to preserve a system of quasi-automatic mutual recognition in criminal matters, which will enhance inter-state cooperation and law enforcement effectiveness across the EU.

Similar considerations apply to the *JZ* case,[32] revolving around the interpretation of 'deprivation of liberty' under Article 26 EAW FD. The provision states

[25] See K Lenaerts and J Gutiérrez-Fons, 'The European Court of Justice and Fundamental Rights in the Field of Criminal Law' in V Mitsilegas, M Bergström and T Konstadinides (eds), *Research Handbook of European Criminal Law* (Edward Elgar, 2015) 7–26; B de Witte, 'Article 53' in S Peers, T Hervey, J Kenner and A Ward, *The EU Charter of Fundamental Rights. A Commentary* (Hart Publishing, 2014).

[26] Case C-168/13 PPU *Jeremy F* EU:C:2013:358 judgment of 30 May 2013.

[27] Lenaerts and Gutiérrez-Fons (n 25).

[28] *Jeremy F* (n 26) para 74.

[29] *Jeremy F* (n 26) para 38.

[30] Mitsilegas (n 21).

[31] According to Besselink, attaching this importance to secondary legislation as 'harmonisation of EU fundamental rights' risks erasing the difference between the primary law nature of fundamental rights and secondary law as the subject of these rights. Besselink (n 1) 542.

[32] Case C-294/16 PPU *JZ v Prokuratura Rejonowa Łódź – Śródmieście* EU:C:2016:610.

that periods already spent in deprivation of liberty before the surrender, may be deducted from the final sentence in the issuing state. The CJEU found that Article 26 EAW FD establishes a minimum level of fundamental rights protection. The Court acknowledged the issuing judge the possibility to apply its own higher standard of protection (based on a more generous interpretation of 'deprivation of liberty') to a situation like that of Mr JZ, where he had been subject in the executing state to a regime that the CJEU found to be as 'restriction' rather than 'deprivation of liberty'.[33]

These cases show that the degree of harmonisation is indeed important for deciding the extent of leeway enjoyed by national authorities. They also confirm, however, that such an assessment must be carried out through the lens of EU law effectiveness and judicial cooperation in criminal matters specifically.

The existence of harmonisation of rights at EU level is key to the *Melloni* ruling and its follow-up. The Charter constitutes the benchmark for mutual recognition and EU law has primacy over national constitutional law – even if the latter offers a higher level of protection. This is so especially in cases where rights have been harmonised at EU level and secondary EU law exists. The importance of harmonisation in this context has been since highlighted by CJEU President Koen Lenaerts, according to whom it follows

> from the existence of EU legislation harmonizing the level of fundamental rights protection that the executing Member State may never impose its own domestic standards on the issuing Member State, as this would call into question the premise that those two Member States are equally capable of providing effective judicial protection of those rights.[34]

It can be argued that the emphasis on harmonisation – regardless of its nature and degree – may actually be counter-productive for the protection of fundamental rights within the system of mutual recognition. As noted earlier in the commentary, the Court in *Melloni* placed great emphasis on the standards agreed in the FD on judgments *in absentia*, without scrutinising the legal nature (third pillar) or the politics (adoption right before the entry into force of the Lisbon Treaty) behind the instrument.

The EU legislative follow-up to the *Melloni* case in the specific area concerned – conviction *in absentia* – seems to have addressed part of these concerns. This occurred by the adoption of related rules post-Lisbon in the presumption of innocence Directive.[35] Articles 8 and 9 of the Directive provide that conviction *in absentia* are possible on condition that: the suspect or accused

[33] *Ibid*, paras 55–57.

[34] K Lenaerts, 'La Vie Après l'Avis: Exploring the Principle of Mutual (yet not Blind) Trust' (2017) 54 *Common Market Law Review* 805–40, 821.

[35] EU Parliament and Council, Directive 2016/343/EU on the strengthening of certain aspects of the presumption of innocence and of the right to be present at the trial in criminal proceedings [2016] OJ L65/1.

person has been informed, in due time, of the trial and of the consequences of non-appearance; or that they, having been informed of the trial, are represented by a mandated lawyer, who was appointed either by the persons concerned or by the state.[36] If those conditions cannot be met, a decision can be taken and enforced as long as the persons are informed of their right to a new trial, or to another legal remedy, which allows a fresh determination of the merits of the case.[37] Even in this case, an over-emphasis on harmonisation disregards the fact that this Directive, along with the other post-Lisbon directives on procedural rights in criminal proceedings, only introduce minimum rules. Importantly, the directives allow Member States the possibility to offer a higher level of protection under national law. This is enshrined in the text via the introduction of non-regression clauses, affirming that nothing in the directives must be construed as limiting or derogating from any of the rights and procedural safeguards that are ensured under the Charter, the European Convention on Human Rights (ECHR), or other relevant provisions of international law or the law of any Member State which provides a higher level of protection.[38]

The existence of non-regression clauses renders the applicability of the *Melloni* ruling in cross-border cases contested. *Melloni* requires national authorities not to expect other systems to offer similarly high standards of fundamental rights protection to their own domestic standards, as long as the standard of protection in the Member State of the issuing authority is compatible with the Charter. This applies in particular in cases where there has been harmonisation at EU level. As the Preamble to the access to a lawyer Directive states expressly, a higher level of protection by Member States should not constitute an obstacle to the mutual recognition of judicial decisions that those minimum rules are designed to facilitate.[39] This seems to confirm that effectiveness of mutual recognition is a game changer in the relationship between harmonisation and the applicable standard of protection.

It is questionable whether minimum harmonisation in the field of procedural rights, coupled with non-regression clauses, is sufficient to justify such

[36] *Ibid*, Article 8.

[37] *Ibid*, Article 9.

[38] EU Parliament and Council, Directive 210/64/EU on the right to interpretation and translation in criminal proceedings [2010] OJ L280/1, Art 8; EU Parliament and Council, Directive 2012/13/EU on the right to information in criminal proceedings [2012] OJ L142/1, Art 10; EU Parliament and Council, Directive 2013/48/EU on the right of access to a lawyer in criminal proceedings and in European arrest warrant proceedings, and on the right to have a third party informed upon deprivation of liberty and to communicate with third persons and with consular authorities while deprived of liberty [2013] OJ L294/1, Art 14; EU Parliament and Council, Directive 2016/1919/EU on legal aid for suspects and accused persons in criminal proceedings and for requested persons in European arrest warrant proceedings [2016] OJ L297/1, Art 11; EU Parliament and Council, Directive (EU) 2016/800 on procedural safeguards for children who are suspects or accused persons in criminal proceedings [2016] OJ L132/1, Art 23; EU Parliament and Council, Directive 2016/343/EU on the strengthening of certain aspects of the presumption of innocence and of the right to be present at the trial in criminal proceedings [2016] OJ L65/1, Art 13.

[39] Directive 2013/48/EU (n 38), Preamble, Recital 54.

an approach. In terms of the interaction between national authorities trying to establish mutual trust, it may be a challenge to accept lower standards in fundamental rights in another Member State when EU law provides only for minimum harmonisation (which can constitute the lowest common denominator for protection at times) and leaves a considerable margin of discretion for the adoption of higher standards by Member States. This is particularly the case in this kind of legislation, where the law in the books is inextricably linked with law in action, and the effective protection being dependent on how the provisions of the directives are actually implemented on the ground.

IV. Primacy

Melloni's constitutional importance lies in the assertion of the primacy and autonomy of EU law vis-à-vis national constitutions. It is a case where European criminal law becomes constitutional law, with questionable effects for the protection of fundamental rights.

In the post-*Melloni* era, a dynamic has materialised in which the CJEU has refined – but never really questioned – the findings stated there, whereas other actors (the ECtHR and Member States' courts especially) have tried to react to the Court's stance. While autonomy is an important argumentative pattern used by the CJEU vis-à-vis Member States,[40] its powerful expressions materialised towards international law – as exemplified by the *Kadi* saga[41] – and the ECHR through *Opinion 2/13*.

The Court's main priority and focus appears to have been the assertion of primacy rather than a detailed examination of the broader fundamental rights implications of the ruling. The CJEU has since transposed this internal reasoning to the EU's external relations, and most notably in its relations with the legal order of the ECHR. In *Opinion 2/13*, the CJEU, based on *Melloni*, asserted the primacy and autonomy of EU law, stating that Article 53 CFREU must be understood as meaning that the application of national standards of protection of fundamental rights must not compromise the level of protection provided for by the Charter or the primacy, unity and effectiveness of EU law. One of the CJEU's arguments to set aside the EU accession to the ECHR was the absence, in the draft agreement, of a coordinating mechanism between Article 53 ECHR and Article 53 CFREU. The former reserves the power of the contracting parties to lay down higher

[40] See, eg, the use of the autonomous concept. L Mancano, 'Judicial Harmonization through Autonomous Concepts of European Union Law: The Example of the European Arrest Warrant Framework Decision' (2018) 43 *EL Rev* 69–88.

[41] Joined cases C-402/05 P and C-415/05 P *Yassin Abdullah Kadi and Al Barakaat International Foundation v Council of the European Union and Commission of the European Communities* EU:C:2008:461.

standards of protection of fundamental rights than those guaranteed by the ECHR. The CJEU found that, in case of accession, the Member States' exercise of the powers under Article 53 ECHR might have jeopardised the primacy, unity and effectiveness of EU law.[42] Furthermore, the Strasbourg Court in the case of *Tarakhel* had insisted on its approach based on an individualised assessment of human rights compliance even in systems claiming to be based on mutual trust.[43]

The CJEU's approach has caused concern in both national constitutional courts and the Strasbourg Court regarding not only the level and manner of protection of fundamental rights, but also ultimately regarding questions of primacy and *Kompetenz-Kompetenz.*

At national level, the divergence of approach was in particular evident in the case law of the German Federal Constitutional Court (*Bundesverfassungsgericht* or BVerG), which intervened regarding the scrutiny of fundamental rights in the execution of an EAW in a case of trial *in absentia* where the defendant's lawyer had not been notified.[44] The BVerG did not go all the way towards confirming a direct clash between EU law and the German Constitution. It however evoked an identity review under the Basic Law and put forward its own detailed scrutiny system, which executing authorities should follow when fundamental rights concerns were raised in relation to a EAW.[45] As will be seen elsewhere in this volume, the BVerG ruling has had a marked influence on the development of the substance of the scrutiny of mutual recognition and mutual trust by the CJEU in the case of *Aranyosi and Căldăraru*, which can also be seen in the light of a more conciliatory approach on mutual recognition by the Strasbourg Court and the BVerG.[46]

While direct and indirect judicial dialogue has had an impact on the evolution of fundamental rights protection in the operation of mutual recognition in criminal matters, the unfolding of the recent *Taricco* saga[47] – in particular between the CJEU and the Italian Constitutional Court – confirm that questions of primacy, constitutional identity and *Kompetenz-Kompetenz* in the constitutionally sensitive field of European criminal law remain contested.

[42] Opinion 2/13, EU:C:2014:2454, para 188–89.

[43] *Tarakhel v Switzerland* App no 29217/12 (ECtHR, 4 November 2014).

[44] BVerfG, Order of the Second Senate of 15 December 2015 – 2 BvR 2735/14 – paras 1–126.

[45] For a critical evaluation, see F Meyer, '"From Solange II to Forever I": The German Federal Constitutional Court and the European Arrest Warrant (and how the CJEU Responded)' (2016) 7 *New Journal of European Criminal Law* 277–94, at 283.

[46] Joined Cases C-404/15 and C-659/15 PPU *Pál Aranyosi and Robert Căldăraru* ECLI:EU:C:2016:198. See also Mitsilegas' and Lazowski's commentaries on *Aranyosi and Căldăraru* in chapter 15 of this volume.

[47] See Case C-105/14 *Ivo Taricco and others* EU:C:2015:555. See also Allegrezza's and Manes' commentaries on *Taricco* in chapter 6 of this volume.

V. Concluding Remarks

The *Melloni* case is one of the most important CJEU rulings of the last few decades, from both a constitutional and criminal law perspective. The case brought to the fore the clashes that can emerge from different standards of protection in an area so close to national sovereignty. It marked the beginning of a new era, the seed of which had been planted by the adoption of mutual recognition to judicial cooperation in criminal matters. The priority given to the primacy of EU law and the effectiveness of judicial cooperation over fundamental rights protection prevents Member States applying the higher standard of protection. The post-*Melloni* era has seen significant development, in legislative and judicial terms. In no case, however, has the Court seriously considered revising the main principles stated in that judgment. The leeway left to Member States on the implementation of the EAW FD occurred in the situation where – unlike in *Melloni* – full harmonisation of EU law had not been carried out. Most importantly, that flexibility was granted on the – explicit or implicit – presuppose that the proper operation of the system was not put in jeopardy. The same holds true for the directives on procedural rights, where the non-regression clause sits next to the warning that the effectiveness of mutual recognition should not be undermined.

Other institutional actors – such as the ECtHR and Member States' constitutional courts – have voiced their uneasiness, if most of the time through engaging in constructive dialogue with the CJEU. The CJEU's judgments in *Taricco* and *LM*[48] show that, if anything, the story is far from over and other landmark chapters are forthcoming in the difficult balance between standards of protection, cross-border law enforcement and individual safeguards.

[48] Case C-216/18 PPU *LM* EU:C:2018:586.

Bypassing or Intensifying the Dialogue between Courts? The Impact of Melloni *at the National Level*

LORENA BACHMAIER WINTER

I. Introduction

It is certainly not surprising that legal scholarship has paid much attention to the landmark ruling of the European Court of Justice (CJEU) in the *Melloni* case.[1] This judgment addresses one of the most debated issues in European constitutionalism, namely the level of protection of fundamental rights that must prevail when there is a conflict between the protection given by national constitutions and by secondary harmonised EU law. The judgment is directly linked to the content and meaning of Article 53 of the Charter of Fundamental Rights of the European Union (hereinafter 'EU Charter'), and the role that national constitutional courts play in the protection of fundamental rights within the EU legal system.[2] This is indeed one of the most difficult and discussed topics,[3] because balancing the unity required of EU law with the respect to the diversity of the legal traditions of the Member States, is not an easy task.[4]

Five years have passed since the judgment of the CJEU on the *Melloni* case was delivered and a huge amount of interesting scholarly analysis and critical comments

[1] C-399/11 *Stefano Melloni v Ministerio Fiscal* EU:C:2013:107.

[2] Much has been written on this constitutional interplay. Only recently, J Komarek, 'Why National Constitutional Courts Should not Embrace EU Fundamental Rights' in S de Vries, U Bernitz, S Weatherill (eds), *The EU Charter of Fundamental Rights as a Binding Instrument. Five Years Old and Growing* (Oxford, Hart Publishing, 2015) 75–92. In the same volume, see J Gerards, 'Who Decides on Fundamental Rights Issues in Europe? Towards a Mechanism to Coordinate the Roles of the National Courts, the ECJ and the ECtHR', 47–74; and also C Rauchegger, 'The Interplay' Between the Charter and National Constitutions after Akerberg Fransson and Melloni. Has the CJEU Embraced the Challenges of Multilevel Fundamental Rights Protection?', 93–131.

[3] See, among others, B De Witte, 'Article 53' in S Peers, T Hervey, J Kenner and A Ward (eds), *The EU Charter of Fundamental Rights: A Commentary* (Oxford, Hart Publishing, 2014) 1523–38, 1527.

[4] On the diverse mechanisms introduced in the Treaty of Lisbon to respect the national diversity within the EU, see V Mitsilegas, *EU Criminal Law After Lisbon* (Oxford, Hart Publishing, 2016) 14–19.

have been published discussing its impact on EU constitutionalism.[5] It is time to analyse what has been the impact of the *Melloni* judgment at national level. Has this CJEU judgment contributed in changing the approach towards the primacy of European law? Has it been interpreted as a positive step for initiating a constitutional dialogue between the CJEU and the constitutional courts? Could it be affirmed that the *Melloni* case has had a significant impact upon the level of protection granted to fundamental rights by the Spanish Constitutional Court (SCC)?

These are some of the questions that will be addressed in this contribution. The aim is to analyse what has been the impact of the *Melloni* judgment at the national level, focusing mainly on the Spanish legal system. To that end it is necessary to go into the legal arguments in detail, put forward by the Plenum of the SCC in the judgment 26/2014 of 13 February deciding on the individual complaint filed by Melloni.

As both the proceedings that triggered the preliminary referral before the CJEU and the content of the *Melloni* judgment of 26 February 2013 are well known, I will only reflect on them here very briefly.[6]

II. The *Melloni* Judgment

In 1996, the Criminal Chamber of the Spanish National Court decided on the surrender of Melloni to the Tribunal of Ferrara, where he was to be tried for a grave fraud bankruptcy offence. After the hearing on his surrender while he was released on bail, he fled. In 1997 the Ferrara Court continued the proceedings

[5] See among others, M Pérez Manzano, 'El Tribunal Constitucional español ante la tutela multinivel de derechos fundamentales en la Unión Europea. Sobre el ATC 86/2011, de 9 de junio' (2012) *Revista Española de Derecho Constitucional* 95, 311–45; J Vervaele, 'The European Arrest Warrant and Applicable Standards of Fundamental Rights in the EU' (2013) *Review of European Administrative Law* 2, 37–54, 41–47; A Tinsley, 'Note on the Reference in Case C-399/11 Melloni' (2012) 3–1 *New Journal of European Criminal Law*, 19–30; N de Boer, 'Addressing Rights' Divergences under the Charter: Melloni' (2013) *Common Market Law Review* 50, 1083–1104; JH Reestman and L Besselink, 'After Akerberg Fransson and Melloni: editorial' (2013) 9 *European Constitutional Law Review* 2, 169–75; P Martín Rodríguez, 'Crónica de una muerte anunciada: comentario a la sentencia del Tribunal de Justicia de 26 de febrero de 2013, Stefano Melloni, C-399/11' (2013) *Revista General de Derecho Europeo* 30, 1–45; W Weiss, 'Grundrechtschutz durch den EUGH: Tendenzen seit Lissabon' (2013) *Europäische Zeitschrift für Wirtschaftsrecht*, 287–92; L Besselink, 'The Parameters of Constitutional Conflict after Melloni' (2014) *European Law Review* 4, 531–52; A Torres Pérez, 'Melloni in Three Acts: From Dialogue to Monologue' (2014) *European Constitutional Law Review* 10, 308–31; V Mitsilegas, *Justice and Trust in the European Legal Order. The Copernicus Lectures* (Napoli, Jovene Editore, 2016) 112–16; L Bachmaier, 'Dealing with European Legal Diversity and the Luxembourg Court: Melloni and the Limits of European Pluralism' in R Colson and S Field (eds), *EU Criminal Justice and the Challenge of Diversity* (Cambridge, Cambridge University Press, 2016) 160–78; L Mancano, 'A New Hope? The Court of Justice Restores the Balance between Fundamental Rights Protection and Enforcement Demands in the European Arrest Warrrant System' in C Briére and A Weyembergh (eds), *The Needed Balances in European Criminal Law. Past, Present and Future* (Oxford, Hart Publishing, 2017) 285–312, 294–96.

[6] In more detail, see Besselink (n 5) 533 *ff*; Bachmaier (n 5) 162 *ff*.

in absentia and all further notifications were sent to the lawyers who had been chosen and appointed by the defendant.

In 2000, the Court of Ferrara sentenced the defendant to a custodial penalty of 10 years. The judgment was appealed in the second instance and later also in cassation before the Italian Supreme Court. Both appeals confirmed the conviction. Once the sentence became final, a European Arrest Warrant (EAW) was issued against Melloni for serving the prison sentence. On September 2008 the Spanish *Audiencia Nacional* ordered the execution of the EAW, which was challenged by Melloni before the SCC, claiming that it violated his constitutional rights of defence recognised under Art 24 of the Spanish Constitution (SC). The Constitutional Court, before deciding on this individual complaint (*recurso de amparo*), filed the preliminary reference to the CJEU.[7]

The SCC first asked if Art 4a (1) EAW after the Council Framework Decision (FD) 2009/299/JHA[8] precluded the national authorities of making the surrender conditional to the possibility of the conviction being open to review/retrial.[9] The second question referred to the compatibility of Art 4a (1) FD EAW with Arts 47 and 48 of the EU Charter. And finally, the third question, which was to be answered only if the second had been responded to in the affirmative, dealt with the meaning and scope of Art 53.2 of the EU Charter in conjunction with Arts 47 and 48, where the Constitutional Court asked if a Member State could provide a higher level of protection than that deriving from the EU law and so preserve the fundamental rights recognised in the National Constitution.

This is the first preliminary reference filed by the SCC to the CJEU, opening the door to a new dialogue between both courts.[10]

[7] Order (*auto*) of the Grand Chamber of the Constitutional Court 86/2011, of 9 June 2011 paras 1–5. On the content and significance of the preliminary reference, see, among others, JM Arias Rodríguez, 'Sobre las cuestiones prejudiciales planteadas en el auto del Tribunal Constitucional de 9 de junio de 2011 sobre la orden de detención europea' (2011) *La Ley* 7726, 1–7; A Torres Pérez, 'Constitutional Dialogue in the European Arrest Warrant; The Spanish Constitutional Court Knocking on Luxembourg's Door? (2012) *European Constitutional Law Review* 8, 105–27.

[8] Council Framework Decision (FD) 2009/299/JHA of 26 February 2009 amending Framework Decisions 2002/584/JHA, 2005/214/JHA, 2006/783/JHA, 2008/909/JHA and 2008/947/JHA, thereby enhancing the procedural rights of persons and fostering the application of the principle of mutual recognition to decisions rendered in the absence of the person concerned at the trial [2009] OJ L81.

[9] The issue was contentious in Spain because the Criminal Chamber of the Spanish National Court (*Audiencia Nacional*) and the Constitutional Court (*Tribunal Constitucional*) maintained clearly divergent positions, the former being in favour of the execution of these EAWs and the latter taking a more protective approach, applying the same standards of protection of fundamental rights *ad extra* as in domestic cases. The stance of the SCC had caused a problematic side effect: by preventing the execution of EAW when the issuing state did not guarantee the retrial in cases of custodial sentences rendered *in absentia*, Spain risked being considered a safe haven for offenders sentenced by Italian courts *in absentia*.

[10] The filing of the preliminary reference was received positively by the majority of the Spanish scholarship. See M Revenga Sánchez, 'Rectificar preguntando. El Tribunal Constitucional acude al Tribunal de Justicia (2011) *Revista Española de Derecho Europeo* 41, 139–50, 139; Rodríguez (n 5) 22. See also the separate Opinion of Judge P Pérez Tremps to preliminary referral of the Constitutional Court, ATC 86/2011.

Much was expected from this newly initiated – and risky – dialogue.[11] However, the judgment in the *Melloni* case has probably not satisfied those high expectations, mainly because of the lack of elaborated arguments when reaffirming the absolute primacy of EU secondary law[12] and the absence of general guidelines on essential questions important for understanding and interpreting human rights in the EU.[13]

The CJEU's answer to the first question underlined that allowing additional grounds for refusal of an EAW would run counter to the principle of mutual recognition and the uniformity and effectiveness of the surrender proceedings. In answering the second question, the CJEU concluded that the rule at stake – Article 4a(1) of FD EAW – 'does not disregard either the right to an effective judicial remedy and to a fair trial or the rights of the defence guaranteed by Articles 47 and 48(2) of the Charter respectively' (para 53).[14]

Regarding the third question, which is the crucial one for the development of the EU constitutional architecture, the CJEU utterly rejects the SCC's interpretation of Article 53 of the Charter, as such interpretation – the possibility to apply a higher standard of protection than the one provided in harmonised secondary EU law – would undermine the principle of the primacy of EU law (paras 56–58), and in this precise case also the unity and the efficacy of EU law (para 63).

III. The Impact of *Melloni* in Spain

It is clear that the *Melloni* CJEU ruling has not gone unnoticed and the number of articles and commentaries on this judgment evidences it. In such context it can be affirmed that the impact among constitutional scholarship has been immense.

At the legislative level, it has to be noted that shortly after the *Melloni* judgment, the Italian *Codice di Procedura Penale* was amended in order to facilitate the review of criminal convictions rendered *in absentia*. While Italy took that step forward in favour of raising its level of protection of fundamental rights, the Spanish Law on Mutual Recognition of Criminal Decisions in the EU[15] adopted in 2014 follows the exact wording of the amended Art 4.1 of the FD EAW. However, these amendments cannot be interpreted as a direct impact of the *Melloni* judgment.

[11] This was not perhaps an appropriate case to ask the Luxembourg Court on how to interpret Article 53 of the Charter and initiate a dialogue on the limits of the primacy of EU harmonised secondary law. And it is certainly doubtful that for entering its decision the Constitutional Court needed to file a preliminary ruling to the CJEU.

[12] Torres Pérez (n 5) 328; Rauchegger (n 2) 13.

[13] Bachmaier (n 5) 166–71.

[14] The CJEU judgment follows strictly the reasoning of the Opinion of the Advocate General, referring directly to its paras 65 to 70.

[15] Ley 23/2014, of 20 November.

At the practical level, the execution of EAW has not experienced significant changes: the problematic cases were those where Italy was the requesting state and only at the constitutional level, because the National Court was already executing the EAWs in accordance with the interpretation provided in the *Melloni* judgment. Indeed, once the SCC has 'reconsidered' its interpretation on the execution of EAW to serve sentences rendered *in absentia*, the 'disagreements' between those two courts have yielded, and proceedings are solved in a swifter way, not having to wait any longer for the last say at the constitutional level.

Beyond the scholarly debate, it is interesting to see what the impact has been, especially on the constitutional courts. The most visible and direct impact of the *Melloni* case is to be found in the follow-up judgment rendered by the SCC, which is why it will be analysed next.

A. The Reaction of the Spanish Constitutional Court

The Spanish Court faced in this case a difficult dilemma: either to accept plainly the CJEU decision, which would contravene its own case law on trials *in absentia* and its position about the primacy of EU law expressed in Declaration 1/2004 (DCC);[16] or reaffirm its own doctrine defending the higher standard of protection of fundamental rights, and by doing so, cause a direct clash between courts. Instead, it compromised and made an intelligent move, which consisted of presenting those contradicting positions as compatible.[17] The Court decided on the individual complaint agreeing to revise its own doctrine on extradition proceedings and criminal trials *in absentia*, whilst avoiding recognising that this was the result of the principle of primacy of EU law. The Court invokes its own Declaration of 2004 as legal reasoning of this judgment and at the same time states that a conflict with the CJEU will not exist, in so far as the CJEU will safeguard in an effective manner a high level of fundamental rights protection.[18] As will be seen later, this is precisely criticised in two of the concurring opinions, as far as it bypasses the crucial issue of the effects of the CJEU ruling at national level and the primacy principle of EU law.

DCC 1/2004 is a crucial element in understanding the decision of the SCC in the *Melloni* case and it is not by chance that its most important reasoning contained

[16] The Declaration was issued upon the request of the Government, before signing the Treaty laying down a Constitution for Europe, in application of Article 95 SC. The Constitutional Court was requested to issue a binding Opinion on: 1. The existence or inexistence of a contradiction between the Spanish Constitution and Article I-6 of the Treaty which lays down a Constitution for Europe. 2. In view of the provisions set forth in Article 10.2 SC, the existence or inexistence of a contradiction between the Spanish Constitution and Articles II-111 and II-112 of the Treaty which lays down a Constitution for Europe, which form part of the Charter of Fundamental Rights of the European Union.

[17] See R Alonso García, *El Juez Nacional en la Encrucijada Europea de los Derechos Fundamentales* (Madrid, Civitas, 2014) 187; Bachmaier (n 5) 172–74.

[18] Para 5 of FJ 3.

in the third paragraph (*fundamento jurídico*, FJ) begins by saying that the response of the CJEU has to be 'completed" with the Declaration, and literally reproduces parts of it.[19] Such Declaration – which is not an opinion and is binding[20] – was requested by the Government precisely to clarify the doubts of the possible clash of the Treaty establishing a Constitution for Europe and the Spanish constitutional system.

The DCC 1/2004 expresses that 'the constitutional transfer enabled by Art. 93 SC is subject to material limits imposed on the transfer itself'.[21] These limits derive implicitly from the Constitution and consist of 'the respect for the sovereignty of the State, of our basic constitutional structures and of the system of fundamental principles and values set forth in our Constitution, where the fundamental rights acquire their own substantive nature'.[22] After recognising the primacy principle of the EU law, the Declaration also insists that the EU legal order is built upon the common values of Member States' constitutions and constitutional traditions, which EU law itself must guarantee.

In the unlikely case of an unsolvable conflict between the EU law and the Spanish Constitution, 'the preservation of the Spanish people's sovereignty and of the supremacy of the Constitution … could lead this Court to approach such problems, which at present seem inexistent, through the relevant constitutional procedures'.[23] The Declaration also shows that the Constitutional Court understood Article 53 of the Charter (then Article II-113 of the Treaty) in the meaning of Art 53 of the European Convention on Human Rights (ECHR), ie that the Charter contained *minimum* standards on human rights that had to be respected but not *maximum* limits of protection of fundamental rights that could not be trespassed if it affected the primacy, effectiveness and unity of EU law. In other words, Article 53 of the Charter was not to be interpreted as allowing a 'downwards' interpretation of fundamental rights protection.[24]

Once the Court has explained and reaffirmed its position – which remains unchanged since the DCC 1/2004 – it reconsiders its own previous case law: 'we must revise how this Court has conceived the right to a fair trial so far',[25] and without any further explanation on the reasons why the previous standard has to be revised now, it accepts that the right to reopen a conviction rendered *in absentia* is no longer part of the constitutional right of defence in EAW proceedings.

Following this 'reconsideration' of its own case law, the level of protection of fundamental rights to be applied *ad extra* will be determined, as provided by

[19] Four of the five paragraphs of the FJ 3 transcribe the text of the DCC 1/2004.

[20] See DCC 1/2004, para 1.

[21] *Ibid*, para 2.

[22] *Ibid*.

[23] *Ibid*, para 4, clearly inspired in the judgment of the German Federal Constitutional Court (*Bundesverfassungsgericht* or BVerfG) of 22 October 1986, known as '*Solange II*' (BvR 197/83).

[24] DCC 1/2004, para 6. In the same vein, see De Witte (n 3) 533 *ff*. On the different interpretations of Article 53 of the Charter in the context of the *Melloni* case, see generally, Besselink (n 5) 540 *ff*.

[25] STC 26/2014, FJ 4.

Article 10.2 of the Constitution,[26] by international conventions and by the Charter of Fundamental Rights of the EU, as interpreted by their respective judicial bodies. And this leads the Constitutional Court to rule against the defendant in the *recurso de amparo* and to confirm the decision on the execution of the EAW against *Melloni*.

In its ruling, the Court abandons its previous case law and agrees to lower the level of protection of fundamental rights in extradition procedures, but does not explicitly recognise the primacy of EU harmonised secondary law:[27] the Court says that the reply of the Grand Chamber of the CJEU will be 'very useful' in interpreting the right to a fair trial, under Article 24 SC and by doing so implicitly conveys the message that, if there were a frontal conflict in the future, the constitutional standards should prevail, for this is the meaning of Art 93 SC (FJ 3, last paragraph).[28]

B. Different Voices at the Spanish Constitutional Court

As seen, the SCC judgment has tried to live up to the supremacy of the national Constitution without explicitly questioning the primacy of the EU law. However, the concurring opinions show that the discussion on 'supremacy versus primacy' in the multi-level system of protection of fundamental rights is more than alive. Perhaps these separate opinions were not necessary for deciding the instant complaint, as the underlying issue did not pose any doubts on the protection of the rights of *Melloni*. Nevertheless some judges seized the opportunity to make their stance in the constitutional interplay of the CJEU and the national constitutional systems.[29]

The first Opinion,[30] while accepting that the surrender of Melloni to serve the conviction sentence would not violate the Spanish Constitution, argues that the Court should have 'entirely suppressed the reasoning under point 3 (FJ 3)', in which the supremacy of the Constitution is reaffirmed and the substantive limits on the cession of sovereignty in favour of the CJEU are mentioned. Judge Asúa criticises the Court's reasoning, because in her view the judgment should have

[26] Article 10.2 SC: 'The principles relating to the fundamental rights and liberties recognised by the Constitution shall be interpreted in conformity with the Universal Declaration of Human Rights and the international treaties and agreements thereon ratified by Spain.'

[27] In the same sense, Torres Pérez (n 5) 321–23.

[28] This had also been the approach in the earlier SCC judgment 61/2013, of March 14 (FJ 5), where it recalled that although EU law does not integrate the constitutionality canon, notwithstanding both international treaties and agreements, as well as the secondary EU law can constitute 'valuable hermeneutical criteria of the meaning and scope of the rights and freedoms that the Constitution recognizes', a value that is attributed on the basis of Art 10.2 SC.

[29] FJ Matia Portilla, 'Primacía del derecho de la Unión y derechos constitucionales. En defensa del Tribunal Constitucional' (2016) *Rev Española de Derecho Constitucional* 106, 479–522, 519 regrets that this division within the SCC is made visible, casting doubt upon the role of the Constitutional Court in the Spanish Constitution.

[30] Concurring separate Opinion of Judge A Asúa Batarrita.

been based on the CJEU interpretation of the primacy of the EU harmonised law and not on its own constitutional provisions, giving the impression that the SCC is not satisfied with the answer of the CJEU to the reference.[31] This Opinion also quotes the ruling in *Akerberg Fransson*, to reassure that when implementing EU law, Member States shall abide by EU fundamental rights.[32]

The second concurring Opinion[33] is more elaborate, but it shares with the previous one the idea that it was not necessary to refer to international conventions in order to justify the review of the level of protection of fundamental rights *ad intra*. Judge Roca states that if the Constitutional Court admits that the CJEU has acted within the limits of its competences and that its interpretation of Arts 47 and 48.2 of the Charter does not affect the material limits of the Spanish Constitution, it is unnecessary to reaffirm the supremacy of the Constitution. By doing so – in the Judge's view – the Constitutional Court 'puts into question basic principles of the European construction' and does not contribute to the dialogue between jurisdictions in a positive way. She considers that the Spanish Court in applying the 'equivalent protection' doctrine set out in *Solange II*[34] and in the ECtHR *Bosphorus* doctrine,[35] should have based its decision on the reasoning of the CJEU. By not doing so, this Judge considers that crucial issues for understanding the logic of the EU architecture have been overlooked.

Finally, this separate vote also affirms that the 'EU law is not international law in the territory of the Member States' (FJ 6). The process of constitutionalisation of the EU law has created a different type of legal order that does not fit into a traditional classification of international law. In order to put an end to many useless discussions, it might be adequate to define the EU as 'an on-going international law experiment'.[36]

The third concurring Opinion,[37] in contrast with the other two, adheres to the stance adopted in the DCC 1/2004, although admitting that the statement in certain parts could be revisited as a consequence of the effects of EU legislation. At the same time, the Judge does not find 'any reason to extend the exceptional treatment deriving from Art. 93 CE' to the extradition procedures with respect to countries that are not members of the EU. The Charter of the European Union is applicable when implementing EU law, and domestic courts often rely on EU fundamental law even if it is not strictly applicable[38] and, on the other hand, differentiating the level of protection of fundamental rights by lowering the protection in

[31] This Opinion has been criticised for contradicting Article 10 SC. See Portilla (n 29) 513–14.

[32] C-617/10 *Aklagaren v Hans Akerberg Fransson* EU:C:2013:105.

[33] Concurring separate Opinion of Judge E Roca Trías.

[34] *Solange II* (n 23).

[35] *Bosphorus v Ireland* App no 45036/98 (ECtHR, 30 June 2005).

[36] The expression is used by B De Witte, 'The EU as an International Legal Experiment' in G de Burca and JHH Weiler (eds), *The Worlds of European Constitutionalism* (Cambridge, Cambridge University Press, 2012) 19–56, 21 *ff*.

[37] Concurring separate Opinion of Judge A Ollero Tassara.

[38] See T Marguery, 'European Union Fundamental Rights and Member States Action in Criminal Law' (2013) 20 *Maastricht Journal of European and Comparative Law* 2, 298–300.

cases of EAW and keeping a higher standard for all the other cases of extradition, might not sound very consistent either.

The intriguing question that triggered the *Melloni* case was precisely what would have happened if the Spanish Constitutional Court had opposed to follow the CJEU ruling? The next paragraph will deal with the consequences that might be traced back to the *Melloni* judgment in the Spanish legal system. The attitude of the German and Italian constitutional courts will also be mentioned.

IV. Bypassing or Intensifying the Dialogue between Courts?

The impact of the *Melloni* 'dialogue' – or lack of dialogue as the SCC judgment 26/2014 betrays –, might have caused the SCC to avoid any further clashes of the two courts in different ways: first by giving precedence to CJEU preliminary references when filed simultaneously with a constitutional question to the Constitutional Court; and second, through the use of the *acte claire* doctrine.

The possibility of giving precedence to the CJEU request when filed together with the constitutional question was not exercised until now and, although it cannot be affirmed that this is a consequence of *Melloni*, in fact, it was only after the *Melloni* judgment that several inadmissibility orders of the SCC moved in this direction.[39] The SCC comes to this solution through an interesting interpretation of Art 35.1 and 2 of the law of the Constitutional Court. This provision requires that the constitutional question refers to a rule 'applicable to the instant case'. Therefore, in case the national judge should have doubts on the compatibility of a rule with EU law and the Constitution, it is for the CJEU to first state if the rule is in accordance with EU law. Only then would it be 'applicable' to the case, and could be questioned before the Constitutional Court. Following these recent decisions on admissibility of constitutional questions, it has become clear that simultaneous referrals to both courts are not permitted. By doing so the Court underlines the primacy of the CJEU in interpreting EU law[40] and reduces also the risk of clashes.[41]

Another possible mechanism for avoiding collisions is to not refer preliminary rulings at all. In fact, since the preliminary request in the *Melloni* case, the SCC has not referred any other case to the CJEU even though there might be cases

[39] On this possibility of giving precedence to the preliminary ruling filed to the CJEU, see Alonso García (n 17) 141–47.

[40] See SCC Orders 168/2016, of 4 October and 183/2016 and 185/2016, both of 15 November declaring inadmissible the constitutional questions submitted by Spanish courts simultaneously with EU preliminary references.

[41] As M García says: the SCC wants the CJEU to speak first, in 'Cautious Openness: The Spanish Constitutional Court's Approach to EU Law in Recent National Case Law' (*European Law blog*, June 7 2017), available at http://europeanlawblog.eu/2017/06/07/cautious-openness-the-spanish-constitutional-courts-approach-to-eu-law-in-recent-national-case-law/.

where it could appear that the *CILFIT criteria* would apply.[42] An example might be found in the SCC Judgment 13/2017, of 30 January, where the Court is dealing directly with EU law in a constitutional complaint filed for denying the defence lawyer access to the file while the defendant was under police arrest. In this case, the Constitutional Court stated that Art 7.1 of EU Directive 2012/13,[43] which ensures the right to access the file, was directly applicable,[44] as Spain had infringed the deadline for its transposition into domestic law.

The Constitutional Court in this case applied the *acte clair* doctrine[45] and did not even consider asking the Luxembourg Court whether the scope of the right of access to the arrest file is as broad as the SCC judged, or as narrow as the Court deciding the *habeas corpus* had originally interpreted.[46] It is known that only when there is a question of interpretation of EU law and the guidance of the ECJ is necessary to resolve such questions in order for the national judge to be able to reach his or her decision, a Constitutional Court is obliged to file the request.[47] But, in the end, it is for the Court itself to take the final decision on the question of whether it will submit a request.[48] This system relies on trust upon the national judges. A too lenient application of the *CILFIT criteria* would not only break such trust, but would also undermine the legal foundations of the EU and its uniform interpretation. I do not state that the SCC is not complying with its obligation to refer for preliminary ruling under Art 267 TFEU, but it would not be unreasonable to think that it might prefer a broad interpretation of the *acte clair* doctrine.

[42] Case 283/81 *CILFIT v Ministry of Health* [1982] ECR I-3415. As it is known, the *acte clair* doctrine is used to resolve the question under Art 267 of the Treaty on the Functioning of the European Union (TFEU) whether a national court has to submit a question for a preliminary ruling to the CJEU. This question is of particular importance in a procedure before national courts making final decisions against which there is no further appeal. The third paragraph of Art 267 TFEU imposes on such courts the obligation to submit a request for a preliminary ruling unless the answer is so obvious that it leaves no scope for any reasonable doubt. Before coming to the conclusion that the act is clear under EU law, the national court must be convinced that the issue is also obvious to the courts of the other Member States and to the CJEU.

[43] EU Directive 2012/13, of 22 May 2012, on the right to information in criminal proceedings [2012] OJ L142/1.

[44] See FJ 7.

[45] On the interpretation of Article 267 TFEU and the more flexible assessment of the *acte clair*, see A Limante, 'Recent Developments in the *Acte Clair* Case Law of the EU Court of Justice: Towards a more Flexible Approach' (2016) 54 *Journal of Common Market Studies* 6, 1384–97.

[46] In this case the police alleged that at the moment when the defence lawyer asked for access to the file, they could not provide it, because there was no file, as the police officers were writing it down in precise detail at that point. The Constitutional Court, however, finds in favour of the applicant on the basis that some materials should have been available and ready to be handed to the defence. It does not even question the legal interpretation of Art 7.1 of Directive 2012/13, in which case the preliminary reference would be obviously needed. By relying on the precise facts of the case, and not questioning the clarity of the EU rule, avoids the referral to Luxembourg.

[47] See N Fennelly, 'The National Judge as Judge of the European Union' in A Rosas et al (eds), *The Court of Justice and the Construction of Europe: Analyses and Perspectives on Sixty Years of Case-Law* (Berlin, Heidelberg, Springer, 2013) 61–79, 77.

[48] Obligation to refer to the CJEU that was emphasised in Case C-224/01 *Köbler* EU:C:2003:513, and later again in Case C-160/14 *Ferrera da Silva* EU:C:2015:565, both related to civil disputes.

The constitutional courts of other Member States have also taken account of the *Melloni* case.[49] The reactions have been diverse, although presenting similarities in defending the role of the constitutional courts in applying their own higher standards of fundamental rights. However, whilst the German Constitutional Court has expressed reluctance – if not opposition – against the firm stance of the primacy of secondary EU law and the lack of dialogue of the CJEU, the Italian Court has moved towards the fight at the open battlefield, by asking the CJEU to revisit its own ruling.

The German Constitutional Court Decision of 15 December 2015, in another EAW execution case known by some already as *Solange III*, clearly states that it would subject to its own constitutional identity check (*Identitätskontrolle*) cases covered by determined secondary EU law.[50] The German Constitutional Court, after recognising the principle of primacy of EU law, asserts that precedence only applies in so far as the Basic Law and the Act of Assent permit or provide for the transfer of sovereign rights. Its scope is limited by the Basic Law's (*Grundgesetz* or GG) constitutional identity that, according to Art 23, s 1, sentence 3 in conjunction with Art 79 s 3 GG, is neither open to constitutional amendment nor to European integration. And 'the identity review conducted by the Federal Constitutional Court safeguards the constitutional identity. As with ultra vires reviews, [identity] reviews may ultimately result in Union law having to be declared inapplicable in exceptional cases'.[51]

The content of this decision is in line with the SCC judgment 16/2014, in so far as it reaffirms the limits of the EU law and mutual recognition principle, but it does it in a more robust way. It states that it will keep its review power and undertake *always* the check of compliance with human dignity, according to the level of protection of the national Constitution.[52] Although in this case the German Constitutional Court, not finding any room for reasonable doubt on the application of the EU law (*acte clair*), concluded that there was no need for a preliminary request to the CJEU under Art 267 TFEU.[53]

[49] On the concerns in applying EU law – precisely FD EAW – in national constitutional courts, see Mitsilegas (n 5) 21–26.

[50] BVerfG Order of 15 December 2015 (2 BvR 2735/14). On this Order, see HH Kühne, 'Auslieferung nach Abwesenheitsverurteilung (Italien) – Solange III' (2016) *Straverteidiger* 5, 299–302; H Satzger, 'Grund- und menschenrechtliche Grenzen für die Vollstreckung einer Europäischen Haftbefehls? – "Verfassungsgerichtliche Identitätskontrolle" durch das BVerfG vs. Vollstreckungsaufschub bei "aussergewöhnlichen Umständen nach dem EuGH' (2016) *NStZ* (9), 514–22; F Mayer, 'From Solange II to Forever I. The German Federal Constitutional Court and the EAW (and how the CJEU responded)' (2016) 7 *New Journal of European Criminal Law* 3, 277–94); J Nowag, 'EU Law, Constitutional Identity, and Human Dignity: A Toxic Mix?' (2016) *Common Market Law Review* 53, 1441–54.

[51] BVerfG Order of 15 December 2015 (2 BvR 2735/14), para 42.

[52] The question of constitutional identity was also the core point in Case C-62/14 *Gauweiler and others* EU:C:2015:400.

[53] As noted by Nowag (n 50) 1450–51, it is debatable whether the issue in this case 'could actually be considered *acte clair*', taking into account that 'the question to what extent national courts have to investigate the procedural laws of other Member States in the context of Article 4(a) of the FD EAW interpretation' is not obvious.

In this case the German Constitutional Court rather acted in quite the opposite way as the Spanish Court towards the dialogue with Luxembourg. Instead of asking and then having to step back from its own standards, the German Court seized the opportunity of an extradition case – that did not present any conflicting area with the primacy of the EU law – to send a message to the CJEU but without entering into the risky territory of the 'dialogue' with Luxembourg. The German Constitutional Court makes a statement against the *Melloni* doctrine, warning that it will not accept lowering their own constitutional standards of protection of fundamental rights if it is against the identity principle. The message of the German Constitutional Court is clear: the EU constitutionalism is to be built from the bottom-up. Sending this warning shot,[54] the German Constitutional Court bypassed the dialogue and sent quite a strong message, which might have 'the potency to be lethal for the EU's legal order'.[55] For the Constitutional Court itself, the strategy appears to be cleverer than the one that was chosen by the SCC in attempting a dialogue with the CJEU and receiving an answer that in no way met the expectations of the Spanish Court, and was almost received as a slap in the face.

Since then, the *Bundesverfassungsgericht* has followed the same parameters in other EAW cases, declaring that the check of the identity principle according to its own constitutional standards is to be done even when applying harmonised secondary EU law, and such a check is not against the loyal cooperation obligation.

However, not every contradiction with German constitutional rights will lead to the refusal of an EAW. The German Constitutional Court has stated that only if such contradiction infringes the *core content* of the fundamental right, would there be a violation of fundamental rights that could lead to the refusal of the execution of a EAW.[56]

In the Constitutional Court Order of 6 September 2016, the applicant was opposed to the execution of the EAW based on the possible violation of his fundamental right against self-incrimination. The Court again undertakes here the check of compliance of the level of protection of fundamental rights in conformity with the notion of human dignity as provided under Article 1 of the Basic Law.

In this decision, the Court concludes that the possibility under British criminal procedural law to use the accused's silence to his or her detriment under certain circumstances is in contradiction of the right not to incriminate oneself as applicable under German criminal law and enshrined in the *Grundgesetz*. However, it does not violate the constitutional principles that are beyond the reach of European integration (*integrationsfest*). Only where the core content of the right not to incriminate oneself, which is inherent to human dignity, is affected, Art 1 of the

[54] Expression used by Mayer (n 50) 284.

[55] Nowag (n 50) 1453.

[56] BVerfG Order of 6 September 2016 (2 BvR 890/16), para 36): 'Nur wenn der unmittlebar zur Menschenwürde gehörende *Kerngehalt der Selbstbelastungsfreiheit* berührt ist, liegt auch eine Verletzung von Art. 1 des Grundgesetzes vor'.

GG is violated:[57] an extradition based on a EAW is not to be refused on the mere grounds that the right not to incriminate oneself is not safeguarded in the requesting state to the same extent as in Germany.

This decision is relevant, in so far as it softens the strong statement made before in the judgment of December 2015: only when the 'core content' of the fundamental right is affected, there would be a violation of the national Constitution, and such standard would have precedence over EU harmonised secondary law.

In its decision of 19 December 2017, the German Constitutional Court also gave precedence to the CJEU, but unlike the Spanish Constitutional Court, it followed this approach on the basis of the fundamental right of the judge predetermined by the law: by not filing the preliminary referral to the CJEU in a case where the *Oberlandesgericht* of Hamburg expressed doubts as to the application of an EAW, the Constitutional Court considered that the applicant had been deprived of his right to the natural judge as recognised under Article 101 of the *Grundgesetz*.[58]

Although not directly linked to the *Melloni* case, in the context of the debate on the powers of constitutional courts in reviewing the EU harmonised law under their own constitutional parameters, it is necessary to mention, albeit very briefly as this judgment will be commented on elsewhere,[59] the *Taricco* case.[60] In the *Taricco* saga, as it is well-known, the Italian Constitutional Court, after the preliminary ruling of the CJEU in 2015, filed another preliminary ruling regarding the enforcement of the first. The Italian Constitutional Court claimed that the enforcement of the CJEU ruling would run against the Italian 'constitutional identity' and therefore requested further clarification via a second preliminary ruling.[61] The Italian Constitutional Court, instead of directly applying its own *contro-limiti* doctrine – and refusing to enforce the CJEU judgment –, gives Luxembourg a last chance to revisit the reasoning in *Taricco* and 'interpret Article 325 TFEU in a way that would make the conflict with the supreme constitutional principle of legality, less strong and evident, albeit without removing

[57] BVerfG Order of 6 September 2016 (2 BvR 890/16), inadmissibility decision, not entering into the merits. See later also BVerfG Order of 18 August 2017 (BvR 424/17), suspending the execution of a EAW against a Romanian citizen, while deciding on the merits of the compliance of the German *Grundgesetz* in the extradition proceedings.

[58] BVerG Order of 19 December 2017 (2 BvR 424/17).

[59] See Allegrezza's and Manes' commentaries on the *Taricco* case in chapter 6 of this volume.

[60] Case C-105/14 *Ivo Taricco and Others* EU:C:2015:555. In its judgment on the fight against VAT fraud, the CJEU concluded that the national court must give full effect to Art 325(1) and (2) TFEU, if need be by disapplying the provisions of national law, the effect of which would be to prevent the Member State concerned from fulfilling its obligations under Art 325(1) and (2) TFEU. The debated questions relate to the statute of limitations regarding the criminal offences for fraud in this ambit.

[61] F Fabbrini and O Pollicino, 'Constitutional Identity in Italy: European Integration As the Fulfillment of the Constitution' (*EUI Department of Law Research Paper No 2017/06*, 9 March 2017) 11, available at http://cadmus.eui.eu/bitstream/handle/1814/45605/LAW_2017_06.pdf?sequence=1&isAllowed=y.

the same'.[62] This second request for a preliminary ruling is seen as a last-ditch attempt to avoid a constitutional collision between the two legal orders. This case was particularly relevant for the whole EU legal architecture, because unlike in *Melloni*, the Italian Court expressly affirmed that a question of 'constitutional identity' was at stake.

After much expectation, the CJEU decided on this second preliminary ruling on 5 December 2017[63] making a compromise and avoiding the clash: the CJEU confirmed the ruling given in the first preliminary question, and stated that the statute of limitations should be shorter, but considered that the national rules should be disapplied

> unless that disapplication entails a breach of the principle that offences and penalties must be defined by law because of the lack of precision of the applicable law or because of the retroactive application of legislation imposing conditions of criminal liability stricter than those in force at the time the infringement was committed.[64]

Looking at the actions and reactions of the three constitutional courts mentioned, it is fair to say that *Melloni* had an impact on the attitude each of them adopted towards the constitutional dialogue with the CJEU. It is interesting to see how differently these three courts reacted in this playground of the multi-level protection of fundamental rights and within the definition of the limits of Article 53 of the Charter.

The Spanish Constitutional Court, after referring to the CJEU, and having to reconsider its own standard – albeit only for the specific case at stake –, does not seem to be very enthusiastic in continuing the dialogue on the national identity exception. By recognising that the concrete facts in *Melloni* did not affect the national identity principle, it has stepped back in order to avoid a clash but leaving the door open for possible future conflict regarding the identity principle exception.

On the other hand, the German Constitutional Court has not been afraid to mark its boundaries in a preventive or anticipatory way: without asking Luxembourg it has decided itself how it will address the constitutional identity exception when confronted in the future with a case where its own standard collides with the EU level of protection.

Finally, the Italian Constitutional Court accepted the challenge and did not shirk the fight, by specifically asking Luxembourg about the 'rules of the game' when it came to the identity principle in the second *Taricco* preliminary ruling, which also fortunately came to an end without an overt clash between the courts.

[62] See M Bassini and O Pollicino, 'The Taricco Decision: A Last Attempt to Avoid a Clash between EU Law and the Italian Constitution' (*Verfassungsblog*, 28 January 2017), available at http://verfassungsblog.de/the-taricco-decision-a-last-attempt-to-avoid-a-clash-between-eu-law-and-the-italian-constitution/.

[63] Case C-42/17 *MAS* EU:C:2017:936.

[64] *Ibid*, para 62.

V. Conclusions

The balance between the systems of judicial protection of fundamental rights established, respectively, by the CJEU and by the Constitutional Court was founded upon the recognition of EU law's primacy, although not in a *carte blanche* way but, on the contrary, assuming implicitly that the Court of Luxembourg would ensure a higher level of protection of fundamental rights.[65] However, the *Melloni* judgment has shown that this will not always be the case and that secondary EU harmonised legislation shall prevail over higher levels of protection of fundamental rights if these are deemed to compromise the primacy, unity and effectiveness of EU law.

Absolute primacy of EU harmonised secondary law is not an uncontroversial issue and dialogue is needed to support the normative authority of the CJEU in the field of fundamental rights.[66] Dialogue is especially important in criminal matters, where the states have always been reluctant to give away sovereign powers and issues affecting the national identity principle might be seen as more relevant. The CJEU should be aware that the area of freedom security and justice (AFSJ) is a more sensitive area of fundamental rights than common market freedoms, and the same parameters used in the economic field may require more mutual understanding in the AFSJ.

As for the future, Member States might not always be willing to accept the primacy principle in an unlimited way. This has been clearly set out by the *Bundesverfassungsgericht*, sending the message that national constitutional courts might not be prepared to give away their role as gatekeepers of the identity principle in favour of the unity and efficacy of the EU law.

While the *Melloni* SCC judgment has brought to the surface the fact that there are single constitutional judges that indeed are in favour of giving unlimited powers to the CJEU in determining the level of protection of fundamental rights when applying EU law, it might have also caused another side-effect: that the constitutional courts tend to limit the direct dialogue with Luxembourg, and by doing so, avoid being subject to a compliance that they are not willing to accept when it comes to the core element of the protection of fundamental rights according to their own constitutional identity. However, such attitudes might end up damaging the EU architecture, its unity and effectiveness, and in the end, also losing the much needed trust.

[65] García (n 17) 189.

[66] A Torres Pérez, *Conflicts of Rights in the European Union. A Theory of Supranatinal Adjudication* (Oxford, Oxford University Press, 2009) 109, accepting that a shortcoming of dialogue is an increase in legal uncertainty. Against this dialogue, however, Portilla (n 29) 505, who argues that the dialogue cannot only lead to conflict, but also to the fact that some constitutional courts, through their dialogue-influence upon the CJEU case law, end up setting the tone on the interpretation of constitutional standards of other countries.

The risks of conflicting interpretations of fundamental rights between the ECHR, the EU Charter and the national constitutions are unavoidable, as the *Taricco* saga shows. It seems that either by expanding the concept of *acte clair* and limiting the dialogue or through an improved dialogue between the CJEU and the national courts, open clashes can be reduced. What the *Melloni* case has shown is that imposing an up-down lower level of protection of fundamental rights, might not be acceptable in the future in terms of the peaceful interplay between the CJEU and the national constitutional courts.

15

Joined Cases C-404/15 and C-659/15 PPU – *Pál Aranyosi and Robert Căldăraru v Generalstaatsanwaltschaft Bremen*

Resetting the Parameters of Mutual Trust: From Aranyosi *to* LM

VALSAMIS MITSILEGAS

I. Introduction

The application of the principle of mutual recognition in the field of criminal law has been a key driver of European integration in criminal matters. Based upon the presumption of a high level of mutual trust across the European Union, mutual recognition has been applied to cover a wide range of judicial decisions extending to all stages of the criminal justice process. However, the application of the principle of mutual recognition on that basis has not been without controversy. A key question which has exercised policy makers, legislators, judges and citizens alike is the extent to which the European Union can introduce an automatic system of recognition based solely on presumed, uncritical trust. At the heart of this debate lies the question of the position of fundamental rights within the general scheme of mutual recognition in EU criminal law, and more specifically the question whether fundamental rights considerations should be allowed to pose limits to the automaticity of mutual recognition, resulting in a greater role for executing authorities in scrutinising the fundamental rights implications of compliance with the request to recognise and ultimately to refusal to execute if fundamental rights concerns persist. Nowhere has this debate arisen more forcefully than in the operation of the emblematic mutual recognition instrument in the field of criminal law, the Framework Decision on the European Arrest Warrant.[1] There, and

[1] Council Framework Decision 2002/584/JHA of 13 June 2002 on the European arrest warrant and the surrender procedures between Member States [2002] OJ L190/1.

after a rocky path, we witnessed recently a paradigmatic change by the Court of Justice in resetting the parameters of mutual trust underpinning mutual recognition and granting greater space to fundamental rights – and ultimately rule of law – concerns to be raised and considered meaningfully at the stage of the execution of the European Arrest Warrant. This contribution aims to assess and evaluate the transformative impact of these rulings – *Aranyosi*[2] and *LM*[3] – in reshaping the principle of mutual trust for the purposes of mutual recognition. In order to do so, the complexities of the perceived wisdom of presumed, uncritical trust will first be highlighted.

II. The Starting Premise: Automatic Mutual Recognition based on Presumed, Uncritical Trust

The fundamental premises of the application of the principle of mutual recognition in criminal matters have been the presumption of a high level of mutual trust in the criminal justice systems of EU Member States, leading to the aim of establishing a system of judicial co-operation based on automaticity and speed. Grounds to refuse execution of a judicial decision were limited and did not at first include concerns regarding the fundamental rights implications of surrender – leading thus to what I have characterised as a 'journey into the unknown' for executing authorities in accepting and enforcing the outcome of a legal system of another EU Member State without asking any questions about its substance.[4] This model of co-operation has been embodied in the Framework Decision on the European Arrest Warrant (hereinafter 'FD EAW'),[5] where non-compliance with fundamental rights is not included as a ground to refuse to execute a EAW, with a general provision – Article 1(3) – rather including the statement that 'this Framework Decision shall not have the effect of modifying the obligation to respect fundamental rights and fundamental legal principles as enshrined in Article 6 of the TEU'.[6] The system established by the text of the FD EAW reflects a view under which membership of the EU *as such* is sufficient to justify a generalised presumption that all Member States comply with fundamental rights, a presumption which in turn is sufficient to justify a no questions asked, high level of mutual trust in the operation of the system. While in the implementation of the FD EAW this presumption has been questioned by a number of Member States, which added non-compliance of surrender with fundamental rights as an express ground of

[2] Joined Cases C-404/15 and C-659/15 PPU *Pál Aranyosi and Robert Căldăraru* ECLI:EU:C:2016:198.

[3] Case C-216/18 PPU *Minister for Justice and Equality (Défaillances du système judiciaire)* ECLI:EU:C:2018:586.

[4] V Mitsilegas, 'The Constitutional Implications of Mutual Recognition in Criminal Matters in the EU' (2006) 43 *Common Market Law Review* 1277–1311.

[5] FD EAW (n 1).

[6] See also Recital 12 of the Preamble to the FD EAW.

refusal in their national law implementing the FD EAW,[7] in its early case law the Court of Justice of the European Union (CJEU) demonstrated strong support for the system established by the FD EAW.[8] The entry into force of the Lisbon Treaty, bringing with it the communitarisation of the third pillar, the constitutionalisation of EU criminal law and of the Charter of Fundamental Rights of the European Union,[9] has raised hopes that the CJEU would modify its stance regarding fundamental rights scrutiny in the operation of the EAW. These hopes were increased by CJEU case law in the field of mutual recognition in asylum law: in the case of *NS and ME*, the CJEU ruled that a transfer under the Dublin Regulation would be incompatible with fundamental rights

> 'if there are substantial grounds for believing that there are systemic flaws in the asylum procedure and reception conditions for asylum applicants in the Member State responsible, resulting in inhuman or degrading treatment, within the meaning of Article 4 of the Charter, of asylum seekers transferred to the territory of that Member State'.[10]

The CJEU approach constituted a paradigmatic shift on mutual recognition based on automaticity: the Court stated expressly that the presumption of compliance with fundamental rights in the receiving Member State is rebuttable[11] and it placed specific duties to sending authorities to examine fundamental rights compliance.[12]

It has been argued that the paradigm change to the operation of mutual trust in *NS* and *ME also* would be applicable in transfers of individuals under the EAW, thus establishing a horizontal benchmark of fundamental rights protection across the area of freedom, security and justice (AFSJ).[13] Yet in its first major post-Lisbon cases on the EAW, and also notwithstanding parallel developments in post-Lisbon EU criminal law,[14] the CJEU appeared reluctant to do so. In *Radu*,[15] and notwithstanding the attempt by Advocate General (AG) Sharpston to bring the protection

[7] On the implementation of the FD EAW, see V Mitsilegas, 'The Area of Freedom, Security and Justice from Amsterdam to Lisbon: Challenges of Implementation, Constitutionality and Fundamental Rights' in J Laffranque (ed), *The Area of Freedom, Security and Justice, Including Information Society Issues: Reports of the XXV FIDE Congress* (Tallinn, 2012) Vol 3, 21–142 and national reports included therein.

[8] V Mitsilegas, *EU Criminal Law* (Hart Publishing, 2009) Ch 3.

[9] V Mitsilegas, *EU Criminal Law After Lisbon* (Hart Publishing, 2016).

[10] Case C-411/10 *NS v Secretary of State for the Home Department* ECLI:EU:C:2011:865, para 85.

[11] *Ibid*, para 104.

[12] *Ibid*, para 94.

[13] V Mitsilegas, 'The Limits of Mutual Trust in Europe's Area of Freedom, Security and Justice. From Automatic Inter-State Cooperation to the Slow Emergence of the Individual' (2012) 31 *Yearbook of European Law* 319–72.

[14] The post-Lisbon mutual recognition Directive on the European Investigation Order (EIO) has introduced an optional ground for non-recognition or non-execution where there are substantial grounds to believe that the execution of the investigative measure indicated in the EIO would be incompatible with the executing state's obligations in accordance with Article 6 on the Treaty on European Union (TEU) and the Charter (Article 11(1)(f)). Directive 2014/41/EU of the European Parliament and of the Council of 3 April 2014 regarding the European Investigation Order in criminal matters [2014] OJ L130/1.

[15] Case C-396/11 *Radu* ECLI:EU:C:2013:39.

of fundamental rights into the fore (notably by advancing arguments based on proportionality),[16] the CJEU continued to focus on the effectiveness of the EAW. *Radu* was followed by the much-discussed *Melloni*,[17] where the CJEU found that Member States cannot refuse to execute a EAW on the basis of a level of fundamental rights protection provided under their national constitution which is higher than the level of protection provided in the Charter. By casting doubt on the uniformity of the standard of protection of fundamental rights as defined in the FD, Member States would undermine the principles of mutual trust and recognition which that Decision purports to uphold and would, therefore, compromise the efficacy of that FD.[18] *Melloni* was followed by the questionable elevation of mutual trust to a fundamental principle of EU law in *Opinion 2/13*.[19]

The reasoning of the CJEU in both *Melloni* and *Opinion 2/13* can be explained from a constitutional law perspective as the Court sending a clear message to the Strasbourg Court and to national constitutional courts of its determination to uphold the primacy and autonomy of EU law.[20] Yet the implications of the Court's reasoning for a meaningful fundamental rights scrutiny in the process of mutual recognition are profound. The CJEU elevated the inherently subjective concept of mutual trust into a fundamental principle of EU law[21] adopting a version of mutual trust which is to be taken at face value and to be presumed, with cracks in the façade of trust appearing only in exceptional cases. In defending the primacy and autonomy of EU law, the CJEU has thus however undermined the credibility of the EAW system in the eyes of national courts and the Strasbourg Court. The CJEU rulings appeared increasingly at odds with the Strasbourg approach, focusing on the individualised assessment of fundamental rights violations. This discrepancy was evident in the case of *Tarakhel*,[22] involving Dublin transfers from Switzerland to Italy, where the European Court of Human Rights (ECtHR) found a breach of the European Convention on Human Rights (ECHR) with regard to specific individuals *even in a case where generalised systemic deficiencies in the receiving state had not been ascertained*.[23] The CJEU approach vis-à-vis the protection of fundamental rights as enshrined in national constitutions has also raised alarm bells in national constitutional courts. These concerns have been

[16] Case C-396/11 *Radu* ECLI:EU:C:2012:648. See in particular para 103.

[17] Case C-399/11 *Melloni* ECLI:EU:C:2013:107.

[18] *Ibid*, para 63.

[19] Case *Opinion 2/13 of the Court, Opinion pursuant to Article 218(11) TFEU* ECLI:EU:C:2014:2454, paras 191–92.

[20] See also the CJEU reiterating in *Opinion 2/13* the Melloni requirement to uphold the primacy, unity and effectiveness of EU law in para 188.

[21] V Mitsilegas, 'The Symbiotic Relationship between Mutual Trust and Fundamental Rights in Europe's Area of Criminal Justice' (2015) 6 (4) *New Journal of European Criminal Law* 460–85.

[22] *Tarakhel v Switzerland* App no 29217/12 (ECtHR, 4 November 2014).

[23] *Ibid*, para 115, emphasis added. As Halberstam has noted, *Tarakhel* was a strong warning signal to Luxembourg that the CJEU's standard better comport either in words or in practice with what Strasbourg demands or else the Dublin system violates the Convention. See Halberstam, '"It's the Autonomy, Stupid!" A Modest Defense of Opinion 2/13 on EU Accession to the ECHR, and the Way Forward' (Michigan Law School, Public Law and Legal Theory Research paper Series, 2015) 432, 27.

expressed by the German *Bundesverfassungsericht* (BVerG) in a ruling delivered in 2015, where it intervened regarding the scrutiny of fundamental rights in the execution of a EAW in a case of trial *in absentia* where the defendant's lawyer had not been notified.[24] The BVerG found that mutual trust has its limits and 'can be shaken'[25] 'if there are indications based on facts that the requirements indispensable for the protection of human dignity would not be complied with in the case of an extradition'.[26] The BVerG focused on the principle of individual guilt, placed within the context of the protection of human dignity, which it asserted is 'beyond the reach of European integration',[27] and found that it also applies to extraditions that take place on the basis of the FD EAW.[28] In a landmark ruling, it introduced the requirement of identity review of measures implementing the EAW when the principle of human dignity is at stake. While the BVerG ultimately found that the system established by EU law was not unconstitutional, it put forward a mechanism of scrutiny of fundamental rights concerns by the executing authority on an individualised basis.[29] While the evocation of the identity review by the BVerG has rightly been criticised,[30] the intervention by the German Constitutional Court has been of considerable significance in raising alarm bells in Luxembourg regarding the implications of continuing to uphold a version of presumed, uncritical, 'blind' trust for the credibility of the EAW system in the eyes of the authorities which are called upon to operate it and in the eyes of national constitutional courts.

III. Revisiting Automaticity: *Aranyosi* and its Impact

The Court of Justice had the opportunity to examine directly the relationship between fundamental rights, mutual recognition and mutual trust in the joined cases of *Aranyosi and Căldăraru*,[31] both referred for a preliminary ruling by the Higher Regional Court of Bremen. The reference was another opportunity for the CJEU to specifically address the question of whether the execution of an EAW could be refused on the grounds of concerns over the violation of fundamental rights. The cases involved both prosecution and conviction warrants issued by Romania and Hungary. The concerns of German authorities centered on the impact of execution on Article 4 of the Charter in view of the existence of pilot

[24] BVerfG, Order of the Second Senate of 15 December 2015 – 2 BvR 2735/14 – paras 1–126.
[25] *Ibid*, para 67.
[26] *Ibid*, para 74. See also para 83.
[27] *Ibid*, para 76.
[28] *Ibid*, para 72.
[29] *Ibid*, paras 63–72.
[30] Meyer has noted that the emphasis on identity review did not fit the facts of the case, as EU secondary law was compliant with the German Constitution: Meyer, '"From Solange II to Forever I": The German Federal Constitutional Court and the European Arrest Warrant (and how the CJEU responded)' (2016) 7 *New Journal of European Criminal Law* 277–94 at 283.
[31] *Aranyosi and Căldăraru* (n 2).

judgments by the ECtHR attesting breaches of Article 3 ECHR on the grounds of the unacceptable state of prison conditions in both countries.[32] The German Court raised two broad questions at the heart of the discussion on defining the parameters of mutual trust: on the extent to which serious fundamental rights concerns could lead to the inadmissibility of a EAW and on the legal framework and content related to the provision of assurances by the issuing authorities asserting compliance with fundamental rights. The CJEU started by reiterating the importance of mutual recognition and mutual trust as highlighted in previous EAW judgments and by placing mutual recognition within a fundamental rights protection framework,[33] also as developed in *Opinion 2/13*.[34] Limits to the principles of mutual recognition and mutual trust between Member States could appear 'in exceptional circumstances';[35] the FD EAW was not meant to have the effect of modifying the obligation to respect fundamental rights encompassed in the Charter of Fundamental Rights.[36] The CJEU noted that Article 4 of the Charter is absolute in nature in that it is closely linked to respect for human dignity as enshrined in Article 1 of the Charter.[37] This is further confirmed by Article 3 ECHR, to which Article 4 of the Charter corresponds.[38]

In a departure from earlier judgments, the CJEU proceeded to provide detailed guidelines to executing authorities on how they must proceed when assessing the existence of a risk of inhuman or degrading treatment arising from the execution of a EAW. The CJEU put forward a two-step approach. First, a general assessment of the risk must take place. Where the judicial authority of the executing Member State is in possession of evidence of a real risk of inhuman or degrading treatment of individuals detained in the issuing Member State, it is bound to assess the existence of that risk when it is called upon to decide on the surrender to the authorities of the issuing Member State of the individual sought by a EAW.[39] To that end, the national court may rely on information that is objective, reliable, specific and properly updated on the detention conditions prevailing in the issuing Member State and that demonstrates that there are deficiencies, which may be systemic or generalised, or which may affect certain groups of people, or which may affect certain places of detention. Sources may include judgments of international courts, such as judgments of the ECtHR, judgments of courts of the issuing Member State, and also decisions, reports and other documents produced by bodies of the Council of Europe or under the aegis of the UN.[40] National authorities are under a positive obligation to ensure that any prisoner is detained in conditions which guarantee

[32] *Aranyosi and Căldăraru* (n 2), paras 43–44 and 60–61.
[33] *Aranyosi and Căldăraru* (n 2), paras 75–78.
[34] *Opinion 2/13* (n 19). See para 78 of the judgment.
[35] *Aranyosi and Căldăraru* (n 2), para 82.
[36] *Aranyosi and Căldăraru* (n 2), para 83.
[37] *Aranyosi and Căldăraru* (n 2), paras 84–85.
[38] *Aranyosi and Căldăraru* (n 2), paras 86–87.
[39] *Aranyosi and Căldăraru* (n 2), para 88.
[40] *Aranyosi and Căldăraru* (n 2), para 89.

respect for human dignity, that the way in which detention is enforced does not cause the individual concerned distress or hardship of an intensity exceeding the unavoidable level of suffering that is inherent in detention and that, having regard to the practical requirements of imprisonment, the health and well-being of the prisoner are adequately protected.[41]

However, a finding by the executing judicial authority that there is a real risk of inhuman or degrading treatment by virtue of general conditions of detention in the issuing Member State does not automatically signify that the execution of the EAW must be refused.[42] Therefore, in addition to a general assessment of the risk, it will also be necessary for the executing judicial authority as a second step to proceed to a further assessment, specific and precise, of whether there are substantial grounds to believe that the individual concerned will be exposed to that risk because of the conditions for his detention envisaged in the issuing Member State.[43] The executing authority is bound to determine whether, in the particular circumstances of the case, there are substantial grounds to believe that, following the surrender of that person to the issuing Member State, he will run a real risk of being subject in that Member State to inhuman or degrading treatment.[44] Central to the assessment of risk at this stage is the establishment of a co-operative mechanism of interaction between the executing and the issuing authorities, in accordance with Article 15(2) of the FD EAW. A request must be made as a matter of urgency regarding all necessary supplementary information on the conditions in which it is envisaged that the individual concerned will be detained in that Member State.[45] Such request may also relate to the existence, in the issuing Member State, of any national or international procedures and mechanisms for monitoring detention conditions, linked, for example, to visits to prisons, which make it possible to assess the current state of detention conditions in those prisons.[46] A time limit for the receipt of the supplementary information may be fixed, which must be adjusted to the particularities of each case, must equally respect time limits set in Article 17 of that FD.[47] The issuing judicial authority is obliged to provide that information to the executing judicial authority.[48] If on the basis of the information provided the executing judicial authority finds that there exists a real

[41] *Aranyosi and Căldăraru* (n 2), para 90.
[42] *Aranyosi and Căldăraru* (n 2), para 91.
[43] *Aranyosi and Căldăraru* (n 2), para 92. According to the CJEU, this is because the mere existence of evidence that there are deficiencies, which may be systemic or generalised, or which may affect certain groups of people, or which may affect certain places of detention, with respect to detention conditions in the issuing Member State does not necessarily mean that, in a specific case, the individual concerned will be subject to inhuman or degrading treatment in the event that he is surrendered to the authorities of that Member State (para 93).
[44] *Aranyosi and Căldăraru* (n 2), para 94.
[45] *Aranyosi and Căldăraru* (n 2), para 95.
[46] *Aranyosi and Căldăraru* (n 2), para 96.
[47] *Aranyosi and Căldăraru* (n 2), para 97.
[48] *Aranyosi and Căldăraru* (n 2), para 97.

risk of inhuman or degrading treatment for the individual in respect of whom the EAW was issued, then the execution is postponed, but it cannot be abandoned.[49] Until the point of obtaining supplementing information that would discount the existence of a risk of inhuman or degrading treatment, a decision on the surrender must be postponed, but if the existence of that risk cannot be discounted within a reasonable time, the executing judicial authority must decide whether the surrender procedure should be brought to an end.[50]

Aranyosi is a landmark judgment and a turning point in the CJEU approach on mutual trust. It confirms a shift from automatic mutual recognition based on uncritical mutual trust (or, as the CJEU President, Koen Lenaerts, has put it 'blind trust'[51]) to earned trust on the basis of an individualised assessment of the fundamental rights consequences of surrender on the ground.[52] *Aranyosi* is significant here in two respects: in departing from the CJEU mantra of 'systemic deficiencies' in confirming the requirement for the executing authority to examine the impact of the surrender on an individual basis; and in emphasising (as it has done in its case law on asylum, and in particular in *NS*), the need for an assessment not only of the law, but also of the practice of fundamental rights protection as regards the individual concerned. In both respects, the CJEU approach becomes increasingly aligned with the approach of the ECtHR in scrutinising mutual trust – with the Strasbourg Court also adopting a more conciliatory tone towards its scrutiny of EU mutual recognition measures.[53] *Aranyosi* is also significant in the CJEU setting detailed parameters for the co-operative relationship between national authorities responsible for operating the EAW. The CJEU has provided reasonably detailed guidance on the dialogue between authorities under Article 15 of the FD EAW under a two-stage approach. In this context, the CJEU appears to have been inspired by the fundamental rights review approach adopted by the BVerG, an approach which has been based, as with the BVerG, on the recognition that the right in question is an absolute right linked human dignity.[54] Although *Aranyosi* is not the outcome of a direct dialogue between the CJEU on the one hand and the BVerG or the ECtHR on the other, its reasoning and outcome can be seen as a recognition by the CJEU of the approach taken by both these courts

[49] *Aranyosi and Căldăraru* (n 2), para 98.

[50] *Aranyosi and Căldăraru* (n 2), para 104.

[51] K Lenaerts, 'La Vie Après l'Avis: Exploring the Principle of Mutual (yet not Blind) Trust' (2017) 54 *Common Market Law Review* (2017) 805–40, at 806. According to President Lenaerts, mutual trust is not to be confused with blind trust.

[52] Writing on the need for earned trust before *Aranyosi*, see Mitsilegas (n 9) Ch 5.

[53] *Avotiņš v Latvia* App no 17502/07 (ECtHR, 23 May 2016); ECtHR, *Pirozzi c. Belgique* App no 21055/11 (ECtHR, 17 April 2018). For further details, see section IV below.

[54] See also G Anagnostaras, 'Mutual Confidence is Not Blind Trust! Fundamental Rights Protection and the Execution of the European Arrest Warrant: *Aranyosi and Caldararu*' (2016) 53 *Common Market Law Review* 1675–1704, at 1702. The author notes that, 'the recognition that the rights that are closely linked to respect for human dignity must be considered as absolute … seems to echo the position of the constitutional court'.

regarding mutual trust.[55] As a first step in a change of direction for the CJEU, *Aranyosi* leaves a number of questions unanswered or creates further questions: is the adopted approach applicable only to cases involving challenges to Article 4 of the Charter, only to absolute rights, or to any fundamental right? Is the approach in *Aranyosi* applicable to other areas of EU law, and in particular Dublin transfers in EU asylum law? What is the extent of the obligations of the authorities operating the EAW under the co-operative mechanism following Article 15 FD EAW? In particular (a question which was left unanswered by the CJEU in Aranyosi), what is the role of assurances in this co-operative paradigm? And what is the extent of these obligations if there are broader systemic concerns on the protection of fundamental rights in the Member State where the issuing authority is based, raising underlying rule of law issues? The CJEU has since had the opportunity to provide answers to some of these detailed questions – especially on the intensity of scrutiny and assurances – in the case of *ML*.[56] The subsequent sections will highlight the broader impact of *Aranyosi* in other areas of EU law and in extending fundamental rights scrutiny from Article 4 of the Charter to effective judicial protection and ultimately the rule of law.

IV. Extending *Aranyosi*: Towards a Fundamental Rights Scrutiny Benchmark across European Public Law

The CJEU in *Aranyosi* not only took into account developments in other courts, but has since applied its reasoning in other areas of European public law, related both to EU internal and external action. In terms of the AFSJ, the CJEU applied *Aranyosi* in the context of Dublin transfers in the case of *CK*.[57] *CK* is important in that it involved a situation whereby it was claimed that a Dublin transfer would be in breach of Article 4 of the Charter even in cases where there are substantial grounds for believing that there are systemic flaws in the asylum procedure and the conditions for the reception of asylum seekers in the receiving Member State.[58] In an important departure from the logic of systemic deficiencies put forward in *NS*, the Court found that it cannot be ruled out that *the transfer* of an asylum seeker may, *in itself*, result, for the person concerned, in a real risk of inhuman or degrading treatment within the meaning of Article 4 of the Charter, *irrespective of the quality of the reception and the care available in the Member State responsible for examining his application*.[59] While the CJEU does not refer to the Strasbourg

[55] Lenaerts (n 51) 807. According to President Lenaerts, the contours of principle are not carved in stone, but will take concrete shape by means of a constructive dialogue between the European Court of Justice, the ECtHR and national courts.

[56] Case C-220/18 PPU *Generalstaatsanwaltschaft* ECLI:EU:C:2018:589.

[57] Case C-578/16 PPU, *CK, HF, and AS* ECLI:EU:C:2017:127.

[58] *Ibid*, para 71.

[59] *Ibid*, para 73. Emphasis added.

ruling in *Tarakhel* in this context, this finding represents a substantial alignment of its case law on Dublin transfers with the approach of the Strasbourg Court in focusing on the examination of the fundamental rights implications on an individual basis. In developing this approach, the CJEU used its findings extensively in *Aranyosi* which it applied by analogy in this case. The Court reiterated in this context that national authorities cannot ignore evidence of the negative consequences of a transfer for the individual, and are *under an obligation to assess the risk* that such consequences could occur when they decide to transfer the person concerned or, in the case of a court, the legality of a decision to transfer.[60] It is, therefore, for those authorities to eliminate any serious doubts concerning the impact of such transfer.[61] The CJEU subsequently mentioned a model of co-operation between the authorities in the two Member States[62] and ultimately allowed for the suspension of the transfer if measures taken do not eliminate the real risk for the individual to be transferred.[63] In its conclusion to *CK*, the Court left no doubt regarding the change in its approach. It expressly rejected the Commission's argument that it follows from Article 3(2) of the Dublin III Regulation (which is an attempt to incorporate the *NS* ruling in EU secondary law[64]) that only the existence of systemic flaws in the Member State responsible is capable of affecting the obligation to transfer an asylum seeker to that Member State.[65] According to the Court, nothing in the wording of that provision suggests that the intention of the EU legislature had been to regulate any circumstance other than that of systemic flaws preventing any transfer of asylum seekers to a particular Member State. That provision cannot, therefore, be interpreted as excluding the possibility that considerations linked to real and proven risks of inhuman or degrading treatment, within the meaning of Article 4 of the Charter, might, in exceptional situations such as those envisaged in the present judgment, have consequences for the transfer of a particular asylum seeker.[66] The Court has placed this expansive interpretation within the broader contours of defining the parameters of mutual trust.[67] Importantly, the Court states in no uncertain terms that the responsibility for fundamental rights violations in case of a transfer in situations whereby such transfer would result in inhuman and degrading treatment would be attributable directly or indirectly to the authorities of the Member State authorising the transfer alone.[68] The Court thus extends its approach taken in the context of EAW transfers in *Aranyosi* to Dublin transfers in *CK*. In this manner, it establishes a

[60] *Ibid*, para 75.
[61] *Ibid*, para 76.
[62] *Ibid*, para 80.
[63] *Ibid*, para 82–89, in particular para 85.
[64] Regulation 604/2013 [2013] OJ L18/31 For an analysis, see V Mitsilegas, 'Solidarity and Trust in the Common European Asylum System' (2014) 2 Comparative Migration Studies 231–53.
[65] *CK, HF, and AS* (n 57), para 91.
[66] *CK, HF, and AS* (n 57), para 93.
[67] *CK, HF, and AS* (n 57), para 95.
[68] *CK, HF, and AS* (n 57), para 95.

benchmark of fundamental rights protection in the evolving paradigm of inter-state cooperation based on mutual trust in EU law.[69] This new benchmark is based on a developed concept of mutual trust based on earned trust under scrutiny and on the articulation of clear fundamental rights responsibilities for the authorities of the issuing/sending Member State.

While *CK* focused on the internal functioning of the AFSJ, there has also been an alignment in the degree of scrutiny of fundamental rights between EU internal and external action. The CJEU has applied *Aranyosi* in extradition requests by third states when the matter has fallen within EU law. In *Petruhhin*,[70] the CJEU stated unequivocally that the existence of declarations and accession to international treaties guaranteeing respect for fundamental rights in principle *are not in themselves sufficient* to ensure adequate protection where reliable sources have reported practices resorted to or tolerated by the authorities which are manifestly contrary to the principles of the ECHR.[71] The duties set out to judicial authorities by the CJEU in *Aranyosi* in internal EAW cases also apply to requested authorities of EU Member States in extradition requests by third countries.[72] In setting up its judgment, the Court reiterated that in its relations with the wider world, the European Union is to uphold and promote its values and interests and contribute to the protection of its citizens, in accordance with Article 3(5) TEU.[73]

V. From a Fundamental Rights to a Rule of Law Scrutiny Benchmark: The Impact of *LM*

In March 2018, and dealing with the question of the fundamental rights compatibility of the execution of a EAW to Poland, the Irish High Court requested the Court of Justice to decide whether the *Aranyosi* test could apply to cases of violations of the rule of law.[74] Building on the Reasoned Proposal of the Commission in accordance with Article 7(1) TEU and on the Opinions of the Venice Commission of the Council of Europe regarding the situation in Poland,[75] the Irish Court argued

[69] Lenaerts (n 51) 837. Here, President Lenaerts refers to a process of public policy convergence.
[70] Case C 182/15 *Petruhhin* ECLI:EU:C:2016:630.
[71] *Ibid*, para 57.
[72] *Ibid*, paras 58 and 59.
[73] *Ibid*, para 44.
[74] *Minister for Justice and Equality v Artur Celmer* [2018] IEHC 119, 2018-03-12.
[75] The European Commission for Democracy through Law (Venice Commission) has adopted the following Opinions concerning Poland: CDL-AD(2017)031, 'Opinion on the Draft Act amending the Act on the National Council of the Judiciary, on the Draft Act amending the Act on the Supreme Court, proposed by the President of Poland, and on the Act on the Organisation of Ordinary Courts', Venice, 8–9, 2017; CDL-AD(2017)028-e, 'Poland – Opinion on the Act on the Public Prosecutor's Office as Amended', Venice, 8–9, 2017; CDL-AD(2016)026-e, 'Opinion on the Act on the Constitutional Tribunal', Venice, 14–15, 2016; CDL-AD(2016)012-e, 'Opinion on the Act of 15 January 2016 amending the Police Act and certain other Acts', Venice, 10-11, 2016; CDL-AD(2016)001-e, 'Opinion on amendments to the Act of 25 June 2015 on the Constitutional Tribunal of Poland', Venice, 11–12, 2016.

that 'the rule of law in Poland has been systematically damaged by the cumulative impact of all legislative changes that have taken place over the last two years'.[76] The Court noted that the Polish Ministry of Justice has a disciplinary role over the presidents of courts, and this may have 'a chilling effect' on them, with consequential impact on the administration of justice.[77] Due to the recent reforms, the Polish Ministry of Justice is also the Public Prosecutor, entitled to play an active role in prosecutions.[78] This 'amalgamation between political and prosecutorial functions'[79] did not sit well with the principle of the rule of law and with the basic features of the EAW proceedings. According to the case law of the Court of Justice, the term 'judicial authority' used in the FD EAW should be interpreted as an autonomous concept of EU law and it is not limited to courts and tribunals, as it may extend to the other national authorities required to participate in administering justice.[80] Nonetheless, it cannot cover an organ of the executive such as a ministry for this would violate the principle of the separation of powers, which 'characterises the operation of the rule of law',[81] and would bar the necessary *judicial* supervision on the respect of the fundamental rights of the person whose surrender is sought.[82]

Against this backdrop, the Irish Court found that the threats to the rule of law in Poland are not theoretical but are 'very real and quite systemic'.[83] As the respect for the rule of law is 'essential for mutual trust in the operation of the European arrest warrant',[84] the Court wondered how the principles of mutual trust and mutual recognition can operate when there are such systemic and inherent defects in the Polish legal system. Engaging with the *Aranyosi* test and its admittedly uneasy application to the case at stake, the Court acknowledged that it appears unrealistic to require a requested person to demonstrate how, in his individual cases, those systemic defects may affect his trial.[85] The two-step approach envisaged in *Aranyosi* also required the executing authority to seek all the necessary information from the issuing authority as to the protections for the individual concerned. However, in circumstances such as those concerning the Polish system, 'it is difficult to see how individual guarantees can be given by the issuing judicial authority as to fair trial when it is the *system of justice itself* that is no longer operating under the rule of law'.[86] The Irish Court therefore required clarification from the Court of Justice on how to handle similar cases.

[76] *Minister for Justice and Equality* (n 74), para 124.
[77] *Minister for Justice and Equality* (n 74), para 128.
[78] *Minister for Justice and Equality* (n 74), para 128.
[79] CDL-AD(2017)028-e, 'Poland – Opinion on the Act on the Public Prosecutor's Office as Amended' (n 75), para 110.
[80] Case C-452/16 PPU *Poltorak* EU:C:2016:858, paras 31–33; and Case C-477/16 PPU *Kovalkovas* EU:C:2016:861, paras 32–34.
[81] *Kovalkovas*, *ibid*, para 36.
[82] *Kovalkovas*, *ibid*, para 37.
[83] *Minister for Justice and Equality* (n 74), para 138.
[84] *Minister for Justice and Equality* (n 74), para 136.
[85] *Minister for Justice and Equality* (n 74), para 141.
[86] *Minister for Justice and Equality* (n 74), para 142 (emphasis added).

Addressing the question raised by the Irish High Court in *LM*, also known as *Minister for Justice and Equality (Défaillances du système judiciaire)*,[87] the Court of Justice extended the two-stage *Aranyosi* test to cases where the rule of law is at stake, under the perspective of the right to a fair trial. In keeping with its case law, and notably with *Opinion 2/13*, the Court first recalled that EU law is based on the fundamental premise that the Member States share a set of common values, as stated in Article 2 TEU.[88] This implies and justifies the existence of mutual trust between the Member States that those values will be recognised.[89] Mutual trust underpins the principle of mutual recognition and they both are 'of fundamental importance given that they allow an area without internal borders to be created and maintained'.[90] However, in exceptional circumstances, limitations may be placed on both these principles, as it is the case when the right not to be subjected to inhuman or degrading treatment is at stake (Article 4 of the Charter).[91] The Court has now extended these limitations when the respect of Article 47 of the Charter, which enshrines the right to an effective remedy and to a fair trial, is jeopardised. The Luxembourg Court points out that judicial independence

> forms part of the essence of the fundamental right to a fair trial, a right which is of cardinal importance as a guarantee that all the rights which individuals derive from EU law will be protected and that the values common to the Member States set out in Article 2 TEU, in particular the value of the *rule of law*, will be safeguarded.[92]

The Court then referred back to its judgment of February 2018 concerning the reduction in the remuneration of Portuguese judges, where it lingers over the notion of the rule of law.[93] In this ruling, the Court provided the first interpretation of Article 47 of the Charter and highlights that 'the very existence of effective judicial review designed to ensure compliance with EU law is of the essence of the rule of law'.[94] This requires the independence of courts and tribunals, which is essential to the proper working of the judicial cooperation system embodied by the preliminary ruling mechanism.[95] It is also essential, the Court added in *LM*, in the context of the EAW mechanism.[96] Recalling some previous judgments on

[87] *LM* (n 3).
[88] *LM* (n 3), para 35.
[89] *LM* (n 3), para 35.
[90] *LM* (n 3), para 36.
[91] *Aranyosi and Căldăraru* (n 2).
[92] *Aranyosi and Căldăraru* (n 2), para 48 (emphasis added).
[93] Case C-64/16 *Associação Sindical dos Juízes Portugueses* EU:C:2018:117.
[94] *LM* (n 3), para 51, with reference to para 36 of *Associação Sindical dos Juízes Portugueses, ibid.*
[95] *LM* (n 3), paras 53–54, with reference to paras 41–43 of *Associação Sindical dos Juízes Portugueses* (n 93). In the latter ruling, the Court of Justice also provides a set of conceptual features determining the extent to which a judicial authority is 'independent' for the purposes of EU law: '… the factors to be taken into account in assessing whether a body is a "court or tribunal" include, inter alia, whether the body is established by law, whether it is permanent, whether its jurisdiction is compulsory, whether its procedure is inter partes, whether it applies rules of law and whether it is independent' (*Associação Sindical dos Juízes Portugueses* (n 93), para 38).
[96] *LM* (n 3), para 55.

the rationale behind the FD EAW, the Court concludes that the high level of trust between Member States underpinning the EAW mechanism is founded on the premise that the criminal courts of the other Member States 'meet the requirements of effective judicial protection, which include, in particular, the independence and impartiality of those courts'.[97]

When the person whose surrender is sought pleads that there are systemic deficiencies in the issuing Member State that are liable to affect the independence of the judiciary, the executing judicial authority is thus required to assess whether there is a 'real risk' that the individual concerned will suffer a breach of his fundamental right to a fair trial if surrendered.[98] This assessment should follow the two-step procedure set out in *Aranyosi*. First, the executing judicial authority must assess whether such a right may be breached because of a lack of independence of the courts in the issuing Member State on account of *systemic* and generalised deficiencies of its legal system.[99] This assessment should be carried out on the basis of material that is 'objective, reliable, specific and properly updated'[100] and must look both at the external independence of judicial authorities from any undue pressure[101] and at their internal independence – which requires equal distance from the parties to the proceedings and the absence of any interest in the outcome of the proceedings.[102] If the executing judicial authority finds that there is a real risk of breach of the essence of the fundamental right to a fair trial on account of systemic or generalised deficiencies concerning the judiciary of the issuing Member State, the executing authority must move on to the second step of its assessment. The executing authority is required to assess 'specifically and precisely whether, in the *particular* circumstances of the case, there are substantial grounds for believing that, following his surrender to the issuing Member State, the requested person will run that risk'.[103] In particular, the executing authority should take into account the personal situation of the individual concerned, as well as the nature of the offence and the factual context that forms the basis of the EAW.[104] As in *Aranyosi*, the Court reminds us that the executing authority should engage in a dialogue with the issuing judicial authority to better assess the threats to the fundamental rights of the individual whose surrender is sought.[105] Within such a dialogue, the issuing judicial authority may provide the executing judicial authority with 'any objective material on any changes concerning the conditions for protecting the guarantee of judicial independence in the issuing Member State, material which may rule out the existence of that risk for the individual concerned'.[106] If this information is not

[97] *LM* (n 3), para 58.
[98] *LM* (n 3), para 59.
[99] *LM* (n 3), para 61.
[100] *LM* (n 3), para 61.
[101] *LM* (n 3), paras 63–64.
[102] *LM* (n 3), paras 65–66.
[103] *LM* (n 3), para 68 (emphasis added).
[104] *LM* (n 3), para 75.
[105] *LM* (n 3), para 76.
[106] *LM* (n 3), para 77.

sufficient to discount the existence of a real risk that the right to a fair trial of the individual concerned will be breached in the issuing Member State, the executing authority must refrain from giving effect to the EAW relating to him.[107] It is also worth noting that the Court of Justice requires the executing authority to embark upon the second stage of the *Aranyosi* test even when the Commission has already adopted a reasoned proposal in accordance with Article 7(1) TEU regarding the issuing Member State.[108] It is only when the European Council has determined that there is a serious and persistent breach of the principles set out in Article 2 TEU that the executing authority is exempted from the assessment of whether systemic deficiencies end up affecting specifically and precisely the individual concerned.[109]

The Court's ruling in *LM* is of far-reaching significance as it paves the way for rule of law scrutiny in Member States via the examination of the fundamental rights concerns underpinning the execution of a EAW. The dialogue between the Irish Court and the CJEU constitutes a key example of bottom-up scrutiny of the rule of law across the European Union. This bottom-up scrutiny can go a long way in addressing the shortcomings of law and practice in relation to the operation of Article 7 TEU and the role and limits of EU institutions in scrutinising effectively rule of law compliance in Member States.[110] National courts can escalate their concerns to the CJEU and invite the Court of Justice to make an assessment. This scrutiny is central for the credible and effective operation of the EAW system, involving cross-border co-operation based on mutual trust. Rule of law scrutiny here occurs in a mechanism involving courts, rather than the executive. It is a mechanism which promotes dialogue and horizontal interactions, and which stresses the importance of rule of law compliance and scrutiny on the ground. The CJEU can act as the enabler of a dialogue between national authorities, providing avenues of communication and co-operation not only at the level of the highest courts, but importantly also in the context of the operation of the EAW at the level of the lower courts. In terms of the scope of fundamental rights scrutiny, *LM* is of importance as it confirms that such scrutiny is not confined to Article 4 of the Charter but extends also to other rights (in the present case Article 47 rights) when linked to the operation of the rule of law. Elements of ambiguity however remain. The link between fundamental rights and the rule of law seems to bring back to the debate the extent of scrutiny by the executing authority on the issue of systemic deficiencies. In this context, the emphasis of the CJEU in *LM* on the need to respect the two-step *Aranyosi* approach may be challenged: it may be increasingly difficult for the executing authority to proceed to the second step if it has been established from the outset that there are breaches of the rule of law in the

[107] *LM* (n 3), para 78.
[108] *LM* (n 3), para 69.
[109] *LM* (n 3). In para 70, the Court mentions Recital No 10 to the FD EAW.
[110] V Mitsilegas and S Carrera, "Upholding the Rule of Law by Scrutinising Judicial Independence' (*CEPS Commentary*, 2018), www.ceps.eu/publications/upholding-rule-law-scrutinising-judicial-independence-irish-courts-request-preliminary (last accessed 20 March 2019).

first step of its scrutiny. In these cases, it seems difficult to see how a sufficient level of trust can be established to allow for the execution of a EAW.

VI. Resetting the Parameters of Mutual Trust: From Presumed to Earned Trust

In resetting the parameters of mutual trust, the two rulings analysed in this contribution undoubtedly constitute landmark judgments for the development of EU criminal law, and arguably EU law more broadly. In *Aranyosi*, the Court of Justice listened to its interlocutors – notably at national level – and their concerns regarding the unsustainability of insisting on the uncritical application of a model of presumed, 'blind' trust in such a fundamental rights-critical field. The ruling in *Aranyosi* is of significance here in three respects: in introducing for the first time in express terms in the EAW system a fundamental rights ground for refusal; in requiring a critical and substantive review of fundamental rights compliance on the ground in the Member State where the issuing authority is based; and, importantly, by moving from a monolithic model of automaticity to a deliberative, dialogical model of co-operation entailing constant communication between the national authorities entrusted to operate the EAW system where fundamental rights concerns arise. While elements of uncertainty will inevitably remain pending further clarification, this dialogical model of co-operation has since become the norm in the operation of the EAW system across the EU. The second judgment analysed in this chapter, *LM*, builds upon *Aranyosi* but offers three further significant constitutional elements in fundamental rights protection in a system which claims to be based on mutual trust: it extends the scope of fundamental rights scrutiny from the absolute right in Article 4 of the Charter to effective judicial protection more broadly, thus opening the door for an across-the-board fundamental rights benchmark in the operation of mutual recognition in criminal matters; it extends fundamental rights considerations to broader rule of law considerations, by stressing the importance of judicial independence as the very basis of a legal system which is capable of ensuring trust; and it demonstrates that fundamental rights scrutiny in the operation of mutual recognition in criminal matters in a dialogical relationship between national authorities can effectively become a powerful mechanism for a decentralised (rather than a top-down) rule of law scrutiny across the EU. In this manner, *Aranyosi* and *LM* pave the way for a fundamental re-direction of EU criminal law from a system aiming primarily and instinctively at boosting the capacities and powers of law enforcement to a system – like any constitutional system – which places the values of the EU and the individual and her rights at its heart.

Aranyosi and Căldăraru *through the Eyes of National Judges**

ADAM ŁAZOWSKI

I. Introduction

The joint case of *Aranyosi and Căldăraru* is – without doubt – a turning point.[1] Prior to the judgment of the Court of Justice, several national courts refused to surrender individuals on human rights grounds. Furthermore, the German Constitutional Court conducted its Constitutional identity review, whereby it sent strong signals into the legal stratosphere.[2] For the domestic courts the judgment in *Aranyosi* and *Căldăraru* very much offers an overdue clarification on how the national judges should proceed when faced with argumentation and evidence, proving that at the receiving end the person being subject to a European Arrest Warrant (EAW) may be exposed to inhuman treatment at detention facility(ies).[3] The Court has ruled that even though the system is based on presumption of mutual trust and mutual recognition, in extraordinary circumstances, and subject to a number of preliminary procedural steps, a domestic court may decide to bring the surrender procedure to an end.[4] This is not, however, a straightforward affair by any stretch

* This chapter draws from an earlier article 'The Sky is Not the Limit: Mutual Trust and Mutual Recognition apres Aranyosi and Caldararu', (2018) 14 *Croatian Yearbook of European Law and Policy*, pp 1–30.

[1] Joined Cases C-404/15 and C-659/15 PPU *Pál Aranyosi and Robert Căldăraru v Generalstaatsanwaltschaft Bremen*, ECLI:EU:C:2016:198. For an academic appraisal, see *inter alia*, G Anagnostaras, 'Mutual Confidence is not Blind Trust! Fundamental Rights Protection and the Execution of the European Arrest Warrant: Aranyosi and Caldararu' (2016) 53 *CML Rev* 1675–1704; Sz Gáspár-Szilágyi, Joined Cases Aranyosi and Căldăraru: Converging Human Rights Standards, Mutual Trust and a New Ground for Postponing a European Arrest Warrant' (2016) 24 *European Journal of Crime Criminal Law and Criminal Justice* 197–219; F Korenica and D Doli, 'No More Unconditional "Mutual Trust" between the Member States: An Analysis of the Landmark Decision of the CJEU in Aranyosi and Căldăraru' (2016) 21 *European Human Rights Law Review* 542–55.

[2] Order of 15 December 2015, 2 BvR 2735/14. For an academic appraisal see, *inter alia*, F Meyer, '"From Solange II to Forever I" the German Federal Constitutional Court and the European Arrest Warrant (and How the CJEU Responded)' (2016) 7 *New Journal of European Criminal Law* 277–94; M Hong, 'Human Dignity, Identity Review of the European Arrest Warrant and the Court of Justice as a Listener in the Dialogue of Courts, Solange-III and Aranyosi: BVerfG 15 December 2015, 2 BvR 2735/14, Solange III, and ECJ (Grand Chamber) 5 April 2016, Joined Cases C-404/15 and C-659/15 PPU, Aranyosi and Căldăraru' (2016) 12 *European Constitutional Law Review* 549–63.

[3] See, *inter alia*, A Łazowski, S Nash, 'Detention' in N Keijzer, E van Sliedregt (eds), *The European Arrest Warrant in Practice* (The Hague, TMC Asser Press, 2009) 33–50.

[4] *Aranyosi and Căldăraru* (n 1), para 104.

of the imagination. Inevitably, the matter in question has eventually reached the Court of Justice *qua* the preliminary ruling procedure.[5] As it is frequently the case with landmark and groundbreaking judgments of the Court, further references from national courts have followed. Cases *LM*[6] and *ML*[7] are presented in turn.

II. *Aranyosi and Căldăraru*: Can We Trust Your Detention Conditions?

A. Introduction

From the point of view of national judges, at least three aspects of this judgment are problematic and merit attention. To begin with, the legal quagmire of the relationship between Articles 3-4a (grounds for refusal to surrender), Article 1(3) (fundamental rights) of the EAW Framework Decision[8] and Article 4 of the Charter of Fundamental Rights comes to the fore. The key question is: do we now have an additional ground for refusal to surrender? If so, why were fundamental rights not included either in the catalogue of mandatory grounds, or on the list of discretionary grounds as good law-making principles would dictate? It is very instructive to look at how the Court of Justice framed this issue and what it means for the national authorities in charge of executing the EAWs. Second, the procedural *modus operandi* developed by the Court of Justice is plausible at first sight. When in doubt, the national court should first make a general determination of the situation at the receiving end and, should that be necessary, also seek a clarification from its counterpart in the requesting country. The key questions, however, are what kind of information may be used in the first instance, and, in turn, what sort of clarification may be requested from a counterpart in another Member State and how comprehensive it should be. Third, under what circumstances can the national court refuse to surrender, or, as euphemistically put by the Court of Justice, may bring the surrender procedure to an end.

B. *Aranyosi and Căldăraru*: A New Ground for Non-Execution of the European Arrest Warrant?

The substantive part of the judgment starts, as one would expect, with a truncated exposé covering the foundations of the mutual recognition principle in

[5] In the early case law, see Case C-396/11 *Ciprian Vasile Radu* ECLI:EU:C:2013:39 and, especially, Opinion of Advocate General Sharpston in Case C-396/11 *Ministerul Public – Parchetul de pe lângă Curtea de Apel Constanţa v Ciprian Vasile Radu*, ECLI:EU:C:2012:648.

[6] Case C-216/18 PPU *LM* ECLI:EU:C:2018:586.

[7] Case C-220/18 PPU *ML* ECLI:EU:C:2018:589.

[8] Council Framework Decision 2002/584/JHA of 13 June 2002 on the European arrest warrant and the surrender procedures between Member States [2002] OJ L190/1.

criminal matters. The picture drawn by the judges at Kirchberg seems to be clear: the system is based on mutual trust and benefits from the presumption that the Member States provide 'equivalent and effective protection of the fundamental right recognized at EU level, particularly in the Charter'.[9] The trouble starts if one reads paragraph 80 of the judgment in a literal fashion. The Court emphasises that an authority, which executes a EAW may refuse to do so on grounds 'exhaustively listed' in Articles 3, 4-4a of Framework Decision 2002/584/JHA. The choice of words employed by the Court of Justice makes it unequivocally clear that the list of grounds is exhaustive. To put it differently, it is the limit. If such a reading were to be correct, it would mean that national authorities may not, at least as per the EAW Framework Decision, refuse to surrender on human rights grounds. Then, however, the Court of Justice ventures away from the Framework Decision itself and continues its analysis by putting the focus on Article 4 of the Charter of Fundamental Rights.[10] In this respect Article 1(3) of the Framework Decision serves as the bridge between these legal acts. It provides, that the EAW Framework Decision, does not modify the obligation to respect fundamental rights enshrined in Article 6 of the Treaty on European Union (TEU). This, as clarified by the Court of Justice in the commented case, also comprises the Charter of Fundamental Rights. The judges confirm, in turn, that the Charter applies to the case at hand as application of national provisions transposing the EAW Framework Decision constitutes implementation of EU law, which – as per Article 51(1) – is *conditio sine qua non* for application of the Charter.[11] For a national judge confusion may allegedly arise from comparative analysis of the interpretation of Article 1(3) of the EAW Framework Decision by the Advocate General Bot and the conclusions of the Court.[12] Arguably, it is one of those examples where it would have served national judges if the Court of Justice openly agreed or disagreed with its own Advocate General.[13] While Advocate General Bot claimed that the provision in question may not serve as a ground for refusal to surrender, the Court of Justice used it as a vehicle to a conclusion, which offers a mixed bag of legal bases. The judges' final conclusion is based on Article 1(3), 5 and 6(1) of the EAW Framework Decision. It is notable that Articles 3, 4 and 4a covering the grounds for non-execution of the EAW are nowhere to be seen. This, as argued later in this commentary, may have been the reason behind a very cautious wording employed by the Court of Justice to describe options available to a national court, should its doubts not be discounted after clarification from the requesting country.

[9] *Aranyosi and Căldăraru* (n 1), para 77.

[10] For an academic appraisal of Article 4 of the Charter see, *inter alia*, M Nowak, A Charbord, 'Article 4' in S Peers, T Hervey, J Kenner, A Ward (eds), *The EU Charter of Fundamental Rights. A Commentary* (Oxford and Portland, Oregon, 2014) 61–99.

[11] See further, *inter alia*, A Ward, 'Article 51' in *ibid* 1413–54.

[12] See also Opinion of Advocate General Sharpston in *Radu* (n 5).

[13] For an academic appraisal of Advocates General and their role at the Court of Justice, see *exempli gratia*, N Burrows and R Graves, *The Advocate General and EC Law* (Oxford, Oxford University Press, 2007).

C. Towards a Creative Interpretation of the EAW Framework Decision

Voltaire acutely observed that 'doubt is an uncomfortable condition'.[14] It is particularly so when a national judge doubts the respect for fundamental rights in the requesting country and considers whether to surrender an individual or not. Arguably, the references in joint cases *Aranyosi and Căldăraru* also put the Court of Justice in an uncomfortable position as it forced the judges to engage in a balancing act of reconciling the mutual trust and mutual recognition with risks to respect for fundamental rights. At this stage of the analysis it is fitting to focus on how the Court of Justice interpreted the Charter of Fundamental Rights and the way it designed a procedure that national judges should follow when they find themselves in the same predicament as *Hanseatisches Oberlandesgericht* in Bremen (from which both references originated).

To begin with, the Court of Justice emphasised that when national authorities deal with the execution of the EAW, they need to take into account Article 4 of the Charter, which prohibits inhuman and degrading treatment or punishment.[15] Since it is modelled on Article 3 of the European Convention on Human Rights (ECHR) it has to be interpreted accordingly, that is taking into account the jurisprudence of the European Court of Human Rights (ECtHR).[16] The question that emerged in cases *Aranyosi* and *Căldăraru* is how to square the circle, taking into account the EAW Framework Decision and Article 4 of the Charter of Fundamental Rights. To put it differently, how a national judge should proceed when, on the one hand, Articles 3-4/4a of the Framework Decision provide for an exhaustive catalogue of grounds for refusal to surrender and yet, on the other hand, such a surrender may not expose a person concerned to inhuman and degrading treatment. In this respect the Court of Justice has proven to be quite creative, developing a two-tier test that should be followed. As will be argued below, it provides some clarity as a matter of principle, but at the same time, a fair degree of uncertainty when it comes to national courtrooms. This is further elaborated in turn.

As a first step, the executing judicial authority must establish whether there is a risk of degrading treatment at the detention conditions in the receiving country. Such argumentation with evidence is likely to be submitted by defence lawyers aiming at non-surrender of their clients. The question is what kind of evidence must be submitted to prove the point. In this respect, paragraph 89 of the judgment is very instrumental. The Court of Justice ruled that:

> the executing judicial authority must, initially, rely on information that is objective, reliable, specific and properly updated on the detention conditions prevailing in the issuing Member State and that demonstrates that there are deficiencies, which may be

[14] Complete Works of Voltaire, Volume 12, Part 1.
[15] For an academic appraisal see, *inter alia*, Nowak and Charbord (n 10) 61–99.
[16] As per Article 52 of the Charter.

> systemic or generalised, or which may affect certain groups of people, or which may affect certain places of detention.[17]

The test is not only about the categories and quality of information that will be employed to make the assessment, but also about the substantive criteria to be used to determine what is specific enough. In this respect the following paragraph of the judgment is crucial as the Court of Justice elaborates further on the detention standards developed in its jurisprudence by the ECtHR. It held:

> it follows from the case-law of the ECtHR that Article 3 ECHR imposes, on the authorities of the State on whose territory an individual is detained, a positive obligation to ensure that any prisoner is detained in conditions which guarantee respect for human dignity, that the way in which detention is enforced does not cause the individual concerned distress or hardship of an intensity exceeding the unavoidable level of suffering that is inherent in detention and that, having regard to the practical requirements of imprisonment, the health and well-being of the prisoner are adequately protected (see judgment of the ECtHR in *Torreggiani and Others v. Italy* [...].[18]

All the above is plausible as far as the principles are concerned. Yet, when one looks at it through the eyes of national judges several questions emerge. While it is true that it gives the domestic courts discretion and flexibility, at the same time it merely provides vague indications and puts the uniform application of EU law at risk. First, the test laid down in paragraph 89 of the judgment is characterised by rather vague wording. The adjectives employed by the Court of Justice are quite open-ended. The test requires a national judge to base the assessment on data, which is: 'objective, reliable, specific and properly updated'. The first three notions are largely linked to the source and quality of information, where the assessment of a national judge will be rather subjective. The fourth criterion requires a more objective evaluation and, thus, it remains the easiest in this set. In practical terms, the key dilemma that the domestic judges face is who to trust. To put it differently, which sources may be treated as trustworthy, so as to guarantee that information meets the discussed requirements? The Court of Justice, seemingly aware of the matter in question, indicated that judgments of international courts as well as national courts may be taken into account. This, obviously, includes the judgments of the ECtHR. Furthermore, documents produced by the Council of Europe or UN related authorities will also serve the purpose. Surely, the reports of the Committee for Prevention of Torture, operating within the Council of Europe, can be of use. It should be noted, however, that the list laid down in paragraph 89 of the judgment is non-exhaustive. Hence, it is for national judges to make a selection of sources of information when acting *ex officio* and to decide what kind of material submitted by defence lawyers should be treated as credible. It leaves it open as to whether sources coming from non-governmental organisations, local or international, should be considered by national judges as 'objective' and 'reliable'.

[17] *Aranyosi and Căldăraru* (n 1), para 89.
[18] *Aranyosi and Căldăraru* (n 1), para 90.

From an academic point of view, one may conclude that the Court of Justice found the balance between providing assistance to national courts and leaving them a solid margin of discretion. In reality, however, the conclusions of the Court are based on a rather optimistic presumption that national judges are *au courant*, for instance, with jurisprudence of the ECtHR or outputs of such outlets as already mentioned such as the Committee for Prevention of Torture. It is also based on a presumption that national judges and their clerks are fluent in foreign languages. This is particularly relevant for the matter at hand as the language regime of the Council of Europe is rather modest when compared to the European Union. To put it differently, judgments or reports are not – as a rule – translated *en masse* into the languages of all Council of Europe members. A reminder is fitting, that the EAW proceedings are subject to a very tight time regime, leaving very little room for translation.

As already mentioned, the Court of Justice requires the information to be 'specific', which – again – may be considered as problematic. A simple question emerges as to what is specific enough to satisfy the test. Would the level of detail required by national judges depend on a particular requesting country? For instance, should the level of detail correspond to the level of trust in the judiciary, law enforcement apparatus and detention conditions in the requesting country? To put it differently, should less trust translate into a higher level of detail required to meet the test? It has been left to the national practice to decide.

Once the 'objective, reliable, specific and properly updated [information] on detention conditions' is collected, the executing authority needs to determine whether there is 'a real risk of inhuman or degrading treatment by virtue of general conditions of detention in the issuing Member State'. If there is no such risk, then the domestic authority has to proceed with the execution of the EAW (providing there are no other grounds for refusal to surrender). If, however, systemic or generalised deficiencies exist, their existence is not *per se* an indication that a person, who is the subject of a EAW, will be exposed to a treatment that would be in breach of Article 4 of the Charter of Fundamental Rights. This needs to be determined by the executing authority separately by liaising with its counterparts in the requesting country. For that purpose, the procedural mechanism laid down in Article 15(2) of the EAW Framework Decision should be employed. The Court of Justice clarified, in a very general fashion, that the evidence obtained must, again, be 'objective, reliable, specific and properly updated' in order to verify if there are 'substantial grounds' to believe that a person in question 'will run a real risk' of being subject to inhuman or degrading treatment.[19] It may include information about *modi operandi* for monitoring of detention conditions. However, all other details are left to the decision of national judges, which – in itself – opens up a host of problems and challenges. For instance, how detailed such a request for supplementary information should be and should the national court of the requesting

[19] *Aranyosi and Căldăraru* (n 1), para 94.

country be trusted blindly? Not surprisingly, the matters in question have returned to the Court of Justice like a boomerang in cases discussed later in the present commentary.

Once all necessary general and individualised information is in place, it is for the national executing authority to decide whether to surrender the person in question or not. In this respect, the Court of Justice has provided general guidance on how the domestic judges should proceed. Should the conclusion be that there is a 'real risk of inhuman or degrading treatment', the execution of the EAW must be postponed. However, as the Court of Justice phrased it, the execution 'cannot be abandoned'.[20] On the one hand, the postponement of surrender gives the executing authority a chance to seek further clarification from the requesting court, and, for the latter, one more opportunity to discount the doubts as to the existence of the risk of inhumane or degrading treatment of the person subject to the EAW. On the other hand, the solution preferred by the Court of Justice triggers numerous challenges for the national courts related to, for instance, the detention of the person concerned during the period of suspension. Furthermore, it is entirely unclear how long such a suspension should last. The Court of Justice has only provided an indication that the time period should be 'reasonable'.[21] This is a blessing and a curse. On the one hand, it gives the national judges discretion but, on the other hand, it painfully lacks detail and offers limited guidance, especially in regards to the next step a national court may take in its final decision to refuse to surrender.

As already mentioned, the Court of Justice has confirmed its earlier jurisprudence in joint cases *Aranyosi and Căldăraru* that limitations of the principles of mutual recognition and mutual trust are on the menu, however only in exceptional circumstances. As the present judgment clarifies, such exceptional circumstances may occur when the national court in charge of the execution of a EAW cannot discount doubts as to the risk of inhuman or degrading treatment that a person subject to EAW may face. Should that be the case, the domestic judges may bring the procedure to an end. The already mentioned euphemistic language employed by the Court is a departure from the statutory vocabulary used by the EU legislator in the EAW Framework Decision. The *raison d'être* behind the decision not to call a spade a spade will remain locked behind the doors of the deliberation room at Kirchberg. It is, however, worth emphasising that the Court of Justice deliberately talks about bringing procedures to an end, instead of refusal to surrender. Perhaps this is related to the fact that neither Article 3, nor Articles 4-4a of the EAW Framework Decision (which deal with grounds for non-execution of the surrender requests) are mentioned in the final conclusions of the Court. Does this mean that the Court has developed a parallel *modus operandi* on top of the existing grounds for non-execution? Alas, this is not clear from the judgment at hand.

[20] *Aranyosi and Căldăraru* (n 1), para 98.
[21] *Aranyosi and Căldăraru* (n 1), para 104.

D. Conclusions

Overall, the judgment in joint cases *Aranyosi and Căldăraru* triggers – not surprisingly – mixed emotions. On the one hand, it offers a long overdue clarification, and, in a way, it brings EU *acquis* in sync with the domestic practice in some of the Member States. Furthermore, it eases the loyalty conflicts discussed above, which face the national judges in such cases. As argued earlier, while providing clarification this judgment also triggers a host of new challenges and questions for national judges. Not surprisingly some of them have found their way to the Court of Justice *qua* subsequent references for preliminary ruling, which are analysed in turn.

III. Case C-220/18 PPU *ML*: Can We Really Trust Your Detention Conditions?

A. Introduction

Case C-220/18 PPU *ML* is surely a follow-up to joined cases C-404/15 and C-659/15 PPU *Aranyosi and Căldăraru* and proves the point made by W Van Ballegooij and P Bárd that the latter case was just the beginning of the dialogue between national courts and the Court of Justice.[22] The judgment in case *ML* also fits into a more general trend that whenever the Court of Justice delivers a groundbreaking judgment setting a principle, it frequently shies away from giving it a satisfactory level of detail.[23] Consequentially, domestic courts follow with further references, seeking clarification of the earlier jurisprudential output.[24] The *ML* case is ideal in demonstrating the phenomenon in question and no doubt further references are due to follow. The facts of the *ML* case are presented in the previous commentary of this chapter and deserve no rehearsing. For the purposes of the analysis that follows it is enough to provide a reminder that the gist of the reference was centred around two main issues.[25] First, whether the *Aranyosi and Căldăraru*

[22] W Van Ballegooij, P Bárd, 'Mutual Recognition and Individual Rights. Did the Court Get it Right?' (2016) 7 *New Journal of European Criminal Law* 439–64, at 462.

[23] Many a time, this is a consequence of the way in which the Court of Justice operates. As frequently discussed in the academic literature, the rules governing functioning of the Court of Justice do not allow for dissenting opinions, therefore the judgments, as well as opinions or orders of the Court, are the products of compromise between judges forming a particular chamber. Allegedly, this may have impact on the quality of judicial discourse and, by the same token, the judgments of the Court. See further, *inter alia*, M Adams, H de Waele, J Meeusen, G Straetmans (eds), *Judging Europe's Judges: The Legitimacy of the Case Law of the European Court of Justice* (Oxford and Portland-Oregon, Hart Publishing, 2013).

[24] In this respect a good example is the judgment in Case C-34/09 *Gerardo Ruiz Zambrano v Office national de l'emploi (ONEm)* ECLI:EU:C:2011:124.

[25] It is notable that the referring court submitted over a page's worth of questions to the Court of Justice. ML (n 7), para 40.

test requires verification of information regarding all detention conditions in the receiving countries or, alternatively, only those detention centres where the person covered by the EAW is likely to be transferred to. Second, the question was how detailed the request for information should be. As explained earlier in the present commentary, on the one hand, the judgment in *Aranyosi and Căldăraru* gives the national authorities discretion to determine what kind of information is specific enough to meet the test. On the other hand, the question emerges if there are limits to the discretion. Arguably, the latter may be inextricably linked to the level of trust in the judicial system at the receiving end. To put it differently, the less trust, the more information may be required and considered to be desirably specific. It could, of course, also work the other way around: the more trust, the less information is required.

B. How Deep is Your Trust?

In the *ML* case the levels of trust in the Hungarian detention centres were, perhaps, not particularly impressive. This was hardly surprising bearing in mind the evidence available to the referring court, comprising, *inter alia*, judgments of the ECtHR.[26] Yet, when looking at the requests for clarification submitted to the Hungarian authorities, it may well be that the case was handled by overzealous judges, who wished to know as much as possible about the Hungarian detention facilities. Either way the Court of Justice was asked for clarification of the judgment in *Aranyosi and Căldăraru*. The preliminary observations made by the judges at Kirchberg offer domestic judges, including the referring court, nothing new. The Court of Justice has provided the systemic background of the principles of mutual trust and mutual recognition, which is well-known from its previous jurisprudence.[27] However, the parts of the reasoning that follow are undoubtedly very useful from the perspective of national judges.

To begin with, the Court of Justice has attended to the relevance of a new legal remedy available as per Hungarian law to challenge the legality of detention conditions. The judges clarified that the existence of such remedy may not, *per se*, rule out the risk of inhuman and degrading treatment at detention centres. By the same token, it does not free the executing judicial authority from the obligation to conduct the general assessment required by the *Aranyosi and Căldăraru* test. The Court in turn proceeded to clarify how much information may be required as a supplementary clarification by the executing authority. It is

[26] For instance *Varga and Others v Hungary* App no 14097/12 (ECtHR, 10 March 2015), paras 79–92.

[27] The only exception are paras 68–71 where the Court of Justice reacts to submissions of the Hungarian Government, disputing the existence of deficiencies in the Hungarian detention centres. The Court of Justice, rightly so, concludes that the existence of such deficiencies is neither the subject of the reference for preliminary ruling, nor determination of their existence is a task for the Court of Justice.

notable that in the case at hand the German authorities sent a total of 78 questions to their Hungarian counterparts. This, as argued earlier, may be the evidence of limited trust combined, perhaps, with a pinch of overzealousness. Nevertheless, it allowed the Court of Justice to provide a necessary clarification of its earlier ruling in *Aranyosi and Căldăraru*. First, the executing judicial authority should make enquiries only related to the detention conditions in prisons, where the person subject to the EAW may be detained. This includes outlets where the surrendered person will be detained on a temporary or transitional basis. *Au contraire*, this precludes general requests covering all national prisons. Second, only conditions of detention which are relevant for determination of a real risk of inhuman or degrading treatment should be enquired about and used for the assessment. In this respect, the Court of Justice has relied – as indicators – on relevant standards developed by the ECtHR.[28] Bearing in mind a lack of relevant EU standards, this is the most obvious choice, which – among others – provides domestic judges with a useful clarification of interaction between EU law and ECHR standards. By the same token, it helps them to navigate the multifaceted legal environment they are exposed to.

IV. Case C-216/18 PPU *LM*: Are You Independent Enough to be Trusted?

A. Introduction

Case C-216/18 PPU *LM*[29] was delivered against a very precarious political background of a Member State, which has downgraded its rule of law standards in a staggering anti-democratic blitz. Ever since the elections in 2015, the Polish Government, the Parliament and the President, driven by the right-wing nationalist *Prawo i Sprawiedliwość* (Law and Justice)have implemented a series of reforms, which largely de-activated the country's Constitutional Tribunal and heavily undermined the independence of the entire judiciary, including most recently also the Supreme Court.[30] To put it differently, the reforms have considerably blurred the boundaries between the executive and the judiciary, raising the fundamental question of whether Poland was still meeting the standard laid down in Article 2 TEU. Not surprisingly this attracted the attention of

[28] *ML* (n 7), paras 90–100.

[29] *LM* (n 6).

[30] For an overview see, *inter alia*, P Filipek, 'Challenges to the Rule of Law in the European Union: The Distressing Case of Poland' (2017) 17 *Revista do Instituto Brasileiro de Direitos Humanos/Journal of the Brazilian Institute of Human Rights*, pp.

several international actors[31] and triggered the alarm bells around the European Union. Alas, it has also raised the questions whether the existing *modi operandi* employed by the European Union to remedy breaches of EU law by the Member States are fit for purpose and whether they can be utilised when the rule of law is at stake.[32] When this commentary was completed, the European Commission was at the stage of testing the waters to see if the standard infringement proceedings based on Article 258 of the Treaty on the Functioning of the European Union (TFEU) could be invoked. It has already submitted two infractions to the Court of Justice where it openly challenged the compatibility of the changes in the Polish law with, among others, Article 19 TEU.[33] At the same time, it has triggered the *par excellence* political procedure based on Article 7 TEU.[34] In course of this, the European Commission identified several threats to the respect for the EU values laid down in Article 2 TEU and as per procedural requirements laid down in Article 7(1) TEU it issued a reasoned proposal.[35] Furthermore, several Polish courts, including the Supreme Court, have proceeded with references for preliminary ruling aiming for a clarification of the alleged reforms, which led to a purge in the judiciary, were compatible with EU law.[36] Not surprisingly, questions were also raised in national courts across the European Union whether the Polish judicial system should continue to benefit from principles of mutual trust and mutual recognition. This matter, too, reached the Kirchberg courtroom in *LM*.

[31] For instance, the Commission for Democracy through Law of the Council of Europe (usually referred to as the Venice Commission) issued several critical reports about the reforms in Poland. See, *inter alia*, Poland – Opinion on the Act on the Constitutional Tribunal, adopted by the Venice Commission at its 108th Plenary Session (Venice, 14–15 October 2016), available at www.venice.coe.int/webforms/documents/?pdf=CDL-AD(2016)026-e; Poland – Opinion on the Draft Act amending the Act on the National Council of the Judiciary; on the Draft Act amending the Act on the Supreme Court, proposed by the President of Poland, and on the Act on the Organisation of Ordinary Courts, adopted by the Commission at its 113th Plenary Session (Venice, 8–9 December 2017), available at www.venice.coe.int/webforms/documents/?pdf=CDL-AD(2017)031-e.

[32] See, *inter alia*, D Kochenov and L Pech, Monitoring and Enforcement of the Rule of Law in the EU: Rhetoric and Reality (2015) 11 *European Constitutional Law Review* 512–40; D Kochenov, *On Policing Article 2 TEU Compliance – Reverse Solange and Systemic Infringements Analyzed*, XXXIII PoLYBIL (2013) 145–170; A Von Bogdandy, M Kottmann, C Antpöhler, J Dickschen, S Hentrei, M Smrkolj, 'Reverse Solange – Protecting the Essence of Fundamental Rights against EU Member States' (2012) 49 *CML Rev* 489–519; M Schmidt, P Bogdanowicz, 'The Infringement Procedure in the Rule of Law Crisis: How to Make Effective use of Article 258 TFEU' (2018) 55 *CML Rev* 1061–1100.

[33] For instance, pending case C-619/18 *Commission v Poland*. See Order of the Vice President of the Court of Justice C-619/18P *Commission v Poland* ECLI:EU:C:2018:852.

[34] For an appraisal of Article 7 TEU and its progeny, see, *exempli gratia*, W Sadurski, 'Adding Bite to a Bark: The Story of Article 7, E.U. Enlargement, and Jörg Haider' (2010) 16 *Columbia Journal of European Law* 385 *ff*.

[35] Proposal for a Council Decision on the determination of a clear risk of a serious breach by the Republic of Poland of the rule of law COM (2017) 835 final.

[36] See, *inter alia*, pending references for preliminary ruling submitted by the Polish Supreme Court: C-522/18 *DŚ v Zakładowi Ubezpieczeń Społecznych Oddział w Jaśle*; C-537/18 *Krajowa Rada Sądownictwa*; C-585/18 *Krajowa Rada Sądownictwa*.

B. The Quagmires of the High Court of Ireland

The reference in the *LM* case was submitted by the High Court of Ireland, which received a number of EAWs issued by the Polish authorities with the view of conducting criminal prosecution of a Polish national, who was accused of drug trafficking. It should be noted that at the material time the already mentioned Article 7 TEU procedure was already triggered by the European Commission and its recommendations made available to the public. Bearing this in mind the referring court faced the dilemma whether to clear the surrender of the person in question to Poland or, alternatively, whether to refuse to do so, taking into account the fact that Polish courts are no longer independent. The latter, potentially, could expose the person surrendered to an unfair trial. Not surprisingly, the High Court of Ireland proceeded with a reference for preliminary ruling to the Court of Justice. The referring court not only analysed *in extenso* the situation in Poland, but also questioned whether the *Aranyosi and Căldăraru modus operandi* was fit for purpose in the case at hand. According to the High Court of Ireland, it is questionable whether any clarification received from the requesting judicial authority should be treated as acceptable. To put it differently, would assurances of independence issued by a national court that is not independent, discount the doubts of a court asked to entertain a request for surrender?[37] Not surprisingly, the Court of Justice decided to employ the urgent preliminary ruling procedure and, bearing in mind the gravity of the situation and importance of the legal issues raised, the case was assigned to the Grand Chamber.

C. *Aranyosi and Căldăraru* Revisited

The judgment rendered by the Court of Justice raises a plethora of legal issues and merits a comprehensive analysis. This, no doubt, is likely follow in the academic literature.[38] The present commentary, as outlined in the introduction, aims to look at the *Aranyosi and Căldăraru* line of jurisprudence through the eyes of national judges. Hence, the analysis that follows focuses only on selected legal issues raised by the judges at Kirchberg.

To begin with, the Court of Justice made an attempt to draw a line between Article 7 TEU proceedings and the EAW Framework Decision. A reminder is

[37] Irish High Court, *Minister for Justice and Equality v Celmer (No 1)* judgment of 12 March 2018, [2018] IEHC 119. For an academic appraisal, see *inter alia*, M Dorociak, W Lewandowski, 'A Check Move for the Principle of Mutual Trust from Dublin: The Celmer Case' (2018) 3 *European Papers* 857–73; S Carrera, V Mitsilegas, 'Upholding the Rule of Law by Scrutinising Judicial Independence: The Irish Court's Request for a Preliminary Ruling on the European Arrest Warrant' (*CEPS Commentary*, 2018), available at: www.ceps.eu/system/files/SCandVM_ROL.pdf.

[38] For an early appraisal see, *inter alia*, P Bárd, W van Ballegooij, 'Judicial Independence as a Precondition for Mutual Trust? The CJEU in Minister for Justice and Equality v. LM' (2018) 9 *New Journal of European Criminal Law* 353–65.

fitting that the latter provides, albeit only in the Preamble, that the European Council may suspend the application of the EAW machinery only in cases of serious and persistent breach of principles laid down in Article 6 (1) TEU. For that to happen, a unanimous decision of the European Council is required as per Article 7(2) TEU. The Court of Justice clarified that in such event, the executing judicial authority would be required to automatically refuse the execution of a EAW. In the current political constellation this scenario is merely a theoretical proposition that is very unlikely to materialise. The political character of Article 7 TEU proceedings, combined with a dominant role prescribed to the Member States (acting either as the European Council or the Council) and the unanimity requirement for the key decision, as well as the fact that two allied Member States are currently subject to the procedure, makes any determination of serious and persistent breach of EU values a highly illusory exercise. This, in a nutshell, means that the suspension of the EAW mechanism *vis-à-vis* Poland or Hungary is not on the cards. It does not, however, change the fact that in the course of EAW proceedings national courts face the dilemmas similar to those expressed by the referring court in the *LM* case. In this respect the Court of Justice has offered a solution along the lines of the *Aranyosi and Căldăraru* ruling.

The Court of Justice made it clear that until the European Council freezes the EAW mechanism in relation to a particular Member State, the national executing authorities may refuse to give effect to EAWs in exceptional circumstances after a thorough individual assessment if in a particular case the person surrendered could be exposed to unfair trial, resulting from a lack of independence of the domestic court. The Court of Justice has ruled that such a decision may be made on the basis of Article 1(3) of the EAW Framework Decision. This, as compared to the *Aranyosi and Căldăraru* ruling and its constructive ambiguity discussed above, is a welcome clarification. Once again it shows an inventive side of the Court of Justice and the way in which it interprets EU law. It is notable, however, that the judges at Kirchberg again opted for phraseology departing from the language of the EAW Framework Decision. As the Court of Justice put it, the executing authority 'may refrain […] to give effect to a European arrest warrant'.[39] In practical terms there is, if any, very little difference between 'refraining' and 'non-executing' a request for surrender. It seems now confirmed that the Court of Justice has opted to turn Article 1(3) of the EAW Framework Decision into an additional ground for refusal to surrender. The picture emerging from the judgment in question is that such a decision should be neither automatic nor taken lightly. Hence, the bulk of the Court's response to the Irish High Court comprises a detailed account of what amounts to judicial independence and what factors should be taken into account by national courts when applying the *Aranyosi and Căldăraru* test.

There are two central elements in the Courts' reasoning. First, the Court of Justice found it fitting to elaborate *in extenso* on the importance of the rule

[39] Para 73 of the judgment.

of law and, in more general terms, the meaning and the scope of Articles 2 and 19 TEU. Second, the judges at Kirchberg have addressed the impact of rule of law breaches on the EAW mechanism. It is not surprising that the Court of Justice has put so much emphasis on rule of law matters. In many respects the judges operate in a legal lacuna and face competence dilemmas. On the one hand, respect for EU values is a pre-condition for EU membership and it is at the heart of EU integration. On the other hand, the EU operates under the principle of conferral, which – in general terms – precludes interventions into areas not falling within its competences.[40] One of the problems currently faced by the EU and its institutions is that the very generous wording of Article 2 TEU is not matched by extensive competences in rule of law matters. Nevertheless, it is rather obvious that respect for rule of law and the existence of independent national judiciaries are *conditiones sine qua non* for application as well as effectiveness of EU law. This link has been extensively dealt with by the Court of Justice in Case C-64/16 *Associação Sindical dos Juízes Portugueses v Tribunal de Contas*[41] and the discussed judgment in *LM* cements this emerging line of jurisprudence and equips the Court of Justice with legal ammunition to deal with the already mentioned rule of law infringement proceedings against Poland and references from the Polish Courts. One has to agree with Matteo Bonelli and Monica Claes that *Associação Sindical dos Juízes Portugueses* arrived at a perfect time and amounted to judicial serendipity.[42] It allowed the Court of Justice to develop key principles in a case of lesser political gravity. By the same token, it paved the way for highly politicised cases regarding respect for rule of law in Poland and Hungary. As already noted, *LM* has been the first in line. The Court of Justice has emphasised that judicial independence is at the heart of the fundamental right to a fair trial, which is guaranteed by Article 47 of the Charter of Fundamental Rights.[43] The Court of Justice has also brought to the fore Article 19 TEU, which 'gives concrete expression to the value of the rule of law affirmed in Article 2 TEU'.[44] It creates an obligation for national courts to guarantee full application of EU law in the Member States and protect the rights of individuals. This is a well-known treatise, which with entry into force of the Treaty

[40] For an academic appraisal of the principle of conferral after entry into force of the Treaty of Lisbon see, *inter alia*, G Davies, 'The Post-Laeken Division of Competences (2003) 28 *European Law Review* 686–98; M Dougan, 'The Convention's Draft Constitutional Treaty: Bringing Europe Closer to its Lawyers?' (2003) 28 *European Law Review* 763–93; P Craig, 'Competence: Clarity, Conferral, Containment and Consideration' (2004) 29 *European Law Review* 323–44; T Tridimas, 'Competence after Lisbon. The Elusive Search for Bright Lines' in D Ashiagbor, N Countouris, I Lianos (eds), *The European Union after the Treaty of Lisbon* (Cambridge, Cambridge University Press, 2012) 50–51; M Dougan, 'The Treaty of Lisbon 2007: Winning Minds not Hearts' (2008) 45 *CML Rev* 617–703; M Claes, B de Witte, '*Competences: Codification and Contestation*' in A Łazowski, S Blockmans (eds), *Research Handbook on EU Institutional Law* (Cheltenham, Edward Elgar Publishing, 2016) 46–87.

[41] Case C-64/16 *Associação Sindical dos Juízes Portugueses v Tribunal de Contas* ECLI:EU:C:2018:117.

[42] M Bonelli and M Claes, 'Judicial Serendipity: How Portuguese Judges came to the Rescue of the Polish Judiciary: ECJ 27 February 2018, Case C-64/16, Associação Sindical dos Juízes Portugueses' (2018) 14 *European Constitutional Law Review* 622–43.

[43] See further, *inter alia*, A Ward, 'Article 47' in Peers, Hervey, Kenner, Ward (n 10) 1197–1275.

[44] Para 50 of the judgment.

of Lisbon, found a proper legal basis in the EU founding treaties (Article 19 TEU). In this context the independence of national courts is a core requirement, also for the effective functioning of the EAW, based on mutual trust and mutual recognition. The Court of Justice has clarified in turn that the decisions on issuing and on execution of the EAW need to be taken by independent courts. Furthermore, in para 57 the judges have rather boldly emphasised the obvious that even in the areas not covered by EU law the Member States have to observe the ECHR, in particular the right to a fair trial. The Court has in turn provided guidance to national courts as to factors which should be taken into account by the executing judicial authority when conducting an assessment of state of affairs in the requesting country. For instance, the Court of Justice delved into external and internal aspects of judicial independence.[45] This led to the exact *modus operandi* the national courts should follow. The Court of Justice has followed in this respect the test laid down in judgment *Aranyosi and Căldăraru*, requiring the national judges to start with a general assessment and then, should doubts arise, follow-up with an individual analysis based on clarifications received from the requesting judicial authority. The latter is required even, as in the case at hand, when the European Commission publishes a reasoned proposal and, by the same token, triggers Article 7 TEU proceedings. The two-step process has been summarised by the Court of Justice in the following fashion:

> If, having regard to the requirements noted in paragraphs 62 to 67 of the present judgment, the executing judicial authority finds that there is, in the issuing Member State, a real risk of breach of the essence of the fundamental right to a fair trial on account of systemic or generalised deficiencies concerning the judiciary of that Member State, such as to compromise the independence of that State's courts, that authority must, as a second step, assess specifically and precisely whether, in the particular circumstances of the case, there are substantial grounds for believing that, following his surrender to the issuing Member State, the requested person will run that risk.[46]

This amounts to *Aranyosi and Căldăraru* revisited and does not follow the suggestions made by Advocate General Tanchev in his Opinion.[47] Furthermore, it fails to address the concerns raised by the Irish High Court in its reference for preliminary ruling about the second step, which for reasons explained further below, may prove not to be fit for purpose. When it comes to the general assessment, which constitutes the first step, the Court of Justice has followed the test laid down in case *Aranyosi and Căldăraru*. In a nutshell, the executing judicial authority must make its assessment based on information that is 'objective, reliable, specific and properly updated'.[48] The Court of Justice has indicated that the material provided

[45] Paras 63–65 of the judgment.

[46] Para 68 of the judgment.

[47] Opinion of Advocate General Tanchev delivered on 28 June 2018 in Case C-216/18 PPU *Minister for Justice and Equality v LM* (Deficiencies in the system of justice), ECLI:EU:C:2018:517.

[48] Para 61 of the judgment.

by the European Commission in its reasoned proposal is based on Article 7(1) TEU. Although this is not mentioned by the Court, one should assume that reports of other bodies could be taken into account as well. This would include, for instance, reports of the Venice Commission, which operates under the auspices of the Council of Europe.[49] *Prima facie*, the Courts' conclusion is sound, yet, it does not take into account the 'whom to trust' dilemma. Not surprisingly, the reports of the Venice Commission as well as the reasoned proposal of the European Commission have been discredited by the Polish authorities, which prefer and promote an alternative understanding of independence of judiciary and the rule of law. The question is whether this in itself may lead to confusion among the national courts of other Member States. Should they trust on face value the assessments made by international institutions or the national authorities of a Member State concerned? The first phase, however, seems to be a relatively easy step to go through when one looks further at the second procedural step required by the Court of Justice. Indeed, particular challenges may arise when the national executing authority proceeds to engage in dialogue with the authorities of the requesting country. This boils down to a fundamental question whether one can trust an assessment and evidence provided by a national court, which – allegedly – is not independent. In the case at hand, the doubts expressed by the Irish High Court were exacerbated by a rather blunt statement courtesy of the Polish Deputy Minister of Justice, who acted in breach of presumption of innocence by alluding that the person, who is subject to the EAW, is a criminal.[50] This has surely undermined already cracking trust in the Polish judiciary and its independence. In *LM* the Court of Justice concluded that if doubts of the requested court cannot be discounted it may refuse to surrender a person requested under the EAW. This has to happen when the executing judicial authority concludes that there is 'a real risk that the individual concerned will suffer in the issuing Member State a breach of his fundamental right to an independent tribunal and, therefore, of the essence of his fundamental right to a fair trial'.[51] In this respect it is interesting to note the two differences between the discussed judgment and the decision of the Court of Justice in *Aranyosi and Căldăraru*. First, Article 1(3) of the EAW Framework Decision is employed unequivocally as the legal basis for such a decision. Second, the Court uses a different language to describe the actions of executing authorities. While in *Aranyosi and Căldăraru* the Court talks about bringing EAW procedures to an end, in the present case the judges at Kirchberg have instructed their domestic counterparts to 'refrain from giving effect to the European Arrest Warrant'.[52] Irrespective of the phraseology, the end result is, however, just the same.

[49] See n 31.

[50] See Irish High Court, *Minister for Justice and Equality v Celmer (No 4)*, judgment of 1 August 2018, [2018] IEHC 484.

[51] Para 77 of the judgment.

[52] Para 77 of the judgment.

D. Conclusions

The *LM* case arrived at a crucial time and, not surprisingly, it has triggered a lot of commotion. From the point of view of principles of mutual trust and mutual recognition it encapsulates well the evolving legal landscape, which no longer features blind and unconditional trust in judicial systems of other Member States. For many national judges it is a welcome development, even though, as academic commentators put it, the case-by-case *modus operandi* laid down therein requires passing of 'Herculean hurdles'.[53] The High Court of Ireland, which submitted the reference in the present case, eventually ruled on 19 November 2018, that the surrender to Poland should be ordered as, despite systemic and generalised deficiencies in the independence of the Polish judiciary, there was no real risk that the requested person would be exposed to a flagrant denial of its right to a fair trial.[54] This, arguably, is one of the first cases and many will follow. The key question is how domestic courts will proceed in the months to come. Since general suspension of the EAW system is neither politically possible nor desired, the burden to assess how much trust there is left in the Polish judicial system will remain on the shoulders of national judges.

V. Conclusions

What does the judgment in joint cases *Aranyosi* and *Căldăraru* and the follow-up decisions leave us with? To begin with, it has been a breaking point for the mutual recognition and mutual trust in criminal matters. Although carefully worded, and setting the *modus operandi* that should be followed in case of doubts about the respect for fundamental rights at the receiving end, the Court in fact has opened the door for national judges to refuse execution of the EAW. It should be noted that everyday practice will determine whether the door has been made merely ajar or wide open. On the one hand, the discussed judgments are the answers to dilemmas faced in the multifaceted legal environment. On the other hand, they are a challenge to the principle of mutual trust. EU law now allows domestic judges to question openly the trust in their counterparts and the legal systems of other Member States. At the same time, this eases the tensions between the obligations resting on the shoulders of domestic judges, courtesy of national law combined with ECHR and the EAW Framework Decision (and some other mutual recognition instruments). In more general terms, as argued by L Mancano, the shift in the jurisprudence of the Court of Justice 'restores the balance between fundamental rights protection and enforcement demands

[53] Bárd, van Ballegooij (n 38) 353–65.

[54] Irish High Court, *The Minister for Justice and Equality v Celmer (No 5)*, 19 November 2018, [2018] IEHC 639, para 123.

in the European Arrest Warrant system'.[55] By the same token the Court of Justice has moved the centre of gravity from security closer to justice. The question is whether the conclusions reached in joined cases *Aranyosi and Căldăraru* should be now also addressed by the EU legislator. To put it differently, if a revision of the EAW Framework Decision were to materialise, should Articles 3-4a be amended in order to codify the jurisprudence coming from Kirchberg? It should be noted, that a precedent has been set in Directive 2014/41/EU on European Investigation Order, which envisages fundamental rights as a non-recognition ground.[56] Yet, for now, any formal revision of the EAW Framework Decision remains merely a theoretical proposition as there is clearly no appetite to proceed with a revision of the legal act in question. This, in turn means, that the question of whether to surrender or not, when in doubt about the respect for fundamental rights, will remain to be answered solely by national courts (assisted by the Court of Justice). And this will boil down to the fundamental question of whether their counterparts in other Member States can be trusted. Trust has not been lost yet, however, as cases discussed in this commentary demonstrate, it has been put to the test.

[55] L Mancano, 'A New Hope? The Court of Justice Restores the Balance between Fundamental Rights Protection and Enforcement Demands in the European Arrest Warrant System' in Ch Brière and A Weyembergh (eds), *The Needed Balances in EU Criminal Law. Past, Present and Future* (Oxford and Portland, Hart Publishing, 2018) 285–312.

[56] Directive 2014/41/EU of the European Parliament and of the Council of 3 April 2014 regarding the European Investigation Order in criminal matters [2014] OJ L130/1. See further A Erbežnik, 'Mutual Recognition in EU Criminal Law and Fundamental Rights – The Necessity for Sensitive Approach' in Brière and Weyembergh (eds), *ibid*, 185–211, at 197–99.

The Effect of CJEU Case Law Concerning the Rule of Law and Mutual Trust on National Systems

PETRA BÁRD AND WOUTER VAN BALLEGOOIJ*

The EU is founded on a number of values enshrined in Art 2 of the Treaty on the European Union (TEU), of which democracy, the rule of law and fundamental rights are overarching.

The principle of mutual recognition at the heart of EU criminal law is intrinsically linked to the concept of the rule of law and the protection of fundamental rights. This principle in surrender proceedings prescribes that 'the Member States are in principle obliged to give effect to a European Arrest Warrant'.[1]

In its *Opinion 2/13* on the draft accession agreement of the EU to the European Convention on Human Rights (ECHR),[2] the Court of Justice emphasised that a Member State shall presume all other Member States to be in compliance with EU law including the respect for fundamental rights. The Court of Justice also referred to 'exceptional circumstances', which would warrant deviating from the mutual trust principle,[3] but the exact nature of these was left open. In the cases of *Aranyosi* and *Căldăraru*[4] and in *LM*[5] the Court of Justice of the European Union (CJEU) had an opportunity to clarify what those exceptional circumstances might be and what they would entail for the role of the judicial authorities, and the individual subject to a surrender procedure.

* The views expressed in this article are solely those of the authors.

[1] Case C-237/15 PPU *Lanigan* [2015] ECR 474, para 36; Judgment of the Court (Grand Chamber) of 5 April 2016 in Joined Cases C-404/15 and C-659/15 PPU *Pál Aranyosi and Robert Căldăraru* ECLI:EU:C:2016:198, para 79.

[2] Court of Justice of the European Union, *Opinion 2/13* of 18 December 2014, not yet published. Opinion pursuant to Article 218(11) TFEU – draft international agreement – Accession of the European Union to the European Convention for the Protection of Human Rights and Fundamental Freedoms – Compatibility of the draft agreement with the EU and FEU Treaties.

[3] *Ibid* at para 192.

[4] *Aranyosi* (n 1), requests for a preliminary ruling from the *Hanseatisches Oberlandesgericht* in Bremen; W van Ballegoooij, P Bárd, 'Mutual Recognition and Individual Rights, Did the Court Get it Right?' (2016) 7 *New Journal of European Criminal Law* 4, 439–64.

[5] Judgment of the Court (Grand Chamber) of 25 July 2018 in Case C-216/18 PPU *Minister for Justice and Equality v LM* ECLI:EU:C:2018:586, requests for a preliminary ruling from the High Court (Ireland).

In the following, the two judgments will be briefly discussed, with a special emphasis on the rule of law aspects of the case law, then their potential consequences for national judiciaries and for suspects will be summarised, before analysing the national implementation of the judicial tests developed by the Luxembourg forum.

I. The *Aranyosi* and *LM* jurispridence

In the surrender cases *Aranyosi* and *LM*, the CJEU reserves the task of suspending mutual trust exclusively to the Member States, and only if the sanctioning prong of Article 7 TEU was successfully invoked.[6] Judicial authorities, in contrast, may only suspend individual surrenders on a case-by-case basis.[7] The question is under what conditions.

The CJEU first answered this question in *Aranyosi*, which concerned the surrender of individuals to countries with detention conditions that amounted to violations of Article 4 EU Charter (Art 3 of the European Convention on Human Rights (ECHR)) prohibiting torture, inhuman or degrading treatment or punishment. The CJEU established a two-prong test for checking the fundamental rights situation in and the potential risks of human rights violations by the issuing Member State, and for potentially allowing the postponement of surrender. As a first step, the executing judicial authority must assess whether there are deficiencies in general. Once a risk of fundamental rights violation is established, as a second step, the executing judicial authority must determine, specifically and precisely, whether there are substantial grounds to believe that the person concerned by a European Arrest Warrant, issued for the purposes of conducting a criminal prosecution or executing a custodial sentence, will be exposed, because of the conditions of his or her detention in the issuing Member State, to a real risk of inhuman or degrading treatment or punishment, within the meaning of Article 4 EU Charter, in the event of his surrender to that Member State.[8] To that end, the executing judicial authority must request supplementary information to be provided by the issuing judicial authority. The executing authority may further rely on any other information available.[9] If the risk of a human rights violation in general and in the specific case is established, the execution of the warrant must be postponed.[10]

Certain other features of the *Aranyosi* case made it questionable whether it would make a strong precedent. The fact that an absolute right was at stake and

[6] Council Framework Decision 2002/584/JHA of 13 June 2002 on the European arrest warrant and the surrender procedures between Member States ('FD EAW') [2002] OJ L190/1, Recital 10.

[7] *LM* (n 5), para 73.

[8] *LM* (n 5), para 92.

[9] *LM* (n 5), para 95–97.

[10] *LM* (n 5), para 98.

that its violation was established beyond doubt made the case a relatively easy one. A further element that made the case easy is that the evidence presented substantiating the general fundamental rights violations was a solid one, namely a pilot judgment vis-a-vis one of the issuing states,[11] and a series of European Court of Human Rights (ECtHR) judgments against the other.[12] Importantly, it remained unclear whether and to what extent the case law would be applicable if not merely a potential (absolute) fundamental rights violation was at stake, but also if an element of the rule of law was in jeopardy in the issuing state. In the case of Artur Celmer referred to as LM, the CJEU got a chance to answer these questions.[13]

The issue concerned whether LM, a crime suspect, should be surrendered from Ireland to Poland when the executing judicial authority has serious doubts as to whether the suspect would receive a fair trial in the issuing state, due to the lack of independence of the judiciary resulting from changes to the Polish judicial system.[14] The CJEU had a chance – and we have previously argued[15] for making use of it – to go beyond its case law and frame the case primarily as a rule of law problem. The CJEU however constructed the case as a possible violation of a fundamental right, in this case the right to a fair trial ex. Article 47 EU Charter, the essence of which includes the requirement that tribunals are independent and impartial.[16] The CJEU ruled that the two-step test in *Aranyosi* needs to be followed by the executing judicial authority when making decisions on surrenders. When discussing the first prong of the test in relation to judicial independence, the CJEU relied on the case *Associação Sindical dos Juízes Portugueses*,[17] and emphasised that both judicial independence and impartiality are crucial for the right to fair trial to be respected.[18] Second, if the first element of the test is satisfied, the executing

[11] *Varga and others v Hungary* App nos 14097/12, 45135/12, 73712/12, 34001/13, 44055/13 and 64586/13 (ECtHR, 10 March 2015).

[12] *Stanciu v Romania* App no 35972/05 (ECtHR, 24 July 2012).

[13] See *LM* (n 5).

[14] High Court of Ireland decision of 12 March 2018, *Minister for Justice and Equality v Celmer* [2018] IEHC 119. For the final version of the preliminary reference, see High Court of Ireland decision of 23 March 2018, *Minister for Justice and Equality v Celmer* [2018] IEHC 119.

[15] Petra Bárd and Wouter van Ballegooij, 'Judicial Independence as a Pre-Condition for Mutual Trust? The CJEU in Minister for Justice and Equality v LM' (2018) 9 *New Journal of European Criminal Law* 3, 353–65; P Bárd and W van Ballegooij, 'Judicial Independence as a Precondition for Mutual Trust' (*Verfassungblog*, 10 April 2018), available at https://verfassungsblog.de/judicial-independence-as-a-precondition-for-mutual-trust/; P Bárd and W van Ballegooij, 'The AG Opinion in the Celmer Case: Why Lack of Judicial Independence Should Have Been Framed as a Rule of Law Issue' (*Verfassungsblog*, 2 July 2018), available at https://verfassungsblog.de/the-ag-opinion-in-the-celmer-case-why-lack-of-judicial-independence-should-have-been-framed-as-a-rule-of-law-issue/; W van Ballegooij and P Bárd, 'The CJEU in the Celmer case: One Step Forward, Two Steps Back for Upholding the Rule of Law Within the EU' (*Verfassungsblog*, 29 July 2018), available at https://verfassungsblog.de/the-cjeu-in-the-celmer-case-one-step-forward-two-steps-back-for-upholding-the-rule-of-law-within-the-eu/.

[16] *LM* (n 5), paras 47–48.

[17] Judgment of the Court (Grand Chamber) of 27 February 2018 in Case C-64/16 *Associação Sindical dos Juízes Portugueses v Tribunal de Contas* ECLI:EU:C:2018:117, request for a preliminary ruling from the *Supremo Tribunal Administrativo*.

[18] *LM* (n 5), paras 64–67.

judiciary must specifically and precisely assess whether, in the case at hand, there are substantial grounds for believing that the requested suspect will run the real risk of being subject to a breach of the essence of the right to a fair trial.[19] When making this assessment, the executing court must first check the extent to which the systemic or generalised deficiencies of the judiciary in the issuing Member State have an impact on the court that will decide the surrendered individual's case.[20] Second, the executing court must also assess whether the individual concerned will run a real risk of breach of his fundamental right to an independent tribunal, having regard to his personal situation, the nature of the offence and the factual context.[21]

II. Potential Consequences for National Judiciaries and Suspects

It is submitted that shifting the responsibility for fundamental rights protection to the issuing judicial authority requires first and foremost adequate safeguards and enforcement mechanisms on democracy, the rule of law and fundamental rights protection in the Member States and the development of further minimum standards at EU level, including as regards pre-trial detention.[22] One should also not forget to ensure the proper enforcement of EU measures already adopted, ensuring dual representation and legal aid for those subject to a judicial cooperation measure within the EU.

A monitoring mechanism could address problems, be it with detention conditions or threats to judicial independence, before they escalate. We have sought to tie this idea with that of a mechanism, allowing executing judicial authorities to 'freeze' judicial cooperation[23] in the event that doubts arise as to respect for the rule of law in the issuing Member State.[24] Such a measure should stay in place

[19] *LM* (n 5), para 68. *cf Aranyosi* (n 1), paras 92 and 94.

[20] *LM* (n 5), para 74.

[21] *LM* (n 5), para 75.

[22] W van Ballegooij, 'The Cost of Non-Europe in the Area of Procedural Rights and Detention Conditions' (European Parliamentary Research Service, PE 611.008, December 2017).

[23] See the *Verfassungsblog* entries by Bárd and van Ballegooij (n 15). The need for a freezing mechanism has also been shared by Professors Carrera and Mitsilegas. See S Carrera and V Mitsilegas, 'Upholding the Rule of Law by Scrutinising Judicial Independence: The Irish Court's Request for a Preliminary Ruling on the European Arrest Warrant' (*CEPS*, 11 April 2018), available at < www.ceps.eu/publications/upholding-rule-law-scrutinising-judicial-independence-irish-courts-request-preliminary.

[24] European Parliament Resolution of 25 October 2016 with recommendations to the Commission on the establishment of an EU mechanism on democracy, the rule of law and fundamental rights (2015/2254(INL)), P8_TA-PROV(2016)0409; W van Ballegooij, T Evas, 'An EU Mechanism on Democracy, the Rule of Law and Fundamental Rights', Interim European Added Value Assessment Accompanying the Legislative Initiative Report (Rapporteur Sophie in 't Veld), European Parliamentary Research Service, October 2016, PE.579.328; Annex I, L Pech, E Wennerström, V Leigh, A Markowska, L De Keyser, A Gómez Rojo and H Spanikova, 'Assessing the Need and Possibilities for the Establishment of an EU Scoreboard on Democracy, the Rule of Law and Fundamental Rights'; Annex II, P Bárd, S Carrera, E Guild and D Kochenov, with a thematic contribution by W Marneffe, 'Assessing the Need and Possibilities for the Establishment of an EU Scoreboard on Democracy, the Rule of Law and Fundamental Rights'.

until the matter is resolved in accordance with the procedure provided for in Article 7 TEU or a permanent mechanism for monitoring and addressing Member State compliance with democracy, the rule of law and fundamental rights (DRF) as proposed by the European Parliament.[25]

Second, we have warned against the CJEU's tendency to limit the discretion of executing judicial authorities. Beyond misinterpreting the principle of mutual recognition, this negates the fact that fundamental rights are also a direct source of EU law.[26]

Third, relying on assurances from issuing judicial authorities creates two classes of EU citizens: those that are treated 'better' because they 'benefit' from free movement and those that apparently do not have the right to an independent judge or adequate detention conditions because they remained inside their Member State.[27]

Fourth, an inverse problem might occur. Certain national constitutions offer a higher level of protection than the EU standard, sometimes limited to their own citizens, sometimes not. Distinguishing between those who remain within and those who come from outside will lead to a direct conflict with those constitutions, thereby reinvigorating the conflict over primacy of EU law, and the degree to which higher protections offered by national constitutional provisions may be maintained in accordance with Article 53 of the Charter.[28]

Fifth, there is a wider problem a lack of judicial independence raises for the EU constitutional construct, which relies on national judges to enforce EU law on behalf of individuals, if need be by setting aside conflicting national law. In this regard it would have been more logical for the CJEU to rely on Article 19 TEU directly on the one hand, like in its earlier *Associação Sindical dos Juízes Portugueses* case and the interim measure inflicted on Poland in the controversy around judicial independence.[29] The contradiction in the two sets of cases may be explained by the fact that in cases involving mutual recognition based instruments, the CJEU can share responsibility with domestic courts – notably the judicial authority of the executing Member State – in determining the health status of the issuing state's judiciary, whereas in the cases targeting judicial independence as such, the CJEU is the ultimate judicial body in the EU setting to address the placing in jeopardy of

[25] European Parliament Resolution of 25 October 2016 (n 24); Follow up to the European Parliament resolution on recommendations to the Commission on the establishment of an EU mechanism on democracy, the rule of law and fundamental rights, adopted by the Commission on 17 January 2017, SP(2017)16.

[26] W van Ballegooij, *The Nature of Mutual Recognition in European Law, Re-examining the Notion from an Individual Rights Perspective with a View to its Further Development in the Criminal Justice Area* (Intersentia, 2015) 356: 'Limiting the discretion of executing judicial authorities, claiming that it is good for mutual recognition fails to understand the need to recognise judicial decisions as opposed to enforcing them directly based on compliance with the standards of the home state (home state control).'

[27] van Ballegoooij and Bárd (n 4) 456.

[28] Case C-399/11 *Melloni* ECLI:EU:C:2013:107; German Constitutional Court, Order of the Second Senate of 15 December 2015 – 2 BvR 2735/14 – paras 1–126, available at www.bverfg.de/e/rs20151215_2bvr273514en.html.

[29] Case C-619/18 R *Commission v Poland*.

judicial independence. Also, in *LM* the CJEU entered into a judicial dialogue with a national court, which specifically asked whether the previous jurisprudence in *Aranyosi* was to be followed, and whether it had to move to the second prong of the test in case the issuing court had a rule of law deficiency, whereas in the other (infringement) case it was not bound by questions formulated in a preliminary reference.

Nevertheless, the deference of the CJEU towards the European Council and the distinction between infringement proceedings to uphold the rule of law and surrender proceedings is unjustified.[30] We have furthermore argued that the second prong of which raises Herculean hurdles for both the defence in terms of proving such violations and on judicial authorities to accept them in individual cases. In our view, once the first step of the test is satisfied, the onus should shift to the stronger party, that is, the state accused of rule of law violations, in the light of the bedrock of the principle of equality of arms.[31] Furthermore, we severely doubt whether a captured court could engage in a proper dialogue with the executing judicial authority on its judicial independence, as the issuing court would thereby risk destroying its own reputation and/or criticising the state's executive upon which it is dependent.[32]

III. National Follow-Up to *Aranyosi* and *LM*: Proving the Need for an EU Mechanism on Democracy, the Rule of Law and Fundamental Rights

At the time of writing, several executing judicial authorities in the Member States have engaged with the two-prong test prescribed by the CJEU. Even in light of the very recent and yet therefore limited case law we can already notice some worrying signs confirming the concerns raised in our previous writings and summarised in the above section.

In Hungary, there are still severe concerns with regard to prison conditions, nevertheless as will be further discussed/argued below, the Court's heavy reliance on Council of Europe standards makes it more difficult for executing judicial authorities to postpone surrender cases on that ground.

[30] *cf* M Krajewski, 'Who is afraid of the European Council? The Court of Justice's Cautious Approach to the Independence of Domestic Judges, ECJ 25 July 2018, Case C-216/18 PPU, The Minister for Justice and Equality v LM' (2018) *European Constitutional Law Review* 1–22 at 19: 'The competence of the Court under Article 19(1) TEU and 47 of the Charter and the competence of the European Council under Article 2 and 7 TEU are parallel.'

[31] European Court of Human Rights, 'Guide on Article 6 of the European Convention on Human Rights', 29–31, available at https://www.echr.coe.int/Documents/Guide_Art_6_criminal_ENG.pdf.

[32] Bárd and van Ballegooij (n 15) 360–63; Krajewski (n 30) 14: 'Clearly, any judge who provided a foreign court with information about political pressure being exerted would face disciplinary action.'

In the case of Poland, the national courts that have expressed themselves on the matter so far all came to the conclusion that there are general deficiencies concerning the judiciary following recent legislative changes as evidenced by various sources, including the Commission's Reasoned Proposal for a Decision of the Council on the determination of a clear risk of a serious breach of the rule of law of 20 December 2017.[33] There are several pending cases where national courts currently apply the test laid down in *LM*,[34] whereas in others the assessment already took place and surrender was ordered.

A. Higher Regional Court of Bremen: *ML*

Two aspects of the *Aranyosi* jurisprudence's impact on national courts deserve greater attention. Both issues have been extensively dealt with in *ML*, another surrender case, where – similarly to *Aranyosi* – a German court had doubts as to whether the convict should be handed over to Hungary with still substandard prison conditions. The Higher Regional Court of Bremen asked the CJEU what information it needed to obtain about the conditions in which ML would be detained in Hungary.[35]

First, when assessing the effects of potentially cramped and substandard prisons on the individual suspect, the executing judicial authorities are only required to assess the conditions of detention in the prisons in which the suspect is intended by the issuing authorities to be detained. This means that the application of the second prong of the *Aranyosi* test will in practice not necessarily lead to the effective protection of detainees.[36]

Second, in *ML* the difficulties of the *Aranyosi* test took their toll. *Aranyosi* placed too much of a burden on executing authorities to check possible systemic fundamental rights violations in the issuing Member States. Among others, it was left open as to what pieces of evidence need to be used to prove the general problem.

The judgment in *Aranyosi* heavily depended on the ECtHR judgment *Varga and Others v. Hungary*,[37] holding that prison conditions in Hungary violated Article 4 EU Charter (Article 3 ECHR). But after the judgment in *Aranyosi* had been rendered, Hungary adopted a new law,[38] which provided a combination of

[33] COM (2017)0835, 20 December 2017.

[34] The *Audiencia Nacional* of Spain and District Court of Amsterdam sent questions to Polish-issuing judicial authorities. See District Court of Amsterdam, 4 October 2018, ECLI:NL:RBAMS:2018:7032; and https://wiadomosci.onet.pl/tylko-w-onecie/sad-w-madrycie-pyta-o-niezawislosc-sedziowska-w-polsce-w-tzw-sprawa-celmera/9vh20ef?utm_source=wiadomosci_viasg&utm_medium=nitro&utm_campaign=allonet_nitro_new&srcc=ucs&utm_v=2 for a copy of the questions asked by the Madrid Court.

[35] Judgment of the Court (First Chamber) of 25 July 2018, Case C-220/18 PPU *ML* ECLI:EU:C:2018:589.

[36] *cf* www.fairtrials.org/publication/beyond-surrender.

[37] *Varga and others* (n 11).

[38] Act No CX of 2016 amending Act No CCXL of 2013 on the enforcement of punishments, measures, certain coercive measures and confinement for regulatory offences.

preventive and compensatory remedies, guaranteeing in principle genuine redress for ECHR violations originating from cramped prisons and other unsuitable detention conditions. Therefore, the question in *LM* was whether surrender still had to be postponed in light of the new Hungarian law. To make matters more complicated, in *Domján v Hungary*[39] the ECtHR declared another Hungarian detainee's application – and all others' in his position – complaining about prison conditions premature and therefore inadmissible, saying that Mr Domján should make use of the remedies introduced by the new domestic law before turning to the Strasbourg Court.

The ECtHR's decision in *Domján* led the Advocate General (AG) to believe in the *ML* case that surrender cannot be postponed any longer on the grounds of poor prison conditions in Hungary.[40] In contrast, the CJEU realised that procedures enabling authorities to grant redress for fundamental rights violations cannot rule out the existence of a real risk of a violation, and it is this latter aspect that the executing authority needs to assess. Even though the *Domján* decision is no ultimate proof that detention conditions changed for the better in Hungary, the CJEU also noted that the existence of the new proceedings of preventive and compensatory remedies may be taken into account when deciding on surrender.[41] Despite this refined reliance on ECtHR case law, the Court implies that 'in the absence of minimum standards under EU law regarding detention conditions'[42] the ultimate bar for determining the potentiality of human rights violations remains to be determined by the Strasbourg Court.

Instead of this heavy reliance on Strasbourg jurisprudence, we propose a regular, context-specific, objective, equal and scientifically sound evaluation, possibly in the form of the above-mentioned DRF mechanism, which would not only alleviate the burden from the national judiciaries to assess each other's legal systems, but also be tailored to the expedited intra-EU judicial cooperation based on the principle of mutual recognition requiring higher standards than those established by the Council of Europe, an entity incorporating a number of states with dismal human rights records.

B. High Court of England and Wales: *Pawel Lis et al*

A judgment by the High Court of England and Wales dated 31 October 2018 in the case of three Polish citizens[43] contesting their surrender to Poland, illustrates

[39] *Domján v Hungary* App no 5433/17 (ECtHR, 14 November 2017).

[40] Opinion of Advocate General Campos Sánchez-Bordona of 4 July 2018 in *ML* (n 35), paras 51–54.

[41] *ML* (n 35), para 117.

[42] *ML* (n 35) para 90. *cf* Wouter van Ballegooij, 'Procedural Rights and Detention Conditions: Cost of Non-Europe Report' (PE 611.008, European Parliamentary Research Service, European Added Value Unit, Brussels, 2017), available at http://www.europarl.europa.eu/RegData/etudes/STUD/2017/611008/EPRS_STU(2017)611008_EN.pdf.

[43] *Pawel Lis et al* [2018] EWHC 2848(Admin).

just how difficult it is for the defence to prove that the wanted person will be individually affected by the current threats to the independence of the Polish judiciary to the extent that they would pose a real risk of a breach of their (fair trial) right to an independent tribunal.

First, the High Court accepted the reasoning of the respondents that the second prong of the test developed by the CJEU; 'a real risk of being subject to a breach of the essence of the right to a fair trial',[44] should be understood as the 'flagrant denial of justice' test developed by the ECtHR.[45] The High Court reasoning that this should be the case because the CJEU did not explicitly state otherwise is not convincing. At the very least the High Court could have raised preliminary questions to obtain further clarity from the CJEU on the standard of proof required for executing judicial authorities to accept that the individual

> will run a real risk of breach of his fundamental right to an independent tribunal and, therefore, of the essence of his fundamental right to a fair trial, having regard to his personal situation, as well as to the nature of the offence for which he is being prosecuted and the factual context that form the basis of the European arrest warrant.[46]

In any event, AG Sharpston's opinion in *Radu* should be recalled: 'such a test [...] seems to me unduly stringent. [...] a trial that is only partly fair cannot be guaranteed to ensure that justice is done'.[47]

After assessing the individuals' personal situation, nature of the offence and factual context, the High Court concludes that their individual cases would likely establish any real risk of breach of their fundamental rights to an independent trial.[48] In particular, the individuals are to be surrendered (the High Court still talks about extradition in accordance with the domestic transposition of the Framework Decision on the European Arrest Warrant) 'for ordinary criminal offences, with no political or other sensitive content' which 'would seem unlikely to be able to establish the necessary risk'.[49]

C. District Court of Amsterdam

In an interim ruling of 4 October 2018,[50] the District Court of Amsterdam stayed surrender proceedings regarding a Polish suspect in view of obtaining answers by Polish judicial authorities (the Circuit Court in Poznań). The District Court was particularly persuaded that the first prong was met by evidence 'during [the] first

[44] *LM* (n 5), para 68.
[45] *Pawel Lis et al* (n 43), para 62–63.
[46] *LM* (n 5), para 75.
[47] Opinion of AG Sharpston delivered on 18 October 2012 in Case C-396/11, *Ministerul Public – Parchetul* de pe *lângă Curtea* de *Apel Constanța v Ciprian Vasile Radu* ECLI: EU: C:2012:648, para 83.
[48] *Pawel Lis et al* (n 43), para 67–70.
[49] *Pawel Lis et al* (n 43), para 71.
[50] ECLI:NL:RBAMS:2018:7032.

6 months since the law on composition of common courts was amended, that is until 12 February 2018, the Minister of Justice dismissed 18,6% court presidents and vice-presidents',[51] as well as the lowering of the pension age of Polish Supreme Court justices and shortening the tenure of the justices, including the President of the Supreme Court, by 40 per cent. On this basis, the District Court also found a real risk of breach of an individual's fundamental right to an independent tribunal. To establish whether in this specific case there would be such a risk, the District Court wished for more details on the protection and maintenance of independence at the level of the judicial authorities that will be competent in the proceedings the wanted person will be subject to. It decided to engage in a 'dialogue' with the issuing judicial authority on the matter, by requesting more information regarding any recent changes in personnel since the law regarding the composition of common courts entered into force. This included information on: the replacement of (vice) presidents and judges, rules and procedures regarding the allocation of cases to divisions of judges within the competent court and their treatment; disciplinary measures against (vice) presidents and judges, including in regards to their remuneration; the procedures that will be open to the wanted person to claim violations of his right to an independent tribunal and the safeguards surrounding these procedures; and the possibilities for extraordinary appeal to the Supreme Court.

D. Irish High Court: *Celmer*

Following the CJEU ruling in *LM*, the controversy was returned to the Irish High Court to apply the test developed by the Luxembourg Court.

In its judgment of 1 August 2018, the High Court determined the general concern with regard to judicial independence in Poland and requested the councils submit questions so as to satisfy the second prong of the text in *LM*, as is required by the Court of Justice.[52] The judicial dialogue went on for some time, until in case *Celmer (No 5)* on 19 November 2018 the Irish Court ordered the surrender of Mr Celmer.[53] Even though the outcome of the proceeding may take a turn as his lawyers are considering appeal,[54] it is worth looking at the judgment in greater detail, since it illustrates the problems we summarised earlier.

As a preliminary point, it should be stated that in relation to the first prong of the *LM* test, the generalised and systemic violations to the independence of Poland's judiciary were not contested. The High Court noted on the basis of expert opinion that there were no core changes in the Polish judicial system since the

[51] The Chancellery of the Prime Minister, 'White Paper on the Reform of the Polish Judiciary', available at www.premier.gov.pl/files/files/white_paper_en_full.pdf, 38.

[52] *Minister for Justice v Celmer (No 4)* [2018] IEHC 484, 1 August 2018.

[53] *Minister for Justice v Celmer (No 5)* [2018] IEHC 639, 19 November 2018.

[54] See www.irishtimes.com/news/crime-and-law/courts/high-court/court-orders-surrender-of-polish-man-after-concerns-over-fair-trial-1.3702875.

Reasoned Proposal of the Commission[55] had been published, therefore all the criticism enshrined there still holds true.[56] It also stated that the replies of the issuing authorities were contradictory[57] – and that there was a dispute between two judges as to who was to represent the Warsaw Court[58] –, but that did not change the Irish Court's assessment.

As to the second prong, it shall be remembered that we argued against following the *Aranyosi* test in rule of law violations, due to the difficulties, if not impossibility, of proving how the suspect would be individually affected by rule of law violations. We also argued that at the minimum the onus should shift to the state in question to prove that the suspect will not be infringed. The High Court seemed to have shared our concern in the referral.[59] In *Celmer (No 5)* the High Court restated the Court of Justice's opposing stance in the form of the *LM* test, where the CJEU clarified that systemic deficiencies in themselves do not establish a real risk to the suspect's right to a fair trial.[60] Then the High Court diligently adhered to its EU law obligations applying the two-prong test.[61]

Just like the High Court of England and Wales in *Pawel Lis et al*, the High Court in *Celmer (No 5)* also set the threshold in determining the breach of fair trial very high equating the real risk of a breach of the essence of the applicant's right to a fair trial with the ECtHR's 'flagrant denial of justice', suggesting that this is what the CJEU judgment entails. The Irish Human Rights and Equality Commission (IHREC) in an *amicus curiae* reminded the High Court of the facts that on the one hand the ECtHR treats 'flagrant denial of justice' as a stringent test of unfairness and that the Court never found an expulsion to be in contradiction with the ECHR on that ground. On the other hand it also recalled that the Court of Justice avoided the use of this test, unlike AG Tanchev in his Opinion in the *LM* case.[62,63] The Irish Court rejected these arguments, and was satisfied to use the 'flagrant denial of justice' test first because this is how the council for Mr Celmer positioned the case right from the outset.[64] This argument seems somewhat unfair given that the CJEU had not yet come up with its 'essence of the right to a fair trial' requirement, which only developed as a result of the preliminary reference. Second, the Irish Court noted that the CJEU did not expressly distance itself from the test in the AG Opinion.[65] Third and related to that, the Court of Justice relied

[55] Commission's Reasoned proposal in accordance with Article 7(1) of the Treaty on European Union regarding the rule of law in Poland, Proposal for a Council Decision on the determination of a clear risk of a serious breach by the Republic of Poland of the rule of law, COM(2017) 835 final, para 180 (2–3).

[56] *Celmer (No 5)* (n 53), paras 72–84, 92–93.

[57] *Celmer (No 5)* (n 53), paras 85–89.

[58] *Celmer (No 5)* (n 53), para 88.

[59] *Minister for Justice v Celmer (No 3)* [2018] IEHC 153, 23 March 2018.

[60] *Celmer (No 5)* (n 53), paras 65 and 69.

[61] *Celmer (No 5)* (n 53), para 71.

[62] Opinion of Advocate General Tanchev, delivered on 28 June 2018 in *LM* (n 5).

[63] *Celmer (No 5)* (n 53), paras 13–14.

[64] *Celmer (No 5)* (n 53), para 18.

[65] *Celmer (No 5)* (n 53), para 14.

on Article 6(1) ECHR (and the corresponding Article 47 of the Charter of Fundamental Rights[66]), whereas the test in the Strasbourg setting is the flagrant denial of justice.[67] In the Irish High Court's view, 'it is inconceivable that the CJEU were amending the well settled test by implication'.[68] If the CJEU were to depart from the flagrant denial of justice test, the High Court is satisfied that it would have expressly stated so.[69] Fourth, the High Court also noted that this reading corresponds to the Court of Justice's earlier case law referring to 'exceptional circumstances' to be demonstrated in order to deny surrender.[70]

The High Court then assessed the evidence as to whether the fair trial rights of Mr Celmer individually were threatened, more specifically whether he would face a flagrant denial of justice. The High Court notes that the general rule of law concerns might, but will not automatically lead to a flagrant denial of justice[71] – a statement which is obvious, otherwise the *LM* test would become meaningless. The suspect however could not show individual concerns. Even his lawyers admitted that there is a probability for having Mr Celmer's rights respected, since his fair trial rights will depend on the person who renders the judgment in the case.[72] The High Court also noted that thus far 'there has been no production of statistics or even anecdotal evidence of trials lacking in fairness since the changes regarding the judiciary in Poland'.[73] The High Court concluded that statements against the presumption of innocence could be remedied, or shall be disregarded by the national court respectively.[74]

In sum, the High Court concluded that the systemic and generalised deficiencies in the judicial system of Poland did not amount to a real risk that Mr Celmer's individual right to a fair trial would be endangered. The High Court emphasised that the threshold created by *LM* was a high one and, in light of evidence before the Court, had not been reached.

In *Celmer (No 5)* the Irish High Court essentially stated that it saw the problems of judicial independence, but there was nothing it could do about preventing the potential effects of the problem on the individual suspect, once the Court of Justice came out with an inoperable judicial test in relation to proving the specific risks. In other words, the High Court gave the CJEU a chance to alleviate the

[66] Explanations to the Charter of Fundamental Rights expressly refer to the fact that the second paragraph of Article 47 corresponds to Article 6(1) of the ECHR, see http://fra.europa.eu/en/charterpedia/article/47-right-effective-remedy-and-fair-trial.

[67] Examples of 'flagrant denial of justice' could amount to a violation of Article 48 Charter of Fundamental Rights. See, eg *Al-Moayad v Germany* App no 35865/03 (ECtHR, 20 February 2007) para 101 on deliberate and systematic refusal of access to a lawyer.

[68] *Celmer (No 5)* (n 53), para 24.

[69] *Celmer (No 5)* (n 53), para 67.

[70] *Celmer (No 5)* (n 53), para 31 referring to the High Court in England and Wales in *Pawel Lis et al* (n 43) and subsequent paragraphs, especially para 45.

[71] *Celmer (No 5)* (n 53), para 100.

[72] *Celmer (No 5)* (n 53), para 102.

[73] *Celmer (No 5)* (n 53), para 103.

[74] *Celmer (No 5)* (n 53), paras 105, 107 and 108, 111, 114.

tensions between quasi automatic execution of judicial decisions and Member States' obligation to protect and promote the rule of law, but once the Court of Justice failed to make use of it, it was beyond the control of the referring court to remedy the problem.

At the time of writing it is unclear where the next stage of this rule of law crisis will play out. Will the CJEU get another chance to refine or revisit its test based on another set of preliminary questions, bearing in mind that 'judicial cooperation in criminal matters, where individual fundamental rights are directly at stake, *cannot* function when there are serious concerns regarding the independence of judicial authorities'[75] or will a national court, such as the German Constitutional Court, have to do the job for it on the basis of its constitution?

[75] *cf* COM (2014) 158 of 19 March 2014 at 2.

INDEX

Advocaten voor de Wereld:
admissibility, 336–7, 342–3, 344
assessment, 346–7
CJEU judgment
arguments, 336–40
implications, 340–6
competence, 334–5, 348
double criminality, 208, 334, 338, 339–41, 345, 349
legality principle and, 353–61
effectiveness, 4
equal treatment, 208, 339–40, 342, 344
facts and context, 333–6
issues, 348–9
judicial cooperation, 333, 338, 342, 345
landmark, 345–6
legality principle, 339–40, 341, 342, 344–5, 349–53
double criminality and, 353–61
mutual trust, 4, 208, 333–47
subsequent cases, 341–6
surrender concept, 337–8
Allegrezza, Silvia, 165–87
Ambos, Kai, 227–33
Annoni, Alessandra, 276, 290–304
Aranyosi:
assessment, 444, 453–4
creative interpretation of FD EAW, 440–3
exceptional circumstances, 455
facts, 425–6
fundamental rights, 378, 382
inhuman/degrading treatment, 426–9, 440
level of scrutiny, 402
LM and, 431–6, 450, 452, 453, 455
towards benchmark, 429–31
landmark, 422, 428, 437
LM and, 431–6, 448, 450, 456–8
mature approach, 4
ML and, 444–6, 461–2
mutual trust, 421–36, 456–8
automaticity, 425–9
earning trust, 436
national courts and, 437–54
prison conditions, 426–8, 438–44, 456
Radu and, 346, 374, 376, 378–9
revisiting, 448–52
rule of law, 449–50, 465
solution, 391–2
subsequent national cases, 460–7
Ashworth, Andrew, 187
assimilation principle:
Amsterdam Treaty, 111
Greek Maize, 108, 120–1, 124–6, 134
limits, 112–13
Lisbon Treaty, 111
PIF Convention, 110–11
pre-*Greek Maize*, 109–10
Taricco, 113, 167
TEC, 110
asylum:
CEAS, 365, 368, 369
Dublin transfers, 253, 365, 367, 372, 423, 429, 430
fundamental rights and, 424–5, 429
non-refoulement, 283, 378
NS, 365, 368, 374, 379, 423
Reception Conditions Directive, 369

Bachmaier Winter, Lorena, 404–19
Bárd, Petra, 444, 455–67
Belgium:
Advocaten voor de Wereld, 333–47, 348–61
ne bis in idem, 202
Bergström, Maria, 259–70
Berlusconi:
accounting rules, 61–3, 65
ambiguities, 55–6
analogical thinking, 63–5
assessment, 53–4, 55–65
CJEU arguments, 40–1
direct effect, 37, 50–2
effectiveness, 42, 57–60, 114, 131–2
facts, 38–40
foundation of EU criminal law, 2–3
Kolpinghuis and, 43
legality principle, 17, 37–54
lex mitior, 37–54
ambiguities, 55–6

deeper issues, 61–3
effectiveness and, 57–60
revisiting, 52–3
perspectives, 43–50
legality as multilevel concept, 47, 48
primacy, 44–7
precision principle, 64
primacy, 44–7
domestic constitution and, 60
proportionality, 114
reception and interpretation, 41–3
revisiting, 50–3
direct effect, 50–2
lex mitior, 52–3
Bernitz, Ulf, 268
Bonelli, Matteo, 450
Brexit, 317–18
bribery, 110, 130
Bulgaria: ECtHR cases, 384

Caeiro, Pedro, 348–61
Căldăraru see Aranyosi
certainty *see* **legal certainty**
Charter of Fundamental Rights (CFR):
Advocaten voor de Wereld, 339, 342
Aranyosi and, 425–6, 438, 440, 456–8
Art 53, 174, 175–7, 249, 394–6, 401–2, 404, 407, 409, 417, 459
CS and, 305–6, 312–14
deportation and, 309–11, 315–17
direct effect, 15
fair trial, 450
inhuman treatment, 425–6, 433, 438, 461–2
legality principle, 47–50
Berlusconi, 38
multilevel concept, 47, 48–9
primacy, 79
scope, 80
Taricco and, 181–2, 189
lex mitior, 52
LM and, 433
Melloni and, 394, 395–6, 406–7, 409–12
mutual trust and, 399, 423
ne bis in idem, 3, 200–1, 204–5, 211, 228, 231
ECHR and, 256–8
Fransson, 246–58
Swedish tax proceedings, 262
non-regression clauses and, 400
Radu, 342, 364, 366, 370, 383
right to liberty, 366
scope of application, 47
child abuse:
Lanzarote Convention (2007), 96
Pupino see Pupino
child pornography, 101–2, 117
citizenship:
Brexit and, 317–18
categories, 459
CFR, 309–11, 312–14, 315–17
Citizenship Directive, 307–9, 320–1, 323, 327
CS, 3–4, 305–6, 311–18, 319–29
deportation of foreign offenders, 306–9, 311–18
EU law, 306–9, 320–1
family members, 309–11
good v bad citizen discourse, 309
post-*CS* cases, 314–17
probationary citizenship, 319
public security deportations, 308, 320–4, 329
Ruiz Zambrano, 305, 309–17
Claes, Monica, 450
Commission v Council (C-176/03) see Environmental Crime
competence:
Advocaten voor de Wereld, 334–5, 348
Commission v Council (C-176/03) *see Environmental Crime*
EAW Framework Decision, 334–5
framework decisions, 137–40
German constitutionalism, 73
Greek Maize, 3, 124–6
legislative development, 152–3
post-Lisbon Treaty, 161–3
Taricco see Taricco
competition law, 343–4
Constitutional Treaty (draft), 72, 140, 151, 152, 154, 160
***contra legem* interpretation,** 71, 78, 92, 103
corruption, 111, 112–13
CS:
assessment, 317–18
CFR and, 312–14
citizenship, 3–4, 305–18, 319–29
CJEU arguments, 312–14
deportation of foreign offenders, 305–18
UK approach, 319–29
facts, 311–12
legal context, 306–11
CFR, 309–11
EU citizenship law, 306–9
proportionality, 313, 314
Ruiz Zambrano and, 312, 313–14
subsequent cases, 314–17

Cyprus: EAWs, 334
Czech Republic:
Advocaten voor de Wereld and, 336
European Arrest Warrants, 334

Damaska, Miriam, 187
data protection, 343
Delors, Jacques, 127
democracy, 335, 455, 458, 459, 460–7
Denmark:
Environmental Crime and, 159
opt-outs, 152, 154–5, 170
deportation *see* **irregular migration**
Di Martino, Alberto, 1–4, 55–65
direct effect:
Berlusconi, 37, 50–2
developing, 8
framework decisions and, 83–4
indirect effect and, 90–1
Kolpinghuis, 10–11, 12, 13–15, 37
subsequent cases, 16
primacy and, 44
principle, 21
protection of EU financial interests (PIF), 133
Return Directive, 278
dissuasive penalties:
Environment Crime, 117
Greek Maize, 108, 114–20, 124
domestic violence: Istanbul Convention (2011), 96
double criminality:
Advocaten voor de Wereld, 208, 334, 335, 338, 339–41, 345, 349
extradition, 355–61
extraterritorial jurisdiction, 353–5
legality principle and, 353–61
proportionality, 357
double jeopardy *see ne bis in idem*
draft Constitutional Treaty, 72, 140, 151, 152, 154, 160

effectiveness principle:
Advocaten voor de Wereld, 4
balancing rights and, 3–4, 79–81, 186–7, 375–6
Berlusconi, 42, 57–60, 114, 131–2
El Dridi, 278, 295
Greek Maize, 108, 114–20, 122, 124, 125, 131–2, 134
Melloni, 4, 399
mutual trust and, 74–7
Pupino, 3, 70
Radu, 423–4
rationale, 68
Return Directive, 282–3, 289
Taricco, 119
El Dridi:
CJEU judgment, 277–9, 294–6
effectiveness principle, 278, 295
facts and context, 276–7, 294
free movement and, 279–80
impact, 290–304
immediate impact, 294–7
Italy, 296–303
landmark, 274–5, 288–9, 303–4
loyal cooperation, 278, 295, 296
national sovereignty, 3–4
Return Directive and, 275–81
amendment, 297–9
discretion, 281
fundamental rights, 277, 279
removal process, 277–8, 279
subsequent cases, 281–8
value for EU law, 279–81
Environmental Crime:
choice of legal basis, 154–5
competence, 3, 117, 125, 137–63
constitutionalism, 139, 144–5, 149–50
ECJ judgment
arguments, 140–2
critique, 142–4, 150
EU institutional reactions, 156–8
expediency, 140, 144
facts and context, 137–40
impact on EU law, 144–50
landmark, 137–40, 150
national reactions, 146, 147, 151–2, 158–9
interventions in proceedings, 155–6
post-Lisbon Treaty, 161–3
primacy of Community over Union competence, 140–3
proportionality, 117
rule of law, 140
ship-source pollution and, 159–60
environmental law: equal treatment, 344
equal treatment:
Advocaten voor de Wereld, 208, 339–40, 342, 344
Italian Constitution, 91, 93
Euratom, 109
European Arrest Warrant:
Advocaten voor de Wereld, 333–61
Conventions, 334

deprivation of liberty, 398–9
double criminality, 355–61
framework decision
Advocaten voor de Wereld, 333–47
competence, 334–5, 348
creative interpretation, 440–3
Gözütok and Brügge, 214–15
presumed mutual trust, 422–5
principles, 208–10
Pupino, 99
Radu, 363–80, 380–92
fundamental rights and
Amsterdam Court, 463–4
Aranyosi, 425–9, 448–52, 456–8
Celmer, 464–7
EU law compliance, 385–6
inhuman treatment, 425–9
LM, 431–6, 450, 452, 453, 456–8
Melloni, 395–6
mutual trust, 421–9
national solutions, 384–91
Pawel Lis, 462–3, 465
proportionality, 390–1
Radu, 363–79, 380–2
refusal to surrender, 386–91, 460–7
standard of protection, 396–7
implementation cases, 380
implementation reports, 373
in absentia trials, 393–403
Kossowski, 227–33, 235
legality principle, 355–61
Melloni
national effects, 404–19
primacy over rights, 393–403
mutual trust, 4, 373
Advocaten voor de Wereld, 333–47
Aranyosi, 421–36, 437–54
automaticity, 421–9
functioning, 385
Gözütok and Brügge, 208, 214–15
LM, 431–6, 455, 460
Radu., 364–9
political motivations, 388
prison conditions and
Aranyosi, 425–9, 438–44
ML, 444–6, 461–2
Radu, 363–79
impact, 376–8
Romanian solution, 382–4
refusal to surrender
Aranyosi, 425–9, 438–43, 448–52
case-law grounds, 389–91
creative interpretation of FD, 440–3
exceptional circumstances, 386–7, 433, 443, 449, 455, 466
fundamental rights and, 384–91
national-law based grounds, 387–9
new grounds for, 438–9
Spain, 174
surrender, 337–8
European Charter of Fundamental Rights *see* **Charter of Fundamental Rights**
European Convention on Extradition (1957), 334
European Convention on Human Rights:
absolute rights, 257
Advocaten voor de Wereld and, 342
draft EU accession agreement (Opinion 2/13), 208, 241, 346, 364, 374–6, 401, 424, 455
fair trial, 18, 23, 176, 366, 463, 465–6
indirect effect, 91
inhuman treatment, 440
living instrument, 262
mutual trust, 215
ne bis in idem, 245, 256–8
non-regression clauses and, 400
non-retroactivity, 42–3, 168, 262
Radu, 342, 364
right to liberty, 366
UK deportations and, 327
European Court of Human Rights:
benchmark, 430–1
CJEU and, 426, 428–9, 430–1, 441–2, 445, 446, 457
criminal charges: meaning, 23, 261–2, 264
criminal penalty: meaning, 217
deportation, 424
EU/ECtHR relationship: *Radu*, 374–6
extradition and fundamental rights, 365, 367, 368
fair trial, 176, 463, 465
Italian impunity and, 186
Kadi, 401
legal certainty, 176, 262–3
legality principle, 349–50
lex mitior, 47, 49–50
limitations periods and, 166–7
mutual trust and, 402
ne bis idem: Swedish cases, 261–5
prison conditions and, 462
proportionality, 313
Romanian and Bulgarian cases, 384
extradition *see* **European Arrest Warrant**

fair trial:
Celmer, 465–7
CFR, 450
CJEU jurisprudence, 451
EAW and, 407
ECHR, 18, 23, 176, 366, 463, 465–6
in absentia trials, 202, 394, 394–401, 395–6
judicial independence, 433, 434, 446–53, 452
LM, 457–8
Melloni, 386, 394, 395–6, 407
Poland, 452
presumption of innocence, 195, 399–400, 452, 466
Radu, 363, 364, 366–7, 382, 463
requirements, 18
right to silence, 415
false accounting, 38–40, 62
family and privacy rights, 310, 383
Ferrajoli, Luigi, 187
Finland: ***Advocaten voor de Wereld*** **and,** 336
Fletcher, Maria, 67–82
framework decisions:
competence, 334–5, 348
environmental protection through criminal law, 137–63
EAW *see* European Arrest Warrant
indirect effect, 84
legality principle and, 350–1
Pupino, 88–9
ship-source pollution, 139–40, 151, 159–60, 162
status, 83–4
unanimity condition, 144–5
vulnerable witnesses, 89
France:
Advocaten voor de Wereld and, 336
Environmental Crime and, 146, 147, 157, 158–9
irregular migration, 281–4
referendum on EU Constitution, 140
Fransson:
criminalisation of VAT fraud, 167
critique, 250–1
facts and context, 246, 260–1
fundamental rights, 411
judicial review of Swedish laws and, 267, 270
landmark, 245, 258, 259
national impact, 259–70
assessment, 269–70
ne bis in idem, 3, 245–58
CFR and ECHR, 256–8
CJEU decision, 247–50
implementing EU law, 247–55
sincere cooperation, 248
Spain and, 411
subsequent cases, 251–5
fraud:
assimilation principle, 111–13
EU budget, 109–10
Fransson, 167, 246
Greek Maize, 107, 127–9
protection of EU financial interests, 127–9
Italy, 111–12, 129–31
PIF Directive, 126
Spain, 132
statutes of limitations, 80
Taricco, 165–87
VAT fraud, 165–87, 246–58, 260–70
free movement, 2, 109, 200, 204, 205, 210, 236, 240, 253, 279–80, 306–7, 309–10, 343, 371, 459
Fripp, E, 324, 326
Fuglsang Sørensen, Henning, 333–47

Germany:
Aranyosi and, 425–9, 437
constitutionalism, 417, 467
EAWs and, 334, 387–9, 390, 402
fundamental rights, 425, 428
EU competences and, 73
extradition, 337, 360
FCR and, 250
Fransson and, 250
free movement, 280
Gözütok and Brügge, 199–211, 212–25
in absentia trials and, 425
judicial review of legislation, 251
Kossowski, 227–33, 234–43
Lisbon Treaty case, 149–50, 160, 162
Market Abuse Directive and, 162
Melloni and, 414–16
ML, 444–6, 461–2
ne bis in idem, 204
res judicata, 220
Solange II, 411
Giuffrida, Fabio, 107–21
Gözütok and Brügge:
legacy, 212–25
mutual trust, 3, 203–7, 213–15
ne bis in idem, 199–211
assessment, 210–11, 223–5
clarification of principle, 215–21
competent authority, 218–19

finality, 217–21, 224, 229–30
legacy, 201–3
mutual trust and, 207–10
novel method of interpretation, 221–3
scope of application, 199–201, 203–7
notion of criminal penalty, 216–17, 224
scholarly debate, 201
Greece:
EAWs and, 388, 390
Greek Maize see Greek Maize
ne bis in idem, 205
Greek Maize:
achievements, 123–9
assessment, 133–5
assimilation principle, 108–14, 120–1, 124–6, 134
competence, 3, 124–6
effectiveness principle, 108, 114–20, 122, 124, 125, 131–2, 134
facts, 107–8
fraud, 107, 127–9
impact, 122–35
domestic laws, 129–32
effectiveness principle, 131–2
equivalent protection in Italy, 129–31
national enforcement choices, 122–3, 124
proportionality, 108, 114–20, 124
protection of EU financial interests, 123, 127–9
effectiveness principle, 131–2
Italian legislation, 129–31
significance, 122
sincere cooperation, 107–8, 109, 111–12, 120

Hassermer, Winfried, 187
Hecker, B, 41–2
human dignity, 277, 291, 414, 415, 425, 426–7, 428, 441
human trafficking, 31–3, 36, 273, 304
Hungary: prison conditions, 425–7, 445, 460, 461–2

***in absentia* trials,** 202, 393–403, 395–6, 396–401, 407, 425
indirect effect:
developing, 8
direct effect and, 90–1
Dutch administrative fines, 21–7
Dutch criminal courts, 27–35
framework decisions, 84
Kolpinghuis, 11–12, 15, 21–7, 33–5
limits, 77–82, 103
contra legem interpretation, 71, 78, 92, 103
principles of EU law, 71, 88–9, 91
Pupino, 71–3, 88–9, 90–3
Lisbon Treaty and, 73–7
meaning, 69–70
police and judicial cooperation, 67–9
principle, 21
Pupino, 67–73, 85–6
establishment, 67–9
evaluation, 77–82
limits, 71–3, 77–82, 88–9, 90–3
national consequences, 89–97
vulnerable victims, 95–7
wider implications, 98–102
inhuman/degrading treatment:
Aranyosi, 378, 426–9, 440–3
Radu, 365, 367
International Covenant on Civil and Political Rights (ICCPR): *lex mitior*, 49
International Criminal Court: jurisdiction, 43, 63
Ireland:
Celmer, 464–7
LM, 431–6, 446–53, 460
opt-outs, 154–5, 170
irregular migration:
cases, 3–4
El Dridi, 273–89
belated Italian amendments, 297–9
immediate impact, 294–7
impact, 290–304
Employers' Sanctions Directive, 274
entry ban violations, 286–7, 301–3
EU criminalisation, 273–5, 291–4
Return Directive, 274, 275–6
conditions, 291–2
criticism, 280–1
direct effect, 278
discretion, 281, 287–8
El Dridi, 276–81
free movement and, 279–80
fundamental rights, 277, 279
Italy, 276, 292–303
post-*El Dridi* cases, 281–8
proportionality, 280
re-entry bans, 301–3
removal process, 277–8, 279, 295
Sweden, 270
Italy:
Berlusconi, 37–65
child pornography, 101–2

constitutional cases, 98–101, 133–4
constitutionalism
equality, 91, 93
legality, 91
principles, 91–2, 93
Taricco and, 172–4, 181, 188–9, 191, 416–17
criminal procedures, 86–7
EAW and, 387–8
El Dridi, 276–89
impact, 296–303
Greek Maize and, 129–31
human trafficking, 304
impunity, 186
in absentia trials, 407
irregular migration control, 276, 290–303
re-entry ban violations, 286–7, 301–3
limitation periods, 80–1, 113, 165–95
substantive nature, 194
Melloni and, 407, 417
non-retroactivity, 92
primacy and, 402
protection of EU financial interests, 129–31, 133
Pupino, 67–82, 83–104
Return Directive and, 276, 292–4
Italian changes, 296–303
re-entry ban violations, 286–7, 301–3
Security Package, 276
special inquiry procedure, 87, 90, 93–5
Taricco see Taricco
VAT/tax fraud, 111–12, 129–31
vulnerable victims, 87–8, 95–7

Jackson, Michael, 7
judge-made law, 192–3

Kaiafa-Gbandi, Maria, 137–50
Kelsen, Hans, 186
Klip, A, 42
Kolpinghuis:
Berlusconi and, 43
consistent interpretation, 11–12, 14–15, 17
Dutch criminal courts, 27–35
direct effect, 10–11, 12, 13–15, 21, 37
facts, 9–10
foundation of EU criminal law, 2–3
general principles, 7–20
indirect effect, 11–12, 15
directive-conform interpretation, 21–7, 36
Dutch administrative fines, 22–7
guidelines, 23–7
legacy, 21–7
maximum v minimum norms, 33–5
judgment, 10–12
landmark case, 7–8, 14
legacy, 15–18, 21–36
legal certainty, 7–8, 17, 22, 27, 36
legality principle, 16–17, 19, 51
non-retroactivity, 7–8, 19, 22, 36
protective European criminal law, 19–20
revisiting, 13–15
Kossowski:
CJEU decision, 228–9, 236–7
analysis, 229–33, 238–42
European Arrest Warrant, 227–33, 235
facts and context, 227–8, 234–6
mutual legal assistance, 234–5
national impact, 242–3
ne bis in idem, 3, 227–33
finality, 228–9, 238–42
mutual trust, 231–3, 237, 239–42, 243
national impact, 242
Kourotakis, Antonio, 391

Lanzarote Convention (2007), 96
Latvia: *Advocaten voor de Wereld* and, 336
Łazowski, Adam, 437–54
legal certainty:
Dutch criminal law, 33
ECtHR, 176, 262–3
indirect effect, 71
Kolpinghuis, 7–8, 17, 22, 27, 36
Taricco and, 192–3, 195
legality principle:
Advocaten voor de Wereld, 339–40, 341, 342, 349–53
double criminality and, 353–61
Berlusconi, 17, 37–54
CFR, 38, 47–50
multilevel concept, 47, 48–9
primacy, 79
scope, 80
Taricco and, 189
double criminality and, 353–61
extraterritorial jurisdiction, 353–5
Italian constitution, 91
Kolpinghuis, 16–17, 19, 51
Melloni, 174, 176, 182
non-retroactivity, 181–2
primacy and, 176–7
principle, 1
Pupino, 17

reshaping, 2
Taricco, 80, 166, 168, 170, 173, 176, 189
assessment, 195, 416–17
defining, 180–3
supranational legislation and, 194
UNSC and, 352–3
Lenaerts, Koen, v–vii, 346, 376, 399, 428
lex mitior:
Berlusconi, 37–54
ambiguities, 55–6
revisiting, 52–3
CFR, 52
ECtHR, 47
loyalty principle and, 57
meaning, 49–50
***lex posterior* rule,** 47
liberty: right to, 364, 366, 381, 382, 383
limitations periods:
ECtHR and, 166–7
Taricco, 80–1, 113, 165–95
substantive nature, 194–5
Lithuania: *Advocaten voor de Wereld* and, 336
Lock, Tobias, 245–58
loyalty principle, 42, 57, 70, 75, 79, 81, 143, 214, 444

Mancano, Leandro, 1–4, 319–29, 393–403, 453–4
Manes, Vittorio, 188–95
Marin, Luisa, 7–20
Market Abuse Directive, 162
Melloni:
CJEU ruling, 394–6, 405–7
controversy, 393, 404–5
EAW, 393–403
effectiveness, 4, 399
facts, 405–6
fair trial, 386, 394, 395–6, 407
fundamental rights, 249, 396–401, 418–19
in absentia trial, 386, 394, 395–6, 396–401
issues, 394
landmark, 396, 403, 404–5
legality principle, 174, 176, 182
mutual trust, 385–6, 394–6, 407
fundamental principle, 424
national impacts, 404–19
Germany, 414–16
Italy, 407, 417
Spain, 407–12, 417
non-regression clauses and, 400–1
primacy, 381, 401–2, 403, 418
Radu and, 364, 370–1, 381, 394–5
Spanish impact
Constitutional Court, 408–12, 417
legislation, 407
subsequent cases, 182–4, 249
Taricco and, 174–8
validity, 392
Meyer, Frank, 37–54
Miettinen, Samuli, 151–63
migration *see* **irregular migration**
mineral waters, 9–10
misappropriation, 101, 130, 387
Mitsilegas, Valsamis, 1–4, 393–403, 421–36
money laundering, 32, 34–5, 36, 112–13, 118–19
mutual trust:
Advocaten voor de Wereld, 4, 208, 333–47
Aranyosi to *LM*, 421–36, 456–8
automaticity, 421–5
Aranyosi and, 425–9, 443
uncritical trust, 422–5
blind trust, 346, 368, 425, 428, 436
CJEU cases: effect on national systems, 455–67
controversy, 421–2
double criminality, 208, 334, 338, 339–41, 345, 349, 353–61
earning, 346–7, 436
EAW, 4, 208–10, 333–47, 364–9, 373
automaticity, 421–9
functioning, 385
Gözütok and Brügge, 214–15
Melloni, 394–402
refusal to surrender, 386–91, 421–55
ECHR, 215
effectiveness and, 74–7
exceptional circumstances, 241, 386–7, 391, 426, 433, 443, 455
fundamental rights and, 373–6
Amsterdam Court, 463–4
Aranyosi, 425–9
Aranyosi to *LM*, 4, 421–36
Celmer, 464–7
LM, 431–6, 452, 453, 455, 460
ML, 444–6, 461–2
monitoring, 458–9
national decisions, 460–7
national levels of protection, 459
Pawel Lis, 462–3, 465
recent cases, 460–7
towards benchmark, 429–31
Gözütok and Brügge, 3, 207–10, 213–15
harmonisation and, 209, 391

importance, 375
judicial discretion, 459
judicial independence and, 433, 434, 446–53
Kossowski, 231–3, 237, 239–42, 243
limits, 74
Lisbon Treaty, 200
Melloni, 385–6, 394–6, 407, 424
national solutions to conflicts
diversity, 384–91
EU law compliance, 385–6
refusal to comply, 386–91
ne bis in idem and, 207–10, 231–3, 237, 239–42, 243
new form of cooperation, 1
objectives, 371, 395
primacy and, 371–2
prison conditions and, 424–9, 438–46
Pupino and, 74–7
Radu, 370–4, 383–4
rule of law and, 455–67

Naziris, Yannis, 212–25
ne bis in idem:
CFR, 3, 200–1, 204–5, 211, 228, 231
ECHR and, 256–8
Fransson, 246–58
Swedish tax proceedings, 262
ECHR, 245, 256–8, 263
European Arrest Warrants, 208–10
Fransson, 3, 245–58
CJEU decision, 247–50
critique, 250–1
implementing EU law, 247–55
subsequent cases, 251–5
Gözütok and Brügge, 199–211
clarification of principle, 215–21
competent authority, 218–19
finality, 217–21, 224, 229–30
legacy, 212–25
limits of application, 199–201, 203–7
notion of criminal penalty, 216–17, 224
novel method of interpretation, 221–3
subsequent cases, 201–3
in absentia judgments, 202
Kossowski, 3, 227–33
analysis, 229–33, 238–42
CJEU decision, 228–9, 236–7
facts, 227–8, 234–6
finality, 228–31, 238–42
mutual trust, 231–3, 237, 239–42, 243
national impact, 242–3
mutual trust and, 207–10, 231–3, 237, 239–42, 243
principle, 1
Radu, 383
reshaping, 2, 3
Schengen Agreement, 199–211
scope of application, 199–201, 203–7
Sweden and, 261–7
Netherlands:
administrative fines, 22–7
Advocaten voor de Wereld and, 336
consistent interpretation: criminal courts, 27–35
directive-conform interpretation, 22–7
maximum v minimum norms, 33–5
EAWs and, 463–4
Gözütok and Brügge, 199–211, 212–25
human trafficking, 31–3, 36
Kolpinghuis, 7–20, 21–36
money laundering, 32, 36
ne bis in idem, 202, 203
Nic Shuibhne, Niamh, 305–18
non-retroactivity
see also lex mitior
Berlusconi, 37–54
effectiveness and, 57–60
criminal law analogy, 92
ECHR, 42–3, 168, 262
indirect effect, 71
Italy, 92
Kolpinghuis, 7–8, 19, 22, 36
legality and, 181–2
Taricco, 168, 189
Nowak, Celina, 234–43

OECD: Anti-Bribery Convention, 130
Ouwerkerk, Jannemieke, 21–36

Packer, Herbert, 187
passive personality principle, 360
PIF Convention, 110–11, 116, 130, 132, 167, 169, 170
PIF Directive, 118, 119, 126, 128, 161–2, 169–71, 174, 194
Poland:
Advocaten voor de Wereld and, 336
EAWs and, 334, 337, 386–7
fair trial, 457–8
judicial independence and, 431–6, 446–7, 452, 457, 459–67
Kossowski and, 242
LM and, 431–6, 446–8, 452, 453, 457

presumption of innocence and, 452
rule of law and, 431–6
Venice Commission, 431–2, 447n31, 452
Portugal: ***ne bis in idem*****,** 202
precision principle, 64, 102, 181–2, 355, 417
presumption of innocence, 195, 399–400, 452, 466
primacy:
Berlusconi and, 44–7
domestic constitution and, 60
legality principle and, 79, 176–7
M.A.S. decision, 183–5
Melloni, 381, 401–2, 403, 418
mutual trust and, 371–2
Pupino and, 77–8
Taricco, 168, 176–7, 402, 403
temporal dimension, 46–7
principles of EU law:
consistent interpretation, 11–12
double jeopardy *see ne bis in idem*
effectiveness *see* effectiveness principle
indirect effect *see* indirect effect
Kolphinghuis, 7–20
legality *see* legality principle
loyalty principle *see* loyalty
mutual trust *see* mutual trust
prison conditions, 426–7, 438–46, 456–8, 460, 461–2
protection of EU financial interests (PIF):
direct effect, 133
effectiveness principle, 131–2
Greek Maize, 133–5
PIF Convention, 110–11, 116, 130, 132, 167, 169, 170
PIF Directive, 118, 119, 126, 128, 161–2, 169–71, 174, 194
Spain, 132
Taricco, 165–87
VAT fraud, 165–87
public procurement, 343, 344
public security deportations, 308, 320–4, 329
Pupino:
balancing safeguards and effectiveness, 3, 79–81
CJEU judgment, 69–73
effectiveness principle, 3, 70
facts, 70, 86–8
Framework Decision and, 88
impact, 67–82
indirect effect, 67–73, 85–6
evaluation of principle, 77–82
limits, 71–3, 77–82, 90–3
Lisbon Treaty and, 73–7
national consequences, 89–97
judicial activism, 103
judicial discretion, 103
Kolpinghuis and, 17
landmark, 102–4, 137, 138–9
legacy, 83–104
legality principle, 17
national consequences, 89–97
vulnerable victims, 95–7
wider implications, 98–102
overview, 86–9
standing of victims, 69–70, 85, 95–7, 103

Radu:
AG Opinion, 364–9, 463
Aranyosi and, 346, 374, 376, 378–9
EAW, 363–79
impact, 376–8
effectiveness principle, 423–4
EU/ECtHR relationship, 374–6
fair trial, 363, 364, 366–7, 382, 463
fundamental rights, 4, 342, 363–9, 377–8
proportionality, 423–4
Romanian implementation, 382–4
Melloni and, 364, 370–1, 381, 394–5
missed opportunity, 363–4, 369–70
mutual trust, 370–4, 383–4
diversity of judicial solutions, 384–91
EU law compliance, 385–6
national effects, 380–92
EU law compliance, 385–6
Romanian implementation of CJEU ruling, 382–4, 391
ne bis in idem, 383
NS and, 365, 368–9
paradigm, 391–2
Raffaelli, Rosa, 363–79
res judicata**,** 58, 220, 263
right to liberty, 364, 366, 381, 382, 383
right to security, 364
right to silence, 415
Romania:
EAW and, 389
implementation of *Radu* ruling, 382–4, 391
Radu, 363–79, 380–4
ECtHR cases, 384
fair trial, 382
pre-trial detention, 382
prison conditions, 425–7

rule of law:
Aranyosi, 449–50
subsequent cases, 460–7
effect of CJEU case law on national systems, 455–67
Environmental Crime, 140
EU founding value, 455, 459
extradition and, 356
LM, 431–6, 450, 455, 460
subsequent national cases, 460–7
Taricco, 195

Schengen Agreement, 3, 154, 155, 199–211, 212–25, 227–33, 235–43, 255
security: right to, 364
security deportations, 308, 320–4, 329
self-incrimination, 415–16
separation of powers, 28, 29, 80, 103, 150, 189, 195, 432
ship-source pollution, 140, 147, 151, 159–60, 162
Sicurella, Rosaria, 122–35
silence: right to, 415
social pact, 14
social security, 246, 252, 343–4
Spain
see also Melloni
Advocaten voor de Wereld and, 336
European Arrest Warrants and, 174
in absentia trials, 386
Melloni impact
Constitutional Court, 408–12, 417
legislation, 407
protection of EU financial interests, 132
staff regulations, 343–4
subsidiarity, 129, 161–2, 186, 246, 249, 338, 372
Sundberg, Hans, 268
Sweden:
Fransson, 245–58
national impact, 259–70
fraud sanctions, 261–2
judicial review of Swedish laws, 267, 270
ne bis idem
ECtHR cases, 261–7
Fransson, 245–58, 259–70
PIF Directive and, 161–2
rebellious lower courts, 265–6, 268
Symeonidou-Kastanidou, Elisavet, 212–25

Taricco:
1st ECJ judgment, 165–8
aftermath, 168–71
Italian constitutionalism and, 172–4, 181, 188–9, 191
scholarly debate, 169, 170
2nd judgment, 174–8, 189
assimilation principle, 113, 167
effectiveness, 119
balancing rights and, 3, 68–9, 168, 181, 186–7
facts, 80
Italian constitutionalism and, 79–81, 416–17
judicial discretion, 192–3
Kolpinghuis and, 18
legal certainty, 192–3, 195
legality principle, 166, 168, 170, 173, 176, 189
assessment, 195, 416–17
defining, 180–3
supranational legislation and, 194
limitations periods, 80–1, 165–87
substantive nature, 194–5
M.A.S. decision and, 178–80, 183–5, 194
national courts' power, 190
non-retroactivity, 168, 189
post-Lisbon pluralism and, 183–7
primacy and, 168, 176–7, 402, 403
proportionality, 80
protection of EU financial interests, 133
rule of law, 195
saga, 165–87, 188–95
separation of powers, 189, 195
Taricco II, 178–80
vagueness of rule, 190, 191, 192
taxation: fraud, 246, 252, 260–70

United Kingdom:
2005 terrorism, 319
Advocaten voor de Wereld and, 336
Brexit, 317–18
Citizenship Directive and, 323–4
CS, 305–18, 319–29
deportation of foreign offenders
approach, 319–29
assessment, 328–9
CS, 311–18
discretion, 326
ECHR and, 327
foreign criminal category, 323
fundamental interests, 325
guidance, 325, 327–8
integration level, 324, 325–6
issues, 326–8
legal framework, 322–4
policy approach, 324–6

preventative grounds, 324, 328
proportionality, 323, 325
public good, 322, 325, 326, 327, 329
public security grounds, 321–2, 323–4, 329
immigration law, 322–4
judicial review of legislation, 251–2
liberal tradition, 388
opt-outs, 154–5
Pawel Lis, 462–3, 465
probationary citizenship, 319
right to silence and, 415
United Nations Security Council: legality principle and, 352–3
United States: 9/11, 334

Vagliasindi, Grazia Maria, 83–104
Van Ballegooij, Wouter, 444, 455–67
Van Kempen, PHPHMC, 33
VAT fraud, 165–87, 246–58, 260–70
Vavoula, Niovi, 273–89
Venice Commission, 431–2, 447n31, 452
victims *see* **vulnerable victims/witnesses**
Voltaire, 440
vulnerable victims/witnesses
see also Pupino
Framework Decision 2001/220, 89
Istanbul Convention (2011), 96
Italian criminal procedures, 87–8
post-*Pupino*, 95–7
Lanzarote Convention (2007), 96
standing, 69–70, 85, 103

Wasmeier, Martin, 205
Weyembergh, Anne, 199–211
Wieczorek, Irene, 380–92

Zedner, Lucia, 319
Zetterquist, Ola, 268

Printed by Libri Plureos GmbH in Hamburg,
Germany

9 781509 911172